Abstracts of KENT COUNTY MARYLAND Wills

Volume 2
1816-1867

Christos Christou, Jr.
&
John Anthony Barnhouser

HERITAGE BOOKS
2012

HERITAGE BOOKS
AN IMPRINT OF HERITAGE BOOKS, INC.

Books, CDs, and more—Worldwide

For our listing of thousands of titles see our website
at
www.HeritageBooks.com

Published 2012 by
HERITAGE BOOKS, INC.
Publishing Division
100 Railroad Ave. #104
Westminster, Maryland 21157

Copyright © 1997 Christos Christou, Jr.
and John Anthony Barnhouser

Other Heritage Books by the author:
Abstracts of Kent County, Maryland Wills, Volume 1: 1777–1816
Abstracts of Kent County, Maryland Wills, Volume 2: 1816–1867

All rights reserved. No part of this book may be reproduced or transmitted in any form or by any means, electronic or mechanical, including photocopying, recording or by any information storage and retrieval system without written permission from the author, except for the inclusion of brief quotations in a review.

International Standard Book Numbers
Paperbound: 978-1-58549-418-7
Clothbound: 978-0-7884-9373-7

Introduction

I have been a long-time member of the Sons of the American Revolution and because of this I am always conscious of the lack of published records for the period between the Revolutionary era and the 1850 census making it harder to find or prove families pre-1850. I hope that this book will fill that void.

I have tried to include as much information as possible without the legal language. I hope that this fuller abstract will give a better picture of what property these people owned and cherished and give a clearer picture of the times. Many interesting lines were copied verbatim. Four pages were missing from the microfilm copies and therefore were copied from the originals in Chestertown (WB 11 p. 159-160, WB 12 p. 146-147).

I would like to acknowledge my adopted son John A. Barnhouser's help in the creation of this book. He tolerated many late hours of reading and typing on my part. John's biological line descends from **Capt. William Blackiston Rasin** which was unknown to us until we heard from Carolyn E. Cooper of Chestertown, MD. She has worked 20 years on the Rasin family and is the "town expert" on Worton, Kent Co, MD families. It was through her hard work and freely giving of information that the Children of the American Revolution accepted John's application in their society based on his descent from Capt. Rasin. I cannot thank her enough for all the information she has provided from the original records. She is indeed a treasure to Kent County.

John, through his Blackiston family, descends from **King Edward III of England** and is a cousin to **President George Washington**. Many people of Kent Co share this same ancestry and also may be unaware. We have learned only after looking at the primary records that so much is yet unknown. I am always interested in constructive criticism and look forward to hearing from as many people as possible who are interested in any of these Kent Co families and I can be reached through Family Line Publications or at the following address:

Christos Christou, Jr.
1023-C Old Eastern Avenue
Baltimore, Maryland 21221
(410) 574-5467
EMAIL: CZCHRIST@EMG.COM

Note: The English monetary system, used in the early U.S. was pounds (£). One pound = 20 shillings = 240 pence.

KING EDWARD III OF ENGLAND (1312-1377)	M.	PHILIPPA OF HAINAULT (1312-1369)
↓		
LIONEL OF ANTWERP (1338-1368)	M.	ELIZABETH DE BURGH (1338-)
		↓
EDMUND MORTIMER (1352-1381)	M.	PHILLIPA PLANTAGENET (1355-)
		↓
HENRY PERCY (1370-1403)	M.	ELIZABETH MORTIMER (1375-A1407)
		↓
JOHN CLIFFORD (1390-1422)	M.	ELIZABETH PERCY (1395-1437)
↓		
THOMAS CLIFFORD (1415-1455)	M.	JOAN DACRE (1415-)
↓		
JOHN CLIFFORD (1435-1462)	M.	MARGARET BROMFLETE (1435-)
↓		
HENRY CLIFFORD (1453-1524)	M.	ANNE ST. JOHN (1453-)
		↓
RALPH BOWES (1485-1516)	M.	ELIZABETH CLIFFORD (1490-)
↓		
GEORGE BOWES (1516-1546)	M.	MURIEL EURE (1516-)
		↓
JOHN BLACKISTON (1537—1587)	M.	ELIZABETH BOWES* (1538—)
↓		
MARMADUKE BLACKISTON (1570—1639)	M.	MARGARET JAMES (1575—1636)
↓		
GEORGE BLACKISTON (1611—1669)	M.	BARBARA LAWSON (1620—1668)
↓		
CAPT. EBENEZER BLACKISTON (1650—1709)	M.	ELIZABETH JAMES (1650—B1697)
↓		
WILLIAM BLACKISTON (1685—1737)	M.	ANN PARK (1695—)
		↓
JOHN RASIN (1713—1761)	M.	ROSAMOND BLACKISTON (1730—B1772)
↓		
CAPT. WILLIAM B. RASIN (1760—1810)	M.	MARTHA WROTH (C1760—A1828)
↓		
PHILIP R. RASIN (1790—1841)	M.	SARAH BENNETT (1792—1856)
		↓
JOHN W. CROUCH (1823—1897)	M.	WILHELMINA RASIN (1830—1907)
↓		
CHARLES W. CROUCH (1870—1944)	M.	GRACE F. BLACKISTON* (1875—1948)
		↓
HARRY T. STATES (1910—1985)	M.	BERNICE T. CROUCH (1913—1965)
		↓
BERNARD BARNHOUSER SR. (1928—1996)	M.	LULA GRACE STATES (1931—1978)
↓		
BERNARD A. BARNHOUSER JR. (1949—)	M.	CHARMAINE M. GUY (1952—)
	↓↓↓	

LAURA   JOHN A. BARNHOUSER   DOROTHY
(1975-)   (1977—)   (1979-)

Table of Contents

Book Number	Years Covered	# of Pages	Microfilm #	
Will Book 10	1816-1827	pp. 1-82, 146-472	WK 687-688-3	1
Will Book 11	1827-1835	pp. 1-343	WK 688-689-1	69
Will Book 12	1835-1854	pp. 1-401	WK 688-689-2	114
Will Book 13	1854-1867	pp. 1-375	CR 52	210
Index of Names and Places				279

Abstract of Kent Co, Maryland Wills 1816-1867

Will Book 10   1816-1827   pp. 1-82, 146-472 WK 687-688-3

Benjamin Chambers of Chestertown, Kent Co
Whereas my dau. **Augusta** the wife of **Judge Houston** my sons **Ezekial F. Chambers** and **James Chambers** have each received a partial advancement and are now settled in the world and have generously expressed their willingness that my estate should go to my younger children, I give my estate in the following manner, to my sons **David Chambers** and **Benjamin Lee Chambers** I give my farm near Fanning's Branch called *"Kelly Langford"*, my wife's 1/3 first taken out. To my dau. **Elizabeth Caroline Chambers** and my son **William Henry Chambers** I give my lands in Worton adjoining the lands of **William Barroll, George W. Thomas** and others including all the several parcels which I have purchased of different people being commonly called *"the Home farm"* (excepting the part I have lately given my wife). Whereas my wife and 3 youngest children will probably continue to reside there, then the rest of my estate to be put in a fund at the disposition of my wife and my son Ezekial for the support of this family. At the death of my wife, to my 3 youngest children. My lots lying on Cannon Street in Chestertown and the lot adjoining the almshouse which I purchased of **Peregrine Wilmer** be kept during the life of my wife for the use of the family. At her death to be sold by my son Ezekial and the proceeds to the 3 youngest children and the lot near the almshouse to be given to my son Ezekial after my wife's death. Whereas my son David may deem it advisable to sell his interest in the lands devised to him before my son Benjamin arrives to the age of 21 or in some other event it may become necessary to sell the lands devised to my son Benjamin or to my son William during the minority of my son and it might promote the interest then the same to be sold free of any claim of dower. I empower my son Ezekial on behalf of my son William with my wife as to the value of her 1/3s and the sum to be received by her. Whereas I want my sons Benjamin and William to have an education and the interest of the estate may not be enough, then my wife and son Ezekial may sell any lands for said purpose. My wife and my son Ezekial to be guardians to my sons Benjamin and William

Execs. my wife **Elizabeth** and my son **Ezekial**. Witnesses Dr. Morgan Browne, Dr. James M. Anderson Jr., Sarah E. Van Bibber. Written Dec. 15, 1815 Proved Feb. 1, 1816 p. 1

Charles Browning of Kent Co
All my estate to my grandson **James** and my granddau. **Sofiah**.

Exec. Samuel Ryley. Witnesses Nathaniel Meginniss, Jesse Jerrum, Thomas Griffin. Written Oct. 20, 1816 Proved Dec. 27, 1816 p. 5

David Crane
To be buried near my late wife. To my dau. **Elizabeth** $50 in 5 payments as her brother **William** may think proper so that **John Lamb** is not to receive any part. To my son **William** $50, my watch, my spectacles. To my son **Boyer** £100. To my son **Thomas** my

wearing apparel and the account I have against him for money received of **James Brooks**. To my son **Stephen's** widow $50. To my son **John** $65. To my dau. **Mary** $50. To my son **Jonathan** $150 provided my son **Philip** will comply with this will and let my negro boy **Sam** have his freedom on Jan. 1, 1830 and give him $15 and my mulatto boy **Bill** have his freedom on Jan. 1, 1835 and give him £10. I give to my son Philip Crane all my real and personal estate

Exec. my son Philip Crane. Witnesses Thomas Hayne, John Hayne, Richard Lynch. Written Feb. 26, 1816 Proved Mar. 9, 1816 p. 7

Mary Lamb of Kent Co
To my granddau. **Mary Ann Bowers** dau. of **John** and **Rosamond Bowers** one bed, also one negro girl **Henny** during the term she is to serve according to the will of my son **David Lamb** and if she has children the to be free for males at 21 and girls at 18. To my dau. **Sarah Bowers** wife of **William Bowers** all my wearing apparel. After my death my negro woman **Rachel** to be free. To my dau. **Rebecca Lamb** all my estate

Exec. my dau. Rebecca Lamb. Witnesses Michael Lamb (called Daniel Lamb in acknowledgements), Daniel Lamb Jr. Written Jun 4, 1811 Proved Feb. 24, 1816 p. 9

James Blackiston of Kent Co
To my wife **Jemima Blackstone** 1/3 part of all my real estate during her life. To my wife **Jemima Blackstone** 1/3 part of my personal estate except the slaves and in lieu $700. Having in the past bestowed on my son **Kennard** land and property that amounts to a reasonable part of my estate I give to Kennard $100. Having in time passed bestowed on my son **Ebenezer** goods and cattle to a considerable amount I give $500. Having in the time past bestowed on my son **James** lately deceased land to the reasonable amount of my estate, I give to my grandchildren the heirs of James $100. To my children **Ann Elizabeth, William Henry** and any child who may be born after me all my real estate inclusive of the 1/3 part given to my wife, to be divided among them by **William Spencer, John Wallis,** and **James Brice** when they arrive at age. To my children Ann Elizabeth, William Henry, and child all the residue of my personal estate. If either of my children Ann Elizabeth or William Henry die, then to the survivor of the surviving children born to me by my wife Jemima Blackstone. If all my said children by my wife should die, then to my grandchildren **James, Thomas, Mary, David** and **Catharine** divided by William Spencer, John Wallis, and James Brice as they arrive of age. My slaves to not be sold or hired out but kept on my farm on which I now reside.

Exec. my wife Jemima Blackstone. Witnesses Henry Lyon Davis, Samuel H. Stephens, Elizabeth Johns. Written Feb. 20, 1815 Proved Sep. 18, 1816 p. 11

James Blake of Kent Co
As it appears that my wife **Alphonso Blake** is only entitled to a life estate in a farm called *"Rousby's Recovery"* lying in Kent containing about 500 acres and in a small tract

Liber 10 1816-1827

adjoining it called *"Thomas' Purchase Resurveyed"* containing about 93 acres and also in a farm in Queen Anns Co called *"Park Resurveyed"* and containing about 400 acres, I give the 3 farms to my wife but if the farm in Queen Anns called *"Park Resurveyed"* which in now advertised for sale be disposed of previous to my death by my wife and myself for the payment of her father's debts then I give the remainder of the annual interest to be invested in Bank Stock in Baltimore the interest to her during her life then to the heirs of her body. If not sold then to be sold by my widow and used for said purpose but if my wife has not issue then she may give by her will to such person she chooses. I give my wife the annual interest of 9 shares in the books of the Farmers and Merchants Bank of Baltimore during her life then to her heirs. To my wife the present crops of wheat on said farm for my debts which are but trifling, also the furniture including the plate, books, and two wheel carriage. To her all my negroes or as I call them black people which I own and trust in their good conduct. I recommend to my wife's care **Charley** and **Zeb**. To my wife all the farming utensils. As my wife and myself have misted my sister **Jane** to this country promising our kind protection and have been pleased with her conduct these 5 years during which she resided to us, therefore I give her $200 annually out of my personal estate. I give her the dividend of the 9 shares of the Farmers and Merchants Bank of Baltimore and I leave her to the kind solicitude of my wife who has upon all occasions treated her as a sister. To my brother **Dominick T. Blake** counselor at law at New York my gold watch. To my friend **Richard Bennet Carmichael** Esq a travelling case of handsome razors a little used.

Execs. my wife and William Carmichael Esq and General Philip Reed. Witnesses James Mayniham, Samuel Hodges, Isaac Spencer. Written Aug. 12, 1816 Proved Sep. 30, 1816 p. 14

James Corse of Kent Co

To my son **William Corse** my upper farm known as *"Mount Independence"*, *"the Agreement"*, *"Part of Partnership"*, and *"Partnership Resurveyed"* and to him 4 negroes **Perry, Joseph Butler, Jacob Tobeyo,** and **Rachel** and discharge all claim I have against him for money that I paid him at different times. To my son **Unit Corse** all that part of a tract called *"Batchelder's Resolution"* lying on the NW side of the Stage Road and on the E side of the W fork of the branch that runs between **James Brooks** land and mine so as to divide the farm with the stage road and the N fork and to him the following negroes **Frank, Chester, Sam Butler, Minta;** his riding horse Brandy and the plank and cedar lumber. To my son **Thomas A. Corse** all the remainder of *"Batchelder Resolution"* lying upon the W side of the N fork of the branch and also all that part that lies upon the SE side of the Stage Road adjoining Morgans Creek upon which the dwelling house stands, and the following negroes **Isaac, Robert, Rebecca, Darkey** and **Susan**. To my son **James Corse** my home dwelling plantation known as *"Wright's Rest"* and *"Middle Neck"* and so that my son can have it in his power to transmit the home dwelling without injury down to posterity, I give to him another plantation called *"Sult Martins Allebone"* and *"Addition"* and to him the following negroes **George, Maria** and child and young **Fillis**. To my wife **Jane Corse** to be considered in value $1,206.26½ which I gave my

3

bond for to **Francis A. Rochester** and **John Hanson** for Jane Corse's use if she survived me in lieu of dower, to wit one negro woman **Nell**, one bed, one bureau, one looking glass that hangs over the fireplace, one mahogany tea table, one tea tray, tea cups and saucers, 6 green windsor chairs, one small pine cupboard, two small tables, that stands upstairs, one hare trunk, 6 knives and forks, one horse and carriage, 2 milch cows, all to be deducted from the bond if she takes the property. I give to my son James Corse or rather confirm the following property to my home dwelling my clock and cupboard, two family records of ages and deaths and my old family bible and one old desk. To my son Unit Corse $500 in lieu of commission on settlement of my estate. He is guardian to my son Thomas A. Corse until he is 21. My house woman Fillis shall be free in one month. The rest of my property I give equally to my 4 sons William Corse, Unit Corse, James Corse, and Thomas A. Corse. my friend **Samuel Ringgold** and my brother **Joseph Everitt** to oversight of the guardianship of my son Thomas and management of my son James and the education of both until they are of full age.

Exec. my son Unit Corse. Witnesses John Hepbron, Macall Medford, Thomas Hayne, Thomas Hepbron Jr. Written May 3, 1815 Proved Feb. 1816 p. 18

Marmaduke Tilden

To my dau. **Mary H. Handy** during her life my dwelling plantation and the land I purchased of **Samuel** and **William H. Groome** being part of *"Worton Manor"*. To my granddau. **Mary H. Handy** after her death the two tracts and if she dies then to the eldest son of my dau. Mary that may be living after the death of my granddaughter. If my dau. dies before the marriage of my granddau. then my son in law **George D. S. Handy** shall have the use of my lands until she is marriage allowing her a reasonable support. To my grandson **Thomas B. Tilden** my plantation part of which I bought of Thomas and **William Ringgold** it being part of a tract called *"Great Oak Manor"* and adjoins the lands of the late **John Carville** provided within 6 months of his being 21 that he conveys to my granddau. **Ann Maria Brice** all his part of the real estate which Thomas and Ann Maria are entitled to in right of their mother. If he does not then the plantation to my granddau. Ann Maria Brice. The interest of said land to both Thomas and Ann Maria, until Thomas makes above conveyance. To my granddau. **Ester Ann** and **Susan L. Handy** each $500 charged to land of granddau. Mary was given within 2 years after my granddau. Mary or my grandson **Marmaduke** shall come into position of said land. To my grandson **Marmaduke P. Hardy** $500 put to bank stock and held till he is 21. If he dies under age or comes into possession of land given to granddaughter Mary then the $500 to my granddaughters Ester Ann and Susan. To my dau. **Mary F. Hardy** my negro man **Paul** until Dec. 31, 1818, my negro woman **Tene** until Dec. 21, 1823, my negro boy **Henry** until Dec. 31, 1840, my negro boy **Ewing** until Dec. 31, 1840, my negro boy **Jere** until Dec. 31, 1842, my negro boy **David** until Dec. 31, 1844. To my granddau. Ann Maria Brice my negro man **Perry** and my negro girl **Fanny** until the Dec. 31, 1842, also my negro girl **Hetty** until Dec. 31, 1846. To my grandson **Thomas B. Tilden** my negro girl **Caroline** until Dec. 31, 1821, my negro girl **Sarah** until Dec. 31, 1823 and my negro boy **Thomas** until Dec. 31, 1840. After my debts, the

Liber 10 1816-1827

remainder of my personal estate to my dau. Mary, my granddau. Ann Maria Briscoe (sic) and my grandson Thomas B. Tilden. My negro man **Cuff** and my negro woman **Fanny** free at my death and if unable to support themselves then my dau. Mary to take care of them.

Exec. my son in law George D. S. Hardy. Witnesses Catharine Bordley, Mary Ann Bordley, Thomas Worrell. Written June 9, 1815 Proved Mar. 18, 1816 p. 23

Peregrine Cooper Sr. of Kent Co
To my son **Benjamin Cooper** my dwelling plantation containing about 330 acres. To my dau. **Wilhelmina Maxwell** £1,000 paid by my son **Peregrine Cooper**. To my son Peregrine Cooper my negro man **Tom** for 2 years then free, and my negroes **Daniel, Bill, Sandy, Hannah, Harriet,** and **Nan** with the infant at her breast. To my dau. Wilhelmina Maxwell the negroes **Isaac, Jim, Tempy, Clant,** and **Bill** a boy. My negro woman **Dinah** to my dau. Wilhelmina for 2 years then free. My negro man **Adam** to be free at my death. To my granddau. **Francis Elizabeth Maxwell** the negroes Albert, Ann, and Maria. My negro woman Blanch to be free at my death. To my granddau. Francis Elizabeth Maxwell my new high post bedstead and the bed and furniture belonging to it. To my son Peregrine Cooper my negro woman **Sue** to serve him 2 years then free. To my dau. Wilhelmina Maxwell choice of 4 milch cows. To my sister **Martha Wilmer** my best milch cow after my dau. has made her choice of 4. To my dau. Wilhelmina Maxwell my iron gray mare called Carlo and my bay horse called Pompey. To my son **Peregrine Cooper** my negro boy **Frederick,** and to him the 2 negroes **Jonas** and **Henry**.

Exec. my son Peregrine Cooper. Witnesses Joseph Wickes Jr, Samuel Kerr, Joseph Wickes 4th. Written Dec. 20, 1816 Proved Jan. 18, 1817 p. 27

Mary Vickers of Kent Co
To my son **Jesse Vickers** my bed, 6 tea cups and saucers, 2 bowls, 1 Turene, 1 tea pot and cream pot, 1 mug and 3 tumblers, 1 decanter, 6 small green edged plates and 1 iron pot. To **Elizabeth Ayres** my bureau, one looking glass, one white trunk and all my wearing apparel which shall be in said trunk. The rest of my personal estate to **Nancy Vickers** wife of **James Vickers**. My house and lot in Chestertown where I now live be sold and be used for my debts and the remainder to Elizabeth Ayres to be paid by my executor at the discretion of Mrs. **Sarah Barroll** wife of **William Barroll**.

Exec. Thomas Davis. Witnesses John B. Eccleston, Thomas Anderson, Isaac Cannell. Written Jan. 6, 1817 Proved Feb. 8, 1817 p. 30

Thomas Eccleston of Kent Co
For a valuable consideration by me received, I give to **Mary Fillingame** wife of **John Fillingame** all that lot adjoining to my farm whereon I now live which was conveyed by deed from said Mary and John Fillingame recorded at Kent Co. My right or claim to the

5

farm which was devised by my father **John Eccleston** to my sister **Elizabeth Eccleston** which lies near Chester River shall be sold and applied to my debts. To my dau. **Margaret Sophia Eccleston** my farm whereon I now live and all my real estate, remainder to my wife **Providence Intes Eccleston** for her life, remainder to my nephew **John B. Eccleston**. To my wife after all debts paid, the rest of my personal estate and the money left from sale of above estate, in lieu of her dower on the land devised to Mary Fillingame and the land to be sold but not in bar of her dower on the land I now live or any other estate she is to have during her life.

Execs. my wife and my nephew John B. Eccleston. Witnesses Joseph Brown 4th, Richard Graves, Isaac Caulk. Written Jan. 18, 1817 Proved Feb. 1, 1817 p. 33

Donaldson Yates of the Eastern Shore, Kent Co, MD
Assistant surgeon on board the U.S. Ship Constitution in the harbor of Boston in Massachusetts, to my brother **George Yates** of Kent Co all my real and personal estate in said county. signed as Donaldson Yeates

Exec. my brother George Yates. Witnesses John M. Lyim (Samuel Wethered said he was acquainted with writing of Donaldson Yates). Written June 10, 1812 Proved May 9, 1817 p. 36

Elizabeth Johns of Kent Co
To my dau. **Elizabeth Johns** all my real estate and my personal estate subject to these legacies, to my son **Arthur Johns** $200, to my son **Enoch Johns** $500.

Exec. Not Given. Witnesses Marcellus Keene, James Blackiston, Mary Smith. Written Jan. 11, 1811 Proved Feb. 20, 1817 p. 37

Richard Roach of Kent Co
To my niece **Hannah Roach** (dau. of **James** and **Elizabeth Roach**) $200 and my bed. To my niece **Ann** dau. as above $200. To my nephew **James Roach** $200 and my chest of tools. To my nephew **Benjamin Roach** $200. To my nephew **Philip Roach** (son of **Philip**) my gold watch. The remainder of my estate to my brother **John Roach**.

Exec. my friend William Hines. Witnesses Nathan Smith, George Neal. Written Nov. 12, 1816 Proved May 3, 1817 p. 39

Darius Copper of Kent Co
To my wife **Mary Copper** all the remainder of my estate after my debts are paid.

Exec. my wife. Witnesses George Watts. Written July 28, 1817 Proved Aug. 12, 1817 p. 41

Vachel Keene of Kent Co
To my wife **Eliza Keene** all my real estate lying in Queen Annes Co and all my personal estate.

Exec. my wife Eliza Keene. Witnesses Richard Keene, Jesse Bodle, Alexander B. Hanson. Written Jan. 8, 1817 Proved June 1817 p. 42

Emanuel Jenkinson of Kent Co
To my cousin **Samuel Covington** son of Samuel Covington of DE all my estate with all the debts due me of said Samuel. If he is dead or die before me then to his brother **John Covington**. My black girl **Margaret** who I now suppose to be about 2 shall serve 10 years then free and enjoin it to said Samuel or John which ever it may be to execute a manumission in terms stated.

Exec. my cousin Samuel Covington (or his brother John if he is deceased). Witnesses William Farrell, James Bradshaw. Written June 12, 1817 Proved July 12, 1817 p. 44

Araminta Briscoe
To my grandson **William Alexander Colder** ½ of my estate which I have a right. To my 5 grandchildren **William Newman, Elizabeth Newman, James Newman, Nathan M. Newman** and **Lorenzo Newman** the other ½. My clock shall not be sold but reserved for Nathan M. Newman at the appraisement and deducted of his part of my estate. My bureau and wearing apparel shall not be appraised but given to Elizabeth Newman exclusive of her part of my estate, and she shall have one bed and furniture which shall be deducted out of her part. My bed quilt which I call the new one and my embroidered counterpane shall not be appraised but given to **William A. Calder** exclusive of his part. The money due from **Isaac Spencer** now pending in court be shall be added to my estate when received except the 1/3 part **Benjamin Massey** is to have as compensation for his attention to the business out of which he is to pay the costs of the suit and $150 to **Ezekial Chambers** in part for his fee, and $50 out of my estate to Ezekial Chambers which will be in full of his fee. My negro boy **Noah** who is hired to **Sewel Green** to continue to live with him as long as he pays his wages, and the wages added to my estate. If any of my heirs die before coming of age then to the survivors.

Exec. Sewel Green of DE. Witnesses Daniel F. Massey, John Sollaway. Written Jan. 3, 1816 Proved Aug. 30, 1817 p. 46

Renunciation I hereby resign right to administration. Written Aug. 28, 1817 Sewell Green

Thomas Nicholson of Kent Co
To my wife **Catherine Nicholson** in lieu of her dower her choice of 2 rooms in my house one above and the other below stairs, the two lots adjoining the garden and ½ the garden to be laid off to the large lot during her life. To my wife in lieu of her 1/3, the

choice of 2 horses, 2 cows, 4 hogs, 4 sheep, ½ the poultry, 1/3 of the kitchen furniture, 2 beds, one bureau, 2 tables, 6 chairs on pair of and irons and my double carriage. My wife shall have privilege of cooking in the kitchen, the use of the carriage horse and 2 stalls in the stable and pasturage for her stock. To my dau. **Nancy** my negro boy **Tom**, to my dau. **Maria** my negro boy **Jim** and to my dau. **Elizabeth** my negro boy **Sam**. The remainder to be divided, 1/7 to the children now living of my son **Edward Nicholson**, 1/7 to the children now living of my son **Charles R. Nicholson**, the remaining 5/7 to my 5 daughters **Rachel, Hannah**, Nancy, Maria, and Elizabeth.

Exec. my friend Thomas Worrell Esq. Witnesses Thomas Hynson, John C. Hynson, Martha Hynson. Written June 15, 1817 Proved Aug. 2, 1817 p. 49

Renunciation I renounce claim to any devise made to me under the will of my husband and claim my dower. Written Aug. 15, 1817 Catharine Nicholson

William Gale of Still Pond, Kent Co

My body to be buried in my own graveyard between my wife's and my son **Williams** grave and that no mourning apparel shall be worn by none of my family after my death. I give one acre land square taking my wife's grave as the center of the square acre as a burying ground to my descendants and their family forever with free egress from the main road may at anytime fence, plank or wall in said ground as a burying ground only. To my brother **Thomas Gale** and **Dr. George W. Thomas** of Chestertown all my estate in trust for 10 years to administer for the family as I have done, then I give to my dau. **Martha H. Gale** 3 negroes **Charlotte** born on Feb. 19, 1805 to serve until she is 32, negro girl **Charity** about 4 years old in early part of Jan. last to serve till she is 32, and a negro boy **Perry** born on Jul 21, 1816 to serve until 35; and to her $800 (without interest) to be raised off the land. I also give her my watch and the seal that was her brother Williams as a family piece to her during her life then to be given to her sons if sons she has at her discretion. I also give her a home in my house while she is single to be kept and accommodated by her brother **Rasin**. To my dau. **Mary Ann Gale** 2 negro girls, a girl **Ede** born Nov. 21, 1803 to serve until 32, also a negro girl **Mariah** Sep. 16, 1806 to serve until she is 32. I give to Mary Ann $800 who is to be taken care of as her sister Martha by her brother Rasin. I confirm to my dau. **Sarah Rasin** the servitude of her woman **Temp** until she is 33 and to be free, **Temp** was born Mar. 30, 1794. I extend the servitude of her man Harry until he is 37, these servitudes are extended to my dau. in lieu of all claims against my property on account of her portion of her uncle **John Hodges** estate. Harry was born Sep. 1, 1796. To my son **Levi H. Gale** a negro boy **Isaac** to serve until he is 32. Isaac was born Feb. 8, 1810. I confirm my gift of man Jesse to my son **James Hodges Gale**. Also I give him all my right in land that he may be entitled to from my son **William Gale** which he would have been entitled to had he lived as his county land for enlisting as a soldier in the Light Draggon under Clinton Wright in the late war with England those titles I give to my son James Hodges Gale. To my housemaid **Charity** a home in my kitchen during her life and $10 per year in addition to the usual accommodation she has been accustomed to receive. My negro man **Sandy**

Liber 10 1816-1827

I will a home in my kitchen during his life with $16 to paid him in addition. I will a home to my negro girl Elizer in my kitchen until she is 30 then free with $6 per year after she is 21 in addition to her usual accommodation. **Elizer** was born Jan. 28, 1810. My boy **Harcules** a home in my kitchen until he is 35 and to receive $10 when he is 25 until he is free in addition to his usual accommodation. Hercules was born July 16, 1804. A home in my kitchen to my man **Emory** until he is 32 and $12 in addition. Emory was born in Apr. 1793 on condition that he take care of his mother **Harriet** and prevent my property being chargeable with any maintenance for her. The woman Harriet I will be free Jan. 1, 1818. The time of servitude on the above Charity, Sandy, Elizer, Hercules, and Emory I give my son **Rasin Gale**, he complying with the stipulations in their favor. Shall **Benjamin** that ran away from me on Apr. 6 last if taken up I will that my administrator sell him and apply the money to my debts. My land in Harrison Co, Kentucky that is in the possession of my brother who acted for me under power of attorney to take a deed from **James Rogers** for me and in a letter from my brother **John Gale** now in my desk that the tract is called the *"Cave Spray"* that the land be sold and applied to my debts. My administrator to confirm my title to a lot of land to **Joseph Parsons** whereon he has begun to put up a house beginning at a posimmon tree and running W towards a stone standing at the W side of an old brick on Mr. **Hepbron's** land running up the line north a parallel line to **Macall Medford's** plank fence E of his lot, Joseph Parsons paying $40 per acre. To my son **Rasin Gale** all my lands in Still Pond during his life only and he paying my debts and legacies to his sisters Martha H. Gale and Mary Ann Gale. After my son Rasin Gale's death then to my son James H. Gale provided that if Rasin has male issue then to such eldest male and then to the eldest male heir of that son.

Exec. my son Rasin Gale. Witnesses John Hepbron, John Moore, George Beck. Written May 18, 1817 Proved Aug. 30, 1817 p. 52

<u>Codicil</u> To expand on the powers of my son Rasin Gale and one of the trustees my brother **Thomas Gale**, he can sell the lot E and NE of Parson's lot and adjoining the old meeting house and any part of my land called *"Redmore's Supply"* being part of a tract formerly belonging to **John Gale** and conveyed to his son **Rasin Gale** my father and by him willed to me, also it being part of a tract now belonging to John Hepbron, then the said brother Thomas Gale one of my trustees named in my will co-jointly with my son Rasin Gale can sell any lots for my debts or legacies. I give the Methodist Society first preference to the lot joining if they provide $60 per acre. Further my son Rasin to take boarding, clothing, and education of my nephew **Francis Cann**. Written May 18, 1817. Witnesses John Hepbron, John Moore, George Beck. My son Rasin Gale my administrator to have $120 per year for the administration of my estate.

Hester Dixon of Kent Co
To my son **John Dixon** a negro man **Jarrel**, a negro child **Maria** and a gun. To my dau. **Caroline Dixon** a negro woman **Cate**, a negro boy **James**, a silver cream cup, 6 silver tea spoons, and $50 and the interest to be paid out of a bond on **Capt. Joseph Mann**.

Abstracts of Kent Co., MD Wills

To my son **George Dixon** a negro girl **Emiline**, a negro boy **Jacob**, a pair of silver tumblers and a silver watch. To my dau. **Louisa Anna Maria Dixon** a negro boy **Washington**, a negro girl **Mary**, 6 silver desert spoons, and $100 with interest to be paid of said bond of Capt. Joseph Mann when she is 16. To my 2 sons John Dixon and George Dixon all the reside of said bond. The remainder of my estate to all my children. The money from the hire of my negroes be used for the support of my children until they arrive of age.

Exec. William Gilbert. Witnesses Samuel G. Osborne, John H. Thomas. Written July 26, 1817 Proved Aug. 30, 1817 p. 61

Barney Corse of Chestertown, Kent Co
To the 3 children of **Thomas Corse** deceased named **Barney Corse, Anna Maria Corse,** and **James Corse** 2 shares in the Union Bank of MD each if they die under age then to survivors. The interest to be used for their maintenance by their mother **Eliza Corse** residing in Pittsburgh, PA. To my servant man **Jim Fray** $50 and all my wearing apparel. To my servant woman **Becky** $50. To the little negro **Jim** the grandson of said Beckey $50. To my son Jesse Corse now residing at Apoquinnick my dwelling plantation on the plot of the town *"Lot No. 26"*. If he dies without issue then to **John Howard, James Howard, Gibson Howard** sons of my relation **John Howard** of Kent Co. The residue of my estate to my son **Jesse Corse.**

Exec. my son Jesse Corse. Witnesses James Houston, James Hodges Jr, Joseph Browne 4th. Written Oct. 9, 1806 Proved Sep. 23, 1817 p. 64

Codicil Whereas Jim Fray has died, I give to my son Jesse the said $50 and my wearing apparel. I give to my son Jesse my lot in Chestertown known as *"Lot No. 80"*. Written July 5, 1817. Witnesses William Harris, James F. Browne, Henry Tilghman.

Philip Davis of Baltimore, mariner
Being bound to sea in the Schooner Montrerrat of said place under my command. To my sister **Sarah Davis** all my property.

Exec. Not Given (implied Sarah Davis) (Philip's sister **Mary Bevins** brought will and acknowledged his signature). Witnesses Hugh Lukes, John Wallace. Written July 7, 1806 (at Baltimore) Proved Oct. 3, 1817 Kent Co p. 67

Nathaniel Boyer of Kent Co
To my sister **Terry Boyer** all my real estate consisting of tract or parts of tracts, the plantation whereon I now live part of *"Rich Level"* which piece I purchased of **Augustine Boyer Jr, Thomas Boyer,** and **Richard Boyer** by deed containing about 108 acres, also one piece in New Castle Co, DE called *"the Ponds"* which I also purchased of Augustine Boyer Jr, Thomas Boyer, and Richard M. Boyer by deed containing about 200 acres, also one piece called the *"Adventure"* adjoining *"Ponds"* containing 50 acres purchased

of the same in New Castle Co, DE, also one other piece in New Castle Co, DE adjoining *"Adventure"* containing 25 acres, *"Heath's Range"* and *"Adventure"* one moiety I own as one of my father's heirs, one moiety I purchased of my brother **Hugh Boyer** and one moiety I purchased of my sister **Rugh Hancock**, also a piece in Kent Co, MD and part in New Castle Co, DE containing 38 acres part of *"Heath's Range"* being part of land which my father **Nathaniel Boyer** late of Kent Co deceased purchased of a **Daniel Charles Heath** and which I got in exchange for other land from my nephew **Frederick Boyer** making in the whole 421 acres. My sister **Ann Martin** shall have a life estate in the house where she now lives on the piece called *"Adventure"*. I give her the house and 3 acres where the house stands during her life. To my niece **Temperance Pell** £475 in 5 years and that she live with my sister free of charge until she marries. To my nephew **Nathaniel Martin** $50 when he is 21. My sister shall find my nephew his board and provide for his necessary English education. I also give my niece Temperance Pell 2 feather beds. Whereas my negro man **Bob** being over 45 so that I cannot free him according to law yet it is my desire that he be able to act as a free man as long as he is not inform he shall have a maintenance out of my estate given to my sister. The bed I sleep on shall be one of the beds for my niece Temperance Pell. My negro men **Cezar, Benjamin, James,** and **Samuel** shall be free at the end of this year and my negro boy **Dennis Spencer** who is 4 to be free at 27. All the residue of my personal estate to my sister **Terry Boyer**.

Exec. my sister Terry Boyer (called **Terisia Boyer** in acknowledgment). Witnesses Ephraim Vansant, George C. Saunders, Nathan Vansant. Written Jan. 8, 1815 Proved Oct. 2, 1817 p. 69

Thomas Edwards

To my dau. **Editha Palmer**, wife of **John Palmer Jr.** my house in Chestertown that I bought of **Edward Palmer** to be under the direction of my 2 sons **Peregrine** and **Emory Edward** for her life. After her death to her 5 children now living. My will is that **Hank, Phill, Henry** and **Mary** shall be free 3 years and all the young negroes to age 28. To my sons Peregrine, Thomas, **Benjamin,** Emory, and **Ourn Edward** all the rest of my estate.

Execs. my 2 sons Peregrine and Emory Edwards. Witnesses John Hurtt, William Browne, John Thomas. Written Jan. 19, 1817 Proved Sep. 22, 1817 p. 73

<u>Codicil</u> Whereas my 3 men **Hark, Phill,** and **Henry** to serve 3 years, now Hark is to serve 4 years, Phill to serve 7 years, and Henry to serve 10 years and my dau. **Editha Palmer** to have $50 each year and share alike with my sons in my personal estate. My granddau. **Mary Palmer** to have my silver spoons but if she dies then to my granddau. **Elizabeth Palmer.** My son Emory shall be sole executor. Written Aug. 13, 1817. Witnesses John Hurtt.

Abstracts of Kent Co., MD Wills

Whereas by the will of Thomas Edwards the intent was to provide Editha Palmer with an equal part of the personal estate of her father, without knowing what portion her part of the estate will be she releases all claim to any part greater than an equal share with the others. Written Sep. 22, 1817 Witness John Hurtt. signed **John Palmer, Editha Palmer.** Acknowledged by George Neal, J.P.

Mary Smith widow of Kent Co

To my great granddau. **Mary Elizabeth Knock** my whole estate after my debts are paid. My grandson in law as guardian to Mary Elizabeth.

Exec. my grandson in law **Jesse Knock**. Witnesses Joseph Mann, Jesse Jerrum. Written Oct. 27, 1811 Proved Nov. 15, 1817 p. 77

Peregrine Ringgold of Kent Co

To my dau. **Sophia Luana Ringgold** all that tract of land which was purchased by my father **(William Ringgold)** of **James Stoops** beginning at a stone marked MR JS in the E line of a tract called *"Huntingfield"* and running to the S extremity of what is called the *"White Marsh"* said thence along the bay shore to the division line between the land **Col. Reed** now possesses and myself by title of part of *"Inheritance"* then with the division line until at the original tract of land called *"Huntingfield"* where a stone is fixed then to the beginning. To my son William Smith Ringgold all that tract called *"E. Tovering Lott"* beginning at a cedar part marked with 8 notches which is the original beginning of *"Tovey's Lot"* and running thence to a hickory tree which stands on the W end of the division line between the land formerly owned by **John Williams** but now by James Ringgold thence to the stone which was set as a boundary between the tract of land called *"Inheritance"* and the beginning of the division line between the land that Col. Reed now possesses and myself. I give to my son **Alexander Hamilton Ringgold** all that tract beginning at the said stone, the division line of Col Reed and myself therewith to Gray Inn Creek then to Bury Cove thence to the reversed line of a tract called *"Prevention of Inconvenience"* to a forked chestnut tree at the *"Wolf Cramp"* then to the E bounds of *"Huntingfield"* thence to the beginning. As I don't have an equal division of the woodland, my will is that Alexander Hamilton Ringgold convey 10 acres to be laid off on the S side of the woodland which I have given him and his sister **Sophia Ringgold** 10 acres to W.S.R. on the N part of Sophia's. In addition to my dau. Sophia Luana Ringgold I give her my negro girl **Rachel** and my negro boy **Charley**. In addition to my son **William S. Ringgold** my negro woman **Poll** and my negro boy **Jim**. In addition to my son Alexander Hamilton Ringgold my negro man **Sam** usually called little Sam and my negro boy **Emory**. To my negro man **Sam** usually called Big Sam his freedom with his tools which he has been accustomed to make use of in his shoe-making business recommending him to preserve the honest character he has always born and thence he may say I am not afraid to die.

Liber 10 1816-1827

Execs. my friend General Walter and Joemark Smith of Georgetown, in D.C. Witnesses None Given (James Ringgold said he know her handwriting). Written 1800 Proved Dec. 16, 1817 p. 79

Codicil My personal estate not mentioned to be divided among my children.

[Page numbers separated here. Page 82 stopped then to page 77 which was crossed out and changed to page 145. It does not appear that any wills are missing however as on the new page 145, the will of Peregrine is continued at the top.]

Harriet Buchanan of Kent Co
To my sisters **Anna Tilden** and **Mary Tilden** all my estate.

Exec. Dr. Charles Tilden. Witnesses Ann Briscoe, Hannah Medford, Ann Yeates. Written Nov. 13, 1815 Proved Dec. 20, 1817 p. 145

Philip Taylor of Kent Co
To my wife **Ann Taylor** a negro boy **Isaac**, a negro girl **Cassa**, my horse and carriage, my trunk and all my wearing apparel. The residue of my personal estate (my negroes excepted) to my wife Ann Taylor and my dau. **Mary Ann Wilmer**. To my wife Ann Taylor ½ of the profits of my estate during her life and the other ½ to my dau. Mary Ann Wilmer, and after my wife's death to have all during her life. After their deaths then to the children of my dau. Mary Ann Wilmer. If she has no heirs then to **William B. Wilmer, James Frisby Brown, Thomas J. James** and **Richard J. Frisby's** eldest son. My negroes to be free at age 31 and they may not be sold nor any hired out of the county except as they may select.

Exec. William B. Wilmer. Witnesses Joseph Mitchell, Richard B. Page, James Wheeler. Written Feb. 21, 1818 Proved Feb. 28, 1818 p. 147

James Hodges of Kent Co
I give all my estate to my son **James Hodges** generally called James Hodges Jr. for his life with remainder to **James Ringgold** and Capt. **Thomas Harris** during his life in trust to preserve the contingent remainders. After my son's death then the real estate to the children of my son with a parent's share for any children dying leaving issue. All my personal estate to the children of my son James Hodges. My son James shall have power to sell any part of estate. My son can change the remainder as designated here. To my dau. **Ann Gale** £100 in one year. To the children of my deceased dau. **Martha Gale** £100 in one year.

Exec. my son James Hodges. Witnesses James Collins Sr., Samuel Wickes, James Collins, Jr. Written Sep. 17, 1816 Proved Feb. 17, 1818 p. 150

Abstracts of Kent Co., MD Wills

Samuel Beck of Kent Co
To my dau. **Sarah Beck** her choice of one of either bed, one negro boy **Edwin** $200, her board and home free at **John Beck's** house until death or marriage. If she chooses to live elsewhere John is to give her £20 per year above what is already given. To my 9 grandchildren, the children of my deceased dau. **Elizabeth Hurtt** namely **Henry Hurtt, Mary Hurtt, Samuel Hurtt, Elizabeth Hurtt, Adah Hurtt, Martha Hurtt, Sarah Hurtt, Reulma Hurtt,** and **James Hurtt** $900 divided between them. To my son **Thomas Beck** $50 and no more. To my son **Samuel Beck** $100 and no more. To my dau. **Adah Vickers** the wife of **Joel Vickers** $1,000, one negro boy **Perry**, one negro girl **Beck**. My negroes **Abraham** and **Moses** to be paid 1½ barrels of corn annually. To my granddau. **Augusta Beck** dau. of **John Beck** and **Sophia Beck** a negro boy **James** and negro girl **Hannah**. To my grandson **Horatio Beck** son of John Beck and Sophia Beck one boy **Emory**. To my grandson **Benjamin Franklin Beck** son of John Beck and Sophia Beck one negro boy **Isaac**. All the residue to my son John Beck.

Exec. my son John Beck. Witnesses John C. Hynson, Howard Kennard, Emory Edwards. Written June 20, 1817 Proved Mar. 28, 1818 p. 154

Isaac Redgrave of Kent Co
Feeling myself in advancing years, to my son **John Redgrave** my wearing apparel, the first choice of one bed and one horse, and a negro girl **Rachel** now in the possession of **Dr. John Maxwell** and £100. To my son **William Redgrave** the residue of my personal estate and the whole of my real estate.

Exec. my son William Redgrave. Witnesses Nathaniel Comegys Jr, Eliza Tilla, George Comegys. Written June 3,1815 Proved Feb. 21, 1818 p. 157

Walter H. Miller of Kent Co
All my real estate to my wife **Sarah Miller** during her widowhood. After her death to my brother **Merritt Miller**. All my personal estate to my wife **Sarah Miller**, except my wearing apparel which I give to my friend **Beckington Scott**. To my aunt **Sarah Hodges** £50 in 6 months.

Exec. my wife Sarah Miller. Witnesses Sarah Miller, Joseph Brown 3rd, Edward B. Tilden. Written 1818 Proved Aug. 7, 1818 p. 158

Codicil My silver watch to be considered part of my wearing apparel.

Caroline S. Browne of Kent Co
To my husband **Morgan Browne** all my estate during his life the remainder to the child I may be blessed with. If I have no children then to my husband. My husband Morgan Browne to be executor and to pay all my debts and the legacies under the will of my mother and no appraisement be made. Also my trustees to make provisions as directed under the will of my mother.

Liber 10 1816-1827

Exec. my husband Morgan Browne. Witnesses Joseph N. Gordon, Samuel Kerr, George W. Thomas. Written Aug. 1, 1818 Proved Sep. 28, 1818 p. 160

Mr. Samuel Copper (nunc.)
Mr. Samuel Copper on his death bed about two hours before his death on Oct. 15, 1818 did declare that his wife was to possess the whole of his estate both real and personal during her life except his negro man **Isaac** to be free in 5 years and after her death to the benefit of his children.

Exec. Not Given. Witnesses Jacob Stephens, James Collins, John K. Ayres, Joseph Sintan. Written Oct. 15, 1818 Proved Nov. 14, 1818 p. 162

Elizabeth Ringgold of Kent Co
All my estate to my 3 sisters **Sarah Ringgold, Rebecca Ringgold,** and **Francis Ringgold**

Execs. my 3 sisters Sarah Ringgold, Rebecca Ringgold, and Francis Ringgold. Witnesses James Ringgold, Sally Blunt, Anna Ringgold. Written Feb. 6, 1811 Proved Dec. 2, 1818 p. 163

Thomas Miller of Kent Co
To my son **Richard** all that parcel of land which I purchased of **Ralph Miller** which is described in a deed of Jul 12, 1797. To my son Richard 10 acres of a lot which I purchased of Araminta Hynson (executrix of Richard Hynson) being part of *"Arcadia"* which is described in a deed of Mar. 8, 1803 to be laid off on the E side of said lot by a line drawn from W to E parallel with the N line. The rest of my real estate to my son Thomas provided that he provide a home for his family to my daughters **Sarah, Juliana,** and **Mary** free from any charge while they are single. If he dies without issue or does not comply then to my son William during his life with same stipulations. If he dies or does not comply then to my heirs. To each of my daughters Sarah, Juliana, and Mary and my son Richard one bed, two pair of sheets, 3 blankets and one bed quilt. All the rest of my personal estate to 6 of my children **William,** Richard, **Martha,** Sarah, Juliana, and Mary.

Exec. my son Thomas. Witnesses John Bradshaw, Joseph Wickes 3rd, Joseph Sintan. Written Mar. 5, 1818 Proved Jan. 16, 1819 p. 165

William Skirven of Farloe, Kent Co
To my wife **Elizabeth Skirven** during her widowhood my farm on Mum Creek [or Shivin Creek] and afterward to my son **Thomas** and **Matilda** my dau. during their lives. My personal estate to my wife and all my children

Execs. my wife and her brother John Jeffries. Witnesses Nicholas Spelman, George D.S. Hands. Written Jan. 1, 1819 Proved Jan. 16, 1819 p. 169

Abstracts of Kent Co., MD Wills

<u>Renunciation</u> I Elizabeth Skirven widow of William quit all claim to bequests in the will of my husband and choose my dower. Written Jan. 20, 1819

James Lamb of Kent Co
To my wife **Charloty Lamb** the full use of my estate during her life and after her death to my nephew **William Lamb**.

Exec. my wife Charloty Lamb. Witnesses Patrick P. Kennard, Samuel Smith, Richard P. Kennard. Written Mar. 9, 1819 Proved Mar. 18, 1819 (Richard came Mar. 20) p. 171

William Brown of Joe of Kent Co
To my wife **Martha Brown** all my estate during her life for the maintenance of her and my children **Joseph Corsey, William, Curtis, Benjamin Osborn, James Glanville, Harriet** and **Martha**. After her death the land to be sold and proceeds divided by trustee **James Ringgold** of Eastern Neck.

Exec. my wife. Witnesses Samuel Wickes, William Scone, Pere Whaland. Written Feb. 17, 1819 Proved Apr. 5, 1819 p. 173

Thomas Smyth of Kent Co
All my real estate lying in Eastern Neck consisting of *"Trumpinton", "Brown's part of Smyth's Meadows", "My own part of Smyth's Meadows", "Smyth's Addition",* and *"Part of Huntingfield"* and of that part of *"Huntingfield"* which I purchased of commissioners to sell the real estate of **William Ringgold** late of Kent Co deceased, also of my land in Langford's Bay Hundred called *"Smyth's wood land"* and adjoining the lands of **Thomas Gresham** and **John Glenn** and others all of which I give to my son **Dr. James Smyth** of Baltimore City, if he pays to my executor £8 10 sh. per acre in two annual payments to be divided among my children, but if my son Dr. James Smyth does not accept this condition then to my son in law **Dr. Thomas Wilson** on same condition. If my son in law does not accept then to my son **William Bedingfield Smyth** on same condition. If none accepts then my executor to sell my estate, reserving the graveyard with free ingress and egress for my descendants. To my dau. **Eliza Nichols** my gold watch which I now wear. To all my sons and daughters and to my grandsons **Edward** and **Henry Tilghman**, a handsome mourning ring, or gold locket whichever they may chose. My executor to pay my daughters Eliza Nichols and **Maria Wilson** £158 12 sh. 6 pence in 15 months due the estate of my deceased son **Henry Smyth** as will appear from my book of accounts of my account against my son James Smyth as will appear in my Ledger C folio 37 shall be considered so much of his portion of my estate already advanced to him and the amount against my dau. Marie Wilson as charged in my Ledger D folio 58 shall be considered so much of her portion of my estate already advanced. My negroes not to be sold out of the State and if convenient not out of the county. My negro woman **Betty** free at my death and my negro man **James Biram** be free and that he have his working tools, according to a list in the back folio of my Ledger E.

Liber 10 1816-1827

Execs. my sons William B. Smyth, James Smyth, my son in law **Dr. Thomas Wilson**. Witnesses William Browne, William Scone, Henry Tilghman. Written Aug. 19, 1818 Proved Apr. 28, 1819 p. 175

Codicil Whereas since the writing of my will my dau. **Eliza Nicols** has died, now I give my gold watch to my dau. **Maria Wilson**. I give all that was given to my daughter Eliza Nicols now to my **Margarett Nicols, Henrietta Nicols, William Nicols, Elizabeth Nicols, Thomas Nicols, James Nicols, Mary Nicols,** and **Sarah Ann Nicols**, the children of my said dau. when they shall be 21 for boys and 16 for girls. Written Not Given

William Salisbury Cooper of Kent Co
To my **Ann Cooper** 1/3 of all my property. My negro man **Charles** and his wife **Sarah** shall until Jan. 1, 1822 then free. My colored man **Jacob** until Jan. 1, 1823 then free. To my only dau. **Ann Massey** wife of **Josiah Massey** all the rest of my estate.

Exec. my daughters husband Josiah Massey. Witnesses William Palmer, Lambert Sappington, Michael Smyth. Written Apr. 29, 1819 Proved Aug. 18, 1819 p. 182

William Skirven of Farloe, Kent Co
To my wife **Elizabeth Skirven** during her widowhood and no longer that my farm on Shivin Creek and after unto my son **Thomas** and **Matilda** (my daughter). All my personal estate to my wife and all my children.

Execs. my beloved wife and her brother **John Jeffries**. Witnesses Nicholas Spelman, George D.S. Handy. Written Jan. 1, 1819 Proved Jan. 16, 1819 p. 185 (Repeated above)

James Arthur of Kent Co
After my wife 1/3 $50 to be kept by my executor for repairs to my dwelling house which I purchased of a certain William Ervine. All the remainder of my estate to my dau. **Sophia Arthur**, and unto my grandson **James Arthur**, the son of **David Arthur**. I give all my real estate unto my wife **Elizabeth Arthur** during her life. All my real estate to my dau. Sophia Arthur for her life that after her marriage to my grandson James Arthur son of David Arthur. If he dies under 21 then to my grandson David Arthur son of David Arthur. If both die then to my heirs at law.

Exec. Henry Tilghman Esq. Witnesses Thomas Davis, Benjamin Greenwood, Joseph Redue. Written Aug. 7, 1819 Proved Oct. 5, 1819 p. 186

Robert Dunn of Kent Co
To my dau. **Ann** all my dwelling plantation where I now live consisting of several tracts of land if my dau. Ann and her husband **Thomas B. Hynson** convey all right to part of the *"Forest Farm"* which the said dau. inherits from her mother unto my dau. Elizabeth and upon failure of issue of Ann then to my dau. **Elizabeth**. My dau. Ann and her

husband are burdened with the funeral charges and to charge my home farm for funeral and debts. My crops are to go with the land and not my personal estate. To my dau. Elizabeth my farm in Broad Neck to her. If she dies without heirs then to my dau. Ann.

The above will was not complete and was scratched out. p. 188

[There is a gap in the wills probated here and the wills that follow are not in strict chronological probate order.]

Isaac Harris of Georgetown and Roads, Kent Co
To my wife **Martha Harris** my dwelling house with 1/3 the lot of ground annexed during her life and all my household furniture. After her death then to my son **George** my dwelling house, and the 1/3 of the lot. To my dau. **Eady** the house in which she now lives, including the ground on which it stands and the small yard around it. The remainder to be sold and to pay each of my daughters **Tempe** and **Hesse** $10 and the balance divided between my sons **Abraham, Harny and Eben**.

Exec. my son Abraham Harris. Witnesses Dr. Edward Scott, Gilbert Chrisfield, Thomas Green. Written June 25, 1821 Proved June 30, 1821 p. 190

James Stavely of Kent Co
To my wife **Elizabeth Stavely** 1/3 of my dwelling plantation during her life and my negro boy **Albert** 10 years old to serve 18 years then free, and the time of service of negro **Matilda**, 3 feather beds, and 1/3 part of my personal property. To my son **James Stavely** all my dwelling plantation to him provided he pays legacies and if not part of my plantation be sold to pay legacies, and to him my negro **Ezekiel** 3 years old to serve 25 years then free, one bed. To my dau. **Ann Staveley** $700 paid by my son James one year after he is of age, also a home at my house free board during the time she is unmarried, also negro **George** 7 years old to serve 21 years, and one feather bed. To my dau. **Asenath** $700 paid by my son James, a home in my house while she is unmarried, a negro **Spence** 3 years old to serve 25 years, and a feather bed. To my dau. **Martha Staveley** $700 paid by my son James, a home in my house while she is single, my negro **Edward** 1 year old to serve 27 years, a feather bed, also negro **Mary** 5 years old to serve 23 years then free. To my son James Stavely and my dau. Ann, Asenath, and Martha Stavely each ¼ remainder of my estate.

Exec. my wife Elizabeth Staveley. Witnesses John Maxwell, William Maxwell, Thomas Gale. Written 1820 Proved Aug. 18, 1820 p. 192

Mary Hands of Kent Co
To my grand niece **Mary Ann Bordley** the dau. of **John Bordley** Esq.

Exec. my grand niece Mary Ann Bordley. Witnesses Anna Maria Hackett, Catharine Hands, Joseph Wickes 4th. Written Aug. 12, 1811 Proved Sep. 26, 1820 p. 194

Liber 10 1816-1827

Codicil To my grand niece **Mary Anne Cummins** late Mary Anne Bordley dau. of the late John Bordley Esq of Worton all that tract in Cecil Co whereon resided my late brother **William Jackson** designated in his will *"Daniel's Den"* and all other real estate which I may possess. Written Feb. 10, 1820. Witnesses Joseph Wickes 4th, Rebecca Tilden, Anne E. Tilden

John Frazier of Kent Co

To my dau. **Emily Frazier** all that part of land I purchased of **William Bryan** to the S and E of the following boundaries beginning at a stone standing in Sandy Bottom on the N side of the main road leading from Bell Air to Fairlee and running thence N 66° E 48 perches, then S 73° E 14 perches, then N 72° E 20 perches then N 41½° E 12 perches then N 19° E 10 perches then NW until it shall intersect the middle of a branch leading into Fairlee Creek then with the drain of said branch to the creek and then with Fairlee Creek as far as my land extends. To my dau. **Harriot Frazier** all that part of tract which I purchased of William Bryan lying N and W of the boundaries above. The deed of William Bryan is dated Jan. 3, 1805 and is recorded in Kent. To my dau. **Araminta Frazier** all that parts of tract I purchased of **Gustavus Hanson, Thomas Granger** and **Arthur Bryan** boundaries can be found by deeds from Gustavus to me, me to Thomas Granger and Thomas Granger to me and Arthur Bryan to me and a 2nd deed from Thomas Granger to me all of which were dated between Jan. 1, 1790 and Jan. 1, 1800 recorded in Kent. To my dau. Araminta Frazier the rest of my real estate. Whereas I have transferred a number of my stock in Union Bank of MD and in the Franklin Bank of Baltimore to my son in law **Alexander Yearly** (husband of my dau. **Ann Yearly**) to help him buy a home in Baltimore and it being agreed upon to return said shares of stock to me and whereas I wish for my dau. Ann Yearly to have $2,500 exclusive of my negroes and I have already given sums totaling $1,300 then I give $2,500 but all sums already given them are included in this total and to be deducted and only if my son in law returns title to me of the bank stocks. If he does not return clear title to me of the stocks then my dau. is to receive no part of the $2,500 and what claim I have against them stands in full force. To my daughters Araminta Frazier, Harriott Frazier and Emily Frazier equal share [does not say share of what]. To my two grandson **John Keatting** and **William Keatting** $1,250 each to be kept in bank stock in Baltimore until age 21. If they die then to my daughters Araminta Frazier, Harriott Frazier, Emily Frazier and Ann Yearly. To my dau. Araminta all the plank shingles and nails which are on my farm and my best riding carriage and one set of plated castors, one set of china, one tea board, 4 waiters, 6 bed quilts, 2 bed spreads, 1 toilet glass, 1 bureau, 6 tea spoons, and 3 negroes **Maria, Perry,** and **Temperance.** To my dau. Harriott Frazier the 3 negroes **Charlotte, William** called **Bill** and **Melissa.** To my dau. Emily Frazier 2 negroes **Clarey** or **Clarissa** and **Caroline.** To my dau. Ann Yearley negro **Rachel.** Whereas I have paid for my son **John Frazier** many large debts which he accounted in various ways and several sums of money which I consider his full portion of my estate then I quit all claims to him if he does not claim any part of my estate. If he charges my estate with any sums then all my claims against him stand in full force and he is to receive no part of my estate and that which is collected to be given my daughters Araminta, Harriott,

Abstracts of Kent Co., MD Wills

Emily and Ann. My negroes free at age 30. The rest of my personal estate to my dau. Araminta Frazier, Harriott Frazier, and Emily Frazier.

Exec. my dau. Araminta Frazier. Witnesses Isaac Cannell, Thomas Wilkins, John B. Eccleston. Written Apr. 28, 1818 Proved Oct. 21, 1820 p. 196

Codicil Whereas I willed to my dau. Ann Yearly the sum of $2,500 and she having received $1,300, I instead now give her the bank stock of Baltimore and the negro Rachel and no more of my estate. Written April 5, 1820 Witnessed Thomas Bordley, Edward Taylor signed John Frazier Sr.

Jacob Lamb of Kent Co

To my mother **Rachel Lamb** all my land called *"Friendship"* and lot called *"Batchelers Resolution"* and a wood lot part of *"Worton Manner"* with all my personal estate during her life. My sister **Hannah Atkinson** to have all said land and personal estate devised to my mother during her life if she pays my sister **Sarah Neals** $600 in 3 annual payments after she comes in possession but if Sarah Neales should die then the $600 to her 2 children **Susannah Yarnel** and **Rebecca L. Yarnel**. My sister Hannah Atkinson pay my brother **John Lamb** $30 per year during her life. Hannah Atkinson pay to my nephew **John Neales** $100 within 2 years and to my niece **Sarah Dawson** $100 in 3 years and to my niece **Eliza Dawson** $100 in 4 years and to my nephew **Isaac Dawson** $100 in 5 years in case of my nieces or nephews of the Dawsons dies then to survivors. At the death of my sister Hannah Atkinson then to my niece **Rachel Atkinson**

Exec. my mother **Rachel Lamb**. Witnesses Thomas Maslin, Jacob Maslin, John Maslin. Written Aug. 13, 1813 Proved Oct. 28, 1820 p. 208

James L. Nowland of Kent Co

To my son **Lambert** $500 and to the children of my late dau. **Harriott** $500 in full consideration of a legacy willed to my son and dau. by their grandfather the late **John Hood** of New Castle Co, DE, but the said negro girl **Nan** or **Nance** which I let my dau. Harriott have with any issue constitute a part of said legacy. To my son **John H. Nowland** all my real estate in Kent Co. The residue of my estate shall be held in trust during the life of my relation **Hester Cook** and the interest shall be paid for her maintenance. After the death of Hester Cook the remainder shall be divided in 5 shares, one share to the children of my late son **Dennis**, one share to the children of my son **James**, one share to the children of my late dau. Harriott, one share to my son John, and my son Lambert one part. The estate to the children of my son Dennis and James and my dau. Harriott remain in the hands of the executor until they come of age but the interest to be paid to their parents or guardians. The interest on the estate to my son John shall be given him during his life and after his death the principal to his children by his first wife. The negroes to be free, **Nat** at 10 years from Jan. 1, 1821, **Phil** in 20 years, **Dos** in 24 years, **Tom** in 20 years, **George** son of **Phillis** in 36 years, **Eneas** in 38 years, **Phillis** in 10 years, **Jenny** in 15 years, **Betty** in 15 years, **Julia** in 17 years, and her

Liber 10 1816-1827

child **Ann**, in 32 years, **Cecilia** in 25 years, **Henry** in 25 years, **George** in 30 years, **Albert** in 32 years, **Maria** dau. of **Phillis** in 30 years.

Exec. my son John H. Nowland. Witnesses James Duyer, William Clow, Edward Scott. Written Oct. 17, 1820 Proved Nov. 11, 1820 p. 209

Mary Duyer of Kent Co
To my dau. **Maria Dorney** my negro girl **Rebecca** 2 years old until she is 29. To my dau. **Rosamond Duyer** my negro girl **Eliza** 22 years to serve until she is 29 and my negro boy **Jacob** 10 years old to serve until 30 and if she dies then to my son **James Duyer** the above boy Jacob and to my son **Phillip Duyer** the negro girl **Eliza**. To my dau. **Susana Watts** my negro girl **Elizabeth** 16 years old to serve until age 29. To my James Duyer my negro boy **Peregrine** 12 years old to serve until age 30. To my son Philip Duyer my negro boy **Samuel** 18 years old to serve at age 30. I set free my negro woman **Temperance** 35 years old. The rest of my estate to my sons **John Duyer, Joseph Duyer**, James Duyer, and Phillip Duyer, and daughters **Maria Derney**, Rosamond Duyer, and Susana Watts

Execs. my son James Duyer and my dau. Rosamond Duyer. Witnesses John Howard, James Beck, Temperance Howard. Written May 6, 1819 Proved Nov. 25, 1820 p. 213

Cassandra Dollis wife of Thomas Dollis of Georgetown, Kent Co
To **George William Wilson** the lot I own in Georgetown in trust for **Alexander Tygart** until he is age 21 and applied to the maintenance of my nephew Alexander Tygart during his nonage. If he dies without issue then to **William George Wilson** son of George William Wilson. To my niece **Cassandra Perce** my carriage.

Exec. (assumed George W. Wilson). Witnesses William Bordley, Juliana C. Bordley, James D. Bordley. Written Nov. 12, 1820 Proved Nov. 15, 1820 p. 215

I Thomas Dollis allow my wife to make said will Nov. 12, 1820. Witnesses the same as above.

James Monat Anderson
To my dau. **Emily Kennard** if single at my decease $500. To my son **Edward** in trust for my dau. **Harriet McLean** as she shall direct for herself or children. My boy **David** free Jan. 1 1826, whichever of my children take care of my old woman **Mammy Grace** shall be entitled to services of boy David until he is free. My negro woman **Molly** and **Suke** shall have a life estate in the ground on which their houses stand on my lots in Chestertown as now fenced off and their heirs to be able to move the houses off said premises within one month after their decease. To **William McLean** bond to me for $380 to my dau. Harriet his wife and **William Harris** bond for the surviving children of my deceased dau. **Maria Harris**. My estate to be sold and divided between my children

James, Harriet, Edward and Emily or their representatives and the surviving children of my deceased dau. Maria Harris in right of their mother's fifth share.

Execs. my sons James and Edward. Witnesses Richard Graves, Nathaniel Kennard, William Graves Jr. Written Jan. 6, 1818 Proved Feb. 8, 1821 p. 217

<u>Codicil</u> To **Susanna Baker** which she has nursed me in all my afflictions $100. Written May 9, 1818 Same 3 witnesses.
<u>2nd Codicil</u> My dau. Emily Kennard may be left without a home now I give my dau. a home in the house in which I now reside for one year and during that time she shall have the privilege of cultivating a garden and raising poultry on the premises. My colored man David shall not be free at 25 but at 30. I give my colored woman Grace $10 annually during her life. Written Nov. 24, 1820 Same 3 witnesses.

Rosamond Duyer of Kent Co
To my eldest sister **Mary Dorney** ½ my personal property. To my other sister **Susanna Watts** the other ½, one pair of sugar tongs excepted which I give to my nephew **Daniel Duyer** son of my brother **John Duyer**. To my brother **James Duyer** ½ my real property. To my brother **Phillip Duyer** the other ½.

Exec. my brother James Duyer. Witnesses John Howard, Edward Crew, Macall M. Rasin. Written Jan. 6, 1821 Proved Jan. 21, 1821 p. 220

Elizabeth Chambers widow of Benjamin Chambers late of Chestertown deceased
To my dau. **Augustine Houston** the widow of the late **Judge Houston**, I give one moiety of my dwelling house and lots of ground attached being the property conveyed to me by **Robert Wright** Esq. and to her my double carriage and pair of horses and a suit of curtains now in the house. To my son **Ezekial F. Chambers** I give a choice by lot of four pieces of old family plate: a coffee pot, tank, can and waiter. To my son **James Chambers** I give a choice by lot of the above plate. To my son **David Chambers** a choice by lot of the plate. To my son **Benjamin L. Chambers** a choice by lot of the plate. These bequests are made as a memorial of maternal regard. To my dau. Elizabeth **Caroline Chambers** the remaining moiety of my dwelling house and one moiety of the land conveyed to me by my late husband being an undivided part of the farm in Worton called the *"Home Farm"*. To my son William **Henry Chambers** the remaining moiety of my said lands in Worton. Whereas my late husband had designed to give to my granddau. **Augusta Houston** a negro child **Harriet** but did not perfect said give I desire my children to cause said negro child to be vested to my granddaughter. To my granddau. **Elizabeth Houston** I give my gold watch the large silver ladle and silver spoons. To my grandson **James Bowers Chambers** I give my small silver ladle. My dau. **Augusta Houston** and my dau. **Elizabeth C. Chambers** and my son **William H. Chambers** and my dau. **Elizabeth C. Chambers** shall be tenants in common. My son **Ezekial F. Chambers** to take profits from estate given to my dau. Elizabeth for the education of my son William and Elizabeth for William until the termination of his

collegiate studies and afterward engage in professional studies. Whereas my son David Chambers has sundry negroes which since his removal to Mississippi he may have conveyed to me in part or whole I claim only as executor of the will of my husband but now I devise to my son Ezekial T. Chambers as surviving executor and to complete as per said will. To my dau. in law **Sarah G. Chambers** a mourning ring as a memorial gift. No appraisement or administration of my estate.

Exec. Not Given. Witnesses Augustine Forman, Thomas Whittington, Joseph R. Walker. Written Dec. 7, 1819 Proved Jan. 1, 1821 p. 222

Bedingfield Hands of Kent Co

To my wife my house lots, my real estate in Chestertown during her life and after I give to my brother **Alexander Hands** and if he dies without issue then said real estate to my sister **Sarah Barroll**. All my negroes to my wife during her life and then to be free. All my plate, my silver handled knives and forks to my brother Alexander Hands as an heirloom. As a testimony to my sister and her son, I give to my nephew **William Barroll** one mourning ring and one breast pin of $20 and $25. To my nephew **William A. Spencer** all my law books and duck gun. To my nephew **Bedingfield Hands Spencer** all my other books and bird gun. The rest of my personal property to my wife.

Exec. Isaac Spencer Esq. Witnesses Walter J. Clayton, Jeremiah Nicols, Henry Tilghman. Written Mar. 3, 1821 Proved Mar. 14, 1821 p. 225

Ann Worrell of Kent Co

My negro man **Richard** be free and my negro man **George** too at the end of the year and my executor to pay $150 each. To my niece **Mary Pearce** I give 3 shares in Union Bank of MD. To my sister **Ann Elizabeth Hyland** all the residue of my property.

Exec. my sister Ann Elizabeth Hyland. Witnesses William Pearce, William A. Spencer, Sarah W. Hyland. Written June 11, 1819 Proved Oct. 21, 1819 p. 226

Henry Page

To be interred according to the Protestant Episcopal Church. My whole estate to my wife **Ann Page** in implicit trust of her prudence

Exec. my wife Ann Page. Witnesses Rebecca Brown, Sarah Miller, William B. Everitt. Written Sep. 20, 1819 Proved May 9, 1821 p. 228

Vincent Hatcheson of Kent Co

To my nephew **Vincent Hatcheson** son of my brother **James Hatcheson** my old negro man **Sam** for 3 years. To my nephew Vincent Hatcheson my negro girl **Millicent** during her life, my duck gun, my saddle and bridle and the balance still due me from my father's estate. My brother James Hatcheson shall have the use of said property until my nephew is at age, except old Sam who is to be free at 3 years. To my sister Mary

Abstracts of Kent Co., MD Wills

Hatcheson my negro boy **Abe** a slave for life but if she dies without issue then to my nephew Vincent Hatcheson. All my wearing apparel to my brother James Hatcheson.

Exec. Not Given. Witnesses Samuel M. Sutton. Written May 1, 1821 Proved May 18, 1821 p. 229

Isaac Elbert free man of color of Kent Co
To my son **Isaac** a lot of ground where I now dwell consisting of part of a tract called *"Hurtt's Lot"* and part of a tract called *"Ward Oak"* and to him the lightest colored of my heifer calves and my silver watch, also one cart, 2 pillows, one feather bed on which his mother now lies after her decease. To my 3 daughters **Ann, Rachel,** and **Elizabeth** a loom and tackle each, they are to take what is now called theirs and all the residue of my personal property to my 3 daughters. My son Isaac to pay for support of my grandson **Isaac** at $5 annually for 4 years and to my dau. Rachel ½ the rent of my house near Travellas Wood (sometimes called College) or if not rented $8 per year.

Execs. my wife **Mary** and my dau. Ann. Witnesses Hugh Wallis, Thomas Brooks, Samuel Rasin. Written Jan. 27, 1818 Proved May 26, 1821 p. 230

Sylvester Nowland of Kent Co
To my wife **Elizabeth Nowland** my plantation where I now live being a tract called *"Adventure"* during her widowhood, and after to her son **John Hawkins Pennington.** To my stepson the said John Hawkins Pennington all that tract of land that I purchased from **John Saunders** called *"Part of the Adventure"* adjoining where I now live. To **John Willson** for the use of his children $100 for their schooling. To **John Carty** my sister's son I give one horse called Rock, a sorrel, and one cow called Closs, a red and white cow, one yoke of oxen that is at **Samuel McCoals.** To my wife Elizabeth Nowland all that part of a tract called *"Dalyes Desire"* all my right and claim to said land. To my wife all the legacy coming to me from the estate of **Thomas Nowland** that I hiered by my brother **Jesse Nowland.** To my wife Elizabeth all the residue of the stock of horses, cattle, sheep, and hogs, and the farming utensils, and household furniture for her widowhood and after her decease to go to John H. Pennington. To my wife a colored man **Philip** for her life and after to John H. Pennington. The horse called Backus to be sold and the balance due **Elizabeth Hesse** be paid

Exec. Not Given. Witnesses Solomon Wood, Solomon Semans, William Kirton. Written Apr. 20, 1821 Proved May 29, 1821 p. 231

Sarah Harragan (nunc.)
After my debts and those of my sisters are paid I leave my property to **Martha Brice, Mary Brice, Tamasina Glann,** and **Ann Brice** dau. of **Henrietta Brice.** Thomas Hynson shall take charge of Ann Brice's part. My aunts **Susanna, Sarah** and **Ann Brice** all my mother's clothes.

Liber 10 1816-1827

Exec. Thomas Hynson. Witnesses None Given. Written Not Dated Proved Apr. 19, 1820 p. 233

George W. Thomas did on Mar. 13 last go into her room at the house of **Richard Brice** in Chestertown where she had been confined by severe disposition and took this draft of her will and left intending to make a formal will however on Apr. 2nd instant she became suddenly more ill and died.

Robert Dunn of Kent Co

To my dau. **Ann** all my home farm or dwelling plantation on which I now live consisting of several parts of tracts of land on the condition that my dau. Ann and her husband **Thomas B. Hynson** shall convey all her interest in the *"Forrest farm"* which she inherited from her mother unto my dau. Elizabeth within 9 months. My dau. Ann or her husband to pay my funeral and I burden my home farm. My crops growing shall go with the land and not be part of my personal estate. To my dau. Elizabeth my farm lying in Broad Neck but if she dies without issue then to my dau. Ann. To my dau. Ann the personal property that is my negroes **James** or **Jim**, **Nathan** or **Nace**, **Bill** son of **Dinah**, **Bill** son of **Hannah**, **Tom** son of **Rose**, **Hannah**, let with her children, **Lydia**, **Rachel**, and **Maria**, the piano forte, my wardrobe, clock, two of the high post bedstead, carpet in the hall, hearth rug, billows and brush, and large brass andirons also used in the hall, large gilt frame looking glass, the 12 red chairs, the window curtains of my house, silver tankard marked R.A.D., 6 large silver table spoons marked R.A.D., 12 new tea silver spoons, the cocoa nut shell sugar dish, all my china and earthen ware, ½ the table linen sheets and ½ the kitchen furniture, ½ the barrels hogsheads and powdering tubs, my bay mare, the mare called Silver heels, the mare called Lady legs, and the horse called Sweeper, the old yoke of oxen, the cart which has new wheels, the choice of 6 milch cows, ½ the yearlings, 12 sheep, ½ the hogs and ½ the remainder of the farming utensils, all the debts due me on book bond, also a pair of mahogany dining tables. My book to my daughters Ann and Elizabeth. All the rest of my estate to my dau. Elizabeth (except the following legacies to my grandson **Robert D. Hynson** and to **William Caton**. To my grandson Robert D. Hynson my shaving box and all it contains my sword, my silver watch, my cabinet and all its contains except the title papers of the land. To William Caton my bay horse called Farmer. No division of my personal estate on my farm, until the end of the year for the benefit of my dau. Ann. If they do not convey the *"Forrest farm"* above then my estate to be settled as if I made no will and give my home farm to my daughters Elizabeth and Ann and pay my legacies to my grandson Robert D. Hynson and William Caton.

Exec. my son in law Thomas B. Hynson. Witnesses Henry Page, Thomas Price, George Collins. Written Apr. 5, 1819 Proved Oct. 30, 1819 p. 234

<u>Codicil</u> My growing crops to my dau. **Mary** to be used to pay my debts, are to include all crops whether gathered, secured, stacked of housed. Written Aug. 8, 1819. Witnesses Matthew Tilghman, Isaac Caulk, Ezekial T. Chambers

Abstracts of Kent Co., MD Wills

Banks Wakeman of Mississippi, physician lately resident of MD
To my wife **Araminta** all my property in MD or Mississippi

Exec. my wife Araminta. Witnesses Gideon Pearce, Matthew Tilghman, J. Randolph. Written Feb. 13, 1819 Proved July 21, 1821 p. 240

John Rutter of Kent Co
All my property to my 3 children **Mary, John** and **Francis**. If any die without issue then their part to the survivors. My wife **Elizabeth** shall have my young horse called ball horse and my Gig above the 1/3 dower. My children to be kept in school and the boys put to trades. **William Moffett** guardian to my children.

Execs. my wife and William Moffett. Witnesses Richard Hall, Jonathan Crockett, Moses Tennant. Written Apr. 24, 1821 Proved Aug. 4, 1821 p. 241

Renunciation I being left executrix do relinquish to Mr. **Thomas Wilson** to be administrator. Written Aug. 3, 1821. Eliza Rutter.
Renunciation Being informed by Mrs. Rutter that the Orphans court is to meet for purpose of granting letters of administration on the personal estate of the late Mr. John Rutter of Kent Co, deceased I do hereby renounce to **Capt. Thomas Wilson**. signed William Moffett. Witness C. Hall Esq.

Rachel Lamb of Kent Co
To my dau. **Hannah Atkinson** one bed and furniture set or 6 siling chairs, one bureau, and £50. To my dau. **Sarah Needles** $50. To my grandsons **John Needles** $50. To my granddau. **Sarah Dawson** one bed and furniture, corn pleat, one cow, one chest, £50 but if she dies then to her 2 youngest sisters. To my son **John Lamb** one horse worth £20. To my granddau. **Eliza Dawson** all my plate, one but bed, 2 suits of furniture, stead and curtains, one cow, one bureau, one walnut chest, and £100 and if she dies then to be divided between her two youngest sisters and brother **Isaac Dawson, Susanna Dawson,** and **Rebecca Dawson.** To my granddau. **Rachel Atkinson** $50 when she is of age. To my son **Jacob Lamb** all the remainder of my estate.

Exec. my son Jacob Lamb. Witnesses William Trew, Bartus Trew (Quaker), Rebecca Trew. Written 4th mo. 10, 1813 Proved Sep. 1, 1821 p. 243

Rebecca Corse of Kent Co
To my niece **Mary Flaharty** dau. of my deceased brother **Michael Flaharty,** all my estate. No inventory should be made.

Exec. my niece Mary Flaharty. Witnesses James M. Anderson Jr, Unit Angier. Written Aug. 7, 1817 Proved Oct. 6, 1821 p. 245

Liber 10 1816-1827

William Smith of Kent Co
To my wife **Hannah Smith** during her life my plantation on which I now dwell with the balance after the settlement of my personal estate but she will give support to my children. After the death of my wife, my plantation to be sold and $100 to my dau. **Augusta**, and the balance to all my other children equally divided. To my wife my negro man **Thomas** to serve until Jan. 1, 1827.

Exec. my wife Hannah Smith. Witnesses Sally Ringgold, Ann Elizabeth Nicholson, Benjamin B. Wroth. Written June 1821 Proved Aug. 13, 1821 p. 246

Milcha Ross of Kent Co
To my grandson **William Thomas Atkinson** all my estate, but if he dies under 21 then to my nephew **Henry Urie** and my niece **Martha Scoone**

Exec. my nephew Henry Urie. Witnesses Thomas Hynson, Isaiah Ashley, Elijah Beck. Written Nov. 1817 Proved Oct. 18, 1821 p. 247

Mary Kendal of Kent Co
To my sister **Ann Simmonds** wife of **Samuel Simmonds** all my wearing apparel. To negro **Thomas** formerly the property of Samuel Simmonds £15. To negro **Richard** the property of my sister **Martha Kennard** late deceased £3 per year during life. To negro **James** formerly the property my above said sister the debt that **James Buchanan** owes my sister Martha Kennard's estate. The remainder of my estate be sold and applied to the purchase and freeing my brother **William Kennedy's** negro **Perry** and **Beck,** if they are not freed then the interest to be paid unto Perry and Beck during life.

Exec. Titus Maslin. Witnesses Thomas Baker, Joseph Simmonds. Written Nov. 4, 1809 Proved Oct. 20, 1820 p. 248

George Greenwood of Kent Co
To my brother **William Greenwood** $40. To my brother **Jonathan Greenwood** $40. To my niece **Elizabeth Lee** $10. To my niece **Mary Rush** $10. To my nephew **Thomas Rush** $10 to be paid him at 21. To my nephew **John Greenwood** one large walnut dining table and $50 at age 20. To my brother **James Greenwood** all my estate but if he dies then to my brother William Greenwood's son **John Greenwood.**

Exec. my brother James Greenwood. Witnesses Nathaniel Sappington, William Meeks, William Welch. Written Oct. 29, 1821 Proved Nov. 17, 1821 p. 249

Susanna Brice of Kent Co
To **Mary Aris** (sic) dau. of my sister **Elizabeth Airs** 1/5 part of my estate during her life and after her death to her son **Richard Thomas Airs.** To my 2 nieces **Sarah** and **Ann Harrigan** daughters of my sister **Mary Harrigan** 1/5 part of my estate. To my 2 nieces **Mary** and **Martha Brice** daughters of my brother **John Brice** 1/5 part of my

estate. To my niece **Henrietta Brice** dau. of my sister **Ann Brice** 1/5 part of my estate. To the 3 daughters of my nephew **Richard Airs** 1/5 part of my estate. To my 2 sisters **Ann** and **Sarah Brice** one spice mortar during their life after their death to **Sarah Harrigan** for it to be continued in my family forever. My man **Isaac** shall have as much of my land as will build him a small house and garden and as much wood or timber as will make him a small house. If he is unable to support himself then to be maintained jointly by those to whom I have devised my estate.

Execs. Sarah Harragan and Mary Brice. Witnesses Thomas Hynson, Charlotte Hynson, James Eagle 3rd, Lavinia E. Hynson. Written Oct. 21, 1815 Proved Nov. 28, 1821 p. 251

Peter Jones of Chestertown
To my son **John** my silver watch with 2 gold seals when he shall be 22. **Hannah Jones** my wife all my estate during her life and at her decease that my property be divided between my children **Nancy, George, James, Eliza,** and **John**.

Exec. my wife Hannah Jones. Witnesses James Harris, James Duddell, Samuel W. Canady. Written Not Given Proved Jan. 16, 1822 p. 253

Thomas Corse of Kent Co
To **Samuel Kerr** all my right of the *"Forrest farm"* and in case **Unit** and **James Corse** my brothers shall not relinquish their right to *"Forrest farm"* then Samuel to have 1/3 of my estate. To my brother Unit Corse my farm on Morgans Creek. To my brother James Corse all my personal estate and my negro **Isaac** shall serve until he is 30. Negro **Rebecca** to serve until she is 25. Negro **Levi** to serve until he is 40. Negro **Susan** to serve until she is 21. Negro **Dark** to serve until she is 20. Negro boy **Robert** to serve until he is 21. All the above negroes to my brother James Corse. I also give to Samuel Kerr my negro man **Phil** whom has now run away provided he ever gets him. Samuel Kerr, Unit Corse, and James Corse to pay my debts equally.

Exec. Samuel Kerr. Witnesses Rasin Gale, Richard Swift. Written Dec. 27, 1821 Proved Jan. 9, 1822 p. 254

Thomas Dollis of Kent co
To **Thomas Dollis Hurtt** (son of **Edward Hurtt**) all my estate. If he dies without issue then to **Wayne Anthony** (son of **John Anthony**)

Exec. John Anthony (or if he dies then Henry Hurtt). Witnesses Robert B. Pennington, John Ireland, Lambert M. Sewell. Written Jan. 10, 1822 Proved Jan. 29, 1822 p. 256

Renunciation I relinquish right as executor. Written Jan. 11, 1822 Witness Lambert M. Sewell signed John Anthony

Renunciation I relinquish right as executor to Edward Hurtt. Written Jan. 15, 1822 Witness G. W. Wilson Signed Henry Hurtt

Rachel Vickers of Kent Co
To my son **David Vickers** ½ of the land that I took up being about 16 ¼ acres. To my dau. **Elizabeth Vickers** all the rest of my estate. **Harriett** to serve 2 years, **Emeline** to serve 4 years from May last, **Pere** to serve 9 years from May last, **Artur** to serve 12 years from May last, **Charles** to serve 22 years from Mar. last, **Richard** to serve 22 years from Mar. last, **Minty** to serve 24 years, **Frank** to serve 27 years.

Exec. Not Given. Witnesses John Hurtt, John Adkinson/Atkinson, Margarett Hurtt. Written Aug. 2, 1820 Proved Feb. 5, 1822 p. 257

Edward Light (colored man) of Kent Co
To my dau. **Rebecca Trusty** the lot I bought at sheriff's sale which was deeded to me by Cuthbert Hall Esq. on May 9, 1806 being part of tract called *"Broad Oak"* situated near Georgetown Crossroads. She is to sell the land and divide proceeds between my children. If Rebecca dies then to my next legal heir to be sold and divided among all my children.

Exec. my dau. Rebecca Trusty. Witnesses John C. McGregor, James Malony, John Willis, James Watts. Written Dec. 20, 1816 Proved Feb. 15, 1822 p. 258

[Someone marked through one occurrence of Light and wrote **Lamb** as last name]

James Brooke of Kent Co
To my children **Mary Hester Brooke, Elizabeth Ann Brooke,** and **Henrietta Eleanor Brooke** all my estate. To my wife Mary Ann above her 1/3 two female slaves to be chosen by her. My wife to be guardian to my children. If I recover from my sickness then my will is of no effect.

Exec. my friend Dr. George W. Thomas of Chestertown. Witnesses Jonathan Harris, William R. Stuart, Ezekiel T. Chambers. Written Dec. 21, 1821 Proved Feb. 26, 1822 p. 260

Nathaniel Sappington of Kent Co
My wife **Ruthey** shall have negroes **Vilette, Pat** and **Minty**. My son **William Sappington** shall have negroes **Benjamin, Pere,** and **Harriett**. My dau. **Susan Sappington** shall have negroes **Eben, Bill, Betsy,** and **Mary**. My friend **Charles Willie** of Baltimore to be guardian to my dau. Susan until she arrives at maturity. To my friend **John Turner** the grandson of **James Duncan** of Kent Co deceased shall be my executor. In consideration of the servitude of the negroes given to my children William and Susan Sappington I request negroes to serve until age 40.

Abstracts of Kent Co., MD Wills

Exec. my friend John Turner. Witnesses John Howard, Thomas Wilson. Written Feb. 11, 1822 Proved Feb. 19, 1822 p. 261

William Spencer of Kent Co
To my brother **Isaac Spencer** all my estate on condition that after my debts are paid he is to take the value of my estate and then add the number of his own children then living with the 2 sons of my lamented brother **Jervis Spencer**, **George** and **William Spencer**, and **William Knight** son of my niece **Charlotte Ringgold Knight** to be given a share that would make them divided equally when **George Spencer, William Spencer** and **William Knight** arrive at 21. If any die before 21 then he does not have to give their part. He then is able to give all my estate to whomever he sees proper but I do not enjoin it upon him to give his son Isaac Spencer and to his eldest male heir with a request that he act a kindly brother to his brothers and sisters. My sister Charlotte Ringgold if agreeable to her to have a residence on my estate during her life with one or two own servants to attend her free of charges of diet or fuel, she having ample funds for her clothing. My estate not to be sold as my debts should be paid from my property by 1823 and none of my negroes be sold out of the state except for gross misconduct. As I have sold land that deeds have not been made then I give my brother Isaac Spencer the power to convey said deeds.

Exec. my brother Isaac Spencer (or if he dies then my nephew Isaac Spencer). Witnesses Nathaniel Comegys, John M. Comegys, Ann Nicholson. Written Mar. 3, 1822 Proved Mar. 22, 1822 p. 263

Welthy Ann Fields of Kent Co
To my son **John Fields** a negro boy **Isaac**, my desk, and my corner cupboard. To my dau. **Mary Merritt** all my wearing apparel. To my son **James Fields** the $50 to be settled for between my son John Fields and my son James Fields. To my son **William Fields** Jesse Clark's note to me for $100 and one bed. To my dau. **Hannah Fields** one negro woman **Rose** and her child **Fillis** and my riding carriage. To my granddau. **Juliana Fields** one negro girl **Susan**, and one bed. To my granddau. **Mary Ann Fields** one negro boy **David**. To my granddau. **Martha Ann Fields** one negro boy **Henry**. To my granddau. **Araminta S. Merritt** one negro girl **Luicia**. My negro boy **Adam** shall be free Jan. 1, 1835 but his wages until then to be divided between my dau. Hannah Fields and my son John Fields and my granddau. Julianna Fields and my grandson **William Merritt Fields** and my son William Fields

Exec. my dau. Hannah Fields. Witnesses Edward Wright Esq., James Jones. Written Aug. 11, 1821 Proved Mar. 21, 1822 p. 265

Patrick Parks Kennard of Kent Co
To my sister **Rachel Tolson** 2/3 of my plantation where I now dwell called *"Denby"* and the other 1/3 to my sister **Sarah Everitt**. To **Andrew Tolson** in trust all that part of land I bought of **Edward Wilkins** then sheriff of Kent Co called *"Worton Manner"* recorded

Liber 10 1816-1827

in Kent Co for the sole use of my sister **Jane Ricketts** and her children. To my sister Sarah Everitt and Rachel Tolson all my personal estate.

Exec. Andrew Tolson. Witnesses Morgan Browne, Peregrine Wroth, Samuel G. Kennard. Written Feb. 14, 1822 Proved Apr. 22, 1822 p. 267

Luke Howard Jr. of Kent Co
To my wife my land during her widowhood with remainder to my son **Bazzel Wells Howard**. To my 2 sons **William** and **Risdon** my negro woman **Mill** and her 3 children **Philip, Saul,** and **Harriet** and their increase when my youngest son Risdon shall be 21 and in case of death to the survivor. My 2 sons William and Risdon shall be paid $80 each when 21. To my son **James Eagle** my black boy **Perry** now 7 to serve till 40. To my wife and youngest son Bazzel Walls negro **Ben** now 23, negro **Wilson** now 12, negro **Lewis** now 4, each to serve till 40.

Execs. my brother **William Howard** and my wife. Witnesses Edward Hurtt, Benjamin Merritt, George Spry. Written Apr. 15, 1822 Proved June 17, 1822 p. 268

Renunciation I **Rebecca Howard** widow of Luke Howard Jr renounce any claim made to me by the will of my husband and elect my dower. Written June 12, 1822

John Wethered a citizen of the USA residing in Baltimore
To my wife **Mary Wethered** during her life the interest the property hereinafter named for the purpose of affording to my wife and unmarried daughters **Mary, Sarah** and **Caroline Wethered** a comfortable support. I have advanced to my married daughters **Catherine Ludlow, Matilda Taffrey** and **Harriet Shubrick** to be considered part of my estate. I have $7,847.09 in the 6% stock. I have **Peregrine Wethered's** obligation for $4,000 with **Lewin Wethered** security. I have Samuel Wethered's obligation for $8,000 with Peregrine Wethered's security for the same. I have **William Heverin's** judgment bond for $3,000. I intend this property for the support of my wife and 3 unmarried daughters if my daughters maintain their affectionate conduct to their mother. After her death, one gunia to Peregrine Wethered, **Samuel Wethered,** Lewin Wethered each when demanded by my sons. The final disposition of my property to my daughters well knowing that their brothers would not take any part of my property as they are perfectly independent greatly by their own industry and good management of what I gave them at the commencement of business, I will to my daughters Sarah Wethered, Catherine Ludlow, Matilda Taffrey, Harriet Shubrick and Caroline Wethered of the aforesaid bank stock. If any try to sell their part it is void. If they marry against their mother's wishes then to be cut off. When their mother dies then she cannot marry without her brothers' consent then to be cut off. My guarded and cautious fondness for my daughters arises from my observation through a long life having frequently seen changes from comfort of life to poverty. To my wife **Mary Wethered** all my household furniture. I gave my sons Samuel and Lewin equal help but after they separated in trade, I gave Samuel negroes, horsekind one cost me $150 and $10 additional and also negro **Nelly** a valuable

Abstracts of Kent Co., MD Wills

young woman all this I give him, he surrendering a small note of mine which I gave to another person and is either lost or not handed to me this I mention in case of my son Samuel's death well knowing that he would rather give then receive from my estate. I wish my children to abide by my will and without administration but if necessary to take letters then to name one of my sons and the other two to be bondsmen. They all know my opinion is never to be bound for any man or woman but as this is obliging my whole family I hope they will excuse it, I appoint my son Lewin Wethered my trustee

Exec. my son Lewin Wethered (trustee). Witnesses Evan Poultney, Philip Poultney. Written Nov. 6, 1820 Proved June 17, 1822 (June 3 came Samuel Sutton) p. 270

Codicil Whereas I have willed to my daughters who are married $1,000 less than my 3 unmarried daughters, her child in the event of the death of their parent to receive an equal annuity. My estate in bonds (except that willed to wall in my family grave yard) shall be equal for my 6 daughters. Written Jan. 19, 1822 Witness Samuel M. Sutton

Ann Taylor of Kent Co
To negress **Minta Freeman** her child **Cassa** to serve until 25. To my only child **Mary Ann Wilmer** I give all my property except my negro boy **Isaac** now 14 to serve until Dec. 31, 1833.

Exec. **William B. Wilmer** my son in law. Witnesses Joseph T. Mitchell, Isabella Hynson. Written Sep. 14, 1821 Proved Aug. 7, 1822 p. 275

Thomas Anderson of Chestertown, Kent Co
To my wife **Bathsheba Anderson** all my estate and to make as little trouble I have made statements thereof on the books of Thomas Anderson and Company and those of Thomas and **Robert Anderson** and will show all my old debts are settled and the claims for legacies due by virtue of the will of my brother Robert Anderson on last ledger p. 494 in which the account of my brother **George Anderson** if fully stated. No inventory of my estate.

Exec. my wife Bathsheba Anderson. Witnesses St. Leger Meeks, James Claypoole, James Houston. Written Dec. 12, 1815 Proved Aug. 23, 1822 p. 276

Ann Bagwell of Kent Co
To my two daughters **Ann Bowen** and **Rebecca Bagwell** all my personal estate equally except $100 to my dau. Ann Bowen, $200 to my dau. Rebecca Bagwell and $200 to my son **Richard Bagwell** to be paid to them out of a legacy devised to me by my brother **John Allen**, deceased, the amount of $500 which is still due to me. Also a legacy of $500 devised to me by my nephew **Mordecai Allen** deceased to be divided between my 3 children

Liber 10 1816-1827

Exec. **Levi Bowen** the husband of my dau. **Ann Bowen**. Witnesses Mary Everitt, Lambert M. Sewell, Purnell F. Smith. Written Apr. 15, 1822 Proved Sep. 2, 1822 p. 277

Michael Glenn of Kent Co
To **Ann Kendall** dau. of **Thomas Kendall** $30. To **Tamasina Glenn** and **Harriott Glenn** the remainder of my estate. To **Elizabeth Worton** $20 a year paid out of estate given Tamasina Glenn and Harriott Glenn

Exec. Thomas Hynson. Witnesses John Glenn, Thomas Crouch, Charles R. Hynson. Written Sep. 1822 Proved Oct. 9, 1822 p. 279

John C. Hynson of Kent Co
To my wife **Martha Hynson** all my dwelling plantation on which I now live also 20 acres of woodland in Skinners Neck (or Chestnut Neck) and all my personal estate so long as she remains my widow and to educate and bring up my children. To my son **John Carvill Hynson** all the real property devised to my wife after her death or marriage, or in case of her death after my youngest child **Laura Hynson** comes of age 16 and be kept together until my child **Laura Lavinia Hynson** comes of age and equal distribution to my 4 daughters **Martha Henrietta, Sarah Ann, Harriott Matilda,** and **Laura Lavinia Hynson** of my personal property, my son John Carvill Hynson becomes possessed of the property devised to him he paying $20 to each of his full sisters as long as they remain single. To my dau. **Eliza Rebecca Brivitt** 26 acres of land for which a deed is already given having prevented her property from being sacrificed and being amply provided for I give her $1.

Exec. my wife **Martha Hynson**. Witnesses **Thomas Hynson, Nicholas Spelman, Charles R. Hynson.** Written Sep. 7, 1822 Proved Sep. 21, 1822 p. 281

Jesse Gilbert of Kent Co
To my son **George E. Gilbert** all my estate reserving to my wife **Eliza Gilbert** her right of dower. If my son dies without heirs and before he is of age then to **Ann Thompson, Warner Gilbert, William Gilbert, Thomas C. Gilbert, Caroline J. Gilbert, Thomas Greenwood, Sarah Greenwood, Ann Greenwood,** and **John Greenwood,** giving my executor the power to sell my land if my son dies.

Exec. William Gilbert. Witnesses Thomas J. Harris, Thomas Newcomb, William Wallis. Written Dec. 20, 1821 Proved Nov. 11, 1822 p. 282

William Scott of Chestertown
To my sisters **Ann** and **Kitty Scott** all my estate

Exec. my sister Ann Scott. Witnesses Edward Scott, Thomas Sutton, Alexander C. Cosden. Written Nov. 28, 1822 Proved Dec. 7, 1822 p. 284

Mary Haynes of Kent Co
To my brother **George Haynes** the whole of my estate if he pays unto his brother **Gideon Haynes** $200. All my clothing to **Caroline Kennard, Martha Kennard** and **Mary Kennard**.

Exec. my brother **George Haynes**. Witnesses Philip Brooks, Macall M. Rasin. Written May 24, 1822 Proved Dec. 10, 1822 p. 285

Samuel Smyth of MD
To **Richard Smith** my son all the land I own, except one acre at the cross roads that reserved acre to my dau. **Sarah Smith** and to my dau. **Rachel Smith** a mulatto slave Jean and her increase as they arrive to be women. My wife to possess the land willed to my son Richard during her widowhood and all my movables at the death of Mary Smith my wife to be divided between my 2 daughters Rachel and Sarah Smyth. [On back states, the property to daughters to go to survivor if one dies.]

Exec. Not Given. Witnesses Samuel Beck Jr., Simon Smyth, James Philips. Written Dec. 6, 1794 Proved Jan. 17, 1823 p. 285

Luke Howard of Kent Co
To my dau. **Permilia** a negro boy **Shade** and negro girl **Fanny** and her choice of bed and the black mare and carriage. To my son **William Howard** a black boy **John** and one **Ellick**. To my granddau. **Elizabeth Howard** a black boy **Luis**. To my grandson **James E. Howard** a black boy **Pery Washington**. To my grandson **Basil W. Howard** a black boy **Jacob**. To my grandson **James E. Howard** after he arrives at 24 the farm that I now live on called *"Decent Changlers"* and *"Riding Addition"*. To my dau. **Anny Smith** $80 paid by my son William at 4 annual payments. To my son William my farm lying between **William Maxwell** and **Rebecca Lambs**, and the farm that I now live on until my grandson James E. Howard arrives to age 24 this to raise my grandson. If any of my children present an account against me to be deducted of their legacy.

Exec. my son **William Howard**. Witnesses Philip Crane, William Crew, William Holdson. Written Aug. 3, 1822 Proved Jan. 22, 1823 p. 287

Rebecca Duyer of Kent Co
To my brother **George B. Duyer** $100 as soon as it can be collected. To my mother **Elizabeth Greenwood** the remainder of my whole estate during her life and after her death $100 to my brother **John Duyer** and the balance to my 2 sisters **Mary Ann Greenwood** and **Sarah Emeline Greenwood**. If either sister dies then to survivor.

Exec. my friend Joseph Greenwood. Witnesses Wilson Stavely, Mary Ann Greenwood. Written Sep. 22, 1822 Proved Mar. 4, 1823 p. 289

Liber 10 1816-1827

Elizabeth Comegys of Kent Co
The negroes to be free, **Perry** on Dec. 31, 1821, **Minty** on Dec. 31, 1820, **Emory** on Dec. 31, 1827, **Charlotte** on Dec. 31, 1821, **Simon** on Dec. 31, 28, **Maria** on Dec. 31, 1821, **James** on Dec. 31, 1829. To my dau. **Anna Elizabeth Garnett** my house and lot in Chestertown likewise $1,000. To my granddau. **Anna Elizabeth Garnett** $1,000. To my dau. **Emeline Comegys** $2,000 and the residue of all my estate.

Exec. Not Given. Witnesses William McClean, Unit Chandler, Ann Maria McClean. Written Sep. 1, 1819 Proved Mar. 3, 1823 p. 290

Frederick G. Briscoe of Kent Co
To **Thomas W. Boyer** son (**Frederick Boyer**) ½ all my estate and the remaining to **George W. Wise** son of **William Wise**. I appoint **Frederick Boyer**, William Wise and **George C. Sanders** to be executors.
I give to my brother **William H. Briscoe** $100 also to be paid to **Thomas R. Cooper** $100

Execs. Frederick Boyer, William Wise and George C. Sanders. Witnesses George C. Sanders, John Colwell, James Robinson. Written Jan. 2, 1823 Proved Mar. 4, 1823 p. 291

Jonathan Winters (nunc.)
We were at the house of Mr. Jonathan Winters heard him declare that he desired his wife should have the whole of his property and having considerable conversation with Mr. **Joseph T. Mitchell** relative to his business. The said Jonathan Winters died the next evening about 8 o'clock.

Exec. Not Given. Witnesses Joseph T. Mitchell, Jeremiah Blanch, John Redgrave. Written Feb. 24, 1823 8 o'clock Proved Feb. 27, 1823 p. 293

Ann Massy of Wilmington Borough, New Castle Co, DE
To my niece **Ann E. Massy** the dau. of my sister **Sarah Massy** $1,000 until she arrives at 21. To my 2 nephews **Phillip Lewis** and **George Reynolds Massy** $1,000 each. To **Elizabeth Falconar** dau. of **Sarah Falconar** all the rents of ½ part of a house and lot in Sharp Street in Baltimore during her life and at her death to my sister Sarah Massy. If they dispose of the same the interest to Elizabeth during her life and after to my sister Sarah. All the rest of my estate to my sister Sarah

Exec. my sister Sarah. Witnesses Nicholas G. Williamson Esq, Jacob Crawford. Written Oct. 11, 1821 Proved Mar. 17, 1823 New Castle Co (copy by Evan H. Thomas Reg.) p. 294

Abstracts of Kent Co., MD Wills

Benjamin Howard Sr. of Cecil Co, farmer
To my son **John Howard** whom I make executor all my lands to take care of during his life. My son John after my estate is settled and to draw yearly ½ the profits from my land. To my dau. **Anne Danelly** after my estate is settled to have ½ the profits. After my sons death to his children. After the death of my dau. Anne Danelly her half to her children. (called Benjamin Howard late of New Castle Co, DE)

Exec. my son John Howard. Witnesses James Bevins, William Stavely, James Smith. Written Aug. 25, 1821 Proved May 2, 1823 p. 296

Joseph Browne 4th of Kent Co
All my real estate in Kent being part of a tract called *"Gresham's Collage"* which formerly belonged to **John Frisby** deceased unto my brother **Morgan Browne** and **Henry Tilghman** of Kent Co, in trust to sell the estate. After paying my debts remainder to such persons who may be my heirs.

Exec. my brother Morgan Browne. Witnesses Richard Ringgold, John B. Hackett, James F. Browne. Written May 5, 1823 Proved May 12, 1823 p. 298

Mary Smith of Cecil Co
To my niece **Sarah Elizabeth Smith** my silver cream cup. To my niece **Mary Ann Smith** my bureau. To my niece **Emily Smith** my bed quilt. To my 5 nieces Emily Smith, Mary Ann Smith, **Araminta Smith,** Sarah Elizabeth Smith and **Harriett Smith** the residue of my estate when they arrive at 18 or marriage.

Exec. my friend Elizabeth Johns of Kent Co, DE. Witnesses Peregrine Biddle, George Biddle. Written Mar. 24, 1823 Proved June 25, 1823 p. 299

Renunciation I was appointed administer on the estate of Mary Smith late of Cecil Co deceased renounce my right to administer. Written June 11, 1823. Witness Pere Biddle. signed Elizabeth Johns

Sarah Wilmer of Kent Co, widow of the late Blackistone Wilmer
To be decently buried at the discretion of my son **William B. Wilmer** in a plain manner in a walnut coffin and I give him the small sum of money due by him to me if he does, as this sum should be more than enough to pay my funeral charges and this sum is understood to be different from a larger claim of $3,400 due me and in my son's hands which is to remain a part of my estate. To my 2 executrixes the interest for 2 years of all my money in lieu of administration fees and all my debts. To my dau. **Mary Tate** $600 paid before Jan. 1, 1827, one negro boy **James** to serve until Dec. 25, 1847, one pair of large looking glasses which are now in her parlor in her house in Chestertown. To my 2 daughters **Sarah Rebecca Wilmer** and **Harriett Wilmer** each $800 paid before Jan. 1, 1827 and they shall share my pew in the church in Chestertown. To my son **John Wilmer** and William B. Wilmer $100 each to be paid by Jan. 1, 1827. To my granddau.

Sarah Maria Tate $600 to be paid by Jan. 1, 1827 and to my grandson **William B. Tate** $400 to be paid by Jan. 1, 1827 but if either or both die, then to survivor then to issue or back to my heirs. If my estate is not sufficient to pay my debts and legacies (which I do not presume to be the case), their share to be reduced in proportion.

Execs. my 2 daughters Sarah Rebecca Wilmer and Harriett Wilmer. Witnesses James E. Barroll, Josiah Gears. Written July 13, 1822 Proved July 2, 1823 p. 301

Codicil Whereas I gave $800 to my 2 daughters, if they marry before they receive their legacy then $100 each come out to my sons John and William B. Wilmer. Whereas I gave to my 2 grandchildren Sarah Maria Tate $600 and William B. Tate $400, if they die without issue $100 to each of my sons John and William B. Wilmer. Written July 26, 1822. Witnesses James E. Barroll, John H. Holt

Sarah Ringgold of Kent Co
I give to **Capt. Thomas Harris** one share and 1/3 part of a share in the Bank of Baltimore on condition that he supports my negro slave **Joe** who is blind. To **Rebecca Ringgold** and **Frances Ringgold** the remainder of my estate consisting of only personal property during their lives. To **Mary Blunt** after the Rebecca and Frances Ringgold my negro slave **Harriet** if she will not sell her out of Kent Co without her consent. To **Joseph Harris, Elizabeth Harris,** and **Maria Harris** after the decease of Rebecca and Frances Ringgold, the remainder of my personal estate.

Exec. Capt. Thomas Harris. Witnesses James Ringgold. Written May 13, 1822 Proved July 26, 1823 p. 306

Matthias C. Attwood, purser in the Navy of the US
To my friend **Samuel Blunt** of Georgetown in D.C. the gun and pair of pistols I possess and $100. To my cousin **John Theodore Hurtt** of Kent Co $200 and all my wearing apparel. To my executor and executrix $200 which I request to employ in erecting around the burying ground belonging to Shrewsbury Chappel in Kent where my grandmother, mother, brother and other relations are interred a brick wall as a memorial of my affection and respect for their memory. To my wife **Martha Ann Attwood** the 2 slaves that belonged to her at the time of her intermarriage with me. I give 2/3 of the rest of my estate I give to my wife Martha Ann Attwood in full right of her dower and the other 1/3 part to my aunt **Tabitha Wright.**

Execs. my wife Martha Ann Attwood and Richard Ringgold of Chestertown. Witnesses John A. Dunlap, Esq. of NY. Written July 9, 1822 Southern District of NY Proved Aug. 20, 1823 (before William P. Vanness Judge of District Court of US for Southern NY) p. 307

Mary Hamer of Chestertown
To my aunt **Sarah Beswick** all my estate

Exec. my aunt Sarah Beswick. Witnesses Mary Skirven, Sarah Francis Skirven, Benjamin B. Wroth. Written Jan. 10, 1820 Proved Oct. 27, 1823 p. 309

James Ringgold of Kent Co
To my wife **Sarah Ringgold** all my estate (except my books of law and history) during her life, my children to be supported out of the profits. After her decease, I give all my personal estate to my children **Alexander W. Ringgold, Richard W. Ringgold, William P. Ringgold, Thomas W. Ringgold, Rebecca Ringgold, Mary Ringgold, Jacob Ringgold,** and **George Washington Ringgold** (except my books of law and history. My son Alexander W. Ringgold must bring my personal estate the property which I have advanced him in my life as charged in my account book, amounting to $1,923 before he is entitled to a dividend of my personal estate, and this property advanced him or his dividend of my personal estate to be his full satisfaction of any claim he may have to the personal property of the late **James Williamson** deceased. To my son Richard W. Ringgold all my books of law and history and $1,000 and this is less than those of my other children because of the extra expense I have been at in his education which I hope will more than compensate him for his difference in property. To my son Thomas W. Ringgold $2,000. To my son Jacob Ringgold $2,000. To my son George Washington Ringgold $2,000. To my dau. **Ann Rebecca Ringgold** $2,000. To my dau. Mary Ringgold $2,000. I give the farm on which I now reside consisting of the farm on which the late James Williamson lived and which I have a power of deeding to either of my children by deed bearing date of July 25, 1804 and recorded Liber TW No. 3 p. 171, 172, and 173 and of the farm of which I purchased of **John Williamson** and his sister Mary who married a **Mr. Hyland** of Cecil Co containing in whole 850 acres unto my son Alexander W. Ringgold if he pays to my son Richard W. Ringgold $1,000, to my dau. Ann Rebecca Ringgold $2,000, to my dau. Mary Ringgold $2,000, to my son Thomas W. Ringgold $500 with interest from the time Alexander takes possession and the principal within 6 years. The farm which I purchased of **James Stoops** except the parcels sold to William Ringgold deceased and exchanged with Dr. **Thomas Willson** and a parcel of land adjoining the same which I got in exchange with Dr. Thomas Willson and all that part of a tract called *"Piney Grove"* adjoining Rock Hall belonging to me by deed or will containing in the whole 470 acres unto my son William P. Ringgold on condition that he pay to my son Thomas W. Ringgold $1,500, to my son Jacob Ringgold $2,000 and to my son George Washington Ringgold $2,000 within 6 years and land to be sold if not paid. Whereas my deceased son James W. Ringgold is charged in my account book with cash and property advanced him at the time of his marriage to the amount of $1,200, I give to my dau. in law **Anna W. Ringgold** and her 2 daughters my grandchildren who I hope will be as well provided for from their maternal estate as I am able to provide for the rest of my children. My wife to be guardian to my children during their minority with my sons Alexander W. Ringgold and Richard W. Ringgold and my brother **Richard Ringgold** to advise and assist her.

Exec. my wife Sarah Ringgold. Witnesses Thomas Willson, Thomas Harris, George Neal, William Hines. Written Jan. 11, 1823 Proved Oct. 8, 1823 (Oct 29 came Thomas Harris) p. 310

George A. Hanson of Kent Co

To my son **George Hanson** all my dwelling plantation whereon I reside in Kent Co consisting of part of a tract called *"Ratcliff Cross"* containing 250 acres, also part of a tract called *"Kemp's Beginning"* adjoining the said tract called *"Ratcliff Cross"* containing 69 acres conveyed to me by **Casparus Meginnis** by deed of June 17, 1796, also that part of tract containing 24 ¼ acres conveyed to me by **Richard S. Thomas** by deed dated July 31, 1799, also that part of a tract called *"Kemp's Beginning"* containing 54 acres conveyed to me by **William Sudler** trustee under the will of **Martha Sudler**, his mother by deed bearing date of Jan. 9, 1801 and also that part of a tract called *"Chigwell"* containing 47 acres conveyed by a decree of the Court of Chancery by deed dated Dec. 13, 1815, also 12 ½ acres purchased of **George W. Thomas** appointed trustee by Kent Co court for the sale of the real estate of **Gustavus T. Wright** an infant. To my dau. **Killy** all my right to that part of lands lying in Kent Co called *"Mill Fork"* and *"Tibbits Venture"* containing 220 acres as described by deed dated Feb. 25, 1803 from **Jonas Stoops** and **Anne** his wife, **Jonathan Hodgson** and **Sarah** his wife and **Elizabeth Johns** to me. To my dau. **Kitty** the rent of said farm. Whereas I hold an obligation of **James Frisby** deceased for £96 14 sh. to me dated Jan. 10, 1815 and an obligation of **Thomas Wilson** to me for $50 dated Dec. 14, 1814 my executor to use the bonds and 500 bushels of Indian corn to pay off a judgment of **William Barroll** Esq. as attorney against my son **Alexander B. Hanson**. I give to my dau. **Lavinia Hanson** $2,000 by my son George in 5 years in 5 annual installments and my son George to pay my dau. Sarah $50 annually until the death of her aunt **Sarah Keene**. To my dau. **Sarah** a negro girl **Charlotte** and her brother **Levi** and a bed. My son George shall have **Silvy** and give her $5 per year for life and she not be compelled to work. I give my piano forte to my dau. Killy and my carriage and carriage horse to my dau. Killy and Lavinia there executors. My daughters are to live on my farm devised to my son George while they are unmarried. I forgive my son Alexander my book account against him amounting to $2,324 and he does not charge my estate for an account he has against me for $100. All the rest of my estate to my children **Catharine,** George and Lavinia. I direct a suit of mourning be given to my friend and relation **John Stoops**. The bequests to my children Alexander, George, Lavinia, and Sarah are on condition that those of age shall convey to Killy all the title to the above land devised to Killy and also their right to all part of a tract in New Castle Co, DE called *"Ringgolds part of the Adventure Resurveyed"* containing 77 acres formerly belonging to their mother and also that my dau. Sarah when of age shall convey to my said dau. Killy all her right to said lands.

Execs. my son George and my dau. Killy. Witnesses Thomas Worrell, Jonathan Harris, Edward Freeman. Written Apr. 8, 1823 Proved Oct. 27, 1823 p. 314

Abstracts of Kent Co., MD Wills

Araminta Rasin of Kent Co
I desire to be interred in the graveyard at the Friends Meeting House in Still Pond. To my granddau. **Eliza Riley** formerly **Eliza Mahard** ½ and the other ½ to my grandson **Samuel Rasin Mahard**, also one bed and furniture, one pair of sheets, one pair of new blankets, and one yarn coverled, also a low bedstead with screws, 2 3/4 yards drab cloth not made up. I give to **Margaret Ellers** widow of my grandson **Jesse Ellers** all my wearing apparel excepting one gound and also one pair of old blankets.
Exec. my nephew John Wallis. Witnesses Francis L. Wallis, Jesse Comegys Wallis. Written Sep. 18, 1823 Proved Oct. 23, 1823 p. 317

Sarah Keene of Kent Co
To my niece **Catharine Hanson** my gold Joe and silver slop bowl. To my niece **Lavinia Hanson** my rocking chair. To my niece **Sarah R. Hanson** my bureau. To **Dr. Scanllin's** dau. **Catharine Scanllin** all my wearing apparel and $100. To my negro man **Dennis** his freedom in 12 months. To **Stephan Hodgson** and **Ann Hodgson** his wife all the residue of my personal estate

Exec. Stephen Hodgson. Witnesses James Brice, William Patterson, John Lusby. Written Mar. 3, 1823 Proved Nov. 8, 1823 p. 318

George Beck of Kent Co
All my property to my wife and my son **James Beck** and after her death all to my son James Beck.

Execs. my wife and my son James Beck. Witnesses Joseph Greenwood, Charles Stanley, Cuthbert Hall. Written Nov. 4, 1823 Proved Dec. 15, 1823 p. 319

Codicil My estate shall be accountable for the support of my sister **Rachel Beck** during her life and my nephew **Josiah Beck** be supported until he is 21. Written Nov. 4, 1823. Witnesses same as will

Thomas Baker of Kent Co
To my son **Samuel E. Baker** $400 deducting what I have already given him and what is charged in my account against him. To my son **Richard Baker** $400 when he arrives at 21. To my dau. **Mary Ann Baker** $400 but if she dies then to my daughters **Anna, Emma** and **Amanda**. To my dau. Anna Baker $400 but if she dies to my daughters Mary Anne, Emma and Amanda. To my dau. Emma Baker $400 but if she dies then to my daughters Mary Ann, Anna and Amanda. The rest of my personal estate to my son **Thomas Baker** at age 18. To my son **William Baker** $400 paid at 21 by my son Thomas Baker. To my son **Francis Baker** $400 to be paid at age 21 by my son Thomas Baker. To my dau. Amanda Baker $400 when she is 16 by my son Thomas Baker but if she dies then to my daughters Mary Ann, Anna, and Emma. To my son Thomas Baker every part of my real estate when he is 18 to pay above legacies and support my sons William and

Liber 10 1816-1827

Francis until age 21 and my dau. Amanda until she is 18. If my son Thomas Baker dies, then to my son Samuel E. Baker but still liable to above legacies.

Exec. Samuel E. Baker. Witnesses James M. Anderson, David Jones, John Whalan. Written Feb. 15, 1823 Proved Dec. 11, 1823 p. 321

Ann Thomas of Kent Co
After my debts are paid to **Samuel Thomas, William Thomas, Henry Thomas, James Thomas, Mary Thomas, Anna Thomas, Elizabeth Thomas** and **Susanna Thomas** with full power to deed any of my real estate.

Exec. James Brown. Witnesses Samuel Wales, Rebecca Brown, Rebecca Brown Jr. Written Nov. 13, 1823 Proved Jan. 15, 1824 p. 321

Warner Chance of Kent Co
To **Elijah Chance** son of my brother **Levi Chance** my silver watch. To **Elizabeth Chance** dau. of my brother **Noah Chance** my silver tea spoons. I give to **Mary Shubrook** for her faithful services in nursing me during my confinement all my queensware, china and looking glass with $40 paid in 4 years at $10 each. All the rest of my property with my wearing apparel I give to my friend **Bartholomew Etherington**

Exec. my friend Bartholomew Etherington. Witnesses Joseph Ireland, James Pearce and Robert Kennard. Written Apr. 3, 1822 Proved Feb. 7, 1824 p. 324

William Browne of Chestertown, Kent Co
To my wife **Susan Browne** all my estate.

Exec. my wife Susan Browne. Witnesses John Russell, Auquilla M. Usilton, Isaac Cannell. Written Mar. 6, 1823 Proved Feb. 17, 1824 p. 325

Ephraim Vansant 4th of Kent Co
To my brother **John R. Vansant** 2 negro men **Ruben** and **John**. To my brother **Lemuel Vansant** 4 negroes **James Ferrell, Daniel, Isaac,** and **Amy**. To my brother **George Vansant** 3 negroes **Henry, Emory,** and **Richard**. To my brother **Henry Vansant** 5 negroes **James, Maria, Rachel, Hannah,** and **Isaac Jr**. To **William Clark** the son of **William Clerk** and my sister **Elizabeth Clerk** $500 when he is 25. To my friend **Lambert Wickes** my stud horse Morow. To my brother Lemuel Vansant $1,000. To my brother John R. Vansant all the property I hold under a bill of sale from John R. Vansant and I give the further sum of $500 in 2 years. To **Fredus Vansant** the son of my brother John R. Vansant my house and lot at the head of Sassafras now in the tenure of **Nathan Vansant**. To my brothers Lemuel Vansant and George Vansant all the residue of my estate.

Abstracts of Kent Co., MD Wills

Exec. my friend Lambert Wickes. Witnesses David Davis, Samuel Vansant, John Ireland. Written Jan. 30, 1824 Proved Feb. 21, 1824 p. 326

James Mitton of Kent Co
My daughters **Sarah Ann** and **Martha** be schooled and clothed at the expense of my estate. My son **Samuel** be put out to a trade early in the spring that a sufficiency of clothing be furnished at the expense of my estate. My sister **Margaret** for her faithful services to have a home as long as she sees proper living unmarried. To my son **Richard** $100 at 21. To my son Samuel Mitton $100 at age 21. To my dau. Sarah Ann $100 at age 16. To my dau. Martha $100 to be paid at 16. My land be bound for said legacies. All the rest of my estate to my son **James Mitton**.

Exec. my son James Mitton. Witnesses Joseph Ireland, Nathaniel Kennard, Benjamin Kelley. Written Feb. 11, 1824 Proved Mar. 6, 1824 p. 328

William Moffett of Kent Co
My lands to be sold. My son **Joseph** the horse he usually rides with bridle and saddle not to be reckoned in his part. To my wife **Sarah Moffett** the use of all my estate during her life unless she chooses to take 1/3 or to each of my children ½. To my 5 children Joseph, **Martha, Susan, Bell Jane** and **William** all my estate after the death of my wife. My executor to sell stock not needed. If my dau. Martha should have to **Emeline** a black girl she should have to be reckoned in part. If my dau. Bell Jane should choose my negro boy **Levi** and a negro girl **Ann** to be reckoned in her part. To my son Joseph all the negro children that may be born of my female negroes to be free at age 28 and if any to not be reckoned in my estate.

Exec. my son Joseph. Witnesses James H. Smith, Ebenezer Welch, John Ireland. Written Sep. 13, 1822 Proved Mar. 18, 1824 p. 329

Thomas Sewell of Kent Co
My son **John Sewell** shall inherit the house and garden where he now lives during his life and that he be given all back rents up to this date. To my son **Lambert Sewell** son **William Sewell** (sic) I give my negro boy **Benjamin** to serve 10 years then to be the property of my son **Lorenzo Sewell** to serve 22 years then free. To my son **Edward Sewell** $1 and no more. To my son Richard Sewell's 2 children $1 each. To my son Lorenzo Sewell my negro boys **Henry** for 20 years, **John** and **David** to serve 21 years. The balance of my estate to my son Lorenzo Sewell. If he dies without issue then to my nephew **Thomas Sewell** tanner of Baltimore. To my friend **James Allen** of Frederick Town, Cecil Co. and his son **John Allen** my skift boat and all her apparatus. My old negro woman **Clanth** to have either a maintenance from my estate during her life or select a home where she pleases. My nephew Thomas Sewell shall be guardian to my son Lorenzo Sewell during his minority.

Liber 10 1816-1827

Exec. Samuel Kerr. Witnesses Richard Davis, Jonathan Greenwood, Joseph Morse. Written Nov. 20, 1822 Proved Apr. 3, 1824 p. 331

Benjamin Barger of Kent Co
To my wife **Rebecca Barger** all of my real estate which is in Worton Neck 15 acres of land which I purchased of Timothy Coldwell of Philadelphia and 10 3/4 acres I purchased of **John Curry** of Kent Co during her widowhood and after I give to my dau. **Susan H. Barger**. All my estate to be divided between my children **William Garber, Rebecca Lee, Mary Sloan's** children and Susan H. Barger. Mary Sloan's children in the hands of my son William for their benefit.

Exec. my wife Rebecca Barger. Witnesses Jeremiah Boots, Andrew Watts, Edward Crew. Written Apr. 5, 1824 Proved Apr. 10, 1824 p. 333

James Pearce of Kent Co
To **Joseph Pearce** my eldest son my bay mare and 2 heifers. To my son **James Pearce** my roan colt raising 2 years old. To my dau. **Sarah Pearce** her choice of beds that are downstairs and her choice of one milk cow. To my dau. **Susanah Pearce** the 2nd choice of beds that is to say one bed and one walnut table. To my son **Henry Kennard Pearce** one young bay mare all my wearing apparel and my duck gun. To my dau. **Ann Pearce** one bed and one walnut table. To my youngest 2 daughters **Mary** and **Kitty Pearce** all the remainder of my estate to be sold and applied to their schooling. To my 3 eldest daughters Sarah, Susanah and Ann my 3 linen wheels Sarah first choice and so on also omitted 2 sty hogs I give to Ann the other to be divided between Sarah and Susannah.

Execs. my son Joseph and Francis Lamb. Witnesses Francis Lamb, Eli Plummer. Written Aug. 28, 1821 Proved Apr. 20, 1824 p. 334

Renunciation I Joseph Pearce renounce right to executorship in favor of my brother James Pearce. Witness Francis Lamb

Daniel Lamb of Kent Co
To my wife **Hannah Lamb** my home plantation being part of *"Warner's Adventure"* and *"Warner's Addition"* and part of *"Nancy's Choice"* during her life. After her death to **Ann W. Chew** during her life and after her death to her son **Daniel Lamb Richardson Chew** if living. If no heirs living then to such of her sisters heirs as shall be living. To my wife all that land I bought of the **Foremans** whereon her son **John Edwards** now lives during her life. After her death then to her son John Edwards and his wife during both of their lives and then to my son John Edwards' son **William Edwards**. If my wife refuse to take the above land instead of her right of dower then the lands willed to her son and grandson shall be sold and the money divided between the children of my niece **Rebecca Worthington** deceased. I give my gig and horse to my wife above her 1/3 of my personal estate and the time of all my apprentice boys. To my niece **Lydia Alston** all the lands that I bought of **John A. Woodland** lying on the N side of the road from

43

my home place divided by the road with a small addition from the end of the first line of my purchase from **James McClain** reversed 43 perches to a small white oak and sapling marked with 12 notches standing by the road side and from said white oak 45 perches went 356 perches until it intersect the out line of my land in the branch called the meeting house branch being part of *"Hillings Adventure"* and part of *"Nancy's Choice"* and *"Hales"* running up the branch with the out lines of my land to the main road then with the road to the white oak. To my niece **Mary Ann Alston** all my lands lying on the E and N of the above said N 45° W line beginning at the said white oak and running N 45° W to the meeting house branch and the out line of my purchase from **Charles Tilden** and wife **Mary** and **Robert Buchanan** then with the out lines of the land until it intersects the division line between **John Haynes** and myself then with the division lines as now established to a stone in the main road by **Philip Crane's** then down the road to the said white oak the beginning being part of the following tracts *"Part of Forrester's Delight"* and *"Part of Hillings Adventure"*. To my brother **Joshua Lamb** the use of all that land I bought of **Aquilla Meeks** and **Mary Blay Tilden** in Tripola containing by estimation 300 acres during his life and after his decease my will is that it shall be sold and divided between the 4 children of Rebecca Worthington. All the residue of my personal estate to be sold and divided between my brother Joshua Lamb and the 4 children of Rebecca Worthington deceased and **John** and **Abner Alston**.

Exec. my wife Hannah Lamb. Witnesses Merritt Miller, William Lynch, Thomas Briscoe. Written Nov. 23, 1820 Proved Apr. 28, 1824 p. 336

William Spearman Sr. of Kent Co, farmer

To my son **John Spearman** $20 and no more. To my son **William Spearman** ¼ part of my farm called *"Partnership"* on the S side of said farm during his life but if he dies with issue then to have their father's part but if no issue then to my son **Gideon Spearman** his part of land left to William. To my son Gideon Spearman ¼ part of said farm during his life but if he dies without issue then to my son William. To my dau. **Araminta Hugle** ¼ part of said farm adjoining Gideon's part. To my youngest dau. **Isabel Spearman** the remainder ¼ part to her where my house stands which I call the N side to her. To my dau. Isabel Spearman one negro lad **Pomp** and a feather bed, one young horse 4 years old called Jack, one hand mill, my silver case and lancets. To my granddau. **Rebecca Money** one cow and calf, one feather bed. The residue of my personal property divided between my children and grandchildren living in this county, the grandchildren to have their mother's part.

Execs. my sons William and Gideon Spearman. Witnesses James Meredith, Milcah Clark, Michael Smith. Written Jan. 15, 1817 Proved Apr. 28, 1824 p. 339

Renunciation Whereas we William Spearman Jr. and Gideon Spearman do renounce the executorship to our brother in law **Guilder Huckill** of DE and his having ¼ part of said land as a suitable person to act as administrator. Written Apr. 28, 1824 Witness Josiah Massy

Liber 10 1816-1827

Susannah Baker of Kent Co
To **Edward Anderson Harris** son of my friend **William Harris** all the moneys due me from my friend William Harris or from the estate of late **Richard Simons** deceased and due from **Ezekial F. Chambers** Esq. as trustee on the estate of William Harris for the benefit of Edward Anderson Harris until age 21. To my niece **Ann Baker** my bed and furniture, quilt, 2 pillow cases and 2 pair of sheets. To my niece **Mary Ann Baker** my mahogany table, a bed quilt, 6 china cups and saucers and china bowl. To my niece **Emma Baker** 6 chairs, one bed and my looking glass. To my nephew **Samuel E. Baker** my large walnut chest. The rest of my estate to my sister **Margaret Harris**.

Exec. my friend William Harris. Witnesses William Harris Jr., Isabella Constable. Written Apr. 28, 1824 Proved June 9, 1824 p. 341

James Briscoe of Georgetown, Kent Co
To my wife **Mary** all my estate.

Exec. my wife Mary. Witnesses Edward Scott, David Davis, Thomas Green. Written Apr. 14, 1824 Proved Apr. 26, 1824 p. 343

Codicil My negro boy **James** and his negro girl **Sarah** each to be free at age 40 and give his shop tools to his brother **Benjamin**. Written Apr. 18, 1824. Witnesses Edward Scott, Thomas Green, James Salisbury

Joseph Browne of Kent Co
To my grandson **Joseph Browne, William** the son of **Ann** to serve until Jan. 1, 1854 then his freedom. To my granddau. **Rebecca August Ruth, Maria** the dau. of **Ann** to serve until Jan. 1, 1838 then free, but any children which she may have are to continue in slavery, males until age 35 and females until age 25. To my son **Morgan Browne, Ann** to serve until Jan. 1, 1827 and her children to continue in slavery as above; also **Ann's** dau. **Elizabeth, Kitty** and **Mary Ann**. To my dau. Rebecca Ruth, **Darkey** and her children **Daniel, Lewis, Elizabeth, Edwin, Temperance** and **George**. Darkey to serve until Jan. 1, 1827 and her children to continue in slavery as above. To my dau. **Ann Browne, Esther** and her children **Charlotte, Mary, Caroline, Ester, Milcah** and **Tabitha**. Esther to serve until Jan. 1, 1827 and her children to continue in slavery as above. To my daughters **Rebecca** and **Ann** all the residue of my personal property, **David, Michael,** and **Henry** until my debts be paid, **Stephan** and **Nathaniel** to serve 4 years from Jan. 1, 1825 the rest of my slaves. To my daughters Rebecca and Ann all my estate during their lives and after to my grandson **Charles Tilden Browne** at age 21 but if he dies under 21 then to my grandson **Joseph Browne**. My dau. Ann may make provision for my granddau. **Sarah H. Browne**.

Exec. my son Morgan Browne. Witnesses Thomas Wilkins, Bartus Trew, Edward Comegys. Written July 2, 1824 Proved Aug. 9, 1824 p. 345

[Certificate of freedom granted to negro Daniel Jan. 29, 1842. Pass granted **Lervis** Oct. 31, 1849. Certificate granted **Temperance** Aug. 24, 1855, written in margin] Pass granted to **George** July 25, 1857.

Charles Groome of Kent Co
To my brother **Daniel Groome's** 4 children **Martha, Margarett, Peregrine,** and **Lavinia** my negro man **Joe** to serve during his life, also negroes **Jim** called **Jim boy, Jake, Sall, Emeline** and **Angeline** (the last 2 daughters of **Sinah**) and the last to serve until 35. Also my negro woman **Jane** to serve 5 years. To my brother **James Groome's** 5 children **Isaac, Charles, James, Sarah,** and **William** my negro **Sam** to serve for 5 years. My negro **Step** be free on Jan. 1 next. My negro woman **Sinah** be free at the same time if she pays my executor the sum of her hire which is about $40 or $50. To my brother **John Groome** the times remaining of my bound boys **Bill** and **Perry**. To my brother John Groome my negro Jane's children **Isaac** and **Jim** and any other children she may have till age 35. Children of Jane, Sall, or Sinah to serve until age 35. All claims against me by the children of my deceased brother Daniel Groome and all accounts between my brother James Groome and me are completely settled. If they claim otherwise the above legacies to them are void. To my brother John Groome all the rest of my estate.

Exec. my brother John Groome. Witnesses Ephraim Stoops, James Greenwood, Samuel Elborn (Witnesses James Salisbury attests to signature of Charles Groome, William Greenwood knew the writing of his brother James Greenwood, Samuel Kerr knew writing of Charles Groome and Ephraim Stoops deceased). Written Oct. 22, 1811 Proved July 30, 1824 p. 347

Rachel Hatcheson of Kent Co
My negroes **Mosses, Jenny** and **Suck** shall be free from slavery. To my sister **Ann Hatcheson** during her life the whole of my estate. Then to my nephew **Vincent Hatchison** and my niece **Mary Hatcheson**

Exec. Not Given. Witnesses James Tennant, John Wallis, Sarah Hackett. Written Sep. 23, 1817 Proved Sep. 3, 1824 p. 349

Ann Hatcheson of Kent Co
To my sister **Rachel Hatcheson** during her life the ½ of the tract we now reside and also the personal estate. After the death of my sister Rachel Hatcheson the above land called *"Killingsworth More"* to be divided between my nephew Vincent Hatcheson and my niece Mary Hatcheson.

Exec. Not Given. Witnesses James Tennant, John Wallis, Sarah Hackett. Written Sep. 23, 1817 Proved Sep. 3, 1824 p. 350

James Bevins of Kent Co

To my son **Thomas Bevins** the farm I purchased from **Notty Young** reserving all that point of woods lying to the NE of the house where Thomas Bevins now lives and adjoining the farm which Dr. **Charles Tilden** purchased from Nolly Young which I design for the use of the farm I purchased from the heirs of **Joseph Stavely**. To my son **James William Bevins** all that farm I purchased from the heirs of Joseph Stavely and all that piece of woods lying to the NE of Thomas Bevins dwelling house and adjoining the land Dr. Charles Tilden. My son James William is not to cut more than ten cord a year and is to use of a road to and from and as long as wood on said land, then I give to my son Thomas Bevins. To my dau. **Kitty Ann Bevins** all that tract I purchased from **Isaac Redgrave** and all that parcel of land purchased by Joseph Stavely from **James Stavely** beginning at the main road leading to Turner's Creek, and running across a branch until it intersects Dr. Charles Tilden's land and bounded on the N by the land belonging to the heirs of James Stavely, containing about 29 acres and to her a negro girl **Ann** to serve until she is 28. My executors shall provide to my wife **Ann Mires Bevins** annually in advance for 2 years 1,400 weight of pork, 15 bushels of wheat, 15 barrels of corn, 2,000 weight of good corn blades, and to receive no more until the land is paid for. After 4 years, I give to my wife the whole use of the farm I purchased from Joseph Stavely's heirs and Isaac Redgraves. If she marries, she is to receive only 1/3. To my wife the first choice of 2 beds, one other bed, all the table, clothes and towels, all the china and crockery, all the carpeting, one bureau, one desk, one book case, and all the looking glasses except one, all the tables, one sitter, 2 pair shovels and tongs, also 6 table spoons (of silver), 5 silver tea spoons, one silver soup spoon, one pair sugar tongs, one pair brass and irons and 2 pair irons and irons, 12 chairs, her choice of the kitchen furniture, all the candle sticks and the choice of 2 cows, my large sorrel horse & carriage, pasturage for 1 horse and 2 cows, and my negro girl **Jane** to serve 10 years. After her death to my son **James William Bevins** and to my dau. Kitty Ann Bevins. To my dau. **Rebecca Howard** $1,599 clear of all claims against me to be paid from the farm I purchased from Notty Young in 8 years after my death and to her my negro girl **Maria** (who she now has) to serve until she is 28, also one bed, one looking glass, one pair brass and irons, 6 silver tea spoons, pair of sugar tongs which she now has. The male child of said negro Maria to be free at 30 and the females at 28. To my son Thomas Bevins one yoke, old oxen, and ox cart, 14 sheep, one bed, also my negroes **Perry** and **Isaac** (after my debts are paid) to serve until they are free agreeably to their manumissions, and whatever furniture I have previously given him shall remain his, but he is not to claim to my estate, except what is given him in this will. To **Henry Hurtt's** four children: **Milly Minty Hurtt** $300 when 18, to **Mary Rebecca Hurtt** $300 when 18, to **James Henry Josiah Hurtt** $300 when 21, to **William Thomas Hurtt** $300 when 21, to **Julieta Ann Hurtt** $300 when 18, all to be paid out of land purchased of Notty Young. If **Levi** behaves himself he is to have one year of his time to serve and one year more which I promised his brother John should have provided Levi behaves himself. If my son James William Bevins dies without issue then divided between my son Thomas Bevins, my dau. Rebecah Howard, my dau. Kitty Ann Bevins, and the heirs of Henry Hurtt by my dau. **Juletta Hurtt** (that is ¼ part to her heirs). My executors to straighten the main road from my gate next to Dr. **George Thomas'** farm to the gate at the cross roads leading to Turners Creek provided, the parties holding the adjoining lands wish it. My son James William Bevins shall have my silver watch and a negro boy **Alexander** until he is free. **Kitty Price** shall have a home in my house. Thomas Bevins to cut 10 cords each year for 4 years for the use of my home farm from the farm willed to my son James William Bevins and delivered on the farm I purchased from Joseph Stavely. To my brother **Charles Bevins** 450 acres of land in Greenbrier Co, part of land called *"Walkers Meaddow"* which **James Welch, Richard Wethered** and myself purchased from **Henry Ringgold** and **Ann** his wife in 1800. To my nephew **Joseph Price** 150 acres being part of same tract. To my niece Kitty Price now living in Kent Co 150 acres of the same tract in Greenbrier Co, VA. To **Ann Vachel** formerly **Ann Price** 140 acres of same tract. To **John Price** the son of **Mary Bevins** 100 acres of same tract. To **Samuel Price's** children that he had by **Ann Fagan** his wife 100 acres of same tract. To **Polly Bevins** (dau. of my brother **Charles Bevins** and **Mary** his wife) 43 acres of same tract laid off in the corner of the survey. To **Katherine Calison** (dau. of my brother Charles Bevins and Mary his wife) 50 acres part of same tract. Henry Hurtt and Benjamin Howard to be guardian of my children but my children to remain with their mother during her widowhood but if she marries then to their apprenticeship guardians.

Execs. Henry Hurtt and Benjamin Howard. Witnesses Robert B. Pennington, James Hepbron, John Hepbron. Written May 18, 1824 Proved Aug. 17, 1824 p. 352

<u>Codicil</u> My land to be cleared off the estate of my son Thomas Bevins until the legacies are paid and my son Thomas has the liberty of said land to burn 15,000 bricks. My 2 farms are to be retained for 4½ years to pay debts. My negro girl **Sal** and the household goods that my dau. **Jeletta Hurtt** has now are to remain her. To my son Thomas Bevins $40 to help pay expenses of digging a well. Written May 27, 1824. Witnesses same as above will.

<u>Renunciation</u> I resign all right to executor in will of James Bevins. Signed Benjamin Howard. Written Aug. 17, 1824 Witness Robert B. Pennington

<u>2nd Codicil</u> To my wife $100 out of my present crop of wheat. Written July 12, 1824 Signed James Bevins Witness Kitty Price.
N.B. I also wish her to have the rent from **Rebecca Lamb**. Signed J.B. Witness Kitty Price Proved Oct 5, 1824

Elizabeth Johns of Dover, DE but now of Kent Co, MD
To my niece **Elizabeth Johns** all my real estate situate lying in Kent Co which was devised to me by the will of my mother **Elizabeth Johns** deceased upon the condition that my sister in law Catharine Johns shall not make any claim against my estate. To my niece Elizabeth Johns all my bank stock (10 shares in the Smyrna Bank of DE) and to my niece Elizabeth Johns upon the said condition my bed, 12 silver table spoons, my wardrobe, and wearing apparel, my watch, watch chain and to my brother **Enoch H.**

Liber 10 1816-1827

Johns all my bank stock in the Mechanic Bank of Baltimore and a bond due me from **James Pearce** of Kent Co, and my negro boy **George** until age 35, and to him all my right in the real estate of **Sarah R. Hanson.** I give to my relative **Lavenia Hanson** one mourning ring. All the remainder of my estate to Elizabeth Johns.

Exec. my brother Enoch H. Johns. Witnesses Catharine Hanson, Sarah R. Hanson, A.B. Hanson. Written Nov. 20, 1823 Proved June 18, 1824 Kent Co, DE p. 359

Before John Adams Registrar Letters of administration on intestate estates Lavinia Hanson saw Elizabeth Johns sign said will and believes the signatures of the witnesses who reside in Chestertown in the state of Maryland (out of the jurisdiction of the register). Written June 18, 1824

Codicil I Elizabeth Johns of Dover in Kent Co give to **Sarah Bell** of Dover $20 yearly by said niece Elizabeth Johns during the life of Sarah Bell and to Sarah Bell ½ of my stockings, ½ my pocket handkerchiefs, all my shoes and best comb. Written June 6, 1824. Witnesses John Adams, James Sykes.

Francis Usselton (Usilton) of Kent Co
To my eldest son **John Usselton** $1, to my dau. Hosanna Reed $1, to my 2 grandson **William Howard** and **Risdon Howard** $1 each and no more. To my second son **Robert Usselton** all that tract I bought of **James M. Anderson** and **William Harris** trustees for the sale of real estate of **Henry Kennard** deceased except part devised unto my son **Francis Usselton,** but if my son Robert Usselton dies without issue then divided between my sons John Usselton, Francis Usselton, **Joseph Usselton,** and my dau. **Hosanna Reed.** I give to my third son Francis Usselton my now dwelling plantation that I bought of **Joshua Kennard** and all the lands on the W and N side of a line drawn from a stone marked P.P.K. VII it being at the end of the second line of the land I bought of James M. Anderson and William Harris trustees aforesaid and running to a stone marked VI set up at the end of the 5th line of a tract called *"Wheel Wright Swamps"* and running to a stone marked P.P.K. II set up at the end of the first line of *"Wheel Wright Swamps"* which land was before sold by **Stephen Kennard** to **John Kennard** as by reference to records of Kent Co and also a road 20 feet wide from the stone marked P.P.K. VII along the lands of **Patrick P. Kennard** until it intersects my home farm. If my son Francis Usselton shall die without issue then to be divided between my sons John Usselton, Robert Usseltton, Joseph Usselton, and my dau. Hosanna Reed. To my fourth son **Joseph Usselton** all the lands I bought of **George Hanson** and wife lying on the N side of the main road leading to Worton Point supposing to contain 19 acres, but if he dies without issue then to be divided between my sons John Usselton, Robert Usselton, Francis Usselton and my dau. Hosanna Reed. To my son **Francis Usselton** all my personal estate. Any dispute to be settled by 2 disinterested persons.

Exec. my son Francis Usselton. Witnesses Samuel G. Kennard, Samuel Kennard, Andrew Toulson. Written Sep. 12, 1824 Proved Sep. 23, 1824 p. 362

Abstracts of Kent Co., MD Wills

Darius Dunn of Kent Co
I give all my estate to **William Shaw** son of **Mary Shaw** on condition of paying debts and $16 a year to negro **Ashbery** during his life and to provide the customary clothing for a person in his situation.

Exec. William Shaw. Witnesses Howard Kennard, Philemon Ward, James Davis. Written Jan. 26, 1823 Proved Oct. 27, 1824 p. 365

Joseph Simmonds of Kent Co
To my wife **Sarah Simmonds** all my estate during her widowhood for the bringing up of my minor or 6 youngest children but if she dies then to be sold and used for my minor children, the remainder to all my children. To my son **Robert Simmonds** at the death of his mother part of my mansion farm contained within the following bounds beginning at Chester River at a corner being the beginning line of a tract of land called *"Tilghmans Farm"* and running from the dividing fence between one and **Samuel Merritt** to a marked cedar standing on the S side of the gate that goes into his farm and running a straight course across my field to a stone that stands by the gate opposite my barn and then running with the fence and road that goes down the neck until it comes to a marked gum that stands in a corner of said fence, and then running a straight course to my woods gate, and then the division fence between me and Samuel Merritt to the bounded stone and with the division fence between me and **David Jones** to said river and with that to the beginning. He paying a security of $2,000 to my 6 youngest children namely **Sarah, William, Elizabeth, Joshua, Phillip,** and **Samuel**. To my son Joseph Simmonds all the rest of my land.

Exec. my wife Sarah Simmonds. Witnesses Samuel Wales, Titus Maslin, James Brown. Written 9th mo 5, 1822 Proved Nov. 2, 1824 p. 366

Elizabeth Hewett of Georgetown, Kent Co
To my son **James Mahanna** my house and lot situate lying in Georgetown beginning at an old stone house which is now down in Front Street and running 65 more E then 60 towards Sassafras River then 60 feet W then 60 to the beginning. My husband **Thomas Hewett** to be guardian to rent or sell said house and lot.

Exec. Not Given. Witnesses James B. Collins, James D. Carroll, William Hewett. Written Dec. 4, 1823 Proved Nov. 25, 1824 p. 368

Isabella Freeman of Baltimore City in Baltimore Co, MD
To be decently buried in Shrewsbury Churchyard in Kent Co. To my dau. **Harriott Maria Blair** the wife of **Archibald Blair** of VA my gold watch and a wirk box. The remainder of my estate to my dau. **Catharine Martha Eliza Freeman**.

Exec. my dau. Catharine Martha Eliza Freeman. Witnesses Peregrine Wethered, Lewin Wethered, Thomas Myer. Written Nov. 26, 1823 Proved Dec. 6, 1824 p. 369

Liber 10 1816-1827

Elizabeth Kennard of Kent Co
To my dau. **Nancy Kennard** one feather bed and walnut bed stead and cord, one looking glass, 1 walnut table, 2 windsor chairs, 1 rush bottom chair, one red chest, one big spinning wheel, one iron pot, tea kettle, one small loom to her when lawfully married and to remain in the hands of **Samuel Caleb Jr**. To Samuel Caleb Jr. one bed and trunnel bedstead and cord, walnut chest, 2 windsor chairs and 1 rush bottom chair, one common six dinner pot and dutch oven, 2 pot racks, one pine table house and lot, one acre and 2 perches during while he is single, if he married to take up with any woman as his wife the house and lot is to be sold and equally divided between **Nancy, Unit, Kennard, William, Asbury, Samuel, Westly, Susan, Emily**, the children of **Elizabeth Kennard**. And Unit Kennard is 21 at that time he is to take house and pay the children for their parts said house and Unit Kennard to have the personal property that I left Samuel Caleb Jr. if he marries or has a woman as a wife about him is if he should due first the bed close to be divided between the beds.

Exec. Not Given. Witnesses Thomas Bordley, Bartholomew Etherington, Ann Bordley. Written Feb. 19, 1823 Proved Dec. 21, 1824 p. 370

Richard Brice of Kent Co
To my wife **Rebecca Brice** all my plantation I purchased of **John Wallis** also my houses and lots in Chestertown during her life and after her death to my niece **Martha Brice** but if she dies then to my niece **Mary Brice** but if she dies then to my nephew **Joseph W. Brice** (son of **Joseph Brice**). To my wife Rebecca Brice all my personal property during her life and after to my niece Martha Brice. My negroes all free at 40. If the land descend to Joseph W. Brice at age 21, I then appoint **Philip Brooks** as the guardian and Philip Brooks and Unit Corse to have oversight of my executrix.

Execs. my wife Rebecca Brice and my niece Martha Brice. Witnesses Edward Nicholson, Unit Corse, Philip Brooks. Written Dec. 18, 1824 Proved Dec. 28, 1824 p. 371

William Redding of Kent Co
To my wife **Melicent M. Redding** all my estate

Exec. my wife Melicent M. Redding. Witnesses William Merritt, Cuthbert Hall, James Salisbury. Written Apr. 30, 1818 Proved Jan. 18, 1825 p. 373

William Smith of Kent Co
The profits of my farm called *"Robotham's Park"* lying in Queen Anns Co be applied to maintain my 3 children **Nancy, Hannah Elizabeth** and **Joel** till they be 16 for females and 21 for male, subject to my wife's thirds. When my son Joel is 21 he to have farm and pay my daughters Nancy and Hannah Elizabeth $500 each in 6 equal annual installments. If either dau. dies then to my other daughter. If Joel dies before 21, then the farm to my sister Hannah Elizabeth if she pays $1,000 to my dau. Nancy in 6 annual installments instead of the $500. My personal estate after my wife's 1/3 then to my 3

children Nancy, Hannah Elizabeth, and Joel. If any dies then to survivors. I give my 6 silver table spoons and carriage to my wife **Martha**. To my children **Margaret** and **Thomas** $5 each. My wife Martha guardian to my children.

Execs. my wife Martha and John B. Eccleston. Witnesses James Bowers, William B. Wilmer, John Stoops. Written Dec. 24, 1824 Proved Jan. 12, 1825 p. 374

Edward Wright of Kent Co

To my son **Thomas H. Wright** the several parcels of land 3 3/4 acres being part of tract called *"Simpson's Adventure"* which I purchased from **Isaac Freeman Sr.** and one acre and 90 perches of land, part of the same tract, which I purchased from **Thomas Sappington** and 7 1/8 acres part of a tract called *"Matthias and Saint John's Fields"* which I purchased from **William Ireland** and 7 acres which I purchased from the State of Maryland called *"Wrights Step"* and also about 18 acres of land called *"Castle Cary"* which I purchased from **Thomas Smith Esq.** This land lies to the N and NE of my barn and on which part of my apple orchard now stands, all to him on condition he pays to my granddau. **Melvina Wright** $248.33 when age 18 and to pay $248.33 to the children of my dau. **Julianna Ellis** when they arrive of age. If all the children of my dau. die then my son **Thomas H. Wright** to pay my dau. in 5 equal installments. If she also dies then the $248.33 to all my children. To my son Thomas H. Wright all that piece of woodland being part of a tract called *"Dunstable and Bennets Regulation"* which I purchased from **Archaball McCall**, beginning at a stone near the Neck Gale and on the E side of the road and running as the fence now stands, until it comes to the S E corner of *"Walkers Field"*, then down with the woods and cleared land until it comes to the head of the first branch, then down with that branch until it intersects **Robert Wilson's** land then round with that land to Skigg's land, then with **Skigg's** land to the beginning supposed to contain 40 or 50 acres upon condition he pays the $25 as aforesaid for each acre to my dau. **Hannah B. Wright** ¼ the amount, to the children of my dau. Juliana Ellis ¼ part, to my granddaughters **Ann Eliza Woodland** and **Sarah Emoly Woodland** ¼ part. If my dau. Hannah dies without issue then to my son **William Wright the younger** when he is 21 but if he dies then to the survivor of him or my dau. Hannah to all my children by his mother's side and if my dau. Juliana Ellis' children should all die before age 21 for boys and 16 for girls then to all my children. If my granddaughter Ann Eliza Woodland dies before 18 then her part to her sister Sarah Emoly Woodland when she is 18, and if Sarah Emoly Woodland dies before 18 then to her sister Ann Eliza Woodland but if they both die then to their brothers by their mother's side and if they leave no sister or brothers then to my dau. Eliza Woodland in 5 annual installments. To my son Thomas H. Wright the following tracts, about 10 acres, part of a tract of land called *"Castle Cary"* which I purchased from Thomas Smith Esq and 46 acres part of the same tract which I purchased from **Thomas Shehan** and 20 acres of land part of a tract called *"Scott's Folly"*, which I also purchased from Thomas Shehan and 26 ½ acres also part of *"Scott's Folly"* which I purchased from William Merritt, beginning at Robert Wilson's bank where the division fence between the heirs of the late **Col. Freeman** and myself now strikes the bank and running with the fence S 37 3/4° E 54 ½ perches then

Liber 10 1816-1827

S 39º W 196 perches to the NW corner of *"Skigg's lot"*, now *"Turner's lot"* thence with **Edward Hurtt's** land, to **Richard Skigg's** land thence with that land to Robert Wilson's land and thence with that land to the beginning, on condition he pays to the children of my dau. Juliana Ellis $400 divided among them in 3 years. If they all die under age then to my dau. Juliana Ellis in 8 annual installments and if she also dies then to all my children and my granddau. Melvina Wright. My executor to pay to the children of my dau. **Eliza Woodland** $400 in 3 years but if they die under age then to their mother and if she dies then to all my children and my granddau. Melvina Wright. To my dau. **Sarah Wright** $400 in 4 annual installments. To my dau. **Melvina Wright** $400 in 5 annual installments but if she dies then to Thomas H. Wright and the children of Juliana Ellis and the children of Eliza Woodland and ¼ to my dau. Sarah Wright. To my son Thomas H. Wright my island called *"Joiner's Fancy"* lying in Sassafras River. I give to my son **Norrist Wright** my set of Washington's Life by Marshall. To my dau. **Hannah Brooks Wright** my negro girl **Susan**. To my brother **Benjamin Wright's** son **William Wright** 17 acres of woodland in Queen Anns Co called *"Wright's Addition"* which I obtained a patent of the state of MD in 1815. To my son Thomas H. Wright all my land called *"Dunstable"*, *"Burnetts Regulation"* and *"Stanaway"* which I purchased from Archibald McCall in trust to sell and give to my dau. Sarah Wright $500 and the residue divided between my son **John Wright**, my dau. **Mary Wright**, my son **James Wright**, my dau. **Hannah B. Wright** and my son **William Wright** the younger. If John, Mary, James, Hannah or William die under age then to their brothers and sisters by their mother's side and if Sarah dies then to all my children and grandchildren. My personal property to be sold and divided 1/12 to my son Thomas H. Wright, 1/12 to the children of my dau. Juliana, 1/12 part to my granddau. Melvina Wright, 1/12 to the children of my dau. Sarah Wright, 1/12 to my son Norrist Wright, 1/12 to my son Edward Wright, 1/12 to my son John Wright, 1/12 to my dau. Mary Wright, 1/12 to my son John Wright, 1/12 to my son James Wright, 1/12 to my dau. Hannah B. Wright, 1/12 to my son William Wright the younger. My son Thomas H. Wright guardian to all my minor children.

Exec. my son Thomas H. Wright. Witnesses George Spry, John Fields, Ephraim Vansant 4th, William Turner. Written June 11, 1823 Proved Jan. 4, 1825 p. 375

Codicil I **Edward Wright** I revoke the 1/12 of my personal estate to my son Edward Wright and to be given to all the other children. The 1/12 part to my dau. Sarah shall be liable to any obligation for her husband **John Fields**. Written Dec. 22, 1824. Witnesses Edward Scott, Zedekiah Newton

Renunciation I Thomas H. Wright renounce the guardianship of the minor children and I renounce the trusteeship for the sale of certain lands devised to me. Written Jan. 20, 1825. Witnesses C. Hall

Elizabeth Worrell of Kent Co
To my sons **Edward Hanson Worrell** and **William Henry Page Worrell** all the stock and farming utensils on the farm where I now live. To my son William my negro man

Pere to serve 5 years from Jan 1, 1825 and then free and my negro man **Primas** to serve 21 years from Jan 1, 1825 and then free. My farm lying on Sassafras River near Georgetown Cross Roads be divided into 2 parts in the same manner it was divided between my sister **Sarah Freeman** and myself and when divided I give to my son William his choice of the two parts. To my dau. **Ann Elizabeth Pearce Worrell** the remaining part of said farm. My son William to rent the part given to my dau. as long as she shall please and also give to Elizabeth's part as far as possible an equal chance on these conditions if my son refuses the choice to Elizabeth without condition, but if he accepts the choice and not comply with its terms he shall for every year he is delinquent pay $50. These conditions to my son William and my dau. Elizabeth if they convey their right in my farm to my son Edward. To my dau. **Sarah Maria Schley** $300 within 3 years if she convey her right in the farm called *"Fairy Meadows"* whereon I now live at $20 per acre if my said dau. Maria does not comply then my son Edward shall be released from the payment of $300. To my dau. **Maria** one bed and all the articles now in her possession my reason for making a small provision for my said dau. then for the rest of my children is that she is already settled in life and her prospects much better then the rest of my children. I give to my dau. Ann Elizabeth one bed, one suit of red curtains, one mattress, one mahogany bureau, one mahogany oval table, one shall work table, one large gilt frame looking glass, 6 chairs and 2 small ones, one set dining china, 12 desert spoons and a dessert ladle, 12 teaspoons, and a pair of salt spoons, all marked E.W., her choice of the carpeting and of a pair of andirons and one pair of plated candlesticks. My son to be put in possession of my farm where I now live and in order to make binding but if my son William and my dau. Elizabeth refuse then I give all my lands to my son Edward and if my son Edward refuses to comply with disposition to my 2 daughters and my son William all my land to them. All the rest of my estate divided between my 2 sons and my dau. Elizabeth.

Execs. my two sons. Witnesses Samuel Ringgold, Elizabeth Ringgold, Peregrine Wroth. Written Dec. 31, 1824 Proved Feb. 9, 1825 p. 385

Richard Hall of Kent Co
To my wife **Elizabeth Hall** her lawful proportion of my personal estate. To my 3 children **James Hall, Hester Hall** and **Joseph Hall** all my personal estate. My son James Hall will continue the farm on which I now live and to keep the family together until Jan. 1 next then to be sold and each one may get their proportion.

Execs. my son James Hall and Samuel Kerr. Witnesses James Tennant, James Heighe. Written Jan. 27, 1825 Proved Feb. 22, 1825 p. 388

Thomas Whittington of Queen Anns Co
To my goddau. **Elizabeth C. Chambers** my houses and lot of ground on Church alley and my lot on Fish Street in Chestertown. To my friend Mrs. **Augusta Houston** my houses and lot on Queen Street in Chestertown. The colored man **Charles** who formerly lived with me $200. My old cook **Pat** be comfortably supported on my farm where she

now is during her life at the expense of the owner. So many of my slaves or servants as shall be 25 or upwards to be free and the others to be free at 25. To my friend **Ezekiel F. Chambers** all the remainder of my estate.

Exec. my friend Ezekiel F. Chambers. Witnesses William S. Hambleton, Joseph Porter, Thomas Gooding. Written Sep. 26, 1821 Proved Mar. 1, 1825 p. 389

Codicil Whereas I Thomas Whittington late of Queen Anns Co now of Kent Co to lands conveyed to me by Ezekiel F. Chambers trustee for the sale of the land of **Philip Kennard** deceased shall be considered part of my estate as residuum and pass as part of the residuary clause. Written July 2, 1822. Witnesses John Lucas 3rd, William S. Hambleton, William S. Lassell

James Ridgaway of Chestertown, Kent Co

To my wife **Araminta Ridgaway** everything I became possessed of from my marriage with her, a schedule of which is now in my possession and my horse and old gig, my black woman **Margaret** lately bought out of estate of **Jervis Ringgold** deceased and to her $50 in lieu of her dower and if she does not abide my will then all property to be sold and considered as part of residuary clause to my daughter. To my son **James Asbury Ridgaway** all my land being on Choptank River in Talbot Co, MD known as *"Waste lands"* and if he dies without issue then to my dau. **Mary Louisa Ridgaway** and to him my silver watch, also a black boy called **Standly Murray** who is a brother to a boy **John Murray** who is bound to my brother **Henry Ridgaway** living on said farm to serve until 25 and Standly was born Aug. 1817. All my reading books to be equally divided between my son and dau. before named. To my dau. Mary Louisa Ridgaway to be kept as specie legacies and not to be sold, my mahogany secretary, one silver ladle marked "R", 6 silver table spoons, 12 silver tea spoons, 2 silver salt shovel, one silver mustard spoon, one sugar tongs, also of silver, and my negro boy called John Murray now bound to my brother at my farm till he is 18 and then to my dau. until 25 then to be free. John Murray was born Nov. 15, 1813, also my negro boy **John** or **John Monk** to serve said dau. until Mar. 4, 1835 then free. To **Arabella Bayard** living in Denton in Caroline Co now in her possession which I claim under a bill of sale recorded in Easton, Talbot Co. The rest of my estate to be sold and after debts to my dau. Mary Louisa Ridgaway. Rev. James Thomas of Easton to be guardian to my children **James Asbury Ridgaway** and Mary Louisa Ridgaway.

Exec. George W. Thomas of Chestertown. Witnesses Charles Stanley, James Mansfield, James E. Barroll. Written Jan. 31, 1825 Proved Mar. 10, 1825 p. 392

Renunciation I Araminta Ridgaway widow of James Ridgaway do renounce any bequest made to me by my husband and take my dower. Written Mar. 15, 1825 Witness James E. Barroll

Benjamin B. Wroth of Kent Co

All that part of my plantation in Kent Co purchased by me of **Edward** and **Henry Tilghman** (by deed dated Jan. 5, 1813) which is to the S of the fence which now runs from the main road leading from Chestertown to I.U. Church through the said lands, belonging to the heirs of **Thomas Maslin** deceased and ½ the wood land on said estate and laid out to make an equal division to my dau. **Editha G. Wroth** and if she dies without heirs then to my sons **Benjamin B. Wroth** and **William Wroth**. If they all died without issue then to my brother **Peregrine Wroth**. If my children die within the lifetime of my wife **Mary Wroth** then the lands to her during her life and then to my brother Peregrine Wroth. The other ½ of the said woodland and the other land on the N of the said fence to my wife Mary Wroth for her life and after her decease I give to my sons Benjamin B. Wroth and William Wroth. If they die without issue then to my dau. Editha G. Wroth and if she dies then to my brother Peregrine Wroth. I give ½ of the lot which I purchased of **Levi Wroth** situated in Kent Co to my dau. Editha G. Wroth. Remainder to my sons Benjamin B. Wroth and William Wroth, then to Peregrine Wroth if they have no issue. If my wife is living then to her then to my brother. Remainder ½ of said lot purchased by me of Levi Wroth, to my wife Mary Wroth, during her life then to my sons Benjamin B. Wroth and William Wroth. I give my gold watch and 2 bed quilts of a hexagon figure to my dau. Editha G. Wroth. All my remainder of my personal estate to my wife Mary Wroth. The bequests to my wife in lieu of her thirds. My brother Peregrine Wroth to be trustee to finish and settle the trust given me by a deed from **Hannah Burneston** deceased to me date Jan. 26, 1821. My brother Peregrine Wroth guardian to my dau. Editha G. Wroth.

Exec. my wife Mary Wroth. Witnesses Elizabeth Maslin, Mary A. Ringgold, Josias Ringgold. Written Mar. 12, 1825 Proved Apr. 4, 1825 p. 395

Codicil My dau. Editha G. Wroth relinquish to my 2 sons whatever may be coming to her from the estate of her grandmother Hannah Burneston and the land is devised to her. Considering that the land of my plantation including the woodland purchased of **Edward** and **Henry Tilghman** for better provision of my dau. Editha G. Wroth than I have made for my other children, I give the woodlot purchased of Levi Wroth to my wife Mary Wroth during her life and then to my sons Benjamin B. Wroth and William Wroth. To my 2 servants **Toney** and **Hannah** who are too old to manumit are $8 during their lives. Written Mar. 12, 1825. Witnesses Elizabeth Maslin, Mary A. Ringgold, Josias Ringgold

Joseph Greenwood of Kent Co

To my wife all my estate during her life except 30 acres in lieu of her 1/3 and she to support my 2 dau. **Mary A.**, **Sarah E.** and my mother and she board and cloth my son **Daniel** during her life. I give to my son **Milburn** 30 acres beginning at lower gate post of my our or road gate and running down the side of the road which leads to the house by a strait line from the road to the division fence which divide my fuilas thence with the fence to **William Freeman's** land. To my son **Daniel B. Greenwood** after the death of my wife, all the rest of my estate with 1/3 of my personal estate and my daughters to have a home with their brother and no board while they are single. The remainder of my personal estate to my 2 daughters Mary A. and Sarah E. Greenwood Exec. my wife. Witnesses Samuel Ringgold, Thomas Copper, Thomas Murphey. Written Mar. 3, 1825 Proved Apr. 6, 1825 p. 400

Richard Spencer of Kent Co
To my son **Lambert W. Spencer** for his part of my estate $4,000 as he chose the money instead of the land as he wishes to go in trade as I have already paid him $2,453. To my son **Richard Spencer** that part of my dwelling plantation which is included within the following lines designated on a plot of my said plantation intended to be sealed up with this will, beginning at a stone a the old shipyard in the division line between Mr. Simon Wickes land and mine running N 18° and 15' W 170 perches to a boundary oak between **Simon Weeks** and me now **Richard Brices** N 31° E 142 perches to a stone at a small gum tree N 80° E 120 perches to a stone no. 3 at a hickory tree thence S 19° E 86 perches to another stone marked no. 4 at a ditch then running a cross my land called *"Spencer lot"* to the out or E bounding line to the said tract to intersect that line 44 perches to the S of the double gum a boundary of my land to a stone no. 5 all which land lying to the S of the said crossing down to the stone at the corner of or near **Mr. Glenn** field to the stone put up by **Jacob Glenn** and myself the corner of his land thence S 70° W 103 perches to a stone at pine marsh thence N 87° W 31 perches to the water at the head of a small cove called perch cove thence S 43° 30' W 87 perches to the beginning containing about 330 acres. My son **Richard Spencer** shall pay to his brother **Lambert W. Spencer** $1,000 as his property is of my value then his brother Lambert and this is to balance it out. And my son **Richard** shall pay his brother Lambert W. Spencer $600 if he chooses to keep the 30 acres part of *"Grisham's Discovery"* but if he refuses to give the $600 then to give title to the 30 acres of *"Gresham's Discovery"* lying a long side of Eccleston land. To my dau. Anna Spencer that part of my plantation called *"Spencer Lot"* including the following lines designated on plat beginning at stone at the 2 gums at stone at Tuskey the third boundary of my son Richard and corner of my son land called Spencer lot to a stone at hair bush the corner of the land called *"Hunters Strate line"* from that line to a stone 10 perches to a stone and cedar post to the corner of *"Smyth Park"*, Hunter's line running with Smyth Park and Spencer lot the division line in the road at the head of Davis Crick near the spring N 30' E to such a number of perches as will reach the stone in the road near the spring near the head of Davis Crick then from the stone in the run in the water marked no. 5 running with the water with the Davis Creek down till it reaches the line of **Samuel Eccleston** running to a double gum marked with 8 notches and stone to the corner of Samuel Eccleston land a piece I bought of **Benjamin Chew Esq.** 21½ acres running with Eccleston land S 5° W 44 perches to a stone or tree marked with Eccleston line from thence a cross from that line towards the home plantation to ditch and stone on the other side of the ditch about 50 perches until it comes to the stone at ditch not far from the home plantation thence running from the stone at ditch to hickory tree with stone at the rute (root) marked R.S. the corner of the home plantation called *"Spencer lot"* devised to my son Richard his corner from the

boundary 86 perches to hickory and stone thence running with the line of my son Richard head line the division line between my son Richard and his sister **Anna** to the beginning stone at tuskey the two gums on line by the 4 springs but my son Richard shall have the use of the road where it now is to pass. To my dau. **Anna** a negro girl called **Willey** to serve her until she arrives at age 36 but if she tries to run away then her mistress to determine whether to set he free. If she dies without heirs then to my grandson **Richard Perry Spencer** to have all lands given dau. Anna. To my granddau. **Emma Banning** dau. of **Martha Banning** all that part of my land called *"Spencers Lot"* beginning at the white oak tree between Simon Wickes and mine running N 26° 45' E 78 perches to stone the corner of **Hezekiah Dunn** land and running N 16° W 79 perches to a stone in the road to the corner of William Brices land and mine from the stone N 60° 30' E 142 perches to the stone at Hair Bush to the second stone of my dau. Anna land from that stone to the first line of my dau. Anna land. If she dies without heirs then to my grandson **Samuel Spencer** son of Lambert W. Spencer. All other negroes not particularly named shall be free at 35. To my grandson **Samuel Spencer** son of Lambert W. Spencer a negro boy **Cleanes** the son of **Sarah** a negro woman I had given to my son Lambert when he was married with her children she had and might have until he arrives at 35. My son Richard shall pay to my dau. Anna after her son **Richard Samuel Wickes** attains 10 years old $70 annually for his education until he has paid $500. If they died then before Richard reaches 10 then to my son Lambert for his son **Richard Perry Spencer**. My personal estate divided among my 3 children.

Execs. my sons Lambert W. Spencer and Richard Spencer. Witnesses William Copper, Richard Grant, Thomas Crouch. Written Aug 5, 1822 Proved Apr. 19, 1825 p. 402

Rebecca R. Houston

To my friends **Doctors Wroth** and **Brown** and Mr. **William McClean** any cash that may remain after the house rent as thanks for their kindness and any of my household furniture herein named should they decline it. To my nephew **William Houston** my suit of bed curtains and draperies the high post bed stead that is at **Mrs. Strongs**, the mahogany table tea table and brass andirons, 11 china plates, and 7 chairs. To my nephew **Benjamin Houston** 6 china plates, one large trunk, my tea pots, sugar dish, cream pot, 7 chairs, and my watch (provided Mr. **Peregrine Wilmer** does not call for it). To my relation **Hannah Houston** all the carpet now in my room, best tea tray that stands under the table, and large round walnut table. To my relation **Mary Wickes** the bed I now lie on. To my relation **Mary Wilmer** the cloak her son Mr. **P. Wilmer** presented to me. To my nieces **Augusta** and **Elizabeth Houston** 6 table, 6 desert and 4 silver tea spoons. To Miss **Margaret** and Miss **Ann McClean** each one quilt. To **Mrs. Cruikshanks** the blue pitcher, penciled large mug and a goblet, green edged vegetable and flat dishes and sauce boat to match, brass tops still andirons and shovel and tongs. To **Mary Cruikshanks** my painted glass mugs, the little red waiters, or to **Ann** her sister and also my japanned sugar box. To **Eugenia Wroth** my toilet table, dressing glass, with the 2 table covers, the pink and the white and the netting belonging to it. To my servant **Rachel** my bed and bolster that are at Mrs. Carvill's and 2 pillows, the bedstead I lie on, the old square mahogany table and 2 old chairs that are in Mrs. Besick's passage, all the china and crockery ware, except what is mentioned, my kitchen furniture my double domestic wrapper, my new dark cotton ditto, 3 old muslin sheets, 4 blankets, 3 old blue cotton bed covers, the flat trunk, the tub that is at Mrs. Blake's and all pieces of carpet and stairs. To **Mary** her dau. a small white trunk with H on it.

Execs. Hannah Houston, Mary Wickes, Anna McClean. Witnesses Caroline M. Carvill (Caroline M. Holedy at acknowledgment), Edward Freeman, Alphonsa T. A. Blake. Written Feb. 1, 1825 Proved July 9, 1825 p. 408

Cuthbert Hall Register of Wills for Kent Co
Whereas my son **Wright Hall** wishes that I should give all my estate to his sisters **Araminta Hall** and **Josephine Hall** from a conviction that he can do better in this world than they can do, therefore I give to my dau. Araminta Hall ½ my estate and to my dau. Josephine Hall ½ my estate.

Exec. my son Wright Hall. Witnesses Joseph Hyland (of Stephen) James M. Smithers. Written Mar. 27, 1825 Proved Oct. 7, 1825 p. 411

James Corse of Kent Co
I set free all my negroes **George, David, Jim, Harry** at my death, **Mary, Beck** and **Mary** with their issue and the boys as they arrive to 21 to wit **Isaac** age 18, **Levi** age 15, **Sandy** 14, **Rees** 9, **John** 10, **Bill** 8, old **Ned** 7, **Charles** 2, and the girls at 18 with their issue to wit **Phillis** 14 and **Sally** 12. If my negroes are not enough for my debts then to sell so much of my real estate. To my brother **Unit Corse** the remainder of my estate and the remainder of the time of my negro boys and girls.

Exec. my brother Unit Corse. Witnesses Joseph Turner, John Usilton, Henry Green. Written Jan. 13, 1824 Proved Oct. 27, 1825 p. 412

Codicil I set Big Henry, Big Bill, Deaf Isaac and Hanner all free at my death. Written Jan. 27, 1825

Mary Price Wilmer of Kent Co
To my nephew **Walter C. Wilmer** $1,600, a breast pin and also one of my rings. To my sister **Mrs. Frances Wilmer** the legacy due me from my sister **Ann's** estate, $100, my best bed and ½ of my clothes. To my sister **Elizabeth Frisby** $200, ½ of my clothes, a large trunk and a small table. To my nephew **John Lambert Wilmer** $100 and one of my rings. To my nephew **William D. Wilmer** $300 and one of my rings, also my negro boy **Dick** to serve until age 32. And at age 32 to be given an ax hoe and cradle and $10. To my nephew **Richard W. Frisby** $100 and a ring. I give to my niece **Margaret Elizabeth Briscoe** $66 and to my niece **Henrietta Wilmer** $44 which $44 is due me from her mother Mrs. **Rachel Wilmer**. To the family servant **Betty** a bed quilt, 2

blankets and one part of sheets, and $8. To my nephew **Walter C. Wilmer** all my china and my other bed and all the residue of my estate.

Exec. my nephew Walter C. Wilmer. Witnesses S. Carmichael, Catharine Carmichael, Samuel H. Stephens. Written Aug. 14, 1825 Proved Oct. 31, 1825 p. 414

Mary Thomas of Kent Co

To my son **Samuel Thomas** one large mahogany dining table as a small token of my affection. To my son **Richard S. Thomas** one mahogany sideboard as a small token of my affection. Being desirous that my son **William Thomas** should be secured a living during his life I give my farm near I.U. Church to my friends **Joseph Turner** and **Bartus Trew** in trust for his support forever. At his death to support his issue. If he has no issue then to my sons Richard S. Thomas and John Thomas. To my granddau. **Deborah Jones** one bureau now at her father **David Jones'**, one suit of bed curtains, one silver porringer, and one silver cream cup as a small token of my affection on account of her tenderness to me always. To **George W. Thomas** of Chestertown in trust the balance of a bond due me from Bartus Trew and all the money which the Chancellor of MD and trustee of my late husband Richard S. Thomas' real estate to pay my son William Thomas and the last two to be paid to my granddaughters Deborah Jones, **Mary Louisa Jones** and **Anna Maria Jones** shall arrive at 18 for their education. $40 to my son William Thomas and $222.22 to each of my granddaughters. My negro woman **Harriott** free at my decease. The residue of my estate to my son John Thomas.

Exec. my son John Thomas. Witnesses Lewis Gale, Joseph Usilton, Robert Usilton. Written Nov. 2, 1825 Proved Nov. 15, 1825 p. 416

Sarah Smith of Kent Co

After my debts, to my grandchildren **Nancy Smith, Hannah Elizabeth Smith** and **Joel Smith** children of my son **William Smith** deceased to be managed by my cousin **Major Smith** to the following directions all my household furniture wearing apparel he may loan during his pleasure to my dau. in law **Martha Smith** and may equally divide between my mentioned grandchildren when age 18 for girls and Joel at 21.

Exec. Major Smith. Witnesses William B. Wilmer, Alexander Wheat. Written Oct. 5, 1825 Proved Nov. 23, 1825 p. 419

Sarah Everitt of Kent Co

To my son **Joseph K. Everitt** my negro man **Ned** or **Edward**, one dressing glass, one small trunk and table spoons. To my son **William K. Everitt** my negro man **Sam** and all the money due me from a bond of **Andrew Toulson** when age 21. To my sister **Jane Toulson** all my wearing apparel. The rest of my estate divided between my sons Joseph K. Everitt and William K. Everitt.

Exec. John Wroth. Witnesses Samuel G. Kennard, William Taylor, Andrew Toulson. Written Nov. 24, 1825 Proved Nov. 28, 1825 p. 421

John Sappington of Sassafras Neck, Cecil Co, MD
To my 3 nephews **John, James,** and **Benjamin Roach** sons of my eldest sister **Elizabeth** by **James Roach**, all my wearing apparel. The rest of my estate to my wife **Sophia Sappington**.

Execs. my wife Sophia Sappington and my friend Hance Severson. Witnesses John J. Corse (Cox), Thomas Severson (John Wroth of Cecil Co knew writing of John Sappington). Written Jan. 25, 1812 Proved Nov. 29, 1825 (Dec. 2 Sophia came) p. 422

Christopher Spry of Kent Co
To my **Charlotte Spry** my farm in Kent Co DE on which **George Ward** now lives containing 230 acres, also my farm in Kent Co MD on which **William Stephens** now lives containing 260 acres, my horse and carriage, all the silver spoons and furniture of the cupboard, a mahogany sideboard, mahogany bureau, largest looking glass, mahogany ding and breakfast tables, 3 bedsteads. Also to her my silver watch and all the gold coin found in the house and $100 in cash. To her all the silks, ribbons, shaw, hats, and bandboxes with all the reading books. $250 to the Methodist Preachers for use of the Methodist Episcopal Church as long as the principal for 17 years is not used. I give to **William Lambdin** son of my sister **Lucretia** $200. To **Rachel Mobery** of Dorchester Co 4 bonds of **Daniel W. Young** and a mortgage on a piece on records of Queen Anns Co, and also $300. All the remaining estate to my sisters **Elizabeth, Sarah, Mary Rebecca,** and **Eve**.

Exec. my wife Charlotte Spry. Witnesses David Spry, Elijah Quimby, Ann Dilahunt. Written Feb. 1, 1823 Proved Dec. 9, 1825 p. 424

Renunciation I hereby renounce my right to administer to **Spry Denny**. Written Dec. 9, 1825 Signed Charlotte Spry.

Macall Medford of Fusbury Square, Middlesex Co (England)
To my wife **Maria Medford** all those lands with all houses lying in Kent Co in MD in North America and which lands descend to me from my late father **Macall Medford** of Kent Co and all my estate in America and Great Britain.

Exec. my wife. Witnesses John Mills Copeman, Mary Mertimer, Owen Cecil, David Lamb "Having made this will in England, before a witness in America". Written Feb. 7, 18011 [sic] [David appears to have been the one to sign later, also a 3 appears under his name]. Written Apr. 22, 1802 Proved Dec. 6, 1825 p. 425

Richard Miller of Kent Co

All that part of my farm in Swan Creek in Kent Co between Tavern branch and the Chesapeake Bay (except the road leading from the said branch to the bay) to my friend **Thomas Miller** in trust that he permit my dau. **Ann Eliza Vanlier** to receive rents and profits during her life without the consent of her husband and after her death to her issue. The above charge with payment of $70 annually to my dau. **Maria Evelina Miller** for her life. The residue of my estate to my dau. **Sarah Hester Miller** (except the burial ground which I wish to be used forever for a family burial ground) and except the said road and a road for the use of my dau. Ann Eliza Vanlier. Sarah Hester Miller to pay to my dau. Maria Evelina Miller $90. If Maria cannot find boarding then my dau. Sarah to board her. If my dau. Sarah Hester Miller dies under 21 then to my dau. Maria Evelina Miller and the $160 to be paid to her shall cease. To my dau. Maria Evelina Miller one bed and my negro boy **Tom** and my negro girl **Lucy**. To my dau. Sarah Hester Miller one bed and one negro boy **John** and my negro girl **Mary**. To my granddau. **Mary Virginia Vanlier** my negro girl **Hannah** and **Mary Jane**. The property to my dau. Ann Eliza Vanlier to be in full of her claim against my estate. All the rest of my estate to my 3 daughters. The property to my dau. Ann Eliza Vanlier not be subject to husband's control and on the account of the incapacity of my dau. Maria Evelina to my friend Thomas Miller and the $160 to be applied to her boarding.

Execs. my dau. Ann Eliza Vanlier and my friend Thomas Miller. Witnesses William Barroll, Jeremiah Nicols, Richard Ringgold. Written Dec. 29, 1823 Proved Dec. 16, 1825 p. 426

Edward Lamb (colored man) of Kent Co

To be buried at my wife **Easter Lamb** and to have all my estate.

Exec. Not Given. Witnesses John C. Norris, Benjamin Parrott. Written Feb. 14, 1825 Proved Feb. 6, 1826 p. 430

Sarah Swift of Kent Co

To my nephew **Edward Swift** all my claim to a lot late the property of my father adjoining the lands of *"Carvill's mill lot"* and the lands of the late **Thomas James** containing 10 acres, also my bed

Exec. my nephew Edward Swift. Witnesses Francis Lamb, William Lamb, Richard Warren. Written May 1825 Proved Feb. 18, 1826 p. 431

Sarah Piner in Kent Co

To my niece **Sarah Piner Wickes** all that may be due me from my the personal estate of my mother **Sarah Piner,** also my furniture and 12 silver table spoons, one mirror or looking glass, 2 beds, and my black woman **Betty** and my black boy **Jim**. To my niece all the land due from my deceased mother lying near Chestertown.

Exec. my nephew **Joseph Wickes 4th**. Witnesses P. Wroth, Mathew Tilghman, Ezekial F. Chambers. Written Jan. 7, 1826 Proved Mar. 9, 1826 p. 433

Hosanna Reed, widow of the late Samuel Reed of Kent Co
To my son **John Ashley** of Kent Co $10. To my dau. **Mary Reed** and to my sons **Joseph Reed** and **George Reed** all my land that I purchased of **Joseph Kennard** adjoining the plantation where I now live containing about 24 ¼ acres refer to bond of conveyance dated Sep 10, 1822, and that part of tract of land I purchased of **Rosamond Stein** containing 3 acres, 1 rood, and 5 perches refer to a deed dated Sep. 12 1821. To my son Joseph Reed my negro boy **Ned** or **Edward**. To my son George Reed $120. To my dau. Mary Reed $120. All the residue of my estate to my dau. Mary Reed, to my sons Joseph Reed and George Reed in equal portions.

Exec. William Coburn. Witnesses Samuel G. Kennard, Moses Kennard, Andrew Toulson. Written Feb. 16, 1826 Proved Mar. 9, 1826 p. 435

Hibert B. Price of Kent Co
To my brother **Spencer Price** of New Castle Co, DE ½ of the note of my brother **Isaac Price** for $500 and the other ½ to my brother Isaac. To my nephew **Edward Stoobs** $200. To my sister **Elizabeth Howard** the note I have against **Unit Augier** deceased for $330.40. To my sister **Sarah Wilson** $50. My negro girl **Ann** and her child be free. The remainder of my estate to my brother **Benjamin Price**

Exec. my brother Benjamin Price. Witnesses Thomas C. Kennard, Francis Cann. Written Mar. 4, 1826 Proved Mar. 20, 1826 p. 437

Thomas Hewitt of Kent Co
To my son **William Hewitt** my house and lot in Georgetown containing about 1½ acres and my looms and locking. To my dau. **Mary Sewall** $50. To my dau. **Anna Hewitt** $50 and 2 volumes of Clark's Commentary. To my dau. **Martha Hewitt** my bed. The rest of my estate to my son William Hewitt.

Exec. my son William Hewitt. Witnesses Robert Elliott, Joseph Ireland Jr, William Knight. Written Mar. 26, 1824 Proved Mar. 10, 1826 p. 439

James Wilson of Kent Co
To my son **James Wilson** all my lands lying in Kent Co and my personal estate

Exec. Henry Hurtt. Witnesses John H. Nowland, William Palmer, James Salisbury Jr. Written Apr. 15, 1826 Proved June 14, 1826 p. 441

George Fourman of Kent Co
As I got a greater part of my property from my wife and through her long affection to me during my infirmity, I give her all my estate during her life and after her death my

Abstracts of Kent Co., MD Wills

real estate to my 4 children **Araminta Elizabeth, George Washington, Alethia Ann, Benjamin Franklin** equally.

Exec. my wife **Elizabeth Fourman**. Witnesses Edward Hines, John M. Armstrong, Josiah Massy. Written Mar. 2, 1826 Proved June 27, 1826 p. 442

Rebecca Ringgold of Kent Co
All my estate to my 3 sisters **Sarah Ringgold, Elizabeth Ringgold**, and **Frances Ringgold**.

Execs. my 3 sisters Sarah, Elizabeth and Frances Ringgold. Witnesses James Ringgold, Anna Ringgold, Sally Blunt. Written Feb. 6, 1811 Proved July 13, 1826 p. 443

John Starling of Kent Co
To my wife **Elizabeth Starling** all my property.

Exec. my wife. Witnesses Joseph J. Thomas, Henry Brown, Edward Currey. Written Dec. 1819 Proved July 18, 1826 p. 444

Ann Elizabeth Hyland of Kent Co
To my son **William Hyland** 1 share of stock in Union Bank of MD. To my son **Stephen Hyland** my town lot or *"Harigan's Lot"* and a negro girl **Catherine**, 2 shares in the Union Bank of MD, 1 share in the Bank of Baltimore, one bed, 2 pillows, 2 sheets, 2 coverleds, 4 blankets, 6 silver table spoons, 6 silver tea spoons and one pair silver sugar tongs. To my dau. **Sarah W. Hyland** all the residue of my property consisting of furniture, bank stock, negroes, etc.

Exec. my dau. Sarah W. Hyland. Witnesses John Hyland (of Stephen), William Pearce, Anna W. Ringgold. Written Aug. 12, 1824 Proved Aug. 29, 1826 p. 445

James G. McClean of Kent Co
To **James Frisby Gordon** $500, my horse, saddle, and bridle, my watch and gun. To **Thomas G. Worrell** $200. To **George Gibson** (free negro) $100 and all my chamber furniture. No part of my real estate is to be used to pay above legacies if my personal estate is not enough to pay these legacies. My negroes over 25 shall be free at my death and the others at 25. My real estate to be applied towards payment of my debts so as to make up deficiency and secure the freedom of my negroes for I am anxious on this subject. John B. Eccleston trustee to make sure terms are carried out and to receive $150 to secure freedom of negro **Vincent** commonly called **Vin** and who belongs to the estate of **Thomas Worrell** deceased. ½ of the residue to **Ann Elizabeth F. Gordon** she paying $30 to **Hannah G. Worrell** during her single life. The other ½ to **Sarah N. Tilghman**, wife of **William C. Tilghman** and she paying to **Anna Matilda Worrell** during her single life.

Exec. John B. Eccleston. Witnesses None (Joseph Gordon and Dr. George W. Thomas Chief Judge of Kent Co give accounts). Written July 17, 1826 Proved Aug. 12, 1826 p. 447

Codicil My washstand to Ann Elizabeth F. Gordon and to sell my real estate if personal estate is insufficient. The $100 to George Gibson (free negro) secured by my real estate if my personal estate is insufficient. Written July 17, 1826

(Joseph N. Gordon saith that on Monday afternoon, the July 17, last he called at Mr. James G. McClain and found John B. Eccleston in the room with him and had the paper believed to be the will in the writing of Mr. Eccleston and upon delivering the paper remarked to Mr. McClean that your uncle Dr. Gordon is here and the Captain of the steam boat will be here presently and you can get a third person shortly, he assented at first but said he did not want the captain of the steamboat as a witness but I will take it with me to Baltimore. On Tuesday the next day he called again to see Mr. McClean at his request to assist him in getting on board the steamboat to go to Baltimore when Mr. McClean said uncle come here and he said I have given your son **Frisby** my horse and watch. I have given to Thomas Worrell $200, to George Gibson $100 and my room furniture as the deponent thought in lieu of his account against him or for services rendered and he had been faithful to him for 12 or 15 months. To **Hannah** and **Anna Mathilda Worrell** I have given $30 annually by **Sally Tilghman** and Ann Elizabeth and that the bulk of the estate was given to Sally Tilghman and Ann Elizabeth Gordon and he remarked James I would have done more for those children that are entirely dependent and he replied that his reason for giving the bulk to Sally and Ann Elizabeth was you know they have been my particular favorites. And my washstand I have given to Ann Elizabeth or yourself, I believe to Ann Elizabeth, but it is intended for the family as it was a family piece. The deponent was informed by letter from John Scott Esq. that Mr. McClean died on Fri. July 20 last)

Dr. George W. Thomas Chief Judge of Kent Co said on Monday July 31 last the deponent, Edward Anderson, and John B. Eccleston went to the room lately occupied by the late James G. McClean and after opening a trunk which contained Mr. McClean's clothes, his watch and pocketbook, and which trunk he had with him at the time of his death, we found the annexed will and a paper which the deponent had given to Mr. McClean on July 17 in relation to a transfer of 10 shares of Chester River Bridge.

Catharine Usilton of Kent Co
All my estate divided among my 3 sons that is my 2 oldest sons and my youngest son named **John Usilton, Robert Usilton,** and **Joseph Usilton.**

Exec. my oldest son John Usilton. Witnesses Thomas Alford, Joseph Duyer. Written Sep. 27, 1826 Proved Oct. 3, 1826 p. 453

Abstracts of Kent Co., MD Wills

William Hosier of Kent Co
To my nephew **William H. Dorsey** my farm where I now reside in Kent Co being part of *"Great Oak Manor"* adjoining Rev. **George D. Handy** and the heirs of **George Skirven**, containing 210 acres. To William H. Dorsey all my farm being part of several tracts *"Worton Manner"*, *"Wallis' Choice"*, *"Budd's Discovery"* and *"Carolla"* purchased in part from **Samuel G. Kennard** and in part from **Samuel** and **William Groome** lying in Worton Point in Kent adjoining William Lamb, Samuel G. Kennard and **Andrew Tolson** containing 227 acres if he pays to his mother **Anne Dorsey** $200 annually during her life. My sister the said Anne Dorsey have the privilege to reside in the dwelling house where I now live and using the house and kitchen and to have firewood along with William H. Dorsey. My negroes **Tom** to be free on Oct. 10, 1832, **Aleck** to be free on Jan. 3, 1839, **Adron** to be free Jan. 1, 1856, **Mary** to be free on Jan. 1, 1830, **Bill** to be free on Aug. 1, 1854, **Frisby** to be free on Feb. 28, 1858, **John** son of **Delia** to be free when he is 25. To William H. Dorsey negroes **Washington** about 18, **Delia** and her child **Rachel**, **Moses** and son of **Letty**, **Harriot**, dau. of **Hannah**, **Louisa** and **George** children of **Beck**. To William H. Dorsey the rest of my estate.

Exec. William H. Dorsey. Witnesses George D.S. Handy, Samuel G. Kennard, James J. Kennard. Written May 8, 1826 Proved Oct. 31, 1826 p. 454
[Pass granted to Bill Mar. 3, 1855]

Nathaniel Comegys Jr.
All my estate to my wife **Debba Comegys** during her life. The rest of my estate to my dau. **Millimenty Comegys**.

Exec. my wife Debba Comegys. Witnesses Isaac Hines, Thomas Woodall, Henry Masten. Written Oct. 25, 1826 Proved Nov. 9, 1826 p. 456

James Claypoole of Kent Co
To my wife **Elizabeth Claypoole** during her life and after to my son **James Claypoole** 1/5 part, to my son **John Claypoole** 1/5 part, to my son **Septimous Claypoole** 1/5 part, to my son **William Claypoole** 1/5 part, to my 3 grandchildren **Elizabeth**, **Margarett**, and **Mary Collins** 1/5 part.

Exec. my wife Elizabeth Claypoole. Witnesses William Crane, John Crane, Daniel Collins. Written Mar. 24, 1826 Proved Nov. 13, 1826 p. 457

Bathsheba Anderson of Chestertown, Kent Co
To my relation **Elizabeth Claypool** wife of **James Claypool** of Chestertown all my estate.

Exec. my friend James Claypool. Witnesses James Mansfield, Cuthbert Hall, Joseph Redue. Written Oct. 16, 1822 Proved Nov. 16, 1826 p. 459

Liber 10 1816-1827

Oliver Smith of Kent Co
My real estate to be sold (except the graveyard to be reserved with ingress and egress) and my debts paid, the remainder to my executors until the death of my wife **Anna Minta Smith**. To my wife all my personal estate forever and the interest of my real estate except for $20 to my brother **Edward Smith** during the life of my wife Anna but if my brother dies in the lifetime of my wife then to my 2 nieces **Julian** and **Margaretta Edwards**. After my wife's death to my sister **Margaret Edwards** during her life and after her death the interest on 1/3 to dau. **Mary Ann Edwards** and to my brother Edward Smith 1/3 proceeds, and if he dies without heirs then to my 2 daughters Julian and Margaretta Edwards. To **Jonathan T. Welch** 1/3 the proceeds. My negro woman **Mary** be set free at 27 and my negro girl **Milly** and negro boy **Theodore** to be free at age 30.

Execs. William and Ebenezer Welch. Witnesses James Boon, Arthur Talbott, George Moffett. Written Dec. 23, 1825 Proved Nov. 21, 1826 p. 460

William Anderson of Kent Co
To **Benjamin Hazle**, son of George Hazel and my dau. **Hosanna Hazel**, all that tract being the farm which I now reside on composed of tracts called *"Massy's Venture"*, *"Boardly Gift"*, *"Little Forest"* and all other lands considered attached to the farm. To **James Hazel** son of George and Hosanna Hazel all that farm now occupied by **John Haley** and all land attached thereto. If either dies without heirs then to the survivor and if both dies then equally divided between the other children of my George and Hosanna Hazel. My personal estate to pay my debts or use part of real estate. Any remainder to my wife **Mary Anderson** in addition to what she may be legally entitled to.

Execs. my friend Samuel G. Osborne of the head of Chester and my son in law George Hazel. Witnesses John McDaniel, Joseph Wright, John Beck. Written Nov. 5, 1826 Proved Dec. 6, 1826 p. 462

Sarah Miller of Kent Co
Being old and infirm, I make my will. My negro man **Perry** aged 25 and my negro man **Richard** age 22, my negro boy **John** age 18, all free on Dec. 1 and my negro girl **Mary** aged 22 and my negro girl **Ann Mariah** aged 4 years and my negro girl **Mary Jane** aged 2 years, and my negro child **Perry** aged 6 months to serve until they arrive at age 30. To **Thomas James Blackiston** son of **James** and **Mary Ann Blackiston** my negro child Perry aged 6 months but if he dies without issue then to my niece Mary Ann Blackiston. To my niece Mary Ann Blackiston my negro girl **Mary** age 22, my negro girl **Ann Mariah** aged 4, and my negro girl Mary Jane age 2 to serve until above mentioned. To my niece Mary Ann Blackiston all the residue of my estate.

Exec. James Blackiston husband of my niece Mary Ann Blackiston. Witnesses Nathaniel Meginniss, Mary Ann Meginniss. Written Dec. 7, 1826 Proved Jan. 24, 1827 p. 464

Abstracts of Kent Co., MD Wills

William Wheeler of Kent Co
To my wife **Ann B. Wheeler** all my estate.

Exec. my wife Ann B. Wheeler. Witnesses David Arthur, James Mansfield, Samuel Mansfield. Written Nov. 1, 1826 Proved Dec. 23, 1826 p. 466

Jane Corse of Kent Co
To my dau. **Eliza M. Hanson** $1,000 from a bond due me by her late husband **John Hanson**. To my granddau. **Jane E. Hanson** a bureau now belonging to me. To my granddau. **Martha H. Hanson** my chest and table. To my granddau. **Ann E. Rochester** and **Elizabeth J. Rochester** the balance of the above bond due me by my late son in law John Hanson.

Exec. my dau. Eliza M. Hanson. Witnesses Thomas C. Kennard, Sarah Hambleton. Written Oct. 27, 1826 Proved Jan. 24, 1827 p. 467

Samuel Hall of Kent Co
To my wife **Rebecca Hall** all my estate during her life, my 2 black men excepted. To **Mary Rebecca Hall** dau. of my brother **Christopher Hall** and to **Sarah Elizabeth Millan** dau. of **William Millan** all my house and lot I now dwell in the head of Chester which I bought of **John Turner**. To my nephew **Josiah Hall** son of my said brother Christopher Hall one silver watch, one bed, but to remain in the hands of my wife during her life. To my brother Christopher Hall all my wearing apparel. My 2 negro men **Joseph Doman** and **James Doman** be set free. To my said niece Mary Rebecca Hall and Sarah Elizabeth Millan the residue of my personal estate after paying my nephew Josiah Hall all of which to remain in my wife's possession during her life

Exec. my wife Rebecca Hall. Witnesses John Evans, John Beck, John McDaniel. Written Oct. 4, 1826 Proved Dec. 19, 1826 p. 469

Elizabeth Thomas of Kent Co
My negro man **Isaac** aged 41 and my negro woman **Rachel** aged 42 and my negro woman **Ruth** aged 38 to be free on Jan. 1. My negro man **Stephen** aged 36 to be free on Jan 1, 1827. To my dau. **Emily Thomas** the balance of my estate.

Exec. my grandson **Thomas Jiney Mann**. Witnesses Nathaniel Comegys, Joseph Mann. Written Mar. 25, 1822 Proved Jan. 5, 1827 p. 471

Liber 11   1827-1835

Will Book 11   1827-1835   pp. 1-343 WK 688-689-1

Eliza Reed of Kent Co
My negroes **Jacob, Minta, Moses, Pere,** and whatever children Minta may have to be free at my death. All the residue of my estate (negroes excepted) to **Lavinia Jane Pendleton** dau. of **Joseph T. Ford.**

Exec. Lavinia Jane Pendleton. Witnesses Mary Thomas, John Usilton, George W. Thomas. Written Aug 7, 1826 Proved Feb. 19, 1827 p. 1

William Harris of Chestertown, Kent Co
I give my property in Kent Co or elsewhere (except in Caroline Co) to my wife **Margaret** during her life for support of herself and my 3 youngest children **Mary Maria, Ann Margaret,** and **Edward Anderson Harris** and to educate my 2 youngest **Ann Maria** and **Edward Anderson Harris.** My wife Margaret and my dau. Mary Maria shall continue the store I have heretofore conducted. After the death of my wife I give to my said 3 youngest all the estate aforesaid. If any die under age without heirs then to survivors. If all die then to my 2 eldest sons **James** and **William Harris.** My wife shall rent out the land in Caroline Co where **Clayton** now resides part of which belonged to my brother **Thomas Harris** and part of which I purchased from others to be used to support my said brother during his life and any excess to my 3 youngest children. If my wife dies before my brother then my dau. Mary Maria shall do the same. If my brother Thomas Harris dies then the land to be sold and divided among my 3 youngest children. My friend **Ezekial F. Chambers** trustee to sell the said farm. My wife Margaret and my dau. Mary Maria shall make inventory of my estate and to be guardians of my 2 youngest children and executrixes.

Execs. my wife Margaret and my dau. Mary Maria. Witnesses Thomas Smith, Harriott M. Clane, Ann H. Smith. Written Feb. 6, 1825 Proved Feb. 1, 1827 p. 2

Catharine Belts of Kent Co
To my sister **Sarah Nandain** my best bed, 2 calico quilts, 4 blankets, towels, gig and harness and my wearing apparel, 2 table clothes, a negro boy **Harry** who is 5 until he is 25. To my nephew **Peregrine Granger** of Centreville a black girl **Elizabeth** who is 9, a negro boy **Josiah** who is 10, **James Henry** who is 7 and a negro girl **Maria** about 3 until they are 30. [freedom pass granted to Maria July 28, 1855]. To **Margarett Wroth** dau. of **John Wroth** a negro girl **Sarah** now 6 and a negro boy **Isaiah** now 4 until age 30. To **Louisa Wroth** dau. of John Wroth a negro girl **Harriott** who is 7 and a negro boy **John** who is 2 until they are 30, and my mahogany bureau. To Peregrine Granger 2/3 of money due for rent in Queen Anns Co. To **Richard Kennard** colored man his 2 children by my woman **Ann** named **Editha** and **George** until they are 21. My woman **Minty** to be free in one month. The residue of my estate to be divided in equal shares and that Peregrine Granger to have one share and the other share to the four children of John Wroth.

Abstracts of Kent Co., MD Wills

Exec. my nephew Peregrine Granger. Witnesses Elizabeth M. Briscoe, John Frazier, Dr. Edward Scott. Written Feb. 8, 1827 Proved Feb. 21, 1827 p. 6

Sarah Milward of Kent Co
My negro man **George** to be hired out for 10 years and the wages annually paid to my brother **Janus Milward** and my sister **Mary Sewall**, and then George to be free. My brother **Janus** to have my bed and bedstead, also my 2 trunks. To my cousin **Mary Ryner** my necklace, toilet table. To my sister Mary Sewall all the residue of my estate.

Exec. my uncle **George Spry**. Witnesses John Wallis, Ephraim Vansant 4th. Written June 10, 1822 Proved Jan. 15, 1827 (Oct. 25, 1826 John Sewall witnessed with codicil) p. 9

<u>Codicil</u> My negro man George to be free immediately after my death. Written June 13, 1826. Witnesses David Davis, John Sewall

Sarah Beswick of Chestertown, Kent Co
To **Araminta Lockwood** wife of **Caleb Lockwood** living in DE all my estate and whereas it is doubtful whether my nephew **Daniel Hamer** is living or dead, but if living to have my house and lot wherein I live in Chestertown for his life.

Exec. Caleb Lockwood of DE. Witnesses William Barroll, Robert Hall, Richard P. Seymour. Written Nov. 26, 1825 Proved Apr. 2, 1827 p. 12

Maria Dorney
To my son **Thomas Dorney** $100. To my dau. **Mary Dorney** and to my son Thomas Dorney all residue of my estate. My negro boy **Perry** after he serves 28 years. **Thomas Dorney** of Harford Co to be guardian to my son Thomas Dorney.

Exec. Thomas Dorney of Harford Co. Witnesses Thomas Gale, John Dwyer, Robert Beswicks. Written Apr. 2, 1827 Proved Apr. 11, 1827 p. 13

William Clark [the start of his will crossed out] p. 14

Milbourn Greenwood of Kent Co
To **James Briscoe** son of **Jacob Briscoe** deceased blacksmith by trade all the land willed to me by my father **Joseph Greenwood** with all other property I may be possessed.

Exec. James Briscoe. Witnesses Samuel Ringgold, Thomas Murphey, Janus County. Written Apr. 15, 1827 Proved May 8, 1827 p. 15

Maria Hudson of Kent Co
My negro boy **Bob** is to be free. All my estate divided between **John Hudson** my brother and my sister **Ann M. Numbers** wife of **Edmund Numbers**

Liber 11 1827-1835

Exec. Samuel Kerr. Witnesses None (Temperance Meeks came and knew writing of Maria Hudson). Written 1827 Proved May 11, 1827 p. 16

William Miller of Kent Co
Whereas I am indebted to my aunt **Nancy Dunn** for $200 and she has said that for settlement of my debt I am to give as a legacy to my son William, therefore I give to my son $200. I give all my estate my wife **Elizabeth**
Exec. my wife Elizabeth. Witnesses John B. Eccleston, Edward Wright, Isaiah Ashley. Written May 15, 1827 Proved June 4, 1827 p. 18

Elizabeth Medford of Kent Co
My negro woman **Joyce** be free on Jan. 1 next. My negro man **Sam** to be free Jan. 1, 1829, My negro man **Theodore** to be free on Jan. 1, 1837. My negro man **George** to be free on Jan. 1, 1838. My negro woman **Sarah** to be free Jan. 1, 1837. My negro girl **Ellen** free on Jan. 1, 1843; and agreeably to the act of General Assembly of MD in the Nov. session of 1809 the issue that may be born of my negro woman Sarah and girl Ellen during their period of service to serve until they arrive at 31 for boys and 26 for girls. All my plate, household furniture, wearing apparel, and the negroes (and issue of Sarah and Ellen) to my dau. **Hannah Medford** and if she dies before the end of the negroes service then they to be free at her death, and to her all my real estate near Turners Creek Point during her life and if she marries then to her husband if she dies during his life and after to her children by him. After her death if she has no issue then to **Samuel Wethered** son of **Samuel**. All the rest of my estate to my friends **Lewin Wethered** of Baltimore City and **George W. Thomas** of Kent Co in trust (except that near Turners Creek Point) to sell said property and put to stock and semiannually interest paid to my dau. Hannah Medford during her life and at her death then to whomever she designates by last will. My old negro man **George** to be supported by my dau. Hannah Medford and knowing her goodness but securing his well being if he is dissatisfied then to have executors support him up to $40 per year.

Execs. my friends Lewin Wethered and George W. Thomas. Witnesses Richard Ringgold, Elizabeth Wickes, Ann E. Garnett. Written Apr. 20, 1827 Proved July 21, 1827 p. 20

Renunciation Filed with the administration bond.

Catharine Amanda Blackiston, dau. of late James Blackiston of Kent
All my real estate left to me by my late father and in Kent Co along with 3 negroes **Tilly Ann**, **Persey Hemsley** and **Jim** to my brothers **David Crane Blackiston** in trust for my mother now the wife of **Casperis Meginniss** during her life and after her death to my brother David Crane Blackiston and my sister **Mary Malvina Blackiston**. All my estate not named to David Crane Blackiston in trust for my mother **Mary** during her life and after her death to my sister and brother above named.

Abstracts of Kent Co., MD Wills

Exec. **James Blackiston** residing near Masseys Creek Cross Roads. Witnesses Adam Waldic, David Crane, Joseph H. Sawyer. Written Mar. 9, 1827 at Philadelphia Proved Apr. 13, 1827 (before Joseph Watson Esq and Mayor of Philadelphia, PA the 3 witnesses confirmed will) p. 25

Elizabeth Nicols
To my sister **Mary S. Nicols** all my monies may be in my possession to finish her education under the direction of **Dr. Wroth** and my sister **Margaret** and to my sister Mary all my wearing apparel (except certain articles) with my blue necklace, earrings, and bracelets, the 3 black plumes, to be disposed of and something useful bought for her. To my sister **Sarah A. Nicols** my bed, blankets, wardrobe, dressing table, looking glass, washstand, basin and pitcher, chairs, cabinets, andirons, shovel tongs, and fender, a breast pin, and amber beads, steel necklaces and steel bracelets. To my sister **Henrietta M. Haynard** my part earrings, breastpin, buckle and ring, also suit of bed curtains. To my sister **Margaret S. Nicols** my mattress mahogany stand writing desk and books, also the black merino shaw and bombazine for a dress. To my brother **James Nicols** the mourning breastpin in the form of a leaf the hair now in it to be taken out and replaced by some of mine with the initials of my name on it. To my friend **Harriet B. Hackett** my carpet. My friend **Mrs. Eliza Comptors** my mourning ring containing the hair of my deceased cousin **Mrs. Martha N. Tilghman**. To my cousin **Ellen S. Tilghman** the likeness of her deceased uncle and aunt Mr. and Mrs. **Henry Tilghman**, also my mourning breastpin containing the hair of her deceased aunt Mrs. Henry Tilghman. My sister Margaret should give the articles and she alone should examine my letters and papers such as it may not be necessary to keep she may destroy. Signed E. H. Nicols.

Exec. Not Given. Witnesses William Barroll, Elizabeth Nicols. Written June 17, 1827 Proved July 9, 1827 p. 27

William Clark of Kent Co
All my personal estate sold except my negro boy **Henry**. To my son **James** my negro boy Henry. To my son **Ira** $50 when he is 21. All the rest of my personal estate to my 5 children **Catharine, Elizabeth, James, Julietta,** and Ira. My friend **George Vansant** and **Nathaniel Maginness** to be guardians to my 5 children and my friend Nathaniel Meginness to procure a home as he may approve.

Execs. my friend George Vansant and Nathaniel Maginness. Witnesses George Meginniss, John Hurlock. Written June 3, 1827 Proved June 12, 1827 p. 29

Francina Comegys of Kent Co
To my 2 granddaughters **Sarah Francina** and **Mary Elizabeth Ringgold** 13 shares of Union Bank of MD until they are 18 or married and no allowance is to be made for board as it is intended that their mother shall superintend the same without charge the amount to be divided when they are of age. To Sarah Francina one negro boy **Lewis** and

Liber 11   1827-1835

to Mary Elizabeth one infant negro **Jim**. My dau. and only child **Ann Worrell Ringgold** to have the rest of my estate.

Exec. my dau. Ann Worrell. Witnesses William Pearce, Lambert Wickes. Written Sep. 12, 1824 Proved June 9, 1827 p. 31

John Wroth of Kent Co

My negro man **Charles** to be free at the end of the year and to pay him $20 per year if he shall conduct himself properly. My negro woman **Rachel** to be free at end of year but if she cannot support herself then to be supported out of my estate. My servant **Charlotte** be free end of the present year, **Emmeline** my servant to be free in 1833. My boy **William** to be free at 1830. My boy **Moses** to be free in 1839. My servant girl **Ann** to be free in 1841. My girl **Sarah** to be free in 1841. My boy **George** to be free in 1845. My **Harriet** to be free in 1845. If my personal estate in $1,600 all my land to be divided between my sons to be agreed upon by them when of age. I give my 2 sons the land on condition that my son **Thomas** pay to my dau. **Margaret** $500 within 5 years and my son **Edward** pay to dau. **Louisa** within 5 years. If $1,600 or more of personal estate then divided between my daughters. If not more, then my sons to make up difference in 7 years. My estate to the maintenance of all my children during their minority. My executor and my brother **Peregrine** to guard their morals. A tenant selected to rent my land and continue the improvement and my brother Peregrine to assist in selecting the tenant and if he dies then **Levi Wroth** should take his place. My friend **Peregrine Granger** of Centreville in Queen Anns Co executor and guardian.

Exec. Peregrine Granger of Centreville. Witnesses George Watts, William Wroth, Samuel Elbert. Written July 11, 1827 Proved July 31, 1827 p. 33

Hannah Lamb of Kent Co

To my dau. in law **Elizabeth Edwards** my gig, one bed and bedstead. I give to my grandson **William Edwards** my horse cart. To my son **John Edwards** my colored boys and girls to serve him until age 21 for the boys and 18 for the girls and my ox cart and yoke of oxen. The rest of my estate to be sold and after debts then to be divided between my grandchildren **Thomas, Joseph, James, Hannah, Elizabeth** and **Mary Edwards**. My apparel divided by fine texture being given my dau. in law Elizabeth Edwards and the residue to **Rachel Wiggins, Caroline Davis**, and **Hannah Freeman**.

Exec. my son John Edwards. Witnesses Joseph Turner, Mary Ann Dorney, Martha Draper. Written June 29, 1827 Proved Aug. 7, 1827 p. 34

Codicil Pay to my friend **Joseph Turner** $20 to upkeep the grave yard at Cecil Meeting house. Written July 5, 1827 Witness Ann Elizabeth Bowers

Abstracts of Kent Co., MD Wills

Catharine Parker wife of James Parker Esq. of the head of Chester
By a deed of indenture dated July 11, 1827 between **Ann Thomas** of the first part and said James Parker and me for a lot situate in the head of Chester being part of a tract called *"London Bridge Renewed"* transferred to said James Parker and myself for our natural lives and then to be given by a will, I therefore give to my niece **Mary Cosden** if she pays to her mother **Jannette Cosden** 1/3 part of the yearly value during her life. If she dies without issue then to my nephew **Alexander Cosden**.

Exec. Not Given. Witnesses William Thomas of John, John McDaniel, Samuel W. Trenchard. Written July 11, 1827 Proved Sep. 18, 1827 p. 39

Henry Tilghman of Kent Co
To my cousin **Elizabeth H. Nicols** an annuity of $175 during her life in 2 semi-annual payments and $3,500 to be invested in stock for the annuity above to be taken out of $3,000 in the Bank of Baltimore and $500 to be collected as soon as possible to make the sum. After the death of Elizabeth H. Nicols, the principal to my niece **Eleanor S. Tilghman** if she is living and of age 21 at the time of Elizabeth's death. If she dies without issue then to **John Henry Tilghman** the son of **John Tilghman** of Melfuto, **Arthur T. Jones** the son of **Arthur T. Jones**, **Richard Tilghman** the son of **Matthew Tilghman** of Chestertown, **James Nicols** the son of my aunt **Eliza Nicols** deceased, **Richard Henry Goldsborough** the son of **Nicholas Goldsborough** of Talbot and to **Edward Tilghman** the son of Mrs. **Rebecca Tilghman** of Philadelphia at the time my niece would have turned 21. If Elizabeth H. Nicols dies before my niece Eleanor S. Tilghman before age 21 then $175 to **Margaret S. Nicols**, **Mary S. Nicols**, and **Sarah H. Nicols**. My land called *"Dugan's Delight"* situated near Georgetown Cross Roads shall be sold and I appoint **John B. Eccleston** Esq my trustee for to sell and put to interest said land. To my cousin **Elizabeth Cooke** of Baltimore City $500 in 3 years. To my cousin **Mary Rarole** of Philadelphia $500 in 4 years. To **Rebecca Tilghman** widow of my cousin **Edward Tilghman Jr.** of Philadelphia $1,000, the interest to her and the principal at her death to her children now living. To my niece Eleanor S. Tilghman $500. My negro woman **Harriet** shall be free on May 9, 1837 and be given a new suit of summer cloth and I give the term she has to serve and my negro boy **Henry** for the term he has to serve to the **Rev. Peter Veuleman** so long as he officiates in the Roman Catholic Chapel in Queen Anns Co where he now resides and if he ends his officiating then their terms of servitude to be part of the residuum of my estate. If he must leave for Europe not for more than 2 years then he does not forfeit provided he provides them with a good home during said time. To Elizabeth H. Nicols her choice of my furniture viz one carpet, one mattress, 6 windsor chairs, one toilet table and 2 covers, one toilet looking glass, 3 sheets, 3 blankets, 2 counter pairs, 2 pillows and bolster cases and andirons shovel and tongs, towels, the walnut bureau, washstand basin, pitcher, my writing desk, and mahogany stand and my suit of bed curtains. To **James Nicols** one feather bed, one pair of blankets, 2 Russian sheets, one counterpane and one cot, and to him provided he lives through his apprenticeship $100. A neat marble headstone and footstone shall be placed at the graves of my father, mother and sister as soon as capable out of my estate.

Also the fence around my wife and myself and the tombstones shall be kept in good repair at the expense of my real estate. A priest of the Roman Catholic Church may call upon my estate for $20 to keep the enclosure and tomb in good repair. The persons in the memorandum folder with this will to have the several items. The remainder of my estate to my brother **Edward Tilghman 3rd**. And I transfer to my brother Edward Tilghman 3rd the bond of mortgage of **William H.D.C. Wright, Gustavus W. T. Wright** deceased and **Robert Wright** deceased. To my cousin **Henrietta Hayward** wife of **Thomas Hayward Jr**. my mahogany dining table and breakfast table, my set of white tea china and the dinner set of blue and white china, my best set of waiters, 12 cut glass tumblers, 12 cut glass wine glasses, and 12 cut glass punch glasses, my best set of knives and forks and my table clothes that are of value, my mahogany sideboard and 12 fancy chairs, my mahogany plate tray and stand, my plated candlesticks, snuffers and tray. To Margaret S. Nicols $300 in 2 years. To Mary S. Nicols and Sarah A. Nicols $300 at age 16.

Execs. my friends **Jeremiah Nicols** and William Barroll Sr. Witnesses Richard Ringgold, Dr. Peregrine Wroth, Richard C. Ringgold. Written Feb. 7, 1827 Proved Apr. 10, 1827 p. 42

<u>Codicil</u> The personal property on my farm to my residuary devisee and he to pay the wages of the overseer and hands on said farm. Witnesses same
<u>Memorandum</u> The enclosure around my wife's grave to be put up as the weather permits (the materials at the chapel) and to get more materials to extend the enclosure to my grave. I do not want a tombstone but to have a head and foot stone with the following inscription Henry Tilghman born 1 Mar 1790 died _ 1827. Mr Edward Tilghman can have the materials that are wanting of the same kind and pattern. To my friend **Dr. T. Willson** my set of window curtains and my side saddle to his dau. Ann Maria. To my friend **Dr. M. Browne** my large duck gun. To my friend **J. B. Hackett** my small duck gun and bird gun and gunning chest and gunning apparatus and my gig and harness. My wearing apparel to Margaret Nicols or Elizabeth Nicols for the use of **James Nicols** that is whatever is useful to him. My gold watch to my cousin **Mrs. Julianna Pacca**. My pair of carriage horses shall be sold. I give my books of miscellaneous and polite literature to Elizabeth and Margaret Nicols and my historical books to **Thomas Willson** son of **Dr. Thomas Willson**. To **Catharine Tilden** the 5 silver spoons and brass andirons which were her mothers. To my friend **Jeremiah Nicols** all my set and numbers of the American Farmer and my case of pruning knives. To my cousin Mrs. **S. H. Barroll** my set of cut glass dishes and plates for desert. To Mrs. **Nancy Tilghman** (of Melfield) 12 silver table spoons and to my friend **John Tilghman** (of Melfield) such of my school books and classical dictionary as he may think useful for his children and I give my piece of homemade table linen to said Mrs. Nancy Tilghman.
I agree that Jeremiah Nicols and William Barroll who are left executors may give bond. Written Apr. 10, 1827 Witness William H. Barroll Signed Edward Tilghman.

Mary Vincent
To my niece **Ann M. Cook** all my estate after my expenses for my illness and funeral

Exec. Not Given. Witnesses Augusta Bowers, Elizabeth C. Wickes, Henrietta M. Forman. Written Mar. 30, 1827 Proved Dec. 21, 1827 p. 54

Ann Carvill of Kent Co
My negro man **George,** my negro man **James,** my negro boy **Vincent,** my negro boy **Thomas,** my negro woman **Sarah** and all her children to be free, but if any hired out then to remain so until the end of the year. The rest of my estate to my niece **Martha Ann Attwood**

Exec. my niece Martha Ann Attwood. Witnesses Richard Ringgold. Written Apr. 23, 1827 Proved Aug. 4, 1827 p. 55

Rebecca Hall of Kent Co
To **Parssella Webb** of Kent Co one large cotton shawl, 1 large silk shawl. To **Louisa C. McDaniel** my large cabinet cloak. All the rest of my clothing and furniture to my granddau. **Sarah Elizabeth Millar**

Exec. my friend John McDaniel. Witnesses Robert Curry Jr, William Stant, John Beck. Written Nov. 13, 1827 Proved Nov. 20, 1827 p. 57

Susan Whorton
To my granddau. **Caroline Hynson** one feather bed bolsters, 2 pillows, one bed cover, one pair blankets. To my son **Thomas P. Gresham** all the rest of my estate

Exec. my son Thomas P. Gresham. Witnesses James Hart, James Crouch, George Wilson. Written Dec. 11, 1827 Proved Dec. 29, 1827 p. 59

James Parker of Kent Co
To my wife **Catharine Parker** and my niece **Mary Cosden** my farm part of a tract called *"Partnership"*. To my executrix the occupation of my house store and lot of ground on the main street in Bridgetown for 5 years and then sold with money placed in the U.S. Bank in Philadelphia under the control of the Delaware Co, PA Orphans Court to be distributed to my nephews and nieces, children of my brothers **William Parker** and **Joseph Parker** and my sisters **Elizabeth Levis** and **Hannah Smith** and if none living then to my wife. To my wife all my furniture in my house in town and I give her my cracker and gig harness. To my niece Mary Cosden my piano forte and my mahogany desk and bookcase and one feather bed. To my wife Catharine and to Mary Cosden 250 volumes of books from my library to be selected in lots of 25 each alternating with my wife getting first lot. The remainder to **Joseph H. Calder**. To **Simon Calder** my wearing apparel one full suit to be selected by my wife. To Joseph H. Calder my ducking gun and my holster and pistols. I give the justices of the peace at the head of Kittys Laws

Liber 11 1827-1835

of Maryland published in 1800 to be deposited in charge of the justice oldest in commission for use of the said justices and the public. To **Dr. John T. Rees** all my medical books and also my mahogany shaving case and also the razors and apparatus. To my wife Catharine the negroes **Darky, George, Bill, Steve, Ned, Pere, Henry, Felix, Ledia, Maria** and **Sylvia** subject to limitations of servitude. [Certificate of freedom granted to Maria June 5, 1854 in margin]. To Mary Cosden the negroes **Nan, Tom, Ellick,** and **Martha** subject to limitations of servitude. They shall limit servitudes to age 40 except Darkey and Nan who are over that age. My wife is to make list of their names and ages and record in records of Kent Co and I know she will not extend their servitudes and rely on her indulgence for the two excepted. To **James Calder** and to the children of **Nathaniel Calder** all the right to a piece of land in Lycoming Co, PA purchased of **Benjamin W. Morris**. ½ to James and ½ to the children of Nathaniel and my executrix to give up papers regarding the land. Residue to my wife Catherine and my niece Mary Cosden. My executrix to erect a brick wall around the graveyard in my orchard where the fence now stands and have it covered in a substantial manner and a substantial gate secured by proper fastening. As property often passes into strange hands I enjoin my wife and Mary Cosden to put in title the free privilege of ingress and egress to the enclosure and to keep in good repair a lien placed against the land for said purpose forever.

Exec. my wife Catherine. Witnesses William Thomas of John, Tabitha Wright, Ann Thomas. Written Jan. 20, 1826 Proved Dec. 26, 1827 p. 60

William Blake of Kent Co
All my real estate to my sister **Maria A. V. Blake**. My negro woman **Bet** shall be free. My saddle and bridle to my brother **Thomas Blake**. The rest of my estate to my brother **Joseph Blake**.

Exec. my mother in law **Sarah B. Blake**. Witnesses John B. Eccleston, William S. Lassell, Edward B. Gibbs. Written Nov. 10, 1827 Proved Jan. 10, 1828 p. 67

Nicholas Riley of Kent Co
To my 3 grandsons **Casparus Meginnis Riley, Samuel Riley,** and **John Crow Riley** sons of my deceased son **Samuel Riley** $100 each when they are 21. If any die then to the survivors. To my son **William Riley** all my estate.

Exec. my son William Riley. Witnesses John Ferguson, Thomas H. Boyer, Joseph Mann. Written July 11, 1826 Proved Jan. 12, 1828 p. 69

Dennis Kennard of Chestertown, Kent Co
All my estate after my debts paid then to **John B. Eccleston** of Chestertown in trust to collect money to pay **Rebecca Thompson** for her kindness during my present illness $20 on Jan. 1 and $40 on Sep. 1 yearly during her life and if interest is not enough for said $60 then to take part of principal. After her death then to the legitimate children of my

natural son **Richard Kennard** born of **Maria Sharpless**. Whereas I have not heard from my son Richard for some years, I direct my executor to advertise in one or more of the newspapers published in the City of Baltimore one in each of 4 successive weeks and if no such legitimate minor children should be ascertained to be in existence within 12 months of the advertising then the balance to the maintenance and education of the legitimate children of **Greenbury Gamble** dec who intermarried with my niece **Sarah Kennard**. If John B. Eccleston declines executorship then to appoint whomever he shall recommend. All my wearing apparel, watch, spoons, household furniture to Rebecca Thompson.

Exec. John B. Eccleston of Chestertown. Witnesses David Arthur, James Mansfield, George Watts. Written Aug. 26, 1827 Proved Dec. 28, 1827 p. 71

Robert Brooke of Northern Liberties in Philadelphia, surveyor
To my wife **Charlotte P.** all the estate during her widowhood and she is to support my minor children and no inventory to be taken during her widowhood but if she marries then an inventory to be taken and she to receive her 1/3. My executors to sell my estate excepting my messuage in which I now dwell and the E part of the lot to contain in length W from the W side of Delaware 3rd St 108 feet and my rent of $75 out of the lot on Laurel St for the use of my wife and children.

Execs. my wife Charlotte P. and my brother in law **George B. Porter** Esq. of Lancaster. Witnesses Joseph H. Siddall, Frederick Beates. Written Nov. 1, 1821 Proved Nov. 17, 1821 Philadelphia (copy from Coram Edmund Rogers Dep. Reg. Philadelphia on Dec. 12, 1827) p. 74

Rebecca Rasin of Kent Co
To my nephew **Joseph Rasin** the farm he now has called *"Cammel's Worth More"* containing 120 acres.

Exec. Not Given. Witnesses William R. Stuart, Mary P. Corse, Mary Meeks. Written July 18, 1825 Proved Feb. 28, 1828 p. 77

Amelia Smith
To my niece **Ann Hanson Smith** all my real estate. To my niece **Mary Reddle** $50. To **John Westly Gibbs**. To **William Harris** and **Edward Anderson** $80 in trust for the worn our preachers and their widows belonging to the annual conference of the Methodist church usually held in Philadelphia conference. The residue to my niece Ann Hanson Smith.

Execs. my niece Ann Hanson Smith and my friend **Jonathan Harris**. Witnesses James M. Anderson, John Constable, Richard P. Seymour. Written Apr. 22, 1822 Proved May 12, 1828 p. 78

Liber 11 1827-1835

John W. Carvill of Kent Co
To my brother **Henry** all my farm whereon I reside being part of a tract called *"Saltus Road"* lying in Kent Co laid out for 518 acres as reference to a deed of partition between John W. Carvill, **Caroline M. Carvill**, and **Henry W. Carvill** dated May 4, 1825 on condition Henry convey to my sister **Caroline Hollyday** for her life and after her death to her son **John Henry Holliday** and if he dies then to her eldest male living then or eldest female issue if Henry assigns a good title to all that field which is parcel which is part of a tract called *"Saltus Road"* and 100 acres of woodland lying contiguous to the said field. If my sister dies without issue then the land to my brother. My brother Henry to pay to my nephew John H. Hollyday $1,000 at age 21, but if he dies without issue then to the first male issue of my sister at 21. To my mother my negro woman **Harriet**. In addition to $180 now charged against my farm payable to my mother I leave her $220 annually during her widowhood. All my slaves in Mississippi to be brought into this state if possible to be given to my brother and sister equally and this year's wages to my sister to improve the land. If my slaves cannot be brought into this state, then **Jim, Louisa** and **Minty** to be free at 30, their wages to my sister. My sister shall be able to draw oyster shells from my farm for the purpose of improving the estate. My brother is to convey to my sister his bay horse farmer. The above requests to my sister are on condition that she relinquish any claims to my estate. My mule colt to my brother in law **George S. Hollyday**. To my brother Henry the residue of my estate.

Execs. my brother Henry and the said George S. Hollyday. Witnesses Francis Lamb, John Stoops, William Lamb. Written Jan. 17, 1828 Proved May 30, 1828 p. 80

George Neal of Kent Co
To my wife **Sophia Neal** all my claim in farm known as *"Perkins farm"* lying in Cackaway Neck in Kent Co which I might have come possessed of by my marriage to my said wife Sophia Neal. To my wife all the personal estate I became possessed of by my marriage to her. All the growing crops on the farm I now reside to my wife. The above to her if she relinquishes claim to my estate. The farm I purchased of **Peregrine Wilmer** of Queen Anns Co part of a tract called *"The Plains"* containing 209 ¼ acres and all that lot of woodland which I purchased of Peregrine Wilmer situate in Kent Co being part of a tract called *"Tulip Forrest"* containing 12 acres to my late wife's **Sarah Neal** deceased, nephew **George Neal Hines** at age 21. If he dies without issue then to **Thomas Neal, Ebenezer Neal, Levi Neal,** and **George Neal** the sons of my nephew **Charles Neal**. If they die without issue then to my nephew **Richard Smith**. All my estate in Chestertown being part of 2 lots of ground designated by as *"Lot No. 81"* and *"Lot No. 82"* on the plot of said town and which I purchased of **Alexander Maxwell** of Caroline Co and of **James G. McClane** late of Kent Co containing 12 acres which I purchased of **George W. Thomas** Trustee for the sale of the estate of **Richard S. Thomas** of Kent Co deceased situate in Quaker Neck in Kent Co. My negro girl **Ann** to be free on Jan. 1, 1834, my negro girl **Fanny** to be free on Jan. 1, 1836, my negro girl **Emmeline** to be free on Jan. 1, 1838, my negro boy **Jim** to be free on Jan. 1, 1839, my negro boy **Isaac** to be free on Jan. 1, 1840, my negro **Mary Ann** to be free on Jan.

1, 1842, my negro boy **Felix** to be free on Jan. 1, 1856, my negro woman **Polly Wright** and her infant child **Charles Henry** shall be free at my death. [Felix granted certificate Dec. 29, 1862 in margin] My nephew Charles Neal to have the preference of renting the farm (by me bequeathed to George Neal Hines) at a yearly rent of $200 if he tills as a farmer until 21. To George Neal Hines my gold watch, all my plate, my set of goldsmith's natural history and my box of china. The proceeds of my farm *"The Plains"* and the hire of my negroes to go to payment of debts, then to my nephew Charles Neal and George Neal Hines

Exec. my wife Sophia Neal. Witnesses William Camp, William H. Wickes, William Keatting Jr. Written May 22, 1828 Proved June 10, 1828 (June 30 came Camp and Wickes) p. 85

John Wallis farmer of Kent Co
Being weak in body from an affliction of the throat make my will, to my wife **Sarah E. Wallis** during her life all my personal estate including my negroes except **Phillis, George, Maria** and Phillis' 2 youngest children purchased at the sale of **Pere Cooper's** property, which I have given my son **Francis**. My wife to take into account the accommodations I furnished my son Francis and **Comegys** that be placed on an equal footing with my other children. If my wife wishes to reduce servitude of negroes for good behavior then to her judgment. I recommend my wife to get a male friend to assist the administration.

Exec. my wife Sarah E. Wallis. Witnesses Daniel Jones, David Davis. Written July 12, 1828 Proved Aug. 9, 1828 (Aug. 11 came Daniel) p. 90

Thomas Barrett of Kent Co
To my 3 children **Alexander Barrett, Thomas Barrett,** and **Christianna W. Barrett** the house and lot in Chestertown upon which I reside and purchased by me of **John Hurtt** by bond to convey dated Nov. 15, 1819 under to control of my executor whom I appoint as trustee and to be applied to maintenance of my dau. Christianna W. Barrett until 21. If she dies then to benefit of my 2 sons. My 2 sons Alexander and Thomas to continue in trade at which they have been brought up. The residue of my estate to my children.

Exec. my friend William H. Barroll. Witnesses James Mansfield, David Arthur, Samuel Mansfield. Written Aug. 12, 1828 Proved Aug. 21, 1828 p. 92

William Graves of Kent Co
Whereas I hold a mortgage of the estate of my brother **Richard Graves** it has been my intention to devise to said Richard and his family, I therefore give to my niece **Elizabeth G. Worrell** in trust to permit Richard Graves to receive the rents. At his death Richard may direct by will to whomever the land above stated. If he has not will then to his heirs at law. My debts paid from my estate and not by the mortgage above except as last

resort. My estate except my farm called *"Buck Neck"* and my negroes be sold. Surplus to my sister **Mary Wilmer** one share, my niece **Sarah Chambers** one share, my niece **Eliza J. Clarkson** one share, my niece **Cornelia Clarkson** one share, to **Cornelia Worrell** the dau. of my deceased niece **Mary Clarkson** afterwards **Mary Worrell** and ½ share to my niece **Elizabeth G. Worrell** but if one share is not more than $200 and $100 to my nephew **William Graves** then deficiency to be made by rent of mansion farm and hire of negroes. If not enough estate then to my sister $100, my niece her dau. $50, to my nieces Sarah Chambers, Eliza J. Clarkson and Cornelia Clarkson $100 each and Cornelia Worrell $100 and William Graves $50. My land and negroes to be rented and used to maintain **Caroline** dau. of **Ann Hawkins** who I do hereby recognize and adopt as my child and if excess after her maintenance then to said Caroline and my dau. **Mary** now the wife of my nephew **John Graves**. If my dau. **Caroline** dies without issue under 17 then to my dau. Mary Graves. If my dau. Mary Graves dies then to Caroline. If both die without issue then to my heirs according to laws. My dau. Mary to have a bed. I selling the lot land purchased by me of Solo. Start a life estate reserved to Ann Hawkins in one acre including the house and will with permission get pine wood for fuel from *"Buck Neck"*. Ann Hawkins to have no control of estate given to Caroline, if she attempts then the executors may keep until Caroline is 21.

Execs. my friend Ezekial F. Chambers and John B. Eccleston. Witnesses Francis Lamb, Richard J. Frisby, Darius Gamble. Written Sep. 21, 1828 Proved Sep. 27, 1828 (Darius came Sep 29) p. 95

John Ringgold Wilmer of Philadelphia
To my wife **Ann Elizabeth Wilmer** all my estate

Execs. my wife Ann Elizabeth Wilmer and my brother in law **John Bowers Eccleston** Esq. of Chestertown. Witnesses Elias Marsh, **Ann E. Wilmer** (sister of John R. Wilmer). Written Apr. 4, 1828 Proved July 3, 1828 (Dec. 4 came Elias) p. 104

Matthew Tilghman of Kent Co
All the lands in Louisiana which I bought of **Antonio Dias** be sold and applied to debt for the said land also for the farm in Queen Anns Co now rented to **James Graham** be sold I expect him to give up his lease 1823. The land i hold near the head of Chester called *"Ring's end"* be sold. As many of my negroes in Louisianna that need to be sold to pay debts. Debts I owe and are owed to me are on a list in my traveling trunk among my papers. To my wife Harriett dau. of Richard Hynson late of Kent Co her 1/3 expecting her to release right of dower on lands as are directed to be sold. To her my negro man **Anthony** who I bought of **William Barroll** and his wife **Margaret** with her dau. **Mary**, the negro woman **Ann** one of the house servants, also the coaches and horses with all my plate and household. In a former will I directed my negro be free but I must now alter that. To my eldest son **Richard** my gold watch that I wear which was his grandfathers together with my wearing apparel, all my books except 20 volumes which I leave to his mother to be selected by her, the bible containing a register of my

81

children's ages. The other bible that was given to me by Mrs. **Mary Roberts** I give to my sister **Anna Maria Brice**. To my dau. **Henrietta** my negro man **Bill** or **Bill Henry** who is now hired to **David Webb** for payment on note to her which will be found in my papers of a legacy of £50 left her by her Aunt Roberts which came to me to **Nicholas Brice** of Baltimore. Upon my arrival in Louisianna I expect to sell my land and my negroes to be hired out and I recommend to them **James Thomas** formerly of Cecil Co MD to hire out my negroes for the maintenance of my children and their mother's 1/3. The rest of my estate with my tract of land in Queen Anns Co called *"Smith's Forest"* divided between my children **Richard Lloyd, Henrietta Louisa, Ann Maria, James Bowers, Mary Caroline** and **William Matthews**. Whereas my wife is in a state of pregnancy then her children to be entitled to my estate along with my other children.

Execs. Nicholas Brice of Baltimore and Henry Tilghman of Chestertown and my wife **Harriott Tilghman**. Witnesses Elias Marsh, Mary Louisa Marsh, Mary Jane Brown. Written Nov. 8, 1820 Proved Dec. 4, 1828 (Dec. 5 came Harriett with will) p. 106

Renunciation I N. Brice resign executorship to Mrs. Tilghman or Mrs. Thomas B. Hynson of Kent Co

Margarett Hayward

To the rector of the chapel in Chester Parish of the Episcopalian Church $100. To my niece **Henrietta Nicols** $50. My wearing apparel to my niece **Margarett Nicols**. To my niece **Margarett Hayward** my mahogany wardrobe, my silver tea pot, and my 12 new pocket handkerchiefs. To my niece **Sally Hayward** my mahogany bureau, my silver cream pot and 6 silver tea spoons. My new high post bed and furniture belonging to my bed chamber to my niece Margarett Nicols. One bed and furniture, one pine table and 4 of my yellow chairs to my niece **Mary and Sarah Nicols**. To my nephew **William Hayward** my gold watch and my silver soup ladle. My books of devotion and religious subjects to my niece **Mary Ann Hayward** and **Elizabeth Hayward**. To my **George Wilson** my 12 silver table spoons. To my niece **Mary E. Wilson** my 12 best desert spoons. To my niece **Anna M. Wilson** my 12 best silver tea spoons. My silver cream ladle to my nephew **Thomas Hayward**. My silver sugar dish and sugar tongs to my nephew **Henry Tilghman**. My negro servant man **Frederick** and my woman **Sally** and **Henny** and my negro girl **Kitty** to be free. My negro girl **Sally** and boy **John** the children of my negro woman **Henny** to her and free them. My negro girls **Henrietta** and **Sally** and negro boy **George** children of my negro woman **Sally** to her and to be free. All the rest of my estate to my nephew Henry Tilghman in trust to divide in 3 parts, 1/3 to my niece Margarett Nicols, 1/3 to my niece Mary Nicols when she is 18, and 1/3 to my niece Sarah Nicols when she is 18. If any die then to survivors. $333.33 to be put to interest to pay the $20 to Mrs. **Anna Maria Smyth**. $100 to my nephew **James Nicols** when 21 and $100 to my nephew **Thomas Nicols** when 21. Exec. to determine the amount due me from **Dr. Thomas Willson**. I give what little I possess to those I consider most helpless and destitute and I trust will be satisfactory to my other nephews and nieces who I consider are provided for already.

Liber 11 1827-1835

Exec. my nephew Henry Tilghman. Witnesses Sarah H. Barroll, Morgan Browne, John B. Hackett. Written Jan. 18, 1825 Proved Jan. 26, 1829 p. 111

Sarah Naudain of Kent Co
To my relation **Mary Ann Granger** wife of **Peregrine Granger** and **Louisa Wroth** all my wearing apparel. To my nephew Peregrine Granger my gig and my 2 servants **Margaret** and **Harry** and to him my household furniture, and to him all the money due me both in Delaware and Maryland

Exec. Not Given. Witnesses Catharine Hanson, Lavinia Hanson. Written Jan. 26, 1828 Proved Jan. 20, 1829 p. 117

John Maxwell of Kent Co
To my wife **Rebecca Maxwell** 1/3 of my estate during her life and whereas my negro woman **Henrietta Maria Trusty** belonged to my wife before our marriage then I leave her the said negro, and to my wife 1/3 personal property. My negro woman **Julia** to be free on Jan. 1, 1838, my negro girl **Emeline** (Trusty born in 1825) to be free on Jan. 1, 47, my negro girl **Angelina,** dau. of Julia born in 1827 to be free on Jan. 1, 1849, my negro boy **George W.** Trusty born 1819 to be free on Jan 1 1848, my negro boy **Jefferson Trusty** born in 1821, my negro girl **Harriet Trusty** born in 1828 and my negro boy **George** son of Julia born in 1821 to be free on Jan. 1, 1850. My negro boy **James Monroe** born in 1825 to be free on Jan. 1, 1854 and if my negro woman Julia or girls Emeline Trusty, Harriett Trusty or Angelina a dau. Julia have children then they are to be free at age 28 for males and 21 for females. Whereas my negro man **Abe** has been a faithful servant he is to remain with my wife while she resides on the farm and I know she will take care of him and when she moves then Abe to live where he wants and to keep his wages along with $30 annually paid out of my son **John M. Maxwell, Albert G. Maxwell,** and my grandson **John H. M. Wallis** to pay $10 each. Whereas a deceased relative of my dau. **Sophia Ann Maxwell** having already better provided for her, I only give her $50 and that she purchase a wardrobe, ladies cabinet or other such article as a small token of my affection. The residue of my estate divided between my sons John M. Maxwell and Albert G. Maxwell and my grandson John H.M. Wallis. If any dies then to survivors. If they all die under age and unmarried then to my wife **Rebecca Maxwell** during her life and then to dau. Sophia Ann Maxwell

Exec. my wife Rebecca Maxwell. Witnesses George W. Thomas, Benjamin Price, William Maxwell. Written Jan. 11, 1829 Proved Feb. 7, 1829 p. 118

Codicil My wife Rebecca Maxwell to be appointed guardian to my grandson John H. M. Wallis. Written Jan. 11, 1829. Witnesses George W. Thomas, Benjamin Price, William Maxwell

Abstracts of Kent Co., MD Wills

Rebecca Maxwell of Kent Co
My executor to sell my lot in Cambridge in Dorset Co, also my lot in Anne Arundel Co near the Ferry Branch. To my dau. **Sophia Ann Maxwell** my dining room carpet, hearth rung and cut glass lamps as a small token of my affection, she having been provided for by a deceased relative. To **Sarah Parsons** widow of **Joseph Parsons** one of my cows and one other cow to **Sarah Lamb** widow of **Joshua Lamb**. To my man **Abraham** one pair of blankets, one coverlet, one bail bucket, and middle sized water tub, one iron pot holding 5 or 6 gallons and the axe he uses. To my woman **Henrietta Maria Trusty** one pair of rose blankets, 2 pair of muslin sheets, one bedspread, one bail bucket and tub, one iron pot holding 8 to 10 gallons, my old bureau. The rest of my estate to my sons **John M. Maxwell** and **Albert G. Maxwell** and my little grandson **John H. M. Wallis**. My son **John** to have my old family clock, one large silver soup ladle, one fine ladle, one marrow spoon, 6 desert and 6 teaspoons and the new carpet purchased for me at the vendue of my husband's property. My son Albert G. Maxwell one silver sugar dish and tongs when he is 21 but if he dies then to my grandson John H. M. Wallis.

Exec. George W. Thomas of Chestertown. Witnesses Ann Maxwell, Francis Cann, Benjamin Price. Written Apr. 24, 1829 Proved July 14, 1829 p. 124

Samuel Wethered of Kent Co
All my property called *"Shrewsbury"* lying in Kent containing 1,470½ acres to my son **John Wethered** on condition that he pays to each of my other children **George, Matilda, Lewina, Eliza, Samuel** and **Sally** $4,000. If my son John refuses then to my son George on same terms. If he refuses then to all my children as tenants in common. All my personal estate to my children John, George, Matilda, Lewina, Eliza, Samuel, and Sally. My negro man **Bill** be free on Jan. 1, 1838 and his brother **Dave** be free on Jan. 1, 1830, also my negro women **Phany** wife of Bill and **Nancy** wife of Dave be free Jan. 1, 1833. My son John guardian to my children under age.

Execs. my sons John and George. Witnesses James Pearce, John Stoops, George W. Hanson. Written Jan. 29, 1828 Proved Feb. 17, 1829 (Mar. 20, 1829 Baltimore, codicil proven) p. 128

Codicil. Written Dec. 30, 1828 Baltimore. I authorize my sons John and George to free my negro woman Fanny wife of **Bill Singo** and negro woman **Nancy** of **Dave Singo's** wife, whenever they think proper. They may free negro **Sam Dorrel**, likewise negro man **George** provided they behave themselves. **Will Sam** to serve 2 years, **George** to serve 14. My sons may free negro woman **Milly**. Witnesses Lewin Wethered, Sally J. Wethered

John Braffett of Kent Co
To **Jesse Alford** my natural son by **Millicent Alford** all my estate but if he dies without lawful heirs then to heirs of **George Hicks** of Baltimore City

Liber 11 1827-1835

Exec. Robert Usilton. Witnesses Samuel G. Kennard, Samuel Kennard, Joseph Kennard. Written Apr. 19, 1826 Proved Apr. 22, 1829 (Apr. 27 came Samuel Kennard) p. 131

Richard Freeks of Kent Co
To my son in law George W. Thomas $75 also my wearing apparel and silver watch. The residue of my property to Mary Ann Lamb the dau. of William and Rebecca Lamb when she arrives at 21. If she dies then to George W. Thomas.

Exec. my friend Henry Carvill. Witnesses John Usilton, Richard Lynch, William Edwards. Written Jan. 30, 1829 Proved Feb. 4, 1829 p. 133

John Mason of Kent Co
To my dau. Mary Matilda Mason all my estate except my negro man Thomas and my negro woman Ann who should serve 4 and 7 years, resp. The children of Elizabeth George to be free at age 30 if my dau. dies without heirs but if she has heirs then to serve forever. If my dau. dies without heirs then the children of Hugh and Margaret B. Wallis and the children of Philip B. Travilla and Ann P. Travilla to have my estate with the above exceptions. To my nephews Thomas and John Williams my wearing apparel.

Exec. Hugh Wallis. Witnesses John Mansfield, Philip B. Travilla, John Moody. Written Mar. 9, 1826 Proved May 19, 1829 p. 135

John Urie Jr. of Kent Co
To my brother Henry Urie all my wearing apparel. To my brother William Urie my silver watch. To my brother James Urie all the residue of my estate subject to the payment below, to my brother Thomas Urie $400 and to my brother William Urie $400 at 22.

Exec. my brother James Urie. Witnesses John Usilton, Robert Usilton, Thomas Eaton. Written Apr. 2, 1829 Proved Sep. 3, 1829 p. 136

James Philips of Kent Co
To my dau. Sarah Berry her choice of one bed. To my grandson James Wesley Philips Jones at age 21 all my real estate in Kent Co containing 100 acres called *"Ashley's Lot"*. To my dau. Wealthy Philips the whole of my personal estate and my real estate until James W.P. Jones arrives of age provided she keeps and supports him until 16 when he should be put in trade. At 21 he is to receive the property and support my dau. Wealthy while she remains single. If my grandson dies then to my two daughters Sarah Berry and Wealthy Philips.

Exec. my dau. Wealthy Philips. Witnesses John Ashley, Joseph Porter, Josiah Gears, John R. Ashley. Written June 2, 1825 Proved Nov. 19, 1829 p. 138

Franky, colored woman of Chestertown
My negro girl **Mary Jane** to be free at my death and her issue. As I am indebted to **Thomas Cuff** for rent and have no otherway to pay I give him the rest of my personal estate.

Exec. Thomas Cuff. Witnesses Thomas Davis, John L. Ringgold. Written Oct. 12, 1829 Proved Dec. 18, 1829 p. 140

Jacob and Sary Stevens of Kent Co
To our dau. **Elizabeth Downey** wife of **James Downey** ¼ part of our estate but not to receive until death of James Downey. If she dies first then to her lawful children but to remain in hands of guardian. To our dau. **Araminty Coalman** wife of **Isaiah Coalman** ¼ part of our estate. Isaiah to be guardian of estate of Elizabeth Downey. To our dau. **Sarah Hutson** wife of **James Hutson** ¼ part. To our dau. **Rebecca Stevens** ¼ part. Signed Jacob Stevens and Sarah Stevens

Exec. Isaiah Coalman. Witnesses George Copper, John K. Ayers, Nicholas Dudley. Written July 31, 1822 Proved Sep. 30, 1829 p. 142

Casparis Meginniss of Kent Co
To my dau. **Hannah Riley** and my son **Samuel Osborn Meginniss** all my real estate lying on the W side of the main road leading from the head of Chester to the head of Sassafras called *"Meginniss' Part of Angel's Rest Resurveyed"*, *"Angels Lot"* and *"Smith's Park"* and 20 acres of woodland which belonged to the heirs of **Mary Newnam** adjoining the lot of woodland purchased of **Samuel Hurlock** designated as *"Lot No. 3"*. To my sons **Nathaniel** and **William Meginniss** all that tract of land whereon the said Nathaniel now resides situate on the E side of the main road leading from the head of Chester called *"Smith's Park"* and *"Angel's Lot"* and all the remainder of the woodland purchased of the heirs of Mary Newnam supposed to be 45 acres. My personal estate after my debts to my 2 sons Samuel Osborn Meginniss and William Meginniss and my grandson **Casparus Meginniss Riley**. My 2 slaves **Clement** and **James** to be free and after Dec. 31. My son **George** and Nathaniel guardians to my sons Samuel Osborn and William and executors.

Execs. my son George and Nathaniel. Witnesses Samuel Clother, Stephen Boyer, Thomas R. Cooper. Written Feb. 9, 1828 Proved Dec. 15, 1829 p. 144

Benjamin Hanson of Kent Co
To my son **James Hanson** all the lands lying in Worton which formerly belonged to **Thomas J. James** and which I purchased of **John Hanson** and **James Hanson** as trustees for the sale of **Thomas J. James**. To my grandson **Thomas Hanson James** $1,800 charged of the lands given to my son James. To my sister **Elizabeth Hanson** during her life that part of my plantation which is contained in the following bounds beginning at the main road in the home line of a tract called *"New Forrest"* and running thence N with

Liber 11 1827-1835

the said home line reversed 133 perches to a run or drain then S 72° W 30 perches then N 11° last 70 perches to the N side of a small branch then N 69° W 72 perches to the S line [W 48 perches, then N 81°] of my part of a tract called *"Gresham's Levels"* then S with that line to a stone marked BH-SS standing in the E line of a tract called *"The Addition"* then with the said E line reversed W 76 perches to a stone marked BH standing at the N line and at the beginning of the E line of *"The Addition"* there S with the said N line reversed to a stone then E to a stone on the main road between my land and the land sold by **Thomas B. Hynson** to **Elizabeth Stake**. At the death of my sister then to my grandson Thomas Hanson James 200 acres of that part of my plantation devised to my said sister Elizabeth on the S part of my land called *"New Forrest"*. The residue I give to my 4 grandchildren **John Wesley Webster, Richard Henry Webster, George Smith Webster,** and **Benjamin Franklin Webster**. My old negro woman **Sarah** shall have a home on my plantation during her life and have firewood. The land called *"Arcadia"* which **Samuel Eccleston** and myself purchased from **Darius Dunn Jr.** by a writ of partition was divided between me and the heirs of Samuel Eccleston I give to my 4 grandchildren **Jane Elizabeth Kennard** wife of Dr. **Thomas C. Kennard, Martha Henrietta Hanson, John Wesley Hanson,** and **Ellen Amanda Hopper**. My son **James Hanson** and my son in law **Henry Webster** trustees to sell land. I give my lands in Swan Creek which I purchased of **Edward B. Tilden** and **Nathaniel Hatcherson** unto my dau. **Emeline Reed** and my grandson **Benjamin Thomas Hanson**. To my son in law Henry Webster $50 annually for 10 years provided my dau. **Hannah Snow** shall live for 10 years and not to be subject to her husband **Daniel J. Snow** if she dies under 10 years then no more payment. To my granddau. **Sarah Elizabeth Bradshaw** all the lands called *"Arcadia"* which I purchased of **William N. Williams** and Sarah his wife and **Catharine Dimmit** (excepting 14 acres which I sold to **James Hollis**) also all the land I purchased of **Henry Page** called *"Gresham's Levels"*. Remainder of my lands to my dau. **Martha Webster** wife of **Henry Webster**. My negroes **Edward, Harriett,** and **Sarah** to be free at my death and my other negroes to be free at age 35. My negro man Edward $50. To my sister **Elizabeth Hanson** my negro lad **Bill,** my girl **Deb** or **Deborah,** my riding carriage or gig, my mare Fancy, my horse Jack, one mahogany tea table, and one bed and bedstead. To my dau. Emeline Reed my negro boy **Emory,** my negro **Ann** and all the plate in my house marked with the letter H. To my granddau. Ellen Amanda Hopper my piano forte. To my dau. Martha Webster my negro girl **Levina** or **Levinia** which Martha has already received. To my grandson Thomas Hanson James the negroes **James, Edwin** and **David**. To my grandson **Philip George Reed** my negro boy **Horace** son of Sarah. [Freedom pass granted to James Oct. 23, 1855, Pass granted to **Isaac Scott** Dec. 29, 1857, pass granted **Isaac James** July 13, 1855, written in margin] To my grandson **James Henry Hanson** my negro woman **Alice** and her 2 children **Mary** and **Sarah** and my 2 boys called Isaac. To my granddau. **Sarah Elizabeth Bradshaw** one bed, one mahogany dining table and one milch cow and calf. To my granddau. **Henrietta Eliza Hanson** $300. To my son in law Henry Webster $500 in trust for Hannah Snow (wife of Daniel J. Snow) [Pass granted Sarah Jan. 22, 1864, in margin] The residue of my negroes to my 4 grandchildren Jane Elizabeth Kennard, Martha Henrietta Hanson, John

Abstracts of Kent Co., MD Wills

Wesley Hanson and James Henry Hanson. The remainder of my personal estate to my children James Hanson, Martha Webster, and Emeline Reed

Execs. my son James Hanson and my son in law Henry Webster. Witnesses John B. Eccleston, William Copper, William R. Durding. Written Oct. 18, 1828 Proved Apr. 11, 1829 p. 147

Benjamin Worrell of Kent Co
To my wife **Mary Worrell** the whole of my estate during her life then to my eldest son **John Hynson Worrell** the whole of the real estate. To my dau. **Rebecca Hynson Spelman** wife of **Nicholas Spelman** one negro man **Perry** and he is not to be sold out of MD and she is to get $10 yearly for 5 years paid by my son John. To my son **Benjamin Worrell** $50 a year for 4 years paid by my son John. To my dau. **Sarah Worrel** one negro boy **Gloster** a slave for life and one negro girl **Fanny** a slave for life and boarding provided to her during maidenhood by my son John. All the rest of my personal estate to my sons John Hynson Worrel and Benjamin Worrel and dau. Sarah Worrel. [spelled Worrell and Worrel throughout]

Exec. my wife Mary Worrell. Witnesses William Camp, Clinton Griffith, Martha H. Hynson. Written Feb. 12, 1827 Proved Feb. 10, 1830 p. 156

Susan Watts of Kent Co
To my son **John Watts**, my dau. **Mary Ann Watts** and **Rosa Maria Watts** all my estate. My negro boy **Samuel** shall be free in 22 years, my negro boy **Perry** after 24 years, my negro boy **Henry** after 26 years, my negro boy **Lewis** after 26 years. [Freedom pass granted to Samuel Oct. 18, 1854 and Pass granted to Lewis June 16, 1856, from notes in margin]

Exec. McCall M. Rasin. Witnesses Thomas Gale, Mary Ann Dorney. Written Nov. 11, 1829 Proved Jan. 5, 1830 p. 158 (pp. 158-9 are missing from microfilm copy)

John Clarke of Quaker Neck (nunc.)
On or about Mar. 2, **John Clarke** then lying at the house of **Edward Browne** where he was attacked with sickness about 3 weeks before, being asked who should have his property said that he wished **Ezekial Kelly** son of **Benjamin Kelly** late of Quaker Neck to have it because all that he possesses he had got from the father of said Ezekial, but he did not call on them to bear witness to that declaration and he died 3 or 4 days later. The undersigned judges believe this to be a valid will if the personal property does not exceed $300. Richard Ringgold, Samuel Ringgold, Thomas Willson

Exec. Not Given. Witnesses Edward Browne, James Milton, John Claypole. Written Not Given (3 weeks before) Proved Mar. 2, 1830 p. 159

Thomas Allen of Kent Co

Liber 11 1827-1835

My estate divided between my wife **Eliza Allen**, my son **John Thomas Allen** and my dau. **Hannah Ann Allen**. If my 2 negro boys **Thomas** and **Joseph** who lately run away from me should be caught then my executor to sell for the most. My friend **John Edwards** to be guardian to my children. My son John bound at 15 years old to a trade. Exec. George W. Thomas of Chestertown. Witnesses Major Smyth, Ashbury S. Sappington. Written Feb. 10, 1830 Proved Apr. 2, 1830 p. 161

Temperance Everitt of Kent Co
All those 2 parts of a tract described in deed from myself to **John B. Eccleston** bearing date Mar. 11, 1822 and which were reconveyed to me by John, I give to my son **William B. Everitt** during his life with remainder to **Ezekial F. Chambers** and John B. Eccleston in trust for such person my son by his last will gives and in default to my niece **Anna Maria Brice** during her life not subject to her husband and after her death then to her dau. **Temperance Caroline** (dau. by **Anna Maria Brice** and **Joseph W. Brice**) but if Temperance dies without issue then to **Ann Louisa Wilmer** dau. of my niece **Ann E. Wilmer** forever. To my niece **Mary Ann Hynson** 3 of my best drapes, bed curtains, 4 window curtains of a tea ground. To my friend Mrs. **Elizabeth Gale** a bed and curtains of a pale blue ground. To Mrs. **Elizabeth Adkinsson** wife of **John Adkisson** one bed a bed and patched work bed quilt. To my friend Mrs. **Elizabeth Coxe** of Harford Co (formerly **Elizabeth Caulk**) my double carriage and harness. To my niece Anna Maria Brice my black merino shawl. To Miss **Eliza Kendle** my figured black silk dress. To **Deborah Hudson** one bed. Whereas my nephew **John B. Eccleston** has always transacted business for me without any charge I give to him $200 for his past services and attention. I also give $100 to John B. Eccleston to make a substantial enclosure around the graveyard on the farm where **Samuel Coleman** now resides, it being our family burial ground. To my niece Ann E. Wilmer $200. My negroes **Pere** and **Edwin** to be free, **Emiline** and my 2 women each called **Mary** to be free on Jan. 1. My negro girls to be free at 20 and my negro boys to be free at 21. To my negro Pere my horse called Bob, one cow, one sow, 250 weight pork, one bed, 2 blankets, one iron pot and a dutch oven. The pork to be furnished him by my son William next fall and Pere to get $20 annually during their joint lives but not chargeable to my estate. [Freedom pass granted to **Horrace Frisby** Dec. 29, 1861 written in margin] To my negro **Edwin** $150, one bed, 2 blankets and sheets and one of my new and thickest patched bed quilts. Mrs. Elizabeth Gale and my niece Mary Ann Hynson shall divide my wearing apparel between my 3 negro women and girl **Betsey**. To **James Eaton** the bed he sleeps on, 2 sheets, and my negro **Bill** 2 blankets, and my negro **Emeline** 2 blankets which she uses. All the rest of my estate to my son William B. Everitt.

Execs. my son William B. Everitt and my nephew John B. Eccleston. Witnesses Robert McCoy, James P. Gale, Charles R. Hynson. Written Feb. 15, 1830 Proved Feb. 25, 1830 p. 162

Sarah B. Blake of Kent Co

I am to be buried at the bottom of the garden at the farm called *"Hill Top"* on the orchard side and to be simple with no mourning to be purchased except for my children, the bearers, clergyman and physician as it would take more from my estate than I would wish. All my estate to my son **Joseph Blake** he being left unprovided for by his father under an expectation and promise made by me. To my 2 sons **Thomas** and **Joseph Blake** all my religious books having my name in them. To my son Thomas Blake a white enamelled mourning ring for **John Vandyke** given me by my mother and also my set of white enameled and gilt tea china now in the house and a piano forte which I have lately purchased of Mrs. **William Barroll**. To my son Joseph Blake a mourning ring for Sarah Graves left to me by my grandmother **Sarah Graves**. As I received a silver watch in trust from my deceased husband Dr. **Benson B. Blake** for our son Thomas Blake, I give the said watch to my son Thomas Blake. To my son in law **William Blake** a breast pin containing the hair of his father and mother which his father requested that I would give to him. To my dau. in law **Maria Ann Blake** all my wearing apparel and my blessing to the said William Blake and Maria Ann Blake as that is all I can leave them except the above trifles as their father hath already provided for them and at his request I should give what little I had to my son Joseph Blake. To my son **Thomas Wiesenthall** and my son Joseph Blake a mahogany sideboard, 2 dining tables, 2 card tables, and 2 bedsteads. To my son Thomas Weisenthall my 1/3 part of the library of books which belonged to his father except such as were given me by my mother and which have the name of **Thomas Vandyke** in them which I wish to divide between my sons Thomas Blake and Joseph Blake. My friend William Barroll of Chestertown guardian to my sons Thomas Blake and Joseph Blake and whereas I am entitled to 1/3 part of the debt coming to my son Thomas Blake from his deceased uncle **Thomas Blake** I give the same to my son Thomas Blake.

Exec. my friend William Barroll of Chestertown. Witnesses John B. Hackett, William J. Clowes, Charles F. Hughes. Written Mar. 30, 1824 Proved Jan. 28, 1830 p. 167

Renunciation I William Barroll renounce all right to letters testamentary under the will of Mrs. Sarah B. Blake in favor of Thomas Blake the son of said Mrs. Blake including guardian to Joseph Blake. Written Jan. 11, 1830 Witness William H. Wickes Signed W. Barroll

Mary Wickes of Kent Co

My black woman **Maria** to be free. To my niece **Mary Henrietta Wickes** my mulatto girl **Minta** now 14 to be free at 22. My black girl **Taraham** now 12 to my sister **Hannah Houston** to serve until she is 22. To my sister Hannah Houston my set of tea china. To my niece Mary Henrietta Wickes my bed, bureau, carpet, 6 windsor chairs, andirons, shovel and tongs. To my nephew **Simon Wickes Jr.** all my houses and lots in Chestertown which were devised to me by my deceased father **Simon Wickes**. If he dies without issue then to my nephew **Charles Henry Wickes**. Whereas the farm I now own adjoining the St. Paul's Church was devised to me by my deceased father Simon Wickes and other real estate with a condition that I should pay to **William Wickes Houston** or his representatives £500 within a year after they could demand their share of the estate of **Benjamin Houston** his father and whereas William Wickes Houston has died intestate leaving **Benjamin Franklin Houston** his brother his only representative I now give to said Benjamin Franklin Houston my nephew my said farm instead of the £500 if he makes a discharge of said claim. If he does not choose said farm then the devise to him void and my cousin **Joseph Wickes 4th** trustee to take said farm and collect rents and then sold to paid said £500 with residue to my estate. Rest of my estate to my sister Hannah Houston.

Exec. my sister Hannah Houston. Witnesses James M. Anderson, Benjamin Greenwood, Mary Burns. Written Jan. 19, 1830 Proved May 10, 1830 p. 171

Philip Ward of Kent Co
All my estate to my sister **Ann Ward** during her life and my sister to take care of **Rachael Dudley** and to see that she does not suffer for any nursery thing. After my sister's death then all my estate to **William Hennery Davis**, the son of **James Davis** and Mary his wife.

Exec. Not Given. Witnesses John Maslin, Thomas Vickers, Joseph Maslin. Written Mar. 11, 1827 Proved June 30, 1830 p. 174

Catherine Martha Eliza Freeman of Kent Co
To be buried at Shrewsbury Church. To Mr. **Archibald Blair** of Richmond, VA all my real estate consisting of 2 tracts, one lying in DE near Smyrna and the other near Georgetown Cross Roads in Kent Co MD to hold for the use of my nephew **Edward Freeman Blair**. It being understood that Mr. Blair pay of the proceeds to my cousin **Edward Freeman** the legacy herein. To my niece **Anna Beverly Blair** a single bill due from my uncle **James Pearce** to me dated Sep. 12, 1823 for $261, also 2 large trunks with their contents now at the house of my uncle James Pearce with all my clothing and wearing apparel except those specifically given. To my cousin Edward Freeman $100. To my cousin **Martha Ann Atwood** a bureau now at the house of my uncle James Pearce. To my nephew Edward Freeman Blair all my plate. The rest of my estate to my niece Anna Beverly Blair. To my sister **Harriet Maria Blair** my gold watch and key.

Exec. Archibald Blair of VA husband of my sister Harriet. Witnesses James Alfred Pearce, Ruth C. Tilden, Mary Ann Tilden. Written July 1830 Proved Nov. 19, 1830 p. 176

Charles Rigby of Kent Co
To my wife **Milcah Rigby** all my personal estate in Kent Co. My negro servants, my household and kitchen furniture, my horses, horned cattle, sheep, hogs and bonds, etc provided she relinquish right of dower in my lands and personal property in Talbot Co. To my sister **Elizabeth Rigby** all my lands in Talbot Co provided she pay off money I

owe to **Lucy Ann Spencer** and a note **William H. Groome** holds due from **Robert Rigby** to the estate of the late **Samuel Groome** and provided she gives my brother **Thomas Rigby** a home during his life where he from any cause should be unable to provide for himself and his board to be free of all charges, also she to surrender to my sister **Margaret Leonard** without pay all bonds which she Elizabeth Rigby may hold against my sister Margaret and to pay Margaret $10 annually. My man **Levi** to be free after the death of my wife Milcah Rigby but to serve her during her life.

Exec. Not Given. Witnesses Jacob Fisher, Nathan Hatcheson, William Copper. Written Aug. 13, 1830 Proved Oct. 13, 1830 p. 179

Thomas Hynson of Kent Co
To my son **Charles R. Hynson** my dwelling plantation where I now live if he pays to his 2 sisters an annual maintenance till death or marriage and if they are obliged to leave his family for ill usage or treatment then to provide a reasonable board for them. To my 2 daughters horse and gig and negro boy **Little Jim** as a waiter, also to be supported by my son provided my son Charles R. Hynson provided my son Charles and his 2 sisters join in a sufficient deed to my 2 sons **Thomas H. Hynson** and **George W. Hynson** for their proportion of their mothers landed estate, on their refusing they shall forfeit their part of my estate. My son Charles to provide my dau. **Caroline** with 2 years in a female school.

Exec. my son Charles R. Hynson. Witnesses Benedict S. Brevitt, John C. Hynson, Martha Hynson. Written Aug. 16, 1830 Proved Oct. 1, 1830 p. 180

Avarilla Williams of Kent Co
To my grandson **Samuel Comegys** $20. To my grandson **Washington Comegys** my large looking glass. To my great granddau. **Millementy Comegys** $20 when she is 18. To my great grandson **Joseph C. Mann** my walnut desk. To my great grandson **Samuel Mann** my watch if I have one at my death or $20 if I do not. To my great great granddau. (sic) **Mary Ann Mann** all my property. My executor to have my estate appraised but not sold when my great granddau. Mary Ann Mann shall be 18 to have last appraisement again and if it does not match then my executor to make up difference.

Exec. my friend and connexion **Thomas L. Mann**. Witnesses Rebecca Sewell, William Cornelius. Written 1830 Proved Oct. 5, 1830 p. 182

James C. Morris of Kent Co
My son **Joseph** to pay debts out of his part. As I gave my son **Thomas Morris** his portion I now leave him 1 shilling. To my son in law **William Evans** one old bay mare and colt and one wooden plough. To my son **John** the red and white yoke of oxen and cart. To my son **William** one young bay horse and one cow and calf (not marked), one black spotted sow and pigs, one bed. To my son Joseph 2 mares and colts, one 2-year old colt, one cart and oxen and all the remainder of the stock not willed before,

Liber 11 1827-1835

household and kitchen furniture and 2 young negroes **John** and **Eliza** and all the stock as much as he wants to remain until the present crop is furnished. My wife **Rachael** to be maintained by my son Joseph and if he fails then to pay her $40 annually and if she has to leave the house then to have one bed. If necessary for administration then my son Joseph whole executor.

Exec. my son Joseph. Witnesses Richard Semans, Stephen Boyer. Written June 28, 1830 Proved Sep. 21, 1830 p. 185

Edward Johnson of Kent Co
My wife **Lydia Johnson** all my estate if she does not marry and conducts herself in a decent manner. To my dau. **Temperance Johnson** after the death or marriage of my wife Lydia the house I now live in with 8 acres of land to be laid off around the house. To my dau. **Maria Frazier** the residue of my land

Exec. my wife Lydia Johnson. Witnesses James Brown, Roland Bennett, Ann Bennett. Written Mar. 21, 1830 Proved May 2, 1831 p. 187

Maria Wickes of Kent Co
To my niece **Augusta Wickes** $300. To my niece **Antonietta Wickes** $300. To my niece **Mary W. Coursey** $300. To my niece Leweza W. **Wickes** $100. To my niece **Emeline L. Wickes Davis** $100. To my nephews **William H. Wickes** and **James P. Wickes** $100. To my nephew **Thomas W. Coursey** and **Samuel Coursey** $50. I charge my executor to pay $10 to charitable purposes and $5 for repair of the graveyard at Block town. The balance of my estate to my brother **William Wickes**.

Exec. my brother William Wickes. Witnesses Susan W. Black, Frederick Wilson. Written Nov. 1834 Proved May 3, 1831 p. 189

Samuel Gibson formerly of Baltimore City but now of Kent Co
To **Mary Runnels** of Baltimore City widow of **Richard Runnels** formerly a gunsmith $50. To **Mary Briscoe** of Baltimore City widow of **Alexander Briscoe** formerly of Kent Co $50. All my personal estate to be sold and the residue of my estate to **Bartis Piner** and **Benjamin Merritt** of Kent Co.

Exec. Benjamin Merritt. Witnesses Daniel Jones, Samuel Kerr. Written May 19, 1831 Proved July 16, 1831 p. 191

Hannah Boyer of Kent Co
To **Mary Lavenia Piner, Louisa H. Piner,** and **Ann Rebecca Piner,** children of **Bartis** and **Rebecca Piner,** all the property.

Exec. Not Given. Witnesses George W. Wilson, William A. R. Wilson. Written Aug. 15, 1831 Proved June 11, 1832 p. 192

Abstracts of Kent Co., MD Wills

John Russel
Considering a will merely an instrument of distribution of property I shall abstain from the use of any expression not necessary, Whereas I purchased a mill and tanyard and lands adjoining at the head of Sassafras in Kent and about 15 acres of woodland lying in Appoquinimink Hundred, New Castle Co, DE and on account of my being an alien in the United States I settled the same on my 3 friends **Hyland B. Pennington, Gideon Longfellow** and **Abraham Cole** in trust for me as the deeds will testify. I also purchased a small farm in Mill Creek Hundred, New Castle Co, DE of **John Gordon** containing 41 acres. My executors to pay the balance owed to John Gordon. The rents of my lands at the head of Sassafras and my personal property (except my clothing and books) to apply to my debts. To my brother **Christopher** a suit of clothes every 2 years during his lifetime the cost of which suit shall not exceed $20 the first suit at Christmas 7 years after my decease. If he pays his note to me dated 1815 then he shall share with **Robert, Simeon,** and **Sarah** or his children if he be dead at the time of distribution. To my brother **Richard Russell** nothing if he do not pay the balance of my note dated 1814 nor to his children, but if he pays then he to share with Robert, Simeon, and Sarah. My books and my mathematical instruments to my nephew **John Russel** son of Christopher Russel. I give my clothes to my brother **William Russel**. To the trustees of the Episcopal Methodist Church at the head of Sassafras, the N point of a lot adjoining the yard on the S W corner of the said yard so as to run the fence on the S side of the meeting house yard in a line to the road leading from Chestertown containing about __ perches of lands to them provided they clear said premises. I give a watch which belonged to my father to **Christopher Russel** son of my brother Christopher Russel and this watch must not be sold or given away. To my brother William Russel the ½ of the rent from the farm which I bought of John Gordon for compensation for transacting my business but only during the time of his handling my concerns.

Execs. my brother William, and my nephews Christopher and John Russels sons of my brother Christopher Russel to observe the discharge by William. Witnesses John Butler, William H. Moffett, John Corbett. Written Feb. 14, 1830 Proved Feb. 21, 1831 p. 193

Robert S. Gamble of Kent Co
To my grandson **Robert Adolphus Gamble** all the land devised to me by my late brother **Darius Gamble** by his will dated Mar. 4, 1788, being the plantation on which I now reside and the land adjoining that my late brother Darius Gamble from the late **James Frisby** containing 31 3/4 acres and a tract adjoining that purchased by me of **Richard S. Thomas**, which land formerly belonged to **Marmaduke Tilden** of Kent Co and devised to him by him to his grandson **Thomas B. Tilden** containing 200 acres. To my granddau. **Jane Catherine Scott Gamble** all that farm at Willis's Cross Roads formerly the property of my deceased brother Darius Gamble containing 450 acres. To my grandson **Stansbury Gamble** all that farm at Smiths Crossroads formerly owned by **Samuel W. Smith** of Kent Co and late the property of my deceased son Darius Gamble with my other lands to which I may be entitled adjoining the same and 30 of woodland part of *"Gamble's farm"* and formerly the property of my brother Darius Gamble and all

Liber 11 1827-1835

my real estate in Queen Anns Co. If my grandchildren **Robert Adolphus Gamble** and **Jane C.D. Gamble** lay claim to any property devised by me to my grandson **Stanberry Gamble** then not to have any part of my estate. My negroes **Ann** and **Perry** to be free, my negro **Mary** to be free in a year, and that Ann's children **Maria, Job, David, Sarah, Ann, Elizabeth, Frisby, Brown, Washington** as they arrive at 26. To my grandson Robert A. Gamble my negro boys **Simon** and **Joseph** to serve until 31. To my granddau. Jane C.P. Gamble my negro girl **Mary** aged about 16 to serve until 31. My negro boys **Sam** and **Isaac** to serve until 31. To my dau. in law Sarah Gamble $100. To my wife **Eliza Gamble** my horse and gig. [Freedom pass to Isaac Apr. 13, 1857 in margin]. My personal estate after debts, then to above named grandchildren when they are 21. I limit the right of my grandchildren to receive profits of land and not to have the right of sale until age 30. **William B. Wilmer** guardian to my grandchildren Robert A. Gamble, Jane S. Gamble and Standsberry Gamble.

Exec. William B. Wilmer. Witnesses Lydia Hurst, Elizabeth Jane McGinniss, John Stoops. Written June 21, 1831 Proved Sep. 13, 1831 (Eliza came on 14th) p. 197

Mary Anne Kennard of Kent Co

My debts paid out of bond due me from **Samuel G. Kennard**. The said remainder of bond to Samuel G. Kennard in trust to apply towards maintaining **Sarah E. Kennard**, dau. of **John T. Kennard** till she is 16 then ½ to her; the other ½ to my dau. **Elizabeth M. Kennard** if then a widow but if married only the interest and then principal if she outlive him. If she dies during coverture then to her children. If Sarah E. Kennard dies before 16 then to Elizabeth M. Kennard. If both died before Sep. 10, 1835 without issue then to **John Anderson** and my dau. Sarah Kennard. My negro **Maria** to Samuel G. Kennard in trust for Elizabeth M. Kennard until Maria is 30 then free. To Sarah E. Kennard my negro woman **Matilda** until she is 30, then free. To my dau. Sarah Kennard my negro girl **Henny** until she is 30 then free, and to her my clock and bookcase. To my son **John Anderson** my mahogany dining table and desk. To **Robert** eldest son of John Anderson $35 at age 21. To Elizabeth M. Kennard my bed and 6 silver tea spoons. The residue of my estate to my dau. Sarah Kennard. [Certificate of freedom granted to Henny Mar. 29, 1855. Certificate of freedom granted to Matilda Aug 7, 1855 written in margin]

Exec. Samuel G. Kennard. Witnesses John Stoops, Jane Drew, William H. Dorsey. Written Mar. 14, 1830 Proved Jan. 12, 1831 p. 200

John Edes of Kent Co

To my wife **Margaret** all my estate during her life with the care of my aged mother. To my dau. **Ann Maria Vickers** a part of my plantation beginning at a stone marked A, then to stones marked B, C, and D then to a marked gum tree on the E side of the road leading down to Broad Neck Point then with the line of a tract land *"Broad fields"* between my farm and the said farm to the stone marked A. After my wife's death then my personal estate to my dau. Anna Maria Vickers in the amount of $120. To my son **James H. Edes** after the death of his mother all my plantation where I now live except what is above devised known by the name of *"Broad Nox Creek"* provided that my son James H. Edes deed a tract of land which he holds called *"Maslins Possession"* to my dau. **Ann Edes** and divide said farm in 3 fields with his timber and at his expense. To my dau. Ann Edes a negro girl **Lavena** until she is 25 then free and her issue at same age, also one cow, one bedstead, a table, a stand, a looking glass, and clock, 6 silver tea spoons and my dau. Ann Edes to have board in common with my son James H. Edes while she lives single. To my granddau. **Margaret E. Vickers** my negro girl **Caroline** until she arrives to the age 25 and all issue at same age. If I do not sell my negro boy **Charles** and my negro girl **Bet** to their parents in my lifetime they shall be divided between my 3 children until they are age 25 and all Bet's issue and the remaining personal property to my 3 children. My son James H. Edes shall give bond for payment of my debts without an administration.

Exec. Not Given (assumed James H. Edes). Witnesses Jacob Maslin, George Collins, Joseph Maslin. Written Oct. 4, 1830 Proved Jan. 11, 1831 p. 203

George Hazel of Kent Co
To my dau. **Mary Ann Blackiston** wife of **William Blackiston** of Kent Co DE $50. To my dau. **Elizabeth Spear** wife of **James Spear** of Kent Co DE jointly with my dau. **Susan Hazel** all that tract called *"Blackiston's Fancy Farm"* lying on the N side of the farm on which I now live containing about 460 acres it being the land formerly belonging to **Lewis Blackiston** equally to my 2 daughters Elizabeth and Susan and to them all my personal estate in MD. To my eldest son **William A. Hazel** my farm situated in Kent Co DE but part is in MD in Queen Anns Co and Kent Co, MD but are adjoining said farm and on which he now resides and to him all my personal property in DE. Whereas all my slaves are free except for **George** being lately bought of **Jesse Knock** out of Newman's estate, he is to be free on Jan. 1, 1846. Whereas my sons **James Hazel** and **Benjamin Hazel** have been provided for by their grandfather **William Anderson** I give to each $1.

Execs. my son William A. Hazel and my son in law James Spear. Witnesses Eli S. Pardee, John Whittington, John Hurlock. Written Feb. 27, 1831 Proved Mar. 7, 1831 p. 206

Samuel Thomas of Kent Co
To my brother **Richard S. Thomas** all my estate (in obedience to the request of my deceased father **Richard S. Thomas** that if I have no issue then to his son Richard S. Thomas and that I am influenced by no feelings of ill will to my other brothers).

Exec. my brother Richard S. Thomas. Witnesses William Barroll, Richard Ringgold, William H. Barroll. Written Feb. 19, 1828 Proved Mar. 22, 1831 p. 209

Liber 11 1827-1835

Josiah Newton of Kent Co
As I have assisted my son **Zedekiah Newton** in farming and giving him considerable stock and money that it shall be full compensation of my estate. As my 2 daughters **Ann Blackway** and **Eliza Baldwin** both being married and for the assistance I have given them and the property I have already given them as full part of my estate. The residue of my property after debts to my sons **Thomas Newton** and **Josiah Newton**

Exec. my son Josiah Newton. Witnesses James H. Smith, Jesse Moffet, Josiah Massy. Written Nov. 28, 1830 Proved Mar. 29, 1831 p. 211

James Wilmer, colored man, living near Georgetown Crossroads
To my wife **Hannah** all my estate. After her death to my wife's son **James Welch** and **Julia Fields** dau. of my niece **Rachel Kennard** of City of Baltimore.

Exec. Not Given. Witnesses Edward Scott, Thomas Green, Samuel R. McHand. Written May 1831 Proved June 25, 1831 p. 213

Philemon Coppage of Kent Co
My negro man **Charles** be free. To the children of **William Beck** and **Mary Beck** of Queen Anns Co all my real estate divide among them consisting of land I lately got of **Benjamin S. Elliot** in exchange for land that descended to me from my father to them the said children of William Beck and my aunt Mary Beck. To my cousins **Susan Ratcliff** and **Eliza Ratcliff** the balance of my personal estate

Exec. Matthias George. Witnesses Eli S. Pardee, Hemsley Holling, Mary Thomas. Written May 28, 1831 Proved Aug. 2, 1831 p. 214

Edward Worrell of Wilmington, DE
Having a certain indenture dated 3rd day of the present month assigned to **Caleb Starr** certain bonds in trust during me life and after to my dau. **Elizabeth** I now confirm. To the managers of the Pennsylvania Hospital in Philadelphia, PA all the estate in DE conveyed by the late Col. **Allan McLane** to my son the late **George W. Worrell** in trust for my wife **Rebecca Worrell** during her life and as executor of my son I now hold as trustee. I request the managers of the PA Hosp. to now be trustees to manage for my wife during her life. All the rest to my son **Edward Worrell** and my dau. **Priscilla B. Smith** wife of **William P. Smith** of Baltimore. Having recently disposed of my farm in Kent Co for a provision for my dau. Rebecca and any additional amount from said farm to my son Edward and daughters Priscilla B. Smith and Elizabeth Worrell

Exec. my son Edward Worrell. Witnesses Joseph Baily, Caleb Starr, John W. Taturn. Written July 4, 1829 Proved Dec. 27, 1830 New Castle Co p. 216

Abstracts of Kent Co., MD Wills

Harriett Chapman of Kent Co

To my 2 daughters **Ann Chapman** and **Henrietta Malvina Chapman** all undivided part of a tract of land called *"Ratcliffs Cross"* situate lying near Chestertown, Kent Co. If either dies, then to survivor. To my dau. **Ann Chapman** my negro woman **Sarah** to serve for term of 6 years, she then free. To my dau. **Ann** my highpost bed, one marseilles quilt white and one demoty counterpane. To my dau. **Harriett Malvina Chapman** my bureau and my negro girl **Priscilla**, also my low post bedstead. To my eldest son **William P. Chapman** my negro boy **Alfred** and my other feather bed and one quilted patch work. To my son **John Emory Chapman** my 2 negro boys **Jim** and **Daniel** and my negro girl **Charlotte** and my other 2 quilted patch work quilts. I appoint my sister **Ann Sudler** guardian to my children.

Exec. Not Given. Witnesses Jonathan Harris, James F. Gordon, Emory Sudler. Written Aug. 5, 1831 Proved Feb. 13, 1832 p. 219

William H. Dorsey of Kent Co

All my real estate to **Samuel G. Kennard** during his life with remainder to his dau. **Adaline G. Kennard**. I give **Hannah** and **Delia** (and **Harriet** and **Harriett** (sic), daughters of Hannah) to **Sarah Elizabeth Kennard**, dau. of **John T. Kennard** deceased. If she dies under 18 then to Samuel G. Kennard. I give **Rachel** dau. of **Delia** to **Juliana Ricketts** of Harford Co. I give my negro boy **Bill** to my friend **John Stoops**. I give **Moses** son of **Letty** to **George Philips** after he is 21. The rest of my estate to Samuel G. Kennard

Exec. Samuel G. Kennard. Witnesses Henry W. Carvill, John G. Graves, John Bordley. Written Mar. 10, 1831 Proved Oct. 3, 1831 p. 221

Ann Woodall of Kent Co

To my dau. **Emily Ann Woodall** one bed to be kept as hers in the hands of her friend wherever she may reside, also 6 silver table spoons. To my son **John W. Lusby** the balance of my personal estate and all articles of personal property that I have already given him. None of my personal estate to be disposed of except my gig to pay my debts. My dau. Emily Ann Woodall to have all right to the farm formerly belonging to the late **John Woodall** my late husband, it being ½ the farm, containing 214 acres, and which said ½ owned at the death of my late husband by his son **Joseph Woodall** and which I purchased of Joseph.

Exec. my friend Samuel Comegys (son Nathaniel). Witnesses Samuel Comegys, Joseph Woodall, Isaac Hines. Written Sep. 28, 1831 Proved Nov. 12, 1831 p. 223

Elizabeth Jones of Kent Co

To my brother **Jacub** and **John Jones** all my title to a tract called *"Gambles Purchase"* containing 149 acres. All my personal property to my said brothers Jacub and John Jones

Liber 11 1827-1835

Exec. my brother Jacub Jones. Witnesses Thomas Bordley, Isaac Smith, Francis Lamb. Written Jan. 1, 1832 Proved Feb. 7, 1832 (Thomas came on Mar. 31) p. 225

Samuel Clothier of Kent Co
To my wife Mary Clothier all my estate.

Exec. my wife Mary Clothier. Witnesses Nathaniel Meginniss, Kinnard W. Martin, John Cole. Written Mar. 17, 1830 Proved Feb. 7, 1832 p. 226

Elizabeth Vickers of Kent Co
All my estate to my brother **Joel Vickers** of Baltimore City in trust for Joel Vickers and his heirs during the life of my sister **Mary Voss** (wife of **William Voss**) in trust to permit the said sister to hold and enjoy the same and if she chooses not to occupy then to have the rents and not subject to debts of her present husband or anyone she may be intermarried and after her death then to the use of my nieces **Sophia Vickers Voss, Rachel Elizabeth Voss, Hester Ann Voss,** and **Mary Jane Voss,** and if William Voss the husband of my sister shall survive her then he shall be entitled during his life to live in the house on High Street which I purchased of **Samuel Reed,** if he wishes, but he shall not be able to rent the same. My sister may sell the land if she chooses. And if sold, William Voss not entitled to live in the house in Chestertown. My negro **Pere** shall be free Jan. 1, 1829 and his wages of 1828 to be paid to him. My negro boy **Arthur** shall be free Jan. 1, 1832 and his wages of 1831 to be paid to him. My boy **Charles** to be free Jan. 1, 1942 and his wages for 1841 to be his. My negro girl **Minty** to be free on Jan. 1, 1844 and her wages for 1843 to be his. My negro girl **Hetty** to be free Jan. 1, 1848 and her wages for 1847 to her. The issue of Minty and Hetty to be free at age 21. To my brother **William Vickers** $50. To my sister **Ann Beck** wife of **Samuel Beck** $100. The remainder of my personal estate to my brother Joel Vickers in trust for my sister Mary Voss to hold. After her death to my niece Sophia Vickers Voss to enjoy while unmarried, but if she marries then to my nieces Sophia Vickers Voss, Rachel Elizabeth Voss, Hester Ann Voss, and Mary Jane Voss. If she remains single until her death, then to the other 3 nieces named. If Joel dies or refuses to be trustee then may be chosen by person who is entitled to estate if of age. Joel to be trustee to hold money and executor.

Exec. my brother Joel Vickers. Witnesses John B. Eccleston, John Harrison, Joseph Redue. Written Jan. 24, 1827 Proved Mar. 8, 1832 (William and Samuel came Mar. 9) p. 228

Codicil I make void the bequest of $50 to my brother William Vickers. I make void the bequest of $100 to my sister Ann Beck wife of Samuel Beck. Written Dec. 8, 1828. Witnesses Samuel W. Canady, William Sappington, Thomas E. Dugan.

Abstracts of Kent Co., MD Wills

Ann Thomas of Kent Co

To my nephew **William Blackiston Thomas** in fee all my real estate but if he dies under age, then to my brother **William Thomas**. My negro boy **George** to be free. To Ms. **Tabitha Wright** $100 as a friendly compliment. I give my bureau to **Mary Thomas**, my brother William's present wife. My forte piano to be sold to pay my burial expenses and the balance if any to my nephew.

Exec. my brother William Thomas. Witnesses James H. Smith, Sophia Smith, Elizabeth Wheatley. Written June 9, 1831 Proved Mar. 13, 1832 p. 238

Daniel Dowman of Kent Co

I give all my estate to my wife **Elizabeth Dowman** and my children of her begot jointly and equally.

Exec. Not Given. Witnesses William Millar, John McDaniel, Samuel R. Turner. Written Dec. 7, 1832 Proved Mar. 19, 1832 p. 241

Abraham Wearum of Kent Co

To my son **William Wearum** one bed and my large walnut chest and its contents after the death of my wife **Ann Wearum** all my estate. To my wife Ann Wearum all the residue of my estate during her life.

Exec. my wife Ann Wearum. Witnesses John Hurtt, Francis Benton, James Kelly. Written Jan. 10, 1832 Proved Mar. 27, 1832 p. 241

Ann Brice of Kent Co

To my dau. **Henrietta Stevens** all that part of land which I now live called *"Wedge's Recovery"* which I purchased of my nephew **Joseph W. Brice** containing 10 acres during her life, this tract is described in a deed dated Dec. 1, 1814 from Joseph W. Brice. To my dau. Henrietta Stevens my negro boy **Peregrine Lewis** aged 15 years in June last to serve until age 35 years and the residue to her also consisting of 2 cows, 8 hogs, 6 windsor chairs, 3 beds, 2 tables, 2 desks and a cupboard. To my granddau. **Sarah Ann Brice** after the decease of her mother Henrietta Stevens the 10 acres. If she dies without heirs then to my grandchildren **James Brice Stevens, John Brice Stevens, Mary Henrietta Stevens,** and **Martha Louisa Stevens,** children of Henrietta Stevens and **Jacob Stevens** her husband late of Kent Co

Exec. my dau. Henrietta Stevens. Witnesses Benjamin Crabbin, William Vannort, Sarah Brice, Philip M. Reed. Written Aug. 19, 1830 Proved Mar. 27, 1832 p. 242

Thomas Davis of Chestertown, Kent Co

To my dau. **Henrietta R. H. Davis** all that land which was sold to me by James E. Barroll Esq. trustee for the sale of the estate of Richard Barroll deceased by deed of Feb. 16, 1822 lying in Chestertown being *"Lot No. 15"*. To my dau. **Martha Ann Glenn**

Liber 11 1827-1835

(wife of **Michael Glenn**) all that lot I bought of **Alexander Maxwell** as by a deed dated Feb. 26, 1818 situated in Chestertown being *"Lot No. 23"* and that part of lot lying in Chestertown being *"Lot No. 24"* which I purchased of Dr. **George W. Thomas** (excepting so much as I have sold to Capt. **Robert Constable**) for her life, remainder to her children. If she has no children surviving then to my dau. Henrietta R. H. Davis. To my son **William A. Davis** all that lot in Chestertown being *"Lot No. 30"* conveyed to me by deed by **James Hodges Jr.** dated Aug. 4, 1810. My son **James M. Davis** guardian to my son William. The rents of my estate to my dau. Henrietta R. H. Davis. On whatever part of my estate my dau. Henrietta R. H. Davis shall reside she to remain without charge until Jan. 1 or to rent that part and receive rents. To my dau. Martha Ann Glenn my negro boy **Alexander** born Mar. 15, 1822 to serve until 1846. To my son William A. Davis my negro girl **Mary Ann** (born Mar. 19, 1825) and to be free Jan. 1 after she is 21 and any male issue to serve until 25 and female issue to serve until age 20. My negro woman **Ann** to be free. Her child **Nancy Elizabeth** aged about 9 months I give to my dau. Henrietta in trust for said Ann until she is 20 and any issue born to Nancy during servitude to be held in like manner for said Ann until 21 for male and 20 for female. Having heretofore given to my son James M. Davis nearly a full share of my estate in money and having shown my confidence in him by appointing him guardian to my son William, I give to him and my son William A. Davis to be divided equally between them a note which I hold of Mr. **George S. Hollyday**. To my dau. Martha Ann Glenn the second choice of a bed. To my dau. Henrietta all the rest of my personal estate.

Exec. my dau. Henrietta R. H. Davis. Witnesses George Vickers, William H. Wickes, Benjamin Greenwood. Written Mar. 26, 1832 Proved Apr. 9, 1832 p. 245

James Pearce of Kent Co
To my sister **Catherine Pearce** all my estate during her life and the remainder to whomever she designates but in case she does not them to my nephew **James Alfred Pearce** and my niece **Ann Ophelia Pearce** being understood that if my nephew **George William Pearce** should live to 21 then James Alfred Pearce and Ann Ophelia Pearce shall pay him $1,000. If my sister dies before me then to my nephew James Alfred Pearce and my niece Ann Ophelia Pearce and them paying to George at 21 the above $1,000.

Exec. my sister Catherine (or my nephew James Alfred Pearce if she dies). Witnesses Daniel Jones, Thomas Rasin, William Keatting. Written May 16, 1827 Proved May 1, 1832 (Apr. 25 came Joseph and Peregrine for codicil) p. 250

Codicil In order to modify my will in consequence of my recent marriage I give to my wife in lieu of dower $200 per annum and if I have children then my sister Catherine to provide for them and if she dies then my nephew James Alfred Pearce. Written July 23, 1831. Witnesses Nathan Peacock, Joseph Moffett, Peregrine Wethered Jr.

Abstracts of Kent Co., MD Wills

Renunciation I Mary Pearce widow of James Pearce do renounce the devise made by the will and codicil of my husband. Written June 18, 1832. Witness Bartus Pierce (Pince)

James Martin of Kent Co
To my wife **Hannah Martin** all my estate during her life. After her death then to my sons **Kennard Martin** and **Benjamin Martin** all my real estate.

Exec. my friend Benjamin Money. Witnesses Nathaniel Meginniss, Samuel Clothier, Edward Sanders. Written Oct. 4, 1830 Proved May 19, 1832 p. 254

Robert Dunn of Kent Co
To my niece **Frances H. Wickes** all the estate I have. To my sister **Araminta Dunn** $50. To my niece **Ann Wilmer** $50. To my niece **Sarah Ann Wickes** my Bible, prayer book and breast pin. To my nephew **Jackson Wickes** all my joiners tools, shaving apparatus and cloths or wearing apparel.

Exec. my niece Frances H. Wickes. Witnesses Michael Miller, Horace Kindal, Stephen Kindal. Written July 1, 1832 Proved Aug. 28, 1832 p. 255

Augusta Bowers of Kent Co
To my dau. **Augusta C. Eccleston** all the lots in Chestertown formerly owned by my deceased husband **James Bowers** and which have been conveyed to me by **Ezekial F. Chambers** and **Sarah E. Chambers** his wife and if Ezekial and his wife Sarah should decide to purchase the lots then the purchase money to Augusta. To my dau. **Elizabeth F. Houston** the rest of my real estate in Chestertown. I give to my dau. the mortgage I hold of my brother Ezekial F. Chambers and the furniture belonging to my chamber. If any rent due me for my house on Queen Street in Chestertown to be applied to funeral and debt and any deficiency to be paid by my daughters Augusta and Elizabeth equally. My 1/3 of a judgment from Hannah Houston and my wearing apparel to my daughters Augusta and Elizabeth. The residue of my personal estate to my dau. Augusta C. Eccleston

Exec. my son in law **John B. Eccleston**. Witnesses Joseph Wickes 4th, Nathaniel T. Hynson, A. W. Sparkes. Written Mar. 5, 1832 Proved Aug. 7, 1832 p. 257

Isaac Spencer of Kent Co
All my estate which I hold from my father which I hold from my brother **William Spencer's** will or that I have purchased myself to be equally divided among my children after deducting $1,300 I have advanced to **Isaac Spencer**, $1,500 I have advanced to **William A. Spencer**, $1,500 I have advanced to **John Spencer** and $1,500 to **Jervis Spencer**.

Execs. my sons William A. Spencer and John Spencer. Witnesses Richard Ringgold, Jacob T. Freeman, Samuel Tomlinson. Written Oct. 8, 1832 Proved Oct. 24, 1832 p. 259

Liber 11 1827-1835

James Hyland of Kent Co
To my son Henry Miles Hyland all my lands known as part of a tract called *"Bounty"* containing 40 acres and one tract called *"Sillers Addition"* containing 11 3/4 acres with a lot taken up by Samuel Beck of whom I bought the above tracts containing 62 ¼ acres. To him 3 feather beds, 6 silver table spoons, all the blacksmith tools, and Iron, my debts due me, my 2 apprentice negro boys Hark and William and a negro woman Mary. All the rest of my estate to my 2 daughters Kesiah Love and Ann Hurtt (excepting wheat enough to seed the field that may be for tillage which I give to son Henry). To my son James Hyland $20.

Exec. my son Henry Miles Hyland. Witnesses James Hodges, Samuel Wickes, James Collins. Written Nov. 10, 1823 Proved Sep. 18, 1832 (Nov. 14 came John Hodges p. 261

Codicil To my son Henry Miles Hyland my mahogany desk. Written Aug. 1831. Witnesses James Hodges, Mary Ann Hodges, John Hodges

Catherine Calder of Kent Co
I am entitled to an undivided interest in the real estate of my grandfather William Spearman and to an undivided part of the real estate of my aunt Catherine Parker which was devised to her by her husband James Parker, therefore I give my right in the above real estate to my sister Isabella Conner, along with all of the residue of my estate.

Exec. my brother in law Benjamin Conner. Witnesses William Thomas (of John), Mary Thomas, Elizabeth E. Calder. Written July 15, 1832 Proved Nov. 27, 1832 p. 265

Charles R. Hynson of Kent Co
To my wife Harriet Matilda, all my personal estate, my negroes, and cattle.

Exec. Not Given. Witnesses Jacob Fisher, Martha Hynson, Araminta Crane. Written Nov. 15, 1832 Proved Dec. 11, 1832 p. 266

Mary Smith maiden of Kent Co
To my father Stephen Smith a servant woman Maria who is manumitted at the age of 35 during his life but free at his death. To my cousin James Smith son of my uncle Michael Smith, my negro Henry about 10 years old, also my negro Betsey about 7 years old, also my negro boy Mortimer about 3 years old until they arrive at 30 then free if the laws of the state permit. He to have them if he lets my father use them during his life, if he refuses then to my father. [pass granted June 11, 1862 written in margin]. If the laws will not allow my negro woman Maria to be free then to my cousin James Smith. To my father Stephen Smith my bed, my mantle clock, carpet, 6 chairs, horse and carriage, and all the money in my trunks, also my cow. To Martha Henrietta Griffith, wife of George C. Griffith all my best clothes, 15 silver spoons and sugar

tongs. My negro woman Maria to have my inferior clothes. All other property to my father.

Exec. Not Given. Witnesses Daniel Collins, Averilla Collins, Elizabeth Griffith. Written Feb. 19, 1833 Proved Mar. 12, 1833 p. 267

William Foreman of Kent Co
To **James Briscoe Jr.** in trust for my dau. **Harriet Copper** my lot of land lying to the right of main road leading from Chestertown to Goose Hill containing about 8 acres. To my son **Mark W. Foreman** my lot called *"Friendship"* containing 10 ¼ acres lying to the left of the main road leading from my house to Chestertown but if he dies without heir then to divide between my dau. **Hannah M. Foreman** and my grandson **Thomas F. Copper**. To Thomas Copper as trustee to **Ariminta H.E. Foreman** ½ my home farm adjoining **Samuel Ringgold** land and my personal property except my negro girl **Hester Ann** interest to be paid her during her life. If she dies without heir then to my dau. Hannah M. Foreman and my granddau. **Harriet A. Copper**. To my dau. Hannah M. Foreman all the rest of my home farm and my negro girl Hester Ann to serve until 30. The family burying ground I reserve for the use of my family.

Execs. Mark W. Foreman and Thomas Copper. Witnesses Samuel Ringgold, James Briscoe Jr, John Edwards. Written Jan. 29, 1833 Proved Apr. 27, 1833 (May 1 came James) p. 270

Edward Beck of Kent Co
To my dau. **Matilda Beck** all my estate during her life and then all my real property to my son **Elisha** during his life and after his death my real estate to my grandson **Edward Beck** son of **Elijah Beck**. My negro woman called **Ann**, to serve my dau. Matilda during her life and my negro boy **Thomas** to serve 16 years from Dec. 25 and if my dau. dies first then to be bound out to learn a trade until free at age 21 which is the time he is set to serve. My sister's son **James Crouch** trustee for my daughter

Exec. Not Given. Witnesses John Hurtt, William T. Adkinson, Thomas Bryan. Written Oct. 27, 1831 Proved Nov. 10, 1842 p. 272

Mary Ann Calder of Kent Co
To **Sarah Elizabeth Smith** my niece and dau. of **James H.** and **Sophia Smith** all my right in the personal estate of **William Spearman** the elder of Kent Co deceased and the personal estate of **James Parker** of Kent Co dec'd.

Exec. James H. Smith. Witnesses Isaac Hines, Jesse Moffett. Written May 26, 1833 Proved June 24, 1833 p. 274

Liber 11 1827-1835

Solomon Start of Kent Co
My farm on Langford's Bay shall be divided into 2 equal parts so as to give ½ the house to each part and ½ the cleared land and ½ the woodland. That part formerly occupied Elizabeth Crouch to be allotted to the S part and that part of said house occupied by Richard Start to be allotted to the N half. The S half to my dau. Elizabeth Crouch the widow of William Crouch deceased for her life and after her death to her dau. Jane Crouch. The N half to my dau. Sophia Start. My dwelling plantation situate on Chester River including all the land commonly used as part said plantation I give to my son John Start but if he dies without issue then to my son Solomon Start. Sarah Andrews commonly called Sally Machelor who is now living with me shall during her life be entitled in the dwelling house. My son Solomon Start and my daughters Rebecca Start, Sophia Start, and Sarah Start a room of my dwelling house. To my son Benjamin Start my schooner called Mary Elizabeth and her furniture and tackle and the money he owes me. All the rest of my personal estate to my son Richard Start and Solomon Start and my daughters Rebecca Start, Sarah Start, Mary Gee wife of Cornelius Gee equally.

Exec. my son John Start. Witnesses John B. Eccleston, William G. Seth, John Buchanan. Written Feb. 23, 1832 Proved June 21, 1833 p. 276

Codicil My sons called in my will, John Start, Benjamin Start, Solomon Start and Richard Start and my daughters called or named in my will Rebecca Start, Sophia Start, Sarah Start and Mary Gee are all my children by Sarah Andrews commonly called Sally Machelor. Written Feb. 23, 1832. Witnesses same.

Frances Ringgold of Kent Co
To my sister Henrietta Harris my negro man Nathan and one share of my stock in the Bank of Baltimore. My niece Henrietta Harris $40, a dressing glass, dressing table, and a patchwork bedspread. My niece Juliet Harris $40, a dressing glass, dressing box, and a chintz bedspread. To my niece Maria Harris $40, a case of drawers, and a dark calico bedspread. To my nephew Alexander Harris, my negro man Bill and a silver watch. To my niece Caroline Burgess my negro man Felix, 2/3 of a share of stock in Bank of Baltimore, a pair of looking glasses and half of my clothes. To my great nephew Thomas Harris Burgess my negro man Peter, a silver can and 6 silver teaspoons. To my great niece Frances Ringgold Burgess my negro boy Frederick, a silver can, a pair of silver salt cellars, a bed bolster, 2 pillows and a pair of blankets. To my sister Hester Holland one share of stock in the Bank of Baltimore, a pair of dining tables, 12 windsor chairs and ½ of my clothes. To my nephew John William Holland $40. To my nephew George Washington Holland $40. To my nephew Alexander Holland $40 and a gold watch. To my niece Sarah Blunt $40. The residue of my estate to my sister Henrietta Harris.

Exec. Not Given. Witnesses Richard W. Ringgold. Written Dec. 29, 1832 Proved June 6, 1833 p. 279

Abstracts of Kent Co., MD Wills

William Armstrong of Kent Co
To my son **John M. Armstrong** all that tract called *"McCay's Purchase"* where I now reside containing about 122 acres adjoining Georgetown Cross Roads. To my John M. Armstrong all my forest land adjoining of **Stephen Boyer** and *"Dodson Lot"* containing about 25 acres and to my on my negro girl **Harriett** until she is 35 years and my two boys **Ben** and **Bill** and my son all the balance of my personal estate. My son John M. Armstrong to pay to my dau. **Mary A. Pennington** $25 and unto my grandson **William A. Pennington** $125 and my negro woman **Cate** to serve him 7 years. My son to also pay my grandson **Robert A. Pennington** $125 and my bay mare silver heels and to pay my granddau. **Sarah A. Harper** (formerly **Sarah A. Pennington**) $100 and my negro girl **Sall** to serve until she is 35. My son to pay my granddau. Mary A. Pennington $125 and my negro boy **George** to serve until he is 40. My son to pay my granddau. **Emily A. Pennington** $100 and my negro girl **Jane** to serve until she is 35. My son to pay my granddau. **Rosetta A. Pennington** at age 16 $100 and my negro boy **Charles** to serve until he is 40. To pay my grandson **Edward B. Pennington** $100 and my negro girl **Betts** until she is age 35, all to be paid out of the land given to John.

Exec. my son John M. Armstrong. Witnesses Benjamin Briscoe, William Moffett, Thomas Lusby. Written Mar. 13, 1833 Proved Aug. 21, 1833 p. 281

John Thomas Reese of Kent Co, now of Philadelphia
All my estate to my cousin Dr. **John Thomas** of Louisianna and to my **James Boon** of Kent Co

Exec. my friend James Boon. Witnesses R. Jordan, Henry W. Williamsen, Alexander C. Draper. Written Aug. 20, 1833 Proved Aug. 29, 1833 p. 283

Jacob Clayton of Kent Co
To **Jacob Clayton** my son my plantation whereon I now dwell known in a deed by **Samuel G. Osborn** one of the commissioners of the land containing by patents containing 169 acres and all my personal estate. My dau. **Elizabeth Tippit** $50.

Exec. my son Jacob Clayton. Witnesses Samuel G. Osborn, Benjamin Chivins, George Wilson. Written May 13, 1833 Proved Sep. 19, 1833 p. 284

Richard Bennett G. Mitchell of Kent Co
All my estate to my wife **Sarah Elizabeth C. Mitchell**

Exec. my wife Sarah Elizabeth C. Mitchell. Witnesses John B. Scott, John Scott, T. Parkin Scott. Written Oct. 2, 1828 Proved Dec. 19, 1833 p. 287

Mary S. Nicols
My friends Mrs. **Ann B. Wilmer** and **Harriett M. Coxe** near Alexandria, D.C. one plain mourning ring with my hair in them. To my friend **Jane Eliza Wilmer** near

Alexandria a gold medallion with my hair in it to cost $5. To **Eugenia M. Wroth** my breast pin, one wrought gold, and one plain gold ring and gold heart with my black and white veils and all my books excepting my small testament which I give to my sister **Margaret**. To **Editha G. Wroth** my bead reticula. To **Mary E. Wroth** my large white cashmere shawl and my guards. All the remainder of my clothes to Eugenia M. and Mary E. Wroth under the direction of my sister Margaret. To my cousin **Elizabeth R. Hayward** one wrought gold ring, not to exceed $3. A mourning breast pin with my hair to my cousin **Thomas S. Hayward**, not to exceed $5. To my friends **Dr. P. Wroth** a handsome Bible to be lettered in gilt on the back. My beds and bedding to my brother **James Nicols** and $100. To my brother **Thomas S. Nicols** $50. To **Edward W. Wroth** a handsome vest with a handsome pen knife and ivory pocket comb with his name on each. To my nephew **William Jackson Wroth** a handsome suit of black cloth and small red chair. My better set of china to sister Margaret with my traveling trunk, my wardrobe, rocking chair. To **Mary Oliver** and **Maria Gibson** and a black and white cotton frock and black silk handkerchief. To **Eliza Ann Oliver** one hair trunk and old bonnet. To **James Oliver,** brother of the above, a suit of domestic. All the rest of my estate to my sister **Margaret S. Wroth**.

Exec. my friend Dr. P. Wroth. Witnesses Mary Ann Ringgold, George S. Hollyday. Written Nov. 29, 1833 Proved Dec. 17, 1833 p. 288

David Webb of Kent Co

To my wife **Mary** for her life my lot of woodland in the head of Chester and adjoining to **George Hazel** and **Solomon Smith** and after her death to my son **Joseph W. Webb**. The rest of my estate to my son Joseph W. Webb. If my son dies without heirs then to my son **John Webb**. Whereas I am entitled to a reversion of the lands in which Mrs. **Avarilla Williams** has a life estate. To my son John Webb $200. As I have given my dau. **Elizabeth Ervin** a full share I now give her $1. To my wife Mary my horse called Toney, my gig or riding carriage, one bed, one cupboard, the china and crockery ware, one table and 6 chairs and 1/3 of my personal estate. The rest of my personal estate to my 3 children **Rachel Carter,** Joseph W. Webb, and John Webb.

Execs. my wife Mary Webb and my son Joseph Webb. Witnesses John Urie, James Urie, Thomas Urie. Written Mar. 20, 1829 Proved Dec. 24, 1833 p. 290

Codicil To my son John Webb instead of $200 to have $400. My wife Mary to have instead of my horse Toney to have my young gray horse called Liberty. Written Aug. 18, 1833. Witnesses Thomas J. Mann, John Wesley Clothier.

John Ferguson of Kent Co

To my wife **Elizabeth Ferguson** all my property and her heirs. If she has no heirs then to my brother **Colin Furgeson**. If he dies before my wife then to the children my sister **Elanor Richardson**

Exec. my brother Colin Furgeson. Witnesses William Thomas of William, W. Riley, William Pearce. Written Mar. 1, 1824 Proved Dec. 31, 1833 p. 294

Elizabeth Wales, wife of Samuel Wales of Kent Co
To my husband Samuel Wales the rents of the tract on which I now reside for 3 years, and after 3 years to my son **James Browne**. He is to pay my daughters **Rebecca Simmonds** wife of **Robert G. Simmonds** and **Elizabeth Jones** wife of **David Jones** during James' life each 1/3 interest of said farm. After his death to my 2 granddaughters **Mary Trew Browne** and **Elizabeth Thomas Browne** on same condition. Also to Rebecca Simmonds and Elizabeth Jones $25 each annually.

Exec. Not Given. Witnesses James B. Ricaud, Charles T. Browne, Benjamin F. Houston. Written July 15, 1833 Proved Jan. 30, 1834 p. 295

William Parks of Kent Co
To my son **Thomas R. Parks** one mantle clock to be left in the care of **Mary Parsons** until Thomas is age 21. To my son **William W. Parks** one silver watch. The rest of my estate to my wife **Maria H. Parks** and my 5 sons Thomas R. Parks, William W. Parks, **James D. Parks, Alexander R. Parks,** and **George W. Parks,** when George arrives at 14. James D. to have one year schooling. And the profits to be applied to the 2 younger sons when they arrive at 14.

Execs. Daniel Collins and William Shaw. Witnesses James Brown 3rd, William Yates, Samuel Elborn. Written Jan. 14, 1834 Proved Feb. 10, 1834 p. 301

Thomas Walker of Kent Co
To be buried in a pine coffin and with no badges of mourning as an unmeaning ceremony. My property divided equally between my surviving children, but as my dau. **Elizabeth M. Morian** whom I equally love has had her portion by my consent willed her by the late **Alexander Miller** of Kent Co to the exclusion of my other children so these children **Thomas Alexander Grieves** and **Mary Sophia Walker,** I therefore will after my debts and my wife's thirds to them. My books I exempt from being sold and divided equally between my children Thomas Alexander Grieves and Mary Sophia Walker and Elizabeth M. Morian. My negro boy **Dick** to be free and negro boy **Harry** to be free Jan. 1, 1843. My other negroes are to already manumitted on the Dorchester records viz. **Rachel** and **Charles.**

Execs. my wife and my son Thomas Alexander. Witnesses Morgan Browne, John W. Walker. Written May 13, 1831 Proved Feb. 18, 1834 (Mar. 18 came Morgan) p. 303

William Barroll of Chestertown, Kent Co
To my wife **Sarah H. Barroll** all my estate forever as I have no doubt she will make a disposition at the time of her death. I request that she consult with my brother **James Barroll** and my friend **Jeremiah Nicols** to sell part of my estate. As I know my debts

are considerable and it will be necessary to sell a great part of my estate. It is my desire that my sister and my 2 nieces **Anna M. Barroll** and **Mary C. Barroll** continue to live with my wife and my books will show what I owe to my 2 nieces and this must be paid out of my estate.

Exec. my wife Sarah H. Barroll. Witnesses Richard Ringgold, Samuel W. Spencer, Richard C. Ringgold. Written Jan. 21, 1832 Proved Mar. 15, 1834 p. 305

Renunciation I Sarah H. Barroll renounce any bequest in my late husband's will and elect my dower. Written Apr. 25, 1834. Witnesses Richard T. Earle

Sarah Gooden Lynch of Kent Co
To my sister **Phoebe Lynch** my negro man **Levi** to serve until he is 30, to be free on May 20, 1844 and to her my part of the farm whereon I now dwell know by the name of *"Camples Worth more"* and my part of the woodland laying between here and Goose Hill in other words all the lands heired from my father.

Exec. Not Given. Witnesses William Thomas of William, James Gale, John Turner. Written Jan. 19, 1834 Proved Mar. 21, 1834 (Mar. 27 came James) p. 307

Tabitha Wright of Kent Co
To **Martha Ann Atwood** (dau. of **Isaac Freeman** deceased) all money due me which was willed to me by **Matthias C. Atwood** that is in the hands of **Richard Ringgold** Esq executor of Matthias C. Atwood. To my niece **Temperance Newman** one bed, one pair of large looking glasses and after her death **Sarah Elizabeth Smith** granddau. of said Temperance shall have the above. To my niece **Frances Susanna Isabella Hurtt** one walnut bureau, one small walnut stand, one small walnut chest, one seal skin white trunk. To **Mary Rebecca Hurtt** dau. of **Henry Hurtt** one bed, one mahogany table, one black leather trunk. And $20 to put up a fence around the graveyard on Commodore **Jacob Jones** farm where I wish to be buried to be paid out of the money willed to me by **Ann Thomas** now in the hands of **James Boon** executor of Dr. **John T. Reese**. To Henry Hurtt the balance of the money willed to me by **Mary Thomas**, and the residue of my property.

Exec. Henry Hurtt. Witnesses David Davis, Henry Hurtt. Written Dec. 25, 1833 Proved Mar. 1, 1834 p. 309

William Hynson Hague of Kent Co
To my wife **Hester Hague** 1/3 of my estate. To my dau. **Johanna Lazenby** $1. To my dau. **Elizabeth Elbourn** $1. To my dau. **Sarah Hague** one cow. The remainder to my son **Thomas Hague** 2/3 and my dau. **Hester Hague** 1/3. The black mare called Pidgeon no in my possession is the property of my son Thomas Hague. I appoint ____ executors of my estate.

Exec. Not Given. Witnesses A. W. Ringgold, William Wickes Sr., Lambert Wickes. Written Mar. 25, 1832 Proved June 18, 1834 p. 312

Codicil If either my son Thomas or my dau. Hester dies then to survivor.

James Eagle of Kent Co
To my wife **Rachel Eagle** all the estate I own during her life provided she maintains my granddau. **Catharine Alphonsa Eagle** while she is single and lives with her. After her death, to my granddau. provided she pays unto my granddau. **Martha Shaw** $100 and to my granddau. **Norcissa Eagle** $300 in 3 years. Also $100 to the eldest son of Martha Shaw when he is 21. If they die before coming of age then my granddau. Catharine Alphonsa is exonerated from paying said sums. If my wife dies before my granddau. Catharine Alphonsa arrives at 18 then **Samuel Baker** to be guardian. If Catharine dies then to my granddau. Martha Shaw if she pays Norcissa Eagle $500

Exec. my wife Rachael Eagle. Witnesses William Copper, Peregrine Burgess, Thomas A. Strong. Written May 29, 1834 Proved July 29, 1834 p. 314

James Nicols of Kent Co
To my nephew **William J. Wroth** $100. To **Edward W. Wroth** my silver watch. To **Eugenia M. Wroth** my gold breast pin set in jet. To Mrs. **Tamacina Glenn** "Clarks Commentary on the New Testament" also my pitchers, wash basin and tumblers. Also one dress. **Mary E. Wroth** $50 when she is 16. All my wearing apparel to **William Meginniss**. All the rest of my estate to my niece **Margaret Priscilla Wroth** when she is 16.

Exec. my friend **Dr. Peregrine Wroth**. Witnesses Joseph Osborne Jr., Joseph Osborne Sr. Written Aug. 21, 1834 Proved Sep. 2, 1834 p. 317

Memo J. Nicols directs his executor to his kind friend Miss **Martha Brice** his "History of Methodism", Hymn book, and pocket testament.

William Pearce of Kent Co
One of my debts left by my father to my sister **Mary**, which is about $800. To **John Kinvin Wroth** son of John Wroth $100 to be paid by his guardian when he is 21. My negro woman **Binah** to be free in 6 months. My negro boys **Jefferson** and **George** to my brother **Edward**; Jefferson to serve until 1824 and George to serve until 1829. To my sister Mary I give my negro child **Mary** until 1833. The remainder 2/3 to my sister Mary if she relinquishes any claim to my brother under my father's will. If she does not then 2/3 to my brother and 1/3 to her.

Exec. my sister Mary Pearce. Witnesses Peregrine Wroth, William Mason. Written May 25, 1813 Proved Sep. 19, 1834 p. 319

Liber 11 1827-1835

Codicil **Jim Mechanic** a negro man who lives with me to get my wearing apparel and my saddle and bridle. Any children of my negro child Mary to serve until 16. Written same as will.

John T. K. Skirven
I give my servant **Amanda Malvina** to my aunts Sarah and Mary Skirven until her time of servitude is over according to a deed of manumission duly recorded. The rest of my estate, ¼ to my two aunts named and 3/4 to my brother **Thomas W. Skirven**.

Exec. my said brother. Witnesses Peregrine Wroth, James Mansfield Jr., N. J. Hynson. Written Apr. 27, 1832 Proved Dec. 22, 1834 p. 322

Mary Thomas of Kent Co
To **Mary Loockerman** of Millington, Kent Co $100. To **Joseph Wright** a tract in Kent Co adjoining **Jesse Knock, Washington Comegys**, and others containing 112 acres to **Joseph Wright** and all the rest of my estate to him forever.

Exec. my friend Joseph Wright. Witnesses John McDaniel, William Millan, Thomas H. Horsey. Written Oct. 13, 1834 Proved Dec. 18, 1834 p. 324

James Hanson of Kent Co
In 4 years on Oct. 1, 1834 my executors may sell the tract devised to me by my father **Benjamin Hanson** containing about 400 acres to pay **John Emory** and **Thomas W. Hopper** on an obligatory instrument and the excess to the child or children of my sister **Hannah Snow**. To my nephew **Benjamin T. Hanson** the present growth of the timber of 5 acres of woodland to my nephew, his brothers **John W. Hanson** and **James H. Hanson**. To my 2 nephews John W. Hanson and James H. Hanson 200 acres on the farm on which my father Benjamin Hanson died, after the death of my aunt **Elizabeth Hanson** if they at age 21 they pay $1,000 to child or children of my sister **Emaline Reed**. If my aunt dies before they are 21 then Dr. **Thomas C. Kennard** to receive rents. I give (with reservation of one house and one acre) a tract which I purchased of the heirs of **James Anderson** and **Edward Anderson** containing 30 acres to my niece **Sarah Elizabeth Bradsha**. My servant woman **Hetty** and her children now and future to be free at age 25. At her release I give to her the one of the above houses and one acre (referred to above) during her life then to revert back to the tract. The rest of my estate to be sold for debt and any surplus to my niece **Maria Elizabeth Webster**. My not providing more for my niece does not result from a lack of affection but a knowledge of her having shared a larger portion of the estate of my father Benjamin Hanson.

Execs. John Constable and Philemon B. Hopper of Kent and Queen Annes Co (or Dr. Thomas C. Kennard if they refuse). Witnesses Daniel Evans Reese, Richard H. Merriken, Maybury Parks. Written Aug. 4, 1830 Proved Dec. 22, 1834 p. 326

John Hepbron of Kent Co
To **Thomas Hepbron** a lot of land I once sold to **Gibson Howard** and repurchased running in a straight line with **Capt. James Gale** land in E direction until it intersects with **Mrs. Medford's** land including the land on the N side of the road with the Blacksmith's shop this being part of the home farm that I hereafter will to my grandson **Tewisham Hepbron**. To **John Henry Hepbron** and **Ann Eliza Hepbron**, my grandchildren, ½ acre adjoining a lot that deeded to my son **Sewell Hepbron** in 1830 being also part of my home farm. To my dau. **Elizabeth Hepbron** the first 2 years of rent of my home farm and Rich Neck farm for what I owe her and ½ the rents for life. To John Henry Hepbron and Ann Eliza Hepbron my grandchildren the other ½ of the rents until my grandson Tewisham Hepbron arrives at age 21. If either dies then to the survivor. If both dies then to my granddau. **Margaret Elizabeth Hepbron**. If my dau. Elizabeth dies before my grandson Tewisham arrive at 21 then the ½ rent of my home farm is to go to my granddau. Margaret Elizabeth Hepbron dau. of Sewell Hepbron and the other ½ to my granddau. **Henrietta Hepbron** the dau. of **James Hepbron**. To my grandson Tewesham Hepbron when he is 21 my home farm except what is already disposed and if he dies then to my son Sewell Hepbron. To my granddau. Henrietta Hepbron the dau. of James Hepbron my farm called Rich Neck and if she should die then to my son James. My lot of land adjoining *"Green Oak"* called *"Retaliation"* to be sold. The residue to my grandchildren viz **Mary** the dau. of **Thomas**, John Henry and Ann Eliz. children of Samuel, Henrietta and **Joseph James** children of James, Tewesham, **John Thomas Maslin,** Margaret Elizabeth children of Sewell. One of my sons is to be guardian to my grandchildren John Henry and Ann Eliza and my 3 sons Thomas, James and Sewell to sell my personal estate and the lot adjoining *"Green Oak"*

Execs. (assumed all 3 sons). Witnesses Eben. Blackiston, Henry Blackiston, Anna Smith. Written Sep. 6, 1834 Proved Jan. 13, 1835 p. 331

Mary Tilden of Kent Co
To my grandson **Nathaniel Hynson** one bureau, one square tea table. To my granddau. **Sophia Ann Freeman** one changeable silk dress. To my son **Nathaniel Hynson** 6 large silver table spoons and $200. The silver spoons to go to my grandson Nathaniel after the death of my son Nathaniel. To my grandchildren **Charles E. Tilden, Mary Elizabeth Tilden, Indiana Tilden** and **Virginia Tilden,** children of my son **Charles E. Tilden** my slaves **Tom, Daniel, William, Jack, Abraham, Sarah, Frederick,** and **Jim** with my kitchen furniture upon age 21 and not before my granddau. Virginia Tilden. My son Charles E. Tilden guardian to my said grandchildren and not required to post bond. If any die then to the survivors. To my grandson Charles E. Tilden over his portion one chest of drawers, to my granddau. Mary Elizabeth one bureau, to my granddau. Indana Tilden one set of chine now in the hands of my son Charles E. Tilden. My slave **Mary** to be free in one year and to get $10.

Exec. my son Charles E. Tilden. Witnesses James B. Ricaud, Daniel Perkins. Written Dec. 20, 1834 Proved Jan. 19, 1835 p. 333

Liber 11 1827-1835

Samuel Comegys (of Samuel) of Kent Co
To my brother in law **Thomas J. Mann** all my estate during his life. After his death to my nephew **Samuel Mann**. If he dies before age 21 then to my nephew **Joseph C. Mann** and if he dies under 21 then to my niece **Mary A. Mann** and if she dies under 18 then to my niece **Millementy Comegys**.

Exec. my brother in law Thomas J. Mann. Witnesses Emily Peacock, Samuel Peacock, Thomas S. Wilmer. Written Oct. 18, 1832 Proved Jan. 27, 1835 p. 338

Sandy Bond, colored man of Kent Co
To my wife **Betsy Bond** all my personal estate and my house and lot purchased of **Simon Wickes** adjoining the land of **William B. Wilmer** and **John Blake** during her widowhood, then to my daughters **Rebecca, Adeline, Temperance** and **Anne** and my sons **Alexander** and **Elijah**.

Execs. William B. Wilmer (to settle real estate) and my wife (to settle personal estate). Witnesses William B. Wilmer, Louisa Ann Tate, Mary Ann Wilmer (Sarah R. Wilmer also witnessed addition of sons names). Written Dec. 21, 1826 Proved Feb. 4, 1835 p. 341

Abstracts of Kent Co., MD Wills 1777-1867 (WB 12)

Will Book 12   1835-1854   pp. 1-401 WK 688-689-2

Sarah Brice of Kent Co

My 3 old negroes shall be free at my death and **Thomas** and **Jenny** shall occupy the kitchen part of my house with a garden during their life and at their death to return to my estate. To **Mary Henrietta** and **Martha Louisa Stevens** all my real estate but if they die then to **Sarah Ann Brice** dau. of **Henrietta Stevens**. To Henrietta Stevens all the remainder of my personal estate with the negroes **Charlotte** for 7 years, **Daniel** for 9 years, **Pere** for 12 years, **Mary** for 13 years, **Minty** for 13 years, **Henry** for 15 years, **George** for 22 years, **Sophia** for 17 years, **Henry** for 22 years, **Mary Jane** for 27 years, **Jane Elizabeth** child for 30 years.

Exec. Benjamin Crabin. Witnesses John Hurtt, Benjamin Crabbin, James H. Legg. Written Feb. 22, 1832 Proved Mar. 17, 1835 p. 1

Codicil To **Martha Brice** my brother's dau. all my part and claim to undivided part of land lying in Skinners Neck. Written Apr. 28, 1832. Witnesses John Hurtt, Ann E. Elburn, Henrietta Stevens

Thomas E. Dugan of Chestertown, Kent Co

After my wife's third, all my person estate (except my negro girl **Hannah**) to my children **Thomas E. Dugan, Jr., William W. Dugan, Joseph O. Dugan, Mary Isabella Dugan** and **Marion Dugan**. To my son Thomas E. Dugan Jr. all the house and lot in Chestertown which I purchased of **William Browne** and wife as seen by deed dated Dec. 11, 1815 called *"Lot No. 88"*; also that lot of land I which I purchased of **John Nevin** and others called *"Lot No. 91"* as seen by deed dated Sep. 19, 1829; also that lot I purchased from **Joseph Wickes** Esq trustee for the estate of **Philip Reed** deceased containing 14 acres 1 rood and 6 perches as seen by deed Jul. 29, 1834. To my son William W. Dugan all the houses and lot of land in Chestertown which I purchased of **Joseph Redue, George Watts** and others, commissioners appointed to divide or sell the real estate of **Robert Constable** deceased bearing date Apr. 24, 1826. To my son Joseph O. Dugan all those houses in Chestertown which I purchased of **William Parker** called *"Lot No. 60"* as seen by deed Nov. 30, 1829. Also that lot which was conveyed to me by **David T. McKim** and **Mary McKim** by deed of July 1, 1834 lying in Chestertown. To my dau. Mary Isabella Dugan all that house in Chestertown called *"Lot No. 62"* which was conveyed to the said Thomas E. Dugan by **Rachel Dudley** by deed of July 20, 1833. And that part of lot on plot of said town called *"Lot No. 63"* conveyed to me by **Joseph Acres** and wife by deed dated Oct. 25, 1833. Also my negro girl **Hannah** aged about 6 years to serve until age 35. To my dau. Marion Dugan all those houses and lot in Chestertown which I purchased of a **John L. Reed** and afterwards from **Edward Browne** former collector of Kent. The deed from Edward Browne dated Nov. 28, 1829 and known as part of lots called *"Lot No. 60"* and *"Lot No. 61"*. To my dau. Marion Dugan until Jan. 1, 1839 all that lot know as *"Lot No. 61"* which was conveyed by Edward Browne by deed dated Nov. 28, 1829, and after that time to the heirs **Robert**

Liber 12   1835-1854

Reed formerly of Kent Co deceased as tenants in common. His heirs being such persons by descent would receive if he died intestate. If my dau. **Emeline Prichard** is a widow at the death of any of my children viz Thomas E. Dugan, Jr., William W. Dugan, Joseph O. Dugan, Mary Isabella Dugan, and Marion Dugan and they have no children then my dau. Emeline Prichard to have during widowhood then to my surviving children. If she becomes a widow before any of my children die without heirs then my sons Thomas, William and Joseph to pay her $20 annually. If my dau. Emeline Prichard separates from her husband my 3 sons to support her. No child may not sell any land they inherit until age 30. The rest of my estate to my children Thomas E. Dugan Jr, William W. Dugan, Joseph O. Dugan, Mary Isabella Dugan, and Marion Dugan. My wife Emeline and my son Thomas to carry on the mercantile business. My estate not to be sold as my debts can be paid. If support or education of my children require it then Orphans Court to direct. My wife Emeline Dugan guardian to my children Thomas, William, Joseph, Mary, and Marion Dugan while they are unmarried.

Exec. my wife **Emeline Dugan**. Witnesses David Arthur, James Mansfield, George Vickers. Written Nov. 26, 1834 Proved Apr. 27, 1835 (codicil proved Apr. 29) p. 2

<u>Codicil</u> To make equal distribution part of *"Lot No. 60"* given to son Joseph O, part of same to son William beginning at the end of 25 feet from the S corner of the house belonging to Mrs. **Mary Voss** and her daughters on part of *"Lot No. 60"* on High Street towards Kent Street running down High Street 38 feet 9 inches until it intersects the lot of heirs of **George Watts** then at right angle to High Street towards Calvert Street 135 feet until it intersects Mrs. Mary Voss and daughters, then parallel with High Street near a NW course 38 feet 9 inches then to beginning. To my dau. Marion Dugan all that log I recently purchased of Mrs. Mary Voss and daughters called *"Lot No. 60"*. My dau. Emeline's part or her children's part not changed in anyway. Written Dec. 10, 1834. Witnesses James Mansfield, George Vickers, John Haley

Sarah Glenn of Kent Co
To **Sarah Ann Glenn** dau. of **Martha Crouch** (late **Martha Glenn**) my negro boy **George**, 2 beds, bureau and large trunk, large chest and little spinning wheel and $16 and a half now in the house and $20 that **George Copper** owes me for the hire of my negro girl **Margaret** for 2 years and 5 of my best dresses. To my nephew **James Glenn** my negro boy **Daniel**, my little chest and a note payable to me from George Copper for $20. To Mrs. **Elizabeth Glenn** my old woman **Minta** and my tea board and work basket with the balance of my clothing and a note from **Richard Spencer** for $200. To my niece Mrs. **Rebecca Copper** my negro **Margarett** and a new dress pattern not made up. To my niece Mrs. **Martha Crouch** my little yellow trunk, a bed quilt a pair of sheets, a black cloth shawl and four dresses. To my old woman **Minta** 2 cotton dresses.

Exec. Not Given. Witnesses Jacob Fisher, Thomas P. Gresham, George Wilson. Written Oct. 19, 1833 Proved May 28, 1835 p. 9

Abstracts of Kent Co., MD Wills 1777-1867 (WB 12)

Nathan Smith of Kent Co
To **George Washington Nicols** second son of my kinsman **Jonathan Nicols** late of Queen Anns Co, deceased all my estate, but should my son **James Smith** contrary to my expectation return home from sea then the bequest to be void and the estate to my said son. But if he does not return then my kinsman **Henry Nicols** of Caroline Co guardian to George Washington Nicols

Exec. Henry Nicols of Caroline Co (codicil changed to John W. Walker). Witnesses Susan Strong, Thomas A. Strong, Catharine Wharton. Written Aug. 16, 1828 Proved June 23, 1835 p. 9

Codicil Postscript As my kinsman Henry Nicols is now no more I appoint my friend John W. Walker of Chestertown. Written Apr. 13, 1835

John K. Buchanan of Kent Co
All my estate to my mother **Ann Thompson**

Exec. Not Given. Witnesses Peter Eisenburg, Cyrus Rasin, Samuel G. Kennard. Written Mar. 16, 1835 Proved Dec. 18, 1834 p. 10

Edmund Numbers of Duck Creek Hundred, Kent Co, DE
My negro man slave **Daniel Neal** to be sold for 4 years and my servant girl **Maria** to be sold for 11 years on Apr. 20 next. My executor to sell lot adjoining lands of **James Welch** and the old Presbyterian meeting house and I give to my 2 daughters **Martha Elizabeth** and **Ann Maria Numbers** all the remainder of my estate but if they do not live to age of accountability then the heirs of my brother **Thomas Numbers** shall be their heirs. **James D. Wilds** guardian of my daughters.

Exec. James D. Wilds. Witnesses Mason Bailey, William McGinniss, Robert Clothier. Written Mar. 7, 1832 Proved Mar. 14, 1832 Kent Co DE (copy received Sep. 28, 1835) p. 11

Elizabeth Gale of Kent Co
My body to be interred in St. Pauls Churchyard in Kent Co. To my son **James P. Gale** my negro man **Simon** to serve until Jan. 1, 1837 and my negro girl **Sarah Ann** to serve until Jan. 1, 1857. To my son **John E. Gale** my negro woman **Hannah** to serve during life and my negro woman **Margaret** to serve him until Jan. 1, 1837 and my negro boy **John** to serve until Jan. 1, 1849. To my son John E. Gale one horse (3rd choice), two head of cattle (3rd choice), and two head of sheep and 6 silver table spoons and 4 silver tea spoons. To my son James P. Gale 7 silver table spoons with one silver tea spoon. My household furniture divided between my 2 sons James P. Gale and John E. Gale. My son James P. Gale all the residue of my property of every species.

Exec. my son James P. Gale. Witnesses Margaret Crow, William B. Everitt. Written Aug. 8, 1831 Proved Dec. 1, 1835 p. 13

Ann Matilda Burchinal of Kent Co
To my mother **Martha Whaland** all my part of land now belonging to her and her 3 children of which I am one. All my other property to my mother. If the above land is sold then to my aunt **Eliza Hodges** $50 to be paid by my mother. signed as Anna Matilda Burchinal

Exec. Not Given. Witnesses Samuel Hodges, Eliza Hodges, Albert G. Miller. Written Apr. 22, 1835 Proved Jan. 2, 1836 p. 14

Mary Battershell of Kent Co
To my friend **Emeline Dugan** of Chestertown my negro boy **James Henry Gooseberry** to serve until Oct. 7, 1851. To **Sarah Scott** (free woman of color) now living near Mr. **Rasin M. Gale** all my wearing apparel, bedding, and all my personal estate (except my money). To **James Browne** (free man of color and brother of said Sarah Scott) ½ of the money left and the other ½ to Sarah Scott.

Exec. my friend Rasin M. Gale. Witnesses George Vickers, John Haley. Written June 4, 1835 Proved Jan. 18, 1836 p. 15

Joseph Monjor of Kent Co
To my wife **Sophia Monjor** my house and lot where I now live containing ½ acre and adjoining the lands of **Robert Wilson** and **Cornelius Comegys** and to her all my personal property.

Exec. my wife Sophia Monjor. Witnesses Philip M. Reed, Samuel Tomlinson, Mary Jane Crouch. Written Aug. 21, 1835 Proved Jan. 11, 1836 p. 16

Thomas Adkinson of Kent Co
To my son **Richard Adkinson** all my real estate when he is 21, he paying to my 8 children $160, viz. my dau. **Livenia** $20 in 1 year after 21, my dau. **Elizabeth** $20 in 2 years, my dau. **Phebe** $20 in 3 years, my son **Lemuel** $20 in 4 years, my dau. **Amanda** $20 in 5th year, **Ann Maria** $20 in 6th year, **Robert** $20 in 7th year, and **Alexander** $20 in 8th year. To my 3 children Ann Maria, Robert and Alexander Adkinson all my personal estate.

Exec. my son **William Adkinson**. Witnesses John Hurtt, Alexander Duncan, Elisha Beck. Written Feb. 5, 1836 Proved Mar. 4, 1836 p. 17

Richard Spencer of Kent Co
To my dau. **Charlotte A. Spencer** the farm on which I lately resided part of which was devised to me by the will of my late father **Richard Spencer** dated Aug. 5, 1822 and the

other part which was conveyed to me by **Robert Banning** and **Emma Banning** his wife and 22 acres of land on Langford's Bay purchased by me of **Samuel Tomlinson** and also the 40 acres adjoining thereto which belonged to my late wife. To my daughters **Martha S. Spencer** and **Maria L. Spencer** my farm on Eastern Neck Island heretofore owned by **Thomas Worrell** and sold by **John B. Eccleston** as trustee to **Ezekial F. Chambers**. My daughters Martha and Maria when of age to convey to my dau. Charlotte their right in the above 40 acres. To my daughters Charlotte A. Spencer, Martha S. Spencer, and Maria L. Spencer my farm on Langford's Bay which I purchased of John B. Eccleston. To my dau. Martha my negro man **Isaac**, negro boys **Abe** and **Henry** and girl **Jane**. To my dau. Charlotte negro **Abe Legard**, and **Rachel** his wife, **Joe** and **Minta** his wife and boy **Ezekial**. To my dau. Maria negro man **Jim**, boys **Clinton** and **Stephen** and girl **Vind** or **Lavinia**. Remainder of my estate to my 3 daughters. If my dau. Charlotte dies under age or without issue then to my daughters Martha and Maria. If they are both dead then to my nephew **Peregrine Spencer** son of my brother **Lambert W. Spencer**. If my dau. Martha dies then to Charlotte and Maria. If all are dead then her land to my nephew **Lambert W. Spencer** son of my brother Lambert W. Spencer. If my dau. Maria dies then to Charlotte and Martha. If they are all dead then her part to my niece **Martha Spencer** dau. of Lambert W. Spencer.

Execs. my friends James P. Wickes and Samuel W. Spencer son of my brother Lambert W. Spencer. Witnesses Joseph Wickes, Anna Wickes, William A. Rollison. Written Feb. 11, 1836 Proved Apr. 5, 1836 p. 18

<u>Codicil</u> Whereas my 5 old negroes **Joseph, Abraham, James, Araminta** and **Hannah** will in a few years be unable to labor and my daughters shall make a comfortable living for them and to pay them a total of $12 each. Date. Feb. 18, 1836. Witnesses William A. Rollison, William Wickes

<u>Solomon Smith of Kent Co</u>

To my wife **Sarah Ann Smith** in lieu of her dower the farm whereon I now reside containing 217 acres during her life and after to my dau. **Elizabeth Smith**. To my dau. Elizabeth Smith my farm lying in Delaware containing 143 acres and my farm which I purchased of **Shadrack Maberry** containing 90 acres and my farm the property of the late Jesse Gilbert deceased and Mary Knock which I purchased at the sale made by the commissioner. Any personal property remaining to my dau. Elizabeth and to her brothers and sisters and the above lands divided. If my dau. Elizabeth dies without issue then to be divided between **Thomas Smith, George Smith, George Deal** and **George Bryan**. My executor to provide for my dau. Elizabeth Smith. **Ann** (dau. of my negro woman **Mary** who is now free) to be free after in 19 years from Jan. 1, 1828. **Charlotte** (dau. of said Mary) to serve for 23 years starting from Jan. 1, 1828. **Henry** to be free after 25 years from Jan. 1, 1828. **Mary Ann** dau. of Mary to be free after 23 years from Jan. 1. [freedom pass granted to negro Henry Dec. 27, 1853. Freedom pass granted to Ann and Mary Ann May 29, 1855]

Execs. Piner Mansfield and John D. Perkins. Witnesses Daniel C. Lockwood, Samuel Woodall, John C. Lockwood. Written May 6, 1831 Proved Apr. 19, 1836 p. 22

Cornelius Comegys of Kent Co
To my brother **Edward Comegys** all my estate provided he pays the legacies. To nephew **Hirum Brown** son of **Hirum Brown** $1,200 in 6 months and if he dies then to his brother **Cornelius Brown** (written Corneilu). To my nephew **Cornelius Curry** (Corneilus) $1,200 when 21 and if he dies then to my niece **Rebecca Curry** (Rebecor)

Exec. Not Given. Witnesses John Maslin, Titus Maslin, Roland Bennett. Written Mar. 17, 1836 Proved Apr. 23, 1836 p. 24

Rebecca Smith of Kent Co
To **William Theodore Jester** during his life all the farm in Caroline Co known as *"Partnership"* and *"Bear Garden Addition"* containing 505 acres and after his death to **William Gibson** son of **John Gibson** of Kent Island, Queen Anns Co forever but if dies without heirs then to Little **Lawrence Pike Pryor**, son of **William Pryor** lately of Kent Co deceased. My executor to sell my land in Kent and Queen Anns Co called *"Flowerfields"* and *"Kent Lot"* containing 96 ½ acres. My friend **Jesse Knock** to collect rents. Whereas it may not require all the rents to support William Theodore Jester in the Hospital of Baltimore where I wish Jesse Knock to place him then to be placed in interest. After his death to be divided between the 2 daughters (**Ann** and **Sarah**) of **Susan Kelly** who intermarried with ___ **Winchester** of Kent Island in Queen Anns Co and to the oldest dau. of **Rachel Gibson** who intermarried with **Thomas J. Lynch,** also of Kent Island in Queen Anns, and to **Ruth Elliott** who intermarried with **Dr. Horton** of Harford Co if she the said Ruth Horton be living and if not then to the aforesaid 3 children but the trustee not to pay to ___ Winchester Father of the said children Ann and Sarah Winchester, nor to Thomas J. Lynch father of said dau. of Rachel Gibson nor to Dr. Horton husband of said Ruth Elliott. My personal estate to be sold (negroes and plate excepted) to be divided between the children of Winchester, Thomas J. Lynch and Ruth Horton with the sale of 4 acres which adjoins the lands of **Luke Myers** heirs. To **Eliza Lucinda Knock**, dau. of **Jesse** and **Sarah Knock** of Queen Anns Co all my plate consisting of one pair of tea pots, one coffee pot, one sugar dish and one cream cup. To the before mentioned 3 children of Winchester and Thomas J. Lynch in trust all my silver spoons large and small. To Sarah Knock wife of Jesse Knock my negro girl Harriett until she is 19 and after Sarah to give her cloths and then to be free with their mother. To my negro woman **Sarah** and her increase of children

Exec. my friend Jesse Knock. Witnesses G. Garrettson, Ebenezer T. Massey, Isaac Hines. Written Nov. 26, 1834 Proved Aug. 4, 1836 p. 25

Sarah Sudler of Kent Co

Abstracts of Kent Co., MD Wills 1777-1867 (WB 12)

To my sister **Ann Sudler** for her life all my undivided part of a tract called *"Ratchliff Cross"* near Chestertown and after her death to my two nieces **Ann Chapman** and **Harriett Malvina Chapman** and if either dies then to survivor.

Exec. my sister Ann Sudler. Witnesses James F. Gordon, Charles Gordon, John E. Chapman. Written Apr. 18, 1835 Proved Jan. 3, 1837 p. 27

William Welch of Kent Co
To my brother **John D. Welch** $500. To my brother **Thomas S. Welch** $800. To my sister **Araminta Jacobs** $300. My farm called *"Wallis' Meadows"*, also my interest in the farm late the property of **Robert Garrett** deceased, also the forest farm lying on the left hand side of the main road leading from Chesterville to Millington and 2 undivided interest in the *"Hurtt Lot"* should be sold by my executors. Whereas I hold two negroes **James** and **Wesly** sold to me by **Arnold Jacobs** on account of my being accountable as endorses with my brother **Ebenezer** for said Jacobs to the Easton Bank and after the said claims are paid the negroes James and Wesly to said Arnold Jacobs. To my son **John Thomas Welch** all my property. If he dies then to **John B. Thomas** all the negroes I received of my wife namely **Phil, Clarissa**, and children to $200 to be paid to Mrs. **Martha Wright** and $300 to Miss **Elizabeth Thomas** by the said John B. Thomas. To my brother John D. Welch the farm on which I now reside also all my woodland lying on the S side of the road running from Chesterville to Millington and adjoining the lands of the late Dr. **John Woodall** also the lot near the Presbyterian meeting house called *"Numbers Lot"* subject to the following provisions: To my brother Thomas S. Welch $4,000 paid by said brother John D. Welch. To my brother John D. Welch the remainder of my estate.

Execs. my brothers John D. Welch and Thomas S. Welch. Witnesses James Heighe, J.M. Comegys, Samuel Comegys. Written Jan. 3, 1837 Proved Jan. 7, 1837 p. 28

Daniel Young, a free man of color, of Quaker Neck
To my dau. in law **Eliza Houston** during her life my house and lot where I now reside and which I purchased of Joseph Dublin during her life and after to **Sarah Ann Houston** dau. of said Eliza Houston formerly **Eliza Jacobs** and also my personal property.

Exec. my dau. in law Eliza Houston. Witnesses William Lamb, Thomas Price, George Vickers. Written Apr. 16, 1836 Proved Mar. 20, 1837 p. 30

Thomas Buchanan of Kent Co
All my property to my mother **Ann Thompson**

Exec. my mother Ann Thompson. Witnesses Samuel G. Kennard, Elijah Eliason, Hamilton B. Warren. Written Feb. 3, 1837 Proved Mar. 20, 1837 p. 31

Liber 12 1835-1854

Noble Parsley, citizen of Kent Co
To **Noble B. Gears** my large chest, and my tools, with my architect book. To **Susan Stephens** (dau. of **Thomas** and **Mary Stephens**) all my beds with all the furniture. The balance after debts be paid to Noble B. Gears and Susan Stephens. My colored man **Benjamin** free and to have all my wearing apparel

Exec. Thomas Stephens. Witnesses Dobbs Joiner, Samuel E. Baker, James S. Primrose. Written Mar. 6, 1833 Proved Mar. 28, 1837 p. 31

Henry Lyon Davis, citizen of Maryland, minister
Minister of the Episcopal Church and former principal of St. John's College, Annapolis but now sojourning in the house of my friend **Samuel H. Stevens**. I am to be interred in the nearest Episcopal church. All my slaves free at the end of the year and that they be delivered to the officers of the Maryland Sae Colonisatio Society for the purpose of being sent to Africa. Had the adult ones been willing to go to that country I should have liberated them several years ago. If they do not consent to return to the land of their fathers they are to remain in bondage until they become willing. I wish them to go to Africa where there is a much better prospect of comfort and prosperity for them. Their names are **Minty, Charity, Monica, Sandy, Rachel, Harriet,** old and young **Frank, Celia,** old **Charity,** little **Charity, Charlotte, Hanson, Luke, Daniel, Levy, Alfred, Adam, Henry, Ferry, Phillis, Emma, July, Ally,** and **Sally** with all the children of the females, some names may be omitted but I want them all to be free. My son **Henry** to remain at Kenyon College until he obtains the degree of Bachelor of Arts and my dau. **Jane Mary** to continue to school until she is 19. The remainder to be divided by law.

Exec. Not Given. Witnesses William Thomas Veazey, Samuel Richard Stephens. Written Sep. 13, 1836 Proved May 2, 1837 p. 32

Codicil I appoint Samuel Hynson Stevens and John Thompson Veazy. Written Sep. 13, 1836

Renunciation Samuel Hynson Stevens and John Thompson Veazy decline administration and recommend to **Dr. David Davis**. Written Jan. 6, 1837

Hannah P. Woodland of Kent Co
I give unto the children of my daughters **Hannah, Ann** and **Margaret:** 1/3 to the children of my dau. Hannah, to **Margaret A.W. Ireland** 2/5, and **Louisa P., Emma H. Alletha L.** and **John W.P. Ireland** 3/5; and to the children of my dau. Ann viz. **Mary H.** and **Margaret Travilla** 1/3; and to **Hannah J. Wallis** and **Margaret A. Wallis** children of my dau. **Margaret** 1/3.

Exec. my relative **Hugh Wallis**. Witnesses Joseph Ireland Jr., James Heighe, John Hurtt. Written June 2, 1835 Proved June 15, 1837 p. 33

Abstracts of Kent Co., MD Wills 1777-1867 (WB 12)

Letecia Smith of Millington in Kent Co
To **Louisa Grimes** formerly a resident of said town of Millington and to **Sarah Ann Comegys** dau. of **Samuel L. Comegys** of Kent Co all my estate.

Exec. Not Given. Witnesses G. Garrettson, M. V. Boyer. Written Jan. 9, 1836 Proved June 22, 1837 p. 34

William Perkins of Kent Co
To my wife **Henrietta Perkins** 4 diaper and damask table cloths, my gig and harness and to her 25 acres of wood land at Muddy Branch on this side of the branch during her life and after her death to my daughters **Sally Maria Perkins** and **Ann Perkins,** it being part of the following tracts adjoining the late **Josias Ringgold** deceased and called *"White Marsh"*, *"Richards Adventure"*, *"Warners Addition"*, and *"Warners Levels Resurveyed"* in lieu of her thirds. To my wife Henrietta Perkins 1/3 of the balance of my estate. I give to my children Sally Maria Perkins, **Isaac Perkins, Ann Perkins, Henry Perkins** and **John Perkins** the balance of my estate. Having advanced to my son Isaac $350 deducted from his share. Having received information that my son Isaac Perkins is about to marry a woman worth $30,000 or if she is worth $10,000 then he is to be excluded from my estate. All my lands at Muddy Branch Not Given to my wife to be sold.

Execs. my friend Hugh Wallis and my wife Henrietta Perkins (Thomas H. Osborn if Hugh refuses). Witnesses William H. P. Worrell, Charles T. Betton, Sally Ringgold. Written Apr. 28, 1837 Proved Aug. 1, 1837 p. 35

John Stoops of Kent Co
To my nephew **William Frisby** $100. To my niece **Susan R. Frisby** $100. The residue of my estate to my uncle **James Stoops** and my niece **Elizabeth Frisby**

Exec. my niece Elizabeth Frisby. Witnesses Catharine Hanson. Written Apr. 24, 1837 Proved Aug. 22, 1837 p. 36

Howard Kennard of Kent Co
To **Ann Page Jr.** the first choice of my horses and $50. To **Julia E. Page** the second choice of my horses and $50. To **Jane Louisa Page** the third choice of my horses and $50. To **Elizabeth O. Page** the fourth choice of one horse and $50. In addition to what I have given **Frances C. Page**, I give the fifth choice of my horses. To **Philis Tilghman** free negro, her choice of one of my milch cows. To **Ann Page Sr.** the remainder of my estate.

Exec. Ann Page Sr. Witnesses Henry Page, Anna E. Brown, Mary B. Tilden. Written Sep. 6, 1832 Proved Sep. 5, 1837 p. 37

Liber 12 1835-1854

Robert Cruikshank of Kent Co
To my 6 younger children beginning at **William James Cruikshank, Maria Louisa Cruickshank, Andrew Jackson Cruickshank, George Washington Cruickshank, Lawrence Cruikshank** and **Sarah Cruickshank** all of my personal estate. My blacks to be equally divided and hired out for their support. If any die without issue then to remainder of named children. My wife **Mary Ann Cruickshank** to have the privilege of raising my younger children and as I have no debts she may decide if appraisement is done and her thirds taken to support the children. The money I loaned my dau. **Eugenia J. Cruikshank** to set her up in the millinery business if she dies without issue that the $400 to my 6 younger children to be paid out of her real estate with interest from the day I delivered to her Oct. 4, 1836 [spelling Cruickshank and Cruikshank used in will]

Exec. my friend George Vickers Esq of Chestertown. Witnesses Stephen Denning, John N. Denning. Written Jan. 22, 1838 Proved Mar. 14, 1838 p. 38

William Crane of Kent Co
Nathaniel McGinnes my son in law will be executor. To my son **William Bowers Crane** the farm on which I reside called *"Baxley"*, also a portion of the adjoining farm called *"Providence"*, beginning at a black hart cherry tree standing along the main road a little above the house where the black woman called Betty lives and running in a straight line to *"Sandybelly"* upon Swan Creek from there around Cuckolds Point up Denbigh Creek until it intersects the main road at Denbigh back to the beginning. To my son **Thomas Richard Crane** all the farm called *"Providence"* known as the *"Bradshaw farm"* except the above portion given to William, also a lot of my wood land beginning at a boundary stone standing a little in the woods to the left of the road leading from Denbigh to Rock Hall and near to **John Ayres'** lot running from thence to a boundary stone between my lands and the lands of Mrs. **Elizabeth Walker**, then with the line down to a boundary stone between my lands and the lands of Mrs. **Jane Copper** then to the beginning. If either of them dies then to the survivor and my dau. **Mary Ann McGinniss** to each get half. If both sons die then to my daughter. To my niece **Mary Rickets Crane** my gig and the mare called Pocahontas. All the rest of my personal estate to be sold except my negroes. The field I bought of **Thomas** and **Washington Hynson** to be sold. The remainder of my personalty to my 2 sons. If my sons live to a man's age they to give their mothers part of the farm in Piney Neck to their brother **William Banks Wakeman**.

Exec. Not Given. Witnesses Jacob Fisher, Robert Smith, William B. Everitt. Written Feb. 28, 1838 Proved Mar. 29, 1838 p. 39

He the testator made no disposition of his negroes and when asked he replied that after Mr. Meginnis was done with them on the farm they were to be divided between William and Thomas, to which we subscribed our names after the above interlineation and addition.

Nicholas Slubey of Baltimore City

All my estate to my two natural daughters **Mary McCarty Sluby** and **Eleanor Boyd** now wife of **A. B. Coachmaker** late **Eleanor Sluby**, daughters of **Margaret McCarty**, and the surviving children of my late nephew **William Jones** that is **William Jones, Ann Eliza Jones,** and **Hariet Jones**. If my named executors refuse to administer then the Orphans Court of Baltimore Co. My estate to be sold. My brother **William Slubey**, deceased conveyed to **Benjamin R. Morgan** attorney at law, Philadelphia certain lots on Spruce Street, Philadelphia about 1798 to which he was not entitled to more than half, the said conveyance recorded in Philadelphia as well as a copy among the papers of my late sister **Isabella Jones** deceased and myself were entitled to half and she wishing to convey her half to her nephews and nieces, children of her son William Jones, Benjamin R. Morgan was willing to convey the half of those lots on condition that she and I relinquish claim to the other moiety. My sister by her attorney **David Lapsley** of Philadelphia and me for myself entered into articles with Benjamin R. Morgan but before my sister could complete the transfer she died and a will drawn by her son in law **James Cruikshanks** with a sweeping clause to give those lots to his dau. **Ann Elizabeth Cruikshanks** in exclusion of those she meant to have so I declined to give validity to said articles by avoiding committing them to record but Benjamin R. Morgan has always expressed a willingness to give validity as seen by his letters and knowing him to be a man of great principle and honor I have paid tax of about $600-$700, being taxes paid by him and reimbursed by me, ½ to come out of Ann Eliza Cruikshank's part of the moiety. I have a judgment on records of Baltimore County court for $11,000 of principal against my nephew **Nicholas Slubey Jones** as a partner in the late house of Nicholas Slubey Jones and **David Jones** and I presume a similar judgment against David Jones in Kent Co, Nicholas S. Jones got a handsome estate by his wife **Frances Jones**, late **Frances Brown** by will of her father **John Brown** deceased, he broke the entail by getting her to convey to his brother David Jones and then David Jones reconveyed to Nicholas S. Jones and wife and they conveyed again to **Mary Brown** mother of his wife, no question without valuable consideration although so expressed in the conveyance, that must be tested before the proper court both his and her brother David Jones' life estate in the estates by their wives answerable for my claim, in fact Nicholas S. Jones's whole estate got by his wife as he broke the entail is liable for it, as it become his own, after the entail was broke, I am indebted in England as much as the Jones' owe me which if claimed, which I do not expect will be, must be paid I have about £113 sterling in the hands of Herries Farugher & Co., Bankers, London, which may be drawn for, there are several lottery tickets their numbers given to **Mary M. Slubey** on which I owe $40, there is a bed, bedding, mattress, books, and various articles in my storeroom and lodging at Mrs. Crockets, St. Pauls Lane, to the amount of $300 or $400. I appoint my executors, recommending the judgments against my nephews to be kept alive by **Nicholas Brice** my attorney in Baltimore and **James Houston** in Kent Co.

Execs. Hezekiah Waters, Luke Thomas, and John Harrod. Witnesses W. Barclay, Archibald Henderson, Peter S. Hartshorne (Joseph Redue was familiar with writing of Nicholas Slubey, James Campbell knew writing of Barclay and Henderson, John G.

Liber 12 1835-1854

Proud knew writing of Hartshorne). Written May 2, 1813 Baltimore Proved Apr. 17, 1838 p. 40

<u>Codicil</u> If my nephews Nicholas Slubey Jones and David Jones pay $10,000 the remainder and interest to them. Written May 2, 1813

Margaret McClean of Chestertown
To my sister **Anna Maria McClean** my property. To my said sister my lot in Primrose Ally in Baltimore City called No. 38 and the house thereon during her life and after her death to **Alexander McClean**. To my sister Anna Maria McClean my house and lot in Chestertown during her life and after to **Thomas Lorain McClean**. To **Elizabeth Jones** granddau. of **Elizabeth Young** 6 silver table spoons and 6 silver tea spoons. To Elizabeth Jones my best bedspread [I give to **Edward A. McClean** my plate and furniture, in margin]

Exec. my sister Anna Maria McClean. Witnesses Ann Elizabeth Garnett, Unit Chandler, Joseph Redue. Written Oct. 4, 1830 Proved May 29, 1838 p. 43

<u>Codicil</u> **Rachel Crane** should have my whole wearing apparel. (No witnesses signed but Unit and Joseph confirmed her writing).

Mary Avarilla Cruikshank of Kent Co
To my brother **Guilford D. Cruikshank** all my lands lying in Kent Co paying to my sister **Eugenia J. Cruikshank** $50 annually. To my sister Eugenia J. Cruikshank my bureau and clothing and all my personal estate.

Exec. my brother Guildford D. Cruikshank. Witnesses Horatio Beck, Mary M. Beck, Augusta Camp. Written July 4, 1838 Proved Aug. 8, 1838 p. 44

Hannah G. Smith
To my dau. **Ann H. Wiley** my bed and furniture. All the rest of my estate to my two daughters **Mary A.** and **Margaret G. Smith** and the slaves which are included should be manumitted by them if the present law by which the manumission of slaves is prevented except on certain conditions, should be repealed.

Execs. my dau. Mary A. Smith and my son in law **Nathaniel Wiley**. Witnesses Ann M. Merritt, Peregrine Wroth. Written Feb. 9, 1833 Proved Nov. 27, 1838 p. 45

Edward Curry of Kent Co
To my minor children **Milicia** and **Celina Curry** all my estate. If they both die before age then to my mother if she is living and if not living then to **Robert** and **Thomas Ury**. My negroes **Maria, Henry, Fanny**, and **Amanda** to be at liberty at 28 years old. The above negro Maria to get the house and ½ acre of ground where old **David** now lives when she is 28.

Abstracts of Kent Co., MD Wills 1777-1867 (WB 12)

Exec. Not Given. Witnesses James Browne (Mrs. Browne wife of James Browne it was in her husbands papers who died about 4 years ago and was never out of her possession until brought to court), Edward Comegys (he did not remember signing the will but thinks it is his signature as witness), **Milcah Kennard** (she was called to her brothers room by Mr. Comegys and signed a paper her brother being sick in bed, she saw no other witness. It was a long time ago. In or about July last she heard Mr. Curry say he had an old will at Mr. James Browne which he intended to alter) (James H. Edes said he knew the writing of Edward Curry and that Edward had 2 female children Milica and Celinda living in 1825 and who are still living one about 16 and the other about 14. He has 2 children a son and dau. born since both living one about 8 and the other about 12 years old. Written Nov. 27, 1838). Written Aug. 6, 1825 Proved Nov. 22, 1838 p. 45

Elizabeth Hanson of Kent Co
To my niece **Sarah Elizabeth Bradshaw** my negro woman **Deborah** with the issue of her body to serve until age 30 for females and age 35 for males. To my brother's dau. **Hannah Snow** my bed, pillows, blanket, sheets and one cotton and yarn counterpin, my bonnet cloak and caps. All the rest of my wearing apparel (not wanted by my niece Sarah) to my niece **Berthia Snow**. To my niece **Jane E. Kennard** a mourning ring. The rest of my estate to my niece Sarah Elizabeth Bradshaw.

Exec. Not Given. Witnesses Thomas C. Kennard, Anna Beck. Written Oct. 27, 1838 Proved Dec. 19, 1838 p. 47

Jane Fray colored woman of Kent Co
To be buried at the discretion of my son **Robert** and my dau. **Mary** called **Candis** and to be paid out of my estate given them. To my son Robert and my dau. Mary called Candis the house and lot where I now live which I purchased of **Joseph N. Gordon** during their life and then to my granddau. **Emily Pears**. All my personal estate to my four children Robert, Mary called Candes, **Rachel** and **Maria**

Exec. Not Given. Witnesses Nathaniel Hynson, Thomas Davis, Richard S. Thomas. Written Sep. 12, 1829 Proved Dec. 18, 1838 p. 48

Lancelott Moffett of Kent Co
After my wife's third, to my son **Lancelott Moffett** all my cleared and wood land in Kent Co where my brick dwelling stands and where I now reside, lying on the E side of the main road leading from Georgetown CrossRoads to New Market (except 46 acres of woodland) when he is 25 and until then the rents to my daughters **Sarah Forman** until he is 25. If Lancelott dies under age without heirs then to my son **Stansbury Moffett** he paying $1,000 to my children in equal shares. After Lancelott is of age then to my 2 daughters **Lavinia** and **Charlotte** a comfortable board on said farm while they remain single. If son Stansbury inherits land the board to cease in consideration of the $1,000. All the lands on the W side of Georgetown Cross roads to New Market and 46 acres of woodland on the E side of the main road leading from Georgetown Cross Roads

Liber 12 1835-1854

adjoining the lands of **John M. Armstrong** which he purchased of **Thomas J. Mann** the heirs of Dixon, and also adjoining the land belonging to the heirs of **Samuel G. Osborn** deceased containing about 264 acres, I give to my dau. Sarah Forman for the term of 10 years and after to be sold by Sarah Forman or if dead by Joseph Moffett of Kent Co, and $150 to be paid to my son **William** if living and if dead to his heirs and the rest to my daughters and my 2 grandchildren **Mary Rebecca Bossee** and **Julianna Bossee** and if either of my grandchildren die then to the surviving grandchild. If they both die then to all my children. My grandchildren are to take their portion of their deceased mother's estate not a full share. If any of my children die with children then they are to receive only their parents share. To my son Stansbury Moffett my negro man **Solomon** a slave for life. To my dau. Sarah Forman my negro boy **David** aged about 4 years and a slave for life. To my dau. **Milliminta Redgraves** my negro woman **Ib** or **Ibbe** aged about 18 and slave for life. To my dau. Lavina Moffett my negro woman **Harriett** aged about 16 years and a slave for life. To my dau. **Charlotte** my negro woman **Caroline** aged about 16 and a slave for life. To my son Lancelott my negro boy **Philip** aged about 6 months, and a slave for life. To my dau. **Emily Sanders** $225 annually for 10 years as feme sole. To my son William Moffett $300 out of the personal estate. To **Lewis Bossee** my grandchildren $5 at age 21. To **Sarah Elizabeth Bossee** $50 at age 20 and one cow, 2 heifers and one calf, the increase of a calf presented by her father **John Bossee** and which I have raised for her. If my dau. Sarah Foreman keeps the 4 head of cattle then she may do so and present them with their increase to **Elizabeth Bossee** on her arrival of age 20. To my granddau. Mary Rebecca Bossee $300 at age 20. To my granddau. Julianna Bossee $300 at age 20. If Mary R. and Julianna Bossee before 20, then to the survivor. If they both die then ½ to **Sarah Elizabeth Bossee** and the other ½ to my daughters. Whereas my 2 daughters **Rebecca** and **Mary** are sick and not expected to recover, but if they do recover, then $225. The negroes to be delivered in 1 year. The rest of my personal estate to my dau. Sarah Foreman for 10 years and then to my children Sarah Foreman, Emily Sanders, Milliminta Redgrave, Lavina Moffett, Charlotte Moffett, and if Rebecca and Mary recover then to be included. Whereas I am now erecting a dwelling on the lands devised to be sold in 10 years and I want to have completed before the sale, and I have several unmarried daughters, I gave interest in 10 years of the lands and the surplus of the personal estate in order for my dau. Sarah Foreman to complete the house and provide a home while my daughters are yet single and keep the family together, but out of the surplus to Lancelott $175 at age 25. if Sarah Foreman marries then she is to take account of expenditures. Stansbury to have $200 out of the personal estate as soon as the executrix can and if Stansbury does not heir the land of Lancelott then he is to have $150 out of the land to be sold in 10 years. There shall be free ingress and egress from the burying ground at the old orchard on the W side of the road to the families who have been in the habit of burying there. My negroes not to be sold out of the state.

Exec. my dau. Sarah Foreman. Witnesses Henry Hurtt, George Leary, Thomas E. Gooding. Written Feb. 23, 1838 Proved Jan. 22, 1839 p. 49

Abstracts of Kent Co., MD Wills 1777-1867 (WB 12)

Codicil My dau. Rebecca mentioned in the will was lying dead in my house before and when my will was executed. The $1,000 that my son Stansbury is to pay if he inherits said land is to be a charge against said estate. Written Mar. 12, 1838. Witnesses Henry Hurtt, Thomas E. Gooding, Robert S. Welch
2nd Codicil The $150 to my son William Moffett from my dau. Sarah Foreman shall not be paid to him but to William F. Smith of Millington for same purpose. Instead of the $300 to son William Moffett I give him $50 and the $250 to **William F. Smith.** The above bequests to William F. Smith in trust by him and interest to be paid to Mrs. **Jane F. Moffett** (wife of my son William) as feme sole during her life and at her death to her children by said William. William to have no control over the money and not subject to his debts. Written Sep. 5, 1838. Witnesses Thomas E. Gooding, Henry Hurtt, Joseph Moffett

Margaret Ann Ingram of Kent Co
All my estate to my mother **Sarah Boots**.

Exec. my mother Sarah Boots. Witnesses Samuel G. Kennard, Robert Usilton, James Beck (of George). Written Sep. 31, 1838 Proved Feb. 17, 1839 (Feb. 23 came Robert) p. 55

William Dick Wilmer of Kent Co
After the debts of my brother **John L. Wilmer** are paid, then to my 2 cousins **Mary Elisabeth Briscoe** and **William Frisby Briscoe** children of **Samuel E. Briscoe** and **Margaret E. Briscoe** all my farm where I now dwell also the wood land in the forest belonging to said farm which I got of Samuel E. Briscoe in exchange for a farm I formerly owned on the Sassafras River in Kent Co and to them my all my negroes until age 28. To my cousin **Margaret Elisabeth Briscoe** all the money due me on book account.

Exec. my friend Samuel E. Briscoe. Witnesses John Silcox, Thomas Jefferson Herdman, Frederick S. Boyer. Written Mar. 17, 1839 Proved Apr. 9, 1839 p. 56

Robert G. Simmonds of Kent Co
To my wife **Rebeca B. Simmonds** all my personal estate

Exec. my wife Rebeca. Witnesses James P. Gale, John B. Tilden. Written 1839 Proved May 2, 1839 p. 57

Alexander C.H. Tate of Port Deposit, Cecil Co, formerly of Kent Co
To my mother **Maria Tate** all my estate

Exec. my mother. Witnesses William B. Wilmer, S. J. Wilmer, Sarah A. Wilmer. Written June 16, 1835 Proved July 16, 1839 (July 23 came William) p. 58

Liber 12 1835-1854

Thomas B. Hynson of Kent Co
My body to be interred in the family burying ground on the farm where I now reside according to the Protestant Episcopal Church. If I die in 1839 then my crops to be cultivated. My farm to be sold except the burying ground and my negroes. To pay my dau. **Mary Elizabeth Brown** what she is due of my estate as soon as can be done. To pay my son **Richard Hynson** what is due him of my estate when he is 21. If my dau. Mary dies without heirs then to my other children. My executor to pay my son **Thomas B. Hynson** his quota of my estate at 21. To pay my daughters **Anna Hynson** and **Ann Louisa Hynson** all their interest at 21. The hire of my negroes for support and education of my children but my 2 youngest daughters Anna Hynson and Ann Louisa Hynson shall have $1,000 more than each child. All my interest in the stock of silk Company to my youngest daughters and to surviving sister if either dies. To my dau. Mary E. Brown I give **Bill Glenn** to serve 10 years, also **Lydia** and her 3 children for 10 years, my negro girl **Fanny**. Also having heard of great misconduct on the part of them I give my dau. the right to deprive them of the freedom of Bill Glenn or Lydia or both of them but I recommend caution to my dau. in this power. To my son Richard Hynson I give **Moses, Ann Maria, Affa** and all of her children. To my son Thomas B. Hynson I give **Bill Munson, Charles, Rachel** and all of her children. To my dau. Anna Hynson I give **Jerry, Joe, Letty,** and **Harriett**. To my dau. Ann Louisa I give **Isaac, Jim, Maria,** and **Kitty,** Kitty to serve 10 years. If Kitty during the nonage of my dau. of Ann Louisa misbehaves and deserves punishment my executors will remember that her freedom is dependent upon good conduct alone. I repeat that Bill Glenn, Lydia and Kitty will forfeit their clause to freedom by bad conduct at any time. The rest of my negroes divided between my children. To my son Richard Hynson my gold watch, chain and seals as a memento of his departed father. To my son Thomas B. Hynson I give my duck gun also the silver watch which was willed to his elder brother **Robert D. Hynson** by his grandfather. To my dau. Mary Elizabeth the wardrobe that belonged to her mother. To my dau. Anna Hynson I give my wardrobe. To my dau. Ann Louisa Hynson I give the piano forte, the stool belonging to it and best bureau. To my old friend **William Caton** my bed mattress, blankets and sheets. Preserve from the sale of my land the house occupied by **Peter Glenn** with the privilege of down wood by him during his life. My cousin **John B. Eccleston** to be guardian to my son Richard Hynson and to provide for his education as his means will afford to qualify him for a profession. **G.B. Westcott** guardian to my son Thomas B. Hynson and his education be furnished so as to prepare him for business. My daughters Anna Hynson and Ann Louisa to their eldest sister and therefore I appoint my son in law **Thomas Browne** guardian to them.

Execs. my son in law Thomas Brown, my brother in law **George B. Westcott**, and my cousin John B. Eccleston. Witnesses J. Brown 3rd, James Brown, W.B. Everitt. Written Mar. 10, 1839 Proved July 9, 1839 (July 17 came James Brown, Jul 16 came H.L. Everitt) p. 59

<u>Codicil</u> To my son Thomas B. Hynson one old silver tankard. To my dau. Mary E. Brown one old fashioned silver sugar dish and tongs, 6 silver table spoons, 6 silver

desert spoons, and 12 silver tea spoons. Written May 14, 1839. Witnesses H. L. Everitt, James B. Tilghman.

John E. Chapman formerly at Ratcliff, Kent Co but now at LaPlata, Charles Co, MD
To my aunts **Anne Sudler** and **Sarah Sudler** of Kent Co my 3 negro servants **Charlotte, James,** and **Daniel**. After their decease James to my sister **Ann**, Daniel to my sister **Malvina** and **Charlotte** to both of them if her hire is paid to my brother **William S. Chapman** for 20 years.

Exec. Not Given. Witnesses William Thomas Swann (Thomas Granger knew writing of John E. Chapman). Written Apr. 3, 1836 Proved Sep. 17, 1839 p. 62

Ann Chapman of Kent Co
To my aunt **Anne Sudler** during her life my 2 servant girls **Charlotte** and **Emma**, being 9 and 3, resp. To my sister **Harriet M. Chapman** my negro girl **Anne** aged 20, my negro girl **Annett** aged 6. To my brother **William S. Chapman** my negro boy **Charles Henry** aged 6 to serve until age 35. After my aunt's death to my said brother my negro girl **Charlotte**. To my sister **Harriett M. Chapman** after the death of my aunt my negro girl **Emma** to serve until age 35 and my sister to pay my brother William ½ o her wages. To my friend **Caroline R. F. Gordon** my negro girl **Arianna** aged 3 years to serve until age 35. To **Ann Louisa Gordon** dau. of **James F. Gordon** and **Sarah Maria Gordon** my negro girl **Cloe** aged about 2 years to serve until she is 35. To **Anne Gordon Sudler** dau. of my cousin **Emory Sudler** $150. My sister Harriett M. Chapman to collect $150 and put to interest and pay to Anne Gordon Sudler when she is 17. To my sister Harriett M. Chapman my servants **Julia** and **Ailey** for 6 years from my death to purchase and erect a tombstone at the head and foot of my grave which I desire to be done as soon as possible. After 6 years they are to be free. To my sister Harriet M. Chapman my undivided interest in a negro man **Alexas**, being the 1/3 part of the term of 4 years to raise the above $150. After 4 years, my 1/3 to be paid to said Alexas for his own use. To my sister Harriett M. Chapman my undivided interest in a negro boy **Alonzo**, being 1/3 part, until age 35 then to his own use. No administration on my estate but my sister to pay all my debts. All the rest of my estate to my sister Harriett M. Chapman and she to appoint someone to complete the trusts herein mentioned.

Exec. my sister Harriett M. Chapman. Witnesses Maria Tate, James F. Gordon. Written Mar. 1, 1838 Proved Jan. 15, 1840 p. 62

Elizabeth Thompson of Kent Co
To **Shadrick Thompson** my son the lot of ground now in his possession. To **Zackeriah Thompson** my son the lot of ground now in his possession. To **Richard Thompson** my son the lot of ground now in his possession. To my 2 sons **Ezekial Thompson** and **William Thompson** the lot of ground now in the possession of said Ezekial.

Liber 12 1835-1854

Exec. my son Shadrick Thompson. Witnesses Joseph Ireland, Thomas K. Stephens, William Megee. Written July 19, 1839 Proved Jan. 10, 1840 p. 65

Elizabeth Greenwood widow of Kent Co
To Sarah Elizabeth Briscoe my granddau. and dau. of James Briscoe my black walnut cupboard and one feather bed. To Mary Elizabeth Duyer dau. of George Duyer and my granddau. one feather bed. My servant girl Sarah to be free at 37. To my son John Duyer $50. The reside of my estate to the children of my deceased dau. Emeline Briscoe and my dau. Mary Hepbron, that is ½ to the children of Emeline and ½ to Mary Hepbron wife of James Hepbron.

Exec. my friend and son in law James Briscoe. Witnesses Thomas B. Keating, Hannah M. Forman (Foreman), William S. Lassell. Written Sep. 1, 1838 Proved Jan. 20, 1840 p. 66

William R. Bennitt of Kent Co
To my 2 sons George Henry Bennett and Samuel Bennett and to my dau. Elizabeth Bennett the whole of my estate. signed W. Roland Bennett

Exec. John Hadaway. Witnesses B. F. Houston, Veazey Sutton. Written Jan. 8, 1840 Proved Jan. 21, 1840 p. 67

Rasin Jones of Kent Co
All my personal estate sold. To my sister Mary Bull ½ farm on which I now reside. To my sister Rebecca Elizabeth Meeks the other ½. If my personal estate is not enough for debts, then my 2 sisters make up difference.

Exec. my brother Daniel Jones. Witnesses Joseph Lyzar, Isaac Cordray, Uriah Lynch. Written Jan. 17, 1840 Proved Jan. 25, 1840 p. 67

Rebecca Burgess late of Kent Co
To my 2 daughters Juliet Burgess and Mary V. Burgess all the personal property I have. If either dies then to survivor.

Exec. Not Given. Witnesses Juliet Harris, Thomas C. Yearley, William Camp. Written Mar. 5, 1840 Proved Mar. 31, 1840 p. 68

James Tennant of Kent Co
My body to buried after the ritual of the Protestant Episcopal Church. To James Rayen, son of James T. Rayen and Julia Ann, his wife $1,000 at age 21. If he dies under 21 then to the grandchildren of my two sisters Sarah Kenney and Elizabeth A. Randall. To William Wallis, son of Hugh Wallis and Margaret his wife 6 acres lying on the N side of the public road leading from the head of Chester River to Chestertown beginning at the beginning of the original tract called *"Deptford"*. To my nephew William Rayen

I give all the residue of my estate being the farm called *"Deptford"* lying in Kent Co and a lot of woodland in Queen Anns Co containing 39 acres and to him all my personal estate.

Exec. my nephew William Rayen. Witnesses Hugh Wallis, Thomas Brooks, Stansbury Moffett. Written Dec. 31, 1836 Proved May 7, 1840 (June 3 came Thomas) p. 69

Codicil William Rayen to act as guardian to minor James Rayen. Written same,. Witnesses same.

John Turner of Kent Co

To my wife **Deborah Turner** all my estate during her life, and my negroes to serve her until age 30. After the death of my wife, then to my nephew Dr. **Thomas Owen Edwards** son of my sister **Mary Edwards**. [freedom pass granted to **Daniel** May 26, 1858, freedom pass granted to **Ann Selina** Dec. 26, 1854, freedom pass granted to **Theodore** May 9, 1856, written in margin]

Exec. my wife Deborah. Witnesses George Gale, James Gale, Lemuel Skaggs. Written Feb. 11, 1837 Proved May 12, 1840 p. 71

Elizabeth Thompson

To my 3 granddaughters **Elizabeth A. Spencer, Kitty Spencer,** and **Charlotte Spencer** $100. To my dau. **Kitty Hands** my furniture and one half my negroes. The rest to my dau. **Caroline Thompson**

Exec. my grandson **Isaac Spencer Jr.** Witnesses Jeremiah Nicols, William Carmichael. Written Sep. 25, 1824 Proved May 29, 1840 p. 72

Elizabeth Glenn of Kent Co

To **James** my eldest son my account against **George Copper** $170 for his part of *"Drum Point"*, also my account against the estate of my son **John** amounting to $70 part of his right to *"Drum Point"* also two milch cows, ten head of sheep and their lambs and all the swine with the exception of two sows and their present litter of pigs and one feather bed. To **William Ransallear** my youngest son my account against my son James for which I have his bond amounting to $200, also one feather bed with 2 finished and one unfinished quilts, one pair new muslin sheets and 6 silver table spoons. To **Mary Rebecca Glenn** my granddau. $30 out of the sale of my horse sold by son James. To **John, Margaret,** and **Rebecca Stewart** my grandchildren $10. To **Sarah Ann Wolahan** my granddau. one cow and calf. To **William Glenn** my grandson all cash in the house on *"Drum Point"* also my cherry tree wood tea chest. To **Mary Elizabeth Glenn** my granddau. one negro girl named **Mary Ann** until she arrives to age 30. To **Elizabeth Sterling Glenn** my granddau. one negro girl named **Harriet** until she arrives at age 30. If my granddaughter's death then to **Thomas Glenn** my grandson until she arrives at age 30. To **Michael** and **Frederick** my 2 sons two negro girls named **Phobe** and **Nancy** at age 30 after they served their unexpired term with their present masters. My son Michael and Frederick must pay to grandson **Washington Danskin Glenn** $10 yearly. I free my old negroes **Amy** and **Isaac** and **Emory**. To **Martha Crouch** my dau. the sum of $20. To **Rebecca Copper**, Martha Crouch my daughters and Mary Elizabeth and Emeline Glenn my granddaughters my wearing apparel with the exception of the shawl given me by my son James which I give to **Eliha Glenn** my dau. in law. To Rebecca Copper and Martha Crouch my daughters, 2 pairs of silver spectacles, one pair each. All the remaining property to be sold and with $50 being the hire of **Emory** between Rebecca Copper, Michael Glenn, and Frederick Glenn my children

Exec. George Copper. Witnesses Samuel Coleman, Benedict S. Brevitt. Written Apr. 14, 1840 Proved June 9, 1840 p. 72

John Whittington of Kent Co

As I made considerable advances to my son James and for which I give him $1. To my son **William Whittington** all that farm lying in Kent which William lives on and adjoining **James Smith** (of George). To my son **John Whittington** (subject to legacy of granddau. **Mary Ann Stant**) all my farm upon which I reside called the *"Home farm"*. To my son John Whittington upon the trusts mentioned, all that farm lying in Kent called *"Beck Farm"* to rent out the same for my dau. **Hannah Wood** (wife of **William Wood**) for her life (subject to provision for **Mahaley Hamilton**) and if she has no child living at her death in trust for my sons John and William Whittington and to my son William ½ part of said farm. My son John to pay rents of said farm (subject to Mahaly Hamilton provision) to my said dau. Hannah as her separate estate not to her husband's control. I give $30 for 7 years paid to Mahaly Hamilton provided the child she now has should so long live, but if not then $30 in proportion of the year the child lives in full of the bequest the said Mahaley may have against me. To my granddau. Mary Ann Stant $300 at age 18, to be paid to her by my son John and charged to the real estate. If she dies before 18 then no legacy paid but to lapse into the estate of said John. To my granddau. Mary Ann Stant a negro girl called **Beck**. To my son William Whittington my negro woman **Priss**. To my dau. Hannah Wood my negro girl **Charlotte** as her separate estate not subject to her husband. If she dies without issue then to my sons John and William. To my son William Whittington my sorrel mare called Kit. My debts paid first by personal estate not legacies. The rest of my estate to my son John Whittington.

Exec. my friend William F. Smith. Witnesses Richard Corbaly, C.R. Hackett, John E. Cacy. Written Jan. 15, 1840 Proved July 21, 1840 p. 74

<u>Codicil</u> To my son John Whittington a tract of woodland attached to the farm on which he now resides called *"the Upper Tract"*. Written June 17, 1840. Witnesses Michael Smith, John E. Cacy, Robert Ruth

Abstracts of Kent Co., MD Wills 1777-1867 (WB 12)

Murray Moffett, black man of Kent Co
To **Enoch Moffett** all my estate.

Exec. Not Given. Witnesses Josiah Newton, David Hart. Written July 14, 1840 Proved Aug. 22, 1840 p. 77

On Feb. 23, 1841 John Silcox said he saw William Dick Wilmer the named testator sign the will with Thomas J. Herdman and Frederick S. Boyer. [see page 56]

Anne Washington Trulock of Kent Co
To my nephew **Rasin Moore Gale** all that part of the farm called *"Ricketts farm"* and *"Hales"* with 8 acres of *"Cedar Hill"*. To my nephew **Joseph Everitt Gale** all that part of a farm called *"Nancy's Choice"* with a part of *"Hales"*, running with the present division fence and gully from branch to branch. To my cousin **Benjamin Everitt Smith** the dwelling plantation where I now live. To **George Washington Purnell Smith** my cousin the farm *"Trulock's Adventure"* running with the fence from branch to branch all to the N of said fence. To Rasin Moore Gale my nephew, timber off *"Trulock's Adventure"* sufficient to make 2 fences across the farm, 24 cedar trees and one large poplar. To my cousin Benjamin Everitt Smith one clock, one bed, one large looking glass, and one young bay mare, and one suit of bed curtains. To **Eliza Thomas** my cousin all my wearing apparel, and one gig. To **William Kennard** one desk and book case. To my cousin George Washington Smith one silver watch, 3 silver table spoons and 6 silver tea spoons. To my cousin **Anna Maria Margaretta Smith** one bed and one suit of bed curtains and one silver cream pot. To **Anne Maria Gale** dau. of my nephew Rasin Moore Gale one bed and a suit of bed curtains, and a small looking glass. To my cousin Benjamin Everitt Smith one cupboard and cupboard ware and one saddle. To my cousin **Mary Wright Smith** one saddle mare, one bridle and one side saddle. To my nephew Rasin Moore Gale all the rest of my estate.

Exec. my nephew Rasin Moore Gale. Witnesses John W. Walker, William Vannost, William B. Wilmer Jr. Written Apr. 1, 1840 Proved Feb. 27, 1841 (Mar. 19 came William Wilmer) p. 78

Anna Gilchrist of Kent Co
To be buried by the christian church of which I belong. All my claim to lots at Goose Hill from my mother's last will and in virtue of an inheritance of my brother **James Gilchrist** to **Hannah Elizabeth Lynch**, dau. of **William Lynch** and **Hannah Gilchrist** his wife and my sister. To my niece **Mary Rebecca Lynch** dau. of William and Hannah Lynch my sister all the rents which may be due on Jan. 1. On the note due me by William Lynch for $90 to be reduced by $17 so that only $73 is due me.

Exec. William Lynch. Witnesses William Wroth, Phebe Lynch, Susanna Smith. Written Dec. 2, 1840 Proved Apr. 24, 1841 p. 80

William B. Everitt of Kent Co

To be interred in the family burial ground near my parent's graves. As the last will of my late mother **Temperance Everitt** (recorded in Kent Co) invests me with the power of directing the inheritance of the farm on which I now reside, also a lot of wood land appertaining to the said farm and mentions as near as I can recollect (the will not being at hand) that the trustees named shall hold the land as I appoint by my will, said trustees **Ezekial F. Chambers** and **John B. Eccleston** shall hold the farm for my wife **Henrietta L. Everitt** durante viduitate during her widowhood. I give to my 2 sons **William B. Everitt** and **M. Tilghman Everitt** and if either dies then to survivor subject only to particular estate of his mother. If they die without heirs then to my relative **James B. Tilghman** and if he dies without issue then to **Tench Tilghman** brother of said James B. Tilghman. If he dies then to my relatives **Richard Hynson** and **Thomas B. Hynson**. The devises to be considered as legal estates. All the rest of the estate to my wife Henrietta L. Everitt durante viduitate and at the termination of her estate to my 2 sons. The whole of my personalty to my wife Henrietta L. Everitt then shared by my sons William B. Everitt and M. Tilghman Everitt. To my wife Henrietta L. Everitt I give negro girls **Jane** and **Hannah** also a wardrobe and writing desk. To my son William B. Everitt my negro boy **Henry** and the clock formerly by the property of his grandfather. To my son M. Tilghman Everitt my boy **Thomas** and the watch of his grandfather. If either of my sons shall embrace the legal profession then to have my law books, if not, then my books to be divided between them both. My wife Henrietta L. Everitt executrix as I owe a great deal of money for Mrs. **Elizabeth Hartt** and there remains more due to the creditors of **William Miller** deceased, I direct my executrix if James Hartt fails to fulfil an agreement to sell the land to liquidate the claim. If my debts are higher, I authorize my wife to sell my Swan Creek farm. As the land of my mother can not be bound to my debts, I do not wish it to be used to pay any claim against my estate. My wife guardian of my children.

Exec. my wife Henrietta L. Everitt. Witnesses Horatio Beck, Colin F. Hale, John Boyer. Written Feb. 3, 1840 Proved May 12, 1841 p. 81

Jeremiah Nicols of Kent Co

All my monies to pay my debts, if this is not sufficient then my farm in Queen Anns Co called *"Price's Hill"* which I purchased of **William Godwin** and all my interest under the will of the late **Henry Nicols** in certain lands in NY, PA, and in and near Easton in Talbot Co shall be sold. If not ready in time then my personal estate on my farm in Quaker Neck or elsewhere can be sold. My wife **Elizabeth Nicols** or in her death my son **Richard Lloyd Nicols** or in his death my son **Jeremiah Nicols** if he is 21 to sell land. 1/6 part to my wife and the remainder to my children Richard Lloyd Nicols, Jeremiah Nicols, and **Anna Maria Nicols**. All the remainder of my estate to be divided by laws of MD. My wife guardian to my son Jeremiah and my dau. Maria. If she dies then son Richard Ll. Nicols shall complete settlement and if he dies then Jeremiah Nicols if 18. If all dead then Orphans court to settle.

Exec. my wife Elizabeth Nicols. Witnesses Richard Ringgold, Samuel Clark, Hiram Browne, Hiram Browne Jr. Written Jan. 18, 1840 Proved June 15, 1841 p. 83

Eliza Bowers of Kent Co
To my sister **Mary Ann Bowers** all my estate during her life and then to my brother **James L. Bowers** in trust for my sister **Sarah Rebecca Neal's** child who now resides in Philadelphia, PA. If no child of said Rebecca Neal then to the children of my brother James L. Bowers, but if no children of either then my whole estate to **Martha Maslin** 3rd dau. of **Jacob Maslin**

Exec. my sister Mary Ann Bowers. Witnesses Peregrine Wroth, John C. Norris, Isaac Bull. Written Dec. 24, 1840 Proved June 15, 1841 (June 16 came John) p. 85

Joseph Turner of Kent Co
To my wife **Sarah Turner** my mansion farm lying on the E side of the main road leading from Still Pond Cross Roads to Chestertown containing about 140 acres during her life and after to my son **Joseph Turner** during his life and then to my grandson **Joseph Turner** but if said grandson dies then to his brother my grandson **Richard Townsend Turner**. To my son **Isaac Turner** the farm on which he resides beginning at a stone marked with the initials of my name being the beginning of my mansion house running then with **John Hepbron's** farm until it comes to a stone standing in the line between *"Redmon's Supply"* and my farmed called *"St. Martins"* then at right angles as the fence now runs taking in a piece of land belonging to *"St. Martins"* about 30 acres to a stone at the corner of said fence being a SW course and from that corner running with the fence near a SE course to *"Crane's Lott"* then to the main road with said road a N course to the beginning containing about 125 acres during his life and then to his son **Edward Turner** being my grandson. To my dau. **Sarah T. Mifflin** wife of **Thomas Mifflin** of Camden, DE my farm called *"St. Martin's"* except 30 acres laid off and joined to my son Isaac Turner's farm containing about 200 acres. If my dau. should die without issue then the farm to be sold and divided among my female grandchildren. To my son Joseph Turner my house in the head of Chester. To my wife Sarah Turner all my furniture with my carriages, horses and other stock for the farm during her life and such part of said property that she may not dispose of in her life, the residue to my 3 children Joseph, Isaac and Sarah. As an appendage to my mansion farm a certain wood lot containing about 12 acres and joining land of the late **Thomas Wilson** deceased, **Samuel Ringgold** and **E. F. Chambers** purchased from the estate of the late **Unit Angier** deceased. To my wife Sarah Turner the free use of getting wood from *"St. Martins"* for fuel. That part of my land called *"Long Point"* in Little Creek Hundred, DE which my wife executed a deed to me in which she reserved the privilege of revoking and if it stands as is then my son Thomas Mifflin to sell or convey to pay 5 legacies to our grandchildren as a reference to said instrument will appear and any surplus to my dau. his wife. To my grandson Richard Townsend Turner $400. To my dau. **Rebecca Turner** $300 and to her sister **Cassandra Turner** $300 the whole of the legacies I devise may be placed at interest and paid to them as they come of age.

Execs. my wife Sarah Turner and my son Joseph Turner. Witnesses John C. Norris, Samuel R. Turner, Benjamin Parrott. Written Jan. 18, 1834 (1st mo) Proved June 16, 1841 p. 86

Samuel G. Osborn of Kent Co
After my wife's third, to my wife **Catharine M. Osborn** all my household and kitchen furniture independent of her 1/3. If unmanufactured bark is on hand, then shall the executor shall carry on the operations of unmanufacturing it up into Queencitron bark until the end of the year and after the operation of bark grinding is ended then to dispose of the mill and the land belonging called *"Unicorn Mills"* with all my personal estate then after my wife's third then to my 2 daughters and son. The shop upon the SE corner of the main streets of Millington. My executor to carry on the lease entered into between **John P. Crossley** leasee and my wife and myself leasors

Exec. my brother **William M. K. Osborn**. Witnesses John K. B. Emory, John E. Cacy, John Scott. Written Apr. 20, 1838 Proved June 26, 1838 John Cacy came (June 21, 1841 came John Emory) p. 88

<u>Renunciation</u> **Elizabeth Nicols** widow of **Jeremiah Nicols** do renounce all claim to devise under the last will of my husband and elect my dower. Written Sep. 4, 1841. Witnesses Richard Ringgold [see page 83]

William Parker of Derrick of Kent Co
To my wife **Elizabeth** all my estate with the provision that she shall support her mother **Ann Myers** during her life and if my wife dies first my estate bound to support her mother at $80 annually. Whereas about 140 acres of my farm on which I now reside is entailed land and thereby my wife not be entitled to profits thereof then I devise all other land to my wife and all my personal estate, but if my wife should be entitled to the interest of the entailed land then my wife only to have life estate of all my other lands and at her death the whole of my land to go to my nephew **William D. Salisbury** subject to $80 to Ann Myers so long as she lives. After my wife's death to my brother in law **William V. Myers** except $200 except which I give to his sister **Mary Ann Duyer** all my interest in what is called *"McKay Farm"* being the life estate of **James Salisbury** and conveyed to me by a deed. I give to my sister **Elizabeth Salisbury** the wife of the said James to her.

Exec. my brother in law William V. Myers. Witnesses Thomas J. Mann, James S. Hyrons, William Foster. Written Aug. 25, 1841 Proved Sep. 8, 1841 p. 91

Morgan Browne of Kent Co
To my son **James F. Browne** all that part of my farm situated in Kent Co which is now known as the *"Violet Farm"* which lies to the S and W of the following lines, beginning at a chestnut tree standing in the division line between my land and the land I sold to **William Parks** and running S 31° E 17 perches, then S 3° E 17 ¼ perches to a

gatepost, then out 17 ½° E 160 perches to the division line of my land and **John Beck's** heirs, the land thus devised being part of those parts of a tract called *"Stepney Heath Manor"* which was conveyed to myself and wife by a deed of **Joseph N. Gordon** and wife and **Simon Wilmer** and wife and conveyed to me by a deed from **Richard Frisby** and by a deed from **James F. Browne, Alexander W. Ringgold** and wife, **Richard W. Ringgold** and wife, **Joseph Browne** and **Charles T. Browne**. To my son James F. Browne a right of way over the road as it now runs from the land above to the public road. I give to my son James F. Browne all that part of a tract of land in Kent Co called *"Arcadia"* which I purchased of **James Hanson** as trustee under the will of **Benjamin Hanson** containing 16 acres which I have received no deed and for which the balance of the purchase money is still due which is to be paid out of my personal estate. My son James F. Browne to pay to the Visitors and Governors of Washington College $1,000 part of the mortgage due me to the Visitors and Governors upon the lands devised to my son James. To my son James F. Browne my negro woman **Harriett** and my negro man **Thomas** or **Tom**. To my son **Joseph Browne** all the lands which were conveyed to myself and wife by a deed from Joseph N. Gordon and wife and Simon Wilmer and wife conveyed by a deed from Richard Frisby, and a deed from James F. Browne, Alexander W. Ringgold and wife, Richard W. Ringgold and wife, Joseph Browne and Charles T. Browne excepting what is given to James and what I conveyed to William Parks, thus the land devised to my son Joseph Browne being part of my farm lying N and E of the 3 lines. To my son Joseph Browne a right of way to and from my landing on Langsford Bay over the road running through the lands devised to my son James F. Browne. The lands of Joseph subject to this right of way. To my son **Joseph Richard** or **Dick** all my medical books and surgical instruments. Whereas I sold to **William Barroll** part of a tract called *"New Keys"* containing about 30 acres supposing that I had in fee simple but now it is supposed that one undivided 1/3 part of said landed descended from my wife **Margaret Browne** to her children as her heirs at law which undivided 1/3 has been conveyed to me by James F. Browne, Alexander W. Ringgold and wife, Richard W. Ringgold and wife, Joseph Browne and Charles T. Browne and whereas the land was sold to **Isaac Gale** under a decree of Kent Co Court by **John B. Eccleston** as trustee now I give all title in *"New Key"*. To my son James F. Browne all my undivided interest in a tract lying in Quaker Neck, Kent Co which was devised by my father **Joseph Browne** to my son Charles T. Browne and which has since been conveyed to my son James and myself by deed from Charles T. Browne if James gives rents to Charles during his life and after to whomever Charles designates by a will. All money owed me from Charles is discharged. During the life of my 2 sisters I give my son Charles T. Browne my dwelling house on the farm devised to my son James and to be provided free of charge by James. If Charles marry then not entitled to a home. **James B. Ricaud** to sell the house and lot on Water Street in Chestertown which I bought of **Robert Cruikshanks** and my lot containing 4 acres on the SW side of Chestertown which I purchased of **William Vanlier** and wife but first offered to my son James for $1,600, if not then to my son in law **Alexander W. Ringgold**, then to my son in law **Richard W. Ringgold**, then to my son Joseph Browne. If my son James does not purchase then he can take away the stable and carriage house. If James B. Ricaud should refuse to act as

Liber 12 1835-1854

trustee then **Joseph Redue** trustee in place. To my dau. **Mary Ann Ringgold** my negro boy **Jim** or **James Jones** and my negro girl **Maria** dau. of **Harriett**. To my dau. **Sarah R.** Ringgold my negro girl **Rachel** and several articles of household furniture and plate belonging to me now in her possession. To my niece **Rebecca Augusta Ruth** my negro girl **Grace Ann** for the time she has to serve. To my niece **Sarah Henrietta Browne** my negro girl **Charlotte**. All the rest of my personal estate to my children James F. Browne 1/7, Mary Ann Ringgold 2/7, and Sarah R. Ringgold 4/7. The land given to son James in full for debts from me to him. The 4/7 should be $1,850 as her part of my estate, if less then James to make up difference but not to exceed $400.

Execs. my 2 sons James F. Browne and Joseph Browne. Witnesses John B. Eccleston, Joseph Wickes, Benjamin F. Beck. Written June 28, 1838 Proved Oct. 19, 1841 (Oct. 14 John Eccleston came, Oct. 20 Joseph Gordon Jr. came) p. 92

Codicil Instead of 4/7 of personal estate, I have by deed dated Feb. 11, 1841 to my daughters Sarah R. Ringgold the house and lot in will directed to be sold by James B. Ricaud subject to $120 to me during my life in lieu of any part of my estate. I revoke all bequests to her except the plate and furniture. My debts first to be paid by $1,000 that was to be directed by my son James on mortgage, except the specific legacies of my son James F. Browne, Mary A. Ringgold, my niece Sarah H. Browne, my son Joseph Browne and the furniture and plate given to my dau. Sarah R. Ringgold unless it is insufficient to cover debts. The stable and carriage house to remain on said property now given to Sarah and not to be taken by son James. Written Feb. 12, 1841. Witnesses John B. Eccleston, George B. Westcott, Joseph N. Gordon Jr.

William R. Durding of Kent Co

To my brother **John T. Durding** all my wearing apparel and my large gun called a shot rifle. to my sister **Elizabeth Copper** my silver watch. Whereas my nephew **William Henry Durding** is afflicted with lameness which makes him unable to provide for himself, I give to William Henry Durding who is the eldest son of my brother **John T. Durding** $100. To my beloved mother **Rebecca Durding** all my lands, to wit a tract of land on Eastern Neck Island called *"Hynson's Addition"* containing 150 acres mentioned in deed dated May 9, 1771 between **Charles Hynson** and **William Durding** (this tract my mother owns 1/3 of as a widow's dower), one other tract adjoining *"Hynson's Addition"* called *"Hynson's Division"* containing 63 acres and 25 perches as mentioned in deed dated March 18, 1812 between **Benjamin Hynson** and **William R. Durding**, and one other lot called *"Skinner's Neck"* or *"Part of Smith's Desert"* containing 20 acres in a deed bearing date Jan. 1, 1802 between **Simon Wickes** and **William Durding** (1/3 of said lot belongs to my mother as a widow's dower) and one other tract which I purchased of **Samuel Coleman** lying on Gray's Inn Creek containing 257 acres mentioned in a deed dated Nov. 10, 1834 between Samuel Coleman and his wife **Mary Ann Coleman** to William R. Durding; I give to my mother Rebecca Durding during her life and to her all my personal estate. After my mother's death my brother John T. Durding to have the lands on Eastern Neck Island and the *"Skinner's Neck"* or *"Part of Smyth's Desert"*,

"Hynson's Addition", "Hynson's Division" or his heirs if he is dead at the death of my mother. He paying to my sister **Elizabeth Copper** $50, if living. If she is dead, then to **Hetty Burgess** dau. of **Peregrine** and **Amanda Burgess** but if she is also dead then my brother John T. Durding to keep the sum. After the death of my mother, I want **Marietta Durding** who is my brother John T. Durding's dau. and who is now living with mother and self to have the farm on Gray's Inn Creek which I purchased of Samuel Coleman after the death of my mother, if Marietta Durdings pays $600 to her then surviving brothers and sisters.

Exec. my mother Rebecca Durding. Witnesses Thomas Harris, Thomas D. Burgess, Joseph Harris. Written Jan. 24, 1837 Proved Nov. 16, 1841 p. 99

John Moore of Kent Co
To my wife **Asenath Moore** my land during her life, and all the stock of meats and 35 barrels of corn and one of the black girls whichever she chooses and after her death to **George Thomas Moore**. John Lloyd to have my sorrel colt. The rest of my property be valued and Asenath Moore and each child that is **Elizabeth Martha, Margaret A. Moore, Rachel J. Moore, John Lloyd Moore** each have equal share and my 2 grandchildren **Lloyd** and **Martha Melvina Skaggs** to share one child's part. George Tho. Moore is to have my land when he is 21, he paying to his sister Margaret A. Moore, Rachel J. Moore, and John Lloyd Moore $100 each. If he dies then to John Ll. Moore. None of my blacks to serve more than age 28.

Execs. my wife Asenath Moore and James Gale. Witnesses George Gale, J. Cumming, Hanson Crew. Written May 21, 1840 Proved Jan. 11, 1842 (Jan. 18 came Hanson) p. 103

Thomas Wilkins of Kent Co
To my son **William H. J. Wilkins** all my real estate lying in Quaker Neck and if he dies without issue, then my real estate to my sons **Bartus Wilkins** and **James F. Wilkins**. All my personal estate to my sons Bartus Wilkins and James F. Wilkins except $360 which is deposited in Baltimore Savings Bank which I give to my son Bartus Wilkins. To my son James F. Wilkins $500 to be paid by my son William H. J. Wilkins at 5 annual payments.

Exec. my son James F. Wilkins. Witnesses Hiram Browne, John Hadaway, William A. Rollison. Written Nov. 16, 1841 Proved Jan. 15, 1842 p. 104

George William Willson of Kent Co
To my wife **William Ann** $140 for her life. To my dau. **Susan E. Heigh** $1,000 in 10 annual payments and 5 acres of wood land to be laid off parallel with the road leading to the old field point. To my dau. **Juliann V. Stephens** $1,000 in 10 annual payments and 5 acres of my wood land laid off adjoining the lot given to my dau. Susan. To my dau. Susan my negro girl **Kity**. To my granddau. Olivia V. Stephens my negro girl **Edy**.

To my son **William George** my negro man **Ben** and my negro girl **Ann**. To my dau. **Mary Henry** my negro man **Perry** and my negro girl **Susan**. To my dau. **Maria Deborah** my negro woman **Silvia** and my negro boy **Abe**. After my debts, I give all of my farm which I purchased from **Robert Wilson** and the farm which I purchased from **James Wilson** with all my personal property to my 3 children William George, Mary Henry, and Maria Deborah. The negro girl **Eda's** wages to be used for my granddaughters education

Execs. my dau. Mary Henry and my son William George. Witnesses Henry Hurtt, James Hurtt, William G. Wilson. Written Dec. 26, 1840 Proved Jan. 18, 1842 p. 105

Sarah Hatcheson of Kent Co

I give to my niece **Saleno Jessop** $50, one bureau and one bedquilt. My executor to pay $200 to my nephew **Benjamin Franklin Beck** as trustee and to pay annually the interest to my niece **Sarah Camp** and at her death the principal to her children, not subject to control of her husband. To my niece's son **Samuel Albert Camp** son of **William Camp** $100 when he is 21. To **John Beck** son of my nephew B.F. Beck $150. To **Samuel Beck** son of my nephew B.F. Beck $100. To my brother **Samuel Beck** of Brook Co, VA the bond I hold of his for $300 and at his death to be paid to his dau. Mrs. **Caroline Browning**. My executor to put a head and foot stone at my grave with my dates of death and age inscribed

Exec. my nephew **Horace Beck**. Witnesses James P. Gale, Mary T. Gale. Written Dec. 2, 1841 Proved Feb. 2, 1842 p. 107

Stephen Denning of Kent Co

To my grandson **Thomas Stephen Dodd** all my dwelling house in Chestertown purchased by me of **John F. Smith** known as *"Cloak property"* but my dau. **Mary Jane Dodd** is to have use during her lifetime and if he dies then to the other children of my daugher Mary Jane Dodd. To my granddau. **Augusta Matilda Dodd** my house and lot called *"Davis Property"* adjoining a lot of **James B. Ricaud Esq** reserving interest to my dau. Mary Jane Dodd during her life and if she dies then to the other children of my dau. Mary Jane Dodd. To my grandchildren **Arvis Elizabeth** and **Oscar Rudolph Denning** my negro boy **Benjamin** to be hired out for their use by their father **John N. Denning**, if either dies then to survivor if they both die then any other children my son John N. Denning should have it being understood that all his children should benefit from the hire of the negro Benjamin and if John dies leaving my dau. in law **Mary** a widow then she is to have interest but if she dies or marries then said negro boy to my dau. Mary Jane Dodd. I release all sums of money my son John N. Denning owes me. To my dau. Mary Jane Dodd my negro man **Jack** and the residue of my property.

Exec. my son in law **John T. Dodd**. Witnesses John Usilton, Joseph Redue, John N. Usilton. Written Feb. 2, 1842 Proved Feb. 8, 1842 p. 109

Abstracts of Kent Co., MD Wills 1777-1867 (WB 12)

Rosamond Bowers of Kent Co
To my dau. **Eliza** one bed it being part of my personal estate. The rest of my estate to my dau. **Mary Ann**.

Exec. my dau. Mary Ann. Witnesses Isaac Bull, George Parsons. Written Nov. 3, 1840 Proved Feb. 23, 1842 (Feb. 28 came George) p. 110

George W. Thomas of Kent Co
To my wife Mrs. **Mary S. Thomas** the property in Chestertown that is the house and *"Lot No. 37"*, the blacksmith's shop occupied by Greenwood and Harrison and the dwelling occupied by **Cuff Oliver**, these lots already belong to Mrs. Thomas, the houses built thereon by me I devise to her, also the house and lot part of *"Lot No. 29"* in said town the house being occupied by **Capt. Claypole** and the lot not rented. Also the pasture lot opposite to my dwelling house also the house and lot part of *"Lot No. 24"* with two buildings one of which is now occupied by **Capt. Ozman** and the other is not rented. To my wife all that piece of land called *"Hopewell"* containing 24 ½ acres of land which I purchased of **Richard Graves** also that part of *"Henford"* which I purchased of Jacob Jones heirs containing about 12 ½ acres and that part of *"Providence"* which I purchased of **Dobbs Joiner** containing about 1 ½ acres all which lands now be within Mrs. Thomas' Worton farm. I give to my wife my farm called *"Airy Hill"* containing about 241 ½ acres parts of *"Kemp's Beginning"*, *"Landford"*, *"Thomas Purchase"* and *"Chigwell"* situated in Kent Co all the lands during her widowhood and in lieu of her thirds. My wife to cut from my lands called *"Round Top"* situated in Queen Anns Co for her use in Chestertown during her life. I give my wife all the negroes and personal property on my *"Airy Hill farm"* and my negro **John Bordley** now on the Upper Farm who was the property of Mrs. Thomas before marriage, and all the negroes now here in Chestertown and the furniture, carriages, and horses there, together with the pair of bay horses which she drives. I give to my wife 50 shares of Baltimore and Ohio Stock and $500 per annum during her life in consideration my wife is to permit my executors to get 2,000 chestnut rails from her *"Worton farm"* for the use of my ill farm near Chestertown. None of the negroes given to Mrs. Thomas except John Bordley and **David Matthew** who belonged to her before marriage are intended for her during life only. To **Sarah Perkins, Ann Perkins, Eliza Perkins** and **Caroline Perkins** respectively all my estate and right in Perkin's mill and the lands thereto, along with the lands purchased by me of **Samuel Griffith** called *"Whitfields"* containing from 133 to 140 acres. To Eliza Perkins, Ann Perkins and **Ann Augusta Perkins** $1,000 each and to Caroline Perkins $500 and my account on repairs done on the mill which I hereby remit to them be considered to be in full discharge of all claims which the said Sarah, Ann, Eliza, and Caroline Perkins may have against me. To my executors my wood lot of 16 acres near Rock Hall called part of *"Smyth's Desert"*, also my mill farm near Chestertown called *"Stepney"* containing 90 acres, also 16 acres being part of *"Triangle"* and *"Goosehill"*, 30 acres being part of *"Campbell's Worthmore"* which is wood and timberland, 145 acres being part of *"Forest"* opposite **Dr. Kennard's**, my 1/3 part of the farm where **John Maxwell** died being the undivided third part, 255 acres part of *"Blay's Range"* and

Liber 12 1835-1854

"Addition" commonly called the *"Wethered farm"* whereon **Edward Hartley** now lives and 150 acres part of *"Riley's Beginning"* to my executors in trust to sell for my debts. To Ann Thomas who is now living with **John G. Hollingsworth** in Queen Anns Co $50 annually. To **Henrietta M. Bruff** $500. To my friend **Robert D. Burns** of Baltimore $1,000. To **George W.T. Perkins** the following property in Chestertown part of *"Lot No. 15"* with the brick stable and garden, part of *"Lot No. 44"* treading yard, the office and water lots part of *"Lot No. 9"* and *"Lot No. 10"* purchased of **Robert Wright** and wife and now occupied by myself. To my executors **Stevenson Archer, John B. Eccleston** and **George S. Hollyday** my farm in Kent Co called *"Upper Farm"* and my farm in Queen Anns Co called *"Round Top"* with all the stock of the 2 farms for 10 years in trust to continue the farms under **Edward Hartley**. After 10 years to **George W.T. Perkins** and his heirs if he does not sell until age 31 and he shall pay $1,000 to his brother **James A. Perkins** and to his brother **Francis Perkins** and **Benjamin B. Perkins** each $500. At the charge of my estate my executors to clothe and send George W. T. Perkins to some good college he selects. To Mrs. **Juliana Constable** my negro woman **Mary** and her child **Eliza** for the terms they have to serve and to **Edward Wilkins** his note for about $123 which I hold. All the rest of my estate to George W. T. Perkins.

Execs. my friends Stevenson Archer of Harford Co, John B. Eccleston and George S. Hollyday. Witnesses Joseph Redue, Daniel Collins, James Alfred Pearce. Written Mar. 2, 1842 Proved Mar. 22, 1842 p. 111

Susan Strong of Kent Co

To my dau. **Harriett M. Thomas** my best carpet, andirons, shovel and tongs, one bed and bolster that I sent to my son **Thomas** last summer. To my son **William H. Strong** my silver soup ladle and my large Bible. To my son **John** a pair sugar tongs and salt spoon and the balance of my silver to be divided between Thomas and **Lawrence Strong**. To **Lawrence M. Strong** one bed, one pair of pillows, one quilt, one white counter pin, one pair blankets, 2 pair sheets, and bedstead and one comfort. To my son John Strong one bed, one bolster, one pair pillows, one quilt, one white counter pin, one pair blankets, two pair sheets, one bedstead, one mantle clock, one comfort and my boy **Horrice**. The things I have given to my children Harriett M. Strong, William H. Strong, Lawrence M. Strong, **John A. Strong,** and **Thomas A. Strong** I do not wish to be appraised. All my servants to my 4 sons William H. Strong, Thomas A. Strong, Lawrence M. Strong, and John A. Strong. The balance of my estate to Harriett M. Thomas, William H. Strong, Thomas A. Strong, Lawrence M. Strong, John A. Strong, and **Susan Waltham** my granddau.

Exec. my son William H. Strong. Witnesses John W. Walker, William B. Wilmer Jr. Written Sep. 14, 1840 Proved May 10, 1842 p. 115

<u>Codicil</u> My granddau. Susan Waltham to have the blacks I purchased of her father's estate by her paying $650 when she is 21. If she chooses not to take them then the

Abstracts of Kent Co., MD Wills 1777-1867 (WB 12)

negroes purchased of the estate of Thomas Waltham to go to my sons William H. Strong, Thomas A. Strong, Lawrence M. Strong, and John A. Strong and they to pay my dau. Harriett Thomas and granddau. Susan Waltham $100 out of each sale of negroes. If she takes the negroes then to pay Harriett Thomas $100, John Strong $112.50, William H. Strong $112.50, Lawrence M. Strong $112.50, Thomas A. Strong $112.50. My sons William, Thomas, Lawrence and John to have hire of negroes until Susan Waltham is 21. To Susan Waltham one bed, bedstead and pillow, one bolster, sheets, and one comfort. Written Apr. 7, 1842. Witnesses J.W. Walker, Sarah W. Middleton

Joseph Reed of Kent Co
To my brother **George R. Reed** 2/3 of my estate. To my uncle **John Usilton** the other 1/3.

Execs. my brother George R. Reed and my uncle John Usilton. Witnesses Joseph Browne, Richard F. Graves, Thomas H. Whaland. Written Apr. 14, 1842 Proved May 12, 1842 p. 117

John Hance of MD, being on visit with friends in Salem, NJ
To my dau. **Rebeckah Ann Hance** all my real estate in the town of Salem with the incumbrance that she pay to **Mary Ann Mufford('s)** child $100 when she is 18. This child's name **Milicent**. All my personal estate to my sons **Isaac Hance, James Hance, Edward Hance**, and my dau. Rebeckah Ann Hance that they each pay to my dau. Mary Ann Mulford, exclusive of her husband. My share of the vessel called Mary to my son Isaac Hance if he pays to my son John Hance $100 and to his children $150. To my sons Isaac Hance, James Hance, Edward Hance, and my dau. Rebeckah Ann Hance my farm in Maryland where I now live on condition that they pay to **Rody Mulford's** two children **Margaret Milicent** and **John Edward** $100. If any sue for larger portion to them $1.

Execs. my sons Isaac, Hance, James Hance, and Edward Hance. Witnesses James Bright, Lewis Green, Rachel G. Nicholson, George M. Ward. Written Apr. 13, 1842 (4th mo) Proved June 1, 1842 p. 118

Temperance Newman of Kent Co
To my only son living **George N. Newman** all my plantation adjoining Masseys Cross Roads comprising several tracts known by name of *"Angel's Rest"*, *"Spring Garden"*, and *"Partnership"* containing 129 acres. To my dau. **Mary Money** $661.50 if she does not marry but if she does then to her 3 children and my personal estate after debts paid except one bed and furniture which I give to my son **Joel G. Newman**.

Exec. my son George N. Newman. Witnesses Charles R. Hackett, Richard Corbaly, Richard D. Downing. Written May 4, 1839 Proved June 14, 1842 p. 119

Liber 12 1835-1854

Isaac Spencer of Kent Co
To **Abe Wilson** (son of **Abe Wilson**) the E end of my lot beginning at the E gate post next to the branch running a S course to a small apple tree at the corner of the henhouse or to intersect the line between Dr. E. Scott then by that line to the road then by and with the main road to the gate post, about 1/8 to ¼ an acre. To my dau. **Ann** or **Nancy Brooks** the rest of my estate during her life and after to my 2 grandchildren **William Thompson** and **Eliza Brooks** my said daughter's children.

Exec. William Gooding. Witnesses William Gooding, A. B. Wheatley, Henry Hurtt. Written Aug. 3, 1841 Proved Jan. 18, 1842 p. 121

Henry Graves of Kent Co.
Being advanced in years, I give my wife **Henny Graves** all my personal property and the house on which I now reside, the same land which formerly belonged to the estate of **Richard S. Thomas** deceased during her life and she paying to my dau. **Eliza** 50¢, to my dau. **Emeline** 50¢, to my dau. **Ann** 50¢. After the death of my wife Henny Graves the above mentioned house and lot to my son **William Graves**.

Exec. Not Given. Witnesses James H. Edes, Thomas Baker, Edward Elbern. Written May 26, 1842 Proved June 21, 1842 p. 122

Richard Graves of Kent Co
To my dau. **Elizabeth Graves** that part of the farm on which I live, beginning at a Persimon tree on the hill along the road leading from Willis's Road to Chestertown and running nearly S to a persimmon tree in the bottom W of the house and from thence due E until it intersects the public road leading to Chestertown. The balance of said farm to be sold with my personal property to pay my debts and Mrs. **Elizabeth G. Worrell** shall deed the part willed to Elizabeth Graves to her and the said Mrs. Elizabeth G. Worrell shall deed all the remaining part of said farm to my son **William Graves** for the purpose above. If there is a surplus then to my sons **Richard Graves, John G. Graves**, and **James Graves** and my dau. **Sarah Harris** each the sum of $100 and any extra to my four children last named and my dau. Elizabeth Graves. I reserve 40 feet square for a graveyard with a free way of getting to same for the use of all my children.

Exec. my son William Graves. Witnesses Peregrine Wroth, Nicholas Mensch, Dobbs Joiner. Written June 3, 1842 Proved June 28, 1842 p. 123

Purnell Fletcher Smith of Kent Co
To my son **George Washington Purnell Smith** my gold watch, 6 silver table spoons marked P.F.S., one mahogany secretary, one case mathematical instruments, one mahogany dressing box and his first choice of books out of my library. To my son **Benjamin Everitt Smith** my house and lot in Georgetown containing 3 ½ acres of land bounded on the N by a street called Princes Staf Street and on the S by a lot formerly belonging to **Thomas Dollis** and by a lot belonging to the heirs of **William P. Ireland**

145

and one E by King Street and on the W by lands belonging to **John Hance** and a lot belonging to the heirs of **Rachel Murry**. To my dau. **Anna Maria Margaretta Smith** 7 shares of bank stock in the Merchants Bank of Baltimore, one mahogany bedstead, a best bed, and 2 pillow cases, one pair of best sheets, one pair of blankets, one marsales quilt, 6 windsor chairs painted oak color, one mahogany dinner table, one pair brass andirons, one painted table with 2 drawers in it, 6 silver desert spoons, one best looking glass, my portrait, and my traveling trunk. To my dau. **Arralanta Robins Smith** 5 shares of bank stock in the Merchants Bank of Baltimore 6 windsor chairs painted oak color, one pair brass andirons, one feather bed, one pair sheets, one pair of blankets, one best bed quilt, one bolster, and 2 pillows. To my dau. **Anna Louisa Smith** 5 shares of same stock, one feather bed, one pair of sheets, one pair of blankets, one bed quilt, one bolster and two pillows, 6 windsor chairs, one walnut breakfast table, one looking glass. To my dau. **Andasia Virginia Smith** 8 shares of bank stock in the Farmers and Planters Bank of Baltimore and one share of bank stock in the Merchants Bank of Baltimore and $200 to be paid by her brother Benjamin Everitt Smith when she is 18. Six windsor chairs and one looking glass to be chosen by her mother. My wife **Mary** to hold the estate during her life and during the minority of my daughters except the 2 eldest who may recover at age 18. The annuity that is due me from the Incorporation of the Protestant Episcopal Church to my 4 daughters. My clock to whichever child my wife chooses to give the house and lot upon which I now reside

Exec. my friend Edward Boyer. Witnesses James Boon, T. B. Darrach, J. Darrach. Written May 3, 1842 Proved July 5, 1842 p. 124

Renunciation I **Mary W. E. Smith** widow of Rev. Purnell F. Smith renounce all claim to bequest in the will of my husband and elect dower instead. Written Oct. 11, 1842 Witness **A.M.M. Smith**

Martha Gale of Kent Co
All that tract lying in Still Pond Neck, Kent Co where I now reside to my son **George Gale**. If he dies without issue then to my nephew **George Thomas Moore**.

Exec. Not Given. Witnesses Dr. Thomas C. Kennard, Elizabeth Crew, Ann Kelly. Written May 7, 1840 Proved Aug. 10, 1842 p. 126

Codicil My negro woman Eliza shall be free

Mary A. Smith of Kent Co
To my niece **Margaret A. Wiley** my gold watch, my best bureau, my venetian carpet, and four pair of my best linen sheets and my feather bed. I give my set of silver table spoons to **Margaretta Knox**, dau. of my cousin **Mary Ann Knox** of Philadelphia and my tea spoons and sugar tongs to her sister **Esther Ann Knox**. I give my travelling trunk and $20 to my friend **Mary Stephens** with all my books. All my wearing apparel to my sister Wiley and my cousin Mary Ann Knox. My servant **Jesse** will be free. All the rest

of my personal estate to my cousins **Edward A. Gibbs** and his sister **Mary Ann Knox**. My portion of the farm now belonging to my sister Wiley and myself to my niece **Margaret A. Wiley**. If she dies then to **William B. Kennard** now living in Accomac Co, VA.

Exec. my cousin Edward A. Gibbs. Witnesses Dr. Peregrine Wroth, Mary Stephens, Araminta Stephens. Written July 26, 1842 Proved Aug. 16, 1842 p. 127

Michael Smith of Kent Co

To my wife **Ann** the Cooper farm, my gig and mare with 1/3 of household furniture. To **James H. Smith** my eldest son my plantation where he now lives lying on the old mill branch and which I purchased of **Thomas Pearce** and to him the 2 farms in Queen Anns Co which were bought of **Hollingsworth** and **Pere Wilmer** and for which he already has deeds. I give to him James H. Smith all my negroes that are in his possession except the negro boy Emory. To my son **William F. Smith** all the rest of my estate. My son James H. Smith pay to my dau. **Jane F. Moffett** $50 annually during her life and my son William F. Smith pay to my dau. Jane F. Moffett $50 annually during her life.

Exec. my son William F. Smith. Witnesses Joseph Wright, William M. R. Osborn, N. Garrettson. Written June 16, 1838 Proved Oct. 18, 1842 p. 129

Rachel Bradshaw of Kent Co

All my property to my niece **Mary Bradshaw Meeks**.

Exec. Not Given. Witnesses Jacob Fisher, William B. Wilmer, Colin F. Hale. Written Apr. 22, 1839 Proved Oct. 18, 1842 p. 130

Mary Trew of Kent Co

To my sister **Rebecca Browne** my mahogany table and one bed quilt. To my brother **Thomas Trew** my silver cream urn and one bed quilt. To my nephew **Bartus Trew** son of my late brother **Bartus** $50 at age 21. All the rest of my estate to my sister **Deborah Trew**.

Exec. my brother Trew. Witnesses Dr. Peregrine Wroth, Elizabeth T. Browne. Written Aug. 3, 1842 Proved Oct. 18, 1842 p. 130

Edward Keatting

My negro man **Joseph** to be free. My negro woman **Mary** to my sister **Mary K. Crouch**, the said negro not being able to take care of herself because of age. I give all my right and title (one third) in the farm which formerly belonged to my mother to hands of **Edwin Crouch** as trustee for the use of my brother **Thomas Browning Keating** for his support and at his death to his heirs. If he has none then to my little nephew **Edwin Crouch**. To said Edwin Crouch my nephew my box of dental instruments

Abstracts of Kent Co., MD Wills 1777-1867 (WB 12)

Exec. my brother in law Edwin Crouch. Witnesses David Davis, Dr. T. N. Tayman, Henry Hurtt. Written Feb. 16, 1843 Proved Mar. 7, 1843 p. 131

Gilbert Chrisfield of Kent Co
To my wife **Elizabeth Chrisfield** during her life all the profits of my estate. To my eldest son **James G. Chrisfield** after the death of his mother Elizabeth Chrisfield my plantation whereon he now dwells which I purchased of **Sarah Ellis** and on the N E side of the public road leading from Georgetown Cross Roads to Masseys Cross Roads containing 86 acres. Two wood lots in the forest which I purchased of **John Anthony** called *"Fanny's Slip"* and *"Tobin's Lott"* to James G. Chrisfield he paying $500 as provided below and after the death of his mother to convey to **Etha N. Chrisfield** by deed the house and lot as he may have a claim where I now live. To **George W. Chrisfield** my second son $200 paid by James G. Chrisfield (it being part of $500). To my dau. **Elizabeth Hurtt** wife of **John Hurtt** $140 (at $20 per year). To my son **Other N. Chrisfield** my lot on the N side of the public road leading from Georgetown Cross Roads to New Market which I purchased of John Hurtt and **Thomas Green** adjoining **John M. Armstrong**, containing 2 1/12 acres, he to pay my son **Alfred Chrisfield** $50 after the death of their mother Elizabeth Chrisfield. To **William King** my wife's eldest son my book account which I have against him. If the balance of $160 is not sufficient to pay debts then James to have as much of the personal estate that will reimburse him before there is a division. After the death of my wife Elizabeth Chrisfield all the rest of my estate to my 4 sons James G. Chrisfield, George W. Chrisfield, Otho N. Chrisfield, and Alfred Chrisfield.

Exec. my wife Elizabeth Chrisfield. Witnesses William Medders, Orlando F. Sutton, Henry Hurtt. Written Jan. 29, 1843 Proved Mar. 7, 1843 p. 132

Sarah H. Lamb of Kent Co
To **Samuel Browne** of Queen Anns Co and son of **Pery Browne** $100 and one silver watch. To **Pery Browne Jr.** and son of Pery Browne Sr. $50. To **Everet Gale,** son of **Rasin Gale** $100. To **Hannah A. Norris** dau. of **John C. Norris** I give a 6 silver tablespoons, these spoons are now loaned to Mrs. **Mary Gale**. To **Susan Norris** dau. of John C. Norris I give 6 silver tea spoons, 1 silver sugar tongs, 6 ivory knives and forks. To **Willamina Gale** dau. of Rasin Gale one feather bed. To **Mary C. Gale** wife of Rasin Gale two tables, carpet and hearth rug, the tables are already in her possession, the carpet and rug at Pery Brown. To **Mary Ann Walls** (Mary Ann Brown that was) 6 chairs, 1 large gilt looking glass, one pair of brass andirons. To **Emily Browne** dau. of Pery Brown, one bureau, and some gilt frame pieces. My bed at Rasin Gale's with ½ of my bedding which is at Pery Browne's should be the bed and bedding which Willamina is to have. To my cousin Pery Brown my other feather bed which is now at his house with the other ½ of the bedding at his house. To **Edwin Brown** and son of Pery Brown $20. To **Mary Ann Norris** wife of John C. Norris one large china bowl and $20. To my negro boy **Joseph James** child of **George Tiller** and **Ginny Tiller** his wife, should be free on Jan. 1, 1855. To my friend John C. Norris the said negro, 1/3 of his

Liber 12 1835-1854

wages to his mother Ginny and 1/3 to his father George and 1/3 to John for his trouble. To **Tabitha Brown** wife of Pery Brown all my wearing apparel. To my friend John C. Norris all my negroes until they are 21 then free and he paying $10 to each of them of their wage (except Joseph James Tiller)

Exec. John C. Norris. Witnesses Dr. R. T. Allen, Rebecca Lamb, John C. Norris. Written Jan. 13, 1842 Proved May 8, 1843 p. 134

Maria Tate of Kent Co
Whereas there are several transactions between my brother **William B. Wilmer** and myself and is at this time indebted to me, I cancel all sums due me from him. To my dau. in law **Sarah Maria Gordon** wife of **James F. Gordon** for her life all my estate. My dau. in law to pay in 1850 to her half-brother **Robert B. A. Tate** $100 annually during his life. My negro woman **Dolly** to be free. My other negroes **Jim** to be free on Jan. 1, 1846, my negro man **Jacob** to be free on Jan. 1, 1849, my negro **Pere** to be free Jan. 1, 1852, **Moses** to be free Jan. 1, 1855, **Julia** and **Ann** to be free on Jan. 1, 1848, and **Henry** to be free on Jan. 1, 1867. My executor to have head and foot stones on my grave and on my deceased father and mother's grave, and a slab to be placed over my dau. **Louisa** and my son **Alexander** and my friend **James B. Ricaud** to select, and if my relatives shall desire to make repairs to the enclosure around the family burial ground my executor to contribute my part of the same. To my sisters **Sarah** and **Harriett Wilmer** one pair of white linen sheets marked number 3 and 4. As most of my estate goes to his wife and children, no appraisement needed. [Freedom passes granted to Moses Apr. 28, 1855, Pere Sep. 1, 1856, Jacob Oct. 4, 1864, written in margin]

Exec. my friend and relative James F. Gordon. Witnesses James B. Ricaud, Joseph N. Gordon Jr., Mary Gordon. Written Mar. 27, 1843 Proved May 13, 1843 p. 136

Edward Scott of Georgetown, Kent Co
To my wife **Anna Maria Scott** all my estate

Exec. my wife. Witnesses Joseph Moffett, John W. Palmer, Dr. James Heigh. Written Aug. 4, 1838 Proved May 23, 1843 p. 138

Martha Browne of Kent Co
To my granddau. **Martha Ann Glanvill Browne** (dau. of my son **Joseph Coursey Browne** deceased) my negro boy **Lem** about 15 until he is 44 years. To my granddau. Martha Ann Glanvill Browne my negro girl **Ann Rebecca** now about 11 until he is 44. If she dies then to granddau. **Marian Hellen Brown** dau. of my son **Benjamin O. Brown**, and if she die then said negroes free. To my granddau. Marian Hellen as said 2 milch cows and their increase and my mare Sally. To my grandson **Charles Decorsey Brown** son of my son **James Brown** one cow, one yoke of oxen and my horse Boxer. To my dau. **Martha** wife of **Samuel Clarke** my negro woman **Hanna** a slave for life and my negro girl **Elizabeth** now about 7 seven years to serve until she is 44 and then

149

to be free and in case of the death of my dau. Martha. The said negro girl **Elizabeth** to my granddau. **Harriot Catharine Brown** dau. of my son **William Brown**. My negro girl **Ann** now about 5 years and my negro boy **Isaac** now about 4 years be sold to for funeral expenses. All the rest of my personal property to my granddau. Martha Ann Glanvill Brown.

Exec. John W. Walker. Witnesses William Camp, Richard Ll. Nicols, Isaac Groome. Written Nov. 8, 1842 Proved June 26, 1843 p. 138

Sarah Ringgold of Kent Co
To my 2 nieces **Sarah Maria Perkins** and **Ann Wallis Perkins** all my land and tract containing 80 acres adjoining the land of my sister **Henrietta Perkins** as long as they remain unmarried. If they die or marry then to survivor. To my nephew **Isaac Perkins** my 3 negro men **Alexander, Hynson** and **Emory** and they are not to be sold out of the state. To my nephew **John Perkins** my clock, one bedstead, one bed, also my negro man **Henry** upon the express condition that my said nephew does not sell them out of state.

Exec. my nephew Isaac Perkins. Witnesses William Wroth, William H. P. Worrell, Joseph Redue. Written Feb. 10, 1843 Proved Aug. 8, 1843 p. 140

Sarah Ingram of Kent Co
My black boy **Pere** to be free. **Harry** who is 16, **Frank** who is 16, **Harriet** who is 18, **Emily Ann** an infant; all free at age 29. To **Mary Jane Beck's** dau. **Margarett Ann Ingram Beck** all the interest on my money till she is 21 and she then is to have 1/3 of said money and 2/3 to **George Rasin Beck** son of **Mary Jane Beck**. To Mary Jane Beck all my estate during her life and after to her children. [Freedom pass granted to Frank Apr. 18, 1856, Harry May 12, 1856, Harriet Dec. 9, 1857]

Exec. **James Beck** (of George). Witnesses Robert Usilton, Joseph Usilton, Thomas Toulson, George Reed. Written Apr. 17, 1843 Proved Aug. 19, 1843 (Aug. 22 came Joseph) p. 142

Benjamin Price of Kent Co
To my wife **Ann M. Price** all that property I purchased of **Joseph W. Webb** and **Thomas Hepbron 3rd** containing 34 ½ acres, all that part of land which I received of **Benjamin Howard** in exchange of land where the main road between land of Benjamin Howard and the farm where I now reside was straightened containing one acre, and that part of land which I purchased of Benjamin Howard containing 52 acres it being part of the farm formerly purchased by **James Bevans** of **Notly Young**, and also all that part of land which I purchased of Dr. **George W. Thomas** containing 16 acres and which adjoins the farm whereon I now reside and the lands of **Joseph W. Webb** and **Isaac L. Price**, being part of what is called *"Tilden Land"* to my wife during her life and after to my son **Hyland Benson Price**. If he dies without heirs then to my son **Isaac Lewis Price**. To my wife my 4 negroes the sons of **Ann** who is free named **Richard, Isaac,**

George, and Henry until they are 28. To my wife my 5 good horses, 6 good cows, 50 barrels of corn, 2,500 pounds of pork, 12 sheats (?), 2 breeding sows, 4 tons of corn blades and all the clover hay on the farm whereon I now reside, two carts, 4 ploughs, 3 small harrows, one fallow harrow, 4 weeding hoes, 2 grubbing hoes, 3 axes, one maul, and set of wedges, my 4 wheel carriage and the harness, 30 bags, and all my furniture in the house and on the farm where I now reside to her my wife Ann M. Price during her life and after her death I give to my son Hyland Benson Price except the 4 negro boys, **Richard, Isaac, George** and **Henry**. My crop to be seeded if I die between seeding time and harvest. And to better carry on the above property is in addition to her right of dower. To my son **Peregrine Price** all that farm called and known by the name *"Gunneries"* containing 257 acres and 25 perches as surveyed by **George Gale** Esq. it being part of *"Gunneries"* and *"Yapp"* that he pays to my dau. **Anna Maria Price** $1,200 in 6 equal installments of $200, also that he pays to my 2 granddaughters **Sarah Matilda Cann** and **Mary Cann**, daughters of dau. **Mary Cann** deceased each $100 when they arrive at age 21. The $1,200 and $200 are charged to my estate given to my son Peregrine Price. To my dau. **Sarah Matilda Canby** all that farm known as *"Howard Farm"* containing 229 acres as surveyed and laid down by George Gale Esq. upon the condition that the owner of the farm called *"Stoneton Fishery"* without hindrance from the owner of the farm called *"Howard Farm"* to my dau. Sarah. To my son **Benjamin F. Price** all that farm called *"Yapp"* containing 264 acres and 10 perches as surveyed and laid down by George Gale Esq, also my negro boy **George** (not the boy of that name herein before mentioned) to serve until he is 25. To my son **William Henry Price** all that farm and tract called *"Stoneton"* containing 320 perches or more as surveyed and laid down by **George Gale** Esq also that part of land called *"Pond Island"* if he pays to my dau. **Adeline Houston** $1,200 in 6 annual payments of $200, also that he pays my grandson **Benjamin Price Cann** the son of my dau. Mary Cann $100 when he is 21 also that he permits my relative **Edward Stoops** to occupy the room he now occupies at "Stoneton" so long as Edward remains unmarried and to have fire wood free of any charge. To my son William Henry Price my negro girl called **Rachel** and my negro boy **Isaac** until they arrive at 25. The rest of my estate to my daughter Adeline Houston 1/3 and **Anna Maria Price** 1/3 and my grandchildren, Benjamin Price Cann, **Sarah Matilda Cann** and **Mary Cann** 1/3 to be divided among them. [Granted pass to George devised Benj. F. Price Dec. 26, 1856 in margin]

Execs. my friend Daniel Jones and my son Isaac Lewis Price. Witnesses Joseph Redue, J.W. Walker, and Benj. Vanhorn. Written Dec. 16, 1842 Proved Sep. 26, 1843 p. 143

Rebecca Durding of Kent Co
For the fidelity of my faithful servant men **Clenus** and **Isaac**, I free them. All my stock, money, and all my personal estate I give to **James C. Durding, John T. Durding, Benjamin R. Durding, Edward P. Durding, Mary Ann McCubbin** (all children of my late son **John T. Durding**) and **Hetty Elizabeth Burgess** (daughter of **Peregrine Burgess**) to be divided between them. I wish all my personal estate to be converted into moeny. To my negro man Isaac $20. All the rest of my estate to the **James C. Durding,**

Abstracts of Kent Co., MD Wills 1777-1867 (WB 12)

John T. Durding, Benjamin R. Durding, Edward P. Durding, Mary Ann McCubbin and Hetty Elizabeth Burgess .

Exec. George Vickers of Chestertown. Witnesses Daniel Collins, Horatio Beck. Written June 2, 1843 Proved Oct. 17, 1843 (Horatio came Oct. 24) p. 147

John T. Stephens of Kent Co
All that tract of land called *"Piney Point"* adjoining Rock Hall and Deep Landing, also all my personal estate to my wife **Emily** during her life or during her widowhood, but in case of her death or second marriage the said property to be disposed of. My *"Piney Point"* land and all my personal estate to be sold and divided among my 9 youngest children born of my wife Emily. I leave ¼ acre attached to my graveyard on the Piney Point farm to be forever exempt from being sold and to continue free in my family for a place of interment. My farm called *"Deep Landing"* shall be divided in the following manner, the tillable land in 3 equal parts and the woodland in 3 equal parts and the shores in 3 equal parts and the 1/3 to be the property of each of my sons names **John T. Stevens, Samuel B. Stevens,** and **Jacob Stevens.** If any money is still owed on said land, all three sons to till the farm and make the payments. If they do not they are to have no part of my estate. All the pasture on the farm shall be used for my 3 named sons and the remainder of my family while occupying the *"Piney Point"* farm. To my son John T. Stevens my shot rifle (called mine). I also give to my son Jacob Stevens my shot rifle purchased from **John Durding.** To all my children that I have had by my former wives, $1 having as I conceive done a good part for them already.

Execs. my wife Emily and my son John T. Stevens. Witnesses Nathan Hatcheson, L. W. Morgan, Benedict S. Brevitt. Written Apr. 16, 1842 Proved Oct. 24, 1843 p. 149
N.B. John Topping Stephens married Sophia Woolihand and Emily Brown. The names of others wives have not been found yet by me.

Mary M. Mason of Kent Co
To **Arthur John Wallis** my farm called *"Darnal's Farm"* containing 175 acres. To my cousin **William W. Wallis** my negro man **Jack** with the present year's wages. To my cousin **John Brooks Wallis** my negro boy **Josiah** (or **Joe**). To my cousin and late guardian **Hugh Wallis** the residue of my personal estate and negroes.

Exec. my cousin and late guardian Hugh Wallis. Witnesses Andrew/Anderson W. Melvin, John F. Melvin, Margaret A. Wallis. Written Oct. 11, 1843 Proved Oct. 31, 1843 p. 151

Rayman Biddle of Kent Co
I sell that farm in Kent Co which I purchased of Dr. **Thomas Willson** and the heirs of the late **James Brooks.** The money due from the estate of the late **Abraham Miller** to be divided amongst all my children. To my dau. **Wilhelmina Lusby** $250. My estate to be appraised (my children can take any article at appraised value) then to be divided as

follows, my son **John** to receive 1/8, the remainder divided between my children **Stephen, Mary, Emeline, Martha, Clarisss,** and **Julia Ann.** Whereas my son Stephen has claimed the bay mare, I give him in place of the bay mare he to take the sorrel mare now 5 years old and to have sorrel mare above his share of my personal estate and to be paid $100 for work on the farm during this year. I have not mentioned my wife as the law provides for her. The sale not to take place before Sep.

Execs. my sons **John A.** and Stephen Biddle and my friend James B. Ricaud. Witnesses James Urie, Joseph N. Gordon Jr., Thomas Copper. Written June 6, 1843 Proved Nov. 16, 1843 p. 151

Rebecca Turner free woman of color of Chestertown
To my granddau. **Rebecca Turner** wife of **Alexander Turner** all my wearing. To my grandson **Edward** otherwise called **Edward Boyer** all my beds and bed clothes. All the residue of my furniture and property to my grandsons **James Oliver** and Edward Boyer. To my grandson James Oliver all that part of my lot on Queen Street commencing at the SE corner of the dwelling house in which I now live and running in a straight line N or NW until it intersects a line drawn from the SE corner of the lot of Joseph Wickes, then W until it intersects a straight line drawn from the SW corner of my dwelling house passing through the garden then with said line reversed to the said SW corner of said dwelling house and then with Queen Street to the beginning including the house on condition that my said grandson James Oliver shall permit my dau. **Nancy** to use during her life the kitchen part free of rent. She is to occupy said kitchen and not rent. And my grandson James Oliver shall not lay claim to the house I permitted him to build on part of my ground which house I give to my grandson Edward Boyer. To my grandson Edward Boyer all that part of the lot lying to the W of the straight line with the lot of Joseph Wickes, the lot of Dr. **B. F. Houston** and the heirs of **Jane Fray** and by and with Queen Street. To my grandsons James Oliver and Edward Boyer all that lot and part of the lot situate on the E of the first line mentioned in the devise to my grandson James Oliver and binding on Queen Street and running back to the lot of Dr. **George W. Thomas** to be divided between them by a straight line commencing at the center of the front part of a lot in Queen Street and running back to the lot of Dr. George W. Thomas the part next the dwelling when divided to be held by my grandson James Oliver and the other part to be held by my grandson Edward Boyer and Edward to have the free use of half of the stable and carriage house or to be paid an equivalent by my said grandson James Oliver. The rest of my estate to my 2 grandsons James Oliver and Edward Boyer. If a problem arises with the division of land then to be decided by Dr. **Joseph N. Gordon** and **James B. Ricaud**

Execs. my 2 grandsons James Oliver and Edward Boyer. Witnesses George Vickers, Joseph N. Gordon Jr., James F. Gordon. Written Sep. 15, 1841 Proved Nov. 16, 1843 (Nov. 21 came George) p. 153

Abstracts of Kent Co., MD Wills 1777-1867 (WB 12)

Titus Maslin of Kent Co
To my nephew **Francis Titus Maslin** alias **Titus Maslin,** fourth son of my brother **Joseph Maslin** $500 when he is 21. To my sister **Ann Wilson** the wife of **John G. Wilson** $100 annually during her life and not subject to her husband. To my nephew **John Joseph Maslin,** third son of my brother Joseph Maslin all my real estate whereon I now dwell in Broad Neck containing about 180 acres subject to $100 annually to my sister. All the rest of my estate to my nephew John Joseph Maslin except my wearing apparel and that I give to my brother **Jacob Maslin** should he be living at my death, if not then my wearing apparel to my brother Joseph.

Exec. my nephew John Joseph Maslin. Witnesses William Camp, Augusta Camp, John B. Camp. Written July 7, 1843 Proved Nov. 14, 1843 p. 156

Henry Hurtt of Kent Co
To my dau. **Milla Minta Henry** $300 or to that due from me to my dau. **Mary Rebecca Hurtt** which was willed to her by her grandfather **James Bevins** and afterwards paid to me. To my son **James Clinton Hurtt** $300 or a sum equal to it due from me to my son **William Thomas Hurtt** which was willed to him as a legacy by James Bevins' last will. The money willed to James Clinton to be put to interest until he is 21 and interest to his guardian Mary R. Hurtt and I wish him to be bound out to a trade or placed in a store where he may learn to work. My negro man **James Wilmer** to be set free. To my son William Thomas Hurtt my negro woman **Emoline Carrol** to serve until 30 and my bay colt black hawl, a compensation for his services. To my dau. Mary R. Hurtt my 2 negroes **Ann Turner** and **Eliza** each to serve until age 30. To my dau. Milla Minta Henry 2 negroes **Martha Ann** and her child **Lewesa** or **Lewisir** to serve until age 30. To my son James Clinton my 2 boys **James** commonly called **Buck** (son of **Sara**) to serve until he is 30, also my bound boy **George Harris** until he is 21. All the negroes to be valued and taken as part of their estate. unsigned will

Exec. Not Given. Witnesses Not Given (**James Hurtt** made oath that his brother Henry Hurtt within a week of his death asked him to get his will but he did not and after his death he found it among his papers, and he believes it to be his writing) (Mrs. **Sarah Camp** said she was present when her deceased brother Henry requested James to get his will which he said was alright except **Pat** and her child, but he could not make it any better). Written Not Dated Proved Nov. 21, 1843 p. 157

Thomas Taylor of Kent Co
To my dau. **Mary Ann Milly** $10 but not subject to her husband's debts. To my son **Thomas Taylor** $20, not subject to his debts. To my son **John Taylor** $20, not subject to his debts. My lease hold lot in the precincts of Chestertown it being part of the college grounds of Washington College and all my lot containing 8 acres situate on the main road leading from Chestertown to Goose Hill and adjoining the lot of **Pere Smith** and others formerly a tract owned by **Isaac Cannell** and the residue of my estate to my friend **John W. Walker** in trust for my sons **Alexander Taylor** and my granddau. **Mary Elizabeth**

Milly, 3/4 to my son Alexander and ¼ to my granddaughter. If either dies then to survivor.

Exec. my friend John W. Walker. Witnesses Joseph Redue, Benjamin Vanhorn, James Boon. Written Oct. 3, 1843 Proved Mar. 11, 1844 p. 159

Hezakiah Coleman of Kent Co

To my **Catharine** during her life all that tract whereon I reside purchased of **Simon Wickes Sr.**, also the tracts purchased of **Hiram Jones** and **Richard Spencer** provided she remains single. If she marries then to have only her 1/3. And to her my personal estate during her life. To my grandson **William Henry Coleman** all the land during his life and if he dies without heirs then to my grandson **John Thomas Coleman**, and if he dies then to my grandson **John A. Rollinson**. To my grandson John A. Rollinson one feather bed and one bay gelding called Tryall and if the horse becomes unfit for service then to have $30 in lieu. Residue of my estate to my grandson William Henry Coleman

Exec. my wife Catharine Coleman. Witnesses Samuel Griffith, Philemon Knotts, Benedict S. Brevitt. Written May 13, 1840 Proved Jan. 15, 1844 p. 161

James Briscoe of Kent Co

All my property to my sons **Joseph, Daniel** and **James Alfred** and my dau. **Sarah Elizabeth**. My man **Pere** free at end of the year, **Maria** aged 27 years last April, and **Sarah** aged 26 years last January, free at age 35 provided that they leave the state. My negro man **Perry** must leave the state at the end of the year. [Maria bill of sale since will was made.] My negroes **William Alexander** who was born Oct. 8, 1836, **James** was born Feb. 4, 1838, shall be free at age 34. My negroes **Elizabeth** who was born July 30, 1839, **Sarah** who was born Sep. 1841, to be free at age 1830 provided they leave the state. **George W. Crossley** guardian to my children and my sons may be put to a trade. To **Elizabeth Crossly** $20 per year for taking care of my dau. until age 16.

Exec. my friend **George Washington Crossley**. Witnesses Dr. Peregrine Wroth, Thomas A. Edwards, William L. Lassell. Written June 6, 1842 Proved Mar. 12, 1844 p. 163

John Constable of Kent Co

To my dau. **Elizabeth Walker** the store and dwelling where she now resides beginning 2 feet from the E end of the dwelling on the main street and running back in a parallel line with a lot belonging to **George Westcott**, also a negro girl **Ann** to serve until age 25 she being 7, also 1/3 share of my Whaland farm. To **John W. Walker** in trust for my dau. **Mary Brown** the residue of my lot on the main street with the 2 shops standing thereon, also my house and lot in Water Street with the furniture therein contained, also a negro **Sal** about 6 years old to serve to 25 years old and 1/6 part of my Whaland farm should my dau. Mary Browne die without lawful issue the 2 shops on Main Street shall descend to my dau. Elizabeth Walker the house and lot in Water Street shall be divided equally between my 2 granddaughters children of my son John namely **Mary** and

Isabella Constable. If my dau. Mary dies then 1/6 part of my Whaland farm to my dau. Elizabeth, My man **Bill** to serve to 28 years of age. To my son **Albert Constable** my Forrest farm to him if he pays his brother **John Constable** $600 in 2 years, also my negro boys **Ned** and **Henry** who are each to serve until they are 28, Ned being about 13 and Henry about 8, also a girl **Caroline** to serve until 30 years. To my son John Constable 1/3 part of my Whaland farm, $600 paid by his brother Albert, also ½ my personal estate. To my son **William** 1/6 of my Whaland farm, also ½ my personal estate. To my wife $120 in lieu of her dower, my sons Albert, John, and John W. Walker to pay $40 each. My negro woman **Ann** to be free at my death. My negro woman **Harriot** to be free at my death, her child to be free at 25. [Freedom pass granted to Ned Sep. 23, 1856 & Henry. written in margin]

Exec. John W. Walker. Witnesses A. W. Sparks, Samuel Frazier, N. G. Westcott. Written May 19, 1841 Proved June 3, 1844 p. 164

Edward B. Tilden of Kent Co
To be buried along side my wife. To my son **Lawrence Washington** the farm whereon I now live, also the field which I purchased of **John B. Morris** of Baltimore. To my son **John H. Tilden** all the lands which I possess on the left hand side of the public road leading from St. Pauls church to Fairlee. To my son Lawrence Washington Tilden the lot of woodland which I purchased of the trustee for the sale of the real estate of the late **John Ireland** deceased, also my 8-day clock. My personal estate to be sold and divided among my 2 children **Sarah E. Hubbel** and **Charles Tilden**.

Exec. my son Charles Tilden. Witnesses Dr. Jacob Fisher, Nathaniel Voshell, Richard Gudgeon. Written Apr. 2, 1844 Proved Apr. 9, 1844 p. 166

Benjamin Arnoe of Kent Co
To my wife **Rebecca Arnoe** the whole of my estate and that she will do a mother's part to my adopted son **Benjamin Franklin Cox**.

Exec. Not Given. Witnesses John Spencer, Bedingfield H. Spencer, Edward Vansant. Written Apr. 13, 1844 Proved May 21, 1844 (June 11 came John) p. 167

Thomas Smith of Chestertown, Kent Co
To my cousin **Margarett Thomas** of Baltimore $1,000, with all the furniture of my room and all my wearing apparel. To my **Dr. Peregrine Wroth** $300 for his kindness to me in my sickness. To my much esteemed **Alexander Yearly** of Baltimore $300. To Rev. **Levi Scott** of the Philadelphia Conference $100. To **Mary Cooper** wife of Rev. **Ignatius T. Cooper** $100. To **Louisa Browne** dau. of **Edward Brown** Esq. of Quaker Neck $200. To the Trustees of the Methodist Episcopal Church in Chestertown $200 to paint externally and repairing the meeting house. To the Philadelphia Conference I give my journal to be corrected and printed for the use of the travelling preachers if the

conference shall judge it expedient. The balance to my cousin Margarett Thomas. To **Levi Wroth** my silver watch, saddle and bridle.

Execs. my 2 friends Dr. P. Wroth and Alexander Yearly. Witnesses Nathaniel Wiley, Thomas Baker. Written Oct. 7, 1842 Proved May 28, 1844 (Codicils proved June 1 by Nathaniel Wiley) p. 167

Codicil I give to the Methodist Episcopal Church in Chestertown $200 for the privilege being buried under the alter of the meeting house. Written Oct. 17, 1842 To Mrs. **Elizabeth Punkers** my britchous picture. I deduct from Louisa Browne's legacy $100 and give it to Rev. Levi Scott making his legacy $200.

2nd Codicil To Dr. Wroth $50. To **Mary Ann Blackiston** $25. To **Caty Salter** $25. Written Apr. 1844.

Cornelius Gee of Kent Co
To my wife **Mary Gee** all my estate

Exec. my wife. Witnesses James Gale, James H. Smith, John H. Young. Written Feb. 4, 1844 Proved June 25, 1844 (June 29 came James Smith) p. 169

Charles T. Browne of Kent Co
All my estate to my nieces 2/3 to **Margaret F. Browne** dau. of **James F. Browne** and 1/3 **Mary Catherine Ringgold** dau. of Richard W. Ringgold. If my niece Margaret wants she may purchase the 1/3 of my niece Mary Catherine. My brother James F. Browne shall take the rents for my debts.

Exec. my brother James F. Browne. Witnesses G. M. Gilbert, James Harris Jr., R. T. Browne. Written June 24, 1844 Proved July 1, 1844 p. 170

Martha Hynson
To my dau. **Sarah Ann Hynson** one bed of her choice. To my dau. **Laura Lavinia Hynson** one bed her second choice and 10 silver tea spoons marked J.M.H. To my dau. **Harriot M. Nicols** wife of **James Nicols** 6 table spoons and the rest of my silver tea spoons and one pair of silver sugar tongs, my mahogany breakfast table, my large looking glass in the parlor and one small dressing glass, my set of Britannia Ware, and all the earthen ware in the cupboard, all my carpets, one large nailed trunk, one pine candlestand, one safe and the rest of my personal estate. To my dau. Harriot M. Nicols wife of **James K. Nicols** my sorrel mare and gig and harness at her disposal as if she were not married. To my son **John C. Hynson** to take charge of his two sisters **Sarah Ann** and **Laura Lavinia**.

Exec. my son John C. Hynson. Witnesses William Camp, William Copper, Susan A. Copper. Written July 3, 1842 Proved Sep. 10, 1844 p. 171

Abstracts of Kent Co., MD Wills 1777-1867 (WB 12)

John Humphreys of Kent Co

To my granddau. **Emily Catharine Humphreys** the brick dwelling house wherein I now reside with the kitchen, smoke house and poultry house with the lot attached lying on the SE side of the brick dwelling bounded as the fence now stands dividing it from a small lot situated on the NW side of the said brick house. If she dies then to my grandson **John Thomas Neal**. To my dau. **Catherine Bradshaw** my negro man **Nathan** a slave for life. To my granddau. **Ann Louisa Humphreys** my negro girl **Maria**. To my granddau. **Mary Louisa Neal** my negro girl **Sarah**, also 6 silver table spoons and my silver soup ladle. To my grandson John Thomas Neal my negro man **Henry**. To my grandson **James M. Page** my negro woman **Mary** and negro boy **Thomas**. To my son **John Humphreys** one old fowling piece. To my dau. **Louisa Neal** the house and granary now occupied by **Samuel C. Ozman** with the wharf and all the ground from the margin of the Creek to the plank fence on the N end of the brick building in which I live with the small lot on the NW side of the said brick house none of which is included in the part of land devised to my granddau. **Emily Catherine Humphreys** but a right of wharf and use of the road is reserved to Emily. The rest of my estate to Louisa Neal.

Exec. my son John Humphreys. Witnesses S. C. Ozman, Thomas Miller, William Shaw. Written Dec. 21, 1843 Proved Nov. 4, 1844 p. 172

Ann Rollins late of Baltimore City, but now in Kent Co, merchant

To my grandsons **Theophilus Waters Russell, John Hamer Russell, James Alexander Russell,** and **William George Russell** and my granddau. **Hester Ann Russell**, sons and dau. of my son **John Russell**, my house and lot which I purchased of **Thomas Taylor** situated on High Street in Chestertown, also my house and lot which I purchased of Mrs. **Emeline Dugan** situated in the upper part of Chestertown, also a certain debt due me by their father, my said son John Russell and all the money I have and what I have in the Savings Bank of Baltimore to my said grandchildren. My granddau. Hester Ann Russell my gold watch. To my grandchildren all my estate. My son John Russell trustee for my grandchildren.

Exec. my son John Russell. Witnesses Thomas Edgar, John W. Carroll, Thomas C. Pinkind. Written July 19, 1844 Proved Nov. 11, 1844 (Nov. 12 came Thomas Edgar and John Carroll) p. 174

James Mansfield of Kent Co

To my wife **Ann Mansfield** during her life all my estate as long as she maintains my dau. **Margarett Sullivan** and her child during the life of my wife and to be maintained by her if her husband **James Sullivan** does not maintain them. Part of my estate to be sold for my debts. My wife may take what she may want at the appraisement. I free from slavery my negro boy **Emory** Dec. 25, 1855 [pass granted Dec. 26, 1855]. I free from slavery my negro boy **Joshua** after Dec. 25, 1857. To my children **James Mansfield, Mary Ann Vickers,** Margarett Sullivan, **John Mansfield, Isabella Price,** and my granddau. **Catharine Tomlinson** all my estate upon the death of my wife. My dau.

Margaret Sullivan's part in hands of my son James in trust for her. If she dies then to my other 4 children and grandchild named.

Execs. my son James Mansfield and my son in law George Vickers. Witnesses David Arthur, Daniel Sparklin, John T. Dodd. Written Feb. 24, 1844 Proved Nov. 18, 1844 (David came Nov. 29) p. 176

William Wroth of Kent Co
To my dau. in law **Mary Louisa Cooper** $500 when she is 18. If she dies then to my dau. in law **Martha Amanda Cooper** which was devised to her sister Mary Louisa Cooper. To my wife **Louisa Wroth** all the remainder of my personal estate. To my wife Louisa Wroth my farm or all lands I own during her life, then to my nephew **William Wroth Apsley**.

Exec. my wife Louisa Wroth. Witnesses Sally M. Perkins, Ann W. Perkins, John Perkins. Written Nov. 22, 1843 Proved Feb. 5, 1845 p. 178

James C. Eagle of Kent Co
To my wife **Julia** all my estate except $5 to my son **Solomon Eagle** and $5 to my dau. **Ann Gresham**.

Exec. Not Given. Witnesses Benedict S. Brevitt, Jacob Fisher. Written Jan. 19, 1844 Proved Feb. 11, 1845 p. 179

Sarah Piner Wickes of Chestertown
o my niece **Mary E. Wickes** $100 annually paid by my brother during his life and after his death, my undivided 1/3 part of the farm near Chestertown called *"Piner's Grove"*. To each of my nephews **Benjamin Chambers Wickes, Joseph A. Wickes, Ezekial C. Wickes**, and **Peregrine L. Wickes** a gold watch to be selected by their father when they are 21. To my nieces **Hester Henrietta Van Bibber Wickes** and **Sarah A. Wickes** $500 when they are 18. To my sister Elizabeth C. Wickes a pair of gold spectacles and a gold pencil. To my niece Mary E. Wickes my mahogany wardrobe, marble top washstand, circular table, carpet, best bed, bolster with the Chintz curtains and my girl **Jane** the dau. of **Charlott**. To my niece Hester Henrietta Van Bibber Wickes my mahogany bureau, small highpost bed with the dimity curtains and my girl **Betsey** dau. of Charlott. To my niece Sarah A. Wickes my low post bed, 12 tea spoons, and 6 desert spoons of silver, also my girl **Ann** dau. of **Beckey**. I free my servant woman **Bett** and give her $10 annually. All the remainder to my brother **Joseph Wickes**.

Exec. my brother Joseph Wickes. Witnesses W. R. Maxwell, Frances E. Maxwell, E. F. Chambers. Written July 26, 1844 Proved Feb. 17, 1845 p. 180

Abstracts of Kent Co., MD Wills 1777-1867 (WB 12)

Milcah Rigby of Kent Co
To **John Abbiss** of Baltimore City all that farm lying on the road from Hales Corner to Rock Hall and which I reside containing 72 acres and which I got in the division of my father's estate; upon the following trusts. the net rents to my nephew **James B. D. Hurtt** for his life, not subject to his debts. After his death to his heirs but if none then to **Henry N. Hurtt Jr.** (a son of my nephew Henry N. Hurtt). Out of the money due me from **John T. Stevens** I give Henry N. Hurtt $50, **Richard H. Hurtt** $50, **Walter T. Hurtt** $50, and any surplus to **Frances H. Abbiss** and **Mary Elizabeth Hurtt**. To my niece **Ann Sophia Hurtt** all the money due me from a note of **Nathan Hatcheson** except $100 which I give to my nephew Henry N. Hurtt. I give to my niece Ann Sophia Hurtt her choice of bed and 2 extra bed quilts. I give to Ann Sophia Hurtt my niece, a judgement I have in Kent Co court against **Lodourck W. Morgan** for about $300. To my niece **Sarah Catharine Abbiss** $250 to be paid out of a note of **Joseph Harris**, a silver soup ladle and 6 old fashioned china plates. To my niece **Margarett Frances Hurtt** a note for about $60 due from **William Copper** at age 30 and to my niece Margarett Frances Hurtt (dau. of **John Hurtt**) $50. To my nephew Walter T. Hurtt and Richard H. Hurtt $100 each out of money due me from Joseph Harris. To my nephew **James Alexander Hurtt** $150 out of note due me from **Alexander W. Ringgold**. To my nephew Henry Hurtt $50 out of obligation due me from Alexander W. Ringgold, the balance of said note is given to James Alexander Hurtt. Henry N. Hurtt $100 out of the bond of Nathan Hatcheson, the balance paid to Ann Sophia Hurtt. To my nephew Henry N. Hurtt the further sum of $100. To **Levi Chase** a free man of color, whom I liberated $50 for his faithful services as my slave. All the rest of my estate to my niece Margarett Frances Hurtt and my nephew Walter T. Hurtt, Richard H. Hurtt and Robert M. Hurtt, not to be given until age 30 or marriage.

Exec. John Abbiss of Baltimore City. Witnesses George Vickers, Thomas Price, James F. Gordon. Written Sep. 3, 1842 Proved Mar. 18, 1845 (James came Mar. 22) p. 181

Ann E. Wilmer of Kent Co
By a deed dated Feb. 7, 1800 **Darius Dunn Jr.** conveyed to **Benjamin Hanson** and my father **Samuel Eccleston** a part of a tract called *"Arcadia"* which about 1804 was divided between Benjamin Hanson and the children and heirs of my deceased father Samuel Eccleston by a writ of partition issued from Kent Co. All my right in said tract I give to my brother **John B. Eccleston**. To my dau. **Sarah R. Ramsey** my wearing apparel and all my furniture. To my brother John B. Eccleston $1,000 during his life in trust to pay the interest to my dau. Sarah not subject to her husband. The principal to be paid to her if my brother dies. If she dies while my brother is living then to my son in law **Albert C. Ramsey** if he is then living. The residue of my personal estate including money due me by my brother, to my brother John B. Eccleston.

Exec. my brother John B. Eccleston. Witnesses Peregrine Wroth, Elizabeth C. Wickes, Laura Chambers. Written Mar. 13, 1845 Proved Mar. 25, 1845 p. 184

Liber 12 1835-1854

James P. Gale of Kent Co
To be buried near the remains of my brother's late wife under a white oak tree in St. Paul's Churchyard. To my wife **Mary T. Gale** all the 4 rooms in the high part of my dwelling house, the necessary use of the kitchen, both the yards and garden with all the fruit, half the apple orchard, the carriage and 3 stalls in the stable, 20 barrels of corn and 20 bushels of wheat annually of the best quality raised on the farm, the use of such part of the granary and corn house as may be necessary to keep her grain in as she may need to burn and a 24-hour clock during her life. To my wife all my furniture, first choice of 2 horses, my 4-wheel carriage, first choice of 2 cows, the privilege of raising 5 hogs and pasturage for 2 horses, 2 cows, and 5 hogs and a quantity of coarse provender for same, also my horse cart. I give her a right of way over the road as it now runs from the yard above devised to the public road and all the poultry that belongs to the farm. To my nephew **James H. Gale** a 24-hour clock after the death of wife Mary T. Gale. To **Mary T. Browne** dau. of **James T. Browne** and **Ann E. Browne** first choice of a cow. To my wife my servant woman **Sarah Ann** to serve as the will of my late mother directs until Jan. 1, 1857 then free. Also her child **Jacob** to serve until Jan. 1, 1870 and my servant woman **Lavinia** who is much afflicted and that she may be taken good care of. To **Jim** and **Ben** servants of my brother and children of **Ben** and **Easter** my wearing apparel. To have tombstones placed at the head and foot of my grave and my burial to be paid out of the first grain of my farm. My brother **John E. Gale** to sell my land that was formerly sold to **Bartus Trew** and purchased by me of **John B. Eccleston** trustee for the sale of Bartus Trew described in a plot made by **Thomas Gale** containing 170 acres, 3 roods and 3 perches to be sold. To my brother John E. Gale the remainder of my estate provided he pays my wife Mary T. Gale $200 annually during her life.

Exec. my brother John E. Gale (or my friend James F. Browne if John declines). Witnesses Jacob T. Freeman, Horatio Beck, Emory Sudler. Written Mar. 22, 1845 Proved Mar. 31, 1845 p. 185

Jane Blake of Kent Co
My estate to be sold by my executor. To my sister **Catharine Kelly** now of Baltimore $100 per year for life. To my niece **Mary Jane Hickey** dau. of my said sister $50 a year during her life separate from her husband. To each of the children of my said niece Mary Jane Hickey $100 per annum to educate them from ages 5 to the age to be put to a trade. If my niece Mary Jane has another child then the annuity given to her to the additional children's education. They are to be educated by the Sisters of Charity in Baltimore. To the Rev. **George King** of the Roman Catholic Church in Cecil Co $100. To Dr. **Peregrine Wroth** of Chestertown $100. To my negro woman **Becky** freedom at my death and $20. [freedom pass granted to Becky Apr. 14, 1856] To **Katy Salter** (fn) living in Chestertown my red cow with a short tail. To **Miss Mary Cruikshanks** $100. To my nieces children now living or to be born $100 to set up in their trade and if any die under 21 and then to survivors. A further sum of $500 to be given at age 21 or marriage and if that is before arrival at age then with the approbation of their father and executor. To **John Byram** the present tenant of the farm whereon I now live $100. To

Abstracts of Kent Co., MD Wills 1777-1867 (WB 12)

the Most Rev. **Samuel Eccleston,** Archbishop of the Roman Catholic Church all the residue of my estate to use in a manner consonant to my wishes and to him specifically 2 patch work, bed quilts and all my jewelry.

Exec. the Honorable John B. Eccleston. Witnesses James Alfred Pearce, Ann Cruikshank, Benjamin F. Houston. Written Mar. 26, 1845 Proved Apr. 11, 1845 (Apr. 19 came Benjamin) p. 187

William W. Brown of Kent Co
My servants, men and women, the children of my old woman **Jin, Henry, Tom, Sam, Richard, Mary Ann, Tempy, Jane, William, Harriett, Jim** to be free at the end of the year. The children of my woman **Mary Ann,** now at my nephew Thomas R. Browns to him, my nephew. To **Mary Ann Benton** $700 and the Eagle Town lot upon E side of the road leading to Rock Hall so much as is enclosed. To my nephew Thomas R. Brown all the residue of my estate. I give **Alexander Wheat** $30, $20 of which he has.

Exec. my nephew Thomas R. Brown. Witnesses Jacob Fisher, L.M. Ricaud, Mordicai Dillehunt, Merritt Miller. Written Apr. 4, 1845 Proved Apr. 15, 1845 p. 190

Casar Wilson of Kent Co
To my wife **Araminta** all my personal estate and if I survive her then to my son **Frederick** and my 2 daughters **Caroline** the wife of **Zachariah Thompson** and **Sophia** the wife of **Daniel Roe.** To my son Frederick Wilson that portion of the house and lot situated in Kent on a public road leading to the state road which leads from Georgetown Cross Roads to Chestertown, on one portion of which I now reside and my son Frederick now occupies, the other portion to be divided by a straight line across the said lot and the part adjoining the public road to him and the other part to my dau. Caroline for her assistance and for whatever claim she may have for 3 years and then after 3 years to my dau. Caroline and my dau. Sophia.

Exec. my wife Araminta. Witnesses T. B. Darrach, Thomas K. Stephens, William B. Redgrave. Written Sep. 14, 1843 Proved May 6, 1845 p. 191

William Woodall of Kent Co
To my son **Isaac Woodall** one negro woman **Ann** and her boy **Jacob,** also one bed. To **William Burch** son of **Rachel Burch** or otherwise **William Woodall** one negro man **Bill** and one negro boy **Perry,** one bed, one milch cow, one heifer, one yoke of oxen and yoke and all my horses of both sex young and old, also one ox cart, one bird gun, one crop cut saw, one hand saw, one drawing knife, one grindstone, 2 narrow axes, also all my plows, harrows, cultivation, all scythes, and crafles, plow gears, cart gears, and singletrees. To **Sary Ann Burch** dau. of Rachel Burch or otherwise called **Sary Ann Woodall** one negro woman **Fan** and her child **Lize,** one bed, one choice milch cow and 2 heifers, one Franklin clock, one high top bed, one walnut desk, one mahogany table, 6 large silver table spoons, one blue pine chest, 6 chairs, all my poultry such as geese,

Liber 12 1835-1854

turkeys, ducks and dungle fowls. To **John Samuel Burch** son of Rachel Burch or otherwise **John Samuel Woodall** one negro man **Joseph** and one negro boy **Edward**, one bed and $250 when he is 21. If he dies then to William Burch or Sary Ann Burch. To **Freeman Bishop** son of **Lidia Bishop** or otherwise **Freeman B. Woodall** so called, one milch cow and $100. To my dau. **Ann Dillihunt** one negro woman **Mary** and her son **Alfred** and her dau. **Mary Ellen,** also all rents. To my granddau. **Mary Dillihunt** dau. of Ann Dillihunt and **Thomas Dillihunt** one negro girl **Pris** all the residue of my personal estate divided between my dau. Ann Dillihunt, **Elizabeth Peacock**, and my granddau. **Mary Dillihunt** dau. of **Mordica Dillihunt.** To my son **Jesse Woodall** all my lands situated in Kent Co in the vicinity of New Market or otherwise called *"Chesterville"* called *"Viana"*, *"Stepney"* and *"Stepney Fields"*

Exec. my son Jesse Woodall. Witnesses Hezekiah Masten, Horace F. Roberts, John Newcomb. Written July 12, 1854 Proved May 6, 1845 p. 192

Jane Toulson of Kent Co
To my friends **Joseph Usilton** and **Robert Usilton** all my estate in trust for my dau. **Susan Jane Ashley** wife of **John R. Ashley** during her life. After her death then to her issue.

Exec. Samuel G. Kennard. Witnesses James B. Ricaud, Joseph N. Gordon, J.F. Gordon. Written Sep. 14, 1839 Proved May 14, 1845 p. 194

John Cole of Kent Co
To my brother **Abraham Cole** my house and lot at Masseys Cross Roads during his life and then to his son **John Emory Cole**. To my niece **Eliza Cochran** the residue of my personal estate except my negroes. To **Charles R. Hackett** my house and lot known as the *"Garland Lot"*. Whereas my negroes **Joseph, Stephen, Edwin, Elizabeth,** and her 2 children **Eveline** and **Frances** have serve faithfully, I set them free.

Exec. my brother Abraham Cole. Witnesses Thomas Stewart, Richard D. Downing, Isaac Ryland. Written Sep. 14, 1841 Proved June 10, 1845 p. 195

Araminta J. Gale wife of John E. Gale of Kent Co
To my husband John E. Gale all my undivided right to the moiety or half part of that tract situated on the Bay side in Kent known as *"Gresham College"* and containing 458 3/4 acres which was conveyed by my said husband and me to a certain **James P. Gale** and **Isaac Gale** recorded among the land records.

Exec. Not Given. Witnesses J. Brown 3rd, William W. Brown, James Brown. Written Dec. 25, 1838 Proved June 7, 1845 p. 196

Abstracts of Kent Co., MD Wills 1777-1867 (WB 12)

Renunciation I **Mary T. Gale** widow of **James P. Gale** late of Kent Co renounce all right to the bequests of the will of my late husband and elect my right under the laws of Maryland. Written June 17, 1845. Witnesses James F. Browne [see page 185]

Edward Stoops of Kent Co
I will a bond given by my cousin **Perry Price** to me as part payment of a claim I held against my uncle **Benjamin Price**. To **Mary Hyland Howard** $100 of the money my cousin **Isaac Lewis Price** owes me. To Isaac Lewis Price the balance of his bond to him. To my cousin **Philina Howard** the amount of money due me by her father **Joseph Howard**. To **Anna Maria Price** $50 which my cousin **Benjamin Franklin Price** is to pay her out of what he owes me. To my cousin Benjamin Franklin Price the remainder of his bond. My carpenters tools to **George Washington Price** son of **John Price**. To my cousin **William Henry Price** all the rest of my estate.

Exec. my cousin William Henry Price. Witnesses Dr. Robert T. Allen, Sarah J. Ringgold. Written May 30, 1845 Proved June 14, 1845 p. 197

William M. Redgrave of Kent Co
From 40 to 50 acres of my land on the N and E end of my farm being bounded by the lands of **Hezekiah Masten, Samuel Jarman** and the lands of the late **David Hartt**, with all my personal estate to be sold. The residue to my 3 children **Lancelot W. Redgrave, Millyminta R. Redgrave, Joseph H. Redgrave** and my wife **Millyminta Redgrave**. The heirs of the late **William Moffett** to have the preference in the purchase of the land when sold

Exec. my brother **Lancelot Moffett**. Witnesses William Graves, Parker Selby, Josiah Newton. Written June 7, 1845 Proved June 17, 1845 p. 198

Sarah Jones of Kent Co
To my brother **Jacob Jones** all my estate as well as what may be coming to me from the estate of my deceased sister Temperance

Exec. my brother Jacob Jones. Witnesses William Graves, Joseph Middletown, Rebecca E. Middleton. Written Jan. 31, 1835 Proved July 22, 1845 p. 199

Jacob Jones of Kent Co
I give all my personal estate to my sister **Sarah Jones**. I give all my real estate to my sister Sarah Jones during her life and after her decease to my friend **Joseph Wickes** of Chestertown

Exec. my friend Joseph Wickes. Witnesses David Collins, James B. Parrish, Charles Tilden of William. Written Sep. 2, 1841 Proved July 22, 1845 p. 200

Liber 12 1835-1854

Sophia Neal of Kent Co
To my dau. **Augusta Camp** $1,500 paid in 5 years. To my son **Horatio Beck** the farm which I purchased of **Daniel Perkins'** heirs on which he now resides and one of 3 bonds each for $2,000 due me from my said son, the remaining 2 to my personal estate. To my dau. **Amanda Melvina Hurtt** $2,000. To my dau. **Clementia Riley** $2,000. To my grandson **George William Camp** $500 to be paid in 2 years. My executor to have in trust my negroes **Shadarick** to serve until Jan. 1, 1852, **Rebecca** to serve until Jan. 1, 1858, **Alexander** to serve until Jan. 1, 1867; to be hired for the benefit of my children viz. Augusta Camp, Horatio Beck, **Benj. F. Beck**, Amanda Melvina Hurtt and Clementia Riley. My negroes to get $50 at their release. My lot in Chestertown now in the occupancy of **Simon Wickes Jr.** and all the residue of my estate to my children Augusta Camp, Horatio Beck, Benj. F. Beck, Amanda Melvina Hurtt and Clementia Riley. [freedom pass granted to Shadrick Oct. 28, 1856. written in margin]

Exec. my son Horatio Beck. Witnesses Mary E. Scott, Dr. Thomas H. Whaland, James F. Browne. Written Mar. 10, 1845 Proved Aug. 11, 1845 (Aug. 12 came Dr. Thomas) p. 201

Harriet M. Spencer of Kent Co
I give all my right in and to part of a tract of land called *"Ratcliff Cross"* situated near Chestertown unto my husband **Samuel W. Spencer** for his life and after his life then to any child I may have living but if I have none living then to my brother **William S. Chapman** and if he dies without heirs then to **Ann Sudler** and **Harriet M. Sudler** daughters of my cousin **Emory Sudler**. My negro girl **Annette** to my aunt **Ann Sudler** during her life and after to my husband **Samuel W. Spencer**. To **Anne Sudler** dau. of my cousin Emory my negro girl **Flora** to serve her until she is 35. To Harriett M. Sudler my negro girl **Eliza Ann** or **Ann Eliza** (dau. of my woman **Caroline**). To my brother William S. Chapman my negro boy **James** who will belong to me at the decease of my aunt and who will be free at age 36, that being the term he has to serve under the will of my sister. I give him also my negro girls **Hester** (dau. of **Ailcey**) and **Lavinia** (dau. of Caroline) to serve until age 35. To my husband Samuel W. Spencer my woman Caroline to serve for 8 years. Also to him my negroes **Anna** and **Alonzo** to serve him for the terms of the will of my sister. And to my husband Samuel W. Spencer the negroes **Daniel** (son of **Sally**), **Alick** (son of Caroline), **Clinton**, **Sally**, and **Henrietta** until age 38 and all other servants I may have until they are age 38. Any issue of my slaves to be free at 35 and not to be sold out of state. To my aunt Ann Sudler the choice of my wearing apparel and the remainder to Mrs. **E. Sudler** and my cousins the Miss Sudlers of Annapolis as a token of my affection. My husband to pay my brother William $40 during his life, to start after the decease of my aunt Ann Sudler. My husband to place a tombstone over the graves of my father and mother from the rent of my lands. To my husband Samuel W. Spencer my negro women **Julia** and **Ailcey** for their remaining terms of service as trustee to complete the trusts confided to me by the will of my sister. To my husband my negro man **Alexas** to serve until all my debts paid. If I have children living then the negroes given to Ann Sudler, Anne Sudler, H.M. Sudler

Abstracts of Kent Co., MD Wills 1777-1867 (WB 12)

and my brother William S. Chapman to go to said child and the $40 to my brother null and void. To my husband all the furniture in my chamber and the remainder of my estate.

Exec. Not Given. Witnesses Lawrence M. Ricaud, Joseph N. Gordon, Jr., James Frisby Gordon. Written Apr. 23, 1840 Proved Oct. 6, 1845 p. 203

Sarah Nowland of Kent Co
To my son **Benedict T. Nowland** all my estate, except my negro man **Frisby** who I will free on Dec. 31 next.

Exec. my son Benedict T. Nowland. Witnesses William A. Brice, Simon W. Boyer, John Gonce. Written Sep. 11, 1845 Proved Oct. 8, 1845 p. 205

Samuel Groome Kennard
I give all my real estate to my wife **Sarah** during her life if she shall remain a widow. After her widowhood I give all my real estate to my dau. **Adaline G. Kennard** during her life and after her life to my friends **John B. Eccleston** and **Ezekial F. Chambers** in trust for support of her issue. If she dies without issue, then to divide in 12 and give 5/12 to **Sarah E. Kennard** dau. of my deceased brother **John** and 4/12 to **Harriott Kennard** dau. of my deceased brother **Philip** and the remaining 3/12 to **Mary Ann Kennard** the dau. of my sister **Elizabeth**. Out of 40 acres of my farm on which I reside being that part of my farm lying on the other or E side of the branch or meadow making out of the cove divides the farm of **Emory Edwards** deceased from my own, pursuing said branch until it reaches the division fence between said farm of Emory Edwards deceased and my own to be sold for my debts. All the rest to my wife. My negroes free as stated, my man **Bill** on Jan. 1, 1847, **Jim Madison** on Jan. 1, 1850, my boy **Robert** on Jan. 1, 1855 when he will be about 25, my girl **Editha** on Jan. 1, 1853 when she will be about 25, my girl **Julia Ann** on Jan. 1, 1863 when she will be about 28, my woman **Sarah** on Jan. 1, 1845 when she will be about 33, **George** on Jan. 1, 1870 when he will be 30, **Jacob** on Jan. 1, 1863 when he will be about 35, **Edwin** on Jan. 1, 1861 when he will be about 35, and any child born of said women or of my woman **Henny** (who is manumitted by the will of **Mary Ann Kennard** my deceased mother in law) from and after the date, males to serve till age 28 and females to serve till age 21. [freedom passed granted to **Robert** and **Editha** Mar. 29, 1855]

Exec. my wife. Witnesses John Anderson, Kitty Kennard, Robert M. Anderson. Written Apr. 17, 1841 Proved Jan. 13, 1846 (Nov. 10, 1845 Ezekial came to prove codicil) p. 207

Codicil My man **Bill** shall continue until Jan. 1, after my death in order to serve a minimum of 1 year to benefit my wife. My woman **Sarah** to continue to serve for the benefit of my wife 2 entire years after my death. My wife shall pay Bill and Sarah $10 each. My negro woman **Julia Ann** shall serve till Jan. 1, 1865. Having manumitted

Liber 12 1835-1854

Jacob and **Edwin** at certain times it is not intended to interfere with the rights of my sister Catharine to whom the said boys belong during her life but at her death to be free should she live beyond the period mentioned. Written Sep. 2, 1845. Witnesses Mary Elizabeth Flint, John Hackett, Ezekial F. Chambers

Juliet Burgess maiden of Kent Co
Mr. **Charles D. Warfield** of Anne Arundel Co owes me $500 which I give to **Hetty Maria Warfield** my niece dau. of **Nicholas D. Warfield** of Anne Arundel Co. $100 which is to remain with Mr. Charles Warfield to be used as his best judgment for said child Hetty. To my niece **Lucy** or **Lucretia Warfield** dau. of Nicholas D. Warfield $100 in same manner. To **William Burgess** and **Vachel Burgess** children of my brother Peregrine Burgess each $100 of the same money to be paid by Mr. Charles Warfield to their father Peregrine Burgess at age 21. The remaining $100, to my niece **Frances R. Burgess** dau. of my brother **Thomas D. Burgess** $50 and the other $50 to my niece **Manelia Watkins**. To **Sarah Ann Burgess** wife of my brother Pere my bed, my dining table and shovel and tongs, also my new black silk dress, my other wearing apparel to said Sarah Ann Burgess and my 2 sisters **Harriet** and **Mary** except my cloak which I give to my friend Mrs. **Frances Wickes**. My bureau and looking glass shall be kept for my niece Hellen Burgess and given to her at age 18. My black leather trunk I give to **Rebecca Burgess** child of my brother Pere. My new bed quilt I give to **Henrietta Burgess** dau. of my brother Thomas and a blue shawl. The residue of my property between my 3 brothers Peregrine, Thomas and **Vachel,** and my 2 sisters and Harriet and Mary, except 6 silver table spoons which I give to my brother Vachel.

Exec. my brother Peregrine Burgess. Witnesses Dr. Jacob Fisher, Lambert Wickes, Hetty E. Burgess. Written Aug. 7, 1845 Proved Dec. 23, 1845 p. 210

James Gregory of Kent Co
To my wife during her life all my estate, and after to my son **John Gregory** and if he is not living then to **Elizabeth Bird** my stepdaughter.

Exec. my wife **Margret Gregory**. Witnesses William Lamb, William A. Rollison, Lewis Titter. Written Dec. 24, 1845 Proved Jan. 9, 1846 (Jan. 20 came Lewis) p. 212

John Urie of Kent Co
To my son **Henry Urie** all that tract belonging to me called *"Denby"* containing 62 acres, also the land I received of my father's estate and the land I bought of **James Urie** and no more of my estate. To my son James Urie the farm I now reside called *"Chance"*, also all the crop and the horses, cattle, hogs, farming utensils, corn in the corn house and barn, the hay and fodder and no more. To the heirs of my deceased dau. **Mary Atkinson** $1 and no more. To the heirs of my deceased son **Robert Urie** $1 and no more. To my dau. **Elizabeth Vickers** $1 and no more. To my son **William Urie** all the remainder of my personal estate in bacon, lard, household and kitchen furniture and all the money.

Abstracts of Kent Co., MD Wills 1777-1867 (WB 12)

Exec. my son **James Urie**. Witnesses Thomas Bryan, Thomas A. Strong, Benedict S. Brevitt. Written Jan. 5, 1846 Proved Jan. 27, 1846 (Jan. 28 came Thomas) p. 213

William Downey of Kent Co

To my wife **Mary Ann Downey** the provisions laid up for the support of our family, all my grey mare called Kit, 2 young cows, 6 hogs and all the poultry, the privilege of remaining in the house and cultivating the ground upon the lot where I now reside, and to my wife one equal moiety or child's part of my undivided property. To my son **William Downey** I give the lot beginning at a stone standing S from my house and running thence to a stone S on the line of **John Urie's** land then W around said lot to the beginning, as is more laid out by plat of said lot and to him my colt and my large duck gun that he now has. To my son **John** I give the lot of land on which my houses standing including all my landed property not devised to my son William laid down in a separate plat, provided he does not marry a dau. of **Dennis Vickers**, if he marries contrary to my wishes, this land to be sold and proceeds divided between my other children, and to my son John my old duck gun and all my carpenters tools. To my dau. **Mary** wife of **James Lewis** I give $10 as he has already received a child's part of my property. To each of my daughters **Betsy** and **Nancy** I give a feather bed. My black girl shall be sold and applied to my debts, with surplus to my children. All the residue of my estate to be divided between my children, my wife sharing with them. My household furniture to my wife Mary Ann Downey.

Exec. my son John Downey. Witnesses William T. Adkinson, Gary H. Leverton, Henry Urie Jr. Written Jan. 20, 1846 Proved Jan. 27, 1846 p. 214

Rebecca Barger of Kent Co

To my dau. **Mary's** son **Robert Usilton** one bed. To my dau. **Sarah's** dau. **Emily C. Usilton** 6 silver teaspoons marked F.R.L. To my dau. **Hannah's** dau. **Frances P. Usilton** 6 silver tablespoons marked F.R.L. to my dau. **Hannah's** dau. **Susan Usilton** $25. To **Susan** the black girl now living with me and dau. of **Jacob Worrell** one small bed with a striped tick, one rug, one small iron pot and small kitchen table. All the remainder to my dau. **Mary A. Usilton** during her life and after to my said dau. Mary's son Robert.

Exec. Robert Usilton. Witnesses James W. Skirven, James Beck of George, John T. Skirven. Written Mar. 4, 1843 Proved Jan. 30, 1846 (Feb. 3 came John) p. 216

William Turner of Kent Co

To my wife **Mary P. Turner** all my estate

Exec. my wife Mary P. Turner. Witnesses T. N. Tayman, John W. Palmer, Henry Hurtt. Written Mar. 23, 1842 Proved Feb. 5, 1846 p. 217

Liber 12 1835-1854

John Usilton of Kent Co
To my wife **Sarah Usilton** 1/3 part of my personal estate and her dower in my real estate, and my close carriage and my bay horse. To my son **John N. Usilton** as evidence of my affection for his kindness and attention to me and of my approbation of his conduct as a dutiful son my negro man **Alexander** of **Elick Augustus**. To my son **John N.** Usilton in trust for my dau. **Elizabeth Howard** my negro girl **Delia** and all the property contained in a bill of sale from **William Howard** to me, to permit her to use and then at her death to convey to her children. The remainder of my estate to be divided between my children **John N. Usilton, Thomas E. Usilton, Avis Louisa Usilton,** and **Sarah Frances Usilton**. If my personal estate is insufficient to pay my debts, then my son **John N.** Usilton to have power to sell portion of real estate.

Exec. my son John N. Usilton. Witnesses George Vickers, John T. Dodd, Alexander Barrett. Written Feb. 4, 1846 Proved Feb. 9, 1846 p. 218

Mary Flayhearty of Kent Co
To my sister **Rebecca Barger** all my property during her life and after her death as follows: to **Susan A. Usilton** dau. of **Francis Usilton** and his late wife **Hannah** $400, to **Emily Usilton** dau. of **Joseph** and **Sarah Usilton** 6 table spoons, 12 tea spoons, sugar tongs, one britannia coffee pot, 2 tea pots, 2 tumblers and my large looking glass and one silver soup lade. To Sarah Usilton wife of Joseph Usilton my silver snuff box. To **Adaline Usilton** dau. of **Robert** and **Mary Usilton** the balance of my money and the residue of my estate.

Exec. Not Given. Witnesses Robert T. Allen, William L. Bowers. Written May 19, 1845 Proved Feb. 9, 1846 p. 220

Elizabeth G. Worrell of Kent Co
To my friend **John B. Eccleston** $100 and to his son **John C. Eccleston** $100. All the residue to my adopted dau. **Cornelia Ricaud** wife of **James B. Ricaud**. If she dies without children then to John C. Eccleston my house and lot situated in Chestertown and the shares of stock in the Union Bank of Maryland and if he takes the land under this devise then I revoke the $100 to him. If my adopted dau. Cornelia Ricaud dies during my life then to my friend James B. Ricaud all money due me from **John E. Gale** and money due me on the assignment from John B. Eccleston against **Thomas Titus,** and all my negroes **George Hartohorn, Frank** and **Jim Henry**. If my dau. dies then to James B. Ricaud and John C. Eccleston all the residue of my personal estate, except my negro woman **Sarah** whom I set free and shall be supported by both of them. If my dau. Cornelia Ricaud survives me then the bequests to James B. Ricaud and John C. Eccleston are void, except the $200 and the negro Sarah. At her death my dau. Cornelia to make a will to distribute same.

Exec. James B. Ricaud. Witnesses H. E. Tilghman, Anna M. Tilghman, James F. Gordon. Written Feb. 5, 1846 Proved Feb. 20, 1846 p. 221

Abstracts of Kent Co., MD Wills 1777-1867 (WB 12)

Renunciation **Margarett Gregory** the widow of **James Gregory** renounce any devises in will of my husband dated Dec. 24 last and take my right of dower. Written Mar. 31, 1846 Witness Thomas Price [see page 212]

William Myers of Kent Co
After my wife's third, I give to my sons **John, William, Frisby,** and **Luke,** my plantation whereon I now dwell. To my dau. **Rebecca,** wife of **William Emmerson** 30 acres which she now occupies and which is part of the farm bequeathed to my sons.

Exec. my son John. Witnesses Joseph Wright, John H. Taylor, William McLaughlin. Written Jan. 27, 1846 Proved Mar. 21, 1846 p. 223

William Ann Wilson of Kent Co (female)
Of the debt due me from Mr. John H. Cummins I give to my dau. **Maria Deborah Wilson** $300. To my dau. in law **Margaret P. W. Wilson** $150 with the request that she will use some of it to put a slab over my son **William George Wilson's** grave. To my sister **Julia** $100. The remainder to my dau. **Susan E. Heigh,** my dau. **Mary H. Wilson,** my granddau. **Olivia Virginia Stephens,** my niece **Louisa Redding,** and **James Boon Pierson,** son of my friend Rev. **John W. Pierson.** The money which shall go to Olivia Virginia Stephens and James Boon Pierson to remain in the hands of my executor. signed as W. Ann Miller

Exec. John W. Pierson. Witnesses David Shields, Elijah E. Miller. Written Mar. 24, 1846 Proved May 11, 1846 p. 224

James Frisby Browne of Kent Co
To my wife all my estate during her widowhood and after to all my children. To my brother his choice of my two duck guns and to my son Morgan my double barrel bird gun. To my sister in law **Rebecca B. Tilden** $100.

Exec. my wife **Ann E. Browne.** Witnesses Thomas B. Flower, Lawrence M. Ricaud, Benj. F. Beck. Written May 25, 1846 Proved June 30, 1846 (July 14 came Benj.) p. 225

Sarah Wilson of Kent Co
To my granddau. **Margaret A. Jump** wife of **Henry T. Jump** $30 and wish it were a larger sum. To my dau. **Delia A. Crossley** wife of **George W. Crossly** all the rest of my estate.

Exec. G.W. Crossly. Witnesses Dr. Robert T. Allen, Thomas Titus. Written May 27, 1846 Proved July 7, 1846 p. 226

Frances Jervis of Kent Co
To my dau. **Sophia** all my personal property to remain in the hands of my brother **Joseph Anthony** until she is 16. To my dau. Sophia a tract of land in Kent Co containing

Liber 12 1835-1854

37 acres adjoining the lands of my brother **Wayne Anthony** and the lands of **John Jervis** during her life and then to her heirs or if she dies without heirs then to my 3 brothers Joseph Anthony, Wayne Anthony and **Benjamin Anthony**.

Exec. Not Given. Witnesses John T. Hurtt, Elijah E. Miller, T.N. Tayman. Written May 5, 1846 Proved Aug. 25, 1846 (Oct. 27 came T.N.) p. 227

Samuel Griffith of Kent Co
My negro slave **Perry** to be free in 2 years. My friend Dr. **Laurence M. Ricaud** to be trustee during the said period and to pay him $5 of his wages, and to purchase his freedom with the wages and the surplus to my executor for his trouble.

Exec. my son **George C. Griffith**. Witnesses Laurence M. Ricaud, William Heverson, Arthur B. Wheatly. Written Aug. 14, 1846 Proved Sep. 1, 1846 p. 228

Codicil My executor to pay to Dr. Laurence M. Ricaud $12 in trust for the benefit of **Andrew Chambers** slave of Mr. **Merritt Miller** for his services during my illness. To Mr. **John Miller** my dark brown horse Jack in trust for his (Andrew Chamber's) father Andrew, and to use the old horse wisely. Written Aug. 17, 1846 Witness Arthur B. Wheatly

Perry Hopkins (free man of color)
All the remainder of my personal estate after my debts to my wife Alley Hopkins. My house and lot where I now reside to my wife **Alley Hopkins** for her widowhood, and after her decease to my 4 children one acre each as follows, the acre at the head of the lot where my dwelling house stands to my dau. **Harriett**, the next acre to my dau. **Betsey**, the next to my son **Moses**, the last to my son **Richard**. As my last 3 named children are slaves, my dau. Harriet to enjoy all the lot during their periods of servitude provided she pays $3 annually for use of each.

Exec. my friend Mr. **William T. Skirven**. Witnesses William B. Wilmer, Laurence M. Ricaud, Michael Gosman. Written Aug. 16, 1846 Proved Sep. 15, 1846 p. 230

Joseph Brown of Kent Co
To my brother **James Brown** and **Augusta Brown** his wife my plantation whereon I now dwell containing about 150 acres and also my lot of woodland in the swamp containing about 15 acres for their joint lives and life of the survivor. After their death to my nephew **Thomas R. Brown**. My negroes to be free at age 30 but until then to my brother James Brown and his wife Augusta Brown and after to my nephew Thomas R. Brown. [Freedom pass granted to **Sarah Francis** Mar. 14, 1863, in margin] All the rest of my estate to my brother James Brown.

Exec. my brother James Brown. Witnesses Joseph Wickes, Elizabeth C. Wickes, Ezekial C. Wickes. Written Aug. 22, 1846 Proved Oct. 7, 1846 p. 231

Abstracts of Kent Co., MD Wills 1777-1867 (WB 12)

Ann Hackett of Kent Co
Whereas on July 17, 1841, **John Hackett** and Ann Hackett his wife conveyed to **George Vickers** all that farm in Kent upon which John and Ann then resided called *"Worton Manor"*, *"Cornwallis' Choice"*, *"Budd's Discovery"* and *"Carolla"* containing 208 acres and 24 perches in trust and at her death to confirm by will the devise, to my son **James Buchanan** 30 acres of the farm on which I reside beginning at the corner of my land and the land of **Emory Edward** deceased at the top of Merritt Hill on the road leading into Worton Neck and on the E side of said road and with said road into Worton Neck such a distance as will be necessary to include 30 acres of land by running a straight line from said road until it intersects **Francis Usilton's** or **Thomas Toulson's** lands and until it intersects the other corner of my land. To my son **Philip K**. Buchanan all the rest of my real estate conveyed to George Vickers by deed of trust and he shall board by my son **Laurence** free of charge during his life if he choose to remain or if not then Laurence to have $50 annually during his life or Philip will have the option of paying $200 or the annual sum. To my son **Robert Buchanan** $20 as his full share at his arrival at age.

Exec. my son Philip Buchanan. Witnesses John Anderson, Edward W. Edwards, Robert M. Anderson. Written July 30, 1844 Proved Oct. 7, 1846 p. 232

Benjamin Greenwood of Kent Co
To my son **George Washington Greenwood** my house and lot in Kent Co and adjoining the land of **John C. Norris** and others at his arrival of age. To my dau. **Mary Ann Greenwood** $250 at age of 18. The residue of my estate between my children George W. and Mary A. Greenwood

Exec. John Wilson. Witnesses John Kelley, Henry Kelley, Alexander R. Parks. Written Sep. 24, 1846 Proved Nov. 10, 1846 p. 234

Benjamin Parrott of Kent Co
Whereas my son **John B. Parrott** will be provided for by his grandmother and I have so little to divide, I give my son $1 and my horse Messenger which he now uses. To my wife **Mary R. Parrott** my carriage one of the best horses of which she is to have the choice, one feather bed, my silver spoons, and other silver plate, my glass tumblers and other glass vessels. To my children by my present wife Mary R. Parrott that is to **Sarah L. Parrott, Benj. W. B. Parrott, George R. Parrott, Rachel B. Parrott,** and **Robert T. Parrott** all the rest of my estate.

Exec. my wife Mary R. Parrott. Witnesses Robert T. Allen, William L. Bowers, Thomas L. Bowers. Written Nov. 8, 1846 Proved Dec. 1, 1846 p. 235

Frances H. Wickes of Kent Co
To my dau. **Sarah Ann Burgess** 2 pair of silver shoe buckles, 2 plain gold rings and all my wearing apparel. To my granddau. **Helen Burgess** my negro girl **Polly** a slave for life. To my son **Samuel A.J. Wickes** all the remainder of my estate if he pays my

granddau. Helen Burgess when she is 18 $50 and pay my grandson **Samuel Joseph Wickes** when he is 21 $50.

Exec. Not Given. Witnesses James E. Blackiston, Henry Blackiston, Benedict S. Brevitt. Written Feb. 12, 1844 Proved Dec. 1, 1846 p. 236

James B. D. Hurtt of Kent Co

To **Thomas W. Trew, William Lamb** and **Francis Baker**, trustees of School District No. 7, 1st Election District $50 for the benefit of said school district. To my aunt **Emeline Redue** $99.60 in gold, also all my books. To **Martha Hurtt** dau. of my brother **John D. Hurtt** my desk, silver sugar tongs and $20, also the residue of my property. To **James Brown Baker** my silver watch. To my brother John D. Hurtt all my wearing apparel and trunk. To **Edward Wilkins** 2 pair silver spectacles, also my silver pencil. To **Juliana Wilkins** my breast pin

Exec. Edward Wilkins. Witnesses John Hadaway. Written Nov. 30, 1846 Proved Dec. 12, 1846 p. 237

Philip K. Buchanan of Kent Co

To my brother **Laurence Buchanan** all my estate during his life and after to my brother **James'** children. The account I have against **William T. Skirven** and **John C. Edwards** for $137.50 to my brother **Robert Buchanan**.

Exec. James B. Ricaud. Witnesses Robert Usilton, William Baker, Edward Plummer. Written Dec. 15, 1846 Proved Dec. 19, 1846 p. 238

David Jones of Kent Co

To my wife **Elizabeth Jones** during her life all my personal estate and after to my 3 daughters **Deborah Jones, Mary L. Sparks** and **Ann Maria Jones** and 2 sons **Thomas Jones** and **Oliver P. Jones**. To my wife Elizabeth Jones all that lot which I purchased of Mrs. **Sophia Neal** executrix of **George Neal** deceased and which is described in a deed from said Sophia Neal to me during her life and after her death to my 2 sons Thomas Jones and Oliver P. Jones. After the death of my wife Elizabeth, my sons Thomas and Oliver shall pay to my dau. Deborah Jones $1, to my dau. Mary L. Sparks $1, and to my dau. Ann Maria Jones $1. My 2 sons shall divided my personal estate for my daughters.

Exec. my wife Elizabeth Jones. Witnesses John Byron, Robert G. Simmonds, Philip T. Simmonds. Written Sep. 30, 1834 Proved Dec. 28, 1846 p. 239

Rebecca Lamb of Kent Co

To **Mary Rebecca Parrott** wife of **Benjamin Parrott** one bed, also my silver watch. To **Ann Elizabeth Allen**, wife of Dr. **Robert T. Allen** and dau. of **William** and **Sarah Bowers** all the rest of my estate to her.

Abstracts of Kent Co., MD Wills 1777-1867 (WB 12)

Exec. Dr. Robert T. Allen husband of Ann Elizabeth Allen. Witnesses A.N.H. Meeks, George W. Wilson, Jacob Sutton. Written Feb. 14, 1840 Proved Jan. 12, 1847 p. 241

Renunciation I **Mary R. Parrott** widow of **Benjamin Parrott** do renounce any devise made for me in the will of my husband and do elect my dower. Written Apr. 13, 1847. Mary R. Parrott [see page 235]

Edward Short of Kent Co
To my sons **Edward, George Washington** and **Francis Asbury Short** all my clothes to be packed on a trunk and sent to them. My 3 horses which I gave to my 3 sons Edward, George Washington and Francis Asbury Short are not to be appraised as part of my estate. My 3 said last mentioned sons to go to their elder brothers as soon as convenient and my executor to give them money to effect said object and my son Francis Asbury to have 10 months schooling provided he choose to accept. To my son Francis Asbury Short my negro boy **Isaiah**. To each of my sons Edward Washington (sic) and Francis Asbury Short one bed. To my sons **William Hyland Short** 1/10 of the residue of my estate deducting $73 which he owes me for ½ of a wheat machine purchased for him and his brother Isaac. I give 2/6 of the remaining 9/10 to my executor **Daniel Jones** in trust for 1/6 to Daniel Jones for benefit of my dau. **Elizabeth Norman** during the life of her husband but after his death to be given to her, the other 1/6 to Daniel Jones for the benefit of my granddau. **Elizabeth Corsons** for education until she is 14 and then to provide for her until age 21 and if she dies then to the children of my dau. Elizabeth Norman. The remaining 4/6 of the 9/10 I give to my 4 sons **Isaac Short,** Edward Short, George Washington Short and Francis Asbury at age 24 and only to pay their expenses out to their elder brothers in the W. My 3 younger sons Edward, George Washington, and Francis Asbury Short to remain with their brothers in the W 4 years and he or they refusing then not to receive their part until age 30.

Exec. Daniel Jones. Witnesses Mary T. Ireland, Frances S. Hurtt, Jacob A. Jones. Written Nov. 10, 1845 Proved Apr. 28, 1847 p. 242

Samuel Merritt of Kent Co
To be decently buried by my friends. My negro boy **George Barrol** now 5 to be liberated on Jan. 1, 1867. To my sister **Frances O. Merritt** my grey mare Jarrett and her colt, also such articles of my household furniture as she may choose. The balance of my personal estate to my brother **Arthur M. Merritt** and to my sister Frances O. Merritt. My farm whereon I reside I give to my brother Arthur M. Merritt and my sister Frances O. Merritt jointly.

Exec. Not Given. Witnesses T. H. Whaland, Laurence Miller Strong, Washington Roby. Written May 12, 1847 Proved June 8, 1847 (June 15 came Washington) p. 244

Liber 12 1835-1854

George A. Briscoe of Kent Co
To my wife **Margaret Briscoe** all my estate

Exec. my wife Margaret Briscoe. Witnesses James B. Ricaud, Joseph Redue, Thomas Price. Written July 27, 1846 Proved June 8, 1847 p. 245

Margaret D. Briscoe of Kent Co
After the debts of my late husband **George A. Briscoe** to my negro man **Harry** my forest lot during his life and then to the property devises herein. My negro man **Harry** shall be free on Jan. 1 next. My servant woman **Williy** to be free Jan. 1 and to have $50. My negro men **John, Sandy,** and **Bill** to be free at age 40. My devises shall support my aunt **Sarah Emerson**. To **Henrietta M. Corbaley, Mary A. Corbaley** and **Hannah J. Corbaley** daughters of Richard Corbaley and Hannah M. Corbaley his wife the rest of my estate.

Exec. my friend William F. Smyth. Witnesses Charles R. Hackett, Isaac Ryland, James B. Greenwood. Written May 24, 1847 Proved June 8, 1847 p. 246

William Johnston
To my son **Henry** ½ of my estate allowing my wife **Sarah Ann** her dower and the balance of my estate to the rest of my children **John, Margaret Ann, William Thomas, George Washington,** and **Sarah Amelia**

Exec. Edward Boyer. Witnesses William S. Evans, John Caldwell, Benjamin Hessey. Written May 27, 1847 Proved June 22, 1847 p. 248

Rebecca Brown of Kent Co
All my estate to my dau. **Elizabeth Thomas Brown** she paying my grandson **James Henry Baker** at age 21 $100 annually for 10 years. To my sister **Deborah Trew** $50 To **Mary Trew** dau. of my brother **Bartus Trew** 6 silver table spoons. To **Ann Rebecca Trew** dau. of my brother Bartus Trew $50.

Exec. John B. Eccleston of Chestertown. Witnesses Thomas W. Trew, Charles B. Tilden, Edward Wilkins. Written Feb. 4, 1846 Proved July 6, 1847 p. 249

John Harrington of Kent Co
To my son **John Harrington** the farm on which I reside known as the *"Hurlock farm"*. The farm which I have given to my son John shall be rented until he is 21. The balance of my estate to be used for the boarding and education of my youngest daughters until they are bound to a trade. To my daughters or such as are then alive when my son is 18 to each $1,000 from the rents of my farm and out of the sale of my *"Cyprus farm"* if this is insufficient. My daughters who are over 14 but under age to be bound to a trade and not to receive a part of my estate unless the executor thinks necessary.

175

Abstracts of Kent Co., MD Wills 1777-1867 (WB 12)

Exec. my friend William F. Smyth. Witnesses Richard D. Downing, Joseph Money, T. N. Tayman. Written June 12, 1847 Proved Sep. 21, 1847 p. 250

Benjamin Anthony of Kent Co
To my brother **Wayne Anthony** $300 in 6 annual payments of $50. The residue of my estate to my brother **Joseph Anthony**.

Exec. my brother Joseph Anthony. Witnesses Thomas N. Tayman, John T. Hurtt, Thomas J. Mann. Written 1847 Proved Aug. 10, 1847 p. 252

Sophiah Mongur of Kent Co
I will my house and lot situated in Quaker Neck, bed and wearing apparel all to be **Julia Sutton's**.

Exec. William A. Rollison. Witnesses Albert Winchester, James Haddaway, William A. Rollison. Written Oct. 4, 1847 Proved Feb. 14, 1848 p. 253

Renunciation I renounce all rights to letters testamentary. William A. Rollison. Written Nov. 1847 Witness S.W. Spencer

The annexed will was offered and a caveat entered against its probate by James B. Ricaud attorney for **Ann Start, Benjamin H. Start, Sarah R. J. Start, John W. Start,** and **James M. Start**, infants and after due investigation by the Orphans Courts had on Jan. 26, the Feb 2 as by the minutes will appear delivered the decision on Feb. 11, 1848: Ordered that the will of Sophia Mongur dated Oct. 4, 1847 is the last will of Sophia Monger.

James L. Ruth of Kent Co
All my estate to my brother **John**, sisters **Mary, Rebecca,** and **Temperance**

Exec. my sister Mary. Witnesses Robert Ruth, John Lee, John Spear. Written Oct. 16, 1847 Proved Mar. 14, 1848 p. 255

Arthur M. Merritt
My negroes **Horace** now 30 to serve till Jan. 1, 1853, **Henry** now 5 years to serve till Jan. 1, 1877, **Emory** now 23 to serve till Jan. 1, 1860 and **Jacob** now 2 years to serve till Jan. 1, 1879 then free. To my wife **Juliana Merritt** all my estate during her widowhood and if she marries then to my children.

Exec. my wife Juliana Merritt. Witnesses James H. Wood, Mary A. Russell, Edward Wilkins. Written Aug. 21, 1847 Proved Mar. 16, 1848 p. 256

Liber 12 1835-1854

Washington Comegys of Kent Co
To my 2 sons **Samuel William** and **John Edward Comegys** all that farm on which I reside in Kent Co called *"Embleton Farm"* and which I obtained in the division of the real estate of the late **William Palmer** deceased in right of my wife **Matilda**. To my wife **Lenora Comegys** in lieu of dower in my real estate all that farm 11/12 in the farm known as *"Major Parker farm"* lying near Millington in Kent Co and which I purchased of **Joseph Wright** at the sale of his property and from **John W. Osborn** and others. To my son **Washington Comegys** my negro girl **Charlotte**. To my son **Henry F. Comegys** my negro girl **Susan**. To my son Samuel William Comegys the negroes **Harriett, Louisa, Richard, Abraham, Emory,** and **Nancy** all my furniture and all my farming utensils and my live stock. To my son John Edward Comegys my negroes **Henrietta, Lucy,** and **Charles**, also a note of $853.53 of **William Gooding** to me, also a receipt from **William F. Smyth** for $300 to me. All the residue of my estate to my 2 sons Samuel William and John Edward Comegys. I have faith that my son Samuel will pay the ½ to his brother Edward or to his guardian.

Exec. my son Samuel William Comegys. Witnesses Richard Corbaley, R. C. Johnson, T. N. Tayman. Written Mar. 15, 1848 Proved Mar. 27, 1848 (Richard cam Mar. 28) p. 257

John T. Smith of Kent Co
To my dau. **Mary Jane Stevens** all that part of my home plantation called *"Part of Piney Grove"* and that part of *"Rearden farm"* purchased by me from Capt. **Thomas Harris** bounded at a stone set up on the bay side running with the road to the intersection of post road then to a stone set up at an oak tree at the front gate then a N course to a stone set up in the branch mark 1826 then continuing with a ditch until it joins Capt. Thomas Harris then to the beginning. To my dau. **Sarah Rebecca Taylor** all that part of the farm on which I now reside formerly owned by **Henry M. Hyland** bounded at a stone set up on the post road and running with the **Elizabeth Walkers** line until it intersects **Thomas Strongs** line then running about a SW course to a large stone with a road to the intersection of the property owned by **William Durding** then running with said line until it comes in a straight line with **John Downeys** lot to the head water of Graysien Creek then with the post road to the beginning, to her during her life then to her son **John Smith Taylor**. To my dau. **Ann Catherine Smith** all the remainder of my estate commencing at the stone set up at an oak tree at the post gate of my home place and running to the stone in the branch marked 1826 then with the line of the ditch or Capt. Harris' line to Elizabeth Walker's line to the post road and then to the beginning. To my 2 daughters Mary Jane Stevens and Sarah Rebecca Smith shall pay to my dau. Ann Catherine Smith $400. To my dau. Mary Jane Stevens one negro girl called **Milcah Ann** to serve until 1872. To my dau. Sarah Rebecca Taylor and her son John Smith Taylor one negro girl called **Eliza Ann** to serve until 1870. To my grandson John Smith Taylor my gun and gunning fixture. To my dau. Ann Catharine Smith one negro boy **Noah** to serve until 1880 and to her my bed and all the remainder of my estate.

Abstracts of Kent Co., MD Wills 1777-1867 (WB 12)

Exec. Not Given. Witnesses S. Riley, Samuel P. Wickes, Thomas D. Burgess. Written Sep. 30, 1847 Proved May 9, 1848 p. 259

Araminta Jacobs of Kent Co
Whereas my sons **James William Jacobs** and **Ebenezer Jacobs** have been raised to manhood and can provide for themselves and I have younger children unprovided for, I give them a memento of $10. All the residue of my estate to my 4 children **Mary Rebecca Jacobs, Thomas Arnold Jacobs, Araminta Jacobs** and **Edwin John Jacobs**

Exec. my brother **Ebenezer Welch**. Witnesses George Vickers, A.W. Sparks, Marth Pippin. Written May 20, 1848 Proved p. 261

Thomas Alford of Kent Co
After my wife's third are taken out, I give to my wife **Ann Alford** all my estate. To **James W. Patten** my bay horse Charles, saddle and bridle. After the death of my wife Ann Alford, the property divided to my nephew **Robert Alford** and James W. Patten.

Exec. my wife Ann Alford. Witnesses Robert Usilton, Joseph Usilton, George B. Ford. Written Oct. 10, 1844 Proved July 11, 1848 p. 263

Michael Lyzar of Kent Co
In addition to my wife's third to have a bed and cupboard ware and one rocking chair. To my dau. **Catharine Start** $1. To my son **William Lyzar** all the balance of my estate and if he dies without heirs then to my grandson **Benjamin S. Start** by his paying to my grandson **John J. C. Lyzar** $300 at $60 annually. I have arranged my property so as to deem it unnecessary to appoint an executor.

Exec. Not Given. Witnesses Francis Usilton, Thomas Toulson, James Beck (of George). Written Feb. 3, 1848 Proved Aug. 15, 1848 (Aug. 30 came Thomas) p. 264

Joseph Dodson of Kent Co
To my nephew **John D. Vansant** my house at Massey Cross Roads, a house and lot at Georgetown Cross Roads adjoining **Henry Hurtts** property, also a house and lot in the forrest adjoining the property of Mr. **William Cacy** and to him $156 due me from **George A. Briscoe** estate. My boy **Isaac** free and my boy **Jacob** free

Exec. my nephew John D. Vansant. Witnesses John T. Briscoe, William Morris, Thomas P. Daris. Written July 26, 1848 Proved Aug. 22, 1848 p. 265

Renunciation
I **Lenora E. Comegys** widow of **Washington Comegys** do renounce any devise in the will of my husband and elect my dower. Written Sep. 5, 1848 Witness E. Welch, Registrar [see page 257]

Liber 12 1835-1854

Henrietta M. Corbaley of Kent Co
To my sisters **Mary A. Corbaley** and **Hannah Corbaley** all my right to the farm held jointly by myself and my said sisters, the same being the farm devised to us by the will of **Margarett D. Briscoe** deceased. To my said sisters Mary A. and Hannah Corbaley all my personal property

Execs. my sisters Mary A. and Hannah Corbaley. Witnesses T. N. Tayman, John W. Stoops, R. C. Johnson. Written July 31, 1848 Proved Sep. 21, 1848 p. 267

Henrietta Perkins of Kent Co
To my 2 daughters **Sally Maria Perkins** and **Ann Wallis Perkins** all my land and land to survivor if either dies. My negro man **Simon** about 28 to my daughters and if he becomes infirm they are to maintain him. To my 2 grandsons **Levi Wroth Perkins** and **William Perkins** and to my granddau. **Margaret Elizabeth Perkins** the children of my son **Isaac Perkins** $100 at age 21 for boys and at 16 for my granddaughter. To my dau. Sally Maria Perkins a piece of fancy work or canvass in a piece representing a stag trees etc. To my dau. Ann Wallis Perkins a pair of glass lamps and 2 profile likenesses in pauces one of my brother the late **Josias Ringgold** and the other of my son Isaac Perkins. My negro woman **Elizabeth** or **Betty** and my negro girl **Mary Helen** (the dau. of my negro Elizabeth) and my carriage horse, my bed with all the residue of my personal estate be used to pay my debts and if a sufficiency then to my granddaughters **Elizabeth Ann Perkins** and **Catharine Emma Perkins** daughters of my son **Henry Perkins** my said negro woman **Elizabeth**. To my son Isaac Perkins my negro girl Mary Helen if she is not sold for debts.

Exec. my son Isaac Perkins. Witnesses Joseph Redue, Samuel L. Sappington, William Thomas of William. Written May 8, 1846 Proved Jan. 2, 1849 (William came Jan. 9) p. 268

Darius Butter of Kent Co
To my brother **Nathaniel Butter** of Caroline Co, MD my silver watch, a large walnut table at my father's and a corn at **William Williamson,** also of Caroline. To my niece **Ann Jane Williamson** a brindle con at her father William Williamson's. All the residue of my estate to my brother **James Butter** during his life and after to his 2 daughters the said **Nancy Jane** and the other **Mary Virginia Butter.**

Exec. my brother James Butter. Witnesses William B. Wilmer, Thomas H. Hagill (called Thomas H. Hayne too). Written Sep. 28, 1848 Proved Nov. 28, 1848 p. 270

Joseph Coleman of Kent Co
To my son **Thomas Coleman** $8. To my son **James Coleman** and **Mary Willier Coleman** all the balance of my property

Exec. **Richard Coleman.** Witnesses Joshua H. Dulany, Darias Coleman, David A. Price. Written Nov. 15, 1847 Proved Dec. 27, 1847 p. 271

Elizabeth Walker of Kent Co

To my grandson **Alexander B. Morian** 170 acres of the farm left me by my brother **Alexander Miller** and by my breaking the entail of the land gives me a right to will as I think right, I require him to pay his __ $100 while she lives but to keep in his hands and **Dr. Hardtner** her husband not to gave a right and after his mother's death to be his. And I give $250 to his mother for her use. To my dau. **Mary S. Hynson** after the death of **Mrs. Wroth** and after my death the farm that was **William Wroth's** and that I bought the reversionary right of his nephew **William Apsley** and **Ann Apsley** which is recorded. I wish my dau. Mary to have the whole use of it while she lives, her husband to have no part of the rents and at her death my grandson **Christopher Columbus Hynson** and he to pay his sister **Virginia W. Hynson** and his sister __ $10 a piece to them yearly and if the dies then to be divided between his two sisters. I also will 50 acres of land to my dau. Mary on the farm I reside beginning at the Wesleyan Chapel and so down taking in the field and house until she gets 50 acres, she can rent or sell. If it is not sold then if she has another dau. then I wish her to have it and if not divided between the two daughters she now has or their survivor. She to have my household furniture and the other things in my house except my best bed, which I will to my son **Grieves** for his dau. **Mary A. E. Walker** and to my son Grieves Walker 50 acres of woodland joining that left his sister Mary also $250 that is now in **Dr. Whaland's** hands, 5 silver desert spoons to my granddau. Mary A. E. Walker. My wearing apparel I wish my dau. E. **M. Hardter** to have some of the best, my son Grieve's wife to have some and my dau. Mary to have the balance. If any money left after my debts and burial then to my dau. E. M. Hardter to have $50 to be in her son's hands for her to correct the memoirs of my life if I should ever finish writing it. I wish it to be printed for the benefit of my children each of them to have a copy and if they are sold then my dau. E. M. Hardtner to have what they bring, the balance after my grandson A. B. Morian takes $50 in charge for his mother to go to my son Grieves. My 4 silver tea spoons to my grandson **Andrew J. Hynson,** my daugher Mary I wish to have Hunter sacred biography, the rest of my books to be divided between her and my son Grieves. Her part to be divided among her children. I will also my dau. Mary to have my double carriage that she may have room and a good way carry her children to meeting to hear the gospel and may the Lord grant to all my children an inheritance that is incorruptible and undefiled and that faded not away. My grandson C.C. Hynson to have my desk and book case and his sisters a bed a piece and the blankets.

Execs. my grandson A. B. Morian and my son Grieves Walker. Witnesses Henry Bryan, Silas Legg, B. S. Brevitts. Written June 8, 1848 Proved Feb. 21, 1849 p. 272

Catharine Ringgold of Kent Co

To my niece **Elizabeth Ann Spencer** my silver coffee pot, my double carriage and harness and my negro woman **Mary** to serve until Jan. 1, 1869, also my negro man **Ned** to serve until Jan. 1, 1856, also my negro man **Sam** to serve until Jan. 1, 1858. To my nephews **Isaac Spencer, William A. Spencer,** and **John Spencer** $20 each. To **Elizabeth Spencer** dau. of my nephew **John Spencer** my work stand and gold watch. My negro woman **Betty** and her children to be free at my decease and my negro Betty $20 per annum during her life. My negro woman **Ann** and her children to be free. All the rest of my estate I give to my sister **Caroline Thompson** during her life and after I give to my niece **Elizabeth A. Spencer**

Exec. my sister Caroline Thompson. Witnesses John B. Eccleston, Anna W. Nicols, Thomas B. Hynson. Written June 3, 1848 Proved Feb. 22, 1849 (Feb. 24 came John) p. 275

Samuel M. Sutton of Kent Co
To **Mary Emma Sutton** dau. of Orlanda F. Sutton $200 at age 18. To my dau. **Ann Virginia Sutton** the following household property which belonged to her mother one bed, one bureau, one dozen cane seat chairs and one pair brass andirons. My other personal property negroes excepted be sold for my debts and then equally divided between my 3 children **Henry Clay Sutton,** Ann Virginia Sutton, and **William Knight Sutton,** and to my 3 said children all my negroes, and all my real estate to them. If they all die without issue then to Orlando F. Sutton. My sons Henry Clay Sutton and William Knight Sutton be bound to learn a trade at 16.

Exec. James B. Ricaud. Witnesses John Frazier Jr, John H. Cummins, John C. Smith. Written Jan. 6, 1848 Proved Feb. 27, 1849 p. 276

Henry Clay Sutton was born Mar. 29, 1832 and William Knight Sutton was born Dec. 29, 1837. signed Samuel M. Sutton. Written Jan. 7, 1848. Ann Virginia Sutton was born Feb. 26, 1835. signed Samuel M. Sutton.

Mary H. Stevens of Kent Co
To **Mary Emily Blackiston** all my right in that tract of land in Kent and adjoining Mrs. **Jane Copper** it being the same that was willed to myself and sister Miss **Sarah Brice.** To **Emily Blackiston** all my estate including my wearing apparel. My negro girl **Jane** shall be free at the end of her term with Mrs. **Emily Stevens** at which time she will be 18. [pass granted to Jane Apr. 28, 1843]

Exec. Not Given. Witnesses Joseph Blackiston, Samuel A. J. Wickes, Samuel B. Stevens. Written Jan. 30, 1849 Proved Mar. 9, 1849 (Joseph Blackiston and Samuel A. J. Wickes came Mar. 10) p. 278

Joseph N. Gordon of Chestertown, Kent Co
To my grandson **Charles Gordon Ricaud** my negro woman **Adeline** and her children to serve 8 years from Jan. 1, 1847 and her male children to the age of 35 and female children to age 31. [freedom pass granted to Adeline July 13, 1855] To my grandson

Abstracts of Kent Co., MD Wills 1777-1867 (WB 12)

Charles Gordon Ricaud my negro girl **Arianna** to be free at age 35 by the will of Miss **Ann Chapman**, if she has children male to serve till age 35 and females to serve till age 31. To my granddau. **Mary Rebecca Ricaud** my negro woman **Sally Jones** dau. of **Charlotte** to serve for 10 years from Jan. 1, 1847. To my son **Joseph N. Gordon** my negro man **Jim** or **James Reynolds** to serve 8 years from Jan. 1, 1847. [James Reynolds pass granted Dec. 26, 1855]. **Ellick** his brother to serve 10 years from Jan. 1, 1847 and **John** a brother to serve 27 years from Jan. 1, 1847. To my son **James F. Gordon** my negro man **Emory** to serve 10 years from Jan. 1, 1847. My servants **Rainy, Charlotte,** and **Sandy Foreman** to be free. My 2 sons and 2 grandchildren to care for my negroes who are advanced in years, and none of the bequests above to take effect until after the death of my dear wife **Mary F. Gordon** who I intend to have all during her life. All the balance of my estate to be divided between my 2 sons and my granddau. Mary Rebecca Ricaud and my grandson Charles Gordon Ricaud. I hope my sons and Mr. **J. B. Ricaud** will assist their mother.

Exec. my wife. Witnesses Joseph Redue, Thomas Price, George W. McKenney. Written Apr. 22, 1847 Proved May 1, 1849 p. 279

Thomas Miller of Kent Co
To my wife **Sarah Miller** and to my children **Sarah Cornelia Miller, Thomas W. H. Miller, Ann Elizabeth S. Miller, Solomon P. W. Miller,** and **Rachel Adelaide Miller** all my estate in common and to pay annual sum of $100 to my dau. **Jane Louisa Wright** for her life. If they die then to their children. To my friend **Hiram Jones** in trust for use of my dau. Jane Louisa Wright during her life $100 annually. I wish no sale of my estate.

Execs. my wife Sarah Miller and my friend James B. Ricaud. Witnesses William B. Wilmer, A. W. Ringgold, James F. Browne. Written May 14, 1841 Proved May 1, 1849 p. 281

Joseph Cotton of Kent Co
My farm on which I live and all the lands I own I give to my wife during her life and the rest of my estate during her life. If my wife has not sold the estate then **Hugh Wallis** Esq to take out administration. To **Sarah Ann Cotton,** dau. of **Rachel Cotton** and grandniece of my wife $5 each year until she is 16. ¼ of my estate to my brother **Isaac Cotton** during his life, then to his 3 daughters **Eliza Ann Cotton, Elizabeth Jones** wife of **Thomas Jones,** and **Hannah Cotton.** To my brother **Daniel Cotton** ¼. To my sister **Elizabeth Smith** wife of **Perry Smith** ¼ during her life and after her death back to my estate and to be divided ½ to my brother Daniel and the other ½ to the daughters of my brother Isaac. The last ¼ to **Rebecca Gattis** wife of **Edward Gattis** during her life and then back to my estate ½ to my brother Daniel and ½ to daughters of my brother **Isaac.**

Exec. Hugh Wallis Esq. Witnesses Peregrine Wroth, Joseph Redue, Benjamin F. Houston. Written Apr. 8, 1843 Proved May 15, 1849 p. 283

Mary Webb widow of David Webb late of Kent Co
To my niece **Mary Meredith** all my wearing apparel. To my nephew **John Wesley Falconar** clothier all my estate

Exec. Not Given. Witnesses G. Garrettson, John E. Cacy, Thomas H. Osborn. Written Mar. 10, 1834 Proved Apr. 3, 1849 p. 285

John Hacket of Kent Co
To my dau. **Cloe Eysenbry** one black boy **John** who is now 18 and to serve until 30 and if she dies then to use of her children, and to her one 4-wheel carriage and one gray horse Tom. To my dau. **Lydia Ann Willis** one black man **Richard** who is 20 and to serve until 30 and if she dies then to use of her children. To my 2 daughters above named all the balance of my moveable property.

Exec. Not Given. Witnesses John E. Gale, B. H. Startt, James H. Rich. Written Apr. 27, 1849 Proved May 30, 1849 p. 286

Matthew Wickes of Kent Co
To my wife the whole of my estate.

Exec. my wife. Witnesses William Hayne, Bartus Boots. Written Oct. 1832 Proved Aug. 3, 1849 p. 287

Samuel Berryman of Kent Co
My wife **Sarah** the remainder of my personal estate and the use of my house and lot during her life after funeral expenses. After the death of my wife my house is to be the property of my brothers and sisters viz. **George, Charles, Richard, John** and **Elizabeth, Hannah,** and **Jane**.

Exec. Not Given. Witnesses William Copper, Susan A. Copper, William J. Dale. Written Jan. 12, 1849 Proved Oct. 12, 1849 p. 288

Maria J. Lyzar of Kent Co
I give all that lot in Worton Heights to my 2 sons **George R. Jones** and **William J. Jones** equally until my son **Ignatius C. Lyzar** to age 21 then the property to go Ignatius. If he dies without heirs then to my 2 above named sons. George R. and William J. Jones are bound to keep property in good repair. To my son Ignatius C. Lyzar one bed. To my son **Octavius H. M. Jones** one feather bed. To my son **Alexander R. Jones** one large looking glass. To my dau. **Velina Caleb** a lot lying in Worton and joining the lands of **Isaac Parsons** and others ¼ acres, also one popular bedstead. To my dau. **Hester A. Long** one bureau. To my son G. R. Jones a lot of ground lying in Worton and joining the lands of **James Beck of John** and others 2 acres, also one large walnut table, also tea board and cupboard ware. To **Isaac N. Younger** a lot of land lying in Worton and

adjoining the lands of **Henry Cohie**, **Samuel H. Hurley** during his life and then to his dau. **Jane**.

Exec. Not Given. Witnesses James Beck of George, Thomas L. Jackson, William Lyzar. Written Nov. 6, 1849 Proved Nov. 27, 1849 p. 289

Ann Sudler of Kent Co
All my undivided right and to all those tracts in Quaker Neck called *"Ratcliffe Cross"* and all parts of woodland to my nephew **Emory Sudler** during his life and after to **William S. Chapman** during his life and after to **Charlotte M. Spencer** and **John Chapman Spencer** children of my late niece **Harriett M. Spencer** and **Samuel W. Spencer**. To my friend **John C. Wilson** the negroes **Chloe** to serve 8 years, little **Charlotte** to serve 8 years, big **Charlotte**, **Charles Henry**, my interest in negro **Alonzo** (being 1/3), big **Jim Bend** now about 12 to serve till 35, one bed, one 8-day clock, one inferior bed, one sorrel mare, in trust for use of my nephew William S. Chapman and in trust. To my nephew Emory Sudler 12 large silver spoons, 12 silver dessert spoons, 12 large ivory handle knives and forks, 12 small ivory knives and forks, 12 napkins for the table, one bed, set of common china and looking glass, the stove and fixtures in my bed room, my 4-wheel carriage. My mortgage of $1,000 due me by my nephew Emory is extended until his death on condition that he pay to my nephew William S. Chapman $30 during his life and after his death the $1,000 to his son **John E. C. Sudler**. To **Anna Gordon Sudler** dau. of my nephew Emory Sudler one small bureau and small travelling trunk. To Charlotte M. Spencer dau. of my late niece Harriet M. Spencer, one cake basket, writing desk, with box, large dressing box, large travelling trunk, gold watch, one bed and writing desk. To John E. C. Sudler son of my nephew Emory Sudler and to John Chapman Spencer son of my late niece Harriet M. Spencer all my bank stock in the Commercial and Farmers Bank of Baltimore applied to education of John E. C. Sudler and John C. Spencer. To Anna Louisa Gordon dau. of James F. Gordon $20 for the purpose of buying a bureau or trinket in token of my regard. To **Thomas Sudler** my dresden quilt and sideboard. To Dr. **John R. Sudler** my large china bowl. All the residue of my estate to my nephews Emory Sudler and William S. Chapman.

Exec. my nephew Emory Sudler. Witnesses James F. Gordon, John T. Wilson, Robert A. Stam. Written Jan. 24, 1850 Proved Jan. 28, 1850 p. 290

<u>Codicil</u> My servant man **Daniel** to be free and if unable to support himself my nephews Emory Sudler and William S. Chapman to do so. To **Sally Sudler** the dau. of my nephew Emory Sudler my negro girl **Mary Josephine** now about 3 years. Written and. Witnesses Same as will

Sarah H. Rasin of Kent Co
To my son **Thomas Rasin** one year services of my negro man **Perry** to commence at the beginning of the year if he has that much service left and if he does not then to have another servant for as long. To my dau. **Sarah Ann Rasin** the whole of my estate

including the negroes during their terms of servitude in accordance with a deed of manumission heretofore executed by me.

Exec. my dau. Sarah Ann Rasin. Witnesses Daniel Haines, Joseph C. Rasin, James Gale. Written 1848 Proved Feb. 27, 1850 p. 294

Joseph Blackiston of Kent Co
To my son **Henry Blackiston** all my lands with all my personal property forever excepting my negro girl **Eliza Ann** under the condition that he pay each of my sons and daughters **James E. Blackiston, John T. Blackiston, William C. Blackiston** and **Henrietta B. Count** $300 at $30 annually. If any die without heirs then to be retained by Henry. To my wife **Ann Blackiston** over and above her right of dower in my estate the above mentioned Eliza Ann during her life and after the death of my wife to be free. [Freedom pass granted to Eliza Ann June 24, 1856, written in margin]. As I have already deeded a part of my farm and given some personal property to my dau. **Sarah J. Ashley** I consider that she has her full portion of my estate. If there shall be brought against my children or accounts then it is to be deducted from legacies of $300 each.

Exec. my son Henry Blackiston. Witnesses Thomas D. Burgess, James H. Edes, Thomas A. Strong. Written Nov. 6, 1849 Proved Jan. 29, 1850 p. 295

N.B. Joseph Blackiston married Henrietta (possibly Eagle) and in 1836 Ann E. Wiggins. All the children apparently by first wife Henrietta.

Francis Usilton of Kent Co
To my dau. **Frances Phelina Reed** wife of **George R. Reed** $5. To my dau. **Susan A. Usilton** $250, one negro boy **Sam** and one negro girl **Maria** and if she dies then to her sisters **Mary E. Usilton** and **Ann R. Usilton**. To my dau. Ann R. Usilton $400 and one negro girl **Hester** and if she dies then to Mary E. Usilton. To my dau. Mary E. Usilton $600 and one negro girl **Ellen** and in case she dies without issue then to Ann R. Usilton. To my son **John Francis Usilton** $1,000, one negro man **Jack,** one boy **Cuff,** one negro woman **Hannah,** one negro woman **Sal** or **Sally,** and one silver watch and old man **Ned** to take care of and is to hold the farm and to have time to pay legacies. If he dies without issue then to **Joseph L. Usilton,** his brothers and sisters to have free of charge with him. To my son Joseph L. Usilton $500 and one negro boy **Bun** or **Hezekiah** and one negro girl **Margaret** and other property belonging to me not named herein and if he dies without issue then to John Francis Usilton.

Exec. James H. Gale. Witnesses Thomas Toulson, James Beck, Sr, Lewis Beck (of George). Written Feb. 25, 1850 Proved Mar. 12, 1850 p. 296

Renunciation I renounce all right to devises in the will of my late husband **Thomas Miller** and elect my dower. signed **Sarah Miller.** Written July 23, 1849 Witness Joseph T. Mitchell [see page 281]

Abstracts of Kent Co., MD Wills 1777-1867 (WB 12)

Joseph Doman of Kent Co
To my son **Daniel L. Doman** $10 and no more as I have already given him a full share. To my dau. **Salina Caulk** $20 to be paid her in one year. To my dau. **Elizabeth Doman** $20 in 2 years. To my dau. **Maria G. Anderson** $20 in 3 years. To my dau. **Eliza Elbert** $120 in 4 years or sooner if my executor prefers. To my dau. **Dorinda Doman** or **Dorinda Ward** $20 in 5 years or sooner. To my son **James Doman** 10 acres of land, it being the land on which he now resides and lying on the right side of the road leading from Millington to Chestertown. To my son **Joseph Doman** $40 in 5 years or sooner. To my son James Doman $130 in 6 years in addition to above land. To my granddau. **Henrietta Offly** $15 as soon as executor has in hand. To my son **Samuel George Doman** the residue of my estate.

Exec. William F. Smyth. Witnesses M. V. Boyer, James F. Gleaves, Robert Ruth. Written Apr. 27, 1849 Proved Mar. 20, 1850 p. 298

Codicil To my dau. Elizabeth Doman in addition to $20 in will give her 10 acres of land to be laid off at the lower end of the farm next to *"Muddy Marsh farm"*. And in addition to James Doman with my brown horse John Richards. Written July 27, 1849. Same witnesses as will

Thomas Harris of Kent Co
To my son **Joseph** my home farm at Rock Hall called *"Piney Grove"* and my other farm adjoining called *"Parson's Poor Lot"* subject to support of my dau. **Juliet** during her single life and to support of my dau. **Eliza** at the Asylum of the Sisters of Charity at Mount Hope Baltimore and if she should be restored to health then to support her during her single life. To my son Joseph my packet with all the tackle and furniture on condition that he pay $150 in 3 installments of $50 to my dau. **Caroline Burgess**. Also to my son Joseph all my other boats at Rock Hall with their tackle and to him the slaves Old man **Nathan**, Old man **Henry**, man **Bill** called **Bill Tilghman**, man **Ben** called **Ben Browne**, man **Sam** called **Sam Freeman**, woman **Sarah**, the house cook, woman **Ann**, dau. of Sarah, and her boy child **Abram**, boy child **Jim** son of **Harriett**. My son to keep the first two named old men servants in comfortable manner. The slaves given to him on condition that he pay $300 in 5 installments of $60 to my dau. **Maria Ewing**. To my son **Alexander** the slaves, man **Sam** called **Tilghman**, man **Solomon** called **Wright**, man **Abram** called **Emory**, woman **Harriett** and her 2 boy children named **Charles** and **Emory**. To my son Alexander one yoke of oxen, one ox cart, and ox chain, one large flushing plough, and one seeding plough, one drag harrow, and one cultivator, one high post bed, bed, now standing in the bar room chamber and one gun, a fowling piece upon the condition that he pay $100 to my dau. Caroline Burgess and $100 to my dau. Maria Ewing. To Caroline Burgess one bed, the same used by her mother and myself, one flag bottom chair and cushion one round topped bureau desk, one silver coffee pot (urn shaped), also $150 by my son Joseph. To my dau. Juliet all the furniture owned by her deceased sister **Henrietta** and one com post maple bed, one bed, also one woman **Mary**, her female child **Sarah Adelade**. To my dau. Juliet a home in the family of my son

Joseph during her single life. To my dau. Eliza 7 shares of stock in the Bank of Baltimore in the named of my deceased wife and I appoint my son Joseph trustee for the support of my dau. Eliza in the Asylum of the Sisters of Charity. After her death then 2 shares in the Bank of Baltimore to my son Joseph and 2 shares to my dau. Juliet, 2 shares to my dau. Maria Ewing and 1 share to my son Alexander. My son Joseph to support my dau. during her insanity. To my dau. Mary Ewing $300 in 5 installments by my son Joseph, also $100 by my son Alexander. To my granddau. **Laura** at the request of her grandmother, one servant girl **Emeline,** also 3 shares of stock of the Union Manufacturing Company of Maryland and I appoint her father to manage said property during her minority, she is the dau. of my son Joseph, and to my granddau. **Maria,** dau. of Joseph 3 shares of Union Manufacturing Co (UMC), and I appoint her father as in the proceeding bequest. To my granddau. **Kate Rossoe** dau. of Joseph, 3 shares of UMC and appoint her father trustee, as in the 2 preceding bequests. To my granddau. **Frances Burgess** 3 shares of the UMC. To my granddau. **Henrietta Burgess** 3 shares of UMC and appoint her father **Thomas D. Burgess** trustee to manage during their minority. To my granddau. **Anna Maria** dau. of Alexander 2 shares of UMC and I appoint her father trustee to manage during her minority. The small articles in my desk and drawers to my son Joseph and Alexander and my son in law Thomas D. Burgess except the punches for leather and my shaving apparatus and razor stone which I give to my son Joseph. I give my books in religion, cookery, gardening and my dictionary to my son Joseph and my dau. Juliet jointly. All my wearing apparel to my dau. Juliet to dispose of as she thinks proper. All the residue of my estate to my son Joseph and as he will receive all the furniture in the house, he shall have the furniture of the public part of the house or the tavern furniture so long as he keeps up the establishment for the accommodation of the travelling public by way of Rock Hall, and if he discontinues said establishment then furniture to be sold and divided between my sons Joseph and Alexander and my daughters Caroline and Maria.

Execs. my sons Joseph and Alexander. Witnesses William Copper, Thomas A. Strong, James E. Blackiston. Written July 19, 1847 Proved Feb. 19, 1850 p. 300

Codicil Whereas I gave my son Joseph my lot called *"Parson's Poor Lot"* for my dau. Juliet during her life and instead give to my dau. Juliet during her life and after her death to my son Joseph. I release my home farm called *"Piney Grove"* which I gave to my son Joseph to support my dau. Juliet during her single life instead he to pay my dau. Juliet $300. And whereas I gave to my dau. Maria Ewing $300 instead I give her $100. And to my son Alexander one silver tea pot and stand and one silver cream pot. Written Nov. 29, 1847. Witnesses James E. Blackiston, James H. Edes, George L. Maslin

Mary S. Thomas of Chestertown of Kent Co
To **Henrietta Maria Bruff** 50 shares of Baltimore and Ohio railroad stock, the certificate thereof in my name cost $5,000, all the furniture, bed, bureau, the carpet on the dining room chamber, 6 windsor chairs, dressing glass, and irons, shovel and tongs, wash table, washbowl, and pitcher belonging to her room, my mahogany work table cover and its

writing box, the writing table and cover, the contents of 3 secretary drawers, the mahogany bureau and its contents except the damask table cloth in the bottom drawer, the mahogany table and covers, 2 pair of new rose blankets, my gold watch, chain and trinkets, whatever jewelry I may have except **Dr. Thomas'** miniature which is in a frame that is intended for my boy **Arthur Burns** son of **Robert Burns** of Baltimore, a hair covered portmanteau trunk and its contents in the 3rd story marked G.W.T., 6 pair Irish linen sheets, bolster cases, 12 pillows, towels and in the bottom drawer of my dressing bureau, 6 towels and 6 napkins and in the small drawers in the dressing bureau, the large chest, the quilts are kept in 2 crickets, all the worsted matts, 2 plated flat bottomed candlesticks and snuffers, one pair of silver sugar tongs at Airy Hill, 12 silver tea spoons marked M, 6 desert spoons marked M, one milk ladle, salt cellar and spoon, silver punch ladle and strainer, the silver cream cup lined with gold, the large blue enameled bowl which was her grandmothers, the set of china purple and luster, all the dining set of liverpool ware in the cupboard, mahogany knife box with 12 dining knives and forks carver and steel, one dozen breakfast, knives and forks belonging to the above set the Britannia ware coffee pot, chocolate pitcher, 3 teapots, cream cup bowl and 12 small new tin plates, two dozen small tumblers in cupboard, spy glass in the parlour all the contents of the closet in the 3rd-story except any cloth for servants, Lowell shirting or yarn for the stockings for the servants, new clothes basket, clothes rack, flat irons, clothesline ironing blanket and sheet, tea kettle, iron pots, gridiron, oven and spider bell metal skillet, iron pot in pantry sifter, flour keg, all flour, brown sugar, coffee, tea, lard, preserves, pickles, ten hams if as many in the meat house, sausage, meal bags, meat tub, all the candles, a pair of small tongs, and shovel, the mantle clock in my room, all the umbrellas and parasols, more particularly the large black silk umbrella, ironing table, kitchen table, safe milk pans, baking pans tin and earthen, all the pining magazines, Harper's edition of the illuminated Bible, 24 small volumes of the history of England, Websters large dictionary, farmer's atlas, to Henrietta M. Bruff $100. To **Peregrine Letherberry Wickes** son of Col. **Joseph Wickes**, the 3-story house on Front Street in which I reside with all its contents except which is devised to other legatees which was devised to me by my father on *"Lot No. 12"* and *"Lot No. 13"*, also the garden with a stone stable on it on the opposite side of the street, the lot in front of the house now in timothy grass between the property where Mrs. **Elizabeth Walker** resides and the stone wall on my garden to him. If he dies without issue then to **Dr. Joseph Wickes** at age 21 subject to use of his father during his minority who will have the emoluments to defray the expenses of his education. To my friend Joseph Wickes my *"Airy Hill farm"* and all wood lots belonging to it, furniture and stock during his life and then to **Benjamin Chambers Wickes**. It should remain in the family forever as the family burying ground is there which must be kept up and attended. If Benjamin dies without issue then to Dr. Joseph Wickes if he has no heirs then to **Ezekial C. Wickes** with the above restrictions to remain in the family forever, should all dies without issue then to my friend **Mary E. W. Green**. To **Mary E. C. Green** wife of **Benjamin F. Green** the 2nd choice of my new bed quilts, the other gifts she received as a bridal one, could Mary have resided in Chestertown she would have had the principal part of my real estate. I give her 6 new damask table cloths out of the drawer of my bureau. To Hester **Van Bibber Wickes** dau.

Liber 12 1835-1854

of Col. Joseph Wickes the contents of drawers 2 and 3 counting from the bottom of my dressing bureau, all the quilts not quilted but lined ready for quilting 5 in number, 6 damask table cloths, the mahogany work table in the 3rd story. To **Sally Agusta Wickes** dau. of Col. Joseph Wickes 3 new bed quilts, 6 pair new muslin sheets, 12 pillow cases, 6 towels, 6 damask table cloths. To **Benjamin C. Wickes** the grass lot in Queen Street where the house stood that I gave to the Protestant Episcopal Chapel at the head of the county. To Dr. Joseph Wickes my grass lot on Fish Street. To **Ezekial C. Wickes** the house and garden on Queen Street where **John Graves** now resides adjoining **Judge Eccleston's** property. To my friend **Elizabeth C. Wickes** wife of Col. Joseph Wickes my carriage and horse Seline. To the trustees of the Methodist Protestant Church for the benefit of the minister who shall reside in the parsonage house, the small lot between the parsonage and Col. Joseph Wickes's garden. To my boy Arthur Burns son of Robert D. Burns, Dr. Thomas' miniature now in a gilt frame during his life and after to Robert Burns his brother, also the American Edition of Dobson's Encyclopedia 36 ½ volumes folio and 1 volume of supplement, 2 paid for but one ever received, vide Dobson rect, To Robert Burns son of Robert the large swing dressing glass in my room which was his mother's, also the volumes of Graham's magazine. To Rev. Dr. **C. F. Jones** Moshiens Ecclesiastical History of the Church 6 vols., Blair's Rhetoric 3 vols. To **Charles Henry Davis** son of **Charles Davis** of this town my milk cow now in town, and 9 vols Humes, Smallet, and Bissetts history of England. To **John Davis** son of Charles my town cart and gear, the Rembler 2 vol., To each of my women namely **Fanny, Rachel, Julia, Sarah Ann,** the beds which they now use, also a suit of black mevino. To Fanny the Bible, prayer book and book of prayers, Dr. Thomas left them to another person after my decease or they all would have been free, To **Ellen** a suit of black mevino, the expenses of the above articles to be paid by my executor Col. Joseph Wickes. To **David Matthews** and **John Bordley**, their freedom. It is my wish that they be hired out and as much of their wages as they can spare be placed in the Savings Bank of Baltimore for their old age. The bank is now kept in South Gay Street near the exchange, President Cushing. To **Samuel Anderson, Margaret Hope** both his children until they arrive at 18 then to be free from their father and not to be sold by him, **Florence Ann** was born Jan. 26, 1844, **Margaret Hope** sister to **Florence Ann** born Jan. 30 1848. To **Henrietta Maria Bruff** the house garden that I purchased of Richard S. Thomas formerly belonging to **Mrs. Atwood** during her life after her decease to **Mary E. Wickes Green.** My Worton farm containing 590 some acres should be sold and divided between Col. Joseph Wickes, Henrietta M. Bruff, Benjamin C. Wickes, and Dr. Joseph Wickes. I wish to be buried at my Airy Hill farm in a walnut coffin and to have a marble pedestal like Dr. Thomas' put up as soon as convenient, the whole of my real estate to be taxed for the funds, with simply my name, age and time of my death. No inventory to be filed.

Exec. my friend Col. Joseph Wickes. Witnesses Peregrine Wroth, Daniel Collins, George S. Hollyday. Written Apr. 26, 1849 Proved Apr. 11, 1850 p. 305

Abstracts of Kent Co., MD Wills 1777-1867 (WB 12)

Thomas Brooks of Kent Co
All my estate including the farm on which I now reside and which was conveyed to me by my late brother **Philip Brooks** by deed dated Mar. 17, 1809 to my niece **Mary Araminta Brooks** and my nephews **John P.D. Brooks** and **George C.M. Brooks** (children of my late brother Philip Brooks) divided among my said niece and nephews

Exec. my sister in law **Araminta A. Brooks.** Witnesses James Alfred Pearce, L. Miller Strong, Daniel Collins. Written Jan. 9, 1840 Proved May 1, 1850 p. 308

Elizabeth Wickes of Chestertown
My servants **Hester Ann Braier, Christiana Norris** and her children and **George Ward** to be free on Jan. 1. The remainder of my property to my niece **Caroline Perkins** who I hereby make my heir. No administration of my estate as my legatee will pay the small amount if any I may owe

Exec. Not Given. Witnesses Edward Wilkins, Juliana Constable, Ann Perkins. Written July 12, 1849 Proved May 28, 1850 p. 309

Samuel Gorman
To my wife **Elizabeth Gorman** (formerly **Elizabeth Pienny**) and to my children **Mary Jane Gorman, William Henry Gorman, Samuel Gorman** all my estate except a mahogany bureau which I give to my oldest dau. **Rebecca Ann Thomas** formerly **Rebecca Ann Gorman.**

Exec. my wife Elizabeth Gorman (formerly Elizabeth Pienny). Witnesses D. C. Blackiston, John Russell, Emory Sudler. Written Sep. 4, 1849 Proved May 7, 1850 p. 310

Temperance Young (col. woman) of Kent Co
To **Thomas Hall** my nephew all my real estate. To the children of Thomas Hall all my personal estate excepting below, To **Mary Jane** dau. of Thomas Hall my best feather bed and also my wearing apparel. To **James Price** my grandson my next best bed.

Exec. Not Given. Witnesses Cornelius J. Scott, William H. Gooding, William T. Miller. Written Mar. 31, 1850 Proved Sep. 11, 1850 p. 311

Samuel Kinard of Farm Bright Helmstead
I wish my wife and 3 small children to have all the household furniture and black mare and then save the crop which is grown, then all the stock and farming implements to be sold and a dividend to be made among all my children **Henrietta Sinclair** if she is living, if dead then her part to be divided among the 3 small children say **Mary Ellen, William Henry,** and **Elizabeth Kenard** and if money left to all my creditors and there is 3 black boys to serve until age 35, they are manumitted in Baltimore and a copy is in my desk. **Bill**'s wages to go to Mary Ellen Kinard, **Perry**'s wages to William Henry Kinard,

Liber 12 1835-1854

Elleck's wages to Ann Elizabeth Kinard. There is 37 shares of Firemans Stock in the Columbia Fire Engine Company which I leave to my son William Henry Kinard, the reason why I make this difference among my children the first gauge of children is Albert and the last is to raise and educate. The farm to be rented out to a good tenant for 10 years. If my wife marries before the 10 years expires then the land to be sold and dividend made among all of the children. No exception in my children's dividend except **Daniel H. Kinard** and this is made be I don't think he would care of it for he went West while he has one cent and I would say give him $100 please be careful to rent the farm to some good man. The gentlemen to settle my estate Mr. **Richard Diggs, Simon W. Boyer.** I have done to the best of my knowledge, if I have done wrong then pardon and forgive me. May the blessed good Lord bless you all. written by Samuel E. Kinard [many spelling mistakes throughout will]

Execs. Mr. Richard Diggs and Simon W. Boyer. Witnesses Joseph Morris, Levin M. Prettyman, George W. Lybrand. Written Feb. 12, 1850 Proved July 9, 1850 p. 312

Renunciation I **Elizabeth Kinnard** widow of **Samuel E. Kennard** do renounce any claim to devises made to me by the last will of my husband and elect my dower. Written Oct. 25, 1850 Witness Nathaniel Meginniss

Mary Dillihunt of Kent Co
To **Sarah Woodall** dau. of Jesse the following negroes to serve till 30, my negro woman **Eliza** born Apr. 24, 1827, my negro boy **George** born in Feb. 1846, and infant **Elizabeth** born last Oct. (1849). To **Editha E. Peacock** dau. of **William Peacock** 4 pairs of linen sheets, one pair of blankets, one comfort, one quilt, 6 silver tea spoons and 6 tablespoons silver and my negro man **Henry Johnson** till he is 30, born on May 24, 1828. **George A. Hines** my bound girl **Rachel** and my negro boy **John** until he is 30 of age when he is free, he was born Dec. 1843. To **Laura Tilden** dau. of **John H. Tilden** $100. To my friend Mrs. **Deborah Turner** one bed quilt. My negro man **Henry Chambers** to be free at my death. My executor to buy tombstones for the graves of my father and mother. The residue of my estate to Mrs. **Louisa McDaniel** wife of John McDaniel [pass granted to Henry Chambers May 14, 1853, pass granted Eliza Jan. 22, 1858]

Exec. John McDaniel. Witnesses Richard Hynson, William B. Wilmer Jr., Emma P. McDaniel. Written July 7, 1850 Proved July 16, 1850 p. 313

Miliscent Toulston
To my niece **Maria Heartly** wife of **Edward Heartly** all my estate. After my estate settled to pay **James Albert Toulston** $10. also written Milliscent Toulson.

Exec. Edward Heartly husband of Maria Heartly. Witnesses R. J. Allen, L.L. Rollison, H.M. Hartley. Written Aug. 8, 1850 Proved Aug. 21, 1850 p. 315

Abstracts of Kent Co., MD Wills 1777-1867 (WB 12)

Elizabeth Burns of Kent Co
To my dau. **Mary Burns** all my estate consisting of the house and lands where I now reside with the condition that she will take care of her sister **Ann Burns** who is idiot at times and unfit to care for herself. To my dau. **Elizabeth Pane** who is married and provided for, I give $1.

Exec. my dau. Mary Burns. Witnesses William T. Skinner, John Bidleman, Julian Bidleman. Written Sep. 12, 1845 Proved Aug. 20, 1850 p. 316

Jacob Jones at present of Baltimore City
All my property and estate to my wife **Ruth Jones** during her widowhood and after my farm situate in Cecil Co to my friend **James Alfred Pearce** to hold in trust for the use of my son **Edward Jones** but I charge $125 to Mrs. **Emily Jones** widow of my son **Richard Jones** during her widowhood but not if she is receiving a pension from the Government of the U.S. If Edward dies without issue then the farm to my grandson **John M. Jones**. If my dau. in law Mrs. Emily Jones dies then the annuity to my grandson John M. Jones during his life. My farm in Kent I give to my dau. **Emily** and is also subject to a charge of $75 to my dau. in law Mrs. Emily Jones and if she dies without issue then to my grandson John M. Jones and the annuity to my grandson if my dau. in law marries or dies. If my grandson succeeds to either farm then the annuities to cease. My 3 negroes **John, Harvey** and **Dave** to be free at my wife's death.

Execs. my wife Ruth Jones and my friend James A. Pearce. Witnesses Eliza Krafft, Charles L. Krafft, Catharine Wise. Written Jan. 8, 1847 Proved Sep. 9, 1850 Baltimore Co (copy dated Sep. 10, 1850) p. 317

Codicil The $200 to be charged to my two farms, $125 to my Cecil Co farm and $75 to my Kent Co farm, at present the farms yielding $600 from Cecil Co and $400 from the Kent Co farm. Written Apr. 7, 1848. Witnesses Francis D. H. Janvier, Augusta C. Twiggs, Augusta Lusby

Renunciation I Ruth Jones appointed executor do renounce right to letters testamentary. Written Aug. 30, 1850 Witness E. S. Jones

Sophia Register of Kent Co
By virtue of a deed executed by my husband **William Register** and myself to **George Vickers** for real estate in Quaker Neck devised to me by my father **Solomon Start** bearing same date as this will, I make this will. To be buried by my husband with a suitable headstone with name etc on the same and if not done in 12 months then to be charge to my real estate. All the lands on Langsford Bay or near the same was devised to me by my father Solomon Start dated Feb. 23, 1832 and proved about June 21, 1833 contained in the deed of trust called *"Bachelor's Choice"* and *"Reardon"* containing 56 acres. To George Vickers of Chestertown in trust to build a brick wall around the graveyard on the farm of my brother **John Start** in Quaker Neck so as to include the

graves of my father, mother, sister **Sarah**, the graves of my 3 children and my own grave and to include 20 feet by 12 feet with a gate and with suitable top or roof on said wall to secure from the weather. To pay my sister **Ann Dryden** $10 as a mark of my regard. To pay over to my husband William Register the balance. Also small stones to be placed at the graves of my children and if not done then charged to my estate. And lastly all my personal property to my husband William Register. [William Register also signed]

Exec. my husband William Register. Witnesses Mary Elizabeth Pinder, William S. Lassell, John Russell. Written Aug. 29, 1850 Proved Oct. 14, 1850 (Oct. 19 came William Lassell) p. 319

Julia Sutton of Kent Co
To my dau. **Susan Porter** all my wearing apparel and my son **Henry Porter** I give 50 cents and to my son **William Thomas Porter** I give 50 cents and to my son **William Veazy Sutton** and my dau. **Sarah Rebecca Sutton** all my estate. My friend **Richard Start** my guardian

Exec. my friend Richard Start. Witnesses G. D. Cruickshanks, Samuel W. Chambers, James Berryman. Written Jan. 15, 1851 Proved Jan. 21, 1851 (Jan 27 came Cruickshanks) p. 322

James Butler free negro of Kent Co
To my son **George** 2 acres of ground and house where he now lives. To my dau. **Mary** 2 acres of ground joining George and after her death to her son **James Reason**, and to my son **Robert** and **Edwin** 3 acres of ground to be laid off between George's lot and the main road each joining Henry Porter's fence, the home and the balance of the lots to my wife during her life and then to my other children **Ellen, Dianna, Araminta, Samuel** and **Francis**. My 2 daughters **Elizabeth** and **Anna** to have a home when out of a home.

Exec. James L. Bowers. Witnesses Henry A. Porter, Charles Copper, James L. Bowers. Written Mar. 1, 1850 Proved Mar. 29, 1851 p. 323

Mary F. T. Handy of Kent Co
The farm where I now reside formerly the property and residence of my deceased father **Marmaduke Tilden** known as *"Green Hill"* to be sold and to be applied to the debt of $2,000 which will be due from me to my dau. **Mary F. McCoy** formerly **Mary F. Handy** in virtue of a deed executed by my said dau. to me dated Aug. 16, 1836 as recorded in Liber TW No. 4 pages 86 and the balance of said sale with $1,000 other land to my son **George** be equally divided all my children Mary F. McCoy, **Esther A.M. Handy, Susan Handy, Marmaduke F. Handy, George D. S. Handy** and **Luther Handy** provided they release all right they may have under the will of their grandfather Marmaduke Tilden or against their father G.D.S. Handy as his executor or against me their mother, or their sister Mary F. McCoy formerly Mary F. Handy arising out of the

said will of their grandfather. If they refuse to relinquish claim then they are to receive nothing of my estate but instead to the other children. To my son George D. S. Handy all that tract lying on Worton Point road and opposite to his residence and formerly the property of my deceased father Marmaduke Tilden containing 117 acres to be his share at $1,000, if more then the excess to a fund of my other real estate, and if less then to have an equal share of the whole. Whereas my dau. Mary McCoy did receive from her father during his lifetime a negro girl valued at $150 without consideration being paid therefore to make an equal distribution, $150 to be deducted from her part.

Execs. my sons George D. S. Handy and Luther Handy. Witnesses William B. Wilmer, John B. H. Anderson, M E. Wilmer. Written Feb. 15, 1850 Proved Apr. 1, 1851 p. 324

Thomas Hepbron of Kent Co

To my nephew **Lewisham S. Hepbron** son of my brother **Sewell Hepbron** all that lot situated at Still Pond Cross Roads with the dwelling, store house (which land was formerly the property of my sister **Elizabeth Hepbron**), also all that lot of land at and near said Cross Roads which was devised to me by my father with the blacksmith shop, taylor's shop and in case of his death without issue then to my brother Sewell Hepbron. To my nephew Lewisham S. Hepbron one negro woman **Maria Wallis** a slave for life with her child **Sally Ann**. To my niece **Ann Eliza Hollingsworth** dau. of my brother **Samuel Hepbron**, all that lot of land near Still Pond Cross Roads which I bought of her and to her one negro girl **Rachel Louisa** a slave for life. To the children of my late brother **James Hepbron** $1,200 divided to **Joseph James Hepbron** $400, to **John Francis Hepbron** $400, to **William Hepbron** $400 at age 21. If either dies under 21 without issue then to the surviving brother. To Joseph James Hepbron my duck gun with the powder horn and shot pouch. To **Henrietta** wife of **Joseph M. Carrow** $10, being less then her brothers because her grandfather **John Hepbron** gave her a tract of land called *"Rich Neck"* making her share more than her brothers. To my brother **Sewell Hepbron** $1,200 including a note of his and also any claim his dau. Margaret Elizabeth may have against me for rents accruing to her prior to May 1, 1851. To my dau. **Mary Ann Elizabeth** now living with me all of my farm and plantation on which I now reside and which I bought of the trustee for the sale of real estate of **Unit Anger** and also all that wood lot I bought of **Judge Eccleston** executor of **George W. Thomas** but if no heir then to my brother Sewell Hepbron and to her the negro woman **Maria Parker** to serve until Jan. 1, 1853, one negro girl **Ellen** to serve until age 35, one negro boy **George** a slave for life, one negro **James Mitchell** a slave for life and one negro man **Isaac** to serve until Jan. 1, 1856 together with all my furniture, cattle, and other property that I may have on the farm. If she has no issue then my personal property to **Joseph J. Hepbron, John F. Hepbron,** and **William Hepbron** sons of **James Hepbron** and **John L. Hepbron, Margaret E. Hepbron, Sewell Hepbron** and **Edward T. Hepbron** children of Sewell Hepbron. I give to **Lewisham S. Hepbron** son of my brother Sewell Hepbron one brown mare Taney, 3 cows, one cart and cart gears, and interest in the grain and if he bring any claim against my estate it to be taken out of his part. The residue of my estate to my dau. Mary Ann Elizabeth

Exec. my dau. Mary Ann Elizabeth. Witnesses George W. Greenwood, John Nelson, Henry Masten. Written Apr. 13, 1851 Proved June 17, 1851 (Codicil proved July 16, 1851) p. 325

Codicil Whereas I gave sundry real estate to my nephew Lewisham S. Hepbron and if he has no issue then to my brother Sewell Hepbron, I mean to Lewisham and if he dies without lawful issue living at the time of his death then to my brother Sewell Hepbron. Whereas I gave my farm and wood lot to my dau. Mary Ann Elizabeth and if she dies without heirs then to my brother Sewell Hepbron, I mean that if she dies without lawful issue living at the time of her death then to my brother Sewell Hepbron. And the personal property to my nephews and niece if she has no lawful issue living at the time of her death. Whereas I gave him my interest in the grain on the farm belonging to him which was devised to him by his grandfather John Hepbron, I mean that he is to have my interest in the grain. The $1,200 to the children of my brother James is without interest. Written May 11, 1851. Witnesses Samuel Kerr, George Vickers, L. L. Price

Jacob T. Freeman of Kent Co
To my wife **Sophia Ann Freeman** for her life all my estate except a tract of wood land lying in Delaware, and at her death to my 2 children **Sophia** and **Martha Ann**. My wife to sell the land in Delaware.

Exec. my wife. Witnesses James B. Ricaud, Cornelia Ricaud, John Butler. Written Mar. 2, 1848 Proved May 3, 1851 (May 10 came Cornelia, May 14 came James, May 3 came Merritt and Thomas) p. 329

Codicil I empower my wife Sophia Ann Freeman to sell all my real estate in Kent if she thinks proper. Written Apr. 24, 1849. Witnesses James B. Ricaud, Merritt Miller, Thomas D. Burgess

Rebecca Wickes of Kent Co
My personal property to all my children. That part of my house in which I live, embracing 2 rooms on the first floor with the rooms above them and the ½ of the lot of ground attached to it, to my dau. **Fanny**. If she dies without issue then to my niece **Charlotte Young**. All that part of my house in which **Nancy Chase** now lives with ½ of the lot of ground attached to my grandson **Samuel Chase**.

Exec. my dau. Fanny. Witnesses Peregrine Wroth, Alexander Barrett, Levi Fiddis. Written Aug. 9, 1845 Proved Nov 29, 1851 p. 331

Mary D. Lamb wife of Daniel Lamb of Kent Co
By power invested in me by deed of trust from **Solomon Eagle** and wife to **Jacob G. Maslin** dated Aug. 4, 1849 and recorded among the land records, I make this will. To my son **Thomas Alexander Lamb** all that farm lying in Broad Neck called *"Maslin's Possession"* containing 65 acres which is mentioned in above deed to hold in trust for my

195

husband **Daniel Lamb** so that he may receive rents during his life and after to Thomas Alexander Lamb and to pay $30 per annum to my dau. **Rebecca C. Stork** wife of **John Stork** during her life and after her death to stop. After 3 years of the death of Rebecca C. Stork I give to my grandson **Daniel Thomas Stork** $50. If Rebecca C. Stork dies, the legacy to Daniel T. Stork to be paid in 3 years after he is 21. Daniel Lamb consents to said will.

Exec. my husband. Witnesses C. Meginniss Riley, John E. Vickers, Thomas Vickers Sr. Written Dec. 6, 1849 Proved July 14, 1851 (July 17 came John and Thomas) p. 332

Samuel Ringgold of Kent Co
To my dau. **Rachel Amanda Ringgold** my farm and mill at Church Hill in Queen Anns Co and she to pay her sister **Elizabeth Ann Sudler Worrell** $100 per annum. To my dau. Rachel Amanda Ringgold my negro man **Peter Davis** to serve 8 years. To my dau. **Martha Ann Rose** my farm on which I now live, which I purchased from **James Boon** called *"Forrest Manor"* containing by recent survey 684 acres. The rest of my property to the said Martha Ann Rose. The negro man George shall serve 4 years. The negro man **Reynolds** shall serve 10 years. Martha Ann Rose to pay all my debts out of the property given. Should my grandson **Samuel Ringgold** and **James Brown Ringgold** return from California, in possession of any funds of mine then to pay my debts.

Exec. my son in law **William Knight**. Witnesses William Miller, John W. Pierson, William Ellis. Written Apr. 5, 1851 Proved Apr. 26, 1851 p. 334

Zachariah Thompson of Kent Co
To my wife **Caroline Thompson** the house and lot where I now reside situate in Kent Co adjoining the lands of **Ezekial Thomas**. I give to my wife my horse and dearborn and corn and household goods during her life and at her death to my brothers **Ezekial Shadrich**, and **Richard Thompson**

Exec. my wife Caroline. Witnesses William A. Miller, Henry Peacock, William L. Hall. Written June 2, 1851 Proved Oct. 7, 1851 p. 336

Sarah Ringgold of Kent Co
To my son **Thomas W. Ringgold** my negro **Simon** on condition that he support my old negroes **Jimmy** and **Perry**. To my son **Richard W. Ringgold** my family Bible. To my son in law **Samuel Comegys** my copy of Scott's Commentaries. To each of my children whatever of mine that they may have in their possession. To my granddau. **Sarah W. Comegys** my room furniture. To my dau. in law **Mary Ann Ringgold** my large black silk shawl. To my dau. **Ann Rebecca Comegys** my alpaca dress, my cloak, and large black cloth shawl. To my dau. **Mary Spencer** the rest of my wearing apparel. To my servant **Jimmy** $10. To my servant **Perry** $5. To my servant **Simon** $5. The remainder of my estate (except $50 to be divided between my daughters Ann Rebecca Comegys and Mary Spencer) consisting of money in consideration of my releasing my life estate in my

Liber 12 1835-1854

2 farms, divided into 5 parts, 1/5 each to the 4 children Richard W. Ringgold, Jacob Ringgold, Ann Rebecca Comegys, and Mary Spencer, and the other 1/5 to Richard W. Ringgold in trust for my dau. in law Mary Ann Ringgold and her children. Execs. my son Richard W. Ringgold and my son in law Samuel Comegys. Witnesses J.M. Comegys. Written July 24, 1849 Proved Sep. 17, 1851 p. 337

Catharine Cuff wife of Thomas Cuff of Kent Co [colored per next will]
To my 2 daughters **Doreas Taylor** and **Deborah Graves** my house situated in Kent (adjoining the land of **Robert Wilson** and farm called *"Tilden farm"*) Exec. my husband Thomas Cuff. Witnesses D. C. Benjamin, John H. Sappington, Prosper M. Davis. Written Feb. 26, 1851 Proved Oct. 2, 1851 (John came Oct. 3) p. 338

John Hankins free man of color of Kent Co
To my wife **Rosetta Hankins** during her life the frame house which I lately purchased and which now stands on part of the lot attached to my dwelling house with land commencing at the back fence running with the cross street 15 feet towards the back then by a line drawn at a right angle to the last line until it intersects the boundary between my premises and those of **Charles Davis**, then to the back fence and the cross street to the beginning. To my dau. **Eliza Hankins** of Baltimore after the death of my wife, the above land given to my wife. If my dau. dies without issue and if my friend **Thomas Cuff**, free man of color of Chestertown shall survive then to him during his life and after to **James Houston Eccleston** son of Judge **John B. Eccleston** of Chestertown. To my dau. Eliza Hankins the house in which I now live and all the lots not devised to my wife. To my dau. Eliza Hankins all my right in lot situate near Chestertown called the *"Brickyard lot"* containing about 4 acres which I purchased of **Samuel E. Baker**. The rest of my estate to my dau. Eliza Hankins. If she dies without issue then to Thomas Cuff during his life and then to James Houston Eccleston.

Exec. Not Given. Witnesses Charles L. Ireland, Alexander Barrett, Aquilla A. Usilton. Written June 11, 1850 Proved Sep. 10, 1851 (Sep. 12 came Charles, Sep. 13 came Aquilla) p. 339

Samuel Hodges of Kent Co
To my wife **Eliza Hodges** my negro woman **Lydia** and her child **Mary**. To **Francis Ann Myers** $400 expended to her education. To my nephew **Walter T. H. Miller** son of **Merritt Miller** all my other negroes in trust to pay my wife Eliza Hodges during her life and after to my nephew Walter T. H. Miller except the following negroes who are to be free, **John** to serve 4 years, **George** to serve 6 years, and **Sam** to serve 10 years. To my nephew Walter T. H. Miller all my real estate. My personal estate to be sold for my debts. My faithful servant **Nannie** to be free at my death and have a home at my bay side farm during her life. [granted negro John a second pass in Feb. 1856]

197

Abstracts of Kent Co., MD Wills 1777-1867 (WB 12)

Exec. my nephew Walter T. H. Miller. Witnesses James B. Ricaud, Rebecca B. Tilden, Mary L. Jones. Written June 5, 1848 Proved Oct. 17, 1851 p. 342

Lavinia Hanson of Kent Co
To my sister **Catharine Wroth** my negro man **Levi** for his unexpired term of service. My negroes **Ezekal, Daniel, Mary, Harriet, William, Allen, Emily** and **Louis** to be free. To my brother **Alexander B. Hanson** during his life and after his death to his children all monies due me except $200 to my said brother in trust if he pays the annual sum of $125 to my sister Catharine Wroth during her life, not subject to her husband. If my nephew **Perry W. Hanson** and my niece **Catharine R. Hanson** children of my late brother **George W. Hanson** die without leaving children I give my reversionary interest in the claim of due me from their late father and existing as a lien on the Ratcliff Farm to my nephew **Edward Alexander Hanson** on condition that he pay my sister Catharine Wroth $50. I give my watch and chain to my niece Catharine R. Hanson when she is 18 and until then to be held by my sister Catharine Wroth. To my sister Catharine Wroth all my household furniture and after her death to my relatives **Susan R. Frisby** and **Elizabeth Anderson** wife of **John B.H. Anderson**. I give my house and lot in Queen Street in Chestertown to my former servant **Rachel Sampson** during her life and after her death to my servants **Harriett** and **Emily**. To my brother Alexander B. Hanson $200 mentioned in the first part to erect a good and substantial enclosure around the family burial ground.

Exec. my brother Alexander B. Hanson. Witnesses J.B. Ricaud, J.F. Gordon, Joseph N. Gordon. Written Apr. 5, 1845 Proved Nov. 11, 1851 p. 343

<u>Codicil</u> To my sister Catharine Wroth 3 shares of stock in the Cotton Factory at Harpers Ferry, separate from her husband. My servant boy **Lewis** son of **Harriet** shall be free. Written May 22, 1849. Witnesses J. B. Ricaud, J. F. Gordon

Philemon Skinner of Kent Co
To my wife **Henrietta Skinner** all my estate during her widowhood having confidence in her attention to our children. After the death of my wife, I give to all my children by my present wife all my estate remaining to said children **Mary Ann, Zebulon, Henrietta, John, Charles, Jane, Harriett, Virginia** and **Alice**, and if they die without issue then to the survivors. My eldest son **Bachellor** and my grandchildren having been heretofore provided for. If my personal estate not enough to pay debts then to sell such part.

Execs. my wife Henrietta Skinner and my son Zebulon Skinner. Witnesses William B. Wilmer, Thomas Stephens, John W. Jones. Written Nov. 27, 1851 Proved Dec. 11, 1851 (Dec. 12 came Thomas) p. 346

Liber 12 1835-1854

Nathaniel Redding of Kent Co
To my wife **Rebecca Redding** all my real estate about 10 ½ acres during her life and after to my dau. **Mary Ann Redding** and my son **Richard Redding**. All my personal property to my wife Rebecca Redding during her life and after to my dau. Mary Ann Redding and my son **James Richard Redding**. To my dau. **Alethia Crouch** $1.

Exec. my son James Richard Redding. Witnesses John L. Briscoe, John W. Lusby, Thomas S. Herdman. Written May 11, 1838 Proved Dec. 12, 1851 p. 347

Probate of **Philemon Skinners** will on page 346. On Dec. 15, 1851 came **John W. Jones** a witness to the will of Philemon Skinner.

William S. Constable of Kent Co
To my wife **Catharine** $1,000 in value of furniture and other property she may choose at appraisement. All my negroes free at age 30 except **Maria** who I free at my death and give her $25 per year during her life with the privilege of procuring fuel for her use out of my woods and pasturing a cow on my premises. One of my 2 log kitchens on the *"Blake Farm"* be removed to the SE corner of said farm near the frog pond farm and 4 acres to be laid off to hold during her life. All my personal estate including my growing crops except my negroes to be sold and to complete the liming of the **Blake** farm in the order in which the fields may come in cultivation at the rate of 50 bushels of lime to the acre and to take 2,000 of chestnut rails purchased of **Parsons** and **Richardson** and 400 posts purchased of **John Gale** to be put on the Blake farm, also to reserve 1,000 chestnut rails with the necessary posts to be put on the main road on the **Whittington** farm and 1,000 chestnut rails for the use of forrest farm and to reserve for the use of the farms all other rails and post. The lot between the Fancy woods and Thomas heirs lands containing about 12 or 13 acres near Oxford Martins and called dry branch lot be sold by my executor. The wood lot adjoining the Blake farm purchased by me of **J. T. Dodd** about 10 acres shall have 25 cords of wood cut from, annually by the tenant of Blake farm who shall sell and the proceeds to the purchase of chestnut rails. The dwelling and barn on the Whittington farm to be finished and a new corn house to be built at the N end of the barn 10 by 20 feet. The dwelling on the forrest farm to be finished and the small dwelling on said farm occupied by James Pearce to be moved to the new house for a kitchen. A new roof to be put on the Blake house and a new barn erected of the size and shape of the one on the Whittington farm. If my personal estate not able to pay debts then as much of my rents and hire of negroes to pay. My family to reside on my home farm for a year after my decease if my wife thinks proper. To my wife Catharine for the term of 12 years, all my estate to be rented out and to keep regular insurance on my houses and the net proceeds for her and my family. After 12 years, subject to my wife's dower, I give all my lands to be divided between all my children. In view of the advanced stage of the season and the difficulty in procuring suitable tenants, I direct my farm *"Fancy"*, *"Forrest"* and *"Blake"* shall be carried on for the benefit of my estate. The farm on the college road to be rented out for the next year, and the stock to be divided between the *"Forrest"* and *"Blake"* farms. My part of the expenses in carrying

on the lime kilns on Fairlee Creek for next year and my proportion of the lime to be applied to the liming my lands.

Exec. my brother **John S. Constable** (if he pays ½ of the commissions to my wife Catharine Constable). Witnesses Thomas H. Whaland, Samuel E. Baker, John D. Cruikshank. Written Nov. 29, 1851 Proved Jan. 7, 1852 p. 349

John Maslin of Kent Co
To my wife **Eliza Maslin** all my estate during her life. After her death then to my son **John Maslin** $300. All the rest of my estate to my son John Maslin and my daughters **Mary Ann Maslin** wife of Jacob G. Maslin, **Sarah Elizabeth Lusby** wife of **John Lusby**, **Amanda Malvina** and **Susan Jemima** in equal portions.

Exec. my son John Maslin. Witnesses William Camp, Thomas Vickers, John B. Camp. Written June 27, 1851 Proved Jan. 26, 1852 p. 352

Hannah Smith of Talbot Co
All my estate including a bond due from **Samuel Ringgold of Edward** of Queen Anns Co for $300 to my 2 daughters **Mary Rebecca Smith** and **Elizabeth Hannah Nicholson Smith**

Exec. Anthony Banning. Witnesses William Townsend, Robert Banning Jr. Written Jan. 25, 1841 Proved Mar. 23, 1852 p. 354

Jane Copper of Kent Co
I wish to be interred at my former residence on the Brice farm. To my granddau. **Jane E. Maslin** all that farm on which she now resides called the Brice farm. To my 2 granddaughters **Mary Ellen Copper** and **Eliza Copper** 2 lots adjoining the Brice farm containing about 40 acres. To my grandson **Samuel G. Copper** my farm situated in Eastern Neck containing 140 acres said farm called the *"Yearley Farm"*. To my granddau. **Christianna Copper** 2 houses situated in Eastern Neck containing 9 acres. To my granddau. **Antonietta Blackiston** one house and lot situated at the head of Rock Hall containing 12 acres. To my great grandson **George L. Maslin** when he is 21 forty acres situated in Eastern Neck formerly owned by **Mary Collins**. To my 2 great granddaughters **Ann R. Maslin** and **Martha J. Maslin** the net rents until my said great grandson George L. Maslin is 21. To my grandson **George T. Copper** the place where I now reside containing 24 acres called *"Part of Pine Grove"* if he pays to his sister **Henrietta Copper** $300 in 3 years. To my son **George Copper** $50. My 3 grand daughters **Sarah Copper** and **Harriett Copper** and **Amelia Copper** monies collected by my executor.

Exec. my son George Copper. Witnesses Stephen Kendall, Nathan C. Satterfield, Benedict S. Brevitt. Written July 8, 1847 Proved Mar. 30, 1852 p. 355

Liber 12 1835-1854

Richard Barroll (a free man of color) of Kent Co
To my sister **Matilda Hynson** $30. To my brother **Abram Freeman** $30. To **Editha Anderson** wife of **William Anderson** a free man of color $30. The rest to my wife **Hester Barroll**

Exec. my wife Hester Barroll. Witnesses John Wilson, John W. Crossley. Written Jan. 10, 1852 Proved Apr. 13, 1852 p. 357

Renunciation I renounce my right to executorship of my husband Richard Barroll deceased and wish Mr. John Wilson to be appointed. Hester Barroll. Written Apr. 13, 1852 Witness William B. Wilmer

Mary Caroline Tilghman of Kent Co
A parcel of land situated in Queen Anns Co which in the will of my father **Matthew Tilghman** is called *"Rings End"* has been sold since his decease and my portion is in the hands of my brother in law **Benjamin F. Houston** with my consent and I give to him forever. To my sister **Harriet Eleis Tilghman** my negro man **Sam** but if she dies without issue then to my niece **Henrietta M. Ll. Everitt**. All the rest of my estate to my niece Henrietta M. Ll. Everitt

Exec. my sister **Henrietta Ll. Everitt**. Witnesses Virginia E. M. Tilghman, James B. Tilghman, Ellen Wills (George B. Westcott and Catherine Eloise Davis confirmed her handwriting). Written June 28, 1844 Proved May 3, 1852 p. 358

George Roeder of Kent Co
My personal estate to my debts and the part of legacies due to such of my children as have not already been paid from the estate of their maternal grandfather. My estate to be rented until my youngest child shall be 21, deducting $150 to my wife and the surplus to my debts and improvement of the farm generally. To my grandson **William Jacobe** $200 at age 21. When my youngest son shall be 21 then my estate sold and divided amongst my children then living, or their children. My wife shall have privilege of a home on my farm with firewood and the privilege of keeping two cows and a part of the fruit so long as the farm shall be rented out. If my wife is living when my estate is sold then the land to be charged $180 during her life in lieu of dower. The part of my estate due my dau. **Maria** to be paid to the Orphans Court in trust for her during her life. Whereas my late son **Aaron Roeder** is indebted to me, then upon the sale of my estate, their portion is to be abated by the indebtedness, being $500.

Execs. my sons **Abraham, George, William F.** and **John A. H. Roeder**. Witnesses J.L. Price, G. W. Price, James F. Taylor. Written Jan. 24, 1852 Proved Apr. 7, 1852 p. 360

Renunciation George P., William F. and Abraham Roeder and the extract of a letter J.A.H. Roeder to his mother Mrs. **Margarett Roeder** dated Mobile Alabama May 2, 1852 "Dear mother, you want me to come home but I am sorry to let you know that I have no money now to come home with". We hereby renounce right to administer to Abraham Roeder and James B. Ricaud. Witnesses George P. Roeder, William F. Roeder, Abraham Roeder. Written May 18, 1852.

Eliza Hodges of Kent Co
To **Frances Ann Meyers** (my adopted child) all my household stuff and furniture. All the rest of my estate to my nephews Capt. **Morgan Browne** and **William Harris**

Exec. Not Given. Witnesses Richard Hynson, Isaac Spencer. Written June 9, 1852 Proved June 24, 1852 p. 363

Mary Ann Bell of Kent Co
Shurlett is now 30 and to be free at age 34. Fanny is 6 and to be free at 30, **Robert** is now 3 and to be free at 35. George is 2 and to be free at 35. To **Ann Bell** $50. The farm where I now reside and also a lot of land a part of *"Boyer's Woods"* containing 26 acres to be sold and divided between my 3 children **William E. C., George Anna** and **John D. Bell**. [pass granted to **Charlotte** Sep. 12, 1857]

Exec. George Vickers, Esq. Witnesses William W. Parks, James Beck of George, James H. Rich. Written Aug. 3, 1852 Proved Sep. 13, 1852 p. 364

Charles H. Black of New Castle Co, DE
To my wife **Ann J. Black** all my lands in Kent Co consisting of one moiety of all that plantation and tract of land held by me as tenant in common with **Nathaniel Wolfe** and which we purchased of **Robert Polk** and **Thomas Clarke**, containing 800 acres. To my wife Ann J. Black all my lands in New Castle Co, DE the lot lying on Union Street in New Castle Co which I purchased of **L. Thomas** and **Elizabeth** his wife with 2 houses erected thereon. All that certain other house and lot situated in the village of Christiana Bridge which I purchased at Sheriff's sale and is now occupied by **Thomas Ogle**. To my wife Ann J. Black all my personal estate. called Charles H. Black M.D. late of town of New Castle in New Castle Co, DE.

Exec. my brother in law **William Janvier**. Witnesses James Cowper, L. T. Bush, James C. Mansfield. Written Feb. 5, 1852 Proved Mar. 29, 1852 New Castle Co, DE (copy from Book V p. 341 on July 17, 1852) p. 366

Joseph Porter of Kent Co
Being old and debilitated, I give to my son **John A. Porter** the house and lot I purchased of **Daniel Denning** and where the said John A. Porter now resides. To my son John A. Porter the privilege of getting wood during his life time off of a piece of pine woods containing about 8 acres running from a middle turning a NW course to the line fence between my farm and Vanorts. My son **Henry A. Porter** and my son **Joseph Porter** trustees. My son Henry A. Porter to annually pay to my son John A. Porter interest of $300 out of my home farm. Whereas my son Henry A. Porter's bond for $900 which

said bond I leave in the hands of my son Henry for the benefit of my son Joseph in the annual sum of $50 until paid out. To my dau. **Mary Primrose** my negro girl **Alsey** now 16 to serve until age 30, also $200 to be paid out of my personal estate. To my grandson **Joseph Henry Primrose** son of **Thomas Primrose** my negro girl **Mary Louisa** now 5 to serve until age 30. To my 2 grandsons **James W. Kenard** and **George H. Kenard** $100 each to be paid by my executor to **James Kenard** their father as their trustee and to James W. Kenard and George H. Kenard my negro girl Ann now 17 to serve until age 30. Their father to hold said negro girl giving $5 to each until James is of age and then to take possession upon his paying George $10 annually. To my son Henry A. Porter all my home farm containing 300 acres during his life and then to my grandson **Joseph Porter** the son of said Henry. And to Henry my negro girl **Henny** now 11 to serve until age 30. To my granddau. **Sarah Temperance Middleton** $100 out of my personal estate. My negro man **Dick** to be free on Dec. 25, 1852. My 2 negro women **Patty** and **Milly** to be free at my death and Patty to occupy the house in the pines during her life with sufficient pine wood for the use of one fire but not to rent the property out without consent of my executor. To my son Henry A. Porter's wife **Ann Maria Porter** my black woman **Jane** now 27 and to be free at 33. To my granddau. **Victoria** the dau. of my son Henry A. Porter my negro girl **Hannah** now 7 to serve until age 30. To my grandson **George Porter** son of Henry A. Porter my negro boy **Joseph Thomas Harris** now 2 to serve until age 30. The balance of my estate to my surviving children.

Exec. my son Henry A. Porter. Witnesses James H. Rich, Moses Kennard, George D. W. Ford. Written May 4, 1852 Proved Jan. 8, 1853 p. 368

Thomas Bordley of Kent Co
To my wife **Ann Bordley** all my personal estate.

Exec. my wife Ann Bordley. Witnesses John R. Stroud, Philemon Skinner (Isaac S. Rogers and John Bordley knew writing of Thomas Bordley and William B. Wilmer Deputy Register of Will also knew writing of Thomas). Written July 7, 1847 Proved Jan. 11, 1853 p. 371

Ebenezer T. Massey of Kent Co
To my wife **Emily Ann Massey** the use of my estate during her life and after her death to my children as follows: to **B.H.C. Massey** my eldest son the farm on which he now lives containing 400 acres. To **Ellen Sophia Crane** wife of Dr. **Thomas H. Crane** my only dau. my farm known as *"White house farm"* containing (by survey and plot made by C.J. Scott on July 2, 1852) 300 acres and 2 roods, and to her my negro woman **Elizabeth** and her son **Hemsley Henry**. To Charles H. B. Massey my second son my 2 farms, one known as *"Brick house farm"* containing 150 acres, the other known as *"Newman farm"* containing 134 acres, also a tract of woodland containing 100 acres lying W of the lands of **Richard Ellis**. To **Thomas G. H. Massey** my 3rd son my farm situated in Queen Anns Co known as *"Tilghman's Friendship"* containing 360 acres with *"Cacy Purchase"* containing 50 acres and 1/3 part of the **Joseph W. Massey** farm

containing 300 acres known as the *"Walker Purchase"* situated in Queen Anns Co near Templeville. To my 4th son **Robert B. M. Massey** my home farm as now laid down with all its right of ways. All the rest of my estate to my sons B.H.C. Massey, Charles H.B. Massey, Thomas H.G. Massey, Robert B.M. Massey and my dau. Ellen Sophia Crane.

Exec. my first son B.H.C. Massey. Witnesses John Lee, Elijah E. Massey, Richard Corbaley Jr. Written 1850 (the witnesses signed Nov. 25, 1852) Proved Jan. 25, 1853 p. 372

Anna Maria Wickes of Kent Co
To **Laura Virginia Dowling** dau. of **James C. Dowling** all my household furniture and wearing apparel. To James C. Dowling my friend all the residue of my estate and at his death to his daughter.

Exec. my son James C. Dowling. Witnesses William B. Wilmer, William T. Skirven, A. W. Skirven. Written Jan. 18, 1851 Proved Feb. 8, 1853 p. 374

Sarah Short of Duck Creek Hundred, Kent Co, DE
To my dau. **Sarah Ann Raughley** wife of **James Raughley** my negro boy **John David White** to serve until age 35, my negro girl **Levina** to serve until age 35. My negro boy **William H. White** to serve until age 25 and then to my granddau. **Sarah Eliza Bell** to serve until age 35. To my granddau. **Mary Gusta Darling** $1. To my son **John Alexander Roche** one feather bed. All the rest of my estate to my dau. Sarah Ann Raughley. called Sarah Short of Little Creek Hundred

Exec. James Raughley. Witnesses Jonathan Brown, John R. Brown. Written Feb. 13, 1851 Proved Jan. 7, 1852 Kent Co, DE (copy from DE June 10, 1853 before John Raughley Register) p. 375

Daniel Lamb of Baltimore City
To my granddau. **Mary W. Stork** one mahogany bureau the one she now has in use. To my wife **Mary D. Lamb** all the residue of my property during her life and after my son **Alexander Lamb** to have the property and be the rightful heir.

Exec. Not Given. Witnesses John Needles, Edward M. Needles. Written June 24, 1848 (6th mo) Proved Apr. 28, 1853 p. 377

Permelia Howard of Kent Co
To my nephew **Asbury Howard** one bed, one trunk, one mahogany table and to my niece **Permelia Howard Price** one bureau, bed, and all my silver and after my expenses then to **Asbury Howard** and **Peregrine Price**.

Exec. Not Given. Witnesses Henry Kelley, William A.M.S. Maxwell. Written Feb. 26, 1853 Proved July 11, 1853 p. 378

Julianna F. Scott, widow, of Kent Co
My negroes to be appraised. To my son **John R. Scott** ½ of these negroes but first my granddau. **Laura Jane Jones**, dau. of **David Jones** my negro girl and to my grandson **David Eugene Jones** son of David Jones my negro boy **John** and the negroes to be hired out and the proceeds to them when they are of age. If they die then to my son John R. Scott. To my said granddau. Laura Jane Jones my bed and my bed furniture including blankets, sheets, and quilts and all my silver ware, my books, my spice box. To my niece Miss **Kitty Wickes** my bureau. To my sister Mrs. **Sarah R. Wickes**, my wearing apparel. The wood lot in the swamp said to contain 5 acres ½ to my son John R. Scott and ½ to interest until my grandchildren Laura Jane Jones and David Eugene Jones are of age.

Exec. David Jones. Witnesses Jacob Fisher, William S. Hammond, Martha A. Bordley. Written June 14, 1852 Proved Aug. 9, 1853 p. 379

Peter Gleen of Kent Co
To my wife **Mariah** all my personal estate in full after my debts.

The said **Peter Gleen** grandson to be free at the age of 21 and his name is Peter Gleen.

Exec. Not Given. Witnesses Lambert Wickes, William Wickes. Written Aug. 29, 1853 Proved Sep. 27, 1853 p. 381

Elizabeth Anderson of Chestertown, Kent Co
To my son **Edward Anderson** my negro servants **Ben Miller, Debby Sudler**, and **Kitty Frisby**, all my household furniture, all the money belonging to me, all my jewelry.

Execs. my son Edward Anderson and James Alfred Pearce of Chestertown. Witnesses Thomas Price, Thomas C. Pinkind. Written Sep. 16, 1845 Proved Dec. 27, 1853 p. 382

Ann Boardly of Kent Co
To my dau. **Sarah C. Rogers** all that lot of ground on which her house stands containing one acre. To my son **Thomas Bordly** $1. To my son **William Bordly** $1. To my son **Samuel Bordly** $1. To my son **John Bordly** $1. To my dau. **Hannah M. Boardly** all my estate while she is single and if she marries then divided among my children equally. To my granddau. **Caroline Sappington** one set of china. To my grandson **James B. Sappington** $1. To my granddau. **Margret M.V.F. Sappington** one large looking glass.

Exec. my son Samuel Bordly. Witnesses Philip Drugan, Samuel E. Baker, John Greenwood of William. Written Mar. 7, 1854 Proved Mar. 14, 1854 p. 383

Abstracts of Kent Co., MD Wills 1777-1867 (WB 12)

William Copper of Kent Co

To my wife **Susan A. Copper** during her life the farm on which I now reside containing 275 acres and to her my 4-wheeled carriage and harness, one bed, 6 chairs, one table, one bureau, all my silver spoons, 6 cups and saucers, the coffee pot that she bought also one tea pot, one sugar dish, and sugar tongs, one carpet, two table clothes, two tools, 6 of each kind of knives and forks. To my wife Susan A. Copper $200, also one negro girl **Hannah, Amelia** born Aug. 27, 1847, to serve until age 21, also one negro girl called **Mary Jane** born July 19, 1842 to serve to age 21, also one negro boy **James** born July 18, 1850 to serve until age 25. The issue of said negro girls Hannah, Amelia, and Mary Jane and all of the other negro girls and of the negro girl called **Hester Henrietta** and sold to **William T. Adkinson** to be free at age 21, also my negro girl **Ann** and her issue to be free at 21. If my wife Susan A. Copper shall marry after my death then have only 1/3 of my estate. No wood or timber sold of my farm. If my death occurs at any season when it may be necessary to provide seed wheat then to my wife Susan A. Copper 40 bushels of wheat. To my niece **Elizabeth Adkinson** dau. of sister **Ann Copper** and **Thomas Brian** $100 to be paid to her by my nephew **Cyrus Copper**. To my brother **Henry Copper** after the death or marriage of my wife Susan A. Copper $20 annually to him during his life by my nephew Cyrus Copper. After the death of my wife, then to my nephew Cyrus Copper all my real estate and one negro boy **Joseph** born Aug. 20, 1850 until age 25. If he dies before 21 then to **John William Copper** and if they both die then to my nephew **Charles Copper**. All the residue of my estate I give to my wife Susan A. Copper to discharge my debts. As my servant woman **Sarah** and her little child **Mary** are afflicted then they are to be supported by my estate and have a home in my kitchen. If they have issue that is not afflicted they to be handled under the residuary clause and free at age 21. My woman **Rachel** was born Aug. 13, 1827 and free at age 30. My wife Susan A. Copper may keep my nephew Cyrus Copper along with her if he maintains himself in a respectful manner to her and if he misbehaves then she may place him at another home. My negro woman **Araminta** be free at age 30, also the negro girls **Hester Henrietta** and **Elizabeth** to be free at 21. Also the negro girl lately sold to William T. Adkinson to be free at the age of 21.

Exec. my wife Susan A. Copper. Witnesses Benedict S. Brevitt, Mary Ann Leary, George Leary. Written Oct. 2, 1852 Proved Apr. 11, 1854 p. 383

Henry Urie of Kent Co

To my son **Henry Urie** all that part of land on which he now resides and half the field next to the main road and to his wife **Sarah** the same during her widowhood. To my son **James Urie** the other half of said field and out to the lines of Capt. **Joseph Harris** and by the cross fence. To my son **John Urie** the field next to the brick dwelling and out houses granary and little corn house excepted and 4 ½ acres of wood land. To my son **Robert Urie** the field and woods adjoining the property of Mr. Parker as the fencing now running with the granary. To my son **Thomas Urie** the field next to Rock Hall with the woods out to Capt. Joseph Harris's line and the little corn house. To my dau. **Mary Ann Warner** $175 out of my personal estate and if not enough then the male heirs to pay balance. To my dau. **Elizabeth Ball** $175 out of my personal estate and if not enough then the male heirs to pay balance. To my wife **Catharine Urie** her 1/3 part of the estate or $33.33 yearly. The road leading from the public road to the crick is to stand as it now does for use of all the heirs and the first that attempt to hinder any of the heirs a free passage shall forfeit his land and it shall be sold and divided among the remaining heirs.

Exec. Henry Urie. Witnesses Samuel G. Copper, Jacob Downey, James U. Coleman. Written Dec. 22, 1853 Proved Apr. 11, 1854 p. 388

In the matter of the will of Henry Urie exhibited on Apr. 11, 1854. Samuel G. Copper aged 26 years says that on Dec. 24, 1853 he received a message from the late Henry Urie to go to his house for the purpose of making his will, he went to the house with Jacob Downey and James U. Coleman and there found Mr. Urie sitting in his room, and after talking some time he asked him what instrument of writing it was that he wanted him to witnesses he was in a hurry to leave to which he rose from his seat and went in an adjoining room and produced the paper now shown. He said that Henry Urie wrote it, he was very nervous, but that it was the best he could do. After 2 hours conversation, he believes Henry Urie was of sound mind. Jacob Downey age 39. James U. Coleman aged 34 years. Joseph Harris aged 40 years was well acquainted with the writing of Henry Urie. James Urie age 55 is a brother of the late Henry Urie and acquainted with the handwriting of Henry Urie.

Mary Gale of Kent Co
My boy **Daniel Johnson** to be free. My boy **James Hinson** to serve my sister **Sarah G. Skirven** until age 35 (he was born Feb. 1, 1830). The balance ½ to my sister Sarah G. Skirven's children or four of them namely **Thomas W. Skirven, Martha E. Skirven, John W. Skirven,** and **Washington G. Skirven,** the other ½ to my brother **James Gale** and to carry my will into effect.

Exec. James Gale. Witnesses John Gale, Mary Jane Skirven, Margaret V. Everitt. Written Apr. 6, 1854 Proved Apr. 20, 1854 p. 392

Phebe W. Rasin of Kent Co
To my grandson **Philip F. Rasin** my small hair trunk and bureau now in his possession, also my silver coffee pot, sugar dish and cream pot each marked with the letter F. they belonged to his father, and if he should sell the plate then to be valued by two people and offered to my son **Edward** at valuation and should he decline then to my other sons in the order of their seniority beginning with the oldest. These legacies not to be reduced by insufficiency of my personal estate and further $500 charged on my real estate in aid of my general personal estate upon an equality with my other children, when the cost of his maintenance and education since the death of his parents and the money I have paid for and on account of his father are taken into consideration. To my granddau. **Mary R. Rasin** $500. To my son **James M. Rasin** $5 in bequeathing to my son this small amount

Abstracts of Kent Co., MD Wills 1777-1867 (WB 12)

I am governed by a sense of duty and justice to the rest of my children, growing out of a certain award made out against me in favor of my son James whereby he will receive more than his fair proportion. I give my 8-day clock to the **Rev. Robert Peggot** of Baltimore City. All the rest as follows, 1/3 to my son **Edward F. Rasin**, 1/3 to my son **Henry H. Rasin**, and the remaining 1/3 to my grandson **Isaac Freeman Rasin** in trust to pay my son **Robert W. Rasin** during his life for his family as he, my son Robert may choose to designate and then in trust to convey the same to his children. I desire my farm called *"Old Field Point"* shall be retained in the family and that it be offered to my son Henry at valuation and if he does not choose it then to my other sons in order of seniority beginning with the oldest first to Robert, then to Edward and then to James. And if necessary to sell then to reserve the graveyard thereon to the use of my family and their descendants. I release my son Edward F. Rasin from all claims I may have against him on account of the professional education I gave him except $500 provided he makes no claim against me for medicine or medical attendance.

Execs. my sons Edward F. Rasin and Henry H. Rasin. Witnesses James Heighe, Samuel E. Briscoe, J. W. Ireland. Written Jan. 28, 1854 Proved Apr. 25, 1854 p. 393

<u>Renunciation</u> I renounce all right to administer under the will of Phebe W. Rasin in favor of Edward F. Rasin. H.H. Rasin. Written May 8, 1854

Philip Reybold of Red Lion Hundred, New Castle Co, DE
To my children **Elizabeth Clark, Ann Clark, Margaret Polk, Susan Murphy, John Reybold, William Reybold, Barney Reybold,** and **Anthony Reybold** full equal 8th parts of 9 equal parts of all the lands in DE, MD, PA or elsewhere of which I am now or at the time of my death seized. To the children of my deceased son Philip Reybold Jr. the remaining 9th part to be managed by John C. Clark and William Reybold whom I appoint trustees during their minority. To my children Elizabeth Clark, Ann Clark, Margaret Polk, Susan Murphy, John Reybold, William Reybold, Barney Reybold, and Anthony Reybold each 1/9 part of my personal estate and the other 1/9 to the children of my son **Philip Reybold Jr.** deceased (to **John C. Clark** and William Reybold, trustees). To my son John Reybold in trust for his 3 blind children **George W. Reybold, Elizabeth Reybold** and **John Reybold** 100 shares of the Capital Stock of the Delaware City Bank standing in my name upon the books of the bank and if any dies unmarried then to survivors. My executors to have power to sell land. The debts owing me by my children or the husbands of either of them and which are secured by their obligations, bonds, etc shall not extinguished by reason of the devises made to them. The 2 bonds executed by John Reybold, Philip Reybold Jr. in his lifetime, William Reybold, Barney Reybold, Anthony Reybold, and **Clayton Reybold** in his lifetime, to pay me $15,000 and the other of said bonds of $8,000 and a note of John Reybold and brothers for $11,251, I direct to be cancelled by my executors and may not be demanded from either of my sons.

Execs. my sons John Reybold, William Reybold, Barney Reybold and Anthony Reybold. Witnesses William O. B. Knight, James S. Rodney, George B. Rodney Esq. Written June 2, 1853 Proved Mar. 9, 1854 New Castle Co (copy made Apr. 7, 1854 by Amos H. Wickersham Register) p. 396

Codicil I revoke the clause regarding the bonds due to me. The 3 blind children of John Reybold, if all the children die then the 100 shares to all my children. Written June 2, 1853

For copy of letters testamentary granted in DE see next book of will on page 31.

Abstracts of Kent Co., MD Wills

Will Book 13   1854-1867   pp. 1-375 CR 52

Mary Sappington of Kent Co
Friend **Mary Hynson** two trunks of wearing apparel and all other wearing apparel. Friend **John Dwyer** who now lives with me, all my farm and plantation, and all remaining estate.

Exec. John Dwyer. Witnesses B. C. Wickes, E.A. Moore, W. J. Hynson. Written Jan. 1, 1851, Proved June 20, 1854, p. 1

Abraham Reading of Kent Co
Son **Isaac Reading** $5 paid by son **Frisby Reading**, Dau. **Margaret Waters** $5 paid by son **Frisby Reading**, Son **Alexander Reading** $5, Dau. **Sarah Ringgold** the house and lot where I now reside, Son **Frisby Reading** the remainder in consideration for his kindness to me and my wife in our old age.

Exec. Not Given. Witnesses Isaac N. Younger, Samuel W. Smith, William J. Owens Date, 1853 (no month or day given), Proved June 24, 1854 p. 2

William Lyzar of Kent Co
James H. Rich my horse called Jim and my carriage, a $100 note held against **Joseph Usilton** and a $99 note held against Union Meeting house. **Benjamin H. Start** all balance of my personal estate. James H. Rich renounced as executor in favor of Benjamin H. Start. witness Wm. Harris

Exec. James H. Rich. Witnesses A. R. Parks, John W. Parsons, James Beck of George. Written June 9, 1854 Proved July 5, 1854 p. 3

Thomas Walker of Kent Co
To be buried at Georgetown and Roads churchyard until such time as my executor can procure a suitable place in a Philadelphia cemetery the one on the Schuylkill if possible. My niece **Anna J. Walker** of Kent Co $350. **Thomas McLoughlin** son of George of Kent Co in consideration of essential service done me by his father during my fire on Jan. 8 1844 my lot known as *"Long Lot"* lying and being upon the road leading from Millington to Smyrna (12 acres) with the exception of a house and a small slip of ground containing 1 acre. My farm in Kent Co formerly the *"New Comb"* farm bought of **Judge Davis** containing 180 acres and my mill property in Queen Annes Co known as *"Unicorn Mill"* and my farm adjacent containing 200 acres to be retained for 5 years and repaired. Incomes arising from property to be divided between my nephew **W. S. Walker** of Kent Co and my niece **Lizzie Archer** of Harford Co and proceeds from final sale after 5 years to nephew and niece. Lizzie Archer's portion retained by W.S. Walker until she is 21.

Exec. W. S. Walker. Witnesses M. V. Boyer, T. L. Cecil, S.L. Blackiston. Written Nov., 1853 (no day given) Proved Jul 11, 1854 p. 4

Liber 13   1854-1867

Benjamin Chambers Wickes of Chestertown
To be decently buried in the yard where those of my family now rest who have gone before me to the world of spirits. To my dear wife all my personal property. To my nephew **Benjamin C. Wickes**, son of my brother **Joseph A. Wickes**, my gold watch and ornaments when he arrives at 21 or upon the death of my wife. To carry out the wishes of my late relative **Mrs. Mary J. Thomas** by preserving *"Airy Hill"* in the family, which I am entitled after the death of my beloved father, to my beloved mother for and during her life and after her death to my brother Joseph A. Wickes and after his death to my nephew Benjamin C. Wickes (wife to received $200 annually for rent until her death).

Exec. my father (**Joseph Wickes** appointed Jul 29). Witnesses Peregrine Wroth, R. Hunter, W.N.E. Wickes. Written Mar. 15, 1854 Proved Jul 25, 1854 p. 7

Codicil The *"Airy Hill"* property with the furniture to my dear mother during her natural life and she paying my wife the annual rent of $200, then to my nephew Benjamin C. Wickes. If Benjamin dies without heirs then to my brother **Joseph A. Wickes**, after his death to my brother **Ezekial C. Wickes**, after his death to my brother **Peregrine L. Wickes**. Written Jul 1, 1854. Witnesses Thomas H. Whaland, Lawrence M. Strong, Wm N.E. Wickes

Abraham Cole of Kent Co
Slaves to be set free on Jan. 1 after my decease: **Pere Ringgold** age about 28, **Sam Sutton** aged about 28, **William Dorsey** aged about 26, and **Pere Bell** aged about 24. My house and lot at the head of Sassafras which I purchased of **John Richardson** and now occupied by **James Cole** my son I leave to James during his natural life and at his death to any of his children that may be living (if one of his children dies but has issue they take interest as if their parent were living). All the rest of estate to my children **Rebecca Thompson** (wife of **John Thompson**), **Alfred Cole**, **Araminta Sherwood** (wife of **William Sherwood**), **John Emory Cole** and **George Hynson Cole**, and my dau. **Mary Eliza Lynch** and their heirs to divide equally. Son-in-law **Thomas Clinton Lynch** trustee for my dau. **Araminta Sherwood** as if she were sole and unmarried and her share not be to be let to the control of her husband.

Exec. Thomas Clinton Lynch. Witnesses George Vickers, C. T. Lusby, Thomas Lusby. Written Aug. 12, 1853 Proved Aug. 29, 1854 p. 10

Codicil Any accounts or advances of money to one of my children or their husbands shall be chargeable against their share. Written June 10, 1854. Witnesses C. T. Lusby, George Vickers, David Staats

Joseph Malsberger of Kent Co
My dau. **Agnes R. Johnson** $2,750 out of personal estate, My dau. **Matilda C. Kraft** $3,750 out of personal estate, My son **Jacob G. Malsberger** $2,750 out of personal estate, My dau. **Catherine Malsberger** $2,750 out of personal estate. All my real estate

lying in the City of Philadelphia and the rest of my estate to my five children, **Elizabeth M. Wooddall,** wife of Edward B. Wooddall; Matilda C. **Kraft,** wife of Henry Kraft; **Agnes R. Johnson,** wife of Richard C. Johnson; Catherine Malsberger and Jacob G. Malsberger and their heirs, but if Jacob or Elizabeth die without issue their share to the other children. I have not made a bequest to my son **Augustus** because I purchased for him the "Davis Farm" and 1/5 of the home farm which will make him worth more than either of my other children. I have also purchased for my daughters Elizabeth and Matilda the *"Spear"* or *"Ozmond Farm"* and for my other children the rest of the home farm.

Execs. son-in-law Richard C. Johnson and George Vickers of Chestertown. Witnesses William Medders, T. N. Tayman, Samuel J. Corbaley. Written Oct. 1, 1854 Proved Oct. 25, 1854 p. 13

William Thomas of William of Kent Co
Beloved wife **Elisa Thomas** all estate during her life except the following: Four children **Alfred T. Thomas, Mary Matilda Thomas, Sarah Elisa Thomas,** and **William Thomas** and my four grandchildren now living of my late dau. **Ann Catharine Wyatt,** their share of their mother's portion. Slaves to be divided: Alfred to have negroes **Peggy** born Aug 7 1846, **Henry** born Jul 11 1848; Mary Matilda to have negroes **Caroline** born Oct 12 1842, **John Thomas** born Sep 2nd 1847; Sarah Elisa to have negroes **Alexander** born Oct 5 1844 and **Agnette** born Sep 12 1849; William to have negroes **James Aron** born Feb 1 1846, **Rose** born May 9, 1850; each to be set free when they turn 35 years old. Negro women **Harriet** and **Emily** to be set free at 35 also (service to wife, then to his children after her death). Harriet to be set free on Jan 23, 1858 and Emily to be set free on Aug 23 1860. Negroes **Jake** born Nov 16, 1852, **Josephine** May, 1851 (no day given) along with any others not named or born after to be divided equally in service to my children. No negroes to pass to my grandchildren now living.

Execs.s wife Elisa Thomas, son Alfred T. Thomas. Witnesses Daniel Jones, Catharine T. Jones, and George Washington Jones. Written Aug. 6, 1853 Proved Oct. 31, 1854 p. 15

Robert Polk of DE City, New Castle Co, DE
Son **William Reybold Polk** to have two plantations one called the *"Middle farm"* on Howells Point containing 443 acres and the other known as the *"Staats farm"* containing 143 acres except the part to the right of the roads which is reserved in common by the owners of the *"Lower farms"* namely Kelley, Spry and Wilson. Son William R. Polk to have land only if bond dated Feb 18, 1854 for the sum of $10,000 be paid and which is then bequeathed to son **John P. R. Polk** (principal of which is to remain in hands of William as long as interest is paid to John while he is in his minority). Son William R. Polk to have all land of a certain plantation in Westmoreland Co, VA known as *"Hollis Marsh Farm"* containing 1,702 acres. Dau. **Anna L. Polk** to have land in St. Georges Hundred in New Castle Co, DE known as the *"Jamison farm"* containing 300 acres and

Liber 13 1854-1867

in case of marriage of my said dau. to make such a settlement in case of misfortune. Son **Robert Polk** to have a certain plantation at Chesapeake City in Cecil Co, MD known as the *"Kibler farm"* containing 300 acres and the ground rent for lots in the village of Chesapeake City. Appoint **George W. Bennett** guardian of son Robert during his minority. George to invest not more than $5,000 in the lumber business. Give the lots in DE City in New Castle Co and brick dwelling house on Market Street in City of Wilmington DE which was conveyed to me by deed of **John O. Bradford** and wife dated June, 1854 and $11,000 to payable 1 year after my decease to **John C. Clark** in trust for my son **Henry C. Polk**. Son **John P. R. Polk** to have lower farm on Howells Point in Kent Co which **Henry Kelley** now lives on containing 555 acres. Dau. **Elizabeth R. Polk** two plantations in Kent Co one of which **George T. Spry** now reside upon called upper farm on Howells Point containing 343 acres and the other called the *"Parks farm"* where **Thomas S. Wilson** now resides containing 202 acres and $10,000 to be paid one year after my death. **John C. Clark** and **William Reybold** to be guardians for Elizabeth during her minority. My dau. **Anna L. Polk** whilst she remains sole (single) and my niece **Amelia H. Polk** shall care for my 3 youngest children: John, Henry and Elizabeth during their minority. If Anna or my son John leave the family the trustee of Henry to increase the income provided to keep the family household together.

Execs. my relation and friend John C. Clark and my son William R. Polk. Witnesses Wm W. Ferris, G.G. Cleaver, George W. Craig. Written July 13, 1854 Proved Oct 26, 1854 at New Castle p. 17

Codicil Niece Amelia H. Polk and son Henry C. Polk to have unexpired time of service of my indented servant girl **Sarah**. Written Aug. 12, 1854. Witnesses Wm. W. Ferris, J.B. Henry

Edward Ringgold of Kent Co

My dear wife **Rebecca Ringgold** during her life a lot of land adjoining her farm being a marsh lot which I purchased of **George W. Thomas** and land adjoining which I purchased of **James Boon**, containing 214 acres and also lands which I purchased of **John B. Armstrong**. After her death to my son **John Fletcher Ringgold**, also to receive land called *"Carvill Farm"* purchased by me from Mrs. **Mary Ann Freeman** and **Harriett W. Carvill**, also to receive lot containing 15 acres and the wood all of which I purchased of **Edwin R. Carvill** (subject to charge of $2,000). My grandson **Samuel Ringgold** (son of my deceased son **Samuel**) all that part of farm on Kent Island in Queen Annes Co upon which his late father resided running up as far as a post now standing on Cox's Creek to the side of a small marsh and lower part of said farm called Cox's Neck (subject to payment of $1,000 to my granddau. **Hannah R. Kemp** wife of **Frederick C. Kemp**) provided however that in the event of my Samuel being compelled to pay to his sister the said Hannah a legacy of $500 under the will of their father my late son **Samuel Ringgold** then the sum of $1,000 be abated by the amount Samuel is compelled to pay his sister. My son **James B. Ringgold** tract called *"Mansion Farm"* on Kent Island on which he now resides. If he has no children living at time of his death to pass to my two grandsons **Edward Ringgold** and **Samuel Ringgold**, children of my late son Samuel, each obliged to pay the widow (if any) of my said son James. James required to pay $12 annually to my negro woman Susan Berry. My dau. **Jane E. Tilden** to have lot situate on Back Street of Chestertown which I purchased of A. W. Sparks and others, and to her children living at the time of her death or to her husband if living at time of her death. If no heirs at time of her death, then land is to be sold and proceeds given to **Robert W. Rasin Jr.**, **Alfred R. Rasin** children of my dau. **Mary R. Rasin** and **Mary J. Cummins** and **Martha R. Cummins** children of my deceased dau. **Martha E. Cummins**, the survivor of each to take the share of their sibling. If dau. Mary living at time of sale of land, she to receive interest as if she were feme sole, and upon her death to Robert and Alfred Rasin. A small piece of land about ¼ acre conveyed to me by **Samuel Osborn** adjoining the lot of the Methodist Episcopal meeting house on Kent Island to the Trustees of the Methodist Episcopal Church or meeting house. To wife Rebecca my negroes **Maria Nicols, Harriett Robinson, James V. Robinson, Frederick Nicols, Richard Hazzard, Selid Nicols** and **Harry**, and **Maria** and **Harriett** to be set free at death of my wife or sooner if they reach age of 30 years and the other negroes to be set free at 30. (Harriett granted manumission Jan 11, 1858) except Harry who is to be set free at end of term for which he was sold to me by executor of **William S. Constable**. To my wife my double and single carriages and all the harness, one big grey horse, one sorrel horse, bay mare Fanny, one horse Harry Croaker, one sorrel mare, one bay mare Lucy, and her colt and also the colt at the *"Carvill Farm"*, one single steer, the choice of 6 milch cows, one ox cart, one horse cart, all the farming utensils, household and kitchen furniture in the dwelling house where I reside, all the crops growing or standing or all crops cut, secured and unsold on the farm whereon I reside near Chestertown and also 15 pounds of pork and 130 bushels of wheat for seed. To my son **John Fletcher Ringgold** my boy Jacob Hazzard to serve him until 30 and then set free. My dau. **Mary R. Rasin** my girl Hannah Robinson until 30. My dau. **Jane E. Tilden** wife of **Charles Tilden** my negro woman Ann and her children (except her child Marion) and my negro Drusilla Hazzard until 30. **Mary J. Cummins** child of my deceased dau. **Martha E. Cummins** my negro girl Stella Robinson until 30. **Martha R. Cummins** child of my deceased dau. Martha my negro girl Athalia Nicols until 30. My son **John Fletcher Ringgold** my negroes John and Emory for the unexpired term of their servitude. My granddau. **Mary Rebecca Ringgold**, child of John Fletcher Ringgold my negro girl Sarah Jane until age 30. My grandson **John E. Ringgold**, son of John F. Ringgold my negro girl Maria Nicols until age 30. Unto **Louisa Ringgold** widow of my late son **George W. Ringgold** my negro woman Harriett Hazzard until age 30. Unto **Elizabeth Smith** the sum of $130 paid by son John F. and to her my negro girl Marion dau. of negro Ann until age 30. I set free at the end of the year next after my decease my negro man **Moses Berry** and to receive $25 annually from son John F. I set free at the end of the year next after my decease my negro woman **Susan Berry** alias **Susan Chase** and paid $12 annually by son James B. I set free at the end of the year next after my death my negroes **Richard Worrell, Washington Smith, Henry Anderson** and **Mary Hazzard**. I give my negro woman Mary Hazzard her child Emily until she is 16 then set free. Split $2,000 with 1/3 to **Robert W. Rasin Jr.** and Alfred

Liber 13 1854-1867

R. Rasin (interest to their mother but not to their father), 1/3 to Jane E. Tilden, 1/3 to Mary J. Cummins and Martha R. Cummins to be paid by John F. after 7 years and not until the death of Mrs. Carvill who is entitled to dower in the *"Carvill Farm"*. Money owed from Henry Jump, Samuel E. Baker and from my deceased son Samuel Ringgold to Mary and Martha Cummins. To sell lot in Chestertown known as the *"Harris Lot"*. In the event Robert W. Rasin preferring any claim against my estate then all bequests to his wife and children are void.

Exec. John F. Ringgold. Witnesses J.B. Ricaud, Daniel Collins, Robert A. Starn. Written May 6, 1854 Proved Dec. 12, 1854 p. 23

Philip Reybold of Red Lion Hund., New Castle Co, DE
Letters of administration (no will given)

Execs. John Reybold, William Reybold, Barney Reybold and Anthony Reybold. Written Mar. 9, 1854 p. 31

Catharine H. Wroth of Kent Co
My dear husband Doctor Peregrine Wroth my farm whereon Edward T. Wroth now resides during his life, then to my nephew George A. Hanson, son of my beloved brother Alexander B. Hanson and to Peregrine $1,000. My cousin Susan Anderson, wife of Dr. Alexanders Anderson of Chestertown $100. All other cash and bonds to my said brother Alexander B. Hanson until my nephew Edward A. Hanson is 25. My servants Maria, Ellen, Thomas Wright, Thomas Worrell, Emory and Harry to be set free at the end of the year in which I may depart this life. I give to Richard Worrell, the husband of my servant Ellen, my servant girls Jane, Emily, Alice Alfred and Louis Jerome, until they arrive at 21 then to be set free. My husband to have all furniture except those articles I held jointly with my late sister Lavinia which things I give to my cousins Ann Elizabeth and Susan Anderson. All remaining estate to my nephew Edward A. Hanson.

Exec. my brother Alexander B. Hanson. Witnesses Thomas B. Hynson, Margaret S. Wroth, R.A. Starn. Written Dec. 27, 1854 Proved Jan. 18, 1855

John Fletcher Ringgold of Kent Co
My mother intends to make her will in conformity with mine, 150 acres owned by my mother devised to me by my father adjoining her lands to be laid off by running a straight line parallel to the new road leading from near Washington College to Morgans Creek being the upper part of said lands nearest the new road running back to Henry's lately *"Gauff's Farm"* to the child or children with which my wife now enceinte and the said farm of my mother (where we now reside) and the adjoining lands devised to me by my father including a marsh lot which he purchased of Doctor George W. Thomas to my dau. Mary Rebecca Ringgold. If child wife is carrying is born alive the lot to dau. Mary Rebecca Ringgold but charged with payment of $3,000 to my son John Edward

Ringgold until Mary is 21. The farm in the First Election District of Kent Co devised by my late father and commonly called the *"Carville Farm"* to be given to son John Edward Ringgold with charge of $500 to unborn child wife is carrying to be expended on the upper part of the farm and lands near Chestertown. No land to be sold until oldest child surviving reaches 21. Exec. to give right of way to **G. B. Westcote** over part of the Carville Farm. To my dear wife **Sarah Catharine H. Ringgold** my negro man **Jeremiah Taylor** and my negro girl **Mary**, slaves which I obtained by my marriage with her, also my negro woman **Lavinia Bright**, a slave for life, and which I purchased of James W. Phillips. All remaining negroes and personal estate to my children. My apprentice boy, **Moses Berry**, I hired out and paid $10 to his father and the balance to said apprentice. My wish is that my wife (who, I am informed, will be entitled to all my apprentices) will act in the same way in reference to Moses and his wages, indemnifying herself against any expense and freedom dues, if any is provided, out of his wages or hire.

Exec. my friend Thomas W. Eliason (surety for guardian bond his brother William C. Eliason). Witnesses George Vickers, Elizabeth H. Smith, Benjamin B. Perkins. Written Jan. 11, 1855 Proved Jan. 30, 1855 p. 34

Elizabeth Jones of Kent Co
To **Thomas Jones** whatever sum of money he may owe me. To **Elizabeth T. Clash** my wearing apparel, bureau, and silver table spoons and silver tea spoons. To **Daphina F. N.** the sum of $15 to be paid by **Oliver P. Jones**. Remainder of estate to Oliver P. Jones

Exec. Oliver P. Jones. Witnesses James Mansfield, William Lamb. Written None given Proved Feb. 23, 1855 p. 38

Anna Maria Medford widow of Still Pond, Kent Co
Satisfy my debts either by bills drawn on my trustees in England or to those whose services I hire. Divide property at Still Pond between my dau. **Anna Maria Hynson** and the children of my deceased daughter, **Mary Anne Medford Welch**, **William Welch** and **Mary Louisa Mann** wife of **Comegys Mann**. After death of my dau. Anna her portion to her children equally, if none living then to the heirs legal of my deceased husband **Macall Medford**. **Anna Maria Hynson** being the oldest heir to have preference of ½. **William Welch**'s part that is ¼ part to be managed by executors during his minority until William is of age which will be on Dec. 2, 1851. ¼ part to **Mary Louisa Mann** wife of Comegys Mann. Land adjoining the farm where I now live which was willed to me by my late husband **Macall Medford** and the house, garden, lot, stable and adjoining building and ground on which a cartwright shop decayed at Still Pond Cross Roads purchased by me of **Rigby Corse** deceased but then of Still Pond may be considered part of that farm. In the event of the death of Anna Maria Hynson, William Welch and Mary Louisa Welch now Mann then to heirs of my late husband. My executors to inform my trustees in England of my death also **Mr. Charles Warden** No. 334 Arch Street Philadelphia.

Liber 13 1854-1867

Execs. Doctor Thomas C. Kennard and James B. Ricaud, Esq. both of Kent Co. Witnesses S. W. Spencer, James Frisby Gordon, T. N. Gordon. Written Sep. 2, 1848 Proved Apr. 17, 1855 p. 39

Jesse Knock of Kent Co
My dear wife Sarah Knock ¼ of farm on which I now reside or ¼ the annual rent and the farm on which Johnathan Chance now resides, also my farm on which Joseph W. Walls now resides, and my farm called *"Clows Hazard"* on which Mr. Holden now resides. also to have bedstead and the necessary bedclothes. My dau. Katherine White my farm on Kent Island, also my farm called *"Clows Hazard"* and my farm on which Joseph W. Walls resides after the death of my wife. My sister in law Elizabeth Thomas and my brother-in-law William Thomas and my friend John C. Turner all my farm in Kent Co on which James Smith now resides in trust for the use of my dau. Ann B. Smith during her life and afterwards to her children by the aforesaid James Smith not to be subject to the control of her husband. To my two granddaughters (children of my dau. Katherine White) viz. Sarah White and Maria Louisa White my house and lot in Baltimore City located on Mulberry Street. To my two grandsons Jesse K. Hines and John Wesley Hines two bonds due from Johnathan Jones for $950. To my dau. Eliza Lucinda Knock my farm near Sudlersville on which Samuel J. Jarman now resides and after the death of my wife my other farm near Sudlersville on which Johnathan Chance now resides. Eliza also to have 2nd choice of my beds, bedsteads and the usual bedclothes. To my son Samuel Henry Knock my farm on which I now reside provided for to the life estate of wife Sarah Knock and Samuel to have remainder of estate.

Execs. my son Samuel Henry Knock and my wife Sarah Knock. Witnesses James F. Gleaves, M.V. Boyer, William F. Smyth. Written Nov. 27, 1854 Proved Apr. 17, 1855 p. 41

John R. Stroud of Kent Co
My beloved wife Eliza Stroud all estate during her life then to all my children as she may feel best to distribute by her own will.

Exec. my wife Eliza Stroud. Witnesses John W. Jones, John W. Coleman (his mark), John A. Rollison, James How Jr., Andrew Hinds. Written Aug. 21, 1851 Proved May Term, 1853 at Stephenson Co, Illinois p. 44

Henry Ware (free man of color) of Kent Co
All estate to James B. Ricaud in trust for my wife and my children share and share alike.

Exec. Not Given. Witnesses James F. Gordon, John N. McDaniel, Joseph N. Gordon. Written Feb. 6, 1854 Proved May 22, 1855 p. 46

Sarah P. Wilson of Millsborough, Washington Co, PA

I, Sarah P. Wilson formerly Sarah P. Vickers and sister of the late Benjamin Vickers, To my friend and relation George Vickers Esq. of Chestertown, Kent Co all my lands which land I purchased from George Vickers as trustee for the sale of the real estate of my deceased brother Benjamin Vickers under a decree of the Chancellor of MD in which I and others were complainants and Glick and others were defendants on July 11 1839 by deed. To Elmore B. Summers a son of Benjamin and Mary Ann Summers a house and lot in Millsborough where I now reside, if he dies without issue to then to William H. Summers and Benjamin Franklin Summers his brothers. Also one mahogany table, bed, bedstead and bedding, one set of chairs, one cupboard and one looking glass. To William H. Summers one bed, bedstead, bedding, one mahogany table, one set of chairs and one looking glass. To Robert W. Summers a son of Benjamin and Mary Ann Summers one bed, bedstead, and bedding, one settee, four windsor chairs and two split bottom chairs, one large dining table and one looking glass. To Benjamin Franklin Summers one bed, bedstead and bedding, one clock, one set of chairs, four of them windsor and two split bottom, his breakfaster table and little stand, his trunk and one looking glass. To Harriett Ann Summers a dau. of Benjamin and Mary Ann Summers one trunk and one rocking chair. If she dies without issue then to her sister Mary Jane Summers. To Mary Jane Summers one trunk and one rocking chair. To her sister Martha Ellen Summers one trunk and one rocking chair. If William H. Summers should die under 21 then to Benjamin Franklin. If Benjamin F. dies under 21 then to William H. All personal estate to Robert W. Summers, Benjamin Franklin Summers, Martha Ellen Summers, Mary Jane Summers and Harriett Ann Summers and to such other children as the said Mary Ann Summers may hereafter have by the said Benjamin Summers. Interest to Mary Ann Summers not subject to her husband. Orphans Court of Washington Co to appoint guardians for the children of Mary Ann and Benjamin. If Mary Ann a widow she to have choice of a room in the said house given to Elmore during her widowhood, all my clothes and wearing apparel to said Mary, all my late husband's wearing apparel to Elmore B. Summers. A suitable head and footstone over my grave at Taylors Meeting house buried by the side of my deceased husband with an inscription as soon as may be.

Execs. My friend and relation George Vickers in MD and my friend Charles W. Bower of Fredericktown PA. Witnesses Freeman Wise, John M. Harford, Esau Powell. Written Nov. 5, 1849 Proved Apr. 11, 1855 p. 47

Codicil If Elmore dies then to William H and Benjamin Franklin Summers. To each of the children of Mary Ann $300, Furniture already given to Elmore. If my friend Charles Bower not be living then my friend James M. Hawthorn of Washington Co PA. Witnesses Isaac N. Carey, John M. Harford, Esau Powell, Date, 1852 (no month and day given, but witnessed July 27, 1852)

2nd Codicil Bond to George Vickers not be considered part of personal estate,. Witnesses George W. Wilson, Nimrod Grabill. Written Sep. 16, 1854. W.W. Hawthorn qualifies. He states Freeman Wise left PA possibly to Illinois and Esau Powell left to California

Liber 13 1854-1867

Sarah H. Barroll of Chestertown
To my grandson **William B. Barroll** my gold watch, To my granddau. **Sarah R. Barroll** my silver cream pot, To my niece **Anna M. Payne** my wrought gold ring, My servant women **Eve** and **Margaret** to be free from all manner of servitude. (Margaret granted pass May 24, 1856) Margaret's son having already been disposed of and manumitted prospectively. All the remainder of my estate to my dau. in law Mrs. **Rebecca Barroll** and her heirs in confidence that she will employ it to the advantage of her children as of herself.

Exec. Not Given. Witnesses H. Tilghman, James F. Gordon, B.F. Houston. Written Aug. 28, 1850 Proved Nov. 20, 1855 p. 56

Antoinette Jones of Kent Co
I, Antoinette Jones, the wife of **David Jones** of the same county settle my worldly affairs with the consent of my said husband first had to my making a last will. Whereas as will by the law of the land with the consent of my husband hereto subscribed as also by the power and authority conferred on me by instrument of writing executed by my said husband in the nature of a post-nuptial settlement I do make and publish this my last will. To my dear husband David Jones and my dear brother **James P. Wickes** the sum of money owed me by bond to my said brother. To my dear husband and his heirs my negro woman **Tempe** and her three children **Henry, Emma,** and **Elizabeth**. To my niece **Charlotte Wickes,** dau. of my brother James, my negro girl **Willie**. To my niece **Mary Wickes,** dau. of my brother James, my negro girl **Martha**. My plate jewelry and apparel to be distributed as expressed in a memorandum in writing left with my will or in the possession of my dear husband. David Jones signed Apr. 16, 1855 that he consented to his wife making this will.

Exec. Not Given. Witnesses William Wickes, M.L. Harris, Lemuel W. Ashley. Written Apr. 16, 1855 Proved Jan. 12, 1856 p. 57

Mary Ann Warner of Kent Co
To my sister **Elizabeth Ball,** in trust, for the benefit of my children, and each to receive an equal share when of age.

Exec. Not Given. Witnesses Martin Allen, Benjamin F. Allen, James E. Blackiston. Written Dec. 18, 1856 Proved Jan. 24, 1856 p. 59

Catharine Knight of Kent Co
To my nephew **William Knight** son of my brother **William Knight** now deceased entire estate

Exec. William Knight. Witnesses George W. Spencer, Edward B. Woodall, Andrew Woodall. Written Dec. 7, 1852 Proved Mar. 18, 1856 p. 60

Abstracts of Kent Co., MD Wills

George Barroll, free man of color, of Kent Co
To my son **Peregrine Barroll**, all the real estate and personal property I may die possessed of, including the land which I now live together with all the buildings and all my personal property provided that my said son shall permit my wife **Sarah Barroll** to remain during the period of her natural life in the house which I now reside and shall furnish her a good and comfortable maintenance. If my said son neglect to refuse to furnish to my said wife the home and maintenance above described, then she will be entitled to $50 annually

Exec. my son Peregrine Barroll. Witnesses Richard S. Thomas, Henry Green, Benjamin B. Wroth. Written June 17, 1851 Proved Apr. 4, 1856 p. 61

Nathaniel Tilman of Kent Co
To my son **Perry Tilman** $5, To my dau. **Aree Ann Tilman** $5, To my dau. **Mary Tompson** $5, To my dau. **May Jane Chase** a part of my land where I now reside starting from two large cedars on the line between the land of **James Graves** and my land and running a straight line across my lot to a big pine tree on the other side of said lot and running back to the line between the land of Mr. **William Vannost** and said lot 1 ½ acres, To my wife **Louisa Tilman** the remainder of my estate during her life and afterwards to my children namely **Nathaniel Tilman, Ezekial Tilman, James Richard Tilman, Ebenezer Tilman,** and **Emely Tilman**. To all my children not now of age they shall serve my wife Louisa until the boys are 21 and the girls are 18. To my son **Henry Tilman** $5, To my dau. **Rebecca E. Tilman** $5.

Exec. Not Given. Witnesses James Wood, Benjamin Middleton (his mark), James Kennard. Written Jan. 16, 1855 Proved Apr. 1, 1856 p. 62

James Weer of Kent Co
To my children **Joseph E. Weer, James H. Weer, Elizabeth J. Weer, Mary Crane,** wife of **William F. Crane, Tacy A. Weer,** and **Emily Weer** all my real estate. To each of my single daughters Elizabeth, Tacy and Emily a home on my farm where I now reside so long as they remain respectively unmarried. To my daughters Elizabeth and Mary I give 7 shares of stock of the Commercial Bank of Philadelphia and to my daughters Tacy and Emily I give 16 shares of the stock. To my son Joseph I give my eight day clock. To my son James I give my silver watch. To my daughters Elizabeth, Mary, Tacy, and Emily I give my household and kitchen furniture. The rest of my estate real, personal or mixed, I give to my sons Joseph E. Weer and James H. Weer.

Exec. my son Joseph E. Weer. Witnesses Richard Hynson, James A. Massey, Stephen K. Toulson. Written Sep. 15, 1854 Proved July 8, 1856 p. 63

William F. Smith of Kent Co
All my estate to my dear sister **Charles Anna Smith** (sic) of the City of Philadelphia

Liber 13 1854-1867

Exec. Thomas J. Britton. Witnesses Jesse K. Hines, M.V. Boyer, Thomas Quimby. Written July 9, 1856 Proved July 22, 1856 p. 64

Joseph Dublin of Kent Co
To my beloved wife **Hannah Dublin** the use of my estate during her life and after her death to my children **Joseph Dublin, Catharine Johnson, Sidney Dublin** and **Matilda Houston.** My dau. Sidney Dublin to have a home with her mother Hannah Dublin during her mothers life.

Exec. my dear wife Hannah Dublin. Witnesses William Lamb, Thomas Baker, William J. Maslin. Written Aug. 5, 1856 Proved Aug. 19, 1856 Proved p. 65

Elijah Dailey of Chestertown, Kent Co
To **James Thomas Lassell,** son of **William S. Lassell** of Chestertown my house and lot situate in Chestertown which I purchased of James B. Ricaud, Esqr and also my house and lot in Chestertown which I purchased of John Russell of Chestertown, to him but to charge $100. The above $100 to my nephew **Edward Daily,** son of my brother **William Dailey** decd.

Exec. William S. Lassill. Witnesses Thomas C. Pinkind, William Parker, William Webb. Written May 20 1848 Proved Aug. 26, 1856 p. 66

Rebecca Elizabeth Meeks of Kent Co
I give and bequeath my interest in the farm lying in Worton which was willed to me and my dear sister **Mary J. Bull** by my brother **Rasin Jones** to my beloved husband **Howard Meeks** during his natural life and after his death to **Daniel W. Bull** and his sister **Mary Elizabeth J. Bull** son and dau. of my sister **Mary J. Bull** and their heirs. I give to **Verlina Caleb** dau. of my brother **Jacob Jones** and wife of **Wesley Caleb** of said Co $50 to be paid by my husband Howard Meeks within 12 months of the execution of this will

Exec. Not Given. Witnesses John Gale, John T. Skinvin, John M. Gale. Written Aug. 16, 1856 Proved Aug. 23, 1856 p. 68

Birdsal Fowler of Kent Co
To my son **William Fowler** $10. To my son **Samuel Fowler** $100 payable by my son **Joseph Fowler** after the arrive at age 21 of my son Joseph. All the rest of my estate to son Joseph Fowler.

Exec. my friend William Watts and guardian of son Joseph. Witnesses George Vickers, George P. Roeder, Joseph G. Briscoe. Written Oct. 20, 1856 Proved Oct. 28, 1856 p. 68

Isaiah Ashley of Kent Co

Son **James David Ashley** my two lots on E side of the public road leading from ChesterTown into Eastern Neck called the *"Big Lot"* and the *"Long Lot"* respectively and my lot of land lying on Rock Hall formerly called *"Rock Point"* also 9 1/6 acres of land called *"Wolf Swamp"* more or less, N of a dividing line to be hereafter made, provided he pay within 2 years from my death a note held by Doctor Thomas Willson for $400 signed in, 1854 by my son James David Ashley as principal and myself as security. If he fail to pay then the above portion of lot called *"Wolf Swamp"* to be bequeathed to my son be sold at public sale and proceeds used to pay note. I also give my son James David Ashley the work shop near my dwelling house and upon a lot of land which I shall hereinafter devise to my son **John D. Ashley** which said workshop he shall remove from off said lot. I also give my carpenter's and other tools connected with the shop and all machinery of whatever kind. I also give to James David Ashley the unexpired term of a negro boy called **Chiners** indented to me and held as an apprentice, also 6 silver teaspoons. I also give to my sons James David and **John Dudley Ashley** my grey horse called Charly to be held jointly. To my son **Lemuel Washington Ashley** 46 square feet of land on which his dwelling now stands and the yard attached, also 11 1/6 acres of my lot of land called *"Wolf Swamp"* on the S side of a dividing line, also my shot moulds and duck gun. To my son **John Dudley Ashley** for his natural life the Blacksmith shop and my lot of land lying to the W side of the public road leading from Chestertown to and down Eastern Neck and extending W from said road down to Rock Hall Creek with the buildings and improvements thereon, except the work shop and also the equal right with himself of my son Lemuel W. Ashley to the use of ½ of the Blacksmith shop and one of the forges and an equal share of the tools and fixtures of the shop in the proper exercise of his vocation as a blacksmith. After the death of my son John Dudley then to John's children **Benjamin Franklin Ashley** and **Mary Elizabeth Ashley.** To my son **Thomas Wroth Ashley** two acres of my lot of land called *"Wolf Swamp"* on the N side of a dividing line between my sons James' and Lemuel's share and $50, and one high post bedstead. To my dau. **Eliza Ann Grant** during her natural life my plantation lying in Kent Co and *"Langford's Neck"* containing 50 acres as if she were a feme sole and not subject to the control of her husband, after her death to **James Alexander Wroth Grant** and **Richard Isaiah Ashley Grant,** her children, equally. To my dau. Eliza Ann 6 large silver spoons, one cherry dining table and one preserving kettle. To my son James David all residue of my estate. Also the graveyard on the lot bequeathed to my son James David, containing 1/8 acre clear of the margin of the marsh shall be reserved as a family burying ground together with a road of ingress and egress to bury the dead. I also will that **Stephen Kendall** (cartwright) have the privilege to said road and bury his dead in said graveyard as his family wish to bury there. My son Lemuel W. Ashley shall have use of the Blacksmith Shop and its appurtenances in common with his brother John D. Ashley during his life after his death the shop to pass to John or John not living to John's children Benjamin Franklin and Mary Elizabeth.

Exec. my son Lemuel W. Ashley. Witnesses Samuel A. J. Wickes, E. W. C. Ireland, Jos. C. Kendall. Written Aug. 13, 1856 Proved Nov. 25, 1856 p. 69

Liber 13 1854-1867

Jacob Stevens of Kent Co
I give to my unborn child or children as the case may be which my wife is now pregnant with all my estate. If my wife **Anna Matilda Stevens** outlive the child or children which she is now pregnant with, I give to my wife forever.

Exec. Lemuel W. Ashley (Lemuel renounced right to administer Nov 25, 1856). Witnesses Samuel Riley, Joseph Middleton, Lemuel W. Ashley. Written Oct. 9, 1856 Proved Nov. 23, 1856 p. 72

John D. Welch of Kent Co
My beloved wife **Sarah E. Welch** the negroes to wit, **Harriet** and her infant child and **Annie**, and such of my household and kitchen furniture she may consider necessary to furnish completely the house on the farm on which my son **William Welch** now resides and also one young brown mare, Erin and her colt, one bay mare Pigeon, one pair brown mules, one second size wagon and harness, one dearbom and harness, one new four wheel carriage and harness, eight head of cattle, eight head of sheep and ten head of hogs, to be selected by my said wife from my general stock and whatever corn, bacon and provender she may require to carry on the farm on which my said son William now resides from the time of my death to the end of the year in which I may die. My dau. **Martha Welch** the following negroes to wit, **Mary Ann, Caroline, Matilda, Lorenzo and George**. My son William Welch my negro girl **Maria**, in trust for my dau. **Louisa Mann**, wife of **J. C. Mann**, for and during her natural life and after her death for her children. My son William all my real estate and personal estate upon the condition that William shall within 6 months after my death convey all the land he now owns to Richard Hynson for the following uses and trust; first in trust for my beloved wife Sarah E. Welch for her natural life, then in trust for my dau. Martha Welch, if she die without leaving issue then in trust for my son William Welch. My will is that my said wife shall release in consideration of the above conveyance to my said son William, any claim she may have to dower and if my wife refuse or neglect to execute such a release within 6 months after my death, then William to have all real estate upon condition that he give his land in trust to **Richard Hynson,** otherwise land to wife during her life then to Martha Welch. William to pay for funeral expenses and to educate my said dau. Martha Welch and if necessary to pay comfortable support for my said dau. Louisa Mann during her life $200.

Exec. Not Given. Witnesses Richard Hynson, T. N. Tayman, George Neal Hines. Written Dec. 28, 1856 Proved Mar. 10, 1857 p. 73

Anna Maria Scott (widow), Georgetown Crossroads, Kent Co
I authorize my executors to complete deed to sale of my mill seat and adjacent lands to **Thomas E. Gooding** for $1,600 upon final payment. To my grandson **Edward Scott** (son of my son **Edward A. Scott**) when he is 21 $100. To all my grandchildren one bible to be paid out of my personal estate. The rest of my estate to my four daughters **Sophia C. Scott, Anna M. Scott, Catharine A. Scott** and **Elizabeth Scott** as long as

either of them shall live sole and unmarried. If they marry then they shall receive $50 per annum. If none of my daughters remain sole or widowed then to my son **Cornelius J. Scott** all my real estate (excepting and reserving the graveyard and square within the garden enclosed on the premises whereon I now reside forever for the purpose of interment for such of my children or descendants as may desire to be laid therein, with free ingress and egress to and from the same) in fee simple. If none of my daughters is sole or unmarried then the rest of my estate amongst all my children (except my son Cornelius J. Scott) and their descendants in loco parenties.

Execs. my son Cornelius J. Scott and my dau. Anna M. Scott. Witnesses John Frazier Jr, Elijah E. Miller, Albert Medders. Written Nov. 19, 1849 Proved Mar. 12, 1857 p. 75

James Urie of Kent Co

To my son **William Thomas Urie** the farm and plantation in Kent Co near Goose hill on which I reside together with all the lots of land, I purchased thereto, and he is to pay $100 a year for 5 years to my son **James Urie**. To my son William Thomas my negro boy **Daniel**, negro girl **Jane**, and negro man **Ned Parker**. Ned Parker to use the small house on the farm which I have erected for his use, so long as Ned shall conduct himself properly as the slave of my said son. Should the bond held against me by **Elizabeth Briscoe** for part purchase of the farm devised to my said son William Thomas Urie, not be paid at the time of my death, then to be paid from farm or by son William. My said son James $100 for 5 years and to James the nursery trees and stalks not planted out as permanent trees at my death on the farm I reside upon. All the rest of my estate I divide between my four daughters namely **Ann Elizabeth, Emeline, Sarah Louisa**, and **Laura**. I appoint George Vickers of Chestertown as executor. If in the event of a revocation of his letters, my will is that my daughters then living shall have the power to designate and appoint a suitable person

Exec. George Vickers of Chestertown. Witnesses G. Jeff Vickers, C. T. Lusby, W. H. Hamilton. Written Apr. 5, 1856 Proved Mar. 26, 1857 p. 77

Washington C. Loockerman, now of Chestertown

My property in Allegheny Co be sold. My negro slaves **John** and **Robert** be set free when age 30. All my books or retained at the discretion of my executor for the use of my son **F. S. Loockerman** and that they be disposed of for protection and secure preservation. The infant dau. **M. A. Waters** of my brother-in-law **D. E. S. Waters** have all the infant clothes found in my drawers or bureaus. To my son F. S. Loockerman all my property of whatever sort except what is devised to my brother-in-law's infant child. I appoint my father-in-law **Rev. F. Waters** sole executor and guardian to my son F. S. Loockerman.

Exec. my father-in-law Rev. F. Waters. Witnesses Andrew Sutton, J.M. Colby, Sarah D. Ballard. Written Mar. 1, 1857 Proved Apr. 4, 1857 p. 79

Liber 13 1854-1867

Richard T. Boyer of Kent Co
My brother **Stephen Boyer** my negro boy named **Wesley** a slave for life. To my nephew **William E. Cacy**, my negro boy named **Lee**, a slave for life. To my (word missing) **Samuel Cacy** my negro girl named **Emily**, a slave for life. To my dear wife **Sophia Boyer** my negro boy named **Lewis** and my negro woman **Amanda**, both slaves for life. also my negro man named **Emory** to serve four years from the date of this my will and at the expiration of the said seven years, I manumit. My farm, plantation and real estate, on which I reside which I purchased of **Samuel E. Briscoe**, which was afterwards conveyed by me to **William Cacy** and reconveyed to me by William Cacy together with all the lands contained in said deeds, and lands conveyed to me by **Peregrine Wethered** I give to my dear wife Sophia Boyer for and during her widowhood afterwards to my two brothers **Stephen Boyer** and **William Boyer**.

Exec. my dear wife Sophia Boyer. Witnesses David B. Griffith, Robert S. Griffith, Thomas P. Davis, J.P. Written Aug. 13, 1856 Proved May 12, 1857 p. 80

Hannah Atkinson
My farm called *"Friendship"* situate in Still Pond, which formerly belonged to my brother **Jacob Lamb** and now in the occupancy of my grandson **John B. Parrott**. My wood lot in Gleaves wood, adjoining the lands of the late **John Turner**, and which said lot also belonged to my said brother Jacob Lamb also to my grandson John B. Parrott. I give the rest of my estate to John B. Parrott.

Exec. my grandson John B. Parrott. Witnesses Henry T. Jump, Thomas L. Bowers, William L. Bowers. Written May 17 1849 Proved Apr. 6, 1857 p. 82

Pere Smith (colored) living near Washington College, Kent Co
To my wife **Elizabeth Smith** during her natural life after her death to my son **Josiah Smith** the house and lots of ground adjoining in which I now live. To my dau. **Kitty Reed** now living in Baltimore, one bed and 13 ½ acres of land on *"Hopewell"* which adjoining the lands of **Stephen Biddle** and **Mr. Goff** and which I purchased of **Judge Eccliston** to her.

Exec. Josiah Smith. Witnesses Peregrine Wroth, James Arthur, Thomas B. Hynson. Written Feb. 9, 1853 Proved July 3, 1857 p. 83

Adeline G. Hammond of Kent Co
To my husband **William S. Hammond** for his natural life my farm and lands in Worton in Kent Co commonly called *"Green Point"*, after his death to my two dear relations **Sarah E. Kennard** and **Mary Ann Kennard**. I give to my said relation Sarah E. Kennard $600 to be paid by my husband William S. Hammond. William S. Hammond consents to the making of the will by his wife Adeline G. Hammond

Exec. my husband William S. Hammond. Witnesses James F. Gordon, Joseph N. Gordon Jr., George Vickers. Written May 13, 1857 Proved Aug. 17, 1857 p. 84

Rebecca Ringgold of Kent Co
To be interred in a plain black coffin, my grave bricked but no gloves or scarfs to be provided for the funeral. To my niece **Elizabeth H. N.** Smith $700 and a bedstead, bed, bolster and pillows, two pair of sheets and two pillow cases. To my nephew **James H. Smith** $200. To my nephew **Thomas Nicholson Smith** $200. To the Missionary Society of the Methodist Episcopal Church, incorporated by an Act of the Legislature of the State of New York passed Apr. 9, 1829 $150. To the American Bible Society formed in New York in 1816 $150. To the Trustees of the Methodist Episcopal Church of Chestertown by their corporate name $200 to be applied to the erection of a new Methodist Episcopal Church in Chestertown or to a remodeling of the present church. To my grandson **William Fletcher Ringgold** a silver ladle, to my grandson **John Edward Ringgold**, 6 silver tablespoons, and to my granddau. **Mary Rebecca Ringgold,** 12 desert spoons, 20 teaspoons, one pair of sugar tongs, one pair of butter knives, and four salt shovels, all silver. The guardian of my granddau. Mary Rebecca Ringgold to pay the sum of $12 annually to the Trustees of the Methodist Episcopal Church in Chestertown until she is 18. My servant man **Harry** to be sold to serve until Jan. 1, 1866 and my servant boy **James** to be sold till he is 28 and then be free. My house and lot in Water Street in Chestertown now occupied by me and which formerly belonged to the late John Constable deceased be sold. So much of the upper portion of my farm near Chestertown to be laid off by a line running parallel to the new road, from near Washington College to Morgans Creek as will with the extension of that line across the land adjoining my farm and devised to me for life by my late husband **Edward Ringgold** according to the direction in the will of my late son **John Fletcher Ringgold,** as shall cut off or leave 150 acres in the upper portion. I give to my grandson **William Fletcher Ringgold** the remainder of my farm and lands on which **William Vansant** resides. I give to my granddau. **Mary Rebecca Ringgold** should William die before 21 lands willed to him, William to have entire land if Mary dies before age 21 and no issue, but charged with a legacy of $3,000 to be paid in 8 years to my grandson **John Edward Ringgold.** No division of lands until the eldest of my said three grandchildren John Edward, Mary Rebecca, and Wm Fletcher (children of my son **John Fletcher Ringgold**) is 21 and interest used for their education and maintenance. The guardian can use sums to keep up buildings. $1,000 to be used to improve lots willed by my son John F. The widow of my said son John Fletcher Ringgold not to have any dower interest in my lands or the income by virtue of the liberty exercised by him in his will. My two servants **Frederick Nicols** and **Delia** I direct to be hired out for my said grandchildren until my granddau. Mary Rebecca Ringgold shall arrive at 18, and if necessary to the erection of a dwelling house on the lower part of my farm devised to her. In case there shall be a deficiency to pay the pecuniary legacies to my niece, nephews, the Missionary and Bible Societies and to the Trustees of the Methodist Episcopal Church, I direct that the deficiency to be made up and paid out by the sale of my servants Harry and James and the proceeds of the sale of my house and lot. I give to my dau. in law, **Sarah Catharine H. Ringgold**

Liber 13 1854-1867

$100 annually. All the rest of my estate to my two grandchildren **Mary Rebecca Ringgold** and **William Fletcher Ringgold**. Exec. Thomas W. Eliason and to take his brother William (Eliason) as one of his sureties and to be guardian for my grandchildren and in case of his death I would desire that Benjamin B. Perkins of Chestertown should succeed him in both offices.

Exec. Thomas W. Eliason. Witnesses Ann Perkins, Eliza Perkins, George Vickers. Written Feb. 7, 1857 Proved Sep. 26, 1857 p. 86

<u>Codicil</u> My niece **Elizabeth H. Smith** shall have the privilege of keeping house, if I die before the end of the present year she is to receive $50. In case she continues to keep house my dau. in law shall have the privilege of living in the family without paying any board from my death.

Rebecca Fox

To my four children **Samuel, Salley, Mary Ann** and **James B.** and my grandchild **Sarah M. Lane**, the child of my deceased dau. Henrietta all my estate share and share alike subject to the following exceptions: To my two sons **Samuel** and **James B.** a horse each selected by them out of my stock of horses

Exec. my friend William T. Spry. Witnesses Samuel Comegys, T.H.W.F. Cornet. Written May 28, 1956 Proved Oct. 27, 1857 p. 92

Henry Mastin of Kent Co

To my dearly beloved wife **Mary Ann Mastin** my personal estate except my negro man **John** and **Amanda** and child. To my nephew **Joseph B. Mastin** my man **John**, and all my real estate in fee simple provided he have lawful issue but if he die without lawful issue then to **Joseph Asbury Mastin**, son of my uncle **William Mastin**. I will my negro woman **Amanda** and her infant child unto **Sarah Ann Moody**, wife of **John Moody**, Amanda to serve 6 years from this date and the child now about 9 months old to serve until 31 years.

Exec. my dear wife Mary Ann Mastin. Witnesses George W. Crossly, James Gale, Joseph C. Rasin. Written Oct. 22, 1857 Proved Nov. 3, 1857 p. 93

Richard Hazzard (of Color)

To my wife **Mary Hazzard** all my personal estate except my gray mare colt which I will to my son **Jacob**. I will my four daughters **Ann, Harriett Jane, Mary Drucilla,** and **Emily,** all the profits of my house and land (after my wife's 1/3) until Jan. 1, 1861. To my son Jacob my house and all my lands to have on Jan. 1, 1861, if he die without issue then to my wife and four daughters.

Exec. Not Given. Witnesses William Graves, Lemuel Skeggs, Levinus E. Graves. Written Aug. 24, 1857 Proved Nov. 4, 1857 p. 94

Hugh Wallis of Kent Co

All my estate to my children or their children if they are deceased. If any of my children are under 18 for girls and 21 for boys, they are to receive $100 till of age for their education and maintenance. The legacies I charge upon all my real estate to equalize as near as may be the gifts to my children, whichever of my children shall be of age shall pay proportionally the said charges of $100 annually to my minor children. In case my personal estate exclusive of my negroes shall be insufficient to pay my debts I give power to sell a tract of land called *"Wyatts Chance"* and *"Plain Dealing"* supposed to contain about 300 acres, formerly part of the middle farm. To my son **William W. Wallis** my farm and land in Kent Co called the Partnership on upper farm, now occupied by **John S. Henlock** containing about 653 acres but charged with the following legacies: to my son **Walter G. Wallis** $5,015, to my dau. **Ruth Ann Wallis** $5,015, to my son **Samuel Wright Wallis** $5,015, to my dau. **Margaret Helen Wallis** $5,015, to my son **Benjamin Franklin Wallis** $25, **Henry Clay Wallis** $8, to bear interest upon my death except the legacy for Ruth Ann shall be paid in 2 years, until each male arrives at 21 and female at 18. To my son **Hugh Maxwell Wallis** my home farm in Morgans Creek Neck in Kent Co called the *"Maiden's Lot farm"*, now occupied by me containing about 500 acres and I charge him with the following legacies: to my son **Benjamin Franklin Wallis** $4,970, to my son **Henry Clay Wallis** $5,006, and to my son **Marion Brooks Wallis** $5,006. To my dau. **Hannah Isabella Wallis,** my farm in Kent Co called *"Darnels Farm"* commonly called the middle farm containing about 210 acres and I charge her with the payment of the following legacies: to my dau. **Elvira Knock** $1,265, to my son **Benjamin Franklin Wallis** $9, **Mary Elvira**'s legacy to be paid in two years and Benjamin's to be paid at age 21. To my dau. **Mary Elvira Knock** (wife of **Samuel H. Knock**) my farm in Kent Co called *"Buckingham"* containing 150 acres. My negroes as follows: To my son **Hugh Maxwell Wallis** my negro **Ferdinand** and my negro woman **Julia** and he is charge with the following legacies to son **William W. Wallis** $197 and my son Benjamin $6. To my son **Walter G. Wallis** my negro boy **Ned** and he is charged with the following legacies to my son **Henry Clay Wallis** $97 and to **Benjamin F. Wallis** $6. To my son **Samuel Wright Wallis,** my negro boy **Amos** and I charge him with the following legacies to my granddau. **Margaret Helen Wallis** $47, **Benjamin Franklin Wallis** $6. To my dau. **Margaret Helen Wallis** my negro woman **Alethea** and my negro girl **Harriett.** To my son **Benjamin Franklin Wallis** my negro woman **Sarah** and her child **Jenny Lind.** To my son **Henry Clay Wallis** my negro woman named **Alethia Waters.** To my son **Marion Brooks Wallis** my negro girl **Lydia.** To my dau. **Mary E. Knock** my negro boy **Joe** and I charge her with the following legacies to Benjamin $3, to Marion $97. My daughters Mary E, Hannah J, and Ruth Ann have heretofore received negroes from me. My three old negroes I dispose of as follows: **Abe** aged about 70 to my son William and his support is charged to William, **Amos** aged about 60, and **Shadrach** aged about 60 to my son Hugh and their support charged to him. The family should be kept together under **Hugh M. Wallis** and his sister **Ruth Ann.**

Liber 13 1854-1867

Execs. Samuel H. Knock, my sons William W. Wallis and Hugh Maxwell Wallis. Witnesses Edward A. Moore, Eben F. Perkins, Joseph N. Gordon Jr. Written June 23, 1855 Proved Dec. 1, 1857 p. 95

Codicil My dear and affectionate wife, **Sarah Ann Wallis** my gray carriage mare, my small carriage and harness and $300 annually in lieu of dower Nov. 23, 1857. Witnesses R. Hynson, A. W. Melvin, William H. Meetur
Renunciation of Widow Widow Sarah A. Wallis renounces claim to dower in lieu of the codicil which provides an annual sum for her.

Hester A. Taylor of Kent Co
To my sister **Salina C. Taylor** during her natural life house and lot situate in town of Millington and my colored woman **Caroline** and her son **Charles** colored boy and all other property, the colored woman to serve till she arrives at 35 and the boy till 28 then both set free. At Salina's death, the estate to pass to my niece **Catherine M. Taylor** and my nephew **William McK. Taylor**, the dau. and son of Dr. **William McK. Taylor** deceased.

Exec. Not Given. Witnesses John E. Stewart, J.A. Edwards, W.J. Anderson. Written Sep. 22, 1857 Proved Dec. 1, 1857 p. 100

Nancy Leaverton of Kent Co
To my son **Charles Leaverton** my negro woman **Susan** aged about 30 to serve for 6 years after my death and then set free, also my negro boy **John Wesley** aged about 5 years to serve until he reaches age 35 years, and a negro boy, an infant, called **Jacob** aged about 9 months to serve until he arrives at 35, and also to have a feather bed, bedding, and bedstead. To my son **William Spencer Leaverton** my negro girl called **George Anna** aged about 7 years to serve until 35 and then set free, also my negro boy called **Adam** aged about 3 years to serve until 35, also my negro boy **Samuel** aged about 2 years to serve until 35, and to have my silver watch, family bible, a feather bed and bedding, bedstead, cupboard and bureau. To my son **James Leaverton** a feather bed, bedding and bedstead. The rest of my estate to my two sons Charles Leaverton and William Spencer Leaverton.

Exec. my son William Spencer Leaverton. Witnesses William S. Lassell, C.H. Kenton, A.F. Fowler. Written Nov. 19, 1857 Proved Jan. 12, 1858 p. 101

Peregrine Wethered of Kent Co
To have my body interred in a decent plain manner no inscription to be placed upon my tombstone except my name and age and the names of my parents **John and Mary Wethered** and to place in my coffin before burial a sufficient quantity of quick lime to prevent the destruction of the body by the maggots or have it wrapped in a well tarred sheet. To my son **John L. Wethered** in fee simple my *"Pools Island"* farm together will all the personal property consisting of negroes, cattle, and farming utensils subject to the

payment of $5,000 to my dau. **Mary Elizabeth Wethered** in $1,000 installments and to release title to his sister interest in the *"Turners Creek Point"* property, and the grain which may be on hand and growing upon said island at the time of my death. To my said dau. the "Turners Creek Point" property consisting of the granary, wharf store house dwelling houses lots gardens and all other houses therein with the brick mansion house containing about 50 acres adjoining land purchased by me as part of real estate of the late **William Blay Tilden** and land purchased at the sale of the estate of **Isaac Stavely** on which the **Rev. John Owen** now resides subject to about 30 acres which I got in exchange with **J.W. Webb** for part of the *"Knock farm"*, together with the remainder of the Knock farm, and also $5,000 paid out of my *"Pools Island farm"*. To my said dau. all my carriages horses, oxen, cows, carts, and farming utensils with ½ of the furniture, plate etc and ½ of the library at my residence and the following servants: Old negro man **Abe**, Old negro woman **Beck**, little **Abe**, all the slaves now at **Samuel Comegys**, all those slaves at **George W. Price**'s, **Peregrine Price**'s, **Isaac L. Price**'s, **Joseph Carrow**'s, **Bill Tinch** and wife and child, a woman and child at **Mr. Lusby**'s, a negro woman at **Mr. Morris**, also a servant girl at **Nathaniel Hynson's**. The whole of the estate shall not be subject to my daughter's husband should she marry. If she die without heirs to my son John L. Wethered, if he die without heirs then to **Samuel** and **George Y. Wethered** sons of my brother Samuel Wethered. My son John L. shall have a right of way from his young farm to some convenient point on the land belonging to the mansion farm free of charge and all the rest of my estate not named herein. To the daughters of **Mrs. Maria Scott** late widow of **Doct. Scott** the negroes woman and children which are now in their possession or which were in the possession of their said mother at the time of her death except the one given by me to one of her daughters on condition that they shall not be removed out of the limits of the state of MD except to Liberia where I have provision that all my slaves may go. I give to my sister **Matilda Jeffries** $100 annually during her life payment thereof I tax from *"Pools Island farm"*. I give to **Elizabeth Eubanks** $100 annually during her life payable from Pools Island farm and also a negro woman which was at Mrs. Maria Scott's Georgetown Cross Roads during her life and thereafter to my dau. Mary Elizabeth. To **Revd John Owen** free rent of the house and premises now occupied by him for and during his continuance as paster of Shrewsbury church and no longer. When any one of my negroes shall arrive at age 40 may be desirous of going to Africa permanently to reside then his or her master or mistress shall surrender them up for that object and furnish them with the aid necessary to enable them to settle in the land of their forefather being impressed with the firm conviction that it would be for their best interests, as to setting them free in this country or prohibiting them from being sold for rebellious conduct I absolutely object to as being an injury to society and equally so to the slave.

Exec. my son John L. Wethered. Witnesses William Thomas Tomlinson, Emeline R. Tomlinson, Joseph E. Weer. Written May 28, 1857 Proved Jan. 12, 1858 p. 103

Liber 13 1854-1867

Mary Boyer dau. of Augustine Boyer late of Kent Co, gentleman
To my beloved sister Susan Boyer all the property I now hold such as Bank stock in Philadelphia and Smyrna the ½ of the slaves which we hold in common, money on mortgage, household furniture, plate, and wearing apparel. (Entire Will of Mary Boyer repeated on page 106)

Exec. my sister Susan Boyer. Witnesses Samuel H. Stephens, William H. Stephens. Written June 1, 1844 Proved Mar. 11, 1858 p. 105

Hezekiah Mastin of Kent Co
To my grandson Joseph Boots Mastin all my estate except the following provisions for my wife Alethea Mastin to have $500 annually out of the proceeds of the farm on which I now reside adjoining the village of Chesterville, if not enough then she to receive no more then the net rents of such farm. To my wife Alethea Mastin my negro girl Susan to serve until 35 years, also a good bed and bedding with it. If my wife survive me, I give to her the several articles of personal property she has bequeathed in her own will with my assent. I also give to her ½ of the books in my library sharing equally with my grandson Joseph Boots Mastin, these bequests in lieu of dower. If my grandson Joseph dies without legal heir then the property to William Harrington Mastin son of my brother James Polk Mastin in fee simple. My 8-day clock, desk and book case and cupboard shall not be sold and shall be the sole use of my grandson after the death of my wife. The tenant occupying the farm before named shall procure fuel and timber for the use of said farm from the tract called *"Grantham"* until my wife's claim on said farm shall cease. It is also my will that the large 8-day clock shall not be sold out of the house where it now stands so long as the property shall remain in the Mastin family. My negro boy Stephen to be set free at 35 years

Exec. John Wesley Pierson (John renounced right to administer Apr. 6, 1858). Witnesses George. W. Medders, Elijah Crossly, John W. Pierson. Written Nov. 1, 1857 Proved Mar. 23, 1858 p. 107

James Gilbert (free man of color) of Kent Co
To David Warren my house and lot of land in Kent Co for 5 years ending Jan. 1, 1862. To my dau. Eliza Scott commencing from Jan. 1, 1862 the said house and lot for her natural life then to my grandson William Richardson. To my said friend David Warren all my farm utensils and my cows until Jan. 1, 1862. The increase will belong to him and one cow absolutely. All my household and kitchen furniture except the beds, bedsteads, and bedding I give equally to David Warren and Maria Hodges (Maria also to receive one cow after 5 years). To Minta Butler one cow after Jan. 1, 1862. To George Bowser one calf. To David Warren one bed, bedstead and bedding. All the remainder of my estate to David Warren and Maria Hodges

Exec. my friend David Warren. Witnesses Thomas Baker, John W. Lond, John W. Jones. Written Feb. 21, 1857 Proved Apr. 14, 1858 p. 109

Sarah Ringgold Wickes of Kent Co
To my son **Joseph Wickes** my negro man **William Doran**, Remainder of my estate to both my daughters **Sarah Jane** and **Catharine**

Exec. my dau. Sarah Jane Wickes. Witnesses Richard W. Jones, William Stevens, Martha A. Bordley. Written Jan. 27, 1858 Proved May 11, 1858 p. 110

Henry Porter of Kent Co
To my beloved wife **Ann Maria Porter** my whole estate during her widowhood. After her death or marriage, then to my eldest son **Joseph Henry Porter,** my home farm containing about 300 acres which I purchased of **Joseph Wickes** as trustee for the sale of the estate of **John Ashley** late of Kent Co, subject to the payment of $3,000 to his sister **Sarah Matilda Porter** and the like sum to his sister **Millicent Henrietta Porter** in three equal installments if he is 21 when he receives land. After the death or marriage of my wife, I give to my second son **George M. Porter** my farm generally known as *"The Gears Farm"* containing about 300 acres which I purchased of **Joseph Wickes** as trustee aforesaid, saving part of the said farm beginning at the corner of said farm at I.U. cross roads and running thence along and with the public road leading from said corner to Chestertown until it reaches a stone set about 280 yards from said corner and then in a straight line in a SW direction until it intersects with the line of division between said *"Gears Farm"* and the manor, then by and with the said division line until it reaches certain lots then with line of division between said lots and the "Gears farm" to the public road leading from Worton Heights to I.U. church, then by and with said road to the beginning supposed to contain about 120 acres subject to the sum of $1,000 to my said dau. **Ann V. Porter** in 5 equal installments. The aforegoing 120 acres to my dau. **Anna V. Porter.** To my son Joseph H. my negro **Pere** now about 20 years and **Bill** about 9 years, each to serve until 35. To my son George M. my negro boy **George** who has a term of years to serve (no number given) and whom I bought of **Moses Kennard** as the administrator of Moses Kennard deceased. To my dau. Anna V. Porter a negro boy **Pere** now about 6 years old until age 38 then set free. To my dau. Sarah M. my negro girl **Sarah Rebecca** about 12 years until she is age 35. To my dau. Millicent H. my negro girl **Charlotte** whom I bought of Moses Kennard as administrator aforesaid and my negro boy **Peter** now about 18 months until age 38. Whereas my said son John has shown an inclination to marry a certain **Rachael Hills**, the dau. of **S. Hills** now the owner of *"Rells Mills"*, if John marries against my consent or the consent of his mother then the farm to go to his brother George and the farm given to George to go to said son Joseph. After the death of my wife, the rest of my estate to all my children equally

Exec. my wife Ann Maria Porter. Witnesses Richard Hynson, R. S. Thomas, John Greenwood. Written Aug. 8, 1856 Proved June 15, 1858 p. 111

Robert T. Allen of Kent Co
Whereas by the last will purporting to be the last will of my wife **Ann E. Allen** I am authorized to charge her real estate devised in trust for my dau. $1,000. To **Wm L.**

Bowers all my estate upon the following uses and trusts, to permit my dau. **Robertine R. L. Allen** for her natural life all my estate and upon her death to her issue, if she have no issue then to whomever dau. would give by her own will, if she shall die without will then to any surviving husband during his life but not the power to cut and sell wood, and after his death then to my father **William Allen**, his heirs or assigns.

Exec. my beloved wife A.E. Allen. Witnesses John L. Bowers, John B. Parrott, Thomas L. Bowers. Written Sep. 2, 1853 Proved July 14, 1858 p. 114

Codicil In addition to my well beloved wife Ann E. Allen's dower in my real estate which I wish her to have I give her all of my stock of every kind, farming utensils and household and kitchen furniture that she may elect to take. Date, 1853 (no month or day given). Witnesses Samuel L. Roeder, Joshua Vansant, Henry Mullikin

Araminta A. Brooks of Kent Co
To my two sons **John P. D. Brooks** and **George C. M. Brooks** all my estate, if either die without issue to the survivor and my plate may be equally divided. If my son George C. M. Brooks be too young at the time of my death to act as one of my executors then son John shall be sole executor

Execs. my sons John P. D. Brooks and George C. M. Brooks. Witnesses David Collins, Thomas B. Hynson, R. A. Starn. Written Apr. 12, 1853 Proved June 18, 1858 p. 117

John M. Armstrong of Kent Co
Orphans Court to value land and divide equally amongst all of my children. To my son **John M. Armstrong Jr.** the home farm upon which I now reside. To my son **William Armstrong** the farm upon which he now resides. The remainder of my estate to my three daughters. My negroes divided amongst my children equally based on their valuation so long as they shall remain slaves under the last will and testament of my father **William Armstrong**. My negro boy **Henry** to my son John and my negro boy **Charles** to my dau. **Sarah A. Armstrong** and my negro girl **Mary Ellen** to my dau. **Ariminta E. Armstrong** and my negro boy **James** to be the slave of my dau. **Ann Louisa Armstrong** and my negro girl **Mary Jane** to be the slave of my son William Armstrong, each to serve until 33 and then set free. My negro **Sarah** to be free during the present year. I give her child now about one year old named **Kate** to serve the said mother until age 21 and then child Kate to be set free. To my 3 daughters my small york carriage and old brown mare. Remainder of estate to all my children.

Exec. my son John M. Armstrong Jr. Witnesses James Heighe, Cornelius J. Scott, T. N. Tayman. Written May 4, 1858 Proved July 27, 1858 p. 118

Josephine Browne
All my estate to my only child **Mary Ann Browne**, but if she die under 18 and without issue then I give to my brothers and sisters now living to be divided equally. If my dau.

arrive at 18 then the property is hers absolutely in fee. The Orphans court to appoint a person to administer my estate

Exec. Not Given. Witnesses Elizabeth C. Frazier, Elise A. Trible, George Vickers. Written July 23, 1858 Proved Aug. 3, 1858 p. 120

Ebenezer Welch of Kent Co

My wife **Margaret T. Welch** $300 annually during her natural life to be paid as follows whereas my brother **John D. Welch** deceased is indebted to me by bond date Sept 25, 1854 for $4,000 plus interest of $826 my will is that my nephew **William Welch** (devisee of the land of my brother **John D.** Welch) that he execute a new bond in his own name secured by mortgage on his real estate and making the interest due semiannually to my wife during her natural life. If the interest shall not amount to $300 per annum then the deficiency to be made up by my nephew **Thomas A. Jacob** charge against the lands hereinafter devised to him. If the interest is more then my wife is to have it. If from unforeseen event my personal estate shall not pay my debts I charge my farm to be given to my nephew Thomas A. Jacobs to pay my said wife. If my nephew William Welch shall decline to secure said bond then my executor to invest the same in landed security. To my wife I also give 12 chairs and the sofa and a horse, carriage and harness, the grey horse, or she prefers another in lieu of it my nephew Thomas A. Jacobs to select a good horse for her, also one bed, bedstead and bedding in parlor chamber and rocking chair. I set free all my negroes on Jan. 1 next after my decease and I charge all my estate even if necessary to sell every property and estate to pay my debts. Any stock or other property that I have given or may give to any of my negroes as presents I wish to be theirs. I liberate all my negro children that may born hereafter. The annuity and legacy to my wife in lieu of any claim of dower. To my negro man **George** and his heirs I give the lot of ground I purchased of **Pearce** which formerly belong to the Swan town property (Mill property) and containing 3 acres. To my negro man **Jacob** I give a lot of ground in the Pines and part of land I purchased of **Samuel E. Briscoe** containing 2 acres and after his death if he has no child then to his two nephews **Arthur** and **Eben** and I give to said Jacob my mare Harriett Ann B. for his attention to my horses. To my negro woman **Caroline** and her children a lot of land containing 2 acres on Herring Branch, a NE course from my dwelling and near to and adjoining the division line between my lands and **Doctor John Frazier**, if she dies then land to children living at that time, born before or after the making of this will. The negroes to receive the land on Jan. 1 after my decease. They shall not sell any land without first offering to nephew Thomas A. Jacobs. Whereas I have contracted to purchase of **C. H. Fairchild** 100 acres of his farm, clear of dower at the price of $1,500 and have paid him in stock etc near $300 the balance to be paid in the present year, the object is to give the said land to a number of my negroes, each to have 6 acres viz, to **Bill Sampson, John Day Piner, William Henry Moore, Sarah Blackiston, Emily Blackiston, Stephen Hardin, Arthur Moore, Alexander Yearly Moore, Andrew Hemphill Carmichael, Maria Carmichael, Kitty Frizby** (now living at Mr. **Stagles**), each part to be laid off and bounded by my nephew Thomas. The remainder of the 100 acres to be held in common by my said negroes. They can not sell except to each other and to pass to their children. Bill Sampson to have first choice of lots and the others appropriately assigned by my nephew Thomas. To **Abe Stanly** and his wife during their joint life a house and lot in Kent Co containing 15 acres which was conveyed to me by **John Lee** and wife on Dec 13, 1857 and after their death to the children of **George Boulden** that may be living but charged with payment of $50. To **George Boulden's** wife and children a house and lot containing 3 acres which was conveyed to me John Lee and wife by deed dated Dec. 13, 1857 but charged with payment of $20. To **George Maguire's** wife and children a house and lot which was conveyed to me by George Maguire and wife dated May 27, 1854 and charged with payment of $75. I give the debt due me from **Wm T. Burgess** and which is intended to be secured by mortgage and amounting to $1,000 as follows: $800 to my grandnephew and grandniece **Sarah Elizabeth** and **Eben Welch**, children of **Richard S. Welch**, and the residue of $200 to **Sarah Elizabeth Welch** their mother, deducting dower rent of **Mrs. Rueter.** My nephew **James Welch** the house and shop in the head of Sassafras which I purchased at constables sale. My undivided ½ part of the Swan Town mill property and property at Swan Town, with machinery, fixtures etc to the mill and divide between my sister **Ann Trenchard** and **Sarah Elizabeth Moffett** (dau. of **William Moffett**). After the death of my wife, the debt due from my brother John D. Welch, I give to all those persons who would be heirs at law at my death as if I had died intestate. To **Annette Tower Vickers**, dau. of my friend **George Vickers**, the sum of $1,000 to be paid by my nephew Thomas. To my old and valued friend George Vickers with whom I have for many years enjoyed uninterrupted friendship and as a mark of my regard for him, I give $1,000, which I am sure he will give a reasonable time to my nephew to pay both these legacies. I give to my nephew Thomas A. Jacobs and his heirs subject to the payment of my debts and legacies, all my farm, plantation, tracts, and parcels of land on which I reside and all the rest of my real estate and all my personal estate (except my negroes and such part before disposed of). The collateral tax on my negroes shall be paid by my nephew Thomas. I give to my nephew **James Welch** $800

Exec. George Vickers. Witnesses William A. Brice, John R. Wilson, Thomas C. Lynch. Written Jan. 29, 1858 Proved Oct. 8, 1858 p. 121

Mary Ann Hamm of Kent Co
All my estate to my sister **Williamina Hamm**.

Exec. my dear sister Williamina Hamm. Witnesses S. J. Bradley, Thomas J. Britton, William F. Smyth. Written Sep. 9, 1858 Proved Oct. 12, 1858 p. 125

Jemima Naudain of Middletown, New Castle Co, DE
Widow of **John A. Naudain** late of Cecil Co, deceased. I give to my son **William Henry Blackiston** of Kent Co for his natural life and no longer my real estate in Kent Co, all my tract of land known by the name of *"Davis' Industry"*, and *"The Forest Farm"*, and all the tract of wood land called *"The Sixty Acre lot"*, or by whatsoever name may be known. The said William keeping all the premises in good order and repair and

after his death to his lawful children (except his dau. **Josephine Blackiston**) to be equally divided and to their children per stirpes if any child is deceased with issue. Josephine excepted because provision made for her in item fourth. To my nephew **Alfred C. Nowland** of Cecil Co land in Cecil Co known by the name of *"Worsell Manor"* in trust for the benefit of my grandchildren of my deceased dau. **Ann Elizabeth Naudain**, late the wife of **Doctor James S. Naudain** of St. Georges Hundred, in New Castle Co aforesaid namely: **Mary Louisa Naudain, James Blackiston Naudain, Alice Schee Naudain, Lydia Eddowes Naudain**, and **Mary Jemima Naudain**. Alfred to collect and manage rents for benefit of grandchildren. At 21 each grandchild to receive his or her full share. At the age of 21 of the youngest grandchild a deed for them as tenants in common to be executed. To Alfred C. Nowland all that certain brick messuage and lot of land situate in the village of Middletown, New Castle Co which John M. Smith and Hannah his wife by date Dec. 24, 1842 and recorded at New Castle Book L. Vol. 5 p. 265 deeded to me in fee simple, in trust for benefit during her minority of granddau. **Anne Matilda Naudain,** a child of my said deceased dau. Ann Elizabeth Naudain, late the wife of the said Doctor James S. Naudain. After Anne is 21, duly executed deed to be issued, if she die under 21 then held in trust for her brother and sisters. To Alfred C. Nowland all the dwelling house and lot of land in Middletown the remainder or reversion whereof in fee simple was granted to me by Maria Moody, by deed of date June 7, 1842 recorded at New Castle Book J. Vol. 5, p 384 in trust for my granddau. Josephine Blackiston aforesaid dau. of my son William. At 21 to be issued a deed, if she die without heirs then to children of William H. Blackiston. To Alfred C. Nowland in trust for my two granddaughters **Anne Jemima Blackiston** and **Emma Blackiston,** children of my said son William, all sums of money my said son William owes me. To Alfred C. Nowland in trust of my granddau. Mary Jemima Naudain all sums of money which Doctor James S. Naudain owes me for rent and for money lent him. If she die under 21 then to her two sisters Anne Matilda Naudain and Lydia Eddowes Naudain. Neither my son William or Doctor James Naudain or any person related to the said doctor by consanguinity be appointed trustee or administrator. For any person attempting hindrance to this will, all provisions for that person are revoked.

Exec. Alfred C. Nowland (revoked by 3rd codicil and replaced by David C. Blackiston). Witnesses Robert A. Cochrane, David McKee, William Wood. Written Apr. 3, 1844 Proved Nov. 11, 1858 p. 126

1st Codicil Doctor James S. Naudain has reduced his debt to me by disposing of some furniture to me which I have attached a schedule. Nephew Alfred C. Naudain (mistake for Nowland) of Cecil Co named in will as trustee shall have every piece of furniture in trust for my grandchildren. Written Apr. 6, 1844. Witnesses Robert A. Cochrane, David McKee, William Wood

Schedule A pair linen sheets, one pair linen pillow cases, a Bolster case for **Maria Louisa Naudain.** A mahogany pier table with marble top, a pier looking glass and two mahogany pedal dining table now at **William Henry Blackiston** for **James Blackiston Naudain.** A pair mantel lamps, a pair mantel ornaments, a mantel looking glass at **Ann**

Liber 13 1854-1867

McIntires, one pair plated candlesticks snuffers and tray, one tea set french china, now at **Ann McIntires**, two linen pillow cases, one pair linen sheets, one Bolster case and one pair venetian blinds for **Ann Matilda Naudain**. One mahogany toilet table, one mahogany wash stand, with marble top, now at Ann McIntires, two pair linen pillow cases, one pair linen sheets, one Bolster case, one calico bed quilt for **Alice Schee Naudain**. One Boston rocking chair, 8 Rush bottom chairs now at William Henry Blackiston, one set granite tea ware now at Ann McIntires, one maple bedstead and feather bed, one pair venetian blinds, one pair linen sheets, two pair pillow cases, one linen Bolster case for **Lydia Eddowes Naudain**. One Marseilles quilt, two damask table clothes, 6 damask napkins, 6 table napkins and cake cover, one pair linen sheets, two pair pillow cases, one linen Bolster case for **Mary Jemima Naudain**
<u>Second Codicil</u> Whereas the real estate belonging to my deceased dau. **Ann Elizabeth Naudain** (formerly **Ann Elizabeth Blackiston**) the same lying in New Castle appears to have been encumbered with debts due to **John Richardson** and **William Richardson** at the time of her death, therefore I have signed over a mortgage of **James S. Naudain** to John Richardson for the sum of $1,500 and to William Richardson a judgement bond to **Jonathan Catlin** and **Catherine Justice** for $1,000. John Richardson's bond against James S. Naudain and wife transferred to Alfred C. Nowland in trust recorded at New Castle in Mortgage Record E Vol 1 p. 406 Nov 20 1846 and a judgement bond from Jonathan Catlin and Catherine Justice for $1,000 given to me on Nov. 29, 1848 for the children of my deceased dau. (all named again). Two shares held by me in the Cantwells Bridge Navigation and Steam Boat Cos to Alfred in trust for my granddau. Mary Jemima Naudain. Written Dec. 9, 1848. Witnesses Robert A. Cochrane, David McKee, William Wood
<u>Third Codicil</u> Since the execution of my will my son William Henry Blackiston hath died leaving a widow **Hannah Maria Blackiston** and nine children, I therefore revoke the two farms for life called *"Davis' Industry"* and *"The Forest Farm"* and *"The Sixty Acre Lot"* and my executor shall sell the land and ½ of *"The Sixty Acre Wood Lot"* shall pay the debts due from my late son William and to save the home or mansion farm of my son in the Upper part of Kent then I authorize the sale of my said farms. Any surplus money to the said H. Maria Blackiston the widow and the following children of my said son **William Henry Blackiston, Samuel Hepburn, Henry Curtis, Anna Jemima, Emma Hepburn, Slater Clay, Clara Leite, Lizzie and Mary Euginia Blackiston**. I have omitted my granddau. **Joseph(ine) Blackiston** from the foregoing since I have made other provision for her in my will. An addition of woodland remaining about 30 acres I have to my H. Maria Blackiston and my grandchildren Samuel H., Henry Curtis, Josephine, Anna Jemima, Emma Hepburn, Slater Clay, Clara Leite, Lizzie, Mary Euginia Blackiston as tenants in common. I revoke the appointment of my nephew Alfred C. Nowland as trustee or executor and appoint my friend David C. Blackiston of Kent Co trustee and executor. Written July 16, 1853. Witnesses Charles Tatman Jr., Edward T. Wroth, Joshua F. Biddle

Perry Price of Kent Co
To my beloved wife **Elizabeth Price** and my real and personal estate in trust for the purpose of keeping and supporting together my present family of children and making her to educate the younger ones until my youngest son **Perry J. Maxwell Price** shall arrive at 21. My estate be sold and the money arising therefrom to be equally divided among all of my children and my said wife if then living to be entitled to her right of dower.

Exec. my wife Elizabeth Price. Witnesses John Wilson, Joshua Clark, William M. A. S. Maxwell. Written June, 1858 (no day given) Proved Jan. 1, 1859 p. 142

Samuel Price Farmer of St. Georges Hund., New Castle Co, Del
To my beloved wife **Lydia A.** Price 1/3 part of all the income of my estate and I give 1/3 part of the income of the purchase money of a farm I sold in Kent Co to a certain William Cacy for the sum of $7,400 and 1/3 part of the annual income of rents paying the taxes at the rate of 20 bushels per acre or 1/5 of the clear or tillable land, also the rent, corn of the farm I sold to **William Cacy** in Kent co in lieu of dower. My son **John Price** my house, lot and stove house in the village of Warwick, Cecil Co, MD now occupied by Hays & Hauston Merchants to his heirs and $400 to be paid from the purchase money for the farm I sold William Cacy and that my said son John Price shall pay to my son **George W.** Price $40 until he arrive at 21. Two sons **Edwin Price** and **George W.** Price the sum of $7,400 to be invested in real estate by my executor. To my son **Richard Lockwood Price** 111 acres of the farm whereon I now reside to be laid off as follows, 96 acres of which shall be of the Reynolds tract next to and binding on the public road leading from Warwick to Middletown, with a line or lines from **John Caudwells** land to **George Reynolds** land and the residue of 15 acres to be laid off adjoining **Alfred Caulk** and wife's land to him. I also give unto my said son Richard L. 10 acres of wood land at Sandy Branch to laid off on the E side of the road leading from Elkton to Warwick situate in Cecil Co except a house and lot or garden where **John Robinson** negro now lives which I have given to said negro during his natural life, and after John's death to my son Richard L. Price and Richard shall pay to my son George W. Price $40 when Richard reached age 21. To my son Richard L. Price ½ of the lot of wood I hold, which lot of wood land I purchased as the real estate of **William Rothwell** Esq. deceased adjoining lands of **Edward Wilson, William Wilson,** and others to be laid off adjoining the lands of Edward Wilson, the division line to run across or the short way of said lot of wood land with the privilege of a road through the other ½ of the said wood lot at all times to go to and return from the said wood land. To my son **Samuel Price** all the residue of the farm I now reside (which I have Not Given to my said son Richard L. Price) with the dwelling, the road running through the said farm where I now live to be for the use of my said two sons Richard L and Samuel from the Middletown Road to the Elkton Road. To son Samuel ½ of the lot of wood land I purchased of William Rothwell deceased to be laid off next and adjoining the public road from the levels to the Sassafras Road and adjoining lands of William and Edward Wilson. I also give the remainder of my wood land by Sandy Branch which I have Not Given to

my son Richard which lies on the W side of the public road leading from Warwick to Elkton adjoining lands of John M. Flintham and others containing 8 acres and shall pay to my son George W. Price when Samuel arrives at 21 the sum of $40 and Samuel to pay Richard $200. All the rest of my personal estate to my dau. **Mary L. Price**, my wife **Lydia A. Price** shall have use of the income until dau. Mary L arrives at age 18. My executor authorized to collect and pay all debts and rents and to execute a good deed to William Cacy for the farm I sold him in Kent Co and to invest $7,400 in real estate for the benefit of my two sons Edwin Price and George W. Price.

Exec. my father in law **Richard Lockwood**. Witnesses Henry Davis, John W. Lynch, Charles Tatman Jr. Written Nov. 21, 1858 Proved Dec. 14, 1858 p. 143

Abram Dolly of Kent Co
My wife **Henny Dolly** all my property during her natural life and then to be divided between my sisters **Hannah Johnson, Nancy Little**, wife of **Joshua Little** and the children of my sister **Sharlotte Williss** and should Hannah not leave any children then to Nancy Little and the children of my sister Sharlotte Williss.

Exec. Not Given. Witnesses Jefferson McWhorten, Robert M. Smyth, William F. Smyth. Written Jan. 3, 1858 Proved Jan. 18, 1859 p. 148

Thomas M. Blackiston of Kent Co
All my real estate to be sold and conveyed in fee to my dau. **Mary E. Blackiston** interest to be payable half yearly. To my dear wife in lieu of dower the sum of $3,000. To my dau. Mary Elizabeth the sum of $2,000. The balance of the proceeds I divide between my son **Thomas Medford Blackiston** and my dau. **Mary Elizabeth Blackiston**. To my dau. Mary E. my negro man Phil to serve five years from my decease and my negro man Dan to serve nine years and my negroes **Rosalia, Henry, Ellen, Martha Ann, Charlotte Ann and Dumb Julia** to serve for life. I give to my son Thomas Medford Blackiston my negro **Louisa** for a term of years according to their manumission in Queen Anns and my negroes **Bill, Lucy**, slaves for life and **Charlotte Ann**'s two children **Mary Elizabeth** aged about __ years and infant **James**. To my dear wife as slaves for life my negroes **Isaac** and **Nelson** and **Ann,** and any matters of household property she may desire. My personal property to be divided between my son Thomas M. and dau. Mary E. I appoint my relation **David C. Blackiston** guardian to my said dau. Mary.

Execs. my son Thomas M. Blackiston and my relation David C. Blackiston. Witnesses George C. Stokes, Margaret Bell, Thomas G. Wroth. Written Jan. 31, 1859 Proved p. 149

Jacob Fisher of Kent Co
Should my brother **Isaac Fisher** of the Town of Huntingdon, Huntingdon Co, PA approve of this will then I bequeath unto my beloved wife **Mary Ann Fisher** all my

estate real personal and mixed except for the following legacies: To my son **Samuel Groome Fisher** my medical and surgical library, all my surgical, obstetrical and dental instruments, my doctor's carriage which he now uses in the practice of his profession, my silver liver watch he now wears, my hickory cane presented to me by my friend **Dr. Birdley** of Baltimore City, one mare with a scald head named Benny which he now drives and one colt without name, two years old in the spring of, 1856, and in consideration of the said bequests for the term of 3 years after my death to pay my wife as natural guardian to my three youngest children the sum of $333 annually, in her death then to the guardian of the said 3 children: **Henrietta Clorinda Cornelia Fisher, Ringgold Williams Fisher**, and **Ella Theodora Fisher**. My son shall reside in the family after my death as long as it may suit his convenience, but should he for any cause remove or separate from the family prior to the expiration of 3 years after my death, then my will is that the above legacies be reduced to $250 annually. To my wife in trust for my son **Jacob F. Fisher**, one mare called Jenny Lind which he claims as his, one colt foaled in the spring of 1856 and any future issue or colts of said mare, also my old mare called Sally, two cows one spotted and with heifers, the other kack and also with heifers, the same I purchased of Joseph Maslin, two bull yearling calves, one horse cart now at the cartwrights to be repaired. My son Jacob will at all times render due respect to his mother and assist her to the best of his endeavors as a dutiful son should do. To my son **Alfred H. Fisher** my sword cane which was presented to me by him some time since, if he should return from the West, directing him at the same time to use said cane with great care and caution, but should said son not return then I give said cane to my son Jacob. To my neighbor and friend **Thomas A. Strong** as a grateful remembrance of his many kindnesses to me, my fig stock cane, which was presented to me by my late friend **Benedict S. Brevitt**.

Exec. My dear wife Mary Ann Fisher and my son Samuel G. Fisher. Witnesses Richard J. Frisby, George Leary, Thomas A. Strong. Written Apr. 21, 1857 Proved Mar 1, 1859 p. 151

<u>Codicil</u> To my son **Jacob Fisher** one bay horse called Charley, the tables, chairs, carpets, table and cupboard furniture, farming utensils etc. purchased by him for me at sale of Mrs. C. Bradshaw's personal property Nov., 1856, also the bed and bedding and farming utensils etc purchased at the sale of Ms. Susan Copper's personal estate Nov., 1856, all of which is hereby given in trust of his mother **Mary A. Fisher** for the sole use of said **Jacob F. Fisher**. To **Samuel G. Fisher** all the medicines, bottles, fixtures, etc appertaining to the apothecary, also ½ of the charges made for services and medicines dispensed since the 9th of Apr., 1856. Written Apr. 21, 1857. Witnesses same as above

<u>Renunciation</u> Widow renounced right as joint executor to Samuel G. Fisher. Mar. 1, 1859

Liber 13 1854-1867

Thomas E. Gooding of Kent Co
To my son **William Henry Gooding** the house situate in Georgetown and Roads between the property known as the Odd Fellow's Lodge and the property belonging to some of the heirs of the late Henry Hurtt to be his during the time of his natural life, and then to descend to the heirs legally begotten of his body but should he leave no lawful issue then to revert to my other children and also I give him $300. To my dau. **Sarah Etta Rogers**, the double house, gardens and premises in one part of which my son in law **William Rogers** now resides situated between the property of **Maria D. Dunlap** and that of **William J. Hall** with the condition that the rents of one of said houses, not occupied by my said dau. and her husband shall during the 3 years after my decease be paid to executor for claims against my estate. I also give my negro girl called **Tempy** to serve her till 35 years old but to remain with wife **Ara Maria Gooding** free of charge for 3 years from Jan. 1, 1858. To my son **Thomas Osborn Gooding** my mill and property attached which I purchased of Mrs. **Anna Maria Scott** but the rents to go into my estate until Thomas arrive at 21.
To my wife **Ara Maria Gooding** all the residue of my estate after legacy to son **William Henry Gooding**, to support my three younger children **Franklin Miller Gooding, Lydia Catharine Gooding, Addison Miller Gooding** for her natural life. If she remarries, she is to have only portion that as the law in such cases gives to the widow of one dying intestate. She is not to receive dower because of property given. If any child dies the surviving ones entitled to such portion, if wife dies then son William not to receive portion in view of bequests. My servant man **George** to serve 12 years from Jan. 1, 1858. My executor should sell my horse called Watchman and also my sorrel mare with ½ of my cattle, towards settling claims against estate. My brother **William Gooding** to be sole executor or if he is not able to then my brother **Aaron L. Gooding**.

Exec. my brother William Gooding. Witnesses Elijah E. Miller, John Frazier Jr, John W. Pierson. Written Dec. 28, 1857 Proved Apr. 12, 1859 p. 154 (Renunciation of Widow of Thomas E. Gooding on p. 164)

Obediah Gleaves free man of color of Kent Co
To my wife **Mary Gleaves** the house I lately built on back street in Chestertown opposite the property **A.W. Sparks** purchased of **William Greenwood** and the garden thereto attached during her natural life and then to my two daughters **Sarah Gleaves** and **Mary Gleaves** as tenants in common. They may use the house while they are single and unmarried in common with my said wife. To my children **Charles Gleaves, Anna Maria Gleaves, Henrietta Gleaves** and **Abram Gleaves,** my house and lot lying on Back Street in Chestertown situate between the house and gardens herein before devised and the house and garden herein after devised to my son **William Gleaves** which is at present occupied by me to the said four children in common. To my son **William Gleaves** my house and lot adjoining the house above devised to my four children and the lot of land now owned by Miss Caroline Thompson

Exec. my son William Gleaves. Witnesses Richard Hynson, John Armstrong, R. C. Wilmer. Written Jan. 24, 1853 Proved May 21, 1859 p. 156

Mary Spencer
To my daughters **Caroline** and **Charlotte** all my silver or plate and my room furniture to be equally divided. Whatever sum may be due me from my mother's estate be also equally divided between my said daughters. In consideration of my dau. Caroline being provided for by her aunt **Caroline** to an amount about equal to the balance of my property and in consideration of being much older than my dau. Charlotte and now nearly educated, I bequeath the rest of my property to my dau. Charlotte.

Exec. Samuel Comegys. Witnesses John M. Comegys, Samuel Comegys, Nathaniel W. Comegys. Written Oct. 6, 1857 Proved June 7, 1859 p. 157

James F. Woodland of Kent Co
To my wife **Margaret W. Woodland** my sole executrix. All my personal property to my wife to sell to satisfy my debts. My real estate shall be held by said wife during her natural life and after her demise to be equally divided between my children except **Samuel** and **Mary**.

Exec. my wife Margaret W. Woodland. Witnesses Nathan Rees Glascow, Joseph T. Crouch, Samuel C. Johnson. Written Mar. 9, 1859 Proved Apr. 28, 1859 p. 159. Witnesses came after the signing by James F. Woodland. Each agreeing that James F. made this will and acknowledged before Henry H. Rasin.

Thomas McLaughlin of Kent Co
To my dearly beloved wife **Jane McLaughlin** during her natural life all my estate and at her death to my son **George McLaughlin**.

Exec. my son George McLauglin. Witnesses Matthew V. Boyer, James H. Hurt, Jesse K. Hines. Written Aug. 19, 1856 Proved June 21, 1859 p. 161

Samuel C. Hamilton of Kent Co
To my dear and affectionate wife **Louisa Hamilton** the whole of my personal estate, except my negro girl **Mary Ellen** forever and the lot I purchased of **George W. T. Perkins** and also a lot bought from **Edward Wilkins** and **George G. Westcott** forever, and all the residue of my real estate during her natural life but after her death to my half brothers **William H. Hamilton, James Hamilton** and **Franklin Hamilton** and unto my half sister **Mary Jane Lambert,** wife of **William H. Lambert**. To my wife Louisa I give my girl Mary Ellen now about 14 years of age until she is 35 years then to be set free, if wife dies then to my half brother William H. Hamilton until she arrives at 35. If Mary Ellen have issue then the males to be set free at 40 years and the females should reach age 35 but to serve my said wife until the age given or upon the death of my wife, to my half brother William H. Hamilton.

Exec. my wife Louisa Hamilton. Witnesses Richard Hynson, Thomas B. Hynson and Jesse K. Hines. Written May 14, 1859 Proved Aug. 15, 1859 p. 162

Richard Corbally of Kent Co
To my wife **Hannah Corbally** all my real estate during her life and no longer. To my two sons **Samuel J. Corbally** and **Richard Corbally** and after the death of their mother Hannah all my real estate. To my daughters **Mary A. Price** and **Hannah M. Corbally** any articles of furniture or household goods that they may want. I have made no other provisions for them because they are already provided for and for no other cause. All the rest of my estate to my two sons Samuel J. Corbally and Richard Corbally.

Exec. Richard Corbally. Witnesses Richard C. Johnson, Jonathan Jones, Agnes R. Johnson. Written Oct. 9, 1858 Proved Aug. 23, 1859 p. 163

Renunciation of Ara M. Gooding widow of Thomas E. Gooding
I **Ara M. Gooding** widow of **Thomas E. Gooding** late of Kent Co deceased do renounce and quit claim to any bequest or devise made to me by the last will of my husband and I elect to take in lieu of thereof my dower or legal share of the estate of my said husband. Witnesses E. E. Miller. Written Aug. 19, 1859 p. 164

John E. Stewart of Kent Co
To my wife **Emily D. Stewart** my dwelling house and lot in Millington during her natural life and at her death to revert to my sister **Martha Ann Stewart**. To **Mary A. Yeates** and **Julia Edwards** my secretary, large looking glass, chairs and silver spoons, and one bed and bedstead. To **William Webb** my apprentice one bed, bedstead, and bedding and also my silver watch and William to be free from all persons whatsoever. To my wife Emily D. Stewart all my undivided right in the Coach shop now in occupation of **James A. Edwards** and myself during her natural life with all the remainder of my personal estate

Exec. James A. Edwards. Witnesses Matthew V. Boyer, William S. Merritt, Thomas J. Britton. Written Sep. 12, 1859 Proved Sep. 27, 1859 p. 165

Ann Cruikshank of Kent Co
To my dau. **Mary Isabella Ringgold** my house and lot in Chestertown to be held during her natural life and after her death to her two daughters **Mary Isabella** and **Sarah Ann** and to my dau. Mary my three servants **Sam, Charles,** and **Polly** until they arrive at age 33 upon the following condition that she may to my son **John**'s three daughters **Kate, Alice** and **Virginia** $100 each when my servant **Sam** shall arrive at age 20 years. I give the following legacies which I hold of my son in law **Thomas W. Ringgold** viz of $450 to each of my son John's daughters Kate, Alice and Virginia when they arrive at age 21. I give $50 to my executors for the purpose of inclosing the grave yard of my husband and family at the old homestead. To my son John's sons **John, Madison,** and **Joel** $20 when they arrive at 20 years old. To my servant **Hannah** $20. To **Robert** servant of my

dau. Mary Isabella Ringgold $5. To my dau. in law **Martha Cruikshank** $10. To **Mary Ann Ringgold** $10. To my granddaughters **Mary Isabella** and **Sarah Ann Ringgold** my secretary (furniture). To my granddaughters **Ann Elizabeth Ringgold** my portable desk. To my grandson **Thomas Ringgold** my picture of Washington's family. To **Joseph H. Hynson** of Louisiana the sample painting of his Aunt **Elizabeth Hickman**. The rest of my property to my dau. Mary Isabella Ringgold.

Execs. my son in law Thomas W. Ringgold and Samuel E. Comegys. Witnesses Vachel Burgess, George H. Willson, Thomas D. Burgess. Written Dec. 16, 1858 Proved Dec. 6, 1859 p. 166

Codicil From the money due from my son **Thomas'** estate to his dau. **Ellen**, interest under 21 years old and principal at age 21. In case of the death of Ellen then the money to my son John's two daughters Kate and Alice. Written Dec. 24, 1858 Witness Richard W. Ringgold.

Elizabeth Read of Kent Co
To be decently interred in the burying ground on *"Delaney Manner"* in DE according to my situation in life. To my son **William McGuire** the sum of $1 and no more. To my dau. **Sarah E. McGuire** all my personal property except the $1 to William and to Sarah all of my land and house forever.

Exec. my esteemed neighbor Joseph Morris. Witnesses David B. Stewart, John S. Morris. Written Aug. 27, 1855 Proved Oct. 5, 1857 p. 169

Pere Pennington of Kent Co
To my affectionate wife **Mary Pennington** and my dau. **Sarah R. Collier** the wife of **Richard S. Collier,** Talbot Co, my real estate in Talbot Co which I purchased of **Col. K. R. Owens** to them forever. To my wife Mary Pennington all the rest of my estate

Exec. Not Given. Witnesses Richard Hynson, William H. Palmer, Charles Stanley. Written Dec. 21, 1859 Proved Jan. 10, 1860 p. 170

James F. Woodland
For a full and consecutive reference to the matters pertaining to the paper purporting to be the will of James F. Woodland see minutes of Orphans Court dated Apr. 28; Aug. 9, 15, 23, 24, 29; Sep. 6, 20, and Jan. 17, 1860.

Thomas Willson of Kent Co
My body is to be interred near the remains of my beloved wives comfortably to my situation and circumstance in life thereof I charge upon my son **Richard Bennet Willson** in consideration of the devisees hereinafter made to him. To my son **Thomas S. Wilson** my houses and lots of land at Queens Town in Queen Annes Co which I bought of **John S. Blake** and which I bought of Dr. **Thomas S. Willson** and a lot of wood land part of

Liber 13 1854-1867

"*Sawyers Forest*" in Piney Neck in Queen Anns Co which I bought of **John Grayson** and I also give to him all the parcel of land adjoining "*Bennets Outlet*" in the said county lines within the following beginning a stone marked no. 1 lying near the public road leading from Beaver Dam Branch towards the Catholic Chapel thence in a straight line south to a marked white oak with a stone near it thence in a straight line W to a stone at the head of Indian Cabbin Branch where strikes one of the lines of "*Bennets Outlet*" and thence with the lines of Bennets Outlet and around with the enclosure to the main road to Beaver Dam Branch and thence with the public road to the beginning at Stone No. 1 and also I give him $500 in addition to the money, stock and negroes already advanced and given to him to the estimated amount of $3,500. To my son **James H. Wilson** all that tract of land called "*Bennets Outlet*" in Queen Annes Co upon which he now resides (lying in the SE or W sides of the adjoining land herein devised to Thomas S. Wilson and also confirm to him the stock, negroes, farming utensils, household furniture and money already advanced him. To my son **George H. Willson** my negro man Henry and his wife Fanny and the several negroes, the stock and money with other property advanced or given to him estimated to amount to more than $8,000. To my dau. **Mary Elizabeth Brown** a negro girl called **Julia** also **Dinah** child of Nancy one of whom is in her possession, and also bonds or notes held by me to be assigned to her to the value of $2,000, in addition to the negroes, money and other effects already advanced to her. To my son **John C. Willson** $3,00 in bond or notes belonging to me and to be assigned to him and all my stock in the Union Bank of MD, in the Union Manufacturing Company, in the Fire Insurance Company in the City of Baltimore and also shares of stock I hold in the Farmers and Mechanics Bank of Kent Co, in addition to the negroes, money, horses and other stock heretofore advanced to him and also negro **Perry** now in his possession to him. To my son **Richard Bennet Wilson** the farm upon which I now reside including "*Trumpington Smyths meadows*", "*Smyths Marsh*", and "*part of Huntingfield*" lying in Eastern Neck in Kent Co on the W and NW side of the public road from the bridge over the narrows towards Rock Hall contiguous on the N side to the lands of George H. Willson, also my woodland near the schoolhouse on the E side of said road containing about 54 acres part of Huntingfield and formerly the property of **William Ringgold**, also the triangular lot of land on the W side of the public road near my lake gate subject to the legacies hereinafter charged and the right of my son **Daniel C. Willson** freely to use the road to the landing on the Bay, the right of way over which said road I hereby devise to said Daniel C. Willson. I also give to my son Richard Bennett Willson 1/3 part of the growing crops and crops remaining unsold on the premises devised to him at my decease and also the negro servants **William**, **David**, **Charles**, **Charlotte**, and **Ann** child of **Eliza**. These bequests in addition to the property already advanced or given. To my son **Daniel Carroll Willson** all the lands now in my possession and lying in Eastern Neck Kent Co which was formerly the property of **William Browne** and also a lot of land lying near the bridge leading to Eastern Neck island and on the E side of the public road passing towards Rock Hall, and also that piece or parcel of land called Crabbins on the E side of said road and all that part of land in church creek part of Huntingfield on the E of the said road (and part of an exchange with the late **James Ringgold**) up to the lands of George H. Willson on the E side of the main road to son Daniel. If the said son should die without leaving issue then said lands to his brother **Alexander H. Willson** and the right of way through the land devised to Daniel to Richard Bennett Willson, and I give all the growing crops and such as remain unsold from the farm devised to him and the sum of $3,000 in money, bond, and notes to be paid by executors. To my dau. **Martha Neal Willson** the sum of $500 to be paid to her by Richard Bennet Willson in 3 annual installments and $500 to be paid by executors, also all my Chester Bridge stock with dividends of which I hold 150 shares, and also 1/3 part of all the growing crops and crops unsold remaining in the Trumpington farm at the time of my decease, in addition to the negroes and other property already given. To my son **John C. Willson** in trust for his brother **Alexander Hookin Willson** $5,000 to be paid by Richard Bennett Willson, and $1,000 to be paid by my executor, and also 1/3 of the growing crops and crops remaining unsold at my decease in the Trumpington farm, held in trust until Alexander of 21, in addition to the negroes and other property already given. The rest to my executors out of which residuum of course their commission must be taken. (Spelling of Willson and Bennett varied in this will)

Execs. my sons John C., Richard B, George H., Daniel C. Witnesses Thomas W. Ringgold, George W. Minnick, Thomas H. Burgess. Written Nov. 23, 1852 Proved Nov. 15, 1859 p. 171

Mary G. Wroth of Kent Co

To my son **Benjamin B. Wroth** my negro man **Perry**, my negro woman **Melvina**, my girl **Maria** and my negro man **Ben** and the young child **Charlotte** that is now at the breast of her mother (Melvina) all of which negroes I leave to my son Benjamin for life, also my stock of horses, cattle, sheep and hogs and all my farming utensils of every description and also all of my household and kitchen furniture of every description excepting such parts thereof as is herein after otherwise disposed. To my son **Josias Ringgold** I leave one bed quilt. To my dau. in law **Mary Wroth** wife of my son **William G. Wroth** of Baltimore I will my negro girl **Hannah** and my negro girl **Margaret** to serve during life, and also a set of silver table spoons. To my dau. **Mary Fisher** all my wearing apparel and a bed quilt with the figure of birds in it. To my granddau. **Mary Matilda Frisby** I bequeath a bed quilt with a wreath on it. To my granddau. **Mary Groome Ringgold** I will a bed quilt and to my grandson **Joseph Rasin** I also give a bed quilt.

Exec. Not Given. Witnesses Levi Wroth, Octavius H. Jones. Written Feb. 9, 1857 Proved Apr. 17, 1860 p. 175

Henry Cottin Free Negro of Kent Co

To be buried in my own burying ground. To my beloved wife **Harriett** one bed and bedding. All the residue of my personal property shall be sold and after paying debts to divide between my widow and children and to rent real estate if not enough to pay debts. To my dau. **Aryan Butler** $100 paid at $10 annually. To my wife Harriet the 1/3 of my landed estate during her natural life. To my children hereafter named all my residue of my estate viz **Janus Henry, Sarah Elizabeth, Anna Eliza, Thomas Ethram, George Washington,** and **Edward Stansbury** equally. Mr. **Henry Kelley** to be executor and that he should care for Thomas Ethram, George Washington and Edward Stansbury my children.

Exec. Mr. Henry Kelley. Witnesses Henry T. Jump, Joseph Howard, Richard H. Harris. Written Mar. 29, 1860 Proved July 10, 1860 p. 176

Abraham Browne (colored)
My dau. **Martha** $4, My dau. **Mary** $4, My dau. **Henny** $4, My dau. **Francis** $4, My dau. **Lettie** $4, To my wife **Caroline Browne** 1/3 of the remainder of my property during her natural life. To my son **Perry Browne** and his heirs all my estate and also my wife Caroline's part after her death.

Exec. Mr. Benjamin F. Beck. Witnesses Isaiah C. Taylor, Damaris V. Comegys, Mary E. Taylor. Written May 15, 1860 Proved Sep. 15, 1860 p. 178

Martha Brice of Chestertown, Kent Co
To **George Henry Brice** (son of **William A. Brice**) of Kent Co $100, To **Perry Price Howard**, son of **Asbury Howard** and **Mary** his wife of Kent $100, To **Perry Price Howard, William Penn Howard, Frank Houstin Howard,** sons of Asbury and Mary Howard of Kent Co all my estate.

Exec. Not Given. Witnesses Benjamin F. Houston, Samuel Franklin Smith, William S. Lapell. Written Jan. 12, 1859 Proved Oct. 16, 1860 p. 179

Codicil Whereas I sold my farm in Kent Co which was devised to me by **Richard Brice** my uncle unto William A. Brice and whereas **Joseph Brice** supposes he has some interest in said farm, now if the said Joseph Brice and his wife shall grant and release unto said William A. Brice in fee simple a deed to be executed by them within 12 months from the date hereof and delivered to said William A. Brice all and every supposed interest in said farm as they may think themselves possessed of then I hereby give and devise unto the children of said **Joseph Brice** and **Mary Jane** his wife $1,000. If they fail to execute such deed then I give the $1,000 to William to defend any suit that they may institute against him. I hereby give William A. Brice $500. Written Jan. 13, 1859. Witnesses Tamasina Glenn, John W. Usilton, and William S. Lapell

James G. Chrisfield of Kent Co
Whereas **Gilbert Chrisfield** (my father) by his last will devised a certain farm containing 86 acres and also two certain tracts of woodland situated in the forest also described in the said will of Gilbert Chrisfield to (my mother) his wife **Elizabeth Christfield** during her natural life and whereas I have purchased the interest of (my said mother) Elizabeth Christfield in the said farm at an annuity of $55, that I have not sold to my brother

George W. Chrisfield and annuity to cease at the death of my mother. I require my executor upon my death to sell the said farm subject to the conditions named in the last will of **Gilbert Christfield** (and not complied with by me). Also after the death of my mother I require my executor to sell the two wood lots. To my wife **Sarah R. Christfield** $500 in place of her dower in my real estate, all of my household and kitchen furniture, and the sum of $600. To afflicted dau. **Sarah E. Christfield** the sum of $500 but the executor can use the principal if necessary and in the event of her death before the principal is paid it will become a part of the residue of my estate. To the children of my wife Sarah R. Christfield living and post humus the residue of my estate. (Spelling of Christfield and Chrisfield interchanged throughout this will)

Exec. Cornelius J. Scott. Witnesses John G. Miers, William A. Miller, Alfred Christfield. Written Apr. 1, 1860 Proved Oct. 30, 1860 p. 181

Richard Wilson a freeman of Kent Co
To my daughters **Susana** and **Rachel** all personal estate. To my son **Richard** to sole executor

Exec. my son Richard. Witnesses William S. Lassell, Charles H. Kenton, James A. Russell. Written Oct. 16, 1857 Proved Nov. 13, 1860 p. 183

John B. Eccleston of Kent Co
My dear wife **Augusta C. Eccleston** all my real estate forever. To my dear wife all my negroes, all my household and kitchen furniture including my plate, and I also give and bequeath to her so much of the remaining portion of my personal estate which will amount to 1/3 of my whole personal estate. To my son **John C. Eccleston** my watch and $1,000. To my dau. **Augusta C. Shoemaker** $1,000. To my son **James Housten Eccleston** all my law books, my guns and $2,000 except the law books I give to my dear wife. All the rest of my personal estate I give to my son in law **Samuel M. Shoemaker** in trust for my dau. **Mariam Eccleston** during her natural life and then to whomever she gives in her last will. If she fails to execute a will then to such child or children, (if more than one) of my said dau. Miriam as may be living at the time of her decease, if she have no issue then to my children John C., Augusta C, and James Houston.

Exec. my son James Houston Eccleston. Witnesses Richard Hynson, William Harris, Nicholas G. Westcott. Written Dec. 12, 1859 Proved Nov. 20, 1860 p. 184

Clementine Lowe of Kent Co
To my nieces **Margaret Ann McDaniel** and **Sarah E. McDaniel** jointly, my negro girl called **Martha**, until 36. To my brother **John W. McDaniel**, my girl called **Jestina** until she is 36. To my niece **Margaret Ann Wilkinson** my four negroes: **Alexander, Marian, Sharlot,** and **Elizabeth,** and their issue, until 36, if they fail to be obedient they shall not be set free and shall remain in the hands of **Christopher Wilkinson,** until Margaret Ann Wilkinson arrives at 16 or married.

Liber 13 1854-1867

Exec. Christopher Wilkinson. Witnesses John Downey, John A. Hirsch, John E. Eisenberg. Written Apr. 15, 1859 Proved Dec. 27, 1860 p. 186

Isaac Elbert of Kent Co, free negro
To my dear sons Joseph Doman Elbert, Samuel Cortney Elbert, my lot of ground called *"Hurts Lot"* adjoining the Brooks lands. To my beloved dau. **Mary Ann Elbert** the farm on which I now reside called Pardonership, by paying the following legacies: To my dear daughters **Eliza Jane Posey, Catharine Editha Elbert, Salina Elizabeth Elbert, Araminta Augusta Elbert**, my son **Isaac Elbert** and **Susan Rebecca Elbert** $70 each, except to my dau. Catharine Editha Elbert to receive $50, they are to be paid in order of their names, two years apart.

Exec. Not Given. Witnesses Elizabeth Thomas, S.H. Boyd, Joseph Boyd. Written Dec. 8, 1860 Proved Jan. 1, 1861 p. 187

Julia Anna Virginia Stephens of Kent Co
The dwelling house, buildings and lot of land containing about a ½ acre of land which was formerly the property of **Samuel Sappington** lying in Galena in Kent Co now occupied by me and which was purchased by me on or about Dec. 30, 1843 from **Thomas Lusby** collector of taxes at a collectors sale for taxes which was conveyed to me Thomas Lusby former collector on Mar. 13, 1860 to be sold by my executor. Out of the sale I give to my eldest dau. **Olivia Virginia Stephens** $900. The interest of a mortgage I hold from **George W. Spencer Esq** for $1,200 of which $300 of the principal has been paid leaving $900 to my second dau. **Anna Louisa Stephens**. To my youngest child **Jenney Jerrildeen Stephens** all the rest of my estate over and above the $900 to Olivia from the sale. To my son **Henry R. Stephens** a 5-acre wood lot which was devised to me by my father **George William Wilson**. Until the sale of my dwelling house my three daughters may enjoy its use. (She was examined away from her husband)

Exec. my friend Caleb Wright Spry. Witnesses E.E. Miller, Joseph P. Ireland, A. Medders. Written Apr. 7, 1860 Proved Apr. 15, 1861 p. 189 C.W. Spry renounced right to admin. for the late Mrs. Julian Anna V. Stephens

Robert Ward free man of color of Kent Co
To my wife **Charlotte Ward** for and during her natural life my house and lot of ground and at her death to be divided between **Mary Hopkins** wife of **Perry Hopkins** free man of color and **Maria Ellen**, dau. of **Joseph** and **Susan Washington** (fr.), Maria Ellen, dau. of Joseph and Susan Washington (fr.) is to have the E part of the lot of ground with the house. Mary Hopkins wife of Perry Hopkins (fr) is to have the W part of the lot of ground. To my wife Charlotte Ward all my personal estate

Exec. Not Given. Witnesses James M. Ayres, Oliver P. Beck, William H. Ayres. Written Dec. 31, 1859 Proved Apr. 16, 1861 p. 191

Abstracts of Kent Co., MD Wills

Ann Perkins of Kent Co
To my dear sister **Caroline Perkins** all my interest in the house and lot in Chestertown where I now reside being part of *"Lot No. 10"* and all the rest of my estate.

Exec. my sister Caroline Perkins. Witnesses Eben F. Perkins, Benjamin B. Perkins, James A. Perkins. Written June 15, 1857 Proved June 14, 1861 p. 191 Caroline Perkins renounces right to administer to my nephew Eben F. Perkins

Thomas S. Corey of Kent Co
To sell my real estate and pay ½ to my dear wife **Ellen P. Corey** for her natural life and the other ½ to **John W. Corey, Albert L. Corey** of Kent Co, **Cyrus Piper Jr** of the State of New Hampshire whom I appoint as guardians of my beloved son **Maro V. Corey** until he is 21. After my wife's death her estate to my son Maro V. Corey. If my son dies without heirs to my brother **John W. Corey, Albert L. Corey** and my sister **Lydia E. Diehl** of New Castle Co, DE except for benefit of wife during her natural life.

Exec. John W. Corey, Albert L. Corey of Kent Co, and William B. Diehl of New Castle Co, DE. Witnesses John Greenwood of William, William Bacchus, Richard C. Smyth. Written May 16, 1861 Proved June 15, 1861 p. 193 William B. Diehl declines to administer. Port Penn, DE Jun 15, 1861.

Ezekiel C. Wickes of Kent Co
To my wife **Augusta Wickes** my entire estate during her natural life and after her death to my children to be equally divided

Exec. my wife Augusta Wickes. Witnesses Melvina Forman, John R. Gray, William H. Meeteer. Written Dec. 22, 1860 Proved July 29, 1861 p. 196

Mary Tryford of Kent Co
To my brother **William Elbert** $300. To my nephew **James William Greenwood** all my negroes males and females until age 36 or until his death and no longer, and after to be set free and to him all the rest of my estate, in the event of his not leaving lawful issue then to William Elbert $1,000

Exec. Not Given. Witnesses Thomas H. Whaland, George W. Robson, Edward Mansfield. Written Sep. 26, 1860 Proved Sep. 24, 1861 p. 197

Hannah M. Corbaley of Kent Co
To my husband **Richard Corbaley** all my real estate during his life and no longer. To my two sons **Samuel J. Corbaley** and **Richard Corbaley,** after the death of their father Richard Corbaley. To my two daughters **Mary A. Price** and **Hannah M. Corbaley** any articles of furniture

Liber 13 1854-1867

Exec. Not Given. Witnesses Richard C. Johnson, Jonathan Jones, Agnes R. Johnson. Written Oct. 9, 1858 Proved Dec. 17, 1861 p. 198

Joseph Allen of the City of Trenton in New Jersey
To **William Allen** (son of my brother Jacob W. Allen deceased) all my wearing apparel of every description. To **Christianna Appleton** (widow of Richard Appleton deceased) $150. To **Harriet Fennel** (wife of Justice Fennel) $150. To **Jonathan B. Wright** of the village of Tully town all my interest in what is called C. B. Loveless patent portable gas generator which I purchased of O.O. Gibson and John J. Forman (agents for the said C.B. Loveless for the Counties of Mercer, Atlantic, Salem, Cape May and Cumberland in the state of New Jersey. To the 3 daughters of my said brother **Jacob W. Allen** deceased namely **Amanda, Alice** and **Rilly** my lot of land in Kent Co containing about 6 ½ acres of land which I purchased of James B. ___ The balance of my estate I give unto the sons of my said brother Jacob W. Allen deceased

Exec. Anthony Burton. Witnesses Theadore Windes, Justice Fennel. Written Dec. 18, 1860 Proved Jan. 19, 1861 p. 199

Giles Lambson of New Castle Hundred, New Castle Co, DE
All my estate to my 8 children however my dau. **Mary H. Townsend** wife of **Solomon Townsend** shall be held in trust by my son **Moses Lambson** and son in law **James Crippen** in trust to be divided equally among her children.

Execs. my son Moses Lambson and son in law James Crippen. Witnesses Lucas Alrich, Allen Voorhees Lesley, William G. Whiteley. Written Sep. 15, 1861 Proved Sep. 20, 1861 p. 201 Letters granted from DE

Emory Sudler of Kent Co
To my son **John Emery E. Sudler** my negro man **Richard** a slave for life and my bay mare Jane and colt to be full payment for a legacy due him from the estate of his late Aunt **Ann Sudler**. To my dear wife **Elizabeth G. Sudler** for and during the period of her natural life all the rest of my estate and after her death to be equally divided amongst my children and the portion due to my dau. **Ann Valk** shall not be liable to debts of her husband. If any of my children die during the lifetime of their mother and not leave issue then their portion to the survivors.

Exec. my wife Elizabeth G. Sudler. Witnesses James B. Ricaud, Benjamin G. Wroth, Thomas G. Wroth. Written Dec. 17, 1861 Proved Mar. 6, 1862 p. 204

William Harris of Kent Co
In the event of my dying without a will then this present writing then I will my gold watch be given to Miss **Ann Elizabeth Ringgold** immediately after my death. I give her the said watch as a slight proof of my love and affection and because of the tender relations existing between us.

Exec. Not Given. Witnesses James Arthur attested that he was acquainted with William's writing. Written Sep. 24, 1859 Proved Apr. 8, 1862 p. 206

We renounce the right to administer the estate of our late brother William Harris and recommend letters to be granted to Richard Hynson. E. G. Harris, Francis Cann Apr. 2, 1862

Samuel Jarman of Kent Co

To my wife **Sarah Ann Jarman** her dower right in my real estate in lieu of the 1/3 of my estate and one negro man **George Hinds**, one negro boy **John Warner**, one negro girl **Elizabeth Warner**, one negro boy **William Tilison**, one negro girl **Sharlotte Warner**, my household furniture, my best carriage and harness, 12 sheep, 6 cows, 4 horses, 10 hogs, one wagon and harness, one cart and harness, one fan, one drag harrow, 7 plows and $700. To my dau. **Mary Ann Rolph** $50 and note of hand of hand against her son **Samuel J. Rolph** $25, and the share of my estate that I already set aside for her. To my grandson **Franklin Jarman** $50 (son of **Samuel J. Jarman** who is now dead), having already had from me his share of my estate. To my dau. **Arsula Moffitt** one negro boy **Henry Warner** and $700 but she must pay $636.38 back to estate for account of her husband **Jeremiah N. Moffett**. To my dau. **Sarah Eliza Jarman** 6 silver teaspoons, one bed, bedstead and clothing and one negro woman **Matilda Tilison** and $1,000. To my son **John Wesley Jarman** ½ of my farm, including all the buildings and the granary, the dividing line at the E corner of a wood lot owned by **John Black** and to run a SE direction, by and with a fence dividing the fields of said farm, leading to the buildings, thence by and with said fence continued to the woodland of said farm, thence to a straight line through said woodland until it intersects land owned by the heirs of H. Masden, being the W side or half of said farm containing about 112 acres to John. If he dies without heirs then to my son **Thomas George Jarman**, and if he dies then to my son **Washington Jarman**. Also John to have one bed, bedstead, and clothing and one silver watch. To my son Thomas George the remaining ½, but if he die without heirs then to son John, then to Washington. And to Thomas one bed, one bedstead, and clothing and $600. To my son **Washington Jarman** 6 silver dessert spoons, 6 silver tablespoons (his mother to have the use of them during her life) and on bed, bedstead, and clothing, one negro girl **Mary Rebecca Tilison**, one negro boy named **William H. Warner** and $2,000. Remainder of money from sale of personal estate to my wife **Sarah E**, my daughters **Arsula Moffett** and **Sarah Eliza**, and my sons John Wesley, Thomas George, and Washington.

Execs. my wife Sarah E. and my nephew Samuel J. Jarman. Witnesses Thomas J. Britton, M.V. Boyer, J. Lambert Dulaney. Written Apr. 13, 1861 Proved May 6, 1862 p. 207

Abraham Dobbs of Kent Co

Liber 13   1854-1867

To my wife **Mary Anne Dobbs** $100 annually. To my son **Absolom Dobbs** $5. To my son **Sampson Dobbs** $5. To my brother **Samuel B. Dobbs** $100 for my son **William Dobbs**. To **James C. Dobbs** (no relationship given) the rest of my personal estate.

Execs. James Bolter (declined right to administer) and James C. Dobbs. Witnesses Stephen Kendal, James Rodness, James E. Blackiston. Written July 13, 1859 Proved May 6, 1862 p. 210 Mary Ann Dobbs and William Dobbs renounce right to admin. Apr. 1862 witness James C. Dobbs; James C. Dobbs renounced right to administer Apr. 10, 1862 witness George Vickers; and Absolom Dobbs renounced right to administer to William H. Smith Apr. 25, 1862 witness George Vickers.

Hannah Wallis Woodland Ireland of Kent Co
My remains to be buried with the remains of my deceased husband. To my son **John William Pope Ireland** all my real personal and mixed estate. To the children of my deceased dau. **Margaret Ann Wallis Woodland Ireland Brown** $800 when they become of age. To **Sarah Elizabeth** the dau. of my deceased dau. **Louisa Perkins Ireland Moffett** $800 when she becomes of age, if she has no issue then to my son John. To my dau. **Alethea Lavinia Woodland Nivin** $800. To my dau. **Emma H. Perkins Ireland Warfield** $150.

Exec. John William Pope Ireland. Witnesses Albert Medders, C.F. Taylor, Joseph P. Ireland. Written July 8, 1858 Proved June 10, 1862 p. 212

James Brown of Kent Co
For the great love of my wife **Augusta Brown** I give her all my estate, negroes, horses, carriages, cattle, hogs, stock of every other kind whatever, household and kitchen furniture, farming utensils, grain, bonds, notes, open accounts and other evidences of indebtedness of other to with also the money which my brother **William W. Brown** owes me which I loaned for the purchase of *"Grisham Hall"* farm upon which he resides money or ½ farm.

Exec. James P. Wickes (renounced right to Mrs. Augusta Brown). Witnesses Thomas R. Brown, Mary W. DeCoursy now Mary W. Gibson, Jacob Fisher. Written Nov. 24, 1854 Proved Nov. 4, 1862 p. 214

Francis Biddle of Kent Co
To my grandson **John T. Lusby** $3,000 at age 21 charged to my real estate. My real estate to all my children: my son **Stephen A. Biddle**, daughters **Emeline**, **Martha**, **Clarissa**, and **Julianna**. Stephen can take part of *"Ringgold farm"* where he now lives and my unmarried daughters may elect part of my *"Brooke farm"* and to my 3 single daughters my carriages and carriage horses and the residue of my personal to Stephen and his sisters.

Abstracts of Kent Co., MD Wills

Exec. my dau. Emeline. Witnesses James Alfred Pearce, Charlotte A.L. Pearce, J.A. Pearce Jr. Written Oct. 28, 1861 Proved Dec. 23, 1862 p. 216

Samuel Kerr of Kent Co

To my niece **Sarah A. Pearce** my negro girl **Julia** now about 18 until she is 30 and my negro boy **Abe** now about 11 until he is 30. To my niece **Adeline K. Merrit** my negro boy **Abe** formerly belonging to the estate of Francis Rutter now about 9 until he is 24 and my negro **Patty** now about 10 until she is 30. To my brother **Andrew Kerr** my negroes **David** now about 25 and **Amos** now about 22 to serve until 35. I set my negroes **Bob, Ben, Jake** and **Ellen** free on Jan. 1 next and $30. I set my negro woman **Clara** free and give her $30 annually charged to the proceeds of my estate. To my nieces **Sarah A. Pearce** and **Adeline K. Merritt** all my household and kitchen furniture and my large carriage and their choice of a pair of my horses and my negro woman **Willie** for 3 years and then set free. To my nephew **George A. Merritt** $300. And my afflicted negro girl **Ann** charge her support to my nieces. To Adeline my negro girl **Maria** now about 3 the child of my said Willie to serve until 25 and then set free. To my niece Sarah A. Pearce my little girl **Sarah** 14 months old the child of my said Willie until she is 25 and then free. To my brother Andrew Kerr all my right and interest in my negro **Gustavius** now about 15, bound until he is 19 to **Jesse Wilson**, until he is 24. To my young friend **John C. Groome, Jr.** my negro boy **George** about 11 and now living with **Mrs. Eliza Merritt** until he is 24 and then set free. All other negroes set free at 25. To my sister **Charlotte Hossenger** $500 free of her husband's use, and then to her children. To my sister **Mary K. Sharp** $100 annually. If nieces marry then to have $1,500. After payment of $100 to my nephew **William K. Merritt** then 1/3 to my brother **Andrew**, 1/3 to my sister **Mary K. Sharpe**, 1/3 held for my sister **Charlotte Hossinger** and upon her death to whomever she chooses by will or her children.

Execs. My brother Andrew Kerr and my friend John C. Groome. Witnesses William Kennedy, Peter Broes, Thomas H. Boyd. Written Aug. 18, 1855 Proved Dec. 11, 1862 p. 218

Codicil my negro boy **Lewis** a child of my said Willie to my niece **Sarah Ann Pearce** until he is 25 according to a deed of manumission already executed in Kent Co Circuit Court. Written June 23, 1861. Witnesses Mary S. Groome Proved July 25, 1863

James Alfred Pearce of Kent Co

My body to be buried at the burial grounds at my farm. A certificate for 26 shares of Union Bank stock which shares belong to my sister Mrs. **Ann O. Wharton**. Debts due me from **Dr. J. Burris** and two bonds of $1,000 each from the Northern and Central Railroad Company for my dau. **Catharine J. Burriss**. To my dear dau. **Lottie** in addition to the bond of the Northern and Central railroad Company for $1,000 already given her two other bonds of the same company of $1,000 and 33 shares of my Union Bank stock and debts due from **James T. Earl Esq** on a bond for $1,500 and shares of Chester Bridge stock. To my little dau. **Mary Clementine** $2,000 out of my personal estate, with what her mother will be able to give her will make a full share of my estate other than that I derived from the mother of Kate, Lottie, and Alfred. To my wife I give the house in which I reside and the stabling and premises including a lot in front of the house and also my old garden lot on Cannon Street and my lot near Chestertown commonly called the *"Ringgold lot"* and also the furniture, except from my office which I give to **Alfred** and the secretary which was my mother's which I give to Lottie, for my wife during her life then the real estate to my son Alfred and my furniture to my daughters Lottie and my son **James Alfred** except the furniture of my chamber to my dau. Mary Clementine. To my wife 1/3 part of my personal estate except what was given to my daughters Kate, Lottie and Mary Clementine then upon her death to my son Alfred. To my wife the servants used and employed in our house then to my son and my double carriage and horses and my cows. The rockaway carriage to my son. To my son Alfred my farm subject to 1/3 dower of my wife and also the lots near Chestertown not hereinbefore devised and after my wife's decease the house and garden and lots devised to her for life with the payment of $600 to my dau. Mary. To my son my plate and my books expecting him to give his sister Lottie and Mary a few of them such as they would desire. The rents of my estate to my wife for support of my three children now at home. To my son Alfred my slaves **Aaron** and **Simon** and my other slaves after the death of my wife. The residue to my son and my daughters Lottie and Mary. No claim against my estate are to be allowed by my children except $35 to Lottie and $40 to Alfred which are to be paid. My dear wife **Matilda C. Pearce** executrix and my son Alfred executor.

Execs. my wife Matilda C. Pearce and my son Alfred Pearce. Witnesses E.F. Chambers, W.W.E. Wickes, J.A. Wickes. Written Sep. 2, 1862 Proved Jan. 9, 1863 p. 225

<u>Codicil</u> To my wife instead of what was given in will from 15th to 23rd line, $1,000 and the Tide Water Canal Bonds now in the possession of **Robert Mickle Esq.** and 33 shares of Union Bank of MD stock. To son **James Alfred Pearce Jr.** in trust for his sister **Kate** $1,000 due me from **Rev. D. M. Wharton** of VA. Upon her death to my daughters Lottie and Clementine. Son James Alfred Pearce Jr. $500. Written Oct. 10, 1862. Witnesses George Vickers, Pere L. Wickes, W. G. Westcott

<u>2nd Codicil</u> Cancel the clause rents from estate to wife for support of three children at home and replace with to my executors to pay for support of my wife and three children at home. Cancel $500 to son James Jr. from Codicil. I charge $100 to real estate given James for support of my dau. **Mary Clementine** during the period of her education at home but if away from home then $200 annually during the period of her education. Written Oct. 11, 1862. Witnesses George Vickers, W. G. Westcott, Pere L. Wickes

<u>3rd Codicil</u> Revise clause where I gave my carriage and carriage horses to my wife and now to my wife and son James Alfred Pearce Jr. The provisions, coal, fuel, hay and provender and 20 barrels of corn from my lots and a quantity of wood to be furnished to my and for the use of my family. Instead of 1/3 dower then 7/16ths of annual rents. Because of increase to wife, I revoke the charge from 2nd codicil to James for education of my dau. **Mary Clementine**. Written Oct. 11, 1862. Witnesses George Vickers, W. G. Westcott, Pere L. Wickes

4th Codicil The remainder of my estate instead of to my three daughters to my wife and my son and my daughters Lottie and Mary. To my wife all the provender including the firewoods contracted for but not yet delivered the killing pigs, the corn fodder and provender from my lots in Town whether on the dwelling house or in the granaries on the wharf for the corn for support of family. All my oats in the granary and the wines and liquors equally divided between my wife and son Alfred. Written Nov. 1, 1862. Witnesses E.F. Chambers, W. H. Meeteer, Pere L. Wickes.

William Smith
To my adopted dau. **Louisa Foreman** all my estate including my house and lot fronting on Main Street and running back to (word missing) adjoining the lands of **George C. Adkinson, Thomas Hudson** and others and the household and kitchen furniture. To Henry Brown the right to till the lot for one half so long as Louisa and him can agree, Louisa having the privilege of annulling the contract any time from Christmas and Mar. not after. James Vickers attests to seeing William Smith (fu) [or fn = free negro?] sign will.

Exec. Not Given. Witnesses Thomas N. Whaland, James M. Vickers, William A. Rollison. Written May 4, 1863 Proved June 16, 1863 p. 233

Eliza Cochran of Kent Co
To my daughters **Hannah C. Sweatman**, my dau. **Sarah A. Cleever**, and my granddau. **Emily Eliza Banthum**, all my parcel on the E side of the road leading through the village of the head of Sassafras divided between the 3 children named and all my real estate consisting of a store house and dwelling house attached at the head of Sassafras to be sold and proceeds divided equally between the 3, after $20 to my little grandson **James Davis**

Exec. John T. Briscoe (renounced right to administer). Witnesses D.B. Stewart, R. A. Frazier, E.B. Caulk. Written Nov. 16, 1861 Proved May 19, 1863 p. 235

Joseph Hill of the City of Wilmington, DE
For the future comfort and happiness of my dear wife and daughter. To the Wilmington and Brandywine Cemetery Company $100 in trust to keep in good order my burial lot. To my wife **Mary Ann Hill,** all my household goods and furniture, house and carriage and harness during her life, then to my dau. **Hannah Ann.** I give my dwelling house in the City of Wilmington on the W side of King Street between 7th and 8th Streets unto my esteemed friend **Joseph Bringhurst** and **Edward Bringhurst Sr.** of DE and **Joseph C. Grubb** of Philadelphia in trust for my wife and then daughter. From the residue of my estate, purchase of $1,000 insurance to the trustees of the Wilmington City Loan for the house and if injured must be repaired. To my wife $1,200 annually, reduce to $400 if remarried, if she is a widow again then $1,000. To my dau. **Hannah Ann** wife of **Joseph C. Grubb.** My dau. may request $6,000 of the capital to be applied to a dwelling house selected by her. My daughter's husband to receive $600 during his life if she dies.

Liber 13 1854-1867

Execs. Joseph Bringhurst, Edward Bringhurst Sr., Joseph C. Grubb. Witnesses Mahlon Betts, Daniel W. Bates. Written Mar. 20, 1860 Proved Mar. 30, 1863 p. 237

Codicil Income to support my brother **Robert Hill** during his lifetime not to exceed $10 per month, to my sister **Elizabeth**, wife of **Robert Maull** of the City of Philadelphia $60 annually, to my sister **Rebecca**, wife of **Cuthbert Hall** of Kent Co, DE $60 annually. If my wife and dau. do not survive, then two shares of my estate to my brother **James Hill** and after his death to his dau. **Margaret Ann Hill**, but if she dies then to her mother **Mary Hill**, during her lifetime. One share to my brother **Robert Hill**, then to his issue. One share to my brother **Thomas Hill** during his life then to his issue. One share to my brother **Henry**, then to his issue. One share to my sister **Rebecca Hall**, then to her issue except her 2 sons, then to her dau. **Emily**. And remaining share to my sister **Elizabeth Maul** during her lifetime. Written Mar. 20, 1860. Witnesses Mahlon Belts, Daniel M. Bates.

William F. Smyth of Kent Co

After my wife's 1/3, to my dear wife **Anna Smyth** my black mare and Rockaway carriage and my negro woman **Charlotte**. To my son **Robert M. Smyth**, the lot of ground running back to the Mill Race out which my store and house stands together with the buildings, also the dwelling house where I reside known as the Bank property and the upper end of the *"Timothy lot"* or so much as may be cut off by a line drawn running straight from the end of the fence on the Back Street to the land of the heirs of **John E. Cacy** deceased together with the house and blacksmith shop attached. Also the stock of goods on hand in my store and he is to pay for the last stock of goods lately purchased about $1,100 and my negro man **Isaac**. To my son **John T. Smyth**, the farm and plantation on which he now resides known as the Spearman farm, as also all the stock and farming implementation and negro woman **Susan** and her children and also my cartwright shop and lot now occupied by John Taylor. To my dau. **Harriet Augusta Smyth** my farm known as the *"Brown farm"* and the land I bought of the silk company and my negro girl **Mary** and my house and lot known as the *"Spry property"*. To my dau. **Annie Elizabeth Crane** the lot and dwelling and improvement now occupied by Rev. M. Watson and also the lot and blacksmith shop nearly off-site and not now occupied and my farm known as the *"Forest farm"* and the lower end of my *"Timothy lot"* lying on the Mill Race and Back Street. To my dau. **Ella G. Smyth** my farm known as the *"Webb farm"*, also the lot of ground with the improvement running as the fences and paling now run known as the *"McDaniel lot"* in the town of Millington, also the small lot on the S side of Sharper Street and negro girl **Sally**. As it is not probable that my son William F. Smyth will ever be competent to do business I direct my sons Robert M. and John T. Smyth to pay him $100 annually. If he ever exhibits the ability to conduct business then his brothers should assist him in some business. My bank stock to be sold. The servants that came from the late **Mrs. Ruth** or her son **Samuel Ruth** into my possession shall form no part of my personal estate and shall be under the control of my wife **Anna Smyth** and subject to her disposal. All the residue of my estate to my children equally except my son **William F. Smyth** who is already provided for.

Exec. my sons Robert M. and John T. Smyth. Witnesses M.W. Boyer, Thomas J. Britton, Richard C. Johnson. Written Oct. 10, 1863 Proved Nov. 3, 1863 p. 251

Merritt Miller of Kent Co
To my son **Walter F. H. Miller** all my real estate in Kent Co and to my granddau. **Maria L. Gamble** $1,000 when of age with interest from age 12 on and if my son Walter Miller without issue living then I devise said real estate to my grandson **Merritt Miller Beck** the son of **Horatio Beck** subject to the $1,000 to my granddau. Maria L. Gamble. Unto my dau. Maria L. **Brown** $7,000 to be paid out of bonds due me to be expended on a purchase of a farm. To my son Walter my negroes old **Perry, Delia, Sam, Jess,** and **Margaret** and request him to take good care of my old negroes. To my dau. **Mary Matilda Beck** my negro woman **Eliza** and her children, my negro woman **Fanny** and her children except **Maria**. To my dau. **Ann E. Gamble** my negro woman old **Charlotte** and **Charlotte Ward** and all her children **Alexine, Sam, Emory, Henry** and a female infant child and any child she may have living at my death and also my negro **Ned** and **Perry**, and all the stock and furniture and property that I have already given to her, all the property she purchased at the sale of **Robert A. Gamble** and all sums due me as the administrator of the late Robert A. Gamble for overpayments upon my estate. To my daughters Mary Matilda Beck and **Sarah E. S. Page** as tenants in common all my real estate in Queen Anns Co To my dau. Sarah E. S. Page my negroes **Pompey, Clinton,** and **Joseph** and **Maria** dau. of **Fanny**. To my dau. **Maria L. Brown** my negroes **Ellen** and her children **Eliza** and her children, and **Jim** and **Alonzo**. Remainder to all my children.

Exec. my son Walter T. H. Miller. Witnesses James B. Ricaud, Cornelia Ricaud, Oliver P. Beck. Written July 22, 1858 Proved Nov. 3, 1863 p. 254

<u>Codicil</u> Whereas I gave to my dau. **Maria L. Browne,** wife of **Morgan Browne** and I have given her certain bonds of more than $6,000 and the negroes **Ellen** and her children, negro **Eliza** and her child and negroes **Jim** and **Alonzo** I remove any devises given to her. Written Nov. 17, 1859.

Joseph Wickes of Kent Co
To my dear wife **Elizabeth C. Wickes** who has been my greatest earthly comfort through many year of my long life, 52 shares of stock in Union Bank of MD, 55 shares of stock of the Merchants Bank of Baltimore, 17 shares of stock of the Chesapeake Bank, my slaves **Charles** and **Edwin** (the children of her woman **Sylvia**), all my household and kitchen furniture and my double carriage and harness and carriage horses and all the provisions put up for the use of the family and 5 of my best cows and one horse at *"Airy Hill"*. To my wife my servants **John, Abe, Joe, Charlotte, Besse** and **Jane** and all my plate, my ice house and stabling, carriage house and premises adjoining the property we now occupy during her life then to my two sons **Joseph A. Wickes** and **Pere L. Wickes**. To my wife my lot of woodland adjoining "Airy hill" containing about 20 acres purchased of Richard B. Carmichael trustee for her life and after to my grandson

Liber 13 1854-1867

Benjamin C. Wickes, if he has no heirs to my son Pere L. Wickes. My wife to have full power to cut from my farm called *"Piner's Grove"* situated near Chestertown wood for her full use in Chestertown during her life. To my two sons Joseph and Pere L. Wickes my farm called *"Piners Grove"* near Chestertown and containing about 500 acres. To my son Joseph the dwelling house in which he now lives situate on High Street Chestertown and the frame dwelling house adjoining the house in which he lives. To my son **Joseph A. Wickes** my negro servants **Sam, Mike, Tom, George, Frederick, Mary, Maria** and **Betsy** and also my small carriage and harness. To my son **Pere L. Wickes** my negro servants **Pere Cotton, Jim, Henry, Boy Pere, Beckey, Pat,** and **Isabel**. To my dau. in law **Ann Rebecca Wickes** $500. To my 3 grandchildren **Augusta M. Wickes, Frances C. Wickes,** and **Mary E. Wickes,** the children of my deceased son **Ezekial C. Wickes** to whom I made considerable advances during his life, my dwelling house and premises on the corner of Front Street and Fish Street, Chestertown subject to the life estate of **Henrietta M. Bruff**. To Henry Welsh of York, PA $8,000 in trust for my dau. **Sarah A. Welsh** for her life free from debts or control of her present or any future husband and after her death for the use of such child or children of said Sarah as may be living. If no issue then the said Henry Welsh will pay 1/3 to **William H. Welsh** the husband of my dau. Sarah and the residue to my sons Joseph and Pere Wickes.

Execs. my sons Joseph A. Wickes and Pere L. Wickes. Witnesses W.G. Westcott, Thomas B. Hynson, John L. Stam. Written July 23, 1863 Proved Jan. 25, 1864 p. 258

Codicil I omitted the dower to my wife in my *"Piners Grove"* farm which I devise to her. The interest of $8,000 to my dau. Sarah to be paid every 6 months to be paid by the trustee Henry Welsh Esq. The garden lot on Queen Street being necessary for the house in which we dwell I give to my wife and my son **Peregrine** during my wife's life then to my son Peregrine. Written Jan. 12, 1864. Witnesses E.F. Chambers, W.G. Westcott, B.F. Houston

Caroline Strong of Kent Co
Sale of my estate except servants. My servants **Milcah** and **Isaac** to the care of my children.

Exec. my friend William T. Adkinson. Witnesses L.M. Ricaud, James Kendall, G.M. Hart, Thomas H. Strong. Written Mar. 26, 1864 Proved Apr. 14, 1864 p. 262

Elizabeth Nicols of Kent Co
To my dau. **Anna Maria Nicols** my negroes **Fanny** and **Hester,** my bureaus, silver coffee pot, work table, large trunks, and all the articles. To my son **Jeremiah Nicols** my negroes **Sam** and **Emory,** my bed and mattress. To my grandson **Harry Nicols** son of **Richard L.L. Nicols** my negro girl **Lucy** child of Negro **Ellen**. To my son Richard L.L. Nicols my negroes **Daniel, Ellen,** and **John,** all my interest in the household goods, furniture, farming utensils and stock on the farm

259

Exec. my son Richard L.L. Nicols. Witnesses James B. Ricaud, Cornelia C. Ricaud. Written Apr. 11, 1860 Proved Apr. 15, 1864 p. 264

Thomas S. Murphy of Kent Co
My farm of 277 acres on Davis Creek in Pine Neck which I purchased from Mrs. Stickney and Mr. Ward her son together with the remainder of my estate to my wife **Dorothy Murphy** for her natural life. After her death to my dau. **Dorothy E.** wife of **Andrew T. Hubbard** for her life. After her death to her children or descendants.

Exec. my wife Dorothy Murphy. Witnesses George W. Thompson, William J. Leary, William S. Elburn. Written May 26, 1862 Proved May 10, 1864 p. 265

John L. Deputy of Hundred of New Castle, DE
A farm in the Hundred containing 80 acres which I purchased from **James T. Bird** and whereon I now reside and my house in Wilmington which I purchased of **William McCaulley** to be sold. My wife **Mary Deputy** $300 annually during life in lieu of dower. The mortgage of $22,500 which I hold against my two sons **Charles M. Deputy** and **Elias Deputy** upon their lands in Kent Co To my son **Solomon Deputy** in trust for each of my other children to wit **Charles M. Deputy, Elias Deputy, Anthony Deputy, Samuel Deputy, James K. P. Deputy, Mary Jane** wife of **William Gale, Susan** wife of **Samuel McCall** and **Elizabeth Deputy** the $22,500. To my wife such articles of household furniture that she may select not to exceed $200. To my granddau. **Catharine Deputy** the dau. of my son Elias $500. To my grandsons, **John** the son of Charles M. Deputy, **John** the son of Solomon Deputy, and **John** the son of **Susan McCall** each $100. The rest of my estate to my children.

Exec. my son Solomon Deputy. Witnesses George B. Rodney, William H. McCullough, Westleigh Robesson. Written Dec. 10, 1862 Proved Jan. 15, 1863 p. 267

Codicil The $22,500 mortgage should be transferred as soon as possible to Solomon Deputy in trust. Written Dec. 10, 1862 same witnesses
2nd Codicil To my wife my brick house and lot on Pine Street in Wilmington, DE. Written Jan. 5, 1863. Witnesses Roderick Sutherland MD, James Couper

Joseph Boyd of Kent Co
My son **Bedford B. Boyd** the farm on which he now resides with the mortgage I hold on said farm according to the lines and fenced by me. To my sons **Joseph** and **Samuel C. Boyd** the farm on which I now resided subject to $1,000 to their brother **John**. To my dau. **Henrietta Dodd** my Butcher Neck farm lying on Chester River and now occupied by one William Folkner as tenant. To my son **Henry L. Boyd** my Wallace farm containing about 161 acres and a legacy of $500 from Henrietta to my son Henry when he is 21. To my son **John Boyd**, my negro boy **Bill** and a legacy of $1,000 to be paid by sons Joseph and Samuel C. Boyd. To my wife Henrietta Boyd my negro woman **Rebecca** and her child **Jane** and not counted against her dower. To my dau. Henrietta

Liber 13 1854-1867

Dodd my negro girl **Ruth**. After my wife's dower, my son **Henry L. Boyd** the rest of my estate.

Exec. Richard Hynson attorney at law of Chestertown. Witnesses Thomas C. Ringgold, Joseph O. Rasin, Samuel D. Turbutt. Written Nov. 11, 1863 Proved May 13, 1864 p. 272

Daniel L. Doman of Kent Co
My wife **Betsy** the house and lot which I purchased of Mr. **William Whittington** where I now live during my widowhood except the right of way from my back lot that I purchased from Mr. **J. Horsey** and at her marriage or death of my wife to my daughters **Mary** and **Emily**. I also give to her my best bed and bedding. My other lot to my sons **Isiah** and **Samuel** and they are to pay to my sons **James**, **Joseph** and my daughters **Hannah** and **Tempy** $30 each. To my dau. **Emily** my watch. The rest of my estate to be sold to pay my debts.

Exec. Moses Caulk (FN). Witnesses John W. Fowler, John T. Thornington. Written May 17, 1864 Proved July 4, 1864 p. 274

William Peacock of Kent Co
After my debts, I give to my dau. **Editha Elizabeth Powell** $300. To my dau. **Sarah Mason** $300. To my dau. **Catharine Ann Hanes** $300. The rest of my estate to dau. **Milliminta** and my son **John W.** equally.

Exec. my son Richard Peacock. Witnesses D.C. Blackiston, Thomas Woodall, Eben Neal. Written July 19, 1864 Proved Sep. 13, 1864 p. 275

Samuel E. Baker of Kent Co
My home farm and lands whereon I reside which I purchased of the **Harris** and **Lewis** heirs containing 290 acres to my two children **Richard Whaland Baker** and **Sarah R.L. Baker**, but if they die under 21 without heirs the survivor receives the whole. To my dau. **Margaret Ann Baker** the Pippin or Broxon farm adjoining **Josiah Ringgolds** and **Henry W. Carvills** farm containing about 160 acres on which **James Pearce** resides. To my dau. **Juliett Parsons** for life the *"Yearly farm"* which I purchased of **John F. Yearly** containing 234 acres now occupied by my said dau. and her husband **John Parsons** adjoining the *"Hollyday farm"* and *"Fennimous lands"* and the house and lot adjoining occupied by Joseph Ford. To my dau. **Henrietta French** for her life the **Joseph Browne** farm which I purchased of **William T. Skirven** adjoining the lands of **William Crow**, **William Tomlinson**, **Comegys Cosden**, and the **Fletcher Ringgold** and Carville farm, and which said *"Browne farm"* is occupied by **William French**. To my dau. **Frances Ann Sparks** for her life the *"Jacobs"* or *"Gordon farm"* containing 224 acres on which **Solomon Sparks** now resides adjoining the land of **William Bowman**, **Jacob Highly**, and **R.S. Thomas Jr.** and the farm late the Wiley now **Margaret Ann Thomas'** farm. The lands given to my said daughters Juliett Parsons and Henrietta French and Frances

261

Ann Sparks shall not be liability to the debts of their respective husbands and shall go to their children after their mother's death. The land given my dau. Juliett Parsons I charge $1,000 to be paid to the children of my dau. **Susan Sparks**. The land given my dau. Henrietta French I charge $1,265 to be paid to the children of my dau. Susan Sparks. The land given my dau. Frances A. Sparks I charge $1,000 to the children of my dau. Susan. The interest to be paid to my dau. Susan Sparks during her life. The land given to my dau. Frances A. Sparks $1,000 to be paid my granddau. **John Anna Dickinson**. My wife **Mary Ann Baker** is entitled to her dower, my personal estate to be sold except the choice of household and kitchen furniture up to $300 my wife chooses. The Brice or Hendrix farm in Queen Annes Co containing 243 acres to be sold. My houses, shops and lot of land in Chestertown occupied by **Robert Morris, Charles Estes** as tenants to be sold and applied to the payment of my debts and to sell the house and lot at Harrisburgh adjoining Henry W. Carvill's farm and occupied by Henry N. Simms. My home farm to be charged with $2,000 to pay debts. Debts due from James Pearce. In the sale of the Carville Farm to my son **William Thomas Baker** I abated the price I asked for said land several thousand dollars considering it his portion of my estate. I now give to my son William $1 and no more. To my dau. **Margaret Ann Baker** I give bed, bedstead, and bedding. The family grave yard on the farm of my brother **Thomas Baker** to be enclosed with a plain iron fence and that my children and the other relatives and person interested to contributed rateably to accomplish the same.

Exec. my friend George Vickers (and my wife Mary Ann Baker added in codicil). Witnesses R.S. Thomas, Jr., John Brice, John T. Toulson. Written Jan. 26, 1864 Proved Nov. 19, 1864 p. 276

Codicil I give my wife all the rest of my household and kitchen furniture and my old horse John, carriage and harness and the choice of two cows. Execs. to convey by deed the Brice and Hendrix Farm in Queen Annes Co to Dr. Samuel V. Mace of Cecil Co. Written Oct. 29, 1864. Witnesses Henry W. Earnest, James Lamb, Edward Plummer, Thomas N. Whaland

John Francis Usilton of Kent Co
All my personal estate to wife **Rachel Usilton**

Exec. my friend John Thomas Skirven. Witnesses Martha J. Parson, Mary E. Shuster, George T. Moore. Written Feb. 11, 1865 Proved Feb. 21, 1865 p. 282

Isaac Hopkins of Kent Co
My wife **Caroline Hopkins** the right to live in the dwelling house where I now dwell during her natural life to be paid by my friend Daniel Roe $20 annually. I give land unto my friend Daniel Roe my house and lot whereon I now dwell known of the *"Brown property"* about 4 3/4 acres as long as he allows wife Caroline Hopkins to live there.

Liber 13 1854-1867

Exec. Not Given. Witnesses John T. Hodgkin, Asbury Ruth, Thomas N. Salloway. Written Dec. 29, 1864 Proved Mar. 18, 1865 p. 283

Robert Wilson of Kent Co

To my dear wife **Martha Amanda Wilson** 1/3 of my estate. To my children **Francis Albert Wilson, Sarah Etta Louisa Wilson,** and **Emma Wilson** all rest of my estate. To my wife Martha Amanda Wilson if she wishes to sell my lands in Queen Annes Co

Exec. my beloved wife Martha Amanda Wilson. Witnesses John N. Usilton, Joseph H. Thompson, Thomas Baker. Written Feb. 18, 1865 Proved Mar. 8, 1865 p. 284

Codicil I appoint my friend Thomas W. Eliason executor in the event of my wife Martha Amanda Wilson. Written Feb. 18, 1865

Benjamin Howard of Kent Co

My son **George W. Howard** all my farm or plantation lying near Turners Creek called *"Youngs Neck"* now occupied by my said son, containing as per survey of **George Gale Esq.** made in the year 1845, a plat and certificate of which now in my possession 252 acres and 31 perches, also all that farm called *"upper Bloomfield"*, containing 201 acres whereon **Dr. James Haman** now resides all of which is subject to free ingress and egress to my *"lower Bloomfield"* lands and subject to legacies. To my dau. **Mary Ellen Haman** all the part of my home farm whereon I now live called Suffold and Green Forest containing by survey for 252 ½ acres. To my son **Joseph James Howard** all residue of my estate whereon he now resides called *"Suffolk"* and *"Green Forest"* containing per a survey 156 acres and two rods and 20 perches: beginning for the same at a stone standing a corner of **Dr. Thomas C. Kennards** lands said stone also being in the road leading to *"Green Oak Farm"* and running thence N 88° and ½° E 129 perches thence N 2° and ½ W 211 perches thence S 84° and ½° W 49 perches thence S 86° W 55½ perches and thence S 16° and ½° W 100 perches and 1/16 perches, thence with a straight line to the beginning and now called Lower Bloomfield containing 201 to be subject to $1,000 grandson **Benjamin Howard** (Haman written sideways) when he shall arrive at 21 (see Release B.F.H. Liber B.F.H. p 423). To wife **Augusta Howard** in virtue of a contract between us before marriage and in lieu of dower in real and personal estate $200 annually during her life charged to my said son George W. Howard. My son charged to furnish my said wife with her board during life and to enjoin all my children to be kind and attentive to my said wife to make her life comfortable. I also give my said wife my York carriage and harness and my horse Boseer. To my dau. **Mary Ellen Haman** the $2,000. All the rest of my estate to my three children.

Execs. my sons Joseph J. Howard, George W. Howard and son in law Dr. James Haman. Witnesses John Wilson, James P. Carothers, Joshua Clark. Written Jan. 5, 1865 Proved Mar. 7, 1865 p. 286

Abstracts of Kent Co., MD Wills

James A. Wood of Kent Co
To my mother **Rebecca Wood** my personal estate. After her death: to my brother **Charles C. Wood** my horse called Braddock and a steel tooth rake, and to my brother **John Wesley Wood** my mare called Kate and a young cow with red color with short horns, to my sister **Mary** my cow called Alice, to my sister **Catharine** my cow called Miss Ricaud, to my sister **Clara Emma** a good bed, bedstead, and bedding, to my sister **Anna**, a good bed, bedstead, bedding and my unfinished quilt called the Beggars quilt, to my niece **Ida**, dau. of my brother Charles $50. To my mother Rebecca Wood all my real estate consisting of my undivided interest in a farm in Cecil Co which descended from my late father **Matthew J. Wood** which is now occupied by John Milburn as tenant and then to my brothers and sisters.

Exec. my mother Rebecca Wood. Witnesses William N. Urian, Howard T. Urian, Samuel W. Curlett. Written Feb. 9, 1865 Proved p. 289

Thomas P. Gresham of Kent Co
To my wife **Ann Gresham** all my estate during her widowhood and no longer. My five sons **Thomas, John, Washington, Valentine** and **Harrison** and my 3 daughters **Sophia, Caroline,** and **Rebecca** shall reside with their mother. To each of my five sons and 3 daughters such board and clothing and other necessaries of the profits while they remain single. If my wife marries, then my estate to be sold and divided between my children.

Exec. my wife Ann Gresham. Witnesses R. W. Ringgold, J.C. Wilson, John A. Rollison. Written Mar. 4, 1865 Proved Apr. 6, 1865 p. 291

Daniel Jones of Kent Co
Whereas a deed of trust to me to my children **Mary Elizabeth, Jacob Alfred, John Wesley** and **George Washington** to carry in effect the desires of their late mother's will, I appoint my son John Wesley trustee. I will my real and personal estate excepting a rose wood piano (belonging to my dau. **Sarah Catharine**) to pay debts. Debts owed to me and which I owe to others are listed separately among my personal papers and are directed to be paid and collected by executor. My children Mary Elizabeth, Jacob Alfred, John Wesley, and George Washington have executed a deed relinquishing their interest in their late mothers property in favor of their other sisters and brother and my son **Washington** shall take the same if he pays Mary E. $1,200, Jacob A. ¼ part or deducting an account I have against him, and to my son John W. ¼ part and the remaining ¼ to be his (George's) part. If George does not want property then to son John under same conditions. If remainder of personal estate, then ½ to my dau. Sarah Catharine if then living, if not then to my dau. Jennie and the other ½ to my son Daniel.

Exec. my son John Wesley Jones. Witnesses George Gale, David W. Hanes, Samuel J. Roseberry. Written Dec. 28, 1864 Proved Apr. 29, 1865 p. 293

Thomas Woodward formerly of Wilmington, DE

Thomas formerly of Wilmington now of the 24th ward of Philadelphia. To my wife **Kate** all my household furniture and articles of domestic use which I have acquired since the death of my former wife **Henrietta**, all articles of furniture remaining which I owned during the life of my said first wife shall be divided among my children. To my wife Kate $1,000 annually so long as she remains my widow in lieu of her dower. All the rest of my estate to my children. If my wife instead chooses dower then all my property to such of my children by my first wife Henrietta that shall survive me. If my two sons are in their minority at my decease then my other adult executors shall have right to administer.

Execs. my sons Brinton Jones Woodward, Garrett Lewis Woodward and my brother in law Joseph J. Martin and my friend Joseph James. Witnesses Joseph B. Townsend, J. Sergeant Price, William H. Townsend. Written Feb. 4, 1864 Proved p. 295

Codicil In addition to my wife Kate I give the house and lot now occupied by me at No. 14 Woodland Terest in West Philadelphia, PA for her until our youngest child shall be 21, if they both die then to my residuary estate. ½ of my entire estate given to the children to go to the executor until each arrives at 30 or if they shall an ability to manage their money then the trustee, **Crosby P. Morton** of Chester, PA, can transfer to them sooner. Written Jan. 17, 1865. Witnesses John W. Bennett, Joseph C. Woodward.

I, **Catharine Woodward,** widow of Thomas Woodward deceased late of Philadelphia do renounce unto Brinton Jones Woodward, Garrett Lewis Woodward, Joseph J. Martin, and Joseph James executors all my claim to estate as contained in will and elect my dower. Written Mar. 2, 1865. Witnesses William Murphy, Thomas R. Elcock.

Philip Jones (free man of color) of Kent Co

To my sons **Richard** and **James Jones** my lot of land I bought of Dr. George W. Thomas and in Chestertown adjoining the lands of Mr. John T. Dodd and others. To my niece **Margaret Ann Shephard** my brick house on *"Schotch Point"* with the lot of land attached. To my three sons **William Henry, Thomas Cuff,** and **William Wesley Jones,** the house in which I now reside. They can reside in or sell interest to the other but not to a stranger unless the other two are willing. My dau. **Ann Maria Hall** my frame house situated on *"Scotch Point"* with the lot of land thereto attached. Expecting that few debts will be left and desiring not to sell my personal estate and it be alienated from my family, use any monies that may be due me or the children to make it up. All my personal estate to my children Richard, James, William H., Thomas C., Wm Wesley Jones, and Ann Maria Hall.

Execs. my sons William Henry and William Wesley Jones. Witnesses L.S. Fowler, P. Stauffer, James A. Shaw. Written 1862 (no month and day) Proved July 29, 1865 p. 301 (William Wesley renounced right to administer. Witness Wm. A. Fisher, Baltimore)

Abstracts of Kent Co., MD Wills

Robert Bogle of Kent Co
To my dear wife **Adelaide R. Bogle** all my estate.

Exec. my wife Adelaide R. Bogle. Witnesses Henry May, Alexander Harris, Richard Norris Jr. Written Nov. 4, 1864 (Executed on Dec. 14) Proved p. 303

Joseph Sinton of Kent Co
My wife **Elizabeth** all my real and personal estate during her life. To my dau. **Mary Ann Downey** $1, To my dau. **Rebecca Williams** $1. To my dau. **Martha A. Coleman** $5 and to have the use of one room in the house during her widowhood. To my dau. **Rachael Webb** $5. After the death of my wife, then to my son **James B. Sinton** all my real estate on which I now reside and also ½ lot called *"Jones lot"*. James shall take care of my dau. Ann Elizabeth Sinton during her lifetime. To my son **Joseph W. Sinton** ½ Jones lot.

Exec. my son James B. Sinton. Witnesses John M. Rodney, John R. Ayres, James E. Blackiston. Written May 8, 1865 Proved Sep. 5, 1865 p. 305

Joseph Usilton of Kent Co
To my son **Lewin Usilton** the farm in Worton, where he now lives called *"The Gale and Waltham Farm"* and commonly called *"Colly Cove"* containing 292 ½ acres (excluding the ten acres hereinafter devised to go with my Rock Point farm) which I purchased of Col. Joseph Wickes and George Vickers trustees and James Beck (of George). I give to my son Lewin my land commonly called *"The Lot Place"* containing about 70 or 80 acres adjoining the Ingram or Bordley farms and at present cultivated and farmed by my said son Lewis, I charge him $1,000 to my dau. **Emily Lusby** without interest. I give unto my dau. **Amanda Edwards** (wife of **Joseph Edwards**) my farm in Worton called *"The Edwards Farm"* which I purchased of **James B. Ricaud Esq.** trustee for the sale of Emory Edward's heirs and conveyed to my. I give to my daughters **Alethea Usilton** my Dorsey Farm where I now live and which I purchased of William Vannoit. I give my farm in Worton in Kent Co commonly called *"Rock Point"* and which I purchased of Whitely and Gibson and others to my dau. **Hester Usilton** and her heirs and 10 acres of Woodland to be laid off from the *"Waltham Farm"* adjoining Rock Point Gate, and to laid off by my son Lewin and the lines to be recorded. To my dau. Emily Lusby (wife of **Josiah Lusby**) $10,000. Whatever interest or property I may have at my death in vessels or boats and their appurtenances I give to my son Lewin. All the rest (subject to bequest to wife) I give to my son Lewin to divide between himself and my four daughters. I charge my five children $40 each (total of $200) to my wife **Mary Usilton** for her life. I also give her a home where I now reside during her life, with a room suitably furnished from my estate according to an arrangement with my wife. Clara Wilson lately my servant $5 annually during her life to be paid by each of my children (total $25).
(On page 309 there is a diagram of the 10 acres of woodland showing G.S. Diehls land on top, road to Rock Point on right, land laid off for Hester Usilton all that part of

Liber 13 1854-1867

woodland of the *"Waltham Farm"* lying W of the public road leading to *"Rock Point"* at a stone near Rock Point Farm Gale.)

Exec. my son Lewin Usilton. Witnesses James H. Edes, Thomas H. Kennard, George Vickers. Written July 4, 1865 Proved Sep. 26, 1865 p. 306

George W. Oldham of Kent Co

To my wife **Susan A. Oldham** and my dau. **Martha Ella Oldham** for the life of my wife, my dwelling house and lots of land in Georgetown in Kent Co where I now reside which I purchased of **George Vickers** trustee for the sale of the late **James Boone** deceased and all provender for family use. After her death, to my daughters **Mary Amanda Massey** and **Martha Ella Oldham**. To my wife and dau. Martha Ella for my wife's life, The Anthony house and lot of land about 10 acres purchased of Mitchell and Pennington, near Anthony's mill and occupied by **Caleb Jarvis** and after her death to my dau. Mary Amanda Massey (wife of **Dr. C.H.B. Massey**) and Martha Ella Oldham. To my grandson **George Oldham Massey** (son of Dr. C.H.B. Massey and my dau. Mary Amanda Massey) The *"Boyer farm"* purchased by me of **John M. Comegys** and **John F. Newman** lying near Chesterville in Kent Co containing about 127 acres and adjoining the lands of the late **Hezekiah Mastin** and others and now carried on by me. 3/4 of rent to pay taxes and ¼ to be invested for 12 years then to erect a suitable building on said farm. Dr. Massey trustee for my grandson. My dear wife Susan A. Oldham a part of land in Cecil Co which I purchased of **James Ford** about 11 acres and a part of land in Cecil Co I purchased of **Benedict Craddock** containing 11 acres these adjoining the farm of my said wife which she derived from her father **Peregrine Biddle**. To my said dau. Mary Amanda Massey the following lands in Cecil Co: my farm commonly called the *"Manor Farms"*, one called the *"Mansion Farm"* at present occupied by **Elias Watson** as my tenant. Also my quarter farm adjoining the Mansion Farm occupied by **William H. Nowland** as my tenant, and all my woodland adjacent to or near said farms (except those stated below) said farms lie in Bohemia Manor. To my dau. **Martha Ella Oldham**, my farm in Sassafras Neck in Cecil Co one called the *"Locust Thickett Farm"* occupied by **Pere Pennington** as tenant, the other called *"Schotchmans Creek Farm"* which I purchased of **James A. Pearce** trustee and occupied by **J. Webb** as tenant. My executors may sell 60 acres of my woodland in Cecil Co adjacent my two Manor Farms devised to my dau. Mary lying farthest from the said farms. All my other land in Kent and Cecil Co to be sold and divided between my wife and two daughters. To my executors $500 for a suitable iron fence or inclosure around my grave and my wife's and a suitable monument to our memory at St. Stephens burial ground in Cecil Co All my moneys in bank or otherwise steamboat stock. $400 to my wife from each of my daughters Mary and Martha in lieu of dower of lands in Cecil Co To my nephew **Hamilton Oldham** $500.

Execs. my wife Susan A. Oldham and my son in law Dr. C.N.B. Massey. Witnesses George Vickers, Thomas N. Hewitt, William T. Betton. Written Dec. 8, 1864 Proved

Abstracts of Kent Co., MD Wills

July 25, 1865 p. 310 (Susan renounced right to administer. Written July 25, 1865 witness William T. Betton)

Susan Frances Skirven of Kent Co
To be buried with a pair of near and plain tombstones placed at my graves. To **Ida S. Stephens** dau. of **George R.** and **Anna E. Stephens** $500 when age 21. If dies under 21, then to my brothers and sisters. To **Anna S. Stephens**, dau. of same, $500 when 21. All the rest of my estate to brothers and sisters. Anything devised to my sister **Sarah Crow** held by executor during the life of her husband C.W. Crow. When Sarah dies without issue then to my brothers and sisters **James A. Skirven, William T. Skirven,** and **Mary E. Skirven.**

Exec. my brother James A. Skirven. Witnesses William Tomlinson, J.A. Harper, William P. Francis. Written Aug. 16, 1865 Proved Oct. 17, 1865 p. 313

Codicil To Ida S. Stephens and Anna S. Stephens 1/10 part of my estate instead of $500 for fear would be more than an equal share of my estate. Written Sep. 11, 1865. Witnesses Mary A. Robinson, Ann E. Skirven, William P. Francis.

Mary Tilden Gale
Rev. Mr. Sutton to take charge of money and effects which he will find in my clothing and about my house and to pay the various students who have paid me for this session's board, he shall pay over the balance to **Mrs. Polly Wilson,** wife of **Alexander Wilson** to whom I also leave all the rest of my estate. To be remembered and settled by Mr. Sutton that **Meginniss** has paid me $25 on this term and **Oregon Benson** has paid up to Xmas or $46.87 both without receipt.

Exec. Andrew J. Sutton. Witnesses C. Beecher Walff, Ralph Wright. Written Oct. 8, 1865 Proved Oct. 18, 1865 p. 316

Edward Comegys of Kent Co
To my niece **A. Rebecca Curry,** my niece Susan C. Brown, my niece **Mary E. Jones** wife of **Oliver P. Jones; Mary C. Brown, Hiram M. Brown, Ann Rebecca Brown,** and **Henry Clay Brown,** the children of my deceased nephew Hiram Brown; **Cornelius Comegys Brown, Thomas Trew Brown, Elizabeth S. Brown, Comegys Brown, Henry Brown,** and **William Trew Brown,** children of my deceased nephew **Cornelius C. Brown; Mary M. Brown, Hiram Brown, William Henry Brown,** and **Arthur M. Brown,** the children of my deceased nephew the late **William H. Brown,** each 1/6 of my whole estate which is to be sold

Exec. Richard Hynson Esq. Witnesses Charles Estes, Thomas B. Trew, Thomas E. Wilkins. Written Nov. 23, 1865 Proved Dec. 5, 1865 p. 317

Liber 13 1854-1867

Rebecca Wood of Kent Co
Whereas my estate being small and my daughters young and experienced and as their estate and income will be small and my two sons being able to provide for themselves, I have concluded to give my estate to my daughters. My affection is the same for all my children, and if my estate was larger I should make no distinction but daughters have not the same opportunity to provide as sons. I give to my daughters **Catharine Jane Wood, Mary Rebecca Wood, Clara Ann Wood,** and **Ann Eliza Wood** all to be divided between them. I desire my son **Charles C. Wood** to be guardian for my two daughters Clara Ann Wood and Ann Eliza Wood, but a legacy of $50 to Ann the youngest. I give to **Sina Jane Wood,** (Tina Jane?) the mother of my late husband $12 annually during her life paid by my daughters at $3 each.

Exec. my son Charles C. Wood. Witnesses George Vickers. Written May 5, 1865 Proved Sep. 12, 1865 p. 319

Margaret F. Harrold of Kent Co late of Baltimore City, MD
To my cousin **Margaret F. Gill** of Kent Co, dau. of **James A.** and **Margaret Thompson** and to my three nieces **Sarah F. Gill** of New Castle Co, DE and **Mary Henderson** of the State of Illinois, dau. of dau. of **John** and **Elizabeth Gilpy** and **Rhoda Reynolds Fenton** of Philadelphia, dau. of **Daniel** and **Ruth McHam,** I give the whole of my estate.

Execs. my friend William S. Thompson and William G. Harrison of Baltimore. Witnesses A. Medders, R. J. Boulden and William McIntyre. Written Dec. 6, 1865 Proved Dec. 19, 1865 p. 320

John C. Ayers
To my wife **Elizabeth Ayers** all the houses, land and tenements and all other goods and cattle during her life, then to be divided between my children equally.

Exec. my brother William H. Ayers. Witnesses John Downey, William H. Ayers. Written Dec. 13, 1865 Proved Jan. 1, 1866 p. 321

Benjamin R. Fiddis of Kent Co
To my beloved wife **Sarah A. Fiddis** all my real and personal estate during her life and after to my two sons **Benjamin W. Fiddis** and **John A. Fiddis**

Exec. my wife Sarah A. Fiddis. Witnesses William H. Lambert, John Hadaway, George W. Hadaway. Written Oct. 8, 1862 Proved Jan. 11, 1866 p. 322

Charles Miller of Kent Co
To **Caroline Price** dau. of my late wife and to her dau. **Mary Price** my house and lot upon which I now reside during her life. After their death, I give to my brother **Norris Miller** all my estate.

Abstracts of Kent Co., MD Wills

Exec. Cornelius J. Scott. Witnesses Jeremiah Peacock, William A. Miller, W.H. Kennard. Written Jan. 14, 1866 Proved Apr. 16, 1866 p. 324

Aaron Benton of Chestertown, Kent Co
To my wife **Mahayla** 1/3 of my real estate during her life or widowhood, and after to my granddau. **Mahayla**. To my daughters **Eliza** and **Harriett** 2/3 of my real estate. My personal estate to be sold.

Exec. James A. Jones. Witnesses Thomas W. Eliason, W.H. Meeteer, Samuel L. Rawleigh. Written Jan. 21, 1864 Proved July 2, 1866 p. 325

Hannah Greenwood of Kent Co
To be decently buried according to the direction of my children. To divide my farm upon which I now reside and also the woodland situated in the Forrest called the DE and MD Forrest, it being conveyed to me by George B. Money by deed dated Oct. 13, 1860 (Liber J.K.H. p 243-5 Kent Co) The first part of farm W of the stream called Quaker Branch upon which is a tenant house and having the said stream of water as its E boundary, 150 acres of land including dwelling house out of buildings and graveyard to be laid off by a line parallel to the division line between my said farm and the land B.H.C. Massey having the boundary Quaker Branch or Division No. 1 and part of the boundary lines of the Mill property known as *"Moffett's mill"* and adjoining my farm and to be called Division No. 2. The other portion of my farm to be divided into two parts by a line drawn from the 17th line of my said farm to its 20th line being the longest line between my farm and the land of the heirs of the late **Commodore Jacob Jones** as will appear by a survey made by **Cornelius J. Scott** in 1860. The woodland in the aforesaid DE and MD Forrest is to be laid off viz. 30 acres to be cut off of the wood lot each (Four divisions). Two persons chosen by my sons **Joshua Vansant** and **Fredus Vansant**. To my grandson **John Clark** 6 sheep, 6 hogs to be selected out of my stock. To my grandson **Thomas Clark** 1 colt horse to be selected out of my stock. To my granddau. **Matilda Wilson** $150 to be paid by my son **Ira Vansant** when she is 20. To my dau. **Rosetta Clark** one bed and bedding shall be selected by my executor. To my dau. **Sarah Scotten** $2,500 to be paid by my son **Joshua Vansant,** but should my dau. Sarah die then to her children. To my dau. Rosetta Clark $2,500 to be paid by my son Fredus Vansant. To my two grandsons John Clark 2/3 of Division 1 and Thomas Clark 1/3 of Division 1. Division 2 to be part of my residuary estate. To my son Joshua Vansant Division 3 but to pay dau. Sarah Scotten $2,500 and if Division 3 is valued higher than Division 4 then Joshua to pay Fredus ½ the difference. To my son Fredus Vansant Division 4 and to pay my dau. Rosetta Clark $2,500. To my son Ira Vansant all the residue of my estate except the graveyard in Division no. 2 which shall be set apart and remain as a place of interment for any of my children and their descendants who desire to lay therein

Exec. Cornelius J. Scott. Witnesses T.C. Meginniss, Alfred Chrisfield, William K. Sutton. Written Dec. 30, 1865 Proved Aug. 13, 1866 p. 327

Liber 13 1854-1867

Caleb W. Spry of Kent Co
To my wife **Sarah Ellen Spry** her 1/3 dower in real and personal estate, I give all my household and kitchen furniture, pictures, and ornaments, a pair of horses and my two carriages and harness for the same. To my niece **Vermadilla Massey** (wife of Robert B.M. Massey) $2,750 and all that farm in Queen Anns Co called *"The Holden Farm"* which I purchased of George Vickers trustee for the sale of George Bramble's real estate containing 300 acres. To my nephew **Thomas Brinkley Spry** son of my late brother **Joshua Spry** of Philadelphia my house and lot on No. 1908 Lombard Street in Philadelphia and he is to pay his sister Mary Spry $1,000 at 22. To my said niece **Mary Spry** $1,000. To my niece **George Anna Spry** dau. of my brother Joshua $2,000. I give to my half sister **Emily Gardiner** wife of **James Gardiner** for her life $1,000 to be divided among her daughters then living. To my nephew **Robert Calder** of Chestertown $333.33. To my niece **Mary Calder** sister to Robert $333.33. To my nephew **Samuel Nickerson** $333.33. If my late servants **Ben Dunn, Eliza Dunn,** and **Kelly Dunn** shall save money to build a house, then to give ¼ to ½ acre for such building and convey the same. The rest of my estate to my son **Caleb Wright Spry**, if he or the other children die under 27, then I give all my lands to the children now living of **William T. Spry** by his former wife **Matilda Spry** formerly **Matilda Holding**, and children now living of **George W. Medders** by his wife **Araminta Spry**; to Thomas Brinkley Spry, George Anna Spry, and Mary Spry children of my late brother Joshua; to **Anna Howard** dau. of the late **James E. Howard** and to **James Henry Spry** (son of **Henry Spry**).

Execs. my wife Sarah Ellen Spry and my friend George Vickers. Witnesses Jesse K. Hines, George B. Westcott, John W. Hines. Written Dec. 16, 1864 Proved Feb. 15, 1866 p. 331

Richard Moffett of Kent Co
To my wife **Louisa Moffett** all my household and kitchen furniture and all my personal estate except a bed, bedstead, and bedding which I give to my dau. **Catharine Matilda Moffett**. Also 1/3 of my real estate for her life. To my son **Richard F. Moffett** all the tract on which he resides containing 126 acres as surveyed by **Charles H. Baker** as per certificate held by Richard being part of my home farm. To him I give the free use of a private road now used from his said land through my home farm occupied by my son **Enoch J. Moffett,** but the road shall not be fenced while the remainder of my home farm shall remain in the family. Being security for my said son Richard to **William J. Hurlock** for $500 I charge the said land so given to him. To my son Enoch J. Moffett during his life all the rest of my home farm on which he now resided and which was conveyed to me by deed from **J.M. Comegys** then to his heirs. I charge the lands for $2,000; $1,000 to my dau. **Louisa Ann Gardiner** wife of the **Rev. Samuel T. Gardiner** for her life and then to her issue, if none then to my children and the other $1,000 to my dau. Catharine Matilda Moffett for her life. I will that my son Enoch J. Moffett shall pay all my just debts. My personal estate exempt from such payment of debts. To my two daughters Louisa Ann Gardiner and Catharine Matilda Moffett my house and lot of land in Millington where I reside and which I purchased of Andrew Woodall, then to the

survivor, or issue of survivor, then to my children. I give to the children now living of my son **Jeremiah N. Moffett** for 25 years 123 acres called *"Palmers Hazzard"* and *"Chester Grove"* where he now resides which formerly belonged to my father **Enoch Moffett**. I appoint my son Jeremiah N. Moffett trustee. After 25 years, then to my son Jeremiah N. Moffett. The graveyard on my said premises to contain ¼ acres to my family and heirs with free ingress and egress.

Exec. my son Richard F. Moffett. Witnesses Samuel Hurlock, Thomas R. Quimby, Charles P. Loper. Written July 19, 1866 Proved Sep. 4, 1866 p. 337

John S. Constable of Kent Co
Whereas I have covenanted in an anti-nuptial agreement entered into with my present wife formerly **Harriett Wilmer** in case she shall survive me to secure to her an annuity of $400. To my son in law Dr. **Samuel Beck** $6,666.66 to pay my wife her annuity. After her death to my dau. **Ellen Beck** (wife of said trustee). To my wife **Harriett Constable** 20 shares of stock of the Union National Bank formerly the Union Bank of Baltimore and whatever parlor or chamber furniture I may have at the time of my death and $2,000. To my son **Stevenson Constable** $3,000. To my dau. **Martha J. Fisher**, wife of **Dr. Samuel G. Fisher** $4,200. To my dau. **Mary Jones**, wife of **Richard W. Jones** $5,000. The rest of my estate to pay my debts and legacies, the surplus to my children Stevenson Constable and my daughters Martha J. Fisher and Mary Jones, except my son **William** who I have advanced more then his full portion.

Exec. my son in law Dr. Samuel Beck. Witnesses Richard Hynson, John W. Collins, Jesse K. Hines. Written Jan. 31, 1866 Proved Aug. 14, 1866 p. 340

Charles Tilden of Kent Co
To my wife **Amelia Octavia Tilden** all my real estate during her life. My wife to pay $50 annually to my sister the wife of **Dr. Peregrine Wroth**. To **Julius Perkins** son of **Henry Perkins** $1,000 when 21. After her death ½ to **Charles T. Ireland** and his youngest son **James Ireland** and the other ½ to **Mary Cecelia World** and **Catharine World**. To my cousin Charles T. Ireland 3 notes totaling $700. All the rest of my personal estate I give ½ to my wife Amelia Octavia Tilden and the other ½ to my sister, the wife of Dr. Peregrine Wroth.

Exec. Dr. Thomas G. Wroth. Witnesses George Gale, William M. S. Maxwell, P.C.A. Clements. Written Nov. 15, 1866 Proved Nov. 27, 1866 p. 343

Mary Ann Norris of Kent Co
In order to make an equal division of my real estate I had a survey and designated Divisions 1, 2, 3, and 4 by Thomas H. Chandler of Kennetts Square, Chester Co, PA which I recorded with this will. To my dau. **Hannah Ann Beck** wife of **Robert Beck** Division No. 1 and contains 111 acres and 143 perches. To my son **John A. Norris** Division No. 2 and contains 154 acres and 139 perches. To my son **William P. Norris**

Liber 13 1854-1867

Division No. 3 and contains 148 acres and 42 perches. To my son **Thomas E. Norris** Division No. 4 and contains 182 acres and 35 perches. In case my said dau. or my said son **John A.** or **William P. Norris** shall die without issue to go over to all my surviving children. I have excepted the real estate of my son **Thomas E. Norris** so that he may make his devise absolutely in fee simple. My personal estate to my children. (Between p. 346-7 has the map surveyed by Thomas H. Chandler, includes names of **Alexander Cheney, Luther Cole, Col. James H. Gail, George B. Westcott**)

Exec. my son John A. Norris. Witnesses Elizabeth Thomas, A. E. Hynson, Richard Hynson. Written June 7, 1865 Proved Sep. 11, 1866 p. 344

John B. Walmsley of Kent Co

I give my real estate consisting of the farm on which I live containing 126 acres to my wife **Martha Jane Walmsley** for her life. After her life, I give to my two brothers **Oliver H. R. Walmsley** and **Benjamin F. Walmsley** and my nephew **John P. Walmsley** son of **George W. Walmsley** deceased.

Exec. my wife Martha Jane Walmsley. Witnesses James Heighe, George W. Chrisfield, John O. Slay. Written Nov. 7, 1866 Proved Dec. 11, 1866 p. 347

George Wilson of the Upper District of Kent Co

All the land that I possess both in MD and DE be left to my dau. **Susanna Wilson** with all the buildings.

Exec. Not Given. Witnesses James McCarter, William J. Lee. Written Oct. 16, 1866 Proved Jan. 8, 1867 p. 347

Milicent Arthur of Kent Co

To my dear husband **David Arthur** all my property including a tract of land in Kent adjoining Dr. Thomas Whaland, John Waibel, and Samuel A. Smith containing 47 acres, 3 roods, 27 perches. A lot of land in Chestertown and designated on the plot thereof *"Lot No. 87"* together with all the buildings, all of which was conveyed to me by deed by my brother **James Wilson** which I give to my husband David Arthur.

Exec. David Arthur. Witnesses John T. Dodd, James A. Burton, Thomas S. Dodd. Written Mar. 18, 1863 Proved Feb. 13, 1867 p. 348

Joseph Howard of Kent Co

To my dau. **Mary Hyland Richardson** $1,000. To my dau. **Philena Clemens** $1,000 but charge $370 which she owes me. I give her my negro girl **Kate** to serve a term of __ years. To my granddau. **Mary Wallis** $200. To my granddau. **Martha Musgrave** $200. To my grandson **Mitchell Price** $50 and $150 which he owes me. To my son **Joseph Wrightson Howard** my farm, plantation and real estate in Kent Co which I now called Cranberry, Adventure, Daletown, Partnership or whatsoever charged with $1,000 to be paid to my youngest dau. **Ann Amelia Howard**. To my wife **Susanna K. Howard** the annual rent of the land devised to my son Joseph Wrightson Howard for her life. To my wife the labor and services of my negroes: **Charles Rolls, John W. Rolls, Ann M. Rolls, Louis Rolls, Becky, Bill** and **Dan** and after my wife's death the unexpired term of servitude of said negroes Dan, Becky, John W. Rolls, and Louis Rolls unto my son Joseph Wrightson Howard and the unexpired term of Charles Rolls, Ann M. Rolls and Bill I give to my youngest dau. Ann Amelia Howard. The rest of my personal estate. My wife **Susanna K. Howard** to be executor

Execs. my wife Susanna K. Howard and my son Joseph W. Howard (son added by codicil). Witnesses Henry T. Jump, Richard H. Harris, George Gale. Written Jan. 28, 1862 Proved Jan. 1, 1867 p. 349

Codicil My wife shall have all the household and kitchen furniture and also her choice of one of my horses and carriage in addition to her 1/3 of my estate. To my son Joseph W. Howard all my stock and farming utensils and implements and all my books. Written Sep. 24, 1866. Witnesses George Gale, Henry T. Jump, Richard W. Harris

Ezekial Foreman Chambers of Chestertown, Kent Co
To be decently buried in the family burial ground in the churchyard. The spot for my grave has been shown to some of my friends and is between my sainted mother and my brother **Thomas** whom I loved most dearly, and is also in the midst of my children who have gone before to the land of rest and peace and who are doubtless in the bosom of their savior awaiting the advent of those loved on earth. Ample provision for my unfortunate son **James** so that he may be clothed and boarded to this end I give to my executor 66 shares of stock held by the Union Bank of Baltimore amounting to $4,950 to set apart for him, or other stock totaling $5,000. After his death, to be part of my personal estate and to my daughters. My two servants **Robert Allen** and **Eliza Blake** to be provided for, by giving Robert to my dau. **Laura** and Eliza to my dau. **Caroline** to whom Eliza was nurse. I give **Becky,** the cook to my dau. Laura to whom Becky was nurse. I have heretofore given **Ellen** (Becky's daughter) to Caroline. The remaining servants to be disposed of agreeable to the wishes of the servant as to the master. By a deed of trust to the late **John B. Eccleston** I am empowered to dispose of the lands, these lands to be sold and proceeds divided between my children. Said land owned by the late **Major James Bowers** being the farm on which **Nathan Voshell** now resides usually called the *"BaySide Farm"* and the *"Outer Farm"* on which **Billy Tilghman** resides including the swamp land and also the farm in Still Pond on which **George A. Rodenhiser** resides called *"Campbell's Worth more"* is to be attached to the property purchased by me and to be included within the enclosures of the said farm. Sell estate and ¼ to be invested for my grandchildren, the children of my deceased dau. **Elizabeth A. Jones**, 1/5 to my dau. Laura for my granddau. **Elizabeth** whom she so affectionately has taken care of from birth, the remaining 4/5 to be paid to my son in law **Rev. Dr. C. F. Jones** to be applied to his four sons, my grandchildren during their minority. ¼ to my dau. **Laura Davis**. ¼ part to my dau. **Caroline**, wife of **George W. T. Perkins** Esq.

Liber 13 1854-1867

¼ part to trustees for use of my dau. **Sarah Maria Louise Owen** for her coverture and to pay to said Maria interest not to exceed $350 annually. If she has other children besides the one she now has then can be increased. If she is made a widow, then to have all interest. If no issue, then 1/3 to heirs of my deceased dau. Elizabeth, 1/3 to my dau. Laura, 1/3 to dau. Caroline. The bank stock to be divided ¼ to the children of my dau. Elizabeth, ¼ to my dau. Laura, ¼ part to my dau. Caroline, ¼ to my dau. **Maria Louise**. A claim due from my esteemed relative and friend Mrs. **H.M. Tilghman** of Hope, Talbot Co which my executor is not to collect during her life. My dau. Laura to have choice of household furniture and ½ of plate and china and dau. Caroline to have household furniture not taken by Laura and ½ plate and china. To my son in law **Dr. Jones** a gold watch to cost $100 to be given to one of his sons he names. To my son in law **G.W.T. Perkins** the gold watch loaned to him. To my grandsons **Ezekial C. Davis, George Perkins** and **Ezekial C. Perkins** a gold watch not to exceed $100. E.C. Davis to take for his the watch and chain I wear and which was owned first by my brother **William** and afterward my brother **David**. George and E.C. Perkins to be procured by their father or to invest the $100 until they are 18 and then purchase the best watch and chain to be had for said money. My two granddaughters **Mary Clare Davis** and **Lilly Jones** to have each a suitable memorial - mourning ring - breast pin or what my dau. Laura may select. My sister **Elizabeth C. Wicks** a mourning ring or breast pin as she may prefer for her devoted kindness during seasons of alarming illness and of yet more painful afflictions which a wise and merciful Providence has found necessary to prepare me for the rest which remaineth for the righteous. Also a breast pin or other such article for my friend and brother in law **Col. Jos. Wickes** with whom I have lived in so much harmony from early childhood to old age. To my dear friend **Samuel J. Donaldson Esq.** of Baltimore a similar mark of my grateful sense of his long, continued, uniform and affectionate regard. Also to my highly esteemed relatives Mrs. Tilghman of Hope and her sister **Miss Foreman** with whom so many pleasant hours of my life have been passed I desire to have a mourning ring and also from the same motives my aunt Mrs. **General Foreman** and to my cousin Miss **Malvina Foreman**. Thanks to many other friends that can never be forgotten. My two sons in law Rev. **C. F. Jones** and **G.W.T. Perkins** Esq and my friend Col. **Joseph Wickes** to be trustees

Exec. my son in law **G.W.T. Perkins**. Witnesses James B. Ricaud, Thomas. DeC. Ruth, S.W. Spencer. Written Jan. 22, 1861 Proved Feb. 9, 1867 p. 353

<u>Codicil</u> My servant man **Billy Tilghman** has died. Billy is in my debt and I take his property but his widow old **Charlotte** to be provided for out of my estate and my daughters are to see to it that this faithful and helpless old servant be not neglected. Written Aug 19, 1862

<u>2nd Codicil</u> My dau. **Maria Louise Owen** has died leaving one child a dau. **Helen Owen**. As she would receive 5 times my other grandchildren, ¼ to my granddau. of what was given to my dau. and ¼ to my granddaughters, ½ to my to my son in law The Rev. Dr. **Clement F. Jones** in trust for his three imbecile children **Marshall, Chambers**

and **Elizabeth**. If Helen dies without issue then to heirs of other daughters. Written Jul 10, 1863. J.B. Ricaud, S.W. Spencer, Thomas DeC. Ruth.
3rd Codicil The debts of Mrs. Tilghman have been paid in full. Whereas since the last codicil to my will events occurred making it necessary to alter the disposition herein made, first by a violation of every just and honest principle that should guide the councils of a free government by the action of a decided minority of those who should (and if military power had not been used to prevent it would have controlled the legislation of the state, the slaves heretofore owned by me as all others in the state have been emancipated very much to the injury of the states, to the comfort of the slaves and to their moral or religious advancement if not ultimately their extinction and certainly to the loss of their owners, from whom this property has been seized and confiscated without one dollar of compensation then lessening my estate by some forty or fifty thousand dollars and secondly by reason of an arrangement made of my farm in Queen Anns which has lately been leased to **Col. Edward Wilkins** and **Mr. -- Shuster** for a term of -- years as a peach orchard. Therefore I wish my farm in Queen Anns to be sold after the lease and distributed to my children and grandchildren as stated in codicil no. 2. The death of my friends Col. **J. Wickes**, Mrs. **H.M. Tilghman**, Mrs. **Genl. Foreman** and **S. J. Donaldson** cause their bequests to be revoked. My former servants Robert and Becky are now dead and Eliza is settled in her own house but if she needs for anything then to be provided. My son in law **George W. T. Perkins** Esq trustee to farm in Queen Anns as landlord proceeds to be divided between heirs. Out of proceeds my granddau. **Lilly Jones** to be provided as my dau. Laura directs to whom she has been a mother from the first hour of birth. And to the completion of the collegiate education of my grandson **Milnor Jones** and providing him proper board and clothing during his college studies and for two years after to be made by my son in law George W. T. Perkins and may confer with my son in law Dr. Jones, the father of Milnor. I hope to re-write my whole will in a more perfect manner but daily demands consume my time and I believe my death to be sudden and soon I have therefore prepared it in its present form. Written Jan. 29, 1866. Witnesses Thomas. DeC. Ruth, N.G. Westcott, S.W. Spencer

John Hurtt of Kent Co
To my wife **Elizabeth Hurtt** my whole estate during her life to maintain family as the affection of a mother ought to dictate. Also my wish that my son **George Hurtt** shall remain with his mother to assist in raising younger children. After the devise of my wife, equally to all my children lawfully begotten with this exception that my son George shall receive $100 extra if he complies with wishes herein expressed.

Exec. Not Given. Witnesses John W. Pearson, John T. Hurtt, William T. Miller. Written Aug. 1, 1853 Proved May 23, 1867 p. 364

Joshua H. Dulaney of Kent Co
My son **William H. Dulaney** $50. To my son **George G. Dulaney** $150. To my son **Joshua L. Dulaney** and my dau. **Adelaide Dulaney** the residue of my estate.

Liber 13 1854-1867

Exec. my son Joshua L. Dulaney. Witnesses Thomas J. Britton, Thomas L. Cecil, S.H. Knock. Written July 16, 1866 Proved Oct. 24, 1867 p. 366

Mary H. Wilson of Kent Co
My niece **Anna Wilson Dunlap** my house and land in Smyrna in DE. My friend **John G. Black** having kindly acted as agent for my mute sister and myself and request he continue his kindness and to place the rents in security for my niece when she is 13 and then to use for her education. If she die under 18, then to her eldest brother **Edwin Wilmer Dunlap** when he is 21. To my sister **Maria D. Dunlap** her note for $250 which bears date of Jan. 1, 1855. The note of Mr. **Edward B. Woodall** for $112.50 dated Jan. 13, 1862 transferred to me by **Eliza E. Miller**, I give to my sister's eldest son **Edwin Wilmer Dunlap**. When he is 12 or 13 the interest to go to his education. If he dies under 21 then to his sister and brother now living. To my niece **Ann Wilson Dunlap** my bed, bedstead, bolster and pillows, with all sheeting and cases and comfortables, my bureaus, wash stand, towels, carpeting, looking glass, cushioned footstools, and books with any and all items in the room I occupy (except my traveling trunk and other articles I otherwise dispose of). My traveling trunk I give to my little nephew **George Wilson Dunlap**. To the infant, called after my father George W. Dunlap, I give my father's cane and a silver fruit knife and regret that I could not do more for him. (to George rising sun bedquilt). To my niece Anna W. Dunlap 6 spoons, marked M.H.W., my gold watch and chain and a watch guard made of my deceased sister's hair, after whom she is named, together with breast pin and all jewelry that I may have. To my niece **Olivia V. Stephens** my silver fork and cameo breast pin. To **Emma D. Stewart** of Philadelphia a box containing a few articles as a memento to be taken care of by sister and forwarded safely to her (Mary H. Wilson I gave the said box to Emma Sep. 1863 myself). To my cousin **Susan Fisher** my silk patchwork chair cushion (N.B. The said cushion I gave during my life). To my cousin **J.G. Black** I give my scarlet pin cushion, bed quilt, as keepsakes from a grateful relative (These two last gifts are handed over by me). To **Edwin Wilmer Dunlap** my large mathematical star quilt. All my other quilts I give to Anna W. Dunlap. If she dies under 18 without issue then to her two brothers now living, except the watch to Edwin with chain. To my sister **Susan E. Heighe** the painting with my name attached with all the other pictures except the Group in an oval frame which I give to Anna W. Dunlap to keep as a remembrance of the originals I so highly esteem. Also to my sister I give my fender and square stand with drawers. To Mary Ellen I give work box with contents for little Maggie. All my clothing, weather hanging, in bureau, trunks or otherwise to Ann Wilson Dunlap and her mother. All the rest to Anna Wilson Dunlap.

Exec. Cornelius J. Scott. Witnesses Elijah E. Miller, A. Medders, William T. Miller. Written Apr. 18, 1863 Proved Nov. 18, 1867 p. 367

<u>Codicil</u> All rents after my funeral expenses for the use of **George Watson Dunlap** at the discretion of my administrator for use of said little nephew. The two quilts have each name attached to them. Written July 12, 1867

Abstracts of Kent Co., MD Wills

<u>2nd Codicil</u> The land in DE to my niece Anna W. Dunlap shall not be sold before she is 25. If she does then to my nephew **Edwin Wilmer Dunlap.** Written Sep. 18, 1866. Witnesses George Vickers, William Gooding, James Willis

Charles Stanley of Kent Co
To my wife **Caroline V. Stanley** during her widowhood or life, then to my children **Charles A.A. Stanley, Araminta F. Stanley, Ezekial F. Stanley,** and **Mary Rebecca Stanley.** My land not to be sold until my youngest child is 18.

Exec. my wife Caroline V. Stanley. Witnesses James B. Ricaud, Samuel W. Spencer, John W. Hines. Written Feb. 4, 1865 Proved Nov. 22, 1867 p. 373

Daniel Ringgold
All my estate to my wife **Sarah A. Ringgold**

Exec. William S. Perkins. Witnesses Henry P. Reading, James F. Cochran, Emma Cochran. Written Sep. 21, 1867 Proved Dec. 20, 1867 p. 374

Mary W.E. Smith
As I commence a trip to Snow Hill Worcester Co this day fearing I may never return and wishing to leave and or make my dau. **Serena L. Smith** independent make the gift of all the contents of the brick dwelling my present residence in Georgetown Kent Co with the exception of one mahogany bedstead and large gilt framed mirror and the portraits of her parents which articles are to be given to my dau. **Anna M.M. Wallis** if the said Serena should marry or leave the said property to Anna M.M. Wallis

Exec. Not Given. Witnesses Richard Sappington, Aralanta R. Sappington, John Henry Bolton. Written Oct. 21, 1857 Baltimore Proved Nov. 11, 1867 p. 375 George W.P. Smith acknowledged that he has seen the writing of Mary W.E. Smith late of Georgetown Kent Co

Index of Names and Places

Note: The witnesses, executors and others named in the will (but not legatees) are indexed by surname only. First names given in the will without surnames are indexed by the testator's surname. Married daughters of male testators are indexed twice, under married names as well as their maiden names (testator's surname). Married daughters of female testators are indexed under their assumed maiden name (testator's surname) which may not be correct since a daughter's maiden name could be different is she were the child of a former marriage by the mother. When in doubt I have indexed under whatever surname is given. Slaves without surnames are indexed under the heading **Slaves**. Names of Tracts and Patents are indexed under the heading **Tracts**.

Abbiss 160
  Frances H. 160
  John 160
  Sarah Catharine 160
Acres 114
Adams 49
Adkinson 29, 104, 168, 256, 259
  Alexander 117
  Amanda 117
  Ann Maria 117
  Elizabeth 117, 206
  Lemuel 117
  Livenia 117
  Phebe 117
  Richard 117
  Robert 117
  Thomas 117
  William 117
  William T. 206
Adkinsson
  Elizabeth 89
Adkisson
  John 89
Africa 121, 230
Airs
  Elizabeth 27
  Mary 27
  Richard 28
  Richard Thomas 27
Alford 65
  Ann 178
  Jesse 84

  Millicent 84
  Robert 178
  Thomas 178
Allegheny Co 224
Allen 42, 149, 164, 169, 170, 172, 191, 219, 233, 274
  Alice 251
  Amanda 251
  Ann 32
  Ann E. 232
  Ann Elizabeth 173
  Eliza 89
  Hannah Ann 89
  Jacob W. 251
  James 42
  John 32, 42
  John Thomas 89
  Joseph 251
  Mordecai 32
  Rilly 251
  Robert T. 173, 232
  Robertine R. L. 233
  Thomas 88
  William 251
Alrich 251
Alston
  Abner 44
  John 44
  Lydia 43
  Mary Ann 44
Anderson 1, 5, 26, 41, 49, 65, 78, 91,

166, 172, 194, 229
  Ann Elizabeth 215
  Bathsheba 32, 66
  Dr. Alexanders 215
  Editha 201
  Edward 21, 78, 111, 205
  Elizabeth 198, 205
  Emily 21
  George 32
  Harriet 21, 22
  Henry 214
  James 22, 111
  James Monat 21
  James Monat Jr. 22
  John 95
  John B.H. 198
  Maria 21
  Maria G. 186
  Mary 67
  Mary Anne 95
  Robert 32, 95
  Samuel 189
  Susan 215
  Thomas 32
  William 67, 96, 201
Andrews
  Sarah 105
Angier 26, 136, 194
Anthony
  Benjamin 171, 176
  Frances 170

John 28, 148
Joseph 170, 176
Wayne 28, 171, 176
Appleton
  Christianna 251
  Richard 251
Apsley
  Ann 180
  William 180
  William Wroth 159
Archer 143
  Lizzie 210
Armstrong 64, 127,
  148, 213, 233, 242
  Ann Louisa 233
  Ariminta E. 233
  Charles 233
  Henry 233
  James 233
  John M. 106, 233
  John M. Jr. 233
  John M. Sr. 233
  Kate 233
  Mary A. 106
  Mary Jane 233
  Sarah 233
  Sarah A. 233
  William 106, 233
Arnoe
  Benjamin 156
  Rebecca 156
Arthur 68, 78, 80,
  115, 159, 225,
  252, 273
  David 17, 273
  Elizabeth 17
  James 17
  Milicent 273
  Sophia 17
Ashley 27, 71, 85,
  219, 222, 223, 232
  Benjamin Franklin
    222
  Chiners 222
  Eliza Ann 222
  Hosanna 63

Isaiah 222
James David 222
John 63
John Dudley 222
John R. Ashley 163
Lemuel Washington
  222
Mary Elizabeth 222
Sarah J. 185
Susan Jane 163
Thomas Wroth 222
Atkinson 29
  Hannah 20, 26, 225
  Mary 167
  Rachel 20, 26
  William Thomas 27
Attwood
  Martha Ann 37, 76
  Matthias C. 37
Atwood 189
  Martha Ann 91, 109
  Matthias C. 109
Augier 63
Ayers 86, 269
  Elizabeth 269
  John C. 269
Ayres 15, 123, 249,
  266
  Elizabeth 5
Baccchus 250
Bagwell
  Ann 32
  Rebecca 32
  Richard 32
Bailey 116
Baily 97
Baker 27, 121, 145,
  157, 173, 200,
  205, 215, 221,
  231, 262, 263, 271
  Amanda 40
  Ann 45
  Anna 40
  Emma 40, 45
  Francis 40, 173
  Henrietta 261

James Brown 173
James Henry 175
Juliett 261
Margaret Ann 261,
  262
Mary Ann 40, 45,
  262
Richard 40
Richard Whaland
  261
Samuel 110
Samuel E. 40, 45,
  197, 261
Sarah R.L. 261
Susanna 22
Susannah 45
Thomas 40, 262
William 40
William Thomas
  262
Baldwin
  Eliza 97
Ball
  Elizabeth 207, 219
Ballard 224
Baltimore ii, 3, 10,
  16, 19, 20, 29, 31,
  35, 37, 42, 49, 50,
  64, 65, 71, 74, 78,
  82, 84, 93, 97, 99,
  105, 119, 124,
  125, 140, 142,
  143, 146, 156,
  158, 160, 161,
  184, 186-190, 192,
  197, 204, 208,
  217, 225, 240,
  245, 246, 258,
  265, 269, 272,
  274, 275, 278
Banning 118, 200
  Emma 58
  Martha 58
Banthum
  Emily Eliza 256
Barclay 124

Index of Names and Places

Barger
 Benjamin 43
 Hannah 168
 Mary 43, 168
 Rebecca 43, 168, 169
 Sarah 168
 Susan H. 43
Barnhouser
 John A. ii
 John Anthony iii
Barrett 169, 195, 197
 Alexander 80
 Christianna W. 80
 Thomas 80
Barrol
 George 174
Barroll 1, 37, 39, 55, 62, 70, 72, 75, 80, 81, 83, 90, 96, 100, 138, 220
 Anna M. 109
 Eve 219
 George 220
 Hester 201
 James 108
 Margaret 81, 219
 Mary 81
 Mary C. 109
 Matilda 201
 Peregrine 220
 Rebecca 219
 Richard 201
 S. H. 75
 Sarah 5, 23, 220
 Sarah H. 108, 219
 Sarah R. 219
 William 5, 23, 81, 108
 William B. 219
Bates 257
Battershell
 Mary 117
Bayard

Arabella 55
Beates 78
Beaver Dam Branch 245
Beck 9, 21, 27, 34, 67, 68, 76, 103, 117, 125, 126, 128, 135, 138, 139, 161, 168, 170, 178, 183-185, 202, 210, 247, 249, 258, 266, 272
 Adah 14
 Amanda Melvina 165
 Ann 99
 Augusta 14
 Benjamin F. 165
 Benjamin Franklin 14, 141
 Caroline 141
 Clementia 165
 Dr. Samuel 272
 Edward 104
 Elijah 104
 Elisha 104
 Elizabeth 14
 Ellen 272
 George 40, 210
 George Rasin 150
 Hannah Ann 272
 Horace 141
 Horatio 14, 165, 258
 James 40, 150
 John 14, 141
 Josiah 40
 Margarett Ann Ingram 150
 Mary 97
 Mary Jane 150
 Mary Matilda 258
 Matilda 104
 Rachel 40

Robert 272
 Samuel 14, 99, 141, 272
 Samuel Jr. 14
 Sarah 14, 141
 Sophia 165
 Thomas 14
 Walter Miller 258
 William 97
Bell 239
 Ann 202
 George Anna 202
 John D. 202
 Mary Ann 202
 Pere 211
 Sarah 49
 Sarah Eliza 204
 William E.C. 202
Belts 257
 Catharine 69
Bend
 Jim 184
 Benjamin 197
Bennett 93, 119, 213, 265
 Elizabeth 131
 George Henry 131
 George W. 213
 Samuel 131
 William Roland 131
Bennitt
 William R. 131
Benson 268
Benton 100
 Aaron 270
 Eliza 270
 Harriett 270
 Mahayla 270
 Mary Ann 162
Berry
 Marion 214
 Moses 214, 216
 Sarah 85
 Susan 214

281

Berryman 193
  Charles 183
  Elizabeth 183
  George 183
  Hannah 183
  Jane 183
  John 183
  Richard 183
  Samuel 183
  Sarah 183
Besick 59
Beswick
  Sarah 38, 70
Beswicks 70
Betton 122, 267
Betts 257
Bevans 150
Bevins 36, 48
  Ann Mires 47
  Charles 48
  James 47, 154
  James William 47
  Juletta 47
  Katherine 48
  Kitty Ann 47
  Mary 10, 48
  Polly 48
  Rebecca 47
  Thomas 47
Biddle 36, 225, 237
  Clarissa 253
  Clarisss 153
  Emeline 153, 253, 254
  Francis 253
  John 153
  John A. 153
  Julia Ann 153
  Julianna 253
  Martha 153, 253
  Mary 153
  Peregrine 267
  Rayman 152
  Stephen 153
  Stephen A. 253
  Susan A. 267

  Wilhelmina 152
Bidleman 192
Bill 59
Bird 260
  Elizabeth 167
  Margret 167
Birdley 240
Bishop
  Freeman 163
  Lidia 163
Black 93, 252
  Ann J. 202
  Charles H. 202
  J.G. 277
  John G. 277
Blackiston 6, 112, 173, 181, 187, 190, 210, 219, 236, 237, 239, 253, 261, 266
  Ann 185, 239
  Ann Elizabeth 2, 236, 237
  Anna Jemima 237
  Anne Jemima 236
  Antonietta 200
  Bill 239
  Catharine 2
  Catharine Amanda 71
  Charlotte Ann 239
  Clara Leite 237
  David 2
  David C. 239
  David Crane 71
  Ebenezer 2
  Ellen 239
  Emily 181, 234
  Emma 236
  Emma Hepburn 237
  Hannah Maria 237
  Henrietta 185
  Henrietta B. 185
  Henry 185, 239
  Henry Curtis 237
  Isaac 239

  James 2, 67, 71, 72, 239
  James E. 185
  James III 2
  James Jr. 2
  Jemima 2, 235
  John T. 185
  Joseph 185
  Josephine 236, 237
  Julia 239
  Kennard 2
  Lewis 96
  Lizzie 237
  Lucy 239
  Martha Ann 239
  Mary 2, 100
  Mary Ann 67, 96, 157
  Mary E. 239
  Mary Elizabeth 239
  Mary Emily 181
  Mary Euginia 237
  Mary Malvina 71
  Nelson 239
  Phil 239
  Rosalia 239
  Samuel Hepburn 237
  Sarah 234
  Sarah J. 185
  Slater Clay 237
  Thomas 2
  Thomas James 67
  Thomas M. 239
  Thomas Medford 239
  Thomas Medford Jr. 239
  William 96
  William C. 185
  William Henry 2, 235, 236, 237
Blackstone
  Jemima 2
  Kennard 2
Blackway

Index of Names and Places

Ann 97
Blair
  Anna Beverly 91
  Archibald 50, 91
  Edward Freeman 91
  Harriet Maria 91
  Harriott Maria 50
Blake 199, 244
  Alphonso 2
  Benson B. 90
  Dominick T. 3
  Eliza 274
  James 2
  Jane 3, 161
  John 113
  Joseph 77, 90
  Maria A. V. 77
  Maria Ann 90
  Mary 59
  Sarah B. 77, 90
  Thomas 77, 90
  William 77, 90
Blanch 35
Blunt 15, 64
  Mary 37
  Samuel 37
  Sarah 105
Boardly
  Ann 205
  Hannah M. 205
Bodle 7
Bogle 266
  Adelaide R. 266
  Robert 266
Bohemia Manor 267
Bolter 253
Bolton 278
Bond
  Adeline 113
  Anne 113
  Betsy 113
  Elijah 113
  Rebecca 113
  Sandy 113

Temperance 113
Bonds
  Alexander 113
Boon 67, 106, 146, 155, 213
  James 106, 109, 196
Boone 267
Boots 43, 183
  Sarah 128
Bordley 5, 20, 21, 51, 98, 99, 142, 203, 205, 232
  Ann 203
  John 18, 189
  Mary Ann 18
  Thomas 203
Bordly 205
  John 205
  Samuel 205
  Thomas 205
  William 205
Bossee
  Elizabeth 127
  John 127
  Julianna 127
  Lewis 127
  Mary Rebecca 127
  Sarah Elizabeth 127
Boulden 235, 269
  George 235
Bowen
  Ann 32
  Levi 33
Bower 218
Bowers 52, 73, 76, 169, 172, 193, 225, 233
  Augusta 102
  Augusta C. 102
  Eliza 136, 142
  Elizabeth F. 102
  James 102, 274
  James L. 136

John 2
  Major James 274
  Mary Ann 2, 136, 142
  Rosamond 2, 142
  Sarah 2, 173
  Sarah Rebecca 136
  William 2, 173
Bowman 261
Bowser
  George 231
Boyd 249, 254
  Bedford B. 260
  Eleanor 124
  Henrietta 260
  Henry L. 260
  John 260
  Joseph 260
  Samuel C. 260
Boyer 35, 77, 86, 93, 106, 122, 128, 134, 135, 146, 166, 175, 186, 191, 210, 217, 221, 225, 231, 242, 243, 252, 258
  Amanda 225
  Ann 11
  Augustine 231
  Augustine Jr. 10
  Edward 153
  Emily 225
  Emory 225
  Frederick 11, 35
  Hannah 93
  Hugh 11
  Lee 225
  Lewis 225
  Mary 231
  Nathaniel 10
  Nathaniel Jr. 11
  Richard 10
  Richard M. 10
  Richard T. 225

Rugh 11
Sophia 225
Stephen 225
Susan 231
Terisia 11
Terry 10, 11
Thomas 10
Thomas W. 35
Wesley 225
William 225
Bradford
  John O. 213
Bradley 235
Bradsha
  Sarah Elizabeth 111
Bradshaw 7, 15, 240
  Catherine 158
  Rachel 147
  Sarah Elizabeth 87, 126
Braffett
  John 84
Braier
  Hester Ann 190
Bramble 271
Brevitt 92, 133, 152, 155, 159, 168, 173, 200, 206, 240
Brevitts 180
Brian
  Thomas 206
Brice 2, 28, 40, 100, 124, 166, 200, 235, 262
  Ann 24, 28, 100
  Ann Maria 4
  Anna Maria 82, 89
  Elizabeth 27
  George Henry 247
  Henrietta 24, 28, 100
  John 27
  Joseph 51, 247
  Joseph W. 51, 89, 100
  Martha 24, 27, 51, 110, 114, 247

Mary 24, 27, 51
Mary H. 181
Mary Jane 247
Nicholas 82
Rebecca 51
Richard 25, 51, 247
Sarah 24, 28, 114, 181
Sarah Ann 100, 114
Susanna 24, 27
Temperance
  Caroline 89
William A. 247
Brices
  Richard 57
Bright 144
  Lavinia 216
Bringhurst 256, 257
Briscoe 13, 44, 70, 104, 106, 178, 199, 208, 221, 225, 234, 256
  Alexander 93
  Araminta 7
  Benjamin 45
  Daniel 155
  Elizabeth 224
  Emeline 131
  Frederick G. 35
  George A. 175, 178
  Jacob 70
  James 45, 70, 131, 155
  James Alfred 155
  James Jr. 104
  Joseph 155
  Margaret 175
  Margaret D. 175
  Margaret E. 128
  Margaret Elisabeth 128
  Margaret Elizabeth 59
  Margarett D. 179
  Mary 45, 93
  Mary Elisabeth 128

  Samuel E. 128
  Sarah Elizabeth 131, 155
  William Frisby 128
  William H. 35
Britain 61
Britton 221, 235, 243, 252, 258, 277
Brivitt
  Eliza Rebecca 33
Broes 254
Brooke
  Charlotte P. 78
  Elizabeth Ann 29
  Henrietta Eleanor 29
  James 29
  Mary Ann 29
  Mary Hester 29
  Robert 78
Brooks 2, 3, 24, 34, 51, 132, 152, 233
  Ann 145
  Araminta A. 190, 233
  Eliza 145
  George C. M. 233
  George C.M. 190
  John P. D. 233
  John P.D. 190
  Mary Araminta 190
  Nancy 145
  Philip 51, 190
  Thomas 190
Brown 6, 14, 23, 41, 50, 64, 82, 93, 108, 122, 129, 163, 204, 253, 256
  Ann Rebecca 268
  Arthur M. 268
  Augusta 171, 253
  Benjamin O. 149
  Benjamin Osborn 16
  Charles Decorsey 149
  Comegys 268

Index of Names and Places

Cornelius 119
Cornelius C. 268
Cornelius Comegys 268
Cornelius Comegys Jr. 268
Curtis 16
Dr. 58
Edward 156
Edwin 148
Elizabeth S. 268
Elizabeth Thomas 175
Emily 152
Frances 124
Harriet 16
Harriot Catharine 150
Henry 268
Henry Clay 268
Hiram 268
Hiram M. 268
Hirum 119
Hirum Jr. 119
James 149, 171, 253
James Frisby 13
James Glanville 16
Joe 16
John 124
Joseph 171
Joseph Corsey 16
Margaret Ann Wallis Woodland 253
Maria L. 258
Marian Hellen 149
Martha 16
Mary 124, 155
Mary Ann 148
Mary C. 268
Mary Elizabeth 129, 245
Mary M. 268
Rebecca 175
Susan C. 268
Tabitha 149
Thomas R. 162, 171
Thomas Trew 268
William 16, 150
William H. 268
William Henry 268
William Trew 268
William W. 162, 253
Browne 1, 10, 11, 17, 31, 36, 45, 75, 83, 88, 108, 114, 117, 126, 136, 138, 140, 144, 147, 157, 161, 164, 165, 182, 245, 261
Abraham 247
Ann 45
Ann E. 161, 170
Ben 186
Caroline 247
Caroline S. 14
Charles T. 138, 157
Charles Tilden 45
Dick 138
Edward 88
Elizabeth 108
Elizabeth Thomas 108
Emily 148
Francis 247
Henny 247
James 108, 117
James F. 137, 138, 157
James Frisby 170
James T. 161
Joseph 45, 138
Joseph 4th 36
Joseph Coursey 149
Joseph Richard 138
Josephine 233
Lettie 247
Louisa 156
Margaret 138
Margaret F. 157
Maria L. 258
Martha 149, 247
Martha Ann Glanvill 149
Mary 247
Mary Ann 139, 233
Mary T. 161
Mary Trew 108
Morgan 14, 36, 45, 137, 202, 258
Perry 247
Pery 148
Pery Jr. 148
Rebecca 45, 108, 147
Samuel 148
Sarah H. 45
Sarah Henrietta 139
Sarah R. 139
Susan 41
Thomas 129
William 41
Browning
Caroline 141
Charles 1
James 1
Sofiah 1
Bruff 259
Henrietta M. 143
Henrietta Maria 187, 189
Bryan 19, 104, 118, 168, 180
Buchanan 105
Ann 116, 172
Harriet 13
James 27, 172, 173
John K. 116
Laurence 172, 173
Philip K. 172, 173

285

Robert 44, 172, 173
Thomas 120
Bull 136, 142
Daniel W. 221
Mary 131
Mary Elizabeth J. 221
Mary J. 221
Burch
John Samuel 163
Rachel 162
Sary Ann 162
William 162
Burchinal
Ann Matilda 117
Burgess 110, 140, 167, 178, 185, 235, 244, 246
Amanda 140
Caroline 105, 186
Frances 187
Frances R. 167
Frances Ringgold 105
Harriet 167
Helen 172
Henrietta 167, 187
Hetty 140
Hetty Elizabeth 151, 152
Juliet 131, 167
Mary 167
Mary V. 131
Peregrine 140, 151, 167
Rebecca 131, 167
Sarah Ann 167, 172
Thomas D. 167, 187
Thomas Harris 105
Vachel 167
William 167
Burneston
Hannah 56
Burns 91
Ann 192

Arthur 188
Elizabeth 192
Mary 192
Robert 188
Robert D. 143
Burris 254
Burriss
Catharine J. 254
Burton 251, 273
Bush 202
Butler 94, 195
Anna 193
Araminta 193
Aryan 246
Dianna 193
Edwin 193
Elizabeth 193
Ellen 193
Francis 193
George 193
James 193
James Reason 193
Mary 193
Minta 231
Robert 193
Samuel 193
Butter
Darius 179
James 179
Mary Virginia 179
Nancy Jane 179
Nathaniel 179
Byram
John 161
Byron 173
Cacy 133, 137, 183, 225, 238
John E. 257
Samuel 225
William 178
William E. 225
Calder 7, 103
Catherine 103
Isabella 103
James 77
Joseph H. 76

Mary 271
Mary Ann 104
Nathaniel 77
Robert 271
Simon 76
Caldwell 175
Caleb
Samuel Jr. 51
Velina 183
Verlina 221
Wesley 221
California 196, 218
Calison
Katherine 48
Camp 80, 88, 125, 131, 150, 154, 157, 200
Augusta 165
George William 165
Samuel Albert 141
Sarah 141, 154
William 141
Campbell 124
Canady 28, 99
Canby
Sarah Matilda 151
Cann 63, 84
Benjamin Price 151
Francis 9, 252
Mary 151
Sarah Matilda 151
Cannell 5, 20, 41, 154
Carey 218
Carmichael 3, 60, 132, 258
Andrew Hemphill 234
Maria 234
Carothers 263
Carroll 50, 158
Carrow 230
Henrietta 194
Joseph M. 194
Carter
Rachel 107
Carty

Index of Names and Places

John 24
Carvill 58, 59, 79, 85, 98, 213, 215
Ann 76
Caroline M. 79
Henry 79
Henry W. 79
John W. 79
Carville 4
Carvills 261
Catlin 237
Caton 129
William 25
Caudwells 238
Caulk 6, 25, 238, 256, 261
   Elizabeth 89
   Salina 186
Cecil 61, 210, 277
Cecil Co 19, 36, 38, 42, 61, 82, 128, 161, 192, 213, 235, 236, 238, 262, 264, 267
Centreville 69, 73
Chambers 7, 25, 29, 45, 55, 63, 69, 81, 89, 102, 118, 135, 136, 159, 160, 166, 167, 171, 193, 255, 256, 259
   Augusta 1
   Benjamin 1, 22
   Benjamin L. 22
   Benjamin Lee 1
   Caroline 274, 275
   David 1, 22, 275
   Elizabeth 22
   Elizabeth A. 274
   Elizabeth C. 22, 54
   Elizabeth Caroline 1, 22
   Ezekial F. 1, 22, 102
   Ezekial Foreman 274
   James 1, 22, 274
   James Bowers 22
   Laura 274
   Maria Louise 275
   Sarah 81
   Sarah E. 102
   Sarah G. 23
   Thomas 274
   William 275
   William H. 22
   William Henry 1, 22
Chance 217
   Elijah 41
   Elizabeth 41
   Levi 41
   Noah 41
   Warner 41
Chandler 35, 125, 272
Chapman 120
   Ann 98, 120, 130, 182
   Charlotte 130
   Daniel 130
   Harriet M. 130, 165
   Harriett 98
   Harriett Malvina 98, 120
   Henrietta Malvina 98
   John E. 130
   John Emory 98
   Malvina 130
   William P. 98
   William S. 130, 165, 184
Chase
   Levi 160
   May Jane 220
   Nancy 195
   Samuel 195
   Susan 214
Cheney 273
Chesapeake City 213
Chester 3, 6, 50, 65, 67, 68, 74, 81, 82, 86, 105, 107, 131, 136, 246, 254, 260, 265, 272
Chestertown ii, 1, 5, 8, 10, 11, 21-23, 25, 28, 29, 32, 33, 35-38, 41, 49, 51, 54-56, 60, 62, 66, 69, 70, 74, 77, 78-82, 84, 86, 89, 90, 94, 98-102, 104, 108, 114, 116, 117, 120, 123, 125, 131, 136, 138, 141, 142, 143, 145, 152-154, 156, 157, 158, 159, 161, 162, 164, 165, 169, 175, 181, 186-188, 190, 192, 197, 198, 205, 211, 212, 214, 215, 216, 218, 219, 221, 222, 224, 226, 227, 232, 241, 243, 247, 250, 255, 259, 261, 262, 265, 270, 271, 273, 274
Chesterville 120, 163, 231, 267, 231
Chew
   Ann W. 43
   Benjamin 57
   Daniel Lamb Richardson 43
Chivins 106

Chrisfield 18, 270, 273
  Alfred 148
  Elizabeth 148
  Etha N. 148
  George W. 148, 248
  Gilbert 148, 247
  James G. 148, 247
  Other N. 148
Christfield 248
  Elizabeth 247
  Gilbert 248
  James G. 247
  Sarah E. 248
  Sarah R. 248
Christou
  Christos Jr. ii
Church hill 196
Clane 69
Clark 44, 136, 213, 238, 263
  Ann 208
  Catharine 72
  Elizabeth 72, 208
  Ira 72
  James 72
  John 270
  John C. 208, 213
  Julietta 72
  Rosetta 270
  Thomas 270
  William 41, 70, 72
  William Jr. 41
Clarke
  John 88
  Martha 149
  Samuel 149
  Thomas 202
Clarkson
  Cornelia 81
  Eliza J. 81
  Mary 81
Clash
  Elizabeth T. 216
Claypole 88, 142

Claypool 66
  Elizabeth 66
  James 66
Claypoole 32
  Elizabeth 66
  James 66
  James Jr. 66
  John 66
  Septimous 66
  William 66
Clayton 23, 69
  Elizabeth 106
  Jacob 106
  Jacob Jr. 106
Cleaver 213
Cleever
  Sarah A. 256
Clemens
  Philena 273
Clements 272
Clerk
  Elizabeth 41
Clother 86
Clothier 102, 107, 116
  Mary 99
  Samuel 99
Clow 21
Clowes 90
Coachmaker
  A. B. 124
Coalman 86
  Araminty 86
  Isaiah 86
Coburn 63
Cochran 278
  Eliza 163, 256
  Hannah C. 256
  Sarah A. 256
Cochrane 236, 237
Cohie 184
Colby 224
Colder
  William Alexander 7
Cole 99, 163, 273

Abraham 94, 163, 211
  Alfred 211
  Araminta 211
  George Hynson 211
  James 211
  John 163
  John Emory 163, 211
  Mary Eliza 211
  Rebecca 211
Coleman 133, 180, 207, 217
  Catharine 155
  Hezekiah 155
  James 179
  John Thomas 155
  Joseph 179
  Martha A. 266
  Mary Ann 139
  Mary Willier 179
  Richard 180
  Samuel 89, 139
  Thomas 179
  William Henry 155
Collier
  Richard S. 244
  Sarah R. 244
Collins 13, 15, 25, 50, 66, 96, 103, 104, 108, 143, 164, 189, 190, 215, 233, 272
  Elizabeth 66
  Margarett 66
  Mary 66, 200
Colwell 35
Comegys 14, 30, 45, 68, 98, 111, 120, 126, 197, 227, 230, 242, 244, 247, 267, 271
  Ann Rebecca 196
  Ann Worrell 73
  Anna Elizabeth 35
  Cornelius 117, 119

Index of Names and Places

Debba 66
Edward 119, 268
Elizabeth 35
Emeline 35
Francina 72
Henry F. 177
John Edward 177
Lenora 177
Lenora E. 178
Matilda 177
Millementy 92, 113
Millimenty 66
Nathaniel Jr. 66
Samuel 92, 113, 196
Samuel L. 122
Samuel William 177
Sarah Ann 122
Sarah W. 196
Washington 92, 177, 178
Washington Jr. 177
Comptors
  Eliza 72
Conner
  Benjamin 103
  Isabella 103
Constable 45, 78, 111, 114, 190, 200, 214, 226
  Albert 156
  Catharine 199
  Elizabeth 155
  Ellen 272
  Harriett 272
  Isabella 156
  John 155, 156
  John Jr. 155
  John S. 200, 272
  Julianna 143
  Martha J. 272
  Mary 155, 272
  Robert 101
  Stevenson 272

William 156, 272
William S. 199
Cook
  Ann M. 76
  Hester 20
Cooke
  Elizabeth 74
Cooper 80, 86
  Ann 17
  Benjamin 5
  Francis Elizabeth 5
  Ignatius T. 156
  Louisa 159
  Martha 5
  Martha Amanda Cooper 159
  Mary 156
  Mary Louisa 159
  Peregrine 5
  Peregrine Jr. 5
  Peregrine Sr. 5
  Thomas R. 35
  Wilhelmina 5
  William Salisbury 17
Copeman 61
Coppage
  Philemon 97
Copper 57, 58, 86, 88, 92, 104, 110, 115, 132, 153, 157, 160, 183, 187, 193, 207, 240
  Amelia 200
  Ann 206
  Charles 206
  Christianna 200
  Cyrus 206
  Darius 6
  Eliza 200
  Elizabeth 139, 140
  George 200
  George T. 200
  Harriet 104

Harriet A. 104
Harriett 200
Henrietta 200
Henry 206
Jane 123, 181, 200
John William 206
Mary 6
Mary Ellen 200
Rebecca 115, 133
Samuel 15
Samuel G. 200
Sarah 200
Susan A. 206
Thomas F. 104
William 206
Corbaley 177, 204, 212
  Hannah 179
  Hannah J. 175
  Hannah M. 175, 250
  Henrietta M. 175, 179
  Mary A. 175, 250
  Mary A. Corbaley 179
  Richard 175, 250
  Richard Jr. 250
  Samuel J. 250
Corbally 243
  Hannah 243
  Hannah M. 243
  Mary A. 243
  Richard 243
  Samuel J. 243
Corbaly 133, 144
Corbett 94
Cordray 131
Corey 250
  Albert L. 250
  Ellen P. 250
  John W. 250
  Lydia E. 250
  Maro V. 250

289

Thomas S. 250
Cornelius 92
Cornet 227
Corse 51, 61, 78, 216
  Anna Maria 10
  Barney 10
  Eliza 10
  James 3, 10, 28, 59
  Jane 3, 68
  Jesse 10
  Rebecca 26
  Thomas 10, 28
  Thomas A. 3
  Unit 3, 28, 59
  William 3
Corsons
  Elizabeth Corsons 174
Cosden 33, 261
  Alexander 74
  Jannette 74
  Mary 74, 76
Cottin
  Anna Eliza 247
  Aryan 246
  Edward Stansbury 247
  George Washington 247
  Harriett 246
  Henry 246
  Janus Henry 247
  Sarah Elizabeth 247
  Thomas Ethram 247
Cotton
  Daniel 182
  Eliza Ann 182
  Elizabeth 182
  Hannah 182
  Isaac 182
  Joseph 182
  Rachel 182
  Sarah Ann 182
Count
  Henrietta B. 185
County 70

Couper 260
Coursey
  Mary W. 93
  Samuel 93
  Thomas W. 93
Covington 7
  John 7
  Samuel 7
  Samuel Jr. 7
Cowper 202
Cox 61
  Benjmain Franklin 156
Cox's Neck 213
Coxe
  Elizabeth 89
  Harriett M. 106
Crabbin 100, 114
Crabin 114
Craig 213
Crane 34, 44, 66, 72, 103
  Annie Elizabeth 257
  Boyer 1
  David 1
  Elizabeth 1
  Ellen Sophia 203
  John 2
  Jonathan 2
  Mary 2, 220
  Mary Rickets 123
  Philip 2
  Rachel 125
  Stephen 2
  Thomas 1
  Thomas H. 203
  Thomas Richard 123
  William 1, 123
  William Bowers 123
  William F. 220
Crawford 35
Crew 22, 34, 43, 140, 146
Crippen 251
  James 251
Crockett 26

Croply 227
Crossley 137, 155, 201
  Delia A. 170
  George W. 155
  George Washington 155
Crossly 227, 231
  Elizabeth 155
  George W. 170
Crouch 33, 58, 76, 117, 242
  Alethia 199
  Edwin 147
  Edwin Jr. 147
  Elizabeth 105
  James 104
  Jane 105
  Martha 115, 133
  Mary K. 147
  William 105
Crow 117, 261
  C.W. 268
  Susan 268
Cruickshank
  Andrew Jackson 123
  Maria Louisa 123
  Mary Ann 123
  Sarah 123
Cruickshanks 193
Cruikshank 162, 200
  Alice 243
  Ann 243
  Charles 243
  Ellen 244
  Eugenia J. 123, 125
  George Washington 123
  Guilford D. 125
  Hannah 243
  Joel 243
  John 243
  John Jr. 243
  Kate 243
  Lawrence 123
  Madison 243

Index of Names and Places

Martha 244
Mary Avarilla 125
Mary Isabella 243
Polly 243
Robert 123, 243
Sam 243
Thomas 244
Virginia 243
William James 123
Cruikshanks 58, 138
  Ann 58
  Ann Elizabeth 124
  James 124
  Mary 58, 161
Cuff 197
  Catharine 197
  Deborah 197
  Doreas 197
  Thomas 86, 197
Cumming 140
Cummins 181
  Martha E. 214
  Martha R. 214, 215
  Mary Anne 19
  Mary J. 214, 215
Curlett 264
Currey 64
Curry 76
  A. Rebecca 268
  Celina 125
  Cornelius 119
  Edward 125
  John 43
  Milcah 126
  Milicia 125
  Rebecca 119
Dailey
  Elijah 221
  William 221
Daily
  Edward 221
Dale 183
Danelly
  Anne 36

Daris 178
Darling
  Mary Gusta 204
Darrach 146, 162
Date 96
Davis 2, 5, 17, 42, 43, 45, 50, 70, 80, 86, 109, 126, 148, 197, 201, 210, 212, 225, 239
  Caroline 73
  Charles 189, 197
  Charles Henry 189
  David 121
  Emeline L. Wickes 93
  Ezekial C. 275
  Henrietta R.H. 100
  Henry 121
  Henry Lyon 121
  James 91, 256
  James M. 101
  Jane Mary 121
  John 189
  Laura 274
  Mary 10, 91
  Mary Clare 275
  Peter 196
  Philip 10
  Sarah 10
  Thomas 100
  William A. 101
  William Henry 91
Dawson
  Eliza 20, 26
  Isaac 20, 26
  Rebecca 26
  Sarah 20, 26
  Susanna 26
DE iii, 7, 10, 11, 20, 35, 36, 39, 44, 48, 49, 61, 63, 70, 91, 94, 96, 97, 116, 136, 202, 204,

208, 209, 212, 213, 215, 235, 244, 250, 251, 256, 257, 260, 265, 269, 270, 273, 277, 278
Deal 118
DeCoursy 253
Denning 123
  Arvis Elizabeth 141
  Daniel 202
  John N. 141
  Mary 141
  Oscar Rudolph 141
  Stephen 141
Denny
  Spry 61
Deputy 260
  Anthony 260
  Catharine 260
  Charles M. 260
  Elias 260
  Elizabeth 260
  James K.P. 260
  John 260
  John L. 260
  Mary 260
  Mary Jane 260
  Samuel 260
  Solomon 260
  Susan 260
Derney
  Maria 21
Dias 81
Dickinson
  Joanna 262
  John Anna 262
Diehl 250
  Lydia E. 250
Diehls 266
Diggs 191
Dilahunt 61
Dillehunt 162
Dillihunt

Ann 163
Mary 163, 191
Mordica 163
Thomas 163
Dimmit
  Catharine 87
Dixon 127
  Caroline 9
  George 10
  Hester 9
  John 9
  Louisa Anna Maria
    10
Dobbs 253
  Abraham 252
  Absolom 253
  James C. 253
  Mary Anne 253
  Sampson 253
  Samuel B. 253
  William 253
Dodd 159, 169, 199, 265, 273
  Augusta Matilda 141
  Henrietta 260
  John T. 141
  Mary Jane 141
  Thomas Stephen 141
Dodson
  Joseph 178
Dollis 145
  Cassandra 21
  Thomas 21, 28
Dolly
  Abram 239
  Hannah 239
  Henny 239
  Nancy 239
  Sharlotte 239
Doman
  Betsy 261
  Daniel L. 186, 261
  Dorinda 186
  Eliza 186
  Elizabeth 186
  Emily 261
  Hannah 261
  Isiah 261
  James 68, 186, 261
  Joseph 68, 186, 261
  Maria G. 186
  Mary 261
  Salina 186
  Samuel 261
  Samuel George 186
  Tempy 261
Donaldson 275
  S.J. 276
Doran
  William 232
Dorney 73, 88
  Maria 21, 70
  Mary 22, 70
  Thomas 70
Dorrel
  Sam 84
Dorsey 95
  Anne 66
  William 211
  William H. 66, 98
Dowling
  James C. 204
  Laura Virginia 204
Dowman
  Daniel 100
  Elizabeth 100
Downey 177, 207, 249, 269
  Betsy 168
  Elizabeth 86
  James 86
  John 168
  Mary 168
  Mary Ann 168, 266
  Nancy 168
  William 168
  William Jr. 168
Downing 144, 163, 176
Draper 73, 106
Drew 95
Drugan 205
Dryden
  Ann 193
Dublin 221
  Hannah 221
  Joseph 221
  Matilda 221
  Sidney 221
Duck Creek 116, 204
Duddell 28
Dudley 86, 114
  Rachel 91
Dugan 99
  Emeline 115, 117, 158
  Joseph O. 114
  Marion 114
  Mary Isabella 114
  Thomas E. 114
  Thomas E. Jr. 114
  William W. 114
Dulaney 252, 277
  Adelaide 276
  George G. 276
  Joshua H. 276
  Joshua L. 276
  William H. 276
Dulany 180
Duncan 117
  James 29
Dunlap 37, 241
  Ann Wilson 277
  Anna Wilson 277
  Edwin Wilmer 277, 278
  George Watson 277
  George Wilson 277
  Maria D. 277
Dunn 87
  Ann 17, 25
  Araminta 102
  Darius 50
  Darius Jr. 160
  Elizabeth 17, 25
  Hezekiah 58

Index of Names and Places

Mary 25
Nancy 71
Robert 17, 25, 102
Durding 88, 152, 177
  Benjamin R. 151,
    152
  Edward P. 151, 152
  Elizabeth 139, 140
  James C. 151
  John T. 139, 151,
    152
  John T. Jr. 151,
    152
  Marietta 140
  Mary Ann 151, 152
  Rebecca 139, 151
  William 139
  William Henry 139
  William R. 139
Duyer 21, 22, 65
  Daniel 22
  Elizabeth 34
  George 131
  George B. 34
  James 21, 22
  John 21, 22, 34,
    131
  Joseph 21
  Maria 21
  Mary 21, 22
  Mary Ann 137
  Mary Elizabeth 131
  Phillip 21, 22
  Rebecca 34
  Rosamond 21, 22
  Susana 21
  Susanna 22
Dwyer 70, 210
  John 210
Eagle 28
  Ann 159
  Catharine Alphonsa
    110
  Henrietta 185

  James 110
  James C. 159
  Julia 159
  Norcissa 110
  Rachel 110
  Solomon 159, 195
Earl 254
Earle 109
Earnest 262
Eastern Neck 16, 118,
  139, 200, 222, 245
Eaton 85
  James 89
Eccleston 5, 6, 20, 52,
  57, 64, 65, 71, 74,
  77, 81, 87-89, 99,
  105, 118, 135,
  138, 139, 143,
  160, 161, 162,
  166, 175, 181,
  189, 194, 248
  Ann E. 160
  Ann Elizabeth 81
  Augusta C. 102,
    248
  Elizabeth 6
  James Housten 248
  James Houston 197,
    248
  John 6
  John B. 6, 89, 102,
    129, 160, 169,
    248, 274
  John Bowers 81
  John C. 169, 248
  Judge John B. 197
  Margaret Sophia 6
  Mariam 248
  Providence Intes 6
  Samuel 57, 160,
    162
  Thomas 5
Eccliston 225

Edes 126, 145, 185,
  187, 267
  Ann 96
  James H. 95
  John 95
  Margaret 95
Edgar 158
Edward 266
Emory 11, 172
  Ourn 11
Edwards 14, 85, 104,
  155, 172, 173,
  229, 243
  Amanda 266
  Benjamin 11
  Editha 11
  Elizabeth 73
  Emory 11, 166
  Hannah 43, 73
  James 73
  James A. 243
  John 43, 73, 89
  Joseph 73, 266
  Julia 243
  Julian 67
  Margaret 67
  Margaretta 67
  Mary 73, 132
  Mary Ann 67
  Peregrine 11
  Thomas 11, 73
  Thomas Jr. 11
  Thomas Owen 132
  William 43, 73
Eisenberg 249
Eisenburg 116
Elbern 145
Elbert 73
  Ann 24
  Araminta Augusta
    249
  Catharine Editha
    249
  Eliza 186

Eliza Jane 249
Elizabeth 24
Isaac 24, 249
Isaac III 24
Isaac Jr. 24
Joseph Doman 249
Mary 24, 250
Mary Ann 249
Rachel 24
Salina Elizabeth 249
Samuel Cortney 249
Susan Rebecca 249
William 250
Elborn 46, 108
Elbourn
  Elizabeth 109
Elburn 114, 260
Eliason 120, 216, 227,
  263, 270
Elkton 238, 239
Ellers
  Jesse 40
  Margaret 40
Elliot
  Benjamin S. 97
Elliott 63
  Ruth 119
Ellis 148, 196
  Julianna 52
  Richard 203
Emerson
  Sarah 175
Emmerson
  Rebecca 170
  William 170
Emory 137
  John 111
England ii, iii, 8, 61,
  124, 188, 189, 216
Ervin
  Elizabeth 107
Estes 262, 268
Etherington 51
  Bartholomew 41
Eubanks
  Elizabeth 230

Evans 68, 175
  William 92
Everitt 4, 23, 33, 117,
  123, 129, 130, 207
  Henrietta L. 135
  Henrietta Lloyd 201
  Henrietta M. Lloyd
    201
  Joseph K. 60
  M. Tilghman 135
  Sarah 30, 60
  Temperance 89, 135
  William B. 89, 135
  William B. Jr. 135
  William K. 60
Ewing
  Maria 186
Eysenbry
  Cloe 183
Fagan
  Ann 48
Fairchild 234
Fairlee 19, 156, 200
Falconar
  Elizabeth 35
  John Wesley 183
  Sarah 35
Fancy 199
Fanny 84
Farrell 7
Fennel 251
  Harriet 251
  Justice 251
Fenton
  Rhoda Reynolds
    269
Ferguson 77
  Elanor 107
  Elizabeth 107
  John 107
Ferrell
  James 41
Ferris 213
Fiddis 195, 269
  Benjamin R. 269
  Benjamin W. 269

John A. 269
Sarah A. 269
Fields 30, 53
  Hannah 30
  James 30
  John 30, 53
  Julia 97
  Juliana 30
  Martha Ann 30
  Mary 30
  Mary Ann 30
  Welthy Ann 30
  William 30
  William Merritt 30
Fillingame
  John 5
  Mary 5
Fisher 92, 103, 115,
  123, 147, 156,
  159, 162, 167,
  205, 240, 253
  Alfred H. 240
  Dr. Samuel G. 272
  Ella Theodora 240
  Henrietta Clorinda
    Cornelia 240
  Isaac 239
  Jacob 239, 240
  Jacob F. 240
  Martha J. 272
  Mary 246
  Mary A. 240
  Mary Ann 239
  Ringgold Williams
    240
  Samuel G. 240, 272
  Samuel Groome 240
  Susan 277
Flaharty
  Mary 26
  Michael 26
  Rebecca 26
Flayhearty
  Mary 169
Flint 167
Flower 170

Index of Names and Places

Folkner 260
Ford 178, 203, 261, 267
Joseph T. 69
Lavinia Jane 69
Foreman 43, 104
  Alethia Ann 64
  Araminta Elizabeth 64
  Ariminta H.E. 104
  Benjamin Franklin 64
  Elizabeth 64
  Foreman 182
  General 275, 276
  George 63
  George Washington 64
  Hannah M. 104
  Harriet 104
  Louisa 256
  Malvina 275
  Mark W. 104
  Miss 275
  Sarah 127
  William 104
Forman 23, 76, 131, 250, 251
  Sarah 126
Foster 137
Fourman
  Elizabeth 64
  George 63
Fowler 229, 261, 265
  Birdsal 221
  Joseph 221
  Samuel 221
  William 221
Fox
  Henrietta 227
  James B. 227
  Mary Ann 227
  Rebecca 227
  Salley 227

Samuel 227
Francis 268
Fray 10, 153
  Candis 126
  Jane 126
  Maria 126
  Mary 126
  Rachel 126
  Robert 126
Frazier 20, 70, 156, 181, 224, 234, 241, 256
  Ann 19
  Araminta 19
  Emily 19
  Harriot 19
  John 19
  John Jr. 19
  Maria 93
Freeks
  Richard 85
Freeman 39, 102, 161, 213
  Abram 201
  Catharine Martha Eliza 50
  Catherine Martha Eliza 91
  Col. 52
  Edward 91
  Hannah 56, 73
  Harriet Maria 91
  Harriott Maria 50
  Isaac 109
  Isaac Sr. 52
  Isabella 50
  Jacob T. 195
  Martha Ann 109, 195
  Minta 32
  Sam 186
  Sarah 54
  Sophia 195

Sophia Ann 112, 195
William 56
French 261
  Henrietta 261
Frisby 36, 81, 138, 240
  Elizabeth 59, 122
  Horrace 89
  James 39, 94
  JOhn 36
  Kitty 205
  Mary Matilda 246
  Richard J. 13
  Richard W. 59
  Susan R. 122, 198
  William 122
Frizby
  Kitty 234
Furgeson
  Colin 107
Gail 273
Gale 18, 28, 60, 70, 88, 89, 109, 117, 128, 132, 138, 140, 141, 151, 157, 163, 183, 185, 207, 221, 227, 263, 264, 272, 274
  Ann 13
  Anne Maria 134
  Araminta J. 163
  Capt. James 112
  Elizabeth 89, 116
  Everet 148
  George 146, 151
  Isaac 163
  James 112, 207
  James H. 161
  James Hodges 8
  James P. 116, 161, 163, 164
  John 9, 199

John E. 116, 161, 163, 169
Joseph Everitt 134
Levi H. 8
Martha 13, 146
Martha H. 8
Mary 148, 207
Mary Ann 8
Mary C. 148
Mary Jane 260
Mary T. 161, 164
Mary Tilden 268
Rasin 8, 9, 148
Rasin Moore 134
Sarah 8, 207
Thomas 8, 9, 161
Willamina 148
William 8, 260
William Jr. 8
Galena 249
Gamble 81
  Ann E. 258
  Darius 94
  Eliza 95
  Greenbury 78
  Jane C.D. 95
  Jane Catherine Scott 94
  Maria L. 258
  Robert A. 258
  Robert Adolphus 94, 95
  Robert S. 94
  Sarah 78, 95
  Stanberry 95
  Stansbury 94
Garber
  Rebecca 43
  William 43
Gardiner
  Emily 271
  James 271
  Louisa Ann 271
  Rev. Samuel T. 271
  Samuel T. 271
Garnett 71, 125

Anna Elizabeth 35
Garrett
  Robert 120
Garrettson 119, 122, 147, 183
Gattis
  Edward 182
  Rebecca 182
Gears 37, 85
Noble B. 121
Gee
  Cornelius 105, 157
  Mary 105, 157
  George 97
  Elizabeth 85
Georgetown 13, 18, 21, 29, 37, 45, 50, 54, 63, 74, 91, 97, 106, 126, 145, 148, 149, 162, 178, 210, 223, 230, 241, 267, 278
Gibbs 77, 147
  Edward A. 147
  John Westly 78
Gibson 251, 253, 266
  George 64
  John 119
  Maria 107
  Rachel 119
  Samuel 93
  William 119
Gilbert 10, 118, 157
  Ann 33
  Caroline J. 33
  Eliza 33, 231
  George E. 33
  James 231
  Jesse 33
  Thomas C. 33
  Warner 33
  William 33
Gilchrist
  Anna 134
  Hannah 134
  James 134

Gill
  Margaret F. 269
  Sarah F. 269
Gilpy
  Elizabeth 269
  John 269
  Mary 269
Glann
  Tamasina 24
Glascow 242
Gleaves 186, 217, 225, 242
  Abram 241
  Anna Maria 241
  Charles 241
  Henrietta 241
  Mary 241
  Obediah 241
  Sarah 241
  William 241
Gleen
  Mariah 205
  Peter 205
Glenn 16, 33, 57, 129, 247
  Bill 129
  Eliha 133
  Elizabeth 115, 132
  Elizabeth Sterling 132
  Frederick 132
  Harriott 33
  Jacob 57
  James 115, 132, 133
  John 132
  Martha 115, 133
  Martha Ann 100
  Mary Elizabeth 132
  Mary Rebecca 132
  Michael 33, 101, 132
  Rebecca 133
  Sarah 115
  Sarah Ann 115
  Tamacina 110

Index of Names and Places

Tamasina 33
Thomas 132
Washington Danskin 133
William 132
Glick 218
Godwin
  William 135
Goff 225
Goldsborogh
  Nicholas 74
Goldsborough
  Richard Henry 74
Gonce 166
Gooding 55, 127, 128, 145, 177, 190, 241, 278
  Aaron L. 241
  Addison Miller 241
  Anna Maria 241
  Ara M. 243
  Ara Maria 241
  Franklin Miller 241
  George 241
  Lydia Catharine 241
  Sarah Etta 241
  Tempy 241
  Thomas E. 223, 241, 243
  Thomas Osborn 241
  William 241
  William Henry 241
Goose hill 104, 109, 134, 154, 224
Gooseberry
  James Henry 117
Gordon 15, 65, 98, 120, 126, 130, 138, 139, 149, 153, 160, 163, 166, 169, 184, 198, 217, 219, 226, 229
  Ann Elizabeth F. 64

Ann Louisa 130
Caroline R.F. 130
James F. 130, 149, 182
James Frisby 64
John 94
Joseph N. 181
Joseph N. Jr. 182
Mary F. 182
Sarah Maria 130, 149
Gorman
  Elizabeth 190
  Mary Jane 190
  Rebecca Ann 190
  Samuel 190
  William Henry 190
Gosman 171
Grabill 218
Graham 81
Granger 19, 130
  Mary Ann 83
  Peregrine 69, 73, 83
Grant 58
  Eliza Ann 222
  James Alexander Wroth 222
  Richard Isaiah Ashley 222
Graves 6, 22, 98, 142, 144, 164, 189, 220, 227
  Ann 145
  Caroline 81
  Deborah 197
  Eliza 145
  Elizabeth 145
  Emeline 145
  Henny 145
  Henry 145
  James 145
  John 81
  John G. 145

Mary 81
Richard 80, 145
Richard Jr. 145
Sarah 81, 90, 145
William 80, 81, 145
Gray 250
Grayson 245
Green 7, 18, 45, 59, 97, 144, 148, 220
  Benjamin F. 188
  Mary E. W. 188
  Mary E. Wickes 189
  Mary E.C. 188
Greenwood 17, 34, 40, 43, 46, 91, 101, 175, 195, 205, 232, 241, 250
  Ann 33
  Benjamin 172
  Daniel 56
  Daniel B. 56
  Elizabeth 34, 131
  Emeline 131
  George 27
  George Washington 172
  Hannah 270
  James 27
  James William 250
  John 27, 33
  Jonathan 27
  Joseph 56, 70
  Mary 131
  Mary A. 56
  Mary Ann 34, 172
  Milbourn 70
  Milburn 56
  Rebecca 34
  Sarah 33
  Sarah E. 56
  Sarah Emeline 34
  Thomas 33
  William 27

Gregory
  James 167, 170
  John 167
  Margarett 170
  Margret 167
Gresham 16, 115, 264
  Ann 159, 264
  Caroline 264
  Harrison 264
  John 264
  Rebecca 264
  Sophia 264
  Susan 76
  Thomas 264
  Thomas P. 76, 264
  Valentine 264
  Washington 264
Grieves
  Thomas Alexander 108
Griffin 1
Griffith 88, 104, 142, 155, 225
  George C. 103, 171
  Martha Henrietta 103
  Samuel 171
Grimes
  Louisa 122
Groome 4, 92, 150, 254
  Charles 46
  Daniel 46
  Isaac 46
  James 46
  John 46
  Lavinia 46
  Margarett 46
  Martha 46
  Peregrine 46
  Samuel 66, 92
  Sarah 46
  William 46, 66
Grubb 256, 257
  Hannah Ann 256
  Joseph C. 256

Gudgeon 156
Hacket
  Cloe 183
  John 183
  Lydia Ann 183
Hackett 18, 36, 46, 75, 83, 90, 133, 144, 167, 175
  Ann 172
  Charles R. 163
  Harriet B. 72
  John 172
Hadaway 131, 140, 173, 269
Haddaway 176
Hagill 179
Hague
  Elizabeth 109
  Hester 109
  Johanna 109
  Sarah 109
  Thomas 109
  William Hynson 109
Haines 185
Hale 135, 147
Haley 115, 117
  John 67
Hall 26, 29, 40, 51, 53, 59, 66, 70, 196, 241
  Ann Maria 265
  Araminta 59
  Christopher 68
  Cuthbert 59, 257
  Elizabeth 54
  Emily 257
  Hester 54
  James 54
  Joseph 54
  Josephine 59
  Josiah 68
  Mary Jane 190
  Mary Rebecca 68
  Rebecca 68, 76, 257

  Richard 54
  Samuel 68
  Thomas 190
  Wright 59
Haman 263
  Benjamin Howard 263
  Dr. James 263
  Mary Ellen 263
Hambleton 55, 68
Hamer
  Daniel 70
  Mary 38
Hamilton 224, 243
  Franklin 242
  James 242
  Louisa 242
  Mahaley 133
  Mary Ellen 242
  Mary Jane 242
  Samuel C. 242
  William H. 242
Hamm 235
  Mary Ann 235
  Williamina 235
Hammond 205, 226
  Adeline G. 225
  William S. 225
Hance
  Edward 144
  Isaac 144
  James 144
  John 144, 146
  Rebeckah Ann 144
Hancock
  Rugh 11
Hands 15, 18
  Alexander 23
  Bedingfield 23
  Kitty 132
  Mary 18
  Sarah 23
Handy 17, 66, 194
  Ester Ann 4
  Esther A.M. 193
  George 193

Index of Names and Places

George D. 66
George D.S. 4, 193
Luther 193
Marmaduke F. 193
Marmaduke P. 4
Mary F. 193
Mary F. T. 193
Mary H. 4
Susan 193
Susan L. 4
Hanes 264
  Catharine Ann 261
Hankins
  Eliza 197
  John 197
  Rosetta 197
Hanner 59
Hanson 4, 7, 19, 49, 83, 84, 122, 138, 198, 215
  Alexander B. 39, 198, 215
  Benjamin 86, 160
  Benjamin T. 111
  Benjamin Thomas 87
  Benjammin 111
  Catharine 39, 40, 198, 215
  Catharine R. 198
  Edward A. 215
  Edward Alexander 198
  Eliza M. 68
  Elizabeth 86, 87, 111, 126
  Emaline 111
  Emeline 87
  George 39, 49
  George A. 39, 215
  George W. 198
  Hannah 87, 111
  Henrietta Eliza 87
  James 86, 87, 111

James H. 111
James Henry 87
Jane E. 68
Jane Elizabeth 87
John 68, 86
John W. 111
John Wesley 87
Killy 39
Kitty 39
Lavenia 49
Lavinia 39, 40, 198, 215
Martha 88
Martha H. 68
Martha Henrietta 87
Perry W. 198
Sarah 39
Sarah R. 40, 49
Hardin
  Stephen 234
Hardter
  E. M. 180
Hardtner 180
Hardy 4
  Marmaduke P. 4
  Mary F. 4
Harford 218
Harford Co 70, 89, 98, 119, 143, 210
Harper 268
  Sarah A. 106
Harragan 28
  Sarah 24
Harrigan
  Ann 27
  Mary 27
  Sarah 27, 28
Harrington
  John 175
  John Jr. 175
Harris 10, 13, 28, 29, 33, 39, 45, 49, 98, 131, 140, 157, 160, 177, 206,

207, 210, 219, 247, 248, 261, 266, 274
  Abraham 18
  Alexander 105, 186, 187
  Ann Margaret 69
  Ann Maria 69
  Anna Maria 187
  Capt. Thomas 37
  Caroline 105, 186, 187
  E. G. 252
  Eady 18
  Eben 18
  Edward Anderson 69
  Edward Anderson' 45
  Eliza 186
  Elizabeth 37
  Francis 252
  George 18, 154
  Harny 18
  Henrietta 105, 186
  Hesse 18
  Isaac 18
  James 69
  Jonathan 78
  Joseph 37, 186, 187, 206
  Joseph Thomas 203
  Juliet 105, 186
  Kate 187
  Laura 187
  Margaret 45, 69
  Maria 21, 37, 105, 186, 187
  Martha 18
  Mary Maria 69
  Sarah 145
  Tempe 18
  Thomas 69, 186

William 21, 45, 69,
  78, 202, 251
Harrison 99, 269
Harrod 124
Harrold
  Margaret F. 269
Hart 76, 134, 259
Hartley 143, 191
Hartshorne 124
Hartt 164
  Elizabeth 135
Hatcherson
  Nathaniel 87
Hatcheson 92, 152,
  160
  Ann 46
  James 23
  Mary 46
  Rachel 46
  Sarah 141
  Vincent 23
Hatchison
  Vincent 46
Hawkins
  Ann 81
  Caroline 81
Hawthorn 218
Haynard
  Henrietta M. 72
Hayne 2, 4, 179, 183
Haynes 44
  George 34
  Gideon 34
  Mary 34
Hayward
  Elizabeth 82
  Elizabeth R. 107
  Henrietta 75
  Margarett 82
  Mary Ann 82
  Sally 82
  Thomas 82
  Thomas Jr. 75
  Thomas S. 107
  William 82
Hazel 67

Benjamin 96
Elizabeth 96
George 67, 96, 107
Hosanna 67
James 67, 96
Mary Ann 96
Susan 96
William A. 96
Hazle
  Benjamin 67
Hazzard
  Ann 227
  Drusilla 214
  Emily 214, 227
  Harriett 214
  Harriett Jane 227
  Jacob 214, 227
  Mary 214, 227
  Mary Drucilla 227
  Richard 214, 227
Heartly
  Edward 191
  Maria 191
Heath 11
Heigh 149
  Susan E. 140, 170
Heighe 54, 120, 121,
  208, 233, 273
  Susan E. 277
Hemsley
  Persey 71
Henderson 124
  Mary 269
Henlock 228
Henry 59, 213
  Hemsley 203
  Milla Minta 154
Hepbron 4, 9, 48, 136,
  150
  Ann Eliza 112, 194
  Edward T. 194
  Elizabeth 112, 194
  Henrietta 112
  James 112, 131,
    194
  John 112, 194

John F. 194
John Francis 194
John Henry 112
John L. 194
John Thomas Maslin
  112
Joseph J. 194
Joseph James 112,
  194
Lewisham S. 194
Margaret E. 194
Margaret Elizabeth
  112, 194
Mary 112, 131
Mary Ann Elizabeth
  194
Samuel 194
Sewell 112, 194
Tewisham 112
Thomas 112, 194
William 194
Herdman 128, 134,
  199
Hesse
  Elizabeth 24
Hessey 175
Heverin
  William 31
Heverson 171
Hewett 50
  Elizabeth 50
  Thomas 50
Hewitt 267
  Anna 63
  Martha 63
  Mary 63
  Thomas 63
  William 63
Hickey
  Mary Jane 161
Hickman
  Elizabeth 244
Hicks
  George 84
Highly 261
Hill

300

Index of Names and Places

Elizabeth 257
Hannah Ann 256
Henry 257
James 257
Joseph 256
Margaret Ann 257
Mary 257
Mary Ann 256
Rebecca 257
Robert 257
Thomas 257
Hills
  Rachael 232
  S. 232
Hinds 217
Hines 6, 39, 64, 66,
  98, 104, 119, 221,
  223, 242, 243,
  271, 272, 278
  George A. 191
  George Neal 79
  Jesse K. 217
  John Wesley 217
Hinson
  James 207
Hirsch 249
Hodges 3, 10, 103,
  117
  Ann 13
  Eliza 117, 197, 202
  James 13
  James Jr. 13, 101
  John 8
  Maria 231
  Martha 13
  Samuel 197
  Sarah 14
Hodgkin 263
Hodgson 40
  Ann 40
  Jonathan 39
  Sarah 39
  Stephan 40
Holden 217

Holding
  Matilda 271
Holdson 34
Holland
  Alexander 105
  George Washington
    105
  Hester 105
Holliday
  John Henry 79
Holling 97
Hollingsworth 143,
  147
  Ann Eliza 194
Hollis
  James 87
Hollyday 107, 143,
  189
  Caroline 79
  George S. 79, 101
Holt 37
Hood
  John 20
Hope
  Margaret 189
Hopkins
  Alley 171
  Betsey 171
  Caroline 262
  Harriett 171
  Isaac 262
  Mary 249
  Moses 171
  Perry 171, 249
  Richard 171
Hopper 111
  Ellen Amanda 87
  Thomas W. 111
Horsey 111, 261
Horton
  Dr. 119
  Ruth 119
Hosier
  William 66

Hossenger
  Charlotte 254
Hossinger
  Charlotte 254
Houston 10, 32, 59,
  108, 124, 131,
  153, 162, 182,
  219, 247, 259
  Adeline 151
  Augusta 22, 54, 58
  Augustine 22
  Benjamin 58, 91
  Benjamin F. 201
  Benjamin Franklin
    91
  Eliza 120
  Elizabeth 22, 58
  Elizabeth F. 102
  Hannah 58, 90
  Judge 1, 22
  Matilda 221
  Rebecca R. 58
  Sarah Ann 120
  William 58
  William Wickes 91
How 217
Howard 21, 22, 30,
  36, 48, 150, 247,
  263, 274
  Ann Amelia 274
  Anna 271
  Anne 36
  Anny 34
  Asbury 204, 247
  Augusta 263
  Basil W. 34
  Basil Wells 31
  Bazzel Wells 31
  Benjamin 263
  Benjamin Sr. 36
  Elizabeth 34, 63,
    169
  Frank Houstin 247
  George W. 263

Gibson 10, 112
James 10
James E. 34, 271
James Eagle 31
John 10, 36
John Jr. 10
Joseph 164, 273
Joseph James 263
Joseph Wrightson 273
Luke 34
Luke Jr. 31
Mary 247
Mary Hyland 164, 273
Permelia 204
Permilia 34
Perry Price 247
Philena 273
Philina 164
Rebecca 31, 47
Risdon 31, 49
Susanna K. 274
William 31, 34, 49, 169
William Penn 247
Howe 217
Howells Point 212, 213
Hubbard
  Andrew T. 260
  Dorothy E. 260
Hubbel
  Sarah E. 156
Huckill
  Guilder 44
Hudson 256
  Ann M. 70
  Deborah 89
  John 70
  Maria 70
Hughes 90
Hugle
  Araminta 44
Humphreys
  Ann Louisa 158

Catherine 158
Emily Catharine 158
Emily Catherine 158
John 158
John Jr. 158
Louisa 158
Hunter 211
Hurley 184
Hurlock 72, 86, 96, 271, 272
Hurst 95
Hurt 242
Hurtt 11, 29, 31, 48, 63, 100, 104, 109, 114, 117, 121, 127, 128, 141, 145, 148, 154, 168, 171, 174, 176, 241, 276
Adah 14
Amanda Melvina 165
Ann 103
Ann Sophia 160
Edward 28, 53
Elizabeth 14, 148, 276
Frances Susanna
  Isabella 109
George 276
Henry 14, 47, 109, 154
Henry N. 160
James 14, 154
James Alexander 160
James B. D. 173
James B.D. 160
James Clinton 154
James Henry Josiah 47
Jeletta 48
John 80, 148, 160, 276

John D. 173
John Theadore 37
Juletta 47
Julieta Ann 47
Margarett Frances 160
Martha 14, 173
Mary 14
Mary Elizabeth 160
Mary Rebecca 47, 109, 154
Milla Minta 154
Milly Minty 47
Reulma 14
Richard H. 160
Samuel 14
Sarah 14, 154
Thomas Dollis 28
Walter T. 160
William Thomas 47, 154
Hurtts
  Henry 178
Hutson
  James 86
  Sarah 86
Hyland 23, 59, 64
  Ann 23, 103
  Ann Elizabeth 23, 64
  Henry M. 177
  Henry Miles 103
  James 103
  James Jr. 103
  Kesiah 103
  Mary 38
  Sarah W. 64
  Stephen 64
  William 64
Hynson 8, 14, 27, 28, 32, 33, 82, 88, 89, 92, 102, 103, 111, 126, 139, 181, 191, 202, 210, 215, 220, 223, 225, 229, 230,

Index of Names and Places

232, 233,
242-244, 248,
252, 259, 261,
268, 272, 273
Andrew J. 180
Ann 17, 25
Ann Louisa 129
Anna 129
Anna Maria 216
Caroline 76, 92
Charles 139
Charles R. 33, 92,
103
Christopher
Columbus 180
Eliza Rebecca 33
George W. 92
Harriet Matilda 103
Harriot M. 157
Harriott Matilda 33
J. M. 157
John C. 33, 157
John Carvill 33
Joseph H. 244
Laura 33
Laura Lavinia 33,
157
Martha 33, 157
Martha Henrietta 33
Mary 112, 210
Mary Ann 89
Mary Elizabeth 129
Mary S. 180
Matilda 201
Nathaniel 112
Richard 129, 135
Robert D. 25, 129
Sarah Ann 33, 157
Thomas 24, 33, 92,
123
Thomas B. 17, 25,
87, 129, 135
Thomas B. Jr. 129
Thomas H. 92

Virginia W. 180
Washington 123
Hyrons 137
Illinois 217, 218, 269
Ingram
  Margaret Ann 128
  Sarah 150
Ireland 28, 41, 42, 52,
  63, 121, 131, 145,
  156, 174, 197,
  208, 222, 249,
  253, 272, 28, 41,
  42, 52, 63, 121,
  131, 156, 174,
  197, 208, 222,
  249, 253
Alethia Lavinia
  Woodland 253
Alletha L. 121
Charles T. 272
Emma H. 121
Emma H. Perkins
  253
Hannah 121
Hannah Wallis
  Woodland 253
James 272
John W.P. 121
John William Pope
  253
Louisa P. 121
Louisa Perkins 253
Margaret A. W.
  121
Margaret Ann Wallis
  Woodland 253
William P. 145
Isaac 59
Jackson 184
  Mary 18
  William 19
Jacob
  Thomas A. 234
Jacobe

William 201
Jacobs
  Araminta 120, 178
  Arnold 120
  Ebenezer 178
  Edwin John 178
  Eliza 120
  James William 178
  Mary Rebecca 178
  Thomas Arnold 178
James 265
  Isaac 87
  Thoams J. 86
  Thomas 62
  Thomas Hanson 86
  Thomas J. 13, 86
Janvier 192
  Ann 202
  William 202
Jarman 164, 217, 252
  Arsula 252
  Arula 252
  Franklin 252
  John Wesley 252
  Mary Ann 252
  Samuel 252
  Samuel J. 252
  Sarah Ann 252
  Sarah E. 252
  Sarah Eliza 252
  Thomas George 252
  Washington 252
Jarvis 267
Jeffries 15
  Elizabeth 15, 17
  John 17
  Matilda 230
Jenkinson
  Emanuel 7
Jerrum 1, 12
Jervis
  Frances 170
  John 171
  Sophia 170

Jessop
  Saleno 141
Jester
  William Theodore
    119
Johns 2, 36, 49
  Arthur 6
  Elizabeth 6, 39, 48
  Enoch 6
  Enoch H. 49
Johnson 177, 179,
  212, 242, 243,
  251, 258
  Agnes R. 211, 212
  Catharine 221
  Daniel 207
  Edward 93
  Hannah 239
  Henry 191
  Lydia 93
  Maria 93
  Richard C. 212
  Temperance 93
Johnston
  George Washington
    175
  Henry 175
  John 175
  Margaret Ann 175
  Sarah Amelia 175
  Sarah Ann 175
  William 175
  William Thomas
    175
Joiner 121, 142, 145
Jones 28, 30, 41, 80,
  93, 101, 151, 174,
  182, 192, 198,
  212, 216, 217,
  231, 232, 243,
  246, 251, 264, 270
  Alexander R. 183
  Ann Eliza 124
  Ann Maria 173, 265
  Anna Maria 60
  Antoinette 219

Arthur T. 74
Arthur T. Jr. 74
C. F. 189, 274
C.F. 275
Chambers 275
Clement F. 275
Daniel 131, 174,
  264
Daphina F. N. 216
David 50, 60, 108,
  124, 173, 205, 219
David Eugene 205
Deborah 60, 173
Dr. C.F. 275
Edward 192
Eliza 28
Elizabeth 98, 108,
  125, 173, 182,
  216, 219, 276
Elizabeth A. 274
Emily 192
Emma 219
Frances 124
George 28
George R. Jones
  183
George Washington
  264
Hannah 28
Hariet 124
Henry 219
Hester A. 183
Hiram 155
Isabella 124
Jacob 109, 164,
  192, 221
Jacob Alfred 264
Jacub 98
James 28, 265
James Wesley
  Philips 85
John 28, 98
John M. 192
John W. 199
John Wesley 264
Laura Jane 205

Lilly 275, 276
Maria J. 183
Marshall 275
Martha 219
Mary 131, 272
Mary E. 268
Mary Elizabeth 264
Mary J. 221
Mary L. 173
Mary Louisa 60
Milnor 276
Nancy 28
Nicholas Slubey 124
Octavius H.M. 183
Oliver P. 173, 216,
  268
Peter 28
Philip 265
Rasin 131, 221
Rebecca Elizabeth
  131, 221
Rev. Dr. D.C. 274
Richard 192, 265
Richard W. 272
Ruth 192
Sally 182
Sarah 164
Sarah Catharine 264
Tempe 219
Temperance 164
Thomas 173, 182,
  216
Thomas Cuff 265
Velina 183
Verlina 221
Washington 264
Wesley 265
William 124
William Henry 265
William J. 183
William Jr. 124
William Wesley 265
Willie 219
Jordan 106
Jump 215, 225, 247,
  274

Index of Names and Places

Henry T. 170
Margaret A. 170
Justice 237
Keating 131
  Thomas Browning 147
Keatting 80, 101
  Edward 147
  John 19
  William 19
Keene 6, 7
  Eliza 7
  Sarah 39, 40
  Vachel 7
Kelley 42, 172, 205, 212, 247
  Henry 213
Kelly 100, 146
  Benjamin 88
  Catharine 161
  Ezekial 88
  Susan 119
Kemp
  Frederick C. 213
  Hannah R. 213
Kenard
  Elizabeth 190
  George H. 203
  James 203
  James W. 203
Kendal 253
  Mary 27
Kendall 200, 222
  Ann 33
  Thomas 33
Kendle
  Eliza 89
Kennard 14, 16, 22, 31, 41, 42, 49, 50, 55, 61, 63, 66, 68, 85, 111, 116, 120, 126, 128, 142, 146, 147, 163, 166, 203, 217, 220, 232, 267, 270
Adaline G. 98, 166
Ann 69
Asbury 51
Caroline 34
Dennis 77
Editha 69
Elizabeth 51, 166
Elizabeth M. 95
Emily 21, 51
George 69
Harriott 166
Henry 49
Howard 122
Jane 31
Jane E. 126
Jane Elizabeth 87
John 49, 166
John T. 95, 98
Joshua 49
Kennard 51
Maria 78
Martha 27, 34
Mary 34
Mary Ann 166, 225
Mary Anne 95
Milcah 126
Nancy 51
Patrick P. 49
Patrick Parks 30
Philip 166
Rachel 30, 97
Richard 69, 78
Samuel 51
Samuel E. 191
Samuel G. 66, 95, 98
Samuel Groome 166
Sarah 30, 78, 166
Sarah E. 95, 166, 225
Sarah Elizabeth Kennard 98
Stephen 49
Susan 51
Thomas C. 87
Unit 51
Westly 51
William 51, 134
Kennards 263
Kennedy 254
  Ann 27
  Martha 27
  Mary 27
  William 27
Kenney
  Sarah 131
Kent Island 119, 213, 214, 217
Kenton 229, 248
Kerr 5, 15, 43, 54, 71, 93, 195, 254
  Andrew 254
  Charlotte 254
  Mary K. 254
  Samuel 28, 254
Kinard
  Daniel H. 191
  Henrietta 190
  Mary Ellen 190
  Samuel 190
  William Henry 190
Kindal 102
King 161
  Elizabeth 148
  William 148
Kinnard
  Elizabeth 191
Kirton 24
Knight 63, 209, 219
  Catharine 219
  Charlotte Ringgold 30
  William 30, 196, 219
  William Jr. 219

Knock 111, 118, 119, 217, 229, 277
  Ann B. 217
  Eliza Lucinda 119, 217
  Elvira 228
  Jesse 12, 96, 119, 217
  Katherine 217
  Mary E. 228
  Mary Elizabeth 12
  Mary Elvira 228
  Samuel H. 228
  Samuel Henry 217
  Sarah 119, 217
Knotts 155
Knox
  Esther Ann 146
  Margaretta 146
  Mary Ann 146
Krafft 192
Kraft
  Henry 212
  Matilda C. 211, 212
L.
  F. R. 168
Lamb 1, 2, 26, 34, 43, 61, 62, 79, 81, 99, 120, 149, 167, 216, 221, 262
  Alexander 204
  Charlotte 16
  Daniel 43, 195, 196, 204
  David 2
  Easter 62
  Edward 29, 62
  Hannah 20, 26, 43, 73, 225
  Jacob 20, 26, 225
  James 16
  John 20, 26
  Joshua 44, 84
  Mary 2
  Mary Ann 85
  Mary D. 195, 204

  Rachel 20, 26
  Rebecca 2, 48, 85, 173
  Rebecca C. 196
  Rosamond 2
  Sarah 2, 20, 26, 84
  Sarah H. 148
  Thomas Alexander 195
  William 16, 85, 173
Lambdin
  Lucretia 61
  William 61
Lambert 269
  Mary Jane 242
  William H. 242
Lambson 251
  Giles 251
  Mary H. 251
  Moses 251
Lane
  Henrietta 227
  Sarah M. 227
Langford 1, 16, 105, 118, 222
Lapell 247
Lapsley 124
Lassell 55, 77, 131, 155, 193, 229, 248
  James Thomas 221
  William S. 221
Lassill 221
Lazenby
  Johanna 109
Leary 127, 206, 240, 260
  George 206
  Mary Ann 206
Leaverton 229
  Adam 229
  Charles 229
  George Anna 229
  Jacob 229
  James 229
  John Wesley 229
  Nancy 229

  Samuel 229
  Susan 229
  William Spencer 229
Lee 176, 204, 235, 273
  Elizabeth 27
  Rebecca 43
Legg 114, 180
Leonard
  Margaret 92
Lesley 251
Leverton 168
Levis
  Elizabeth 76
Lewis 261
  James 168
  Mary 168
  Peregrine 100
Light
  Edward 29
Lind
  Jenny 228
Little
  Joshua 239
  Nancy 239
Lockwood 119, 239
  Araminta 70
  Caleb 70
  Lydia A. 239
  Richard 239
Lond 231
Long
  Hester A. 183
Longfellow
  Gideon 94
Loockerman
  F. S. 224
  John 224
  Mary 111
  Robert 224
  Washington C. 224
Loper 272
Love
  Kesiah 103
Loveless 251

Index of Names and Places

Lowe
  Clementine 248
  Jestina 248
  Martha 248
Lucas 55
Ludlow
  Catherine 31
Lukes 10
Lusby 40, 106, 192,
  199, 211, 224,
  230, 249
  Ann 98
  Emily 266
  John 200
  John T. 253
  John W. 98
  Josiah 266
  Sarah Elizabeth 200
  Wilhelmina 152
Lybrand 191
Lyim 6
Lynch 2, 44, 85, 109,
  119, 131, 134,
  211, 235, 239, 2,
  44, 85, 131, 134,
  211, 235, 239
  Hannah 134
  Hannah Elizabeth
    134
  Mary Eliza 211
  Mary Rebecca 134
  Phoebe 109
  Rachel 119
  Sarah Gooden 109
  Thomas Clinton 211
  Thomas J. 119
  William 134
Lyzar 131, 184
  Catharine 178
  Hester 183
  Ignatius C. 183
  John J.C. 178
  Maria J. 183
  Michael 178

  William 178, 210
Maberry
  Shadrack 118
Mace 262
Machelor
  Sally 105
Madison
  Jim 166
Maginness
  Nathaniel 72
Maguire 235
  George 235
Mahanna
  Elizabeth 50
  James 50
Mahard
  Eliza 40
  Samuel Rasin 40
Malony 29
Malsberger
  Agnes R. 211
  Augustus 212
  Catherine 211, 212
  Elizabeth M. 212
  Jacob G. 211, 212
  Joseph 211
  Matilda C. 211
Mann 12, 68, 77, 107,
  137, 176
  Capt. Joseph 9
  Comegys 216
  J. C. 223
  Joseph 9
  Joseph C. 92, 113
  Louisa 223
  Mary A. 113
  Mary Ann 92
  Mary Louisa 216
  Samuel 92, 113
  Thomas J. 113, 127
  Thomas Jiney 68
  Thomas L. 92
Mansfield 55, 66, 68,
  78, 80, 85, 111,

  115, 119, 202,
  216, 250
  Ann 158
  Isabella 158
  James 158
  James Jr. 158
  John 158
  Margarett 158
  Mary Ann 158
Marsh 81, 82
Martin 99
  Ann 11
  Benjamin 102
  Hannah 102
  James 102
  Joseph J. 265
  Kate 265
  Kennard 102
  Nathaniel 11
Mary 27
Masden 252
Maslin 20, 27, 50, 56,
  91, 96, 119, 187,
  200, 221, 240
  Amanda Malvina
    200
  Ann 154
  Ann R. 200
  Eliza 200
  Francis Titus 154
  George L. 200
  Jacob 136, 154
  Jacob G. 195, 200
  Jane E. 200
  John 200
  John Joseph 154
  John Jr. 200
  John Thomas 112
  Joseph 154
  Martha 136
  Martha J. 200
  Mary Ann 200
  Susan Jemima 200
  Thomas 56

Titus 154
Mason 110
  John 85
  Mary M. 152
  Mary Matilda 85
  Sarah 261
Massachusetts 6
Massey 7, 17, 119, 204, 220, 267, 270
  Ann 17
  B.H.C. 203
  C.H.B. 267
  Charles H. B. 203
  Dr. C.H.B. 267
  Ebenezer T. 203
  Emily Ann 203
  George Oldham 267
  Joseph W. 203
  Josiah 17
  Mary Amanda 267
  Robert B.M. 204, 271
  Thomas G.H. 203
  Vermadilla 271
Massy 44, 64, 97
  Ann 35
  Ann E. 35
  George Reynolds 35
  Phillip Lewis 35
  Sarah 35
Masten 66, 163, 164, 195
Mastin 227, 267
  Alethea 231
  Amanda 227
  Henry 227
  Hezekiah 231
  James Polk 231
  John 227
  Joseph Asbury 227
  Joseph B. 227
  Joseph Boots 231
  Mary Ann 227
  Stephen 231
  Susan 231
  William 227

William Harrington 231
Matthew 142
Matthews
  David 189
Maul
  Elizabeth 257
Maull
  Elizabeth 257
  Robert 257
Maxwell 18, 34, 83, 84, 142, 159, 205, 238, 272
  Albert G. 83, 84
  Alexander 79, 101
  Frances Elizabeth 5
  John 14, 83, 84
  John M. 83, 84
  Rebecca 83, 84
  Sophia Ann 83, 84
  Wilhelmina 5
May 266
Mayniham 3
McCall 52, 53
  John 260
  Samuel 260
  Susan 260
McCarter 273
McCarty
  Margaret 124
McCaulley 260
McClain 65
  James 44
McClane 79
McClean 35, 58, 59, 65
  Alexander 125
  Ann 58
  Anna Maria 125
  Edward A. 125
  Frisby 65
  James G. 64
  Margaret 58, 125
  Thomas Lorain 125
McCoals 24
McCoy 89

Mary F. 193
McCubbin
  Mary Ann 151, 152
McCullough 260
McDaniel 67, 68, 74, 76, 100, 111, 191, 217
  Clementine 248
  John 191
  John W. 248
  Louisa 191
  Louisa C. 76
  Margaret Ann 248
  Sarah E. 248
McGinnes
  Nathaniel 123
McGinniss 95, 116
  Mary Ann 123
  Nathaniel 123
McGregor 29
McGuire
  Elizabeth 244
  Sarah E. 244
  William 244
McHam
  Daniel 269
  Rhoda Reynolds 269
  Ruth 269
McHand 97
McIntires 237
McIntyre 269
McKee 236, 237
McKenney 182
McKim 114
McLane
  Allen 97
McLaughlin 170
  George 242
  Jane 242
  Thomas 242
McLauglin 242
McLean
  Harriet 21
  William 21
McLoughlin

Index of Names and Places

George 210
Thomas 210
McWhorten 239
Mechanic
  Jim 111
Medders 148, 212,
  224, 231, 249,
  253, 269, 277
  Araminta 271
  George W. 271
Medford 4, 9, 13, 112
  Anna Maria 216
  Elizabeth 71
  Hannah 71
  John Edward 144
  Macall 61, 216
  Margaret Milicent
    144
  Maria 61
  Mary Ann 144
  Mary Anne 216
  Milicent 144
  Rody 144
Meeks 27, 32, 71, 78,
  174
  Aquilla 44
  Howard 221
  Mary Bradshaw 147
  Rebecca Elizabeth
    131, 221
Meeteer 250, 256, 270
Meetur 229
Megee 131
Meginnis 77
  Casparus 39
Meginniss 1, 67, 72,
  99, 102, 191, 268, 270
  Casparis 86
  Casperis 71
  George 86
  Hannah 86
  Mary 71
  Nathaniel 86
  Samuel Osborn 86

William 86, 110
Melvin 152, 229
Mensch 145
Meredith 44
  Mary 183
Merriken 111
Merrit
  Adeline K. 254
Merritt 31, 51, 125,
  243
  Adeline K. 254
  Araminta S. 30
  Arthur M. 174, 176
  Benjamin 93
  Eliza 254
  Frances O. 174
  George A. 254
  Juliana 176
  Mary 30
  Samuel 50, 174
  William K. 254
Mertimer 61
Methodist 9, 61, 78,
  94, 156, 157, 189,
  214, 226
Meyers
  Frances Ann 202
Mickle 255
Middleton 144, 164,
  220, 223
  Sarah Temperance
    203
Middletown 164
Miers 248
Mifflin
  Sarah T. 136
  Thomas 136
Milburn 264
Millan 111
  Sarah Elizabeth 68
  William 68
Millar 100
  Sarah Elizabeth 76

Miller 14, 23, 44, 62,
  102, 117, 152,
  158, 162, 170,
  171, 190, 196,
  224, 241, 243,
  248, 249, 258,
  270, 276, 277
  Alexander 108, 180
  Ann E. 258
  Ann Eliza 62
  Ann Elizabeth S.
    182
  Ann Mariah 67
  Ben 205
  Charles 269
  Eliza E. 277
  Elizabeth 71, 180
  Jane Louisa 182
  John 171
  Juliana 15
  Maria Evelina 62
  Maria L. 258
  Martha 15
  Mary 15
  Mary Jane 67
  Mary Matilda 258
  Merritt 14, 171,
    197, 258
  Norris 269
  Rachel Adelaide
    182
  Ralph 15
  Richard 15, 62
  Sarah 14, 15, 67,
    182, 185
  Sarah Cornelia 182
  Sarah Hester 62
  Solomon P.W. 182
  Thomas 15, 62,
    182, 185
  Thomas W.H. 182
  Walter F. H. 258
  Walter H. 14
  Walter T. H. 197

William 15, 71, 135
William Jr. 71
Millington 111, 120,
  122, 128, 137,
  177, 186, 210,
  229, 243, 257, 271
Millsborough 218
Milly
  Mary Ann 154
  Mary Elizabeth 155
Milton 88
Milward
  James 70
  Janus 70
  Mary 70
  Sarah 70
Minnick 246
Mitchell 13, 32, 35,
  185, 267
  James 194
  Joseph T. 35
  Richard Bennett G.
    106
  Sarah Elizabeth C.
    106
Mitton
  James 42
  Margaret 42
  Martha 42
  Richard 42
  Samuel 42
  Sarah Ann 42
Mobery
  Rachel 61
Moffet 97
Moffett 26, 67, 94,
  101, 104, 106,
  128, 132, 149, 272
  Arsula 252
  Bell Jane 42
  Catharine Matilda
    271
  Charlotte 126, 127
  Emily 127
  Enoch 134, 272
  Enoch J. 271

Jane F. 128, 147
Jeremiah N. 252,
  272
Joseph 42
Lancelot 164
Lancelott 126
Lancelott Jr. 126
Lavinia 126
Louisa 271
Louisa Ann 271
Louisa Perkins
  Ireland 253
Martha 42
Mary 127
Milliminta 127
Murray 134
Rebecca 127
Richard 271
Richard F. 271
Sarah 42, 126
Sarah Elizabeth
  235, 253
Stansbury 126
Susan 42
William 26, 42,
  127, 164, 235
William Jr. 42
Moffitt
  Arsula 252
  Jeremiah N. 252
Money 102, 176, 270
  Mary 144
  Rebecca 44
Mongur
  Sophiah 176
Monjor
  Joseph 117
  Sophia 117
Monk
  John 55
Monroe
  James 83
Moody 85, 227, 236
Moore 9, 210, 229,
  262

Alexander Yearly
  234
Arthur 234
Asenath 140
Elizabeth Martha
  140
George Thomas
  140, 146
John 140
John Lloyd 140
Margaret A. 140
Rachel J. 140
William Henry 234
Morgan 124, 152, 160
Morgans Creek 3, 28,
  215, 226, 228
Morian
  Alexander B. 180
  Elizabeth M. 108
Morris 77, 178, 191,
  230, 244, 262
  James C. 92
  John 92
  John B. 156
  Joseph 92
  Rachael 93
  Thomas 92
  William 92
Morse 43
Morton
  Crosby P. 265
Mulford 144
  Rody 144
Mullikin 233
Murphey 57, 70
Murphy 260
  Dorothy 260
  Dorothy E. 260
  Susan 208
  Thomas S. 260
Murray
  John 55
  Standly 55
Murry
  Rachel 146
Musgrave

Index of Names and Places

Martha 273
Myer 50
Myers
  Ann 137
  Elizabeth 137
  Francis Ann 197
  Frisby 170
  John 170
  Luke 119, 170
  Rebecca 170
  William 170
  William V. 137
Nandain
  Sarah 69
Naudain 237
  Alice Schee 236, 237
  Ann Elizabeth 236, 237
  Ann Matilda 237
  Anne Matilda 236
  Dr. James S. 236
  James Blackiston 236
  Jemima 235
  John A. 235
  Lydia Eddowes 236, 237
  Maria Louisa 236
  Mary Jemima 236, 237
  Mary Louisa 236
  Sarah 83
Neal 6, 39, 261
  Amanda Melvina 165
  Augusta 165
  Charles 79
  Clementia 165
  Ebenezer 79
  George 79, 173
  John Thomas 158
  Levi 79
  Louisa 158
  Mary Louisa 158
  Sarah 79
  Sarah Rebecca 136
  Sophia 79, 165, 173
  Thomas 79
Neales
  John 20
Neals
  Sarah 20
Needles 204
  John 26
  Sarah 26
Nelson 195
Nevin
  John 114
New Castle 10, 11, 20, 35, 36, 39, 63, 94, 97, 202, 208, 209, 212, 213, 215, 235-238, 250, 251, 260, 269
New Castle Co 10, 11, 20, 35, 36, 39, 63, 94, 97, 202, 208, 209, 212, 213, 215, 235, 236, 238, 250, 251, 269
New Jersey 251
Newcomb 33, 163
Newman 96, 267
  Elizabeth 7
  George N. 144
  James 7
  Joel G. 144
  Lorenzo 7
  Mary 144
  Nathan M. 7
  Temperance 109, 144
  William 7
Newnam 86
Newton 53, 134, 164
  Ann 97
  Eliza 97
  Josiah 97
  Thomas 97
  Zedekiah 97
Nichols
  Eliza 16
Nicholson 27, 30, 51, 144
  Catharine 7
  Charles R. 8
  Edward 8
  Elizabeth 8
  Hannah 8
  Maria 8
  Nancy 8
  Rachel 8
  Thomas 7
Nickerson
  Samuel 271
Nicols 23, 62, 72, 108, 110, 132, 150, 181, 260
  Anna Maria 135, 259
  Athalia 214
  Eliza 17, 74
  Elizabeth 17, 72, 75, 135, 137, 259
  Elizabeth H. 72, 74
  Frederick 214, 226
  George Washington 116
  Harriot M. 157
  Harry 259
  Henrietta 17, 82
  Henrietta M. 72
  Henry 116, 135
  James 17, 72, 74, 75, 82, 107, 110, 157
  James K. 157
  Jeremiah 75, 135, 137, 259
  Jeremiah Jr. 135
  Jonathan 116

Margaret 72, 107
Margaret S. 72, 74
Margarett 17, 82
Maria 214
Maria Nicols 214
Mary 17, 82
Mary S. 72, 74,
   106
Richard L.L. 259
Richard Lloyd 135
Sarah 82
Sarah A. 72
Sarah Ann 17
Sarah H. 74
Selid 214
Thomas 17, 82
Thomas S. 107
William 17
Nivin
  Alethea Lavinia
    Woodland 253
Norman
  Elizabeth 174
Norris 62, 136, 137,
  149, 172, 266, 273
  Christianna 190
  Hannah A. 148
  Hannah Ann 272
  John A. 272
  John C. 148
  Mary Ann 148, 272
  Susan 148
  Thomas E. 273
  William P. 272
Nowland 63, 236, 237,
  267
  Alfred C. 236
  Benedict T. 166
  Dennis 20
  Elizabeth 24
  Harriott 20
  James 20
  James L. 20
  Jesse 24
  John H. 20
  Lambert 20

Sarah 166
Sylvester 24
Thomas 24
Numbers
  Ann M. 70
  Ann Maria 116
  Edmund 70, 116
  Martha Elizabeth
    116
  Thomas 116
Offly
  Henrietta 186
  Ogle 202
Oldham 267
  George W. 267
  Hamilton 267
  Martha Ella 267
  Mary Amanda 267
  Susan A. 267
Oliver 142
  Eliza Ann 107
  James 107, 153
  Mary 107
Osborn 106, 122, 127,
  147, 183, 214
  Catharine M. 137
  John W. 177
  Samuel G. 137
  William M.K. 137
Osborne 10, 67, 110
Owen 230
  Helen 275
  Maria Louise 275
  Sarah Maria Louise
    275
Owens 210, 244
Ozman 142, 158
PA 10, 72, 76, 77, 97,
  135, 136, 208,
  218, 239, 259,
  265, 272
Pacca
  Mrs. Julianna 75
Page 13, 25, 87, 122
  Ann 23
  Ann Jr. 122

Ann Sr. 122
Elizabeth O. 122
Frances C. 122
Henry 23
James M. 158
Jane Louisa 122
Julia E. 122
Sarah E. S. 258
Palmer 17, 63, 149,
  168, 244
  Editha 11, 12
  Edward 11
  Elizabeth 11
  John 12
  John Jr. 11
  Mary 11
  Matilda 177
  William 177
Pane
  Elizabeth 192
Pardee 96, 97
Parker 206, 221
  Catharine 74, 76
  Catherine 103
  Derrick 137
  Elizabeth 76, 137
  Hannah 76
  James 74, 76, 103,
    104
  Joseph 76
  Maria 194
  Ned 224
  William 76, 114,
    137
Parks 111, 137, 172,
  202, 210
  Alexander R. 108
  George W. 108
  James D. 108
  Maria H. 108
  Thomas R. 108
  William 108
  William W. 108
Parrish 164
Parrott 62, 137, 225,
  233

Index of Names and Places

Benjamin 172-174
Benjamin W.B. 172
George R. 172
John B. 172, 225
Mary R. 172, 174
Mary Rebecca 173
Rachel B. 172
Robert T. 172
Sarah L. 172
Parsley
  Noble 121
Parson 262
Parsons 9, 142, 199, 210
  Isaac 183
  John 261
  Joseph 84
  Juliett 261
  Mary 108
  Sarah 84
Patten
  James W. 178
Patterson 40
Payne
  Anna M. 219
Peacock 101, 113, 196, 261, 270
  Catharine Ann 261
  Editha E. 191
  Editha Elizabeth 261
  Elizabeth 163
  John W. 261
  Milliminta 261
  Richard 261
  Sarah 261
  William 191, 261
Pearce 23, 26, 41, 64, 73, 84, 91, 108, 143, 162, 190, 192, 205, 234, 254, 255, 261, 262, 267
  Alfred 255

Ann 43
Ann O. 254
Ann Ophelia 101
Catherine 101
Catherine J. 254
Edward 110
George William 101
Henry Kennard 43
James 43, 49, 91, 101
James Alfred 101, 254, 255
James Alfred Jr. 255
James Jr. 43
Joseph 43
Kitty 43
Lottie 254
Mary 23, 43, 110
Mary Clementine 254
Matilda C. 255
Sarah 43
Sarah A. 254
Sarah Ann 254
Susannah 43
Thomas 147
William 110
Pears
  Emily 126
Pearson 276
Peggot 208
Pell
  Temperance 11
Pendleton
  Lavinia Jane 69
Pennington 28, 48, 267
  Edward B. 106
  Emily A. 106
  Hyland B. 94
  John Hawkins 24
  Mary 244
  Mary A. 106
  Pere 244

Robert A. 106
Rosetta A. 106
Sarah A. 106
Sarah R. 244
William A. 106
Perce
  Cassandra 21
Perkins 112, 119, 150, 159, 165, 190, 216, 227, 229, 242, 250, 278
  Ann 122, 142, 250
  Ann Augusta 142
  Ann Wallis 150, 179
  Benjamin B. 143
  Caroline 142, 190, 250, 274, 275
  Catharine Emma 179
  E.C. 275
  Eliza 142
  Elizabeth Ann 179
  Ezekial C. 275
  Francis 143
  G.W.T. 275
  George 275
  George W. T. 274, 276
  George W.T. 143
  Henrietta 122, 150, 179
  Henry 122, 179, 272
  Isaac 122, 150, 179
  James A. 143
  John 122, 150
  Julius 272
  Levi Wroth 179
  Margaret Elizabeth 179
  Sally Maria 122, 179
  Sarah 142

Sarah Maria 150
William 122, 179
Philadelphia 43, 72,
    74, 76, 78, 81, 97,
    106, 124, 136,
    146, 156, 210,
    212, 216, 220,
    231, 256, 257,
    265, 269, 271, 277
Philips 34
    George 98
    James 85
    Sarah 85
    Wealthy 85
Phillips 216
Pienny
    Elizabeth 190
Pierce 102
Pierson 196, 231, 241
    James Boon 170
    John W. 170
Pinder 193
Piner
    Ann Rebecca 93
    Bartis 93
    Bartus 93
    John Day 234
    Louisa H. 93
    Mary Lavenia 93
    Rebecca 93
    Sarah 62
Pinkind 158, 205, 221
Piper 250
Pippin 178
Plummer 43, 173, 262
Polk 213
    Amelia H. 213
    Anna L. 212, 213
    Elizabeth R. 213
    Henry C. 213
    John P. R. 212, 213
    Margaret 208
    Robert 202, 212,
        213
    Sarah 213

William Reybold
    212
Porter 55, 85, 193
    Ann Maria 203, 232
    Ann V. 232
    Anna V. 232
    Bill 232
    Charlotte 232
    Charlotte P. 78
    George 203, 232
    George B. 78
    George M. 232
    Henry 193
    Henry A. 202
    Henry Porter 232
    John A. 202
    Joseph 202, 203
    Joseph Henry 232
    Joseph Jr. 202
    Mary 203
    Millicent Henrietta
        232
    Pere 232
    Peter 232
    Sarah Matilda 232
    Sarah Rebecca 232
    Susan 193
    Victoria 203
    William Thomas
        193
Posey
    Eliza Jane 249
Poultney 32
Powell 218
    Editha Elizabeth
        261
Prettyman 191
Price 25, 48, 83, 84,
    120, 160, 170,
    175, 180, 182,
    195, 201, 205,
    230, 238, 265
    Adeline 151
    Ann 48
    Ann M. 150

Anna Maria 151,
    164
Benjamin 63, 150,
    164
Benjamin F. 151
Benjamin Franklin
    164
Caroline 269
Edwin 238
Elizabeth 63, 238
George W. 238
George Washington
    164
Hibert B. 63
Hyland Benson 150
Isaac 63
Isaac L. 150
Isaac Lewis 150,
    164
Isabella 158
James 190
John 48, 164, 238
Joseph 48
Kitty 48
Lydia A. 238, 239
Mary 151, 269
Mary A. 243, 250
Mary L. 239
Mitchell 273
Peregrine 151, 204
Permelia Howard
    204
Perry 164, 238
Perry J. Maxwell
    238
Richard Lockwood
    238
Samuel 48, 238
Sarah 63
Sarah Matilda 151
Spencer 63
William Henry 151,
    164
Prichard
    Emeline 115
    Primrose 121

Index of Names and Places

Joseph Henry 203
Mary 203
Thomas 203
Proud 125
Pryor
  Lawrence Pike 119
  William 119
Punkers
  Elizabeth 157
Quaker 26, 79, 88,
  120, 135, 138,
  140, 156, 176,
  184, 192, 270
Quaker Branch 270
Quaker Neck 79, 88,
  120, 135, 138,
  140, 156, 176,
  184, 192
Queen Annes Co 7,
  111, 210, 213,
  244, 245, 262, 263
Queen Anns Co 3, 51,
  53, 54, 55, 61, 69,
  73, 74, 79, 81, 82,
  95, 96, 97, 116,
  119, 132, 135,
  142, 143, 147,
  148, 196, 200,
  201, 203, 204,
  245, 258, 271
Quimby 61, 221, 272
Ramsey
  Albert C. 160
  Sarah R. 160
Randall
  Elizabeth A. 131
Randolph 26
Ransallear
  Elizabeth 132
  William 132
Rarole
  Mary 74

Rasin 22, 24, 34, 88,
  101, 116, 185,
  227, 242, 261
Alfred R. 214, 215
Araminta 40
Edward 207
Edward F. 208
Henry H. 208
Isaac Freeman 208
James M. 207
Joseph 78, 246
Mary R. 207, 214
Phebe W. 207
Philip F. 207
Rebecca 78
Robert W. 208,
  214, 215
Robert W. Jr. 214
Robert W. Sr. 215
Sarah 8
Sarah Ann 184
Sarah H. 184
Thomas 184
William Blackiston
  ii
Ratcliff
  Eliza 97
  Susan 97
Raughley 204
  James 204
  Sarah Ann 204
Rawleigh 270
Rayen
  James 131
  James T. 131
  Julia Ann 131
  William 131
Read
  Elizabeth 244
Reading 278
  Abraham 210
  Alexander 210
  Frisby 210
  Isaac 210

Margaret 210
Sarah 210
Redding
  Alethia 199
  James Richard 199
  Louisa 170
  Mary Ann 199
  Melicent M. 51
  Nathaniel 199
  Rebecca 199
  Richard 199
  William 51
Reddle
  Mary 78
Redgrave 35, 162
  Isaac 14, 47
  John 14
  Joseph H. 164
  Lancelot W. 164
  Milliminta 127
  Millyminta 164
  Millyminta R. 164
  William 14
  William M. 164
Redue 17, 66, 99, 114,
  124, 125, 139,
  141, 143, 150,
  151, 155, 175,
  179, 182
  Emeline 173
Reed 3, 12, 99, 100,
  114, 115, 117, 150
  Eliza 69
  Emaline 111
  Emeline 87
  Frances Phelina 185
  George 63
  George R. 144, 185
  Hosanna 49, 63
  Joseph 63, 144
  Kitty 225
  Mary 63
  Philip 114
  Philip George 87

Samuel 63
Rees
  John T. 77
  Reese 111
  John T. 109
  John Thomas 106
Register
  Sophia 192
  William 192
Reybold 215
  Ann 208
  Anthony 208
  Barney 208
  Clayton 208
  Elizabeth 208
  George W. 208
  John 208
  John Jr. 208
  Margaret 208
  Philip 208, 215
  Philip Jr. 208
  Susan 208
  William 208, 213
Reynolds 238
  James 182
Ricaud 108, 112, 138,
  141, 149, 153,
  162, 163, 166,
  170, 171, 173,
  175, 176, 181,
  182, 195, 198,
  202, 215, 217,
  221, 251, 258-260,
  266, 275, 276, 278
  Charles Gordon 181
  Cornelia 169
  J. B. 182
  James B. 169
  Laurence M. 171
  Mary Rebecca 182
Rich 183, 202, 203, 210
  James H. 210
Richardson 199, 237
  Elanor 107
  John 211
  Mary Hyland 273

  William 231
Ricketts
  Jane 31
  Juliana 98
  Ridgaway 55
  Araminta 55
  Henry 55
  James 55
  James Asbury 55
  James Ridgaway 55
  Mary Louisa 55
Rigby
  Charles 91
  Elizabeth 91
  Margaret 92
  Milcah 91, 160
  Robert 92
  Thomas 92
Riley 108, 178, 196,
  223
  Casparus Meginnis
    77
  Casparus Meginniss
    86
  Clementia 165
  Eliza 40
  Hannah 86
  John Crow 77
  Nicholas 77
  Samuel 77
  Samuel Jr. 77
  William 77
Ringgold 4, 13, 15,
  16, 27, 36, 37, 39,
  48, 54, 56, 57, 62,
  64, 70, 71, 75, 76,
  86, 88, 96, 102,
  104, 105, 107,
  109, 110, 122,
  136, 137, 138,
  160, 164, 182,
  215, 244-246, 261,
  264
  Alexander Hamilton
    12

  Alexander W. 38,
    138
  Ann 214
  Ann Elizabeth 244,
    251
  Ann Rebecca 38,
    196
  Ann Worrell 73
  Anna W. 38
  Caroline 181
  Catharine 180
  Daniel 278
  Delia 226
  Edward 213, 214,
    226
  Elizabeth 15, 64
  Emory 214
  Frances 37, 64, 105
  Francis 15
  George W. 214
  George Washington
    38
  Hannah R. 213
  Harry 214, 226
  Henrietta 105, 179
  Hester 105
  Jacob 38, 197
  James 38, 226
  James B. 213
  James Brown 196
  Jane E. 214
  Jervis 55
  John 214
  John E. 214
  John Edward 216,
    226
  John Fletcher 213,
    214, 215, 226
  Josias 122, 179,
    246
  Louisa 214
  Marion 214
  Martha E. 214
  Mary 38, 196, 216,
    246

Index of Names and Places

Mary Ann 139, 196, 244
Mary Catherine 157
Mary Elizabeth 72
Mary G. 246
Mary Groome 246
Mary Isabella 243
Mary R. 214
Mary Rebecca 214, 215, 226, 227
Pere 211
Peregrine 12
Rachel Amanda 196
Rebecca 15, 37, 38, 64, 213, 226
Richard 38
Richard W. 38, 138, 157, 196
Samuel 104, 196, 200, 213, 214
Samuel Jr. 213
Samuel Sr. 215
Sarah 15, 37, 38, 64, 150, 196, 210
Sarah A. 278
Sarah Ann 243
Sarah Catharine H. 216, 226
Sarah Francina 72
Sarah Jane 214
Sarah R. 139
Sophia 12
Sophia Luana 12
Thomas 244
Thomas W. 38, 196, 243
William 12
William Fletcher 226, 227
William P. 38
William S. 12
Roach
　Ann 6
　Benjamin 6, 61

Elizabeth 6, 61
Hannah 6
James 6, 61
James Jr. 6, 61
John 6, 61
Philip 6
Philip Jr. 6
Richard 6
Roberts 163
　Mary 82
Robesson 260
Robinson 35, 238, 268
　Hannah 214
　Harriett 214
　James V. 214
　John 238
　Stella 214
Robson 250
Roby 174
Roche
　John Alexander 204
　Sarah 204
Rochester 4
　Ann E. 68
　Elizabeth J. 68
Rock Hall 38, 123, 142, 152, 160, 162, 186, 187, 200, 206, 222, 245
Rodenhiser
　George A. 274
Rodness 253
Rodney 209, 260, 266
Roe 262
　Daniel 162
　Sophia 162
Roeder 202, 221, 233
　Aaron 201
　Abraham 201
　George 201
　George P. 201
　John A.H. 201
　Margarett 201
　Maria 201

William F. 201
Rogers 9, 78, 203
　Sarah C. 205
　Sarah Etta 241
　William 241
Rollins
　Ann 158
Rollinson
　John A. 155
Rollison 118, 140, 167, 176, 191, 217, 256, 264
Rolph
　Mary Ann 252
　Samuel J. 252
Rose
　Martha Ann 196
Roseberry 264
Ross
　Milcha 27
Rossoe
　Kate 187
Rothwell 238
Rueter 235
Runnels
　Mary 93
　Richard 93
Rush
　Mary 27
　Thomas 27
Russel
　Christopher 94
　Christopher Jr. 94
　John 94
　Robert 94
　Sarah 94
　Simeon 94
　William 94
Russell 41, 176, 190, 193, 221, 248
　Hester Ann 158
　James Alexander 158
　John 158

317

John Hamer 158
Richard 94
Theophilus Waters
  158
William George 158
Ruth 133, 176, 186,
  257, 263, 275, 276
James L. 176
John 176
Mary 176
Rebecca 176
Rebecca August 45
Rebecca Augusta
  139
Temperance 176
Rutter 26, 254
  Elizabeth 26
  Francis 26
  John 26
  Mary 26
Ryland 163, 175
Ryley 1
Ryner
  Mary 70
Salisbury 45, 46, 51,
  63, 137
  Elizabeth 137
  James 137
  William D. 137
Salloway 263
Salter
  Caty 157
  Katy 161
Sampson
  Bill 234
  Rachel 198
Sanders 35, 102
  Emily 127
  George C. 35
Sappington 17, 27, 61,
  89, 99, 179, 197,
  249, 278
  Caroline 205
  Elizabeth 61
  James B. 205
  John 61

Margret M.V.F.
  205
Mary 210
Nathaniel 29
Ruthey 29
Sophia 61
Susan 29
Thomas 52
William 29
Sassafras 41, 50, 53,
  54, 61, 86, 94,
  128, 211, 235,
  238, 256, 267
Satterfield 200
Saunders 11
  John 24
Sawyer 72
Scanllin
  Catharine 40
  Dr. 40
Schley
  Sarah Maria 54
Scone 16, 17
Scoone
  Martha 27
Scott 14, 18, 21, 33,
  45, 53, 70, 97,
  106, 137, 156,
  165, 190, 203,
  224, 233, 241,
  248, 270, 277
  Ann 33
  Anna M. 223
  Anna Maria 149,
    223
  Catharine A. 223
  Cornelius J. 224
  Doctor 230
  E. 145
  Edward 149, 223
  Edward A. 223
  Eliza 231
  Elizabeth 223
  Isaac 87
  John R. 205
  Julianna F. 205

Kitty 33
Maria 230
Sarah 117
Sophia C. 223
William 33
Scotten
  Sarah 270
Selby 164
Semans 24, 93
Seth 105
Severson 61
Sewall 70
  Mary 63, 70
Sewell 28, 33, 92
  Edward 42
  John 42
  Lambert 42
  Lorenzo 42
  Richard 42
  Thomas 42
  William 42
Seymour 70, 78
Sharp
  Mary K. 254
Sharpe
  Mary K. 254
Sharpless
  Maria 78
Shaw 50, 108, 158,
  265
  Martha 110
  Mary 50
  William 50
Shehan
  Thomas 52
Shephard
  Margaret Ann 265
Sherwood
  Araminta 211
  William 211
Shields 170
Shoemaker
  Augusta C. 248
  Samuel M. 248
Short
  Edward 174

Index of Names and Places

Elizabeth 174
Francis Asbury 174
George Washington 174
Isaac 174
Sarah 204
Sarah Ann 204
William Hyland 174
Shrewsbury 37, 50, 84, 91, 230
Shubrick
  Harriet 31
Shubrook
  Mary 41
Shuster 262, 276
Siddall 78
Silcox 128, 134
Simmonds 27, 173
  Ann 27
  Elizabeth 50
  Joseph 50
  Joshua 50
  Phillip 50
  Rebecca 108
  Rebecca B. 128
  Robert 50
  Robert G. 108, 128
  Samuel 27, 50
  Sarah 50
  William 50
Simms 262
Simons
  Richard 45
Sinclair
  Henrietta 190
Singo
  Bill 84
  Dave 84
Sintan 15
Sinton 266
  Elizabeth 266
  James B. 266
  Joseph 266
  Joseph W. 266

Martha A. 266
Mary Ann 266
Rachael 266
Rebecca 266
Skaggs 132
  Lloyd 140
  Martha Melvina 140
Skeggs 227
Skigg 52
Skinner 192, 203
  Alice 198
  Bachellor 198
  Charles 198
  Harriett 198
  Henrietta 198
  Jane 198
  John 198
  Mary Ann 198
  Philemon 198
  Virginia 198
  Zebulon 198
Skinners
  Philemon 199
Skinvin 221
Skirven 38, 168, 171, 173, 204, 207, 261, 262, 268
  Elizabeth 15, 17
  George 66
  James A. 268
  John T.K. 111
  John W. 207
  Martha E. 207
  Mary 111
  Mary E. 268
  Matilda 15, 17
  Sarah 111, 268
  Sarah G. 207
  Susan Frances 268
  Thomas 15, 17
  Thomas W. 111, 207
  Washington G. 207
  William 15, 17

William T. 268
Slave
  Mary Ellen 233
Slaves
  Aaron 255
  Abe 24, 83, 118, 141, 228, 230, 254, 258
  Abe Stanly 235
  Abraham 14, 84, 112, 118, 177
  Abram 186
  Adam 5, 30, 121, 229
  Adeline 181
  Adron 66
  Affa 129
  Agnettee 212
  Ailcey 165
  Ailey 130
  Albert 18, 21
  Aleck 66
  Alethea 228
  Alethia Waters 228
  Alexander 48, 101, 150, 165, 169, 212, 248
  Alexander Yearly Moore 234
  Alexas 130, 165
  Alexine 258
  Alfred 98, 121, 163
  Alice 87
  Alice Alfred 215
  Alick 165
  Allen 198
  Ally 121
  Alonzo 130, 165, 184, 258
  Alsey 203
  Amanda 111, 125, 225, 227
  Amelia 206
  Amos 228, 254

Amy 41, 133
Andrew 171
Andrew Hemphill
  Carmichael 234
Angelina 83
Angeline 46
Ann 21, 42, 45, 47,
  63, 69, 73, 79, 81,
  85, 87, 95, 101,
  104, 129, 141,
  149, 150, 154-156,
  159, 162, 165,
  177, 181, 186,
  206, 214, 239,
  245, 254
Ann M. Rolls 274
Ann Mariah 67
Ann Selina 132
Anna 165
Anne 130
Annett 130
Annette 165
Annie 223
Anthony 81
Araminta 118, 206
Arianna 130, 182
Arthur 99, 234
Arthur Moore 234
Artur 29
Ashbery 50
Athalia 214
Beck 14, 27, 59,
  66, 133, 230
Beckey 10, 159,
  259
Becky 10, 161, 274
Ben 31, 106, 141,
  161, 186, 246, 254
Ben Dunn 271
Benjamin 9, 11, 29,
  42, 121, 141
Besse 258
Bet 77, 96
Betsey 89, 103, 159
Betsy 29, 259
Bett 159

Betts 106
Betty 16, 20, 59,
  62, 179, 181
Bill 2, 5, 19, 25,
  29, 46, 59, 66, 77,
  82, 84, 87, 89, 98,
  105, 106, 129,
  156, 162, 166,
  175, 186, 232,
  239, 260, 274
Bill Sampson 234
Bill Tinch 230
Bill's 190
Billy Tilghman 275
Binah 110
Bob 11, 70, 254
Brown 95
Buck 154
Bun 185
Caroline 4, 19, 45,
  96, 127, 156, 165,
  212, 223, 229, 234
Cassa 13, 32
Cate 9, 106
Catherine 64
Cecilia 21
Celia 121
Cezar 11
Charity 8, 121
Charles 17, 29, 54,
  59, 73, 80, 96, 97,
  99, 106, 108, 129,
  130, 177, 184,
  186, 229, 233,
  243, 245, 258
Charles Rolls 274
Charley 3, 12
Charlott 159
Charlotte 8, 19, 35,
  39, 45, 73, 98,
  114, 118, 121,
  130, 133, 139,
  177, 182, 184,
  202, 232, 245,
  246, 257, 258
Charlotte Ann 239

Charlotte Ward 258
Chester 3
Chiners 222
Chloe 184
Clant 5
Clanth 42
Clara 254
Clara Wilson 266
Clarey 19
Clarissa 19, 120
Cleanes 58
Clement 86
Clenus 151
Clinton 118, 165,
  258
Cloe 130
Cuff 5, 185
Dan 239, 274
Daniel 5, 41, 45,
  46, 98, 112, 114,
  115, 116, 121,
  130, 132, 165,
  184, 198, 207,
  224, 259
Dark 28
Darkey 3, 45
Darky 77
Dave 84, 192
David 4, 21, 22,
  30, 42, 45, 59, 87,
  95, 125, 127, 142,
  245, 254
Deb 87
Deborah 87, 126
Delia 66, 98, 169,
  226, 258
Dennis 40
Dennis Spencer 11
Dick 59, 108, 203
Dinah 5, 25, 245
Dolly 149
Dos 20
Easter 161
Eben 29, 234
Eda 141
Ede 8

Index of Names and Places

Editha 69, 166
Edward 18, 60, 63, 87, 163
Edwin 14, 45, 87, 89, 163, 166, 167, 258
Edy 140
Elick 169
Eliza 21, 93, 143, 154, 165, 177, 191, 245, 258
Eliza Ann 185
Eliza Blake 274
Eliza Dunn 271
Elizabeth 21, 45, 69, 95, 149, 150, 155, 163, 179, 191, 203, 206, 219, 248
Elizabeth Warner 252
Elizer 9
Elleck 191
Ellen 71, 163, 185, 189, 194, 215, 239, 254, 258, 259, 274
Ellen Worrell 215
Ellick 34, 77, 182
Emeline 29, 42, 46, 83, 89, 187
Emiline 10, 89
Emily 150, 198, 212, 215, 225
Emily Blackiston 234
Emily Hazzard 214
Emma 121, 130, 219
Emmeline 73, 79
Emoline 154
Emory 9, 12, 14, 35, 41, 87, 133, 150, 158, 176,
177, 182, 186, 214, 215, 225, 258, 259
Eneas 20
Ester 45
Esther 45
Eve 219
Eveline 163
Ewing 4
Ezekal 198
Ezekial 18
Fan 162
Fanny 4, 5, 34, 79, 88, 125, 129, 189, 202, 245, 258, 259
Felix 77, 80, 105
Ferdinand 228
Ferry 121
Fillis 3, 30
Flora 165
Florence 189
Frances 163
Frank 3, 29, 121, 150, 169
Franky 86
Frederick 5, 82, 105, 112, 259
Frederick Nicols 214, 226
Frisby 66, 95, 166
George 3, 18, 20, 21, 23, 45, 46, 49, 59, 66, 69-71, 73, 76, 77, 80, 82-84, 96, 100, 106, 110, 114, 115, 151, 154, 166, 169, 174, 191, 194, 197, 202, 223, 232, 234, 241, 254, 259
George Anna 229
George Hinds 252
Gloster 88
Grace 22, 139
Gustavius 254
Hank 11
Hanna 149
Hannah 14, 25, 41, 56, 62, 66, 98, 114, 116, 118, 135, 185, 203, 206, 243, 246
Hannah Robinson 214
HannahiSlaves 5
Hanson 121
Harcules 9
Hark 11, 103
Harriet 5, 9, 22, 31, 37, 73, 74, 79, 83, 98, 121, 132, 150, 198, 212, 223
Harriett 29, 87, 98, 106, 127, 129, 138, 139, 162, 177, 186, 198, 214, 228
Harriett Hazzard 214
Harriett Robinson 214
Harriot 66, 156
Harriott 60, 69
Harry 59, 69, 83, 108, 150, 175, 214, 215, 226
Harvey 192
Hemsley 203
Henny 2, 82, 95, 166, 203
Henrietta 82, 83, 165, 177
Henry 4, 5, 11, 21, 30, 41, 42, 45, 72, 74, 77, 88, 103, 114, 118, 121, 125, 135,

149-151, 156,
158, 162, 176,
186, 191, 212,
219, 233, 239,
245, 258, 259
Henry Anderson
214
Henry Warner 252
Hester 104, 165,
185, 206, 259
Hetty 4, 99, 111
Hezekiah 185
Horace 87, 176
Horrice 143
Hynson 150
Ib 127
Ibbe 127
Isaac 3, 5, 8, 13,
14, 15, 28, 30, 32,
41, 46, 47, 59, 68,
79, 87, 95, 118,
129, 133, 150,
151, 178, 194,
239, 257, 259
Isaac Jr. 41
Isabel 259
Isaiah 69, 174
Jack 112, 141, 152,
185
Jacob 10, 17, 21,
34, 69, 149, 161,
162, 166, 167,
176, 178, 229, 234
Jacob Hazzard 214
Jacob Tobeyo 3
Jake 46, 212, 254
James 9, 11, 14,
16, 25, 27, 35, 36,
41, 45, 69, 76, 83,
86, 87, 118, 120,
130, 139, 154,
155, 165, 182,
194, 206, 226,
233, 239
James Aron 212

James V. Robinson
214
Jane 46, 47, 106,
114, 118, 126,
135, 159, 162,
181, 203, 215,
224, 258, 260
Jarrel 9
Jean 34
Jefferson 83, 110
Jenny 20, 46, 114
Jenny Lind 228
Jere 4
Jeremiah Taylor
216
Jerry 129
Jess 258
Jesse 146
Jestina 248
Jim 5, 8, 10, 12,
25, 46, 59, 62, 71,
73, 79, 92, 98,
111, 112, 118,
129, 139, 149,
161, 162, 166,
169, 182, 184,
186, 258, 259
Jim boy 46
Jim Fray 10
Jimmy 196
Jin 162
Job 95
Joe 37, 46, 129,
152, 228, 258
John 34, 41, 42,
55, 59, 62, 66, 67,
69, 82, 93, 116,
142, 175, 182,
183, 191, 192,
197, 205, 212,
214, 224, 227,
258, 259
John Day Piner 234
John Robinson 238
John W. Rolls 274
John Warner 252

John Wesley 229
Jonas 5
Joseph 89, 95, 118,
147, 148, 163,
206, 258
Joseph Butler 3
Josephine 212
Joshua 158
Josiah 69, 152
Joyce 71
Julia 20, 83, 130,
149, 165, 166,
189, 228, 239,
245, 254
July 121
Kate 233, 273
Katy 161
Kelly Dunn 271
Kitty 45, 82, 129
Kitty Frizby 234
Kity 140
Lavena 96
Lavinia 118, 161,
165
Lavinia Bright 216
Ledia 77
Lee 225
Lem 149
Lervis 46
Letty 66, 98, 129
Levi 28, 39, 42,
47, 59, 92, 109,
198
Levina 87, 204
Levinia 87
Levy 121
Lewesa 154
Lewis 31, 45, 72,
88, 198, 225, 254
Lewisir 154
Little Abe 230
Lize 162
Lorenzo 223
Louis 198
Louis Jerome 215
Louis Rolls 274

Index of Names and Places

Louisa 66, 79, 177, 239
Lucy 62, 177, 239, 259
Luicia 30
Luis 34
Luke 121
Lydia 25, 129, 197, 228
Mammy Grace 21
Margaret 7, 55, 83, 115, 116, 185, 189, 219, 246, 258
Margarett 115
Maria 3, 9, 19, 21, 25, 35, 41, 45, 47, 69, 77, 80, 90, 95, 103, 116, 125, 129, 139, 155, 158, 185, 194, 199, 214, 215, 223, 246, 254, 258, 259
Maria Carmichael 234
Maria Nicols 214
Mariah 8
Marian 248
Marion 214
Martha 77, 154, 219, 248
Martha Ann 239
Mary 10, 11, 18, 29, 45, 59, 62, 66, 67, 79, 86, 87, 89, 95, 101, 103, 110, 112, 114, 118, 143, 147, 158, 162, 163, 179, 180, 184, 186, 197, 198, 203, 206, 216, 257, 259
Mary Ann 45, 132, 223

Mary Elizabeth 239
Mary Ellen 242
Mary Hazzard 214
Mary Jane 62, 233
Mary Rebecca Tilison 252
Matilda 18, 95, 223
Matilda Tilison 252
Melissa 19
Melvina 246
Michael 45
Mike 259
Milcah 45, 177, 259
Mill 31
Millicent 23
Milly 67, 84, 203
Minta 3, 32, 69, 90, 115
Minty 29, 35, 69, 79, 99, 114, 121
Molly 21
Monica 121
Mortimer 103
Moses 14, 66, 69, 73, 98, 129, 149
Moses Berry 214, 216
Mosses 46
Nace 25
Nan 5, 20, 77
Nance 20
Nancy 84, 101, 132, 177, 245
Nannie 197
Nat 20
Nathan 25, 105, 158, 186
Nathaniel 45
Ned 59, 60, 63, 77, 156, 180, 185, 228, 258
Ned Parker 224
Nell 4

Nelly 31
Nelson 239
Noah 7, 177
Pat 29, 54, 154, 259
Patty 203, 254
Paul 4
Peggy 212
Pere 29, 54, 69, 77, 89, 99, 114, 149, 150, 155, 232, 259
Pere Cotton 259
Peregrine 21, 100
Perry 3, 4, 8, 14, 19, 27, 31, 35, 46, 47, 67, 70, 88, 95, 141, 155, 162, 171, 184, 190, 196, 245, 246, 258
Persey 71
Pery 34
Peter 105, 196, 232
Phany 84
Phil 20, 28, 120, 239
Philip 24, 31, 127
Philis 122
Phill 11
Phillis 20, 21, 59, 80, 121
Phobe 132
Poll 12
Polly 80, 172, 243
Pomp 44
Pompey 258
Primas 54
Pris 163
Priscilla 98
Priss 133
Rachel 2, 3, 12, 14, 19, 25, 41, 58, 66, 68, 73, 98, 108, 121, 129, 139,

323

151, 189, 191, 194, 198, 206
Rainy 182
Rebecca 3, 21, 28, 165, 260
Rees 59
Reynolds 196
Richard 23, 27, 29, 41, 67, 69, 150, 151, 162, 177, 183, 251
Richard Hazzard 214
Richard Worrell 214
Robert 3, 28, 166, 202, 224, 243
Robert Allen 274
Rosalia 239
Rose 25, 30, 212
Ruben 41
Ruth 68, 261
Sal 48, 155, 185
Sall 46, 106
Sally 59, 82, 121, 165, 182, 185, 194, 257
Sam 2, 8, 12, 23, 46, 60, 71, 84, 95, 162, 181, 185, 186, 197, 201, 243, 258, 259
Sam Butler 3
Samuel 11, 21, 88, 229
Sandy 5, 8, 59, 121, 175, 182
Sara 154
Sarah 4, 17, 45, 58, 69, 71, 73, 76, 87, 95, 98, 112, 116, 119, 131, 155, 158, 161, 166, 169, 171, 186, 189, 206, 213, 228, 233, 254

Sarah Blackiston 234
Sarah Jane 214
Sarah Rebecca 232
Saul 31
Selid Nicols 214
Shadarick 165
Shade 34
Shadrach 228
Sharlot 248
Sharlotte Warner 252
Shurlett 202
Silvia 141
Silvy 39
Simon 35, 95, 116, 179, 196, 255
Sinah 46
Solomon 127, 186
Sophia 114
Spence 18
Standly 55
Stella Robinson 214
Step 46
Stephan 45
Stephen 68, 118, 163, 231
Stephen Hardin 234
Steve 77
Suck 46
Sue 5
Suke 21
Susan 3, 28, 30, 53, 141, 168, 177, 229, 231, 257
Susan Berry 214
Susan Chase 214
Sylvia 77, 258
Tabitha 45
Taraham 90
Temp 8
Tempe 219
Temperance 19, 21, 45, 46
Tempy 5, 162, 241
Tene 4

Theodore 67, 71, 132
Thomas 4, 27, 76, 85, 89, 104, 114, 135, 138, 158
Thomas Worrell 215
Thomas Wright 215
Tilghman 186
Tilly 71
Tom 5, 8, 20, 25, 62, 66, 77, 112, 138, 162, 259
Toney 56
Vilette 29
Vin 64
Vincent 64, 76
Vind 118
Washington 10, 66, 95
Washington Smith 214
Wesley 225
Wesly 120
Will 84
Willey 58
William 19, 45, 73, 103, 112, 155, 162, 198, 245
William Doran 232
William H. Warner 252
William Henry Moore 234
William Tilison 252
Willie 219, 254
Williy 175
Wilson 31
Wright 186
Zeb 3
Slay 273
Sloan
  Mary 43
Slubey
  Isabella 124
  Mary M. 124

Index of Names and Places

Nicholas 124
William 124
Sluby
  Eleanor 124
  Mary McCarty 124
Smith 6, 13, 16, 33, 36, 42, 44, 52, 69, 97, 99, 100, 104, 112, 118, 123, 133, 134, 154, 157, 181, 210, 216, 225, 236, 247, 253, 256, 273, 278
  A.M.M. 146
  Amelia 78
  Andasia Virginia 146
  Ann 147
  Ann B. 217
  Ann Catherine 177
  Ann H. 125
  Ann Hanson 78
  Anna Louisa 146
  Anna M.M. 278
  Anna Maria Margaretta 134, 146
  Anna Minta 67
  Anny 34
  Araminta 36
  Arralanta Robins 146
  Augusta 27
  Benjamin Everitt 134, 145
  Charles Anna 220
  Edward 67
  Eliza 17
  Elizabeth 118, 182, 214, 225
  Elizabeth H. 227
  Elizabeth H. N. 226
  Elizabeth Hannah Nicholson 200
  Emily 36
  George Washington Purnell 134, 145
  Hannah 27, 76, 200
  Hannah Elizabeth 51, 60
  Hannah G. 125
  Harriett 36
  James 103, 116, 217
  James H. 104, 147, 226
  Jane F. 147
  Joel 51, 60
  John F. 141
  John T. 177
  Josiah 225
  Kitty 225
  Letecia 122
  Louisa 256
  Major 60
  Margaret 52
  Margaret G. 125
  Maria 17
  Martha 52, 60
  Mary 12, 36, 103, 146
  Mary A. 125, 146
  Mary Ann 36
  Mary Jane 177
  Mary Rebecca 200
  Mary W. E. 146
  Mary W.E. 278
  Mary Wright 134
  Michael 103, 147
  Nancy 51, 60
  Nathan 116
  Oliver 67
  Pere 225
  Perry 182
  Priscilla B. 97
  Purnell Fletcher 145
  Rachel 34
  Rebecca 119
  Richard 34, 79
  Samuel W. 94
  Sarah 34, 60
  Sarah Ann 118
  Sarah Elizabeth 36, 104, 109
  Sarah Rebecca 177
  Serena L. 278
  Solomon 107, 118
  Sophia 104
  Stephen 103
  Thomas 52, 156
  Thomas Nicholson 226
  Washington 214
  William 27, 51, 60, 256
  William F. 128, 147, 220
  William P. 97
Smithers 59
Smyrna 48, 91, 210, 231, 277
Smyth 16, 17, 34, 89, 175, 176, 177, 186, 217, 235, 239, 250, 258
  Anna 257
  Anna Maria 82
  Annie Elizabeth 257
  Eliza 16
  Ella G. 257
  Harriet Augusta 257
  Henry 16
  John T. 257
  Maria 16
  Robert M. 257
  Samuel 34
  Thomas 16
  William Bedingfield 16
  William F. 257

Snow
    Bertha 126
    Daniel J. 87
    Elizabeth 126
    Hannah 87, 111, 126
    Sollaway 7
    Sparkes 102
    Sparklin 159
    Sparks 156, 178, 214, 241, 261
      Frances Ann 261
      Mary L. 173
      Susan 262
    Spear 176
      Elizabeth 96
      James 96
    Spearman
      Araminta 44
      Catherine 103
      Gideon 44
      Isabel 44
      John 44
      William 103, 104
      William Jr. 44
      William Sr. 44
    Spelman 15, 17
      Nicholas 33, 88
      Rebecca Hynson 88
    Spencer 2, 3, 7, 23, 58, 109, 115, 118, 156, 202, 217, 219, 249, 275, 276, 278
      Ann 145
      Anna 58
      Bedingfield Hands 23
      Caroline 242
      Charlotte 132, 242
      Charlotte A. 117
      Charlotte M. 184
      Elizabeth 181
      Elizabeth A. 132, 181
      Elizabeth Ann 180

George 30
Harriet M. 165
Harriett M. 184
Isaac 30, 102, 145, 181
Isaac Jr. 102, 132
Jervis 30, 102
John 102, 181
John Chapman 184
Kitty 132
Lambert W. 57, 118
Lambert W. Jr. 118
Lucy Ann 92
Maria L. 118
Martha 118
Martha S. 118
Mary 196, 242
Nancy 145
Peregrine 118
Richard 57, 117, 155
Richard Perry 58
Richard Sr. 117
Samuel 58
Samuel W. 165, 184
William 30, 102
William A. 23, 102, 181
Spry 31, 53, 61, 212, 227, 249
    Araminta 271
    Caleb W. 271
    Caleb Wright 271
    Charlotte 61
    Christopher 61
    Elizabeth 61
    Eve 61
    George 70
    George Anna 271
    George T. 213
    Georgeanna 271
    Henry 271
    James Henry 271
    Joshua 271

    Lucretia 61
    Mary 271
    Mary Rebecca 61
    Matilda 271
    Sarah 61
    Sarah Ellen 271
    Thomas Brinkley 271
    William T. 271
St. Paul 90, 161
St. Paul's 90, 161
St. Pauls 116, 124, 156
Staats 211
Stagles 234
Stake
    Elizabeth 87
Stam 184, 259
Stanley 40, 55, 244, 278
    Araminta F. 278
    Caroline V. 278
    Charles 278
    Charles A.A. 278
    Ezekial F. 278
    Mary Rebecca 278
Stanly
    Abe 235
Stant 76
    Mary Ann 133
Starling
    Elizabeth 64
    John 64
Starn 215, 233
Starr 97
Start
    Ann 176, 193
    Benjamin 105
    Benjamin H. 176, 210
    Benjamin S. 178
    Catharine 178
    James M. 176
    John 105, 192
    John W. 176
    Mary 105

Index of Names and Places

Rebecca 105
Richard 105, 193
Sarah 105, 193
Sarah R.J. 176
Solomon 105, 192
Solomon Jr. 105
Sophia 105, 192
Startt 183
Stauffer 265
Staveley
  Ann 18
  Martha 18
Stavely 34, 36, 230
  Asenath 18
  Elizabeth 18
  James 18, 47
  James Jr. 18
  Joseph 47
Stein
  Rosamond 63
Stephens 2, 15, 60,
  121, 131, 147,
  162, 198, 231
  Anna E. 268
  Anna Louisa 249
  Anna S. 268
  Emily 152
  George R. 268
  Henry R. 249
  Ida S. 268
  Jenney Jerrildeen 249
  John Toppin 152
  Julia Anna Virginia 249
  Juliann V. 140
  Mary 121, 146
  Olivia V. 277
  Olivia Virginia 170, 249
  Susan 121
  Thomas 121
  William 61

Stevens 100, 114, 181, 232
  Anna Matilda 223
  Araminty 86
  Elizabeth 86
  Emily 181
  Henrietta 100, 114
  Jacob 86, 100, 152, 223
  James Brice 100
  John Brice 100
  John T. 160
  John T. Jr. 152
  Martha Louisa 100, 114
  Mary H. 181
  Mary Henrietta 100, 114
  Mary Jane 177
  Rebecca 86
  Samuel B. 152
  Samuel H. 121
  Samuel Hynson 121
  Sarah 86
  Sarah Ann 114
  Sary 86
Stewart 163, 229, 244, 256
  Emily D. 243
  Emma D. 277
  John 132
  John E. 243
  Margaret 132
  Martha Ann 243
  Rebecca 132
Stickney 260
Still Pond 8, 9, 40, 136, 146, 194, 216, 225, 274
Stokes 239
Stoobs
  Edward 63
Stoops 12, 46, 52, 79, 84, 95, 179

  Anne 39
  Edward 151, 164
  James 38, 122
  John 39, 98, 122
  Jonas 39
Stork
  Daniel Thomas 196
  John 196
  Mary W. 204
  Rebecca C. 196
Strong 110, 116, 168, 174, 177, 185, 187, 190, 211, 240, 259
  Caroline 259
  Harriett M. 143
  John 143
  John A. 143
  Lawrence 143
  Lawrence M. 143
  Susan 143
  Thomas 143
  Thomas A. 143
  William H. 143
Strongs 58
Stroud 203, 217
  Eliza 217
  John R. 217
Stuart 29, 78
Sudler 98, 161, 190, 251
  Ann 98, 120, 165, 184, 251
  Anna Gordon 184
  Anne 130, 165
  Anne Gordon 130
  Debby 205
  E. 165
  Elizabeth Ann 196
  Elizabeth G. 251
  Emory 130, 165, 184
  Harriet M. 165
  John E. C. 184

John Emery E. 251
John R. 184
Martha 39
Sally 184
Sarah 119, 130
Thomas 184
William 39
Sudlersville 217
Sullivan
  James 158
  Margarett 158
Summers
  Benjamin 218
  Benjamin Franklin 218
  Elmore B. 218
  Harriett Ann 218
  Martha Ellen 218
  Mary Ann 218
  Mary Jane 218
  Robert W. 218
  William H. 218
Sutherland 260
Sutton 24, 32, 33, 131, 148, 174, 181, 224, 268, 270
  Ann Virginia 181
  Henry Clay 181
  Julia 176, 193
  Mary Emma 181
  Orlanda F. 181
  Sam 211
  Samuel M. 181
  Sarah Rebecca 193
  William Knight 181
  William Veazy 193
Swan Town 234, 235
Swann 130
Sweatman
  Hannah C. 256
Swift 28
  Edward 62
  Sarah 62
Sykes 49
Taffrey
  Matilda 31

Talbot Co 55, 91, 135, 200, 244, 275
Talbott 67
Tate 113, 130
  Alexander 149
  Alexander C.H. 128
  Louisa 149
  Maria 128, 149
  Mary 36
  Robert B.A. 149
  Sarah Maria 37, 149
  William B. 37
Tatman 237, 239
Taturn 97
Taylor 20, 61, 170, 201, 247, 253, 257
  Alexander 154
  Ann 13, 32
  Caroline 229
  Catherine M. 229
  Charles 229
  Doreas 197
  Dr. William McK. 229
  Hester A. 229
  Jeremiah 216
  John 154
  John Smith 177
  Mary Ann 13, 154
  Philip 13
  Salina C. 229
  Sarah Rebecca 177
  Thomas 154, 158
  William McK. 229
  William McK. Jr. 229
  William McK. Sr. 229
Tayman 148, 168, 171, 176, 177, 179, 212, 223, 233
Tennant 26, 46, 54
  Elizabeth A. 131
  James 131
  Sarah 131

Thomas 1, 8, 10, 11, 15, 29, 35, 48, 55, 60, 64, 65, 69, 71, 74, 77, 79, 83, 84, 89, 97, 103, 108, 109, 124, 126, 143, 145, 153, 179, 194, 199, 202, 212, 213, 215, 220, 232, 249, 261, 262, 265, 273
  Agnettee 212
  Alexander 212
  Alfred T. 212
  Ann 41, 74, 100, 109
  Ann Catharine 212
  Anna 41
  Caroline 212
  Dr. 188
  Elisa 212
  Eliza 134
  Elizabeth 41, 68, 120, 217
  Emily 68, 212
  Ezekiel 196
  G. W. 188
  George W. 25, 39, 60, 85, 101, 142, 150
  Harriet 212
  Harriett M. 143
  Henry 41, 212
  Jake 212
  James 41, 82
  James Aron 212
  John 106, 212
  John B. 120
  Josephine 212
  Margarett 156
  Mary 41, 60, 100, 109, 111
  Mary J. 211
  Mary Matilda 212
  Mary S. 142, 187

Index of Names and Places

Peggy 212
Rebecca Ann 190
Richard S. 39, 60, 94, 96
Richard S. Jr. 96
Rose 212
Samuel 41, 60, 96
Sarah Elisa 212
Susanna 41
William 41, 60, 100, 212, 217
William Blackiston 100
Thompson 241, 260, 263, 269
  Ann 116, 120, 145
  Caroline 132, 162, 181, 196
  Elizabeth 130, 132
  Ezekial 130
  Ezekial Shadrich 196
  James A. 269
  John 211
  Kitty 132
  Margaret 269
  Margaret F. 269
  Nancy 145
  Rebecca 77, 211
  Richard 130, 196
  Shadrick 130
  William 130, 145
  Zachariah 162, 196
  Zackeriah 130
Thomspon
  Ann 33
Thornington 261
Tilden 13, 14, 19, 91, 122, 128, 164, 175, 198, 230
  Amelia Octavia 272
  Anna 13
  Catharine 75

Charles 44, 156, 214, 272
Charles E. 112
Dr. Charles 47
Edward B. 87, 156
Harriet 13
Indiana 112
Jane E. 214, 215
John H. 156, 191
Laura 191
Lawrence Washington 156
Marmaduke 4, 94, 193
Mary 13, 44, 112
Mary Blay 44
Mary Elizabeth 112
Mary F. 193
Mary H. 4
Rebecca B. 170
Sarah E. 156
Thomas B. 4, 94
Virginia 112
Tilghman 10, 17, 23, 25, 26, 63, 82, 130, 169, 201, 219, 274, 276
  Ann Maria 82
  Anna Maria 82
  Aree Ann 220
  Bill 186
  Billy 274
  Charlotte 275
  Ebenezer 220
  Edward 16, 56, 74
  Edward 3rd 75
  Edward Jr. 74
  Eleanor S. 74
  Ellen S. 72
  Ezekial 220
  H.M. 275, 276
  Harriet Eleis 201
  Harriott 82
  Henrietta 82

Henrietta Lloyd 201
Henrietta Louisa 82
Henry 16, 36, 56, 72, 74, 82
James B. 135
James Bowers 82
James Richard 220
John 74, 75
John Henry 74
Louisa 220
Mary 220
Mary Caroline 82, 201
Matthew 74, 81, 201
Mrs. Martha N. 72
Nancy 75
Nathaniel 220
Perry 220
Philis 122
Rebecca 74
Rebecca E. 220
Richard 74, 81
Richard Lloyd 82
Sally 65
Sarah N. 64
Tench 135
William C. 64
William Matthews 82
Tilla 14
Tiller
  George 148
  Ginny 148
  Joseph James 148
Tilman
  Aree Ann 220
  Ebenezer 220
  Emely 220
  Ezekial 220
  Henry 220
  James Richard 220
  Louisa 220
  Mary 220

May Jane 220
Nathaniel 220
Perry 220
Rebecca E. 220
Tinch
  Bill 230
Tippit
  Elizabeth 106
Titter 167
Titus 170
  Thomas 169
Tolson 31
  Andrew 30, 66
  Rachel 30
Tomlinson 102, 117, 118, 230, 261, 268
  Catharine 158
Tompson
  Mary 220
Toulson 49, 61, 63, 150, 172, 178, 185, 220, 262
  Andrew 60
  Jane 60, 163
  Susan Jane 163
Toulston
  James Albert 191
  Miliscent 191
Townsend 200, 265
  Mary H. 251
  Solomon 251
Tracts
  "Addition" 3, 143
  "Adventure" 10, 11, 24
  "Airy Hill farm" 142, 188
  "Airy Hill" 142, 211, 258
  "Angel's Lot" 86
  "Angel's Rest" 144
  "Angels Lot" 86
  "Arcadia" 15, 87, 138, 160
  "Ashley's Lot" 85

"Bachelor's Choice" 192
"Batchelder Resolution" 3
"Batchelder's Resolution" 3
"Batchelers Resolution" 20
"Baxley" 123
"BaySide Farm" 274
"Bear Garden Addition" 119
"Beck Farm" 133
"Bennets Outlet" 245
"Big Lot" 222
"Blackiston's Fancy Farm" 96
"Blake Farm" 199
"Blake" 199
"Blay's Range" 142
"Boardly Gift" 67
"Bounty" 103
"Boxley" 123
"Boyer farm" 267
"Boyer's Woods" 202
"Bradshaw farm" 123
"Brick house farm" 203
"Brickyard lot" 197
"Broad fields" 95
"Broad Nox Creek" 96
"Broad Oak" 29
"Brooke farm" 253
"Brown farm" 257
"Brown property" 262
"Brown's part of Smyth's Meadows" 16
"Browne farm" 261
"Buck Neck" 81

"Buckingham" 228
"Budd's Discovery" 66, 172
"Burnetts Regulation" 53
"Cacy Purchase" 203
"Cammel's Worth More" 78
"Cammels Worth More" 109
"Campbell's Worth more" 274
"Campbell's Worthmore" 142
"Camples Worth more" 109
"Carolla" 66, 172
"Carvill Farm" 213, 214, 215
"Carvill's mill lot" 62
"Carville Farm" 216
"Castle Cary" 52
"Cave Spray" 9
"Cedar Hill" 134
"Chance" 167
"Chester Grove" 272
"Chesterville" 163
"Chigwell" 39, 142
"Cloak property" 141
"Clows Hazard" 217
"Colly Cove" 266
"Cornwallis' Choice" 172
"Crane's Lott" 136
"Cyprus farm" 175
"Dalyes Desire" 24
"Daniel's Den" 19
"Darnal's Farm" 152
"Darnels Farm" 228

Index of Names and Places

"Davis Farm" 212
"Davis Property" 141
"Davis' Industry" 235, 237
"Decent Changlers" 34
"Deep Landing" 152
"Delaney Manner" 244
"Denby" 30, 167
"Deptford" 131, 132
"Dodson Lot" 106
"Drum Point" 132
"Dugan's Delight" 74
"Dunstable and Bennets Regulation" 52
"Dunstable" 53
"E. Tovering Lott" 12
"Embleton Farm" 177
"Fairy Meadows" 54
"Fancy" 199
"Fanny's Slip" 148
"Fennimous lands" 261
"Flowerfields" 119
"Forest Farm" 17, 257
"Forest" 142
"Forrest farm" 25, 28
"Forrest Manor" 196
"Forrest" 199
"Friendship" 20, 104, 225
"Gamble's farm" 94

"Gambles Purchase" 98
"Garland Lot" 163
"Gauff's Farm" 215
"Gears Farm" 232
"Goosehill" 142
"Gordon farm" 261
"Grantham" 231
"Great Oak Manor" 4, 66
"Green Forest" 263
"Green Hill" 193
"Green Oak Farm" 263
"Green Oak" 112
"Green Point" 225
"Gresham College" 163
"Gresham's Collage" 36
"Gresham's Discovery" 57
"Gresham's Levels" 87
"Grisham Hall" 253
"Grisham's Discovery" 57
"Gunneries" 151
"Hales" 44, 134
"Harigan's Lot" 64
"Harris Lot" 215
"Heath's Range" 11
"Henford" 142
"Hill Top" 90
"Hillings Adventure" 44
"Hollis Marsh Farm" 212
"Hollyday farm" 261
"Home Farm" 22, 133
"Hopewell" 142, 225

"Howard Farm" 151
"Hunters Strate line" 57
"Huntingfield" 12, 16
"Hurlock farm" 175
"Hurts Lot" 249
"Hurtt Lot" 120
"Hurtt's Lot" 24
"Hynson's Addition" 139, 140
"Hynson's Division" 139, 140
"Inheritance" 12
"Jacobs" 261
"Jamison farm" 212
"Joiner's Fancy" 53
"Jones lot" 266
"Kelly Langford" 1
"Kemp's Beginning" 39, 142
"Kent Lot" 119
"Kibler farm" 213
"Killingsworth More" 46
"Knock farm" 230
"Landford" 142
"Langford's Neck" 222
"Little Forest" 67
"Locust Thickett Farm" 267
"London Bridge Renewed" 74
"Long Lot" 210, 222
"Long Point" 136
"Lot No. 10" 143, 250
"Lot No. 12" 188
"Lot No. 13" 188
"Lot No. 15" 100, 143

"Lot No. 23"   101
"Lot No. 24"   101, 142
"Lot No. 26"   10
"Lot No. 29"   142
"Lot No. 3"   86
"Lot No. 30"   101
"Lot No. 37"   142
"Lot No. 44"   143
"Lot No. 60"   114, 115
"Lot No. 61"   114
"Lot No. 62"   114
"Lot No. 63"   114
"Lot No. 80"   10
"Lot No. 81"   79
"Lot No. 82"   79
"Lot No. 87"   273
"Lot No. 88"   114
"Lot No. 9"   143
"Lot No. 91"   114
"lower Bloomfield"   263
"Lower farms"   212
"Maiden's Lot farm"   228
"Major Parker farm"   177
"Manor Farms"   267
"Mansion Farm"   213, 267
"Maslin's Possession"   195
"Maslins Possession"   96
"Massy's Venture"   67
"Matthias and Saint John's Fields"   52
"McCay's Purchase"   106
"McDaniel lot"   257
"McKay Farm"   137
"Meginniss' Part of Angel's Rest Resurveyed"   86

"Middle farm"   212
"Middle Neck"   3
"Mill Fork"   39
"Moffett's mill"   270
"Mount Independence"   3
"Muddy Marsh farm"   186
"My own part of Smyth's Meadows"   16
"Nancy's Choice"   43, 44, 134
"New Comb"   210
"New Forrest"   86, 87
"New Key"   138
"New Keys"   138
"Newman farm"   203
"Numbers Lot"   120
"Old Field Point"   208
"Outer Farm"   274
"Ozmond Farm"   212
"Palmers Hazzard"   272
"Park Resurveyed"   3
"Parks farm"   213
"Parson's Poor Lot"   186, 187
"Part of Forrester's Delight"   44
"Part of Hillings Adventure"   44
"Part of Huntingfield"   16, 245
"Part of Partnership"   3
"Part of Pine Grove"   200
"Part of Piney Grove"   177

"Part of Smith's Desert"   139
"Part of Smyth's Desert"   139
"Part of the Adventure"   24
"Partnership Resurveyed"   3
"Partnership"   44, 76, 119, 144
"Perkins farm"   79
"Piner's Grove"   159, 259
"Piners Grove"   259
"Piney Grove"   38, 186, 187
"Piney Point"   152
"Plain Dealing"   228
"Pond Island"   151
"Ponds"   10
"Pools Island farm"   230
"Pools Island"   229
"Prevention of Inconvenience"   12
"Price's Hill"   135
"Providence"   123, 142
"Ratchliff Cross"   120
"Ratcliff Cross"   39, 165
"Ratcliffe Cross"   184
"Ratcliffs Cross"   98
"Rearden farm"   177
"Reardon"   192
"Redmon's Supply"   136
"Redmore's Supply"   9
"Rells Mills"   232
"Retaliation"   112
"Rich Level"   10
"Rich Neck"   194

Index of Names and Places

"Richards Adventure" 122
"Ricketts farm" 134
"Riding Addition" 34
"Riley's Beginning" 143
"Ring's end" 81
"Ringgold farm" 253
"Ringgold lot" 255
"Ringgolds part of the Adventure Resurveyed" 39
"Rings End" 201
"Robotham's Park" 51
"Rock Point" 222, 266, 267
"Round Top" 142, 143
"Rousby's Recovery" 2
"Saltus Road" 79
"Sandybelly" 123
"Sawyers Forest" 245
"Schotch Point" 265
"Schotchmans Creek Farm" 267
"Scotch Point" 265
"Scott's Folly" 52
"Shrewsbury" 84
"Sillers Addition" 103
"Simpson's Adventure" 52
"Skigg's lot" 53
"Skinner's Neck" 139
"Smith's Forest" 82
"Smith's Park" 86
"Smyth Park" 57

"Smyth's Addition" 16
"Smyth's Desert" 142
"Smyth's wood land" 16
"Smyths Marsh" 245
"Spear" 212
"Spencer lot" 57
"Spencers Lot" 58
"Spring Garden" 144
"Spry property" 257
"St. Martin's" 136
"St. Martins" 136
"Staats farm" 212
"Stanaway" 53
"Stepney Fields" 163
"Stepney Heath Manor" 138
"Stepney" 142, 163
"Stoneton Fishery" 151
"Stoneton" 151
"Suffolk" 263
"Sult Martins Allebone" 3
"The Addition" 87
"the Agreement" 3
"The Edwards Farm" 266
"The Forest Farm" 235, 237
"The Gale and Waltham Farm" 266
"The Gears Farm" 232
"The Holden Farm" 271
"the Home farm" 1

"The Lot Place" 266
"The Plains" 79, 80
"the Ponds" 10
"The Sixty Acre lot" 235, 237
"The Sixty Acre Wood Lot" 237
"the Upper Tract" 133
"Thomas Purchase" 142
"Thomas' Purchase Resurveyed" 3
"Tibbits Venture" 39
"Tilden farm" 197
"Tilden Land" 150
"Tilghman's Friendship" 203
"Tilghmans Farm" 50
"Timothy lot" 257
"Tobin's Lott" 148
"Tovey's Lot" 12
"Triangle" 142
"Trulock's Adventure" 134
"Trumpington Smyths meadows" 245
"Trumpinton" 16
"Tulip Forrest" 79
"Turner's lot" 53
"Turners Creek Point" 230
"Unicorn Mill" 210
"Unicorn Mills" 137
"upper Bloomfield" 263
"Upper Farm" 143
"Viana" 163
"Violet Farm" 137

"Walker Purchase" 204
"Walkers Field" 52
"Walkers Meaddow" 48
"Wallis' Choice" 66
"Wallis' Meadows" 120
"Waltham Farm" 266, 267
"Ward Oak" 24
"Warner's Addition" 43
"Warner's Adventure" 43
"Warners Addition" 122
"Warners Levels Resurveyed" 122
"Waste lands" 55
"Webb farm" 257
"Wedge's Recovery" 100
"Wethered farm" 143
"Wheel Wright Swamps" 49
"White house farm" 203
"White Marsh" 12, 122
"Whitfields" 142
"Wolf Cramp" 12
"Wolf Swamp" 222
"Worsell Manor" 236
"Worton farm" 142
"Worton Manner" 20, 30, 66
"Worton Manor" 4, 172
"Wright's Addition" 53
"Wright's Rest" 3
"Wrights Step" 52

"Wyatts Chance" 228
"Yapp" 151
"Yearley Farm" 200
"Yearly farm" 261
"Youngs Neck" 263
Travilla 85
  Ann 121
  Ann P. 85
  Margaret 121
  Mary H. 121
  Philip B. 85
Trenchard 74
  Ann 235
Trew 26, 45, 161, 175, 268
  Ann Rebecca 175
  Bartus 60, 147, 175
  Bartus Jr. 147
  Deborah 147, 175
  Mary 147, 175
  Rebecca 147, 175
  Thomas 147
  Thomas W. 173
Trible 234
Trulock
  Anne Washington 134
Trusty 29
  George W. 83
  Harriet 83
  Henrietta Maria 83, 84
  Jefferson 83
  Rebecca 29
Tryford
  Mary 250
Turbutt 261
Turner 30, 53, 59, 73, 100, 109, 137, 217, 225
  Alexander 153
  Ann 154
  Cassandra 136
  Deborah 132, 191
  Edward 136

Isaac 136
John 29, 68, 132
Joseph 60, 73, 136
Joseph III 136
Joseph Jr. 136
Mary 132
Mary P. 168
Nancy 153
Rebecca 136, 153
Richard Townsend 136
Sarah 136
Sarah T. 136
William 168
Turners Creek 48, 71, 230, 263
Twiggs 192
Tygart
  Alexander 21
Urian 264
Urie 107, 153, 168, 207
  Ann Elizabeth 224
  Catharine 207
  Daniel 224
  Elizabeth 167, 207
  Emeline 224
  Henry 27, 85, 167, 206
  Henry Jr. 206
  James 85, 167, 168, 206, 224
  James Jr. 224
  Jane 224
  John 167, 206
  John Jr. 85
  Laura 224
  Mary 167
  Mary Ann 206
  Robert 167, 206
  Sarah 206
  Sarah Louisa 224
  Thomas 85, 206
  William 85, 167
  William Thomas 224

Index of Names and Places

Ury
  Robert 125
  Thomas 125
Usilton 41, 59, 60, 65, 69, 85, 128, 141, 150, 172, 173, 178, 197, 210, 247, 263, 267
  Adaline 169
  Alethea 266
  Amanda 266
  Ann R. 185
  Avis Louisa 169
  Catharine 65
  Elizabeth 169
  Emily 169, 266
  Emily C. 168
  Frances P. 168
  Francis 49, 169, 185
  Hannah 168, 169
  Hester 266
  Hosanna 49
  John 49, 65, 144, 169
  John Francis 185, 262
  John N. 169
  Joseph 49, 65, 163, 169, 266
  Joseph L. 185
  Lewis 266
  Mary 168, 169, 266
  Mary A. 168
  Mary E. 185
  Rachel 262
  Robert 49, 65, 163, 168, 169
  Sarah 168, 169
  Sarah Frances 169
  Susan 168
  Susan A. 169, 185
  Thomas E. 169
Usselton

Francis 49
John 49
Joseph 49
Vachel
  Ann 48
Valk
  Ann 251
Van Bibber 1
Vandyke 90
  Sarah 90
  Thomas 90
Vanhorn 151, 155
Vanlier 62, 138
  Ann Eliza 62
  Mary Virginia 62
Vanness 37
Vannoit 266
Vannort 100
Vannost 134
  William 220
Vansant 11, 42, 53, 70, 156, 226, 233
  Elizabeth 41
  Ephraim 4th 41
  Fredus 41, 270
  George 41, 72
  Hannah 270
  Henry 41
  Ira 270
  John D. 178
  John R. 41
  Joshua 270
  Lemuel 41
  Nathan 41
  Rosetta 270
  Sarah 270
Veazey 121
Veazy 121
Veuleman
  Rev. Peter 74
Vickers 91, 101, 115, 117, 120, 123, 153, 160, 169, 178, 195, 196,

200, 202, 211, 212, 216, 218, 221, 224, 226, 227, 234, 235, 253, 255, 256, 262, 266, 267, 269, 271, 278
  Adah 14
  Ann Maria 95
  Annette Tower 235
  Benjamin 218
  David 29
  Dennis 168
  Elizabeth 29, 99, 167
  George 159, 172, 192, 218, 235
  James 5
  Jesse 5
  Joel 14, 99
  Margaret E. 96
  Mary 5
  Mary Ann 158
  Nancy 5
  Rachel 29
  Sarah P. 218
  William 99
Vincent
  Mary 76
Virginia 62, 112, 146, 170, 179-181, 198, 201, 204, 243, 249
Voshell 156, 274
Voss 115
  Hester Ann 99
  Mary 99
  Mary Jane 99
  Rachel Elizabeth 99
  Sophia Vickers 99
  William 99
Waibel 273
Wakeman
  Araminta 26
  Banks 26

Dr. Banks 26
William Banks 123
Waldic 72
Wales 41, 50
  Elizabeth 108
  Samuel 108
Walff 268
Walker 23, 108, 116,
  134, 143, 144,
  150, 151, 154,
  155, 177, 210
  Anna J. 210
  Elizabeth 123, 155,
    180, 188
  Elizabeth M. 108
  Grieves 180
  John W. 155
  Mary A.E. 180
  Mary S. 180
  Mary Sophia 108
  Thomas 108, 210
  W.S. 210
Wallace 10
Wallis 2, 24, 33, 40,
  46, 70, 80, 85,
  122, 132, 152,
  182, 229
  Abe 228
  Alethea 228
  Amos 228
  Anna M.M. 278
  Arthur John Wallis
    152
  Benjamin Franklin
    228
  Comegys 80
  Elvira 228
  Ferdinand 228
  Francis 80
  Hannah Isabella 228
  Hannah J. 121
  Harriett 228
  Henry Clay 228
  Hugh 85, 121, 131,
    152, 228
  Hugh M. 228

  Hugh Maxwell 228
  Joe 228
  John 51, 80
  John Brooks 152
  John H. M. 83, 84
  Julia 228
  Lydia 228
  Margaret 121, 131
  Margaret A. 121
  Margaret B. 85
  Margaret Helen 228
  Maria 194
  Marion Brooks 228
  Mary 273
  Mary E. 228
  Mary Elvira 228
  Ned 228
  Ruth Ann 228
  Samuel Wright 228
  Sarah 228
  Sarah Ann 229
  Sarah E. 80
  Shadrach 228
  Walter G. 228
  William 131
  William W. 152,
    228
Walls 217
  Mary Ann 148
Walmsley 273
  Benjamin F. 273
  George W. 273
  John B. 273
  John P. 273
  Martha Jane 273
  Oliver H.R. 273
  Walter 13
Waltham
  Susan 143
Ward 50, 144, 260
  Ann 91
  Charlotte 249
  Dorinda 186
  George 61, 190
  Philip 91
  Robert 249

Warden 216
Ware
  Henry 217
Warfield
  Charles D. 167
  Emma H. Perkins
    253
  Hetty Maria 167
  Lucretia 167
  Lucy 167
  Nicholas D. 167
Warner
  Mary Ann 206, 219
Warren 62, 120, 231
  David 231
Warwick 238, 239
Washington
  George ii
  Joseph 249
  Maria Ellen 249
  Pery 34
  Susan 249
Washington Co 218
Waters 124, 224
  Alethia 228
  D. E. S. 224
  M. A. 224
  Margaret 210
  Rev. F. 224
Watkins
  Manelia 167
Watson 72, 257, 267
Watts 6, 29, 43, 73,
  78, 114, 115, 221
  John 88
  Mary Ann 88
  Rosa Maria 88
  Susan 88
  Susana 21
  Susanna 22
Wearum 100
  Abraham 100
  Ann 100
  William 100
Webb 82, 150, 221,
  230, 267

Index of Names and Places

David 107, 183
Elizabeth 107
John 107
Joseph W. 107, 150
Mary 107, 183
Parssella 76
Rachael 266
Rachel 107
William 243
Webster
  Benjamin Franklin 87
  George Smith 87
  Henry 87
  John Wesley 87
  Maria Elizabeth 111
  Martha 87
  Richard Henry 87
Weer 220, 230
  Elizabeth J. 220
  Emily 220
  James 220
  James H. 220
  Joseph E. 220
  Mary 220
  Tacy A. 220
Welch 27, 42, 48, 67, 116, 128
  Ann 235
  Annie 223
  Araminta 120, 178
  Arthur 234
  Caroline 223, 234
  Eben 234, 235
  Ebenezer 120, 178, 234
  George 223, 234
  Hannah 97
  Harriet 223
  Jacob 234
  James 97, 235
  John D. 120, 223, 234
  John Thomas 120
  Jonathan T. 67

Lorenzo 223
Louisa 223
Margaret T. 234
Maria 223
Martha 223
Mary Ann 223
Mary Anne 216
Mary Louisa 216
Matilda 223
Richard S. 235
Sarah E. 223
Sarah Elizabeth 235
Thomas S. 120
William 120, 216, 223, 234
Welsh 259
Sarah 259
Sarah A. 259
William H. 259
Westcote 216
Westcott 129, 139, 156, 201, 242, 248, 255, 259, 271, 273, 276
  George 155
  George B. 129
Westmoreland Co 212
Wethered 6, 48, 50, 84, 101, 225, 230
  Abe 230
  Beck 230
  Caroline 31
  Catherine 31
  Eliza 84
  George 84
  George Y. 230
  Harriet 31
  John 31, 84, 229
  John L. 229
  Lewin 31, 71
  Lewina 84
  Little Abe 230
  Mary 31, 229
  Mary Elizabeth 230

  Matilda 31, 84
  Peregrine 31, 229
  Sally 84
  Samuel 31, 71, 84, 230
  Samuel Jr. 71, 230
  Samuel Sr. 230
  Sarah 31
Whalan 41
Whaland 16, 144, 165, 174, 180, 200, 211, 250, 256, 262, 273
  Ann Matilda 117
  Martha 117
Wharton 116, 255
  Ann O. 254
Wheat 60
  Alexander 162
Wheatley 100, 145
Wheatly 171
Wheeler 13, 68
  Ann B. 68
  William 68
White
  John David 204
  Katherine 217
  Maria Louisa 217
  Sarah 217
  William H. 204
Whiteley 251
Whitely 266
Whittington 23, 96, 199, 261
  Hannah 133
  James 133
  John 133
  John Jr. 133
  Thomas 54
  William 133
Whorton
  Susan 76
Wickes 5, 13, 15, 16, 18, 19, 59, 71, 73,

76, 80, 90, 101,
102, 103, 110,
113, 114, 118,
139, 153, 155,
160, 164, 165,
167, 171, 178,
181, 205, 210,
211, 219, 222,
232, 250, 253,
255, 259, 266
Ann Rebecca 259
Anna 58
Anna Maria 204
Antoinette 219
Antonietta 93
Augusta 93, 250
Augusta M. 259
Benjamin C. 211, 259
Benjamin Chambers 159, 188, 211
Catharine 232
Charles Henry 90
Charlotte 219
Col. Joseph 188, 275
Dr. Joseph 188
Elizabeth 190
Elizabeth C. 159, 189, 258, 275
Emeline L. 93
Ezekial C. 159, 188, 211, 250, 259
Fanny 195
Frances C. 259
Frances H. 102, 172
Hannah 90
Hester Henrietta VanBibber 159
Hester Van Bibber 188
Jackson 102
James P. 93, 219

Joseph 159, 188, 211, 232, 258, 275, 276
Joseph 4th 63, 91
Joseph A. 159, 211, 258, 259
Kitty 205
Lambert 41
Louisa W. 93
Maria 93
Mary 58, 90, 219
Mary E. 159, 259
Mary Henrietta 90
Matthew 183
Nancy 195
Pere L. 258, 259
Peregrine L. 159, 211, 259
Peregrine Letherberry 188
Rebecca 195
Richard Samuel 58
Sally Augusta 189
Samuel A.J. 172
Samuel Joseph 173
Sarah A. 159
Sarah Ann 102
Sarah Jane 232
Sarah Piner 62, 159
Sarah R. 205
Sarah Ringgold 232
Simon 57, 90
Simon Jr. 90
William 93
William H. 93
Wicks
  Elizabeth C. 275
Wiesenthall
  Sarah B. 90
  Thomas 90
Wiggins 185
  Rachel 73
Wilds 116
Wiley 146, 157
  Ann H. 125
  Margaret A. 146

Nathaniel 125
Wilkins 20, 30, 45, 175, 176, 190, 242, 268
Bartus 140
Col. Edward 276
Edward 143, 173, 276
James F. 140
Juliana 173
Thomas 140
William H. J. 140
Wilkinson 248
Christopher 248
Margaret Ann 248
Williams 12
Avarilla 92, 107
John 85
Rebecca 266
Sarah 87
Thomas 85
William N. 87
Williamsen 106
Williamson 35
Ann Jane 179
James 38
John 38
Mary 38
William 179
Willie
Charles 29
Willis 29, 278
Lydia Ann 183
Williss
Sharlotte 239
Wills 201
Willson 39, 88, 152, 222, 244-246
Alexander H. 246
Alexander Hookin 246
Ann 245
Charles 245
Charlotte 245
Daniel C. 245
Daniel Carroll 245

Index of Names and Places

David 245
Dinah 245
Dr. T. 75
Dr. Thomas 38, 75
Eliza 245
Fanny 245
George H. 245
George William 140
Henry 245
James H. 245
John 24
John C. 245, 246
Julia 245
Juliann V. 140
Maria Deborah 141
Martha Neal 246
Mary Elizabeth 245
Mary Henry 141
Nancy 245
Perry 245
Richard Bennett 244
Susan E. 140
Thomas 38, 75, 82, 244
Thomas S. 244
William 245
William Ann 140
William George 141
Wilmer 1, 13, 52, 60, 81, 95, 113, 128, 134, 138, 143, 147, 171, 179, 182, 191, 194, 198, 201, 203, 204, 242
Ann 32, 59, 102
Ann B. 106
Ann E. 81, 89, 160
Ann Elizabeth 81
Ann Louisa 89
Blackistone 36
Frances 59
Hannah 97

Harriett 36, 149, 272
Henrietta 59
James 97, 154
Jane Eliza 106
John 36
John L. 128
John Lambert 59
John Ringgold 81
Maria 149
Martha 5
Mary 36, 58, 81
Mary Ann 13, 32
Mary Price 59
P. 58
Peregrine 58, 79
Rachel 59
Sarah 36, 149
Sarah R. 160
Sarah Rebecca 36
Walter C. 59, 60
William B. 13, 32, 36, 95, 113, 149
William D. 59
William Dick 128
Wilmington 35, 97, 213, 256, 260, 265
Wilson 16, 17, 29, 30, 39, 52, 76, 93, 106, 115, 136, 141, 172, 174, 184, 201, 212, 218, 235, 238, 254, 263, 264, 266, 268
Abe 145
Abe Jr. 145
Alexander 268
Ann 154
Ann Maria 75
Anna M. 82
Araminta 162
Capt. Thomas 26
Caroline 162

Casar 162
Delia A. 170
Emma 263
Francis Albert 263
Frederick 162
George 82, 273
George William 21, 249
James 63, 141, 273
James H. 245
James Jr. 63
John C. 184
John G. 154
Julia 170
Julia Anna Virginia 249
Margaret P.W. 170
Maria 16, 17
Maria Deborah 170
Martha Amanda 263
Mary E. 82
Mary H. 170, 277
Matilda 270
Milicent 273
Rachel 248
Richard 248
Richard Bennet 245
Richard Jr. 248
Robert 117, 141, 197, 263
Sarah 63, 170
Sarah Etta Louisa 263
Sarah P. 218
Sophia 162
Susana 248
Susanna 273
Thomas 17, 26
Thomas S. 213, 244
William Ann 170
William George 21, 170
Winchester 119, 176
Ann 119

Sarah 119
Susan 119
Windes 251
Winters
  Jonathan 35
Wise 35, 192, 218
  George W. 35
  William 35
Wolahan
  Sarah Ann 132
Wolfe
  Nathaniel 202
Wood 24, 176, 220, 236, 237, 269
  Ann Eliza 269
  Anna 264
  Catharine 264
  Catharine Jane 269
  Charles 264
  Charles C. 264, 269
  Clara Ann 269
  Clara Emma 264
  Hannah 133
  Ida 264
  James A. 264
  John Wesley 264
  Mary 264
  Mary Rebecca 269
  Matthew J. 264
  Rebecca 264, 269
  Sina Jane 269
  Tina Jane 269
  William 133
Woodall 66, 98, 119, 219, 261
  Ann 98, 163
  Edward B. 277
  Emily Ann 98
  Freeman B. 163
  Isaac 162
  Jesse 163, 191
  John 98, 120
  John Samuel 163
  Joseph 98
  Sarah 191
  Sary Ann 162
  William 162
Wooddall
  Edward B. 212
  Elizabeth M. 212
Woodland 242
  Ann 121
  Ann Eliza 52
  Eliza 53
  Hannah 121
  Hannah P. 121
  James F. 242, 244
  John A. 43
  Margaret 121
  Margaret W. 242
  Mary 242
  Samuel 242
  Sarah Emily 52
Woodward 265
  Brinton Jones 265
  Catharine 265
  Henrietta 265
  Kate 265
  Thomas 265
Worcester Co 278
World
  Catharine 272
  Mary Cecelia 272
Worrel
  Sarah 88
Worrell 5, 8, 39, 73, 118, 122, 145, 150
  Ann 23
  Ann Elizabeth 23
  Ann Elizabeth Pearce 54
  Anna Mathilda 65
  Anna Matilda 64
  Benjamin 88
  Cornelia 81
  Edward 97
  Edward Hanson 53
  Edward Jr. 97
  Elizabeth 53, 97
  Elizabeth Ann Sudler 196
  Elizabeth G. 80, 145, 169
  Ellen 215
  George W. 97
  Hannah 65
  Hannah G. 64
  Jacob 168
  John Hynson 88
  Maria 54
  Mary 81, 88
  Rebecca 97
  Rebecca Hynson 88
  Richard 214, 215
  Sarah Maria 54
  Thomas 64, 215
  Thomas G. 64
  William Henry Page 53
Worthington
  Rebecca 43
Worton ii, 1, 4, 19, 20, 22, 30, 33, 43, 49, 66, 86, 142, 172, 183, 189, 194, 221, 225, 232, 266
  Elizabeth 33
Wright 22, 30, 67, 71, 75, 77, 111, 143, 147, 170, 177, 268
  Benjamin 53
  Edward 52, 53
  Eliza 53
  Gustavus T. 39
  Hannah B. 52, 53
  Hannah Brooks 53
  James 53
  Jane Louisa 182
  Jonathan B. 251
  Joseph 111
  Julianna 52
  Martha 120
  Mary 53
  Melvina 52, 53
  Norrist 53

Index of Names and Places

Polly 80
Sarah 53
Tabitha 37, 100, 109
Thomas 215
Thomas H. 52
William 53
William Jr. 52
Wroth 27, 31, 38, 54, 56, 61, 63, 73, 75, 110, 111, 125, 134, 136, 145, 147, 150, 155, 160, 161, 180, 182, 189, 195, 211, 215, 220, 225, 237, 239, 246, 251, 272
Alice Alfred 215
Ben 246
Benjamin B. 56, 246
Benjamin B. Jr. 56
Catharine 198
Catharine H. 215
Charlotte 246
Dr. 58, 72
Dr. P. 107
Dr. Peregrine 110, 156, 215, 272
Editha G. 56, 107
Edward 73
Edward T. 215
Edward W. 107, 110
Ellen 215
Emily 215
Emory 215
Eugenia 58
Eugenia M. 107, 110
Hannah 246
Harry 215
Jane 215

John 69, 73, 110
John Kinvin 110
Levi 56, 73, 157
Louis Jerome 215
Louisa 69, 73, 83, 159
Margaret 73, 246
Margaret Priscilla 110
Margaret S. 107
Margarett 69
Maria 215
Mary 56, 246
Mary E. 107, 110
Mary G. 246
Melvina 246
P. 107
Peregrine 56, 73, 110, 156, 272
Perry 246
Thomas 73
William 56, 159, 180
William G. 246
William J. 110
William Jackson 107
Wyatt
  Ann Catharine 212
Yarnel
  Rebecca L. 20
  Sarah 20
  Susannah 20
Yates 6, 108
Yearley 131
Yearly 156, 261
  Alexander 19
  Ann 19
Yeates 13
  Donaldson 6
  George 6
  Mary A. 243
Young 61, 150, 157
  Charlotte 195

Daniel 120
Elizabeth 125
Notty 47
Temperance 190
Younger 183, 210
Jane 184